"The *Routledge Handbook of African Social Work Education* is a long-awaited book that adds significantly to the knowledge base of international social work. Most significantly, it is an important milestone on the long road to decolonising social work education, research, and practice worldwide. It contains in-depth, contextualised case studies, research findings, and experience-based contributions from various African countries."

Tanja Kleibl, Technical University Würzburg-Schweinfurt (THWS), Germany

"This book provides an in-depth exploration of social work education and fields of practice, with practical examples from diverse contexts across Africa. The book is not only relevant for social work educators, practitioners, students, and social policy makers, but also all those interested in decolonial perspectives in social work and social development."

Janestic Mwende Twikirize, Makerere University, Uganda

ROUTLEDGE HANDBOOK OF AFRICAN SOCIAL WORK EDUCATION

This timely *Routledge Handbook of African Social Work Education* creates a much-needed space to explore what makes social work uniquely African as well as shaping, informing, and influencing a new culturally relevant era of social work. The specific focus on social work education offers approaches to transition away from the hegemony of Western literature, knowledge, and practice models underpinning African social work education. The authors identify what is relevant and meaningful to inform, influence, and reconceptualise culturally relevant social work curriculum.

Covering Botswana, Cameroon, Ethiopia, Ghana, Guinea, Kenya, Malawi, Nigeria, South Africa, Tanzania, Uganda, Zambia, and Zimbabwe, the Handbook comprises both empirical and conceptual chapters, multiple approaches, case studies, and key debates on social work education. It is structured in four parts:

- Approaches to Indigenising, Decolonising and Developing Culturally Relevant Social Work Education
- Social Work Education: Evolution across Contexts
- Embedding Field Practicum into Social Work Education
- Knowledge Exchange between the Global South and Global North.

The range of indigenous, local knowledge that the Handbook presents is crucial to social work evolving and facilitating for reciprocal learning and knowledge exchange between the Global South and Global North. Whilst the context of the Handbook is Africa, the topics covered are relevant to a global audience engaged in social justice work across social work, social welfare, social development, and sustainability.

Susan Levy is Associate Dean International and Senior Lecturer in Social Work, in the School of Humanities, Social Sciences and Law, University of Dundee, UK.

Uzoma Odera Okoye is a Professor in the Department of Social Work at the University of Nigeria, Nsukka.

Pius T. Tanga is a Professor of Social Work at the University of Fort Hare, South Africa.

Richard Ingram is a Professor of Social Work at the University of Dundee, UK.

ROUTLEDGE HANDBOOK OF AFRICAN SOCIAL WORK EDUCATION

Edited by
Susan Levy, Uzoma Odera Okoye,
Pius T. Tanga and Richard Ingram

LONDON AND NEW YORK

Designed cover image: M_D_A © Getty

First published 2024

by Routledge

4 Park Square, Milton Park, Abingdon, Oxon OX14 4RN

and by Routledge

605 Third Avenue, New York, NY 10158

Routledge is an imprint of the Taylor & Francis Group, an informa business

© 2024 selection and editorial matter, Susan Levy, Uzoma Odera Okoye, Pius T. Tanga and Richard Ingram; individual chapters, the contributors

The right of Susan Levy, Uzoma Odera Okoye, Pius T. Tanga and Richard Ingram to be identified as the author[/s] of the editorial material, and of the authors for their individual chapters, has been asserted in accordance with sections 77 and 78 of the Copyright, Designs and Patents Act 1988.

All rights reserved. No part of this book may be reprinted or reproduced or utilised in any form or by any electronic, mechanical, or other means, now known or hereafter invented, including photocopying and recording, or in any information storage or retrieval system, without permission in writing from the publishers.

Trademark notice: Product or corporate names may be trademarks or registered trademarks, and are used only for identification and explanation without intent to infringe.

British Library Cataloguing-in-Publication Data

A catalogue record for this book is available from the British Library

ISBN: 978-1-032-32295-7 (hbk)
ISBN: 978-1-032-32296-4 (pbk)
ISBN: 978-1-003-31434-9 (ebk)

DOI: 10.4324/9781003314349

Typeset in Times New Roman
by Deanta Global Publishing Services, Chennai, India

CONTENTS

List of figures and tables — *xi*
Contributors — *xiii*
Acknowledgements — *xxi*
Foreword — *xxii*
Acronyms and abbreviations — *xxv*

    Introduction — 1
    Susan Levy, Uzoma O. Okoye, Richard Ingram, and Pius T. Tanga

PART 1
Approaches to Diversifying, Decolonising, and Developing Culturally Relevant Social Work Education — **11**

1 Complexities Involved in Establishing a Culturally Relevant Social Work Curriculum in Nigeria — 13
   Mel Gray, Susan Levy, Uzoma Odera Okoye, and Solomon Amadasun

2 The Informality Paradigm in Social Work Practice in Africa: Philosophy, Continuity, and Prospects for Integration into Professional Practice — 26
   Venesio Bwambale Bhangyi, Milliam Kiconco, and Wing Hong Chui

3 Exploring the Potential of an Ecosocial Approach for African Social Work Education — 37
   James Kutu Obeng and Michael Emru Tadesse

4 African Indigenous Knowledge Systems and Theories in Teaching Social Work — 49
   Mmaphuti Mamaleka

5 Translanguaging and Pedagogic Pathways to Culturally Relevant Social
   Work Education   62
   Thembelihle Brenda Makhanya and Susan Levy

6 Faith and Spirituality in Social Work Education and Practice in Ethiopia   74
   Ashenafi Hagos Baynesagn, Tasse Abye, and Emebet Mulugeta

7 Faith and Spirituality in Social Work Education and Practice in Nigeria   86
   Oghenechoja Dennis Veta

8 Social Work and Pastoral Counselling in South Africa: Inter-sectoral Partnership 96
   Selelo Frank Rapholo and Zibonele France Zimba

PART 2
Social Work Education: Evolution across Contexts   **105**

9 Exploring the Challenges of Child Protection in Nigeria   107
   Abiodun Blessing Osaiyuwu

10 Social Work Education: Opportunities and Challenges in Tanzania, East Africa   118
   Johnas A. Buhori

11 Advancing Social Work Education Using Online Learning in South Africa:
   Challenges and Prospects   130
   Ntandoyenkosi Maphosa and Mziwandile Sobantu

12 Insurmountable Barriers to Social Work Education: Experiences of Online
   Learning from Rural South Africa   141
   Eleanor A Hendricks and Richard Ingram

13 Social Worker Role-Taking during Communicable Disease Outbreaks in
   South Africa: The Need for Disaster Management Training   152
   Christo Heunis, Mariëtte Joubert, and Alice Ncube

14 Cyber Counselling Competencies: Implications for Curriculum
   Development and Training of Social Work Practitioners   165
   Cecilia Tutu-Danquah and Lawrence Murphy

15 The Coming of Age of Social Work Education in Zimbabwe: Towards
   Reinforcing the Developmental Social Work Agenda   178
   Tatenda Goodman Nhapi

16 Social Work Education and Training in Francophone Africa: The Case of Cameroon 189
Pius T. Tanga and Gabriel A. Ekobi

17 *A Case Study of the Emerging Social Work Sector in Guinea, West Africa* 200
Marissa Kaloga and Abdoul Karim Camara

18 Culture and Ethnicity in Medical Social Work: Lessons for Future Directions for Social Work Curriculum Transformation in Kenya 217
Wilkins Ndege Muhingi, Ajwang' Warria, and Edwine Jeremiah Otieno

PART 3
Embedding Field Practicum into Social Work Education **229**

19 Social Work Field Practicum: Experiences, Challenges, and Perspectives from Malawi 231
Agnes Gogo Wizi-Kambala

20 Dearth of Standard Social Work Agencies for Field Practicum: Barrier to Social Work Pedagogy in Nigeria 242
Chinyere Onalu, Chinwe Nnama-Okechukwu, Patricia Agbawodikeizu, and Ngozi Chukwu

21 Situational Analysis of Social Work Field Practice in Tanzania Mainland 254
Meinrad Haule Lembuka

22 The Importance and Challenges of Social Work Field Education: The University of Benin Experience 266
Tracy B.E. Omorogiuwa

23 Field Practicum in Social Work Education: The Ethiopian Experience 276
Demelash Kassaye

24 Family Genogram as an Experiential Method to Enhance Training in Social Work Practice in Botswana 288
Tumani Malinga

25 Rethinking Social Work Education in South Africa amidst the COVID-19 Pandemic: Suggestions for Innovative Fieldwork Practice 300
Thabisa Matsea

26 Being a Student Social Worker during Academic Disruptions in South
    Africa: What Do We Need to Prepare for Practice?   311
    Marichen van der Westhuizen, Ronel Davids, and Violet Adonis

PART 4
Knowledge Exchange between the Global South and the Global North   **323**

27 Prioritising Indigenous Knowledge in Social Work Education through
    Experiential Learning: Narratives from Social Workers   325
    Rita Adoma Parry, Elizabeth Onyedikachi George, and Catherine Suubi Kayonga

28 An International University Partnership to Support the Social Service
    Workforce and Strengthen the Child Protection System in Ghana   335
    Bree Akesson and Magnus Mfoafo-M'Carthy

29 Sources of Knowledge Transfer between the Global South and the Global
    North in Social Work Education   346
    Peninah Kansiime, Sharlotte Tusasiirwe, and Diana Nabbumba

30 Social Work Education and Black African Diaspora: Explorations in the
    Republic of Ireland   358
    Washington Marovatsanga and Paul Michael Garrett

31 Social Work and Practice Education, Decolonisation and Ubuntu: Making
    Connections in Malawi   370
    Janet Walker, Simon Cauvain, Felix Kakowa, and Anstance Fometu

32 Challenges and Prospects for Integrating Interprofessional Education and
    Collaborative Practice (IPECP) into Social Work Education across Cultures 382
    Abigail Adubea Mills, Doris A. Boateng, Sevaughn Banks, and Felicia Tuggle

Index   *395*

LIST OF FIGURES AND TABLES

Figures

13.1	Cumulative COVID-19 cases by province, 7 July 2022	156
13.2	Social workers indicating non-delivery of services to vulnerable groups in MMM during COVID-19	158
13.3	Levels of post-traumatic stress	159
14.1	Summary of Ghanaian Counsellors' Competencies of Standard H1–H7	171
14.2	Cyber counselling competency framework	174
17.1	Transmission, indigenisation, and authentisation Continuum, adapted from Walton and El Nasr, 1988	203
17.2	Transmission, indigenisation, and authentisation of social work in Guinea	211
24.1	Lesego family genogram with demographic data	292
24.2	Lesego family genogram showing demographic information and relationships	293

Tables

1.1	Journals Used in Literature Review on Nigerian Social Work	16
1.2	Distribution of Literature Review Papers by Theme and Frequency of Publication	17
1.3	Three Main Themes in the Literature Review Papers Relating to Developing a Culturally Relevant curriculum in Nigeria	17
4.1	African Indigenous Knowledge (AIK) Types of Opportunities and Benefits in Social Work Education	53
10.1	Development of Social Work Education and Training in Tanzania	121
13.1	Checklist for Minimum Competencies and Value Standards for Social Work during Communicable Disease Disasters	161
14.1	Cyber Counselling Training for Counsellors	173
16.1	Social Work Curriculum at National School of Administration and Magistracy (École Nationale d'Administration et Magistracie – ENAM)	195

List of figures and tables

17.1	Constructivist Case Study, Adapted from Boblin et al. (2013)	204
17.2	Qualitative Data Sources	204
17.3	Alignment between AGTS and IFSW ethical principles	208
17.4	Social Work Sector Timeline in Guinea	210
19.1	Patterns of Field Practicum in Malawi	236
21.1	Sample of Social Work Training Institutions in Tanzania	258
30.1	The Four Social Work Educators	360
32.1	Competencies for the Interprofessional and Collaborative Applied Global Health Practice (IPCAGHP) Course	389

CONTRIBUTORS

Tasse Abye (PhD) is Senior Research Associate, Department of Social Work and Community Development, University of Johannesburg, South Africa, and Associate Researcher at Institut des Mondes Africains in Paris, France. Besides teaching and research, Abye works as an advisor and consultant on capacity building, chiefly around issues of social work, higher education, and research.

Violet Adonis is a Lecturer in the Department of Social Work at the University of the Western Cape, South Africa, focusing on fieldwork education and training. Her research interests focus on learning and teaching, psychosocial wellbeing, and fieldwork for preparation for practice in social work.

Patricia Uju Agbawodikeizu is a social researcher and Senior Lecturer in the Department of Social Work, University of Nigeria, Nsukka. She is a research fellow with Health Policy Research Group and H3Africa, Nigeria. Her primary research interests are in the areas of ageing, gender, and public health.

Bree Akesson is Canada Research Chair (Tier II) in Global Adversity and Wellbeing and Associate Professor of Social Work at Wilfrid Laurier University in Canada. Her program of research ranges from micro-level understandings of the experiences of war-affected families to macro-level initiatives to strengthen global social service systems.

Solomon Amadasun, a graduate of the University of Benin, Nigeria, and PhD student at Deakin University, Australia, has published widely on Nigerian social work and related issues, including *Social Work for Social Development in Africa* (September Publishing House, 2020) and *Social Work, Social Welfare and Social Development in Nigeria* (with Mel Gray) (Routledge, 2023).

Sevaughn Banks, Associate Professor in the MSW Department at California State University, Stanislaus, USA, has over two decades of social work leadership. Her research interest is global workforce development. She led numerous research projects, received 14 grants, has authored eight publications, and made over 30 professional presentations at national and international conferences.

Contributors

Venesio Bwambale Bhangyi is Assistant Lecturer in Social Work at Kyambogo University, Uganda. He also works with the Ministry of Health in Uganda as a public health social worker. His research interests are in environmental social work, public social services, social policy, and social development.

Doris A. Boateng is a Social Worker and Senior Lecturer at the Department of Social Work, University of Ghana. Her current research interests examine climate change adaptation models for rural Ghanaian women farmers. Her recent publication discusses attitudes, experiences, and perceptions of Ghanaians towards mental illness, stigma, and treatment beliefs as well as pathways to service utilisation.

Johnas Amon Buhori, The Open University of Tanzania, is a trainer, coach, lecturer, consultant, and researcher with dynamic skills and knowledge, very open to learn and accept constructive criticism. His excellent interpersonal relationships, diligence, and compatible personality traits has facilitated him to take various opportunities in any diverse environment.

Abdoul Karim Camara is a Project Manager and Social Work Specialist with 15 years of experience in the management of community development projects focused on social work, psychosocial care, child protection, support for young people, team and activity management, and training facilitation.

Simon Cauvain, Nottingham Trent University, UK, carries out research that centres on frontline social worker experiences and how they influence retention and 'stay and go' decisions. He visits Malawi to provide post-qualification education. Simon is dedicated to supporting the necessary resourcing of Malawian social work practice through the professionalisation of education, professional standards, creation of an association, and legislation.

Wing Hong Chui is Professor and Head in the Department of Applied Social Sciences at the Hong Kong Polytechnic University. Prior to this, he was a youth social worker who worked with children and juvenile offenders and has continued to seek to build a better world through his varied contributions.

Ngozi Chukwu holds a PhD in Medical/Family Social Work. She is a consummate social work researcher/educator at the University of Nigeria, Nsukka. Her primary research interests are in public health, disabilities, social work pedagogy, maternal and child health, elderly care, and migration, and she has published widely in these fields.

Ronel Davids is a Senior Lecturer and the coordinator of the postgraduate programme in the Department of Social Work at the University of South Africa. Her research interests include supported education for students with physical disabilities, community-based social work within the deaf society, and support to parents with children with hearing loss.

Gabriel Acha Ekobi is a postdoctoral fellow with the Department of Social Work and Social Development, University of Fort Hare, South Africa. He holds a PhD in Development Studies from North West University, South Africa. He is a member of the Council for the Development of Social Science Research in Africa and the Memory Studies Association. His research interests include food security, informal economy, indigenous knowledge systems, and social protection. He has published many papers in peer-reviewed journals.

Anstance Fometu, Children and Families International Foundation (CFIF), is a qualified social worker, learning disability nurse, and Registered Manager. She has worked extensively with children, families, and adults with learning disabilities and complex health needs. She serves as the Chair of CFIF. Anstance is passionate about supporting social work practice in Africa through the IFSW Africa Region.

Paul Michael Garrett, University of Galway, Ireland, is the author of several books and has been described by the *International Journal of Social Welfare*, as 'probably the most important critical social work theorist in the English-speaking world'.

Elizabeth Onyedikachi George is a social worker and academic who currently works as a doctoral research fellow at VID Specialized University (Norway). Her research interests include disability studies, citizenship studies, and anti-oppressive social work, with the goal being to highlight Nigerian and African voices and perspectives.

Mel Gray (PhD), Professor Emeritus (Social Work), has published widely on social work in Africa over the last 40 years, most recently editing the first *Routledge Handbook of Social Work and Social Development in Africa* (2017) and co-authoring *Social Work, Social Welfare and Social Development in Nigeria* (with Solomon Amadasun) (Routledge, 2023).

Ashenafi Hagos Baynesagn (PhD) is an Associate Professor at the School of Social Work, Addis Ababa University, Ethiopia. He teaches social work practice, community development, and research methods courses. Ashenafi has also served in various administrative positions at the university. His research interests include community development, migration, refugees, population movement, and social work education.

Eleanor Hendricks is an Associate Professor at the University of Limpopo, South Africa. Eleanor is a passionate academic whose key research areas include social media, school violence, reproductive health, and gender-based violence. Eleanor has taught an array of undergraduate courses. She has also supervised several students in various fields at Masters and Doctoral level. She has been in the field of academia for 6 years, and practiced as a field social worker for 6 years.

Christo Heunis is an Associate Professor at the Centre for Health Systems Research & Development, University of the Free State, South Africa. He holds a PhD in Sociology. His research interests are from a social and implementation science perspective: health systems and public health programmes for tuberculosis, human immunodeficiency virus, the TB-HIV nexus, and the COVID-19 pandemic.

Richard Ingram is a Professor of Social Work at the University of Dundee. His social work practice background is in the context of children, education, families, and youth work. His principal research interests include relationship-based practice, emotions, student experiences, and international perspectives in social work education. He is the co-editor in chief of *Social Work Education: The International Journal* and is the UK representative on the executive committee of the European Association of Schools of Social Work.

Otieno Edwine Jeremiah, Tangaza University College, Kenya, holds a Bachelor of Arts degree in Sustainable Human Development, currently pursuing an MBA. Otieno holds a diploma in Development Studies and Social Work and has written four book chapters and two journal articles. He also provides youth mentorship. Otieno is undertaking an engagement at Radicle Global under a project.

Mariëtte Joubert holds a B.Soc.Sc. in Social Work and a Master of Social Work obtained from the University of the Free State, South Africa. Joubert is currently enrolled for her PhD in Disaster

Management at DiMTEC. Her research interests focus on forensic social work, professional court reports and disaster social work.

Felix Kakowa is a Senior Lecturer in Social Work at the University of Malawi and former President of the Association of Social Workers in Malawi. He has great passion for the development of professional social work in Malawi and has coordinated training of Practice Educators in collaboration with Children and Families International Foundation.

Marissa Kaloga is a tenure-track faculty member in the School of Social Sciences at the University of Otago in Aotearoa New Zealand. Her global, interdisciplinary research uses qualitative methods, social network analysis, and futuring to explore the potential for innovation and entrepreneurship to advance social, economic, and environmental justice.

Peninah Kansiime (PhD) is a social work lecturer at Edith Cowan University. Prior to becoming an academic, she practiced social work in different geographical contexts. Her research interests include conflict-related sexual violence, decolonisation, religion and spirituality, plus indigenous world views. Peninah trains students to become critically reflective practitioners.

Demelash Kassaye, Dr. Comdr., is an Associate Professor of Social Work and Social Development at the School of Social Work, Addis Ababa University, Ethiopia. Formerly, he was a police officer who served in the Ethiopian police for more than 25 years. His area of research includes policing, crime, social work, peace, and security.

Milliam Kiconco is both a sociologist and an educationist. Milliam is a teacher by profession. She has taught at the university level in Uganda for 18 years. She currently works as a lecturer at Kyambogo University, Uganda, in the Department of Sociology, Anthropology, and Population Studies, Faculty of Social Sciences.

Meinrad Haule Lembuka is a Lecturer in Social Work at The Open University of Tanzania at the Department of Sociology and Social Work. He is a multidisciplinary expert, knowledgeable in the areas of HIV/AIDS, key populations, social work, social welfare policies, international relations, gender, social policies, and Ubuntu. He has published several articles and chapter book contributions in social work, social development, community development, and Ubuntu practice.

Susan Levy is Associate Dean International and Senior Lecturer in Social Work in the School of Humanities, Social Sciences and Law, University of Dundee, UK. Her research centres on international, indigenous, and culturally relevant social work, with a focus on Africa; and the social dimensions of arts-based practices. She recently co-edited with Uzoma Okoye, the special issue: 'New Directions in Social Work Education in Africa: Challenges and Prospects' in *Social Work Education: The International Journal*.

Thembelihle Brenda Makhanya, (PhD) is a senior lecturer and acting program leader at the University of Mpumalanga, South Africa. Makhanya has published widely, is a member of the Ubuntu Research Group, and appointed to the Editorial Advisory Committee of the Social Work/ Maatskaplike Werk (SW/MW) journal. She is a founder and a chairperson of Imbewu Youth Empowerment Centre, an NGO offering pyschosocial needs to young peope. She was runnerup in the Association of South African Social Work Education Institutions (ASASWEI), Emerging Social Work Educator of the Year, 2021.

Tumani Malinga is a Senior Lecturer in the Department of Social Work, University of Botswana. She holds a PhD in Social Work and Minor in Gender Relations in International Development,

University of Illinois at Urbana-Champaign, Urbana, USA. Her interest is exploring experiences of low-income women, mental health issues, and social work education.

Mmaphuti Mamaleka is a Senior Lecturer at the University of Venda, South Africa. Her teaching focuses are supervision, management, as well as fieldwork practice, and she specializes in supervision and management. Areas of interest include parenting, gender-based violence, and Afrocentricity (indigenous knowledge systems). She supervises undergraduate and postgraduate research. She presents at conferences.

Ntandoyenkosi Maphosa (PhD) is a Lecturer at the University of Johannesburg, South Africa. She holds a Bachelors Degree in Social Work, a Masters qualification in Community Development and a PhD in Social Work. Her research interests include gender-based violence, women empowerment issues, community development, and social work teaching and learning.

Washington Marovatsanga holds a PhD from the University of Galway, Ireland. He has worked at Atlantic Technological University (ATU), Ireland, and contributed to graduate social work programmes at University College Cork and University of Galway. He served as an elected board member of the Irish Association of Social Workers (IASW).

Thabisa Matsea is a Senior Lecturer at the University of Venda in Limpopo Province, South Africa. She has more than ten years teaching experience in higher education. Her research interests include mental health in rural settings, teaching and learning in higher education, social work, as well as HIV and AIDS.

Magnus Mfoafo-M'Carthy is a Professor of Social Work at Wilfrid Laurier University in Canada. His research interests include global mental health, disability, and mental illness and stigma among immigrant communities. He is involved in multiple collaborative projects in Canada, Ghana, and other parts of the world.

Abigail A. Mills is a Senior Lecturer at the Department of Social Work, University of Ghana. Her research activities span the fields of disability, education, and health. Her current research explores sexual and reproductive health issues among adolescents with visual or hearing disabilities, and inclusive education for learners with visual disabilities in Ghana.

Wilkins Ndege Muhingi holds a PhD in Social Work, MSc., and a BSc. in Social Work and Health Care, currently a Medical Social Work Lecturer at Jomo Kenyatta University of Agriculture and Technology, Kenya, previously a Lecturer and Deputy Director of graduate studies and research at Pan Africa Christian University.

Emebet Mulugeta (PhD) is an Assistant Professor at the School of Social Work, Addis Ababa University, Ethiopia, and a consultant on issues related to vulnerable and disadvantaged groups and children in contact with the law. Besides teaching and research responsibility, Emebet is also involved in different community service activities aiming to capacitate different government and civil society organisations working to respect children's and women's rights.

Lawrence Murphy is the founder of Worldwide Therapy Online in Canada. He is a clinical practitioner, a pioneer in cyber counselling, and a notable social worker. Lawrence has great expertise in cyber counselling and he trains practitioners worldwide. His research area includes social development, cyber counselling, and mental health.

Diana Nabbumba (PhD) is a social worker practising in home and community aged care. She is a casual academic and adjunct research fellow at La Trobe University, Australia. Her research interests are rural aged healthcare, care for older people, social policy, decolonisation, spirituality, and workforce training.

Alice Ncube is a Senior Lecturer at DiMTEC, UFS, South Africa. Ncube holds a PhD and Master's in Disaster Management and a postgraduate diploma in gender studies. Her research interests are social vulnerability and climate change, international forced migration, gender issues, climate change and adaptation resilience and sustainable livelihoods of disadvantaged communities.

Tatenda Goodman Nhapi holds a Bachelor's degree in Social Work and Graduate, Erasmus Mundus MA Advanced Development in Social Work. Tatenda has experience in Zimbabwe's Department of Social Development. Besides being a UK frontline practitioner, Tatenda is a Research Associate with the University of Johannesburg, South Africa, Department of Social Work and Community Development.

Chinwe Nnama-Okechukwu, University of Nigeria, is an accomplished professional in social work practice and education. Her areas of expertise are child/family welfare, public health, policy/programme review, qualitative research, humanitarian assistance, and technical report writing. Through her expertise and scholarly pursuits, she contributes significantly to the advancement of social work in Nigeria and Africa.

James Kutu Obeng is an Early-Stage Researcher in the ASTRA project. He works as a researcher at the Natural Resources Institute Finland (Luke) and a doctoral researcher at the University of Jyväskylä, Finland. His current research focuses on the use of the natural environment to promote sustainable wellbeing.

Uzoma Odera Okoye is a Professor in the Department of Social Work at the University of Nigeria, Nsukka, and holds a PhD in Social Gerontology. She has authored over a hundred journal articles and chapters on different social issues. She has supervised and graduated over 40 Masters and 20 PhD students. Her current research interests include older adults, climate change, migration, and public health.

Tracy B.E. Omorogiuwa, a quintessential academic, who has pioneered the social work field education of the University of Benin, Nigeria, since 2008. She has to her credit a number of papers and four flagship texts on social work, which are serving the needs of social work students and practitioners in Nigeria.

Chinyere Onalu is a Lecturer and Researcher in the Department of Social work, University of Nigeria, Nsukka, with keen interest in the areas of public health and related issues.

Abiodun Blessing Osaiyuwu is a Lecturer at the University of Benin, Nigeria, with research focused on child labour, child protection, mental health, and gender issues. As a qualified social worker, she has practised in the United Kingdom, within public sector organisations, working with disabled people and in mental health and family and child care.

Rita Parry is a Social Worker from the University of Ghana with work experience in promoting the rights of women and girls in Ghana. In Europe, she has experience with organisations in the area of child welfare. Her research currently focuses on migration studies, exploring the challenges of transnational families.

Selelo Frank Rapholo holds a PhD in Social Work. He is Associate Professor and the Head of Department (HoD) attached to the Department of Social Work, University of Limpopo, South Africa. Dr. Rapholo has taught social work for a number of years and has successfully supervised postgraduate research. He has published a number of articles and book chapters. His niche area is child protection and public health.

Mziwandile Sobantu is an Associate Professor at the University of Johannesburg, South Africa. He obtained his BSW and Masters in Housing and Human Settlement degrees at the University of the Witwatersrand. He also holds a PhD in Social Work from the University of Johannesburg. He writes mainly on housing and social development.

Michael Emru Tadesse is a doctoral researcher in the ASTRA Project at the Free University of Bozen-Bolzano, Italy. He is also a former lecturer and head of the Department of Social Work at Mizan-Tepi University, Ethiopia. He currently studies the social solidarity economy of people of African descent in Europe.

Pius Tanga holds a PhD and is currently a full professor of Social Work at the University of Fort Hare, South Africa. His research interests are in household poverty dynamics, social protection, and social work education. Pius has published extensively, and he is a recipient of many research awards.

Felicia Tuggle is an Assistant Professor in the Department of Sociology, Anthropology, and Social Work at Auburn University, USA. Her research focuses on the role of social work education and practice in advancing sustainable development via interprofessional and multi-sector collaborations in the areas of health, education, and democracy.

Sharlotte Tusasiirwe (PhD) is a Lecturer of Social Work at Western Sydney University, Australia. She is the author of the book *Decolonising and Reimagining Social Work in Africa: Alternative Epistemologies and Practice Models* (Routledge, 2023); co-author of *Re-imagining Social Work: Towards Creative Practice* (Cambridge University Press, 2024), and co-editor of *Ubuntu Philosophy and Decolonising Social Work Fields of Practice in Africa* (Routledge, 2024).

Cecilia Tutu-Danquah is a Lecturer and Counselling Psychologist at the University of Ghana. She is the principal of TUCEE Institute of Counselling and Technology. Cecilia is an expert in pedagogy and andragogy, a distinguished social worker, and an educational technologist. Her research area includes mental health and social development.

Marichen Van der Westhuizen is the Head of the Department of Social Work at the University of the Western Cape, South Africa, with research focus areas including supported education, decolonised social work education and training, ecological social work, intercultural social work and the arts, and substance use disorders.

Oghenechoja Dennis Veta (PhD), University of Ilorin, Ilorin, Nigeria, is a professional social worker. He worked with the Delta State Civil Service Commission, Department of Community Development, Ministry of Women Affairs, Community, and Social Development. He achieved the level of Assistant Chief Community Development Officer, and later left for academia.

Janet Walker is Visiting Professor (International Social Work) University of Lincoln, UK, where she was previously Deputy Head/Head of Social Work. She is a Trustee of the charity Children and Families International Foundation (CFIF), working alongside colleagues in Malawi supporting them in developing their social work education and projects that support communities.

Ajwang' Warria, University of Calgary, Canada, worked in the counter-human trafficking field and practiced as a social worker. She continues to provide her expertise as an advisory board member on a project spearheaded by the International Rescue Committee and UNICEF and as a Think Tank member with the Olympic Refuge Foundation (ORF).

Agnes Gogo Wizi Kambala is a Lecturer in Social Work at the University of Malawi. She holds a Master of Arts in Social Work from Durham University (UK) and a Bachelor of Education from the University of Malawi. Her research interests include social work pedagogy, disability, youth development, and child protection.

Zibonele France Zimba holds a PhD in Social Work. He is a lecturer of community development and leadership at the University of Johannesburg, South Africa. His research agenda currently focuses on cultural practices with implications in social work, social work and technologies, and social work with disabilities.

ACKNOWLEDGEMENTS

The origins of this *Handbook* date back to 2019 and the first meeting between Levy and Okoye in the Social Work Department, University of Nigeria. The meeting covered many issues, including the challenges faced by Nigerian and, more broadly, African scholars in publishing their work and the dominance of Western literature in social work education. Over the intervening years we have been collaborating and working to address the challenges identified in that initial meeting. This has been achieved through a number of initiatives, including British Academy funded African Social Work Writing Workshops, an edited special edition of *Social Work Education: The International Journal*, and this *Handbook*.

We thank the British Academy for funding the African Social Work Writing Workshops that brought together early career researchers from across Africa. All the workshop participants have published at least one paper since the workshops, and most have a chapter in this *Handbook*. We also want to thank Taylor and Francis, the publisher of 'New Directions in Social Work Education in Africa: Challenges and Prospects', the special edition of *Social Work Education: International Journal*, for giving us permission to republish the paper by Kaloga and Camara on social work in Guinea, as Chapter 17 in this *Handbook*. Finally, our thanks are extended to all of our authors for their commitment to this *Handbook* and for driving change and influencing the future of social work in Africa and across the globe.

FOREWORD

Mel Gray

Following on from the special issue of *Social Work Education: International Journal* (Levy and Okoye, 2023), this *Handbook* expands on the diverse discourses influencing contemporary social work education in sub-Saharan Africa. Africa is a vast geographically and culturally diverse continent that has had a marked impact on international social work education. It has initiated various discourses, from launching the worldwide indigenisation debate in the north to introducing developmental social work in the south and, most recently, gifting the concept of Ubuntu to the profession's Global Agenda. The influence of social work education in Africa cannot be overstated. It preceded and shaped practice. As in the West, prior to social work education, volunteers and charity workers and, in Africa, missionaries performed many functions social workers later claimed within their professional repertoire. Though many scholars point to traditional helping and indigenous community care as early social work in Africa, social work, as accepted internationally today, is the professional domain of university-educated practitioners with a four-year bachelor of social work degree. African educators constantly strive to meet internationally prescribed values and ethics, and education and practice standards, and to shape the profession in accordance with international social work definitions. They also replicate and adhere to a professional organisational structure shaped by international social work organisations, constituting one of the five world regions.

Most importantly, social work education is an industry within a knowledge economy that spawns lucrative publications for thriving publishing companies that continue to absorb smaller locally based outlets. These publishing houses play a huge role in internationalising social work with social work educators their main contributors. Likewise, myriad influences shape the practice domain, which, in the face of minimalistic public welfare provision in many African countries, give non-government organisations a major role in the social service sector. Again this is a sector where international organisations exert huge control over policy and areas and methods of service provision, and who provides those services. These two contexts are the main employers of social work practitioners in Africa. There have been constant complaints that social work education does not prepare social workers adequately for practice, that what universities teach them does not fit the requirements of the practice contexts in which they will work. The lack of appropriate, properly supervised field placements exacerbates this situation. Several chapters collectively provide an in-depth account of the challenges of fieldwork education, including resource constraints, non-recognition of the profession, the dearth of social work placement agencies and suitably qualified supervisors, and recommendations to respond to this situation. As Gray et al. (2017, 2018) found in their research on fieldwork in southern and eastern Africa, these persistent issues for African social work educators require innovative solutions.

Equally, social workers complain about poor working conditions, extremely low salaries, their poor status and lack of recognition of the value of their services, retention issues and high staff turnover, and the exodus of social workers to more lucrative foreign countries, creating a large diaspora in North America, Europe, and Australasia. The latter provides evidence that social work education programs train social workers in Western social work theories and methods, which are not suited to culturally diverse African contexts. Nevertheless, universities continue to produce thousands of social work graduates each year, many of whom will leave the profession due to the difficulties of working in the poorly resourced social services sector.

Another factor that continues to plague social work education in Africa is poorly prepared academics, many drawn from related social science disciplines, without any professional training or practice experience in social work. Many begin teaching social work as postgraduate students and, once qualified, carry huge teaching loads. Due to excessive workloads and administrative, educational, and student demands, many educators complain that they do not have time for research and writing, or even for preparing culturally relevant curricula, courses, and teaching materials. They are on a treadmill, trapped in Western knowledge and pedagogical methods, with libraries filled mainly with out-of-date Western texts. Thus, the ongoing themes in the discourse on social work education in Africa: The lingering colonial legacy and dependence on Western curricula; lack of indigenous teaching material and outmoded teaching practices; struggle to reorient the curriculum from remedial casework to community-centred and culturally relevant practice; and underproduction and underuse of social research. Gray et al. discuss these issues in the opening chapter.

I have painted this bleak picture so you can better understand and appreciate the sterling work of social work educators and scholars and the tough challenges they face. This book attests to their stout efforts to improve social work education in Africa. It attests to their important role as critics and commentators, holding politicians and decision-makers to account, questioning unjust policies and practices, and seeking the best for their students and socioeconomic sector.

Traversing 13 of Africa's 54 sovereign African countries, the chapters cover many of the regions and countries where social work education has a presence, including in Cameroon in Central Africa; Ethiopia, Kenya, Tanzania, and Uganda in East Africa; Botswana, Malawi, South Africa, Zambia, and Zimbabwe in southern Africa; and Ghana, Guinea, and Nigeria in West Africa. Absent are Muslim countries in northern Africa, like Egypt, with a long history of social work and from which the indigenisation debate began. Brought to Africa by European colonisers, most countries where social work has obtained a foothold have equally embraced Christianity and, as several of the chapters in this collection show, this is extremely important in African cultures heavily embedded in spiritual beliefs and practices. Social work's Judeo-Christian values are consistent with African cultures heavily steeped in the philosophy of Ubuntu. Absent then are issues relating to Islamic social work's development in northern Nigeria and Egypt, for example.

This aside, the chapters show the huge variations across the countries covered that make the concept of 'African social work' and 'African social work education' as problematic as notions like 'Western social work'. Africa is a linguistically, culturally, ethically, and religiously diverse continent, with divisions that have spawned violence and conflict, and humanitarian problems relating to poverty, hunger, AIDS and HIV, migrants, refugees, trafficked and internally displaced people, and gender-based violence. These are 'wicked problems' that social workers in humanitarian non-governmental organisations (NGOs) encounter, while those in public services are frequently locked into statutory child and youth services. The chapters reflect social work's presence in health and the challenges of responding to the COVID-19 pandemic and its growing role in environmental interventions, especially disaster responses. They show the broad range of issues and problems for inclusion in the social work curriculum. Collectively, they comprise a sound contribution to the discourse and growing literature on social work education in Africa. Most importantly, they highlight persistent problems with professional knowledge transfer and the challenges for those seeking to decolonise African social work education by increasing local content in teaching social work and preparing students for culturally relevant practice. However, African social work educators need to be knowledgeable about, and mindful of, global social work and global issues, by working and developing interdependent relationships with colleagues in the West. Many Northern academics court African universities eager to give their students international social work placements. Resultantly, Northern academics become a voice for African social work education, reinterpreting their experiences through a Western lens. African educators need to be more vocal. They need to make their mark on the global stage, highlighting the complexities of transferring and imposing outside knowledge to address internal problems. African educators and scholars can take the lead in conceptualising social work from an African perspective and blaze a path in social work's response to, inter alia, environmental events, human trafficking, internally displacement, and political and gender-based violence. This collection is a step in this direction as African educators find their voices and speak from their local experiences to a global audience.

References

Gray, M., Agllias, K., Mupedziswa, R., & Mugumbate, J. (2017). The role of social work field education programs in the transmission of developmental social work knowledge in Southern and East Africa. *Social Work Education, 36*(6), 623–635. http://dx.doi.org/10.1080/02615479.2017.1310833

Gray, M., Agllias, K., Mupedziswa, R., & Mugumbate, J. (2018). The expansion of developmental social work in Southern and Eastern Africa: Opportunities and challenges for social work field programs. *International Social Work, 61*(6), 974–987. https://doi.org/10.1177/0020872817695399

Levy, S. and Okoye, U. (2023) 'New Directions in Social Work Education in Africa: Challenges and Prospects', Special Issue *Social Work Education: International Journal*, 165-168, https://doi.org/10.1080/02615479.2023.2181530

ACRONYMS AND ABBREVIATIONS

AASOGUI	Association of Guinean Social Workers
ACRWC	African Charter on the Rights and Welfare of the Child
AfrIPEN	Africa Interprofessional Education Network
AfDB	Africa Development Bank
AGTS	Association Guinéene des Travailleurs Sociaux (Guinean Association of Social Workers)
AIK	African Indigenous Knowledge
ANAS-Guinée	Association National des Assistants Sociaux-Guinee
ANPPCAN	African Network on Prevention and Protection against Child Abuse and Neglect
ART	Antiretroviral Therapy
ASASWEI	Association of South African Social Work Education Institutions
ASSWOT	Association of Schools of Social Work in Tanzania
ASWEA	Association of Social Work Education in Africa
ASWM	Association of Social Workers in Malawi
ASWNet	Africa Social Work Network
ATR	African Traditional Religion
AU	African Union
BSW	Bachelor of Social Work
CBO	Community Based Organisation
CBWCY	Community Based Work with Children and Youth
CCPA	Canadian Counselling and Psychotherapy Association
CCPWs	Community Child Protection Workers
CDOs	Community Development Officers
CENAFOD	African Centre of Training for Development
CHE	Council on Higher Education
CIRD	Center Internationale de Récherche et Documentation
COVID-19	Coronavirus disease (*SARS-CoV-2 virus*)
CP	Collaborative practice
CPD	Continuing Professional Development
CPSS	Child Protection Sub-Sector
CRA	Children's Rights Act (2003)

Acronyms and abbreviations

CSO	Civil Society Organisation
CSWE	Council of Social Work Education
CSWZ	Council of Social Workers of Zimbabwe
DCPWS	Department of Child Protection and Welfare Services
DSC	Department of Correctional Services
DSD	Department of Social Development
DSW	Department of Social Work
ECOWAS	Economic Community of West African States
ELT	Experiential Learning Theory
ENAAS	Ecole Nationale des Assistants des Affaires Sociales
ENAM	Ecole Nationale d' Administration et Magistracie
ENSK	L'Ecole Nationale de la Sante de Kindia
EPAS	Educational Policy and Accreditation Standards
EPRDF	Ethiopian People's Revolutionary Democratic Front
FIDS	Faculty of Integrated Development Studies
FGN	Federal Government of Nigeria
FMWASD	Federal Ministry of Women Affairs and Social Development
FOGUIReD	Italian Guineo Fund for the Reconversion of Debt
FRN	Federal Republic of Nigeria
FSW	Faculty of Social Work
GCCHI	Ghana Cross-Cultural Healthcare Immersion
GOZ	Government of Zimbabwe
HEI	Higher Education Institution
HIV/AIDS	Human Immunodeficiency Virus/Acquired Immuno-Deficiency Syndrome
HKMU	Hubert Kairuku Memorial University
IAC	International Association of Counsellors
IASSW	International Associations of Schools of Social Work
ICSW	International Council on Social Welfare
ICT	Information Communication Technologies
IFSW	International Federation of Social Work
IKS	Indigenous Knowledge Systems
INFTS	Institute National de Formation en Travail Sociale
INGO	International Non-Governmental Organisation
IO	International Organisation
IPCAGHP	Interprofessional and Collaborative Applied Global Health Practice
IPE	Interprofessional Education
IPECP	Interprofessional Education and Collaborative Practice
ISW	Institute of Social Work
LASAG	Sonfonia's Laboratoire d'Analyse Socio-Anthropologique de Guinée
MASCFE	Ministry of Social Affairs, the Promotion of Women and Children
MCP	Malawi Congress Party
MENRS	Ministry of National Education and Scientific Research
MoGCDSW	Ministry of Gender, Children, Disability and Social Welfare
MoHCDGEC	Ministry of Health Community Development Gender, Elderly and Children
MSW	Master of Social Work
NACTE	National Accreditation Council for Technical Education
NAJASOGUI	New Guinean Association of Young Social Workers

Acronyms and abbreviations

NASW	National Association of Social Workers
NCHE	National Council for Higher Education
NDP	National Development Plan
NEPAD	New Partnership for Africa's Development
NGO	Non-Governmental Organisation
NHRC	National Human Rights Commission
NPC	National Planning Commission
NSFAS	National Student Financial Aid Scheme
NNGO	National Non-Governmental Organisation
NQF	National Qualification Framework
NSO	National Statistical Office
NSPPF	National Social Protection Policy Framework for Zimbabwe
PACA	Protection and Affordable Care Act
PE	Practice Educator
PGDSW	Postgraduate Diploma in Social Work
PTSD	Post-traumatic Stress Disorder
PWLE	People With Lived Experience
REPSSI	Regional Psychosocial Support Initiative
SACAP	South African College of Applied Science
SACSSP	South African Council for Social Service Professions
SAQA	South African Qualification Authority
SDG	Sustainable Development Goal
SFDRR	Sendai Framework for Disaster Risk Reduction
SRD	Social Relief of Distress
SSA	Sub Saharan Africa
SSW	Schools of Social Work
SSWIM	Supporting Social Work in Malawi
SWA	Social Welfare Assistant
SWO	Social Welfare Officer
TASWO	Tanzania Association of Social Workers
TCU	Tanzania Commission of University
TESWEP	Tanzania Emerging Schools of Social Work Programme
UB	University of Botswana
UCT	University of Cape Town
UDS	University of Development Studies
UFH	University of Fort Hare
UGLC	Université General Lasana Conté
UKZN	University of KwaZulu-Natal
UN	United Nations
UNCRC	United Nations Convention on the Rights of the Child
UNDP	United Nations Development Programme
UNESCO	United Nations Education Scientific and Cultural Organization
UNICEF	United Nations Children's Fund
UNISA	University of South Africa
UNN	University of Nigeria, Nsukka
USA	United States of America
USAID	United States Agency for International Development

Acronyms and abbreviations

VVF	Vesical-Vaginal Fistula
WIL	Work-integrated learning
WHO	World Health Organisation
WLU	Wilfrid Laurier University
WMO	World Meteorological Organisation
YWCA	Young Women Christian Association

INTRODUCTION

Susan Levy, Uzoma O. Okoye, Richard Ingram, and Pius T. Tanga

Abstract

The Introduction to the *Routledge Handbook on African Social Work Education* contextualises the book within contemporary global shifts to creating social work education that is responsive to local conditions and is culturally relevant. Approaches to transitioning away from the hegemony of Western literature, knowledge, and practice models currently underpinning African social work education are introduced. Ways of working with different knowledge systems and worldviews, different ways of knowing, doing, and seeing social work, are introduced as a foundation for reciprocal learning and knowledge exchange between the Global South and the Global North. Chapters covering Central Africa: Cameroon; East Africa: Ethiopia, Kenya, Tanzania, and Uganda; Southern Africa: Botswana, Malawi, South Africa, Zambia, Zimbabwe; and West Africa: Ghana, Guinea, and Nigeria are introduced under the four themed sections in the *Handbook*: 1. Approaches to Indigenising, Decolonising, and Developing Culturally Relevant Social Work Education, 2. Social Work Education: Evolution across Contexts, 3. Embedding Field Practicum into Social Work Education, and 4. Knowledge Exchange between the Global South and the Global North. The context of the *Handbook* is Africa, yet the topics covered are relevant to ongoing debates in social work, social welfare, social development, and sustainability across the globe.

Social work education across the globe is constantly evolving, reflecting, and aligning with developments in practice, knowledge, and understanding as well as adjusting to social, cultural, and political contextual changes. This responsive and reactive element of social work education occurs in a myriad of ways, sometimes local in nature whilst at other times it can have a global character. This *Routledge Handbook on African Social Work Education* explores, contests, and provides unique insights into contemporary social work education in Africa and the prevailing dynamic process and challenge of knitting the local with the global (Levy et al., 2022; Ragab, 2017). Throughout the *Handbook*, the reader will find the content and focus of African social work education in transition or at a crossroads, as new paths are forged to create a new culturally relevant era of social work. Indigenous knowledge and decolonising curricula are central points, from which the chapters radiate out and coalesce, making visible and connecting social work with the environment through ecosocial work; the arts through traditional cultural practices; development and engagement with the United Nations Sustainable Development Goals (UNSDGs); and through bringing to the fore religion and spirituality as core to everyday African lives. Contemporary and traditional issues are intertwined as discussions cover what is relevant and meaningful for current social work as well as what makes social work uniquely African.

This is a timely book with a unique focus on social work education in Africa with relevance to social work, social welfare, social development, and sustainability in Africa, the Global South more generally, as well as the Global North. Geography does not delineate or divide interest in decolonising and diversifying social work curricula and understanding ways to teach and engage students in issues around race, ethnicity, power, social justice, and cultural understanding. These issues are present across the globe, and they are made manifest through the voices, challenges, and arguments presented here. The book contributes to shaping ways to build a foundation of indigenous literature to facilitate the transition away from the hegemony of Western literature, knowledge, and practice models (Midgley, 1981; Osei-Hwedie, 1995; Shawky, 1972).

The *Handbook* traverses the vast and varied continent of Africa, providing the reader with multiple approaches and insights into social work education in 13 countries with each chapter distilling pathways for change through recommendations. The chapters cover Central Africa: Cameroon; East Africa: Ethiopia, Kenya, Tanzania, and Uganda; Southern Africa: Botswana, Malawi, South Africa, Zambia, Zimbabwe; and West Africa: Ghana, Guinea, and Nigeria.

As a profession, social work is at the forefront of driving and achieving social change and social justice, and addressing the UNSDGs across the globe. The contributions in this *Handbook* evidence similarities and dissimilarities across Africa in terms of social work education, and the same can be said for within the countries covered where consistency is not necessarily the norm. There are chapters based in countries where there is currently no social work training, and where there is little, if any, published literature on social work (Guinea and Cameroon). For others, social work is more established, and the impact and effectiveness of the profession is the key priority (for example, South Africa and Nigeria). The variance across countries is visible in terms of levels of social protection and social welfare, the evolution and status of the social work profession, and the impact this then has on the priorities and pressures facing educators. Some authors question the dominance of urban social work when the majority of Africans live in rural locations (for example, Bhangyi et al. and Lemkuka), whilst, for others, the lack of regulation and professional status leave social work vulnerable to legislative and structural interpretation, whereby the role and purpose of social work is not reserved or protected (for example, Malawi and Ethiopia). As documented in this *Handbook*, the ambition for professional recognition and status is mirrored in academia, with social work courses frequently located within wider academic discipline groupings such as sociology, social policy, criminology, and psychology. This can leave social work education with a less prominent voice within established academic environments, thus adding an additional challenge when seeking to evolve and change.

Social workers wherever they are located in the world are in a privileged position to be able to enter the lives of a range of different people, build relationships, understand diverse lived experiences, and collaboratively co-create positive outcomes. Effective and meaningful change at all levels, whether at the individual, family, community, society, or policy level, emerges from knowing your subject and its context. Social work education is fundamental to building a foundation for future practitioners. That is social workers who can work with complexity, uncertainty, and diversity, but who can also understand cultural touch points and are orientated to what is familiar and local. A central narrative running through the chapters of this *Handbook* is the need to Africanise and indigenise social work education, to break the hegemony of Western knowledge and practice models that have not, and are not, providing a foundation for future practitioners to know their subject and their context (Mwansa, 2011). The language of indigenising, decolonising, diversifying, or developing culturally relevant curriculum all require a base of African research and literature to enable change to happen. This requires new knowledge that is rooted in contemporary African social issues that can lend a greater sense of relevance and applicability to practice (Gray et al., 2008; Rankopo and Osei-Hwedie, 2011; Twikirize and Spitzer, 2019). Whilst centring on

Introduction

Africanism and the need for African solutions to African problems, the authors present a future that transcends the juxtaposing of Western and African knowledge in binary form through acknowledging the strengths, learning, and change that can be achieved through working with different knowledge systems and worldviews, different ways of knowing, doing, and seeing social work.

Along with exploring and providing examples of how African social work education is being indigenised, the *Handbook* advances the discourse on this topic. Through engaging with the emerging tensions arising from traditional cultural practices coming face to face with global social work values and ethics, the book contests what it means to indigenise. Traditional ways of being and doing have a temporality, a social dimension, and spatial roots. Whilst some traditional practices transcend time and place, others now appear out of place in a continent that has experienced colonialism/post-colonialism and globalisation. A key challenge for social work educators is finding ways to work with the given reality through combining African and Western ways of being. The authors acknowledge that Western theory and practice models have proved inadequate in addressing social work educational and practice needs in Africa; however, rather than dismissing Western social work knowledge, the *Handbook* argues for reciprocal learning and knowledge exchange between the Global South and the Global North (Nuttman-Shwartz and Ranz, 2014). This is relevant for social work across the globe as the profession seeks change through the development of more inclusive and culturally relevant curricula based on interdependency, which is the essence of Ubuntu.

We live in a global world, which requires an awareness of, acknowledgement of, and engagement with living and working with interdependency, whether that be between different knowledges and world views, between people, across political borders, or with the environment. Many social problems have origins that are located at a global level but require a local response, and this includes the COVID-19 pandemic (2020–2022). COVID-19 provides a vivid and recent example of a global event which triggered a range of pedagogical challenges for social work education in terms of online provision, compromised field education, ways to respond to disasters, and exacerbation of prevailing social issues. The timing of this *Handbook* offers valuable insights into responses to the COVID-19 pandemic that avoided large fissures in students' learning, and provides examples of ways of working with uncertainty, and in times of large-scale disasters.

The *Handbook* comprises both empirical and conceptual chapters, and it is framed around four parts:

Part 1: Approaches to Indigenising, Decolonising, and Developing Culturally Relevant Social Work Education
Part 2: Social Work Education: Evolution across Contexts
Part 3: Embedding Field Practicum into Social Work Education
Part 4: Knowledge Exchange between the Global South and the Global North

As editors we have worked with the authors to encourage the use of examples to provide you, the reader, with a feel of what social work looks like and how it is experienced as well as key issues that currently make African social work education not only unique, but also familiar and similar to social work in other geographies. We offered authors the choice of submitting an abstract in a local language as a means through which the *Handbook* could engage in the power of language, to contest the prevailing dominance of English in social work education, and to role model alternative ways to present social work knowledge. Abstracts are presented in 14 languages. In addition, we asked authors to move beyond identifying prevailing challenges, to be outcomes orientated, leading to each chapter ending with three recommendations to progress and work towards change in African social work education.

Before moving on to introduce each of the chapters, we want to reflect on some absences, the areas of silence created by things that are not covered in the chapters and yet are ripe for further exploration. These centre on:

1. Theory: there is a growing literature on social work in Africa yet theorising and the development of new ways to conceive of African social work remains peripheral within the literature.
2. Practice Models: following on from the need for more African social work theorising, to enable practice to fully respond to local, contextualised issues, there is also the need for more culturally relevant practice models.
3. Regions: the *Handbook* covers sub-Saharan Africa (Central, East, Southern, and West Africa); we were unable to include the voices and insights from social work in North Africa.

Highlighting these areas of absences is designed to stimulate and drive future developments to extend the work presented here. The *Handbook* creates a much needed space to explore current social work education and to shape and influence its future, as well as to deliver an openness to discuss the persistent challenges and precariousness of social life and social work in the fascinating continent that is Africa.

Part 1: Approaches to Indigenising, Decolonising, and Developing Culturally Relevant Social Work Education

This opening part of the Handbook of eight chapters addresses indigenising, decolonising, and developing culturally relevant social work education. The chapters offer ways to rethink and reimagine African social work education through engaging and reflecting on what and how social work is currently taught in Africa, and where changes could be introduced to unsettle and challenge the legacies of colonialism. The chapters offer innovative and creative approaches from changes to pedagogy, the language/s used in social work teaching, the literature students engage with, and curriculum content.

The starting point for decolonising curriculum is having an alternative, non-Western body of literature that is culturally relevant. Chapter 1, by Gray, Levy, Okoye, and Amadasun, contests the narrative that there is little published literature on Nigerian social work that could be used to create a culturally relevant curriculum. The authors reviewed published literature on Nigerian social work and found 308 papers. With a focus on communal and cultural ways of being, ethics, and ethnicity, they highlight some of the complexities around developing a culturally relevant curriculum.

In Chapter 2, by Bhangyi, Kiconco, and Chui, the authors explore approaches to incorporating traditional informal ways of being and doing social work into social work education. They highlight that the reach of social work is limited across Africa, being largely centred in urban areas, when the majority of the population live in rural settlements. They call for embedding an informality paradigm into social work education, which, they argue, will better prepare students to work more closely with rural communities at a more localised level. Chapter 3, by Obeng and Tadesse, retains a link between the social and the spatial. This time the focus is on ecosocial work and the strong connections African's have with the physical environment and the spirit world. Drawing on data from social work curricula in Ethiopia, Ghana, Nigeria, and South Africa, Obeng and Tadesse demonstrate that there is little integration of the social connections with the environment in social work education, and they highlight the importance of this as a route to indigenous social work.

Introduction

Chapter 4, by Mamaleka, introduces African Indigenous Knowledge Systems (AIKS) and four African theories, which, it is argued, can be used for understanding African social work and the development of culturally relevant interventions that are responsive to local needs. She highlights how indigenous knowledge has been passed down orally through traditional art forms, including storytelling and folklore through the use of local languages, and she calls for the use of these languages in social work education. In Chapter 5, Makhanya and Levy return the reader to the topic of language and how the delivery of social work education in English disempowers. The chapter is situated within South Africa, a country with 11 official languages, and where the majority of people requiring social work support do not have English has a first language. The authors address translanguaging and epistemic injustice, with a focus on the language policy at the University of Kwa-Zulu Natal, which encourages the equal use of English and isiZulu, as a successful pathway for decolonising and creating culturally relevant social work education.

The next three chapters (Chapters 6–8) all cover the importance of religion and spirituality in African's day-to-day lives and the need to integrate this into curricula. Baynesagn, Abye, and Mulugeta focus on Ethiopia (Chapter 6); Veta on Nigeria (Chapter 7); and Rapholo and Zimba on South Africa (Chapter 8). The latter explore ways for social workers to work more closely with pastors who are seen as more accessible and central to supporting people through challenging times. All three chapters focus on Christianity, a religion of colonialism; however, it is an area of people's lives that has been transformed over the decades to become uniquely African, reflecting the deep spirituality of people across the continent. An emerging theme in these three chapters centres on the ethics of using ingenious knowledge when it conflicts with social work values, with calls for ways to develop strategies for social work to blend African and Western approaches that align with global social work values and ethics.

Part 2: Social Work Education: Evolution across Contexts

Part 2 comprises ten chapters, and the chapters are united by their keen sense of a need for change and the complexity of charting a steady course through the turbulent and, at times, contradictory priorities that are faced by social work educators. In many ways this theme reflects the wider messages contained within this *Handbook* in terms of the fluidity and flexibility required of social work practice and the academy. The purpose of social work is to reflect and address contemporary social issues and challenges within the contexts that they arise. The International Federation of Social Workers (IFSW) definition of social work that is referenced regularly throughout this *Handbook* provides a firm foundation for the profession and for social work educators, but the ways in which the vision is delivered and understood varies and evolves in response to external factors and nuances.

The chapters in Part 2 are united in their accounts of how social work education has responded to local and global phenomena. They speak of the need for educators to interface with practitioners, policymakers, and legislators to ensure that the content and pedagogical approach of social work education reflects and facilitates the ever-evolving focus and status of the profession. It is interesting that such responsiveness requires looking forward and backwards as social work educators seek to innovate, whilst maintaining a keen eye on the importance of the cultural context as well as wider social work values. It is inevitable that some of the chapters in Part 2 reference the COVID-19 pandemic and the direct and indirect impact that it has had on requiring change and prompting action. Such need for responsiveness was globally felt, but it is fascinating to see how such a global phenomenon was felt and experienced by social work educators in a range of contexts. Indeed, it has heightened the focus on the social work role in terms of taking a lead at times of profound change and disasters.

Part 2 opens with Osaiyuwu's Chapter 9, which explores the challenges facing child protection in Nigeria. The narrative vividly identifies the need for social work to define itself in the context of a multidisciplinary environment whilst holding onto and articulating its values and purpose. This challenge is viewed through a lens of reaching towards traditional communal conceptions of care whilst also identifying the need for governmental clarity and direction to ensure the safety of children. In Chapter 10, Buhori, writing from the context of Tanzania, similarly identifies a gap between current legislation and workforce capacity and the complexity of social needs requiring intervention. Indeed, the challenges facing social work education in terms of status within the corridors of academia are mirrored by the challenges of status in practice contexts. The traditional construct of *Msaragamba* is identified as a way of understanding the role of community elders in terms of a social work approach that is embedded in indigenous knowledge and, in turn, acts as a way of raising and clarifying the status of social work practice and education in a culturally relevant manner.

Chapter 11 by Maphosa and Sobantu uses the experience of the COVID-19 pandemic and the impact that this had on the pedagogical approaches utilised within social work programmes in South Africa. The chapter charts the historical evolution of social work pedagogy, rightly placing these recent challenges within a continuum of progression and responsiveness of social work education – whereby pedagogies evolve and become embedded whilst holding onto core values and intended outcomes. Hendricks and Ingram in Chapter 12 chart the experiences of educators and students in South Africa in terms of the pivot to the online delivery of social work education during the early stages of the pandemic. They argue that this universal response to the crisis was not equitable in its effectiveness and accessibility. The impact of the COVID-19 pandemic is further explored in Chapters 13 and 14 by Heunis, Joubert and Ncube, and Tutu-Danquah and Murphy, respectively, which cast a light on the implications for practice and the need for social workers to develop a skill set that helps them to respond to profound social disruptions as well as the potential shift to online modes of relationship building that may arise in such circumstances. Both chapters underline the symbiotic relationship between social work education and the external context and the need for adaptations and changes in focus to emerge and be embedded in real time.

Chapter 15 by Nhapi considers the maturation of social work education in Zimbabwe through the lens of developmental social work. This participative community-based approach vividly places social work as a 'front row witness' to social phenomenon and crucially underlines the need to lower barriers between academia and practice to enable social work education to deliver the knowledge and skills that will be most relevant and effective to meet contemporary challenges.

This need for evolution and relevance is further explored in Chapters 16 and 17, which are situated in Francophone Africa: Cameroon (Tanga and Ekobi) and Guinea (Kaloga and Camara). Neither country currently has a social work degree programme, yet the authors provide rich historical context, highlighting the limits of the European roots of social work in the two countries, and they call for an Afro-centric refresh for the future of social work education to reflect the realities of the local context. From the Guinean perspective, Kaloga and Camara frame this transition in the Transmission, Indigenisation, and Authentisation continuum.

The role of culture is further explored in the final chapter of Part 2, Chapter 18 by Muhingi, Warria, and Otieno, which focuses on the complex cultural considerations that need to be incorporated into medical social work education and training in Kenya. The chapter once again stresses the need for indigenous knowledge to be brought to bear on contemporary issues and debates emerging within practice and social work education.

Introduction

Part 3: Embedding Field Practicum into Social Work Education

Field practicum (field education, practice placement, and internship) is an integral component of social work education connecting theory to practice, and, as such, it is core to social work education. Part 3 provides insight into field practicum in Malawi, Nigeria, Tanzania, South Africa, Ethiopia, and Botswana. Whilst central to social work training, the current situation of field practicum across Africa comes with numerous challenges. These include the processes of field practicum, assessment of student learning and competence, and the training of field instructors. Combined, these challenges are presented as constituting a 'crisis' in field practicum in Africa. The authors argue that if these issues are not addressed, they pose a threat to the profession across the continent. Along with highlighting challenges, the chapters in Part 3 also demonstrate the salience of field practicum as a source of indigenous knowledge that students can develop whilst in the field and integrate into their learning journeys.

There are eight chapters in Part 3, and whilst there are chapters in other parts that are jointly written by African and non-African authors, all of the chapters in Part 3 are solely authored by Africans.

The first chapter in Part 3, Chapter 19 by Wizi-Kambala, explores the experiences and challenges of social work field practicum in Malawi where the profession is evolving and developing. The chapter discusses arrangements for field practicum at two of the countries universities, along with outlining challenges confronting field work practicum, focusing on resource constraints and the non-recognition of the profession in Malawi. Chapter 20 by Onalu, Nnama-Okechukwu, Agbawadikeizu, and Chukwu examines the dearth of standard social work agencies for field practicum as stumbling blocks for social work pedagogy in Nigeria. The authors recommend the placement of students during vacations within their localities and regular retraining of agency supervisors to mitigate some of the challenges.

Lemkuka's Chapter 21 deals with the situational analysis of social work field practice in Tanzania Mainland, with a particular focus on rural and developmental social work. The chapter echoes some of the challenges that are encountered in most African countries as well as highlighting concerns that students on field practice frequently undertake low-skilled and routine tasks that are not directly related to social work. The cause of this is situated within the shortage of qualified social work instructors, and the impact on students' future readiness for practice is discussed. The chapter by Omoroguiwa, Chapter 22, is based on a case study of the University of Benin, Nigeria. She introduces the reader to the structure and methods of field education at her university as well as discussing some of the limitations bedeviling this vital component of social work education. Suggestions for change that are presented include enhanced training of staff to support students in field practicum.

From Nigeria, we move to Ethiopia, and the perspectives of Ethiopian stakeholders. Chapter 23, by Kassaye, touches on the exposure of students to the complexities of culturally rich yet sensitive settings with diverse and at-risk populations. He highlights the opportunities for students, through field practicum, to be introduced to indigenous Ethiopian knowledge and traditional communal practices of care. From Botswana, Malinga, in Chapter 24, focuses on the use of a family genogram as an experiential method to enable students to gain an in-depth understanding of people's lives. She presents the genogram as a tool to enhance social work field practicum through using it to address the over-reliance on didactic teaching methods, to support students to build meaningful relationships with clients, to conceptualise concepts, as well as to train students in self-introspection in preparation for field practicum.

The final two chapters in Part 3 come from South Africa and discuss different responses to and perspectives on the impact of COVID-19 on field practicum. In Chapter 25, Matsea examines the impediments that confronted social work institutions during the COVID-19 pandemic and the challenges of adopting a hybrid form of field practicum compared with delivering campus-based hybrid lectures. This chapter reiterates the need for social work to remain agile and receptive to creative and innovative ways of implementing field practicums during future pandemics. Chapter 26 by Westhuizen, Davis, and Adonis discusses students' mental health issues that became apparent during the pandemic and the impact of this on students' readiness for practice. The chapter presents findings from an analysis of students' experiences during the COVID-19 pandemic and highlights the value of lived experiences and experiential knowledge when considering decolonial practice. The chapter recommends changes to fieldwork modules to better prepare students for field practicum when academic life is disrupted.

Part 4: Knowledge Exchange between the Global South and the Global North

In the final part, Part 4, the focus shifts to engaging with the reality that social work education in Africa cannot develop to the level we want it to without collaboration with social work educators from the Global North. Through their chapters, the authors discuss some of these collaborations and the importance as well as the need to bring in local knowledge while imbibing knowledge from the Global North. The chapters (re)confirm that knowledge exchange in social work education is largely one directional, namely, from the Global North to the Global South, which translates into continued dependency rather than interdependency. Whilst some of the authors argue that knowledge produced in Africa can be of benefit to the Global North, there are minimal examples in the chapters of how African knowledge is being used and how it could be integrated into social work education in the Global North. In other words, the prevailing narrative is of continued dependence of African social work on the Global North, which helps explain the essence of the advocacies around decolonisation of social work and reflects why formal social work in Africa has remained emerging and growing despite decades of presence in the region. Rebalancing the wheels of knowledge exchange across the regions of the world must be an agenda for global social work. Trust between regions and the issue of brain-drain through African scholars not returning home after spending time in the Global North is core to this future agenda. It is a conversation emerging from the chapters in Part 4 and should be discussed in subsequent academic platforms.

Part 4 comprises six chapters, opening with Chapter 27 by Parry, George, and Kaypnga, who highlight that social work education in Africa is Eurocentric, with little done to centre the sociocultural context and distinctive conditions of Africa. Drawing on narratives from social workers in Ghana, Nigeria, Uganda, Ethiopia, and Zambia, they demonstrate the importance of experiential knowledge gained through knowledge exchange opportunities, and they call for reciprocal learning between the Global South and the Global North through the rebalancing of a heavily theorised Western education model with everyday African experiences. Chapter 28 by Akesson and Mfoafo-M'Carthy provides an example of knowledge exchange and partnership between a Global South Ghanaian university and a Global North Canadian university, with a focus on child protection. The authors discuss the value of this collaboration, including challenging and contesting commonly held perceptions of African children that are frequently viewed through the lens of poverty, famine, and war, and they call for moving the dialogue forward to support the training of a robust social service workforce.

In Chapter 29, Kansiime, Tusiirew, and Nabbumba draw on personal experiences from studying and working in Ghana and the West. They introduce useful examples of knowledge transfer from the Global South to the Global North and the opportunities for co-constructed knowledge sharing to facilitate decolonisation by social work educators in African culture and indigenous knowledge. They introduce four channels for knowledge transfer: social work education; research; academic publications; and digital information-sharing platforms. The chapter recommends a review of social work curricula globally to examine the origins of the knowledge taught and co-constructed knowledge sharing to facilitate decolonisation attempts by social work educators in Africa. Chapter 30 by Marovatsanga and Garrett continues the theme of the transfer of knowledge from the Global South to the Global North. The chapter is situated in Ireland and highlights the importance of African scholars producing literature to decolonise and diversify curricula in the Global South as well as the Global North. Drawing on the experience of social work academics in Ireland, the authors highlight how the limited inclusion of different perspectives (African literature) in social work curriculum in Ireland constrains students' understanding and preparedness for working with cultural diversity, and they discuss the wider impact of this on service users and their outcomes.

Chapter 31 by Walker, Cauvain, Kakowa, and Fometu takes us back to Africa, specifically Malawi. The chapter examines field practicum in Malawi through the lens of decolonialisation and Ubuntu to offer an alternative approach to preparing students for practice. The chapter reports on a Malawi-UK collaboration on the training of practice educators and highlights knowledge exchange as a multidirectional process that is critical for addressing global challenges. Chapter 32 by Mills, Boateng, Banks, and Tuggle is the final chapter in the *Handbook*, and it focuses on integrating Interprofessional Education and Collaborative Practice (IPECP) into social work education. The authors note that even though IPECP is central to the future of integrated working across social work and health, very few social work programmes offer it in Africa. The chapter describes the collaboration between academics in Ghana and the United States to develop an IPECP curriculum centred on the Ubuntu philosophy. The chapter also provides an overview of inter-professional education in Africa and the United States, and it gives insights into the curriculum design process.

The final chapters all communicate an important narrative that is threaded throughout this *Handbook*. That narrative is focused on the synergies to be achieved from bringing ideas together, and from journeying away from dualist narratives that divide and position knowledges, practices, and ways of living in opposition to each other. Reciprocal learning between the Global South and the Global North, and working with diverse knowledges, will be at the heart of the future of social work.

The authors in this *Handbook* provide unique insights into social work education across Africa, building a foundation of literature to inform, shape, and reconceptualise curricula to move away from the dominance of Western theory and practice models. The chapters provide approaches and case studies, as well as identifying challenges to be confronted and addressed in moving indigenous knowledge of African social work from the periphery to the centre of social work education. We hope this work will enrich and broaden the lens of social work education across the continent of Africa and beyond to influence and impact lives across this world we share.

References

Gray, M., Coates, J., and Yellow Bird, M. (eds) (2008). *Indigenous Social Work Around the World: Towards Culturally Relevant Education and Practice*. Aldershot: Ashgate.

Levy, S., Okoye, U. O., and Ingram, R. (2022). Making the 'local' visible in social work education: Insights from Nigeria and Scotland on (re)balancing and contextualising indigenous and international knowledge. *British Journal of Social Work*, 52(7), 4299–4317. doi:10.1093/bjsw/bcac028.

Midgley, J. (1981). *Professional Imperialism: Social Work in the Third World*. London: Heinemann.

Mwansa, L. J. (2011). Social work education in Africa: Whence and whither? *Social Work Education*, 30(1), 4–16. doi:10.1080/02615471003753148.

Nuttman-Shwartz, O., and Ranz, R. (2014). A reciprocal working model for fieldwork with international social work students. *The British Journal of Social Work*, 44(8), 2411–2425. Available at: http://www.jstor.org/stable/43688069.

Osei-Hwedie, K. (1995). *A Search for Legitimate Social Development Education and Practice Models for Africa*. Lewiston and New York: Edwin Mullen.

Ragab, I. (2017). Has social work come of age? Revisiting the authentisation debate 25 years on. In M. Gray (ed.), *Routledge Handbook of Social Work and Social Development in Africa* (pp. 33–45). London: Routledge.

Rankopo, M. J., and Osei-Hwedie, K. (2011). Globalisation and culturally relevant social work: African perspectives on indigenization. *International Social Work*, 54(1), 137–147. doi:10.1177/0020872810372367.

Shawky, A. (1972). Social work education in Africa. *International Social Work*, 15(3), 3–16. doi:10.1177/002087287201500302.

Twikirize, M. J., and Spitzer, H. (eds.) (2019). *Social Work Practice in Africa: Indigenous and Innovative Approaches*. Kampala: Fountain Publishers, African Books Collective.

PART 1

Approaches to Diversifying, Decolonising, and Developing Culturally Relevant Social Work Education

1
COMPLEXITIES INVOLVED IN ESTABLISHING A CULTURALLY RELEVANT SOCIAL WORK CURRICULUM IN NIGERIA

Mel Gray, Susan Levy, Uzoma Odera Okoye, and Solomon Amadasun

Abstract: English

This chapter discusses findings from an empirical study that explored issues surrounding the development of a culturally relevant social work curriculum for Nigeria. It begins with a focus on conceptualisations of culture within the African social work discourse on indigenisation and culturally relevant social work with reference to 'indigenising' social work education. Second, it contextualises this cultural discourse through a discussion of the findings from a literature review of publications on Nigerian social work and from a focus group with Nigerian social work academics. These findings relate to communal and cultural ways of being, ethics, and ethnicity. They show the complexities involved in developing a culturally relevant curriculum that strives to adhere to international social work standards and values in a context with divergent cultural, religious, and ethnic beliefs and traditions. The chapter closes with a reconceptualisation of a culturally relevant social work curriculum and offers three recommendations for progressing towards achieving this outcome.

Abstract: Igbo

Isi nke a tulere nchọpụta ndị sitere na otu nchọcha e mere nke nyochara isi okwu ndị metụtara imebe kọrịkulum amụmamụ mwulite obodo nke na-emetụta omenala na Naijiria. Nke a ga-amalite site n'ilekwasị anya na nghọta ihe bụ omenala dị ka o si metụta amụmamụ mwulite obodo nke metụtara ime ka ihe bụrụ nke ndị, omenala, nnwere onwe na amụmamụ mwulite obodo mbawanye n'Afrịka, na-atụnyere ime agụmakwụkwọ amụmamụ mwulite obodo ka ọ bụrụ 'nke ndị'. Nke abụọ, ọ na-etinye amụmamụ metụtara omenala n'ọnọdụ site n'itule ihe ndị a chọpụtara site na ntụleghari zuru oke e mere n'agụmagụ ndị e bipụtara maka amụmamụ mwulite obodo na Naijiria, ya na otu mkparịta ụka ajụjụ ọnụ nke e jiri ndị ọkachamara n'amụmamụ mwulite obodo mee. Ihe ndị ahụ a chọpụtara na-emetụta ụzọ mbikọrịta na usoro omenala dị iche iche, usoro ebimndụ, na ebe onye si. Ha na-egosi ihe mgbagwo so n'ihibe kọrịkulum amụmamụ mwulite obodo na-emetụta omenala nke na-agbalị ịgbaso usoro ruru ogogo amụmamụ mwulite obodo na mba ụwa n'ọnọdụ ebe e nwere omenala, okpukpere, na nkwenye sitere n'ebe onye si nakwa ọdịnala dịgasị iche iche. E mechiri isi nke a site n'ịghọtagharị ihe bụ kọrịkulum amụmamụ mwulite obodo na-emetụta omenala ma tụnye aro atọ, ndị ga-enye aka imejupụta mpụtara nke a.

Introduction

Africa is a diverse continent that has had a marked impact on international social work education through the various discourses it has initiated, from launching the worldwide indigenisation debate in the north (Ragab, 1990, 2017; Shawky, 1972) to introducing developmental social work in the south (Patel, 2005; Patel and Hochveld, 2012). Gray et al. (2014) documented the attempts of the Association for Social Work Education in Africa (ASWEA), 1971-1989, to indigenise the social work curriculum. They noted the evolution of social work education in Africa with the first schools emerging in South Africa in Stellenbosch in 1931, and Cape Town and Pretoria in 1933 and 1934 respectively, though, for political reasons, ASWEA excluded South Africa, due to its apartheid policy. Schools to the north followed, in Egypt in 1936, Algeria in 1942, Ghana in 1945, Zambia in 1950, Uganda in 1954, Tanzania in 1958, Ethiopia in 1959, Upper Volta (now Burkina Faso) in 1960, and Tunisia and Zimbabwe in 1964. Other countries followed in the 1960s and early 1970s, including Nigeria in 1976, with latecomers Namibia in 1983 and Botswana in 1985. African institutions for higher education based their programmes on colonial models and many started with basic skills or technical training for welfare officials, hence constant reference to social work training rather than professional social work education reflected in much early literature, and the publicly accessible ASWEA documents[1]. This colonial bias formed the basis for Midgley's (1981) seminal text that became a pivotal catalyst for the indigenisation debate. Most influential in furthering the discourse on indigenisation in social work education was the work of Kwaku Osei-Hwedie (1993, 1995, 1996a, 1996b) and many followed his lead. Midgley also played a major role in the developmental social work turn in southern Africa, while Patel introduced his theory on social development to, and brought it to bear on, South Africa's welfare transformation policy (Patel, 2005). Permeating the African discourse on social work education were persistent themes, highlighted by ASWEA, relating to ongoing challenges to indigenising the curriculum, including the following:

Lingering colonial legacy and dependence on Western curricula.
Lack of indigenous teaching material and outmoded teaching practices.
Struggle to reorient the curriculum from remedial casework to community-centred practice.
Underuse of African social research.

These issues remain firmly embedded in contemporary discourses on social work education, despite many positive developments, especially in the growth of a rich African literature on social work. Most recently, the international social work community has embraced the African concept of *ubuntu*, undoubtedly through the valuable involvement of African social work educators in the development of the Global Agenda for Social Work and Social Development (International Association of Schools of Social Work (IASSW), International Federation of Social Workers (IFSW), and the International Council on Social Welfare (ICSW), 2020). In this chapter, attention focuses first on conceptualisations of culture within the African social work discourse on indigenisation and cultural relevance with reference to social work education. Secondly, we contextualise this cultural discourse in Nigeria through findings from a literature review of published work on Nigerian social work, and a focus group with Nigerian social work academics. Thirdly, we discuss the complexities of developing a culturally relevant curriculum in a context where local values and practices often do not align with international social work standards. The chapter closes with three recommendations for progressing towards a culturally relevant social work curriculum.

'Indigenising' Social Work

Nearly two decades ago, Gray (2005) noted that 'indigenising' social work involves challenging universal knowledge and cultural hegemony to make way for indigenous voices and local ways of knowing. The aim was and still is to enhance culturally relevant education and practice by accepting and promoting contextualised knowledge and local traditions in the belief they play a crucial role in promoting people's wellbeing. Indigenising the curriculum involves strengthening local identities and discourses in social work education settings by teaching indigenous and post-colonial knowledge, research methods, and practice theories that draw critical attention to colonial legacies in contemporary social work (Gray and Amadasun, 2023; Levy et al., 2022; Ranta-Tyrkkö, 2011).

Despite ongoing calls for indigenisation, social work has been slow to adopt local knowledge, traditional forms of assistance, and non-Western and indigenous worldviews. One such worldview is belief in the role of spirits in people's daily lives. Social workers practising with indigenous African communities need to have an understanding of African cultural practices like witchcraft and ancestral worship (Mabvurira, 2016; Ross, 2010). Educators, practitioners, and researchers cannot ignore spiritual issues in culturally relevant education, practice, and research (Mabvurira and Makhubele, 2018), nor can they ignore the conflict arising from ethnic division (Olu-Olu, 2014).

This African worldview is juxtaposed against a Western view of ethically mandated culturally competent practice rooted in core principles relating to client-centred, strengths-based social work practice, in which clients' culturally based values, norms, and diverse ways of knowing are seen as 'unique cultural assets' (Marsiglia and Booth, 2015, p. 424). Working 'within a client's cultural context to address risks and protective factors [and] ... has the potential for increasing the effectiveness of interventions' (Marsiglia and Booth, 2015, p. 424) through a process of *cultural adaptation* or indigenisation within African social work discourse. According to Marsiglia and Booth (2015), 'culturally grounded social work challenges practitioners to see themselves as the *other*' (p. 424) with the process of cultural adaptation a joint responsibility of worker and client that takes place through a relational process of interaction and dialogue or mutual communication.

Contemporary discourse on culturally competent practice implies that it is a universal imperative within social work. From the outset, this is problematic within the African context, given the paucity of research on 'evidence-based interventions' and ways to measure in Afrocentric methodology (Mabvurira and Makhubele, 2018). Scholars have noted the limited scholarly contributions from academics and researchers in the Global South to social work knowledge (Hodge and Kibirige, 2022; Pawar, 2015) and research-based teaching materials (Nilsen et al., 2023). Thus, 'locating interventions that have been designed for and tested with a given cultural group' (Marsiglia and Booth, 2015, p. 425) presents the first challenge to cultural adaptation and, in turn, culturally competent practice. Additionally, it suggests a casework focus (long criticised within the indigenisation discourse) and an emphasis on partnership in which people work cooperatively with one another (Gopalkrishnan, 2019; Marsiglia and Booth, 2015). It also presents a paradoxical view of culture as simultaneously fixed – you can learn about others' culture – and dynamic and flexible – it can be adapted or transformed through interaction (Dean, 2001; Gopalkrishnan, 2019; Nadan and Ben-Ari, 2013). In reality, cast as the *other*, social workers' 'own culture' becomes an important consideration, especially self-awareness and responsibility for beliefs, emotions, and attitudes, as these affect professional functioning.

Nadan's (2017) review of the literature from the Global North on cultural competence revealed that most social work education programmes focused on providing knowledge about cultures; cultivating awareness of, and sensitivity to, cultural differences; and developing skills to work across cultures. They tended to avoid critical power issues, and anti-oppressive and antiracist approaches that invited attention to the culturally aware 'self' (usually from the dominant group and, therefore, part of the problem) rather than the culturally different 'other' (from a minority and oppressed group).

In Africa, where histories of colonisation have disempowered and marginalised cultural groups, the relevance of an apolitical practice framework becomes ever more questionable (Sakamoto, 2007). To counter the hegemonic forces of colonisation, Africans have learnt to switch between different colonialist and African cultural frames and ethnic identities. This applies equally to social workers and clients, who have a generic understanding of African cultures, but have less engagement with issues related to harmful cultural practices, especially in social work education.

Methodology

To identify Nigerian scholars contributing to social work knowledge in Nigeria, this study comprised a comprehensive literature review of social work literature published by Nigerian social work academics in international, African, and Nigerian journals; an online survey, and focus group with Nigerian academics. The focus group held in Lagos, Nigeria, involved 10 Nigerian social work academics from the Universities of Nigeria, Lagos, Ibadan, and Ilorin, it aimed to elicit information for, and academics' ideas on, a culturally relevant curriculum in Nigeria (Levy et al., 2023).

The literature review consisted of a search of Sage Premier, Wiley Online, ScienceDirect, Cambridge Journals, Taylor and Francis Online, Oxford Journals, Springer Online Journals, and Sociology Source Ultimate. Table 1.1 provides a summary of the literature found (n=308) in international, African, and Nigerian social work (n=151) and non-social work journals (n=157). The inclusion criteria were: Nigerian social work authors within and outside Nigeria, papers on social work in Nigeria published in English-language peer-reviewed journals from 2010 onwards, at least one of the authors or co-authors had to be Nigerian, and the subject matter had to relate directly to social work in Nigeria. The papers were automatically included if they were published in a peer-reviewed social work journal. The researchers were particularly interested in literature that addressed local social problems and indigenous and culturally relevant issues.

Table 1.1 Journals Used in Literature Review on Nigerian Social Work

	Journal Category	Journals Searched	Papers Included in Review
Social work	International	79	78
	African	3	20
	Nigerian	5	53
Sub-total		**87**	**151**
Non-social work	International	45	113
	African	12	25
	Nigerian	14	19
Sub-total		**71**	**157**
Total papers included in review		**158**	**308**

The 308 papers were themed and arranged under three categories from most to least published (Table 1.2).

This chapter focuses on the papers relating directly to a culturally relevant curriculum across three themed categories (see Table 1.3):

1. Communal and cultural ways of being
2. Ethics and a culturally relevant curriculum
3. Ethnicity and a culturally relevant curriculum.

Table 1.2 Distribution of Literature Review Papers by Theme and Frequency of Publication

Least Published Papers *< 10*		*Moderately Published Papers* *10–20*		*Most published Papers* *>20*	
Young people	8	Social work profession	16	Health	70
Disability	6	Migration, human trafficking, and IDPs	15	Ageing	44
Crime, conflict, and peacebuilding	6	Social work practice	14	Child welfare, including school social work	42
Environmental issues	5	Social work approaches	11	Social work education	34
Social work research	4	Community development	11	Gender, women, GBV, and LGBTQ+	22
Total	**29**		**67**		**212**

Table 1.3 Three Main Themes in the Literature Review Papers Relating to Developing a Culturally Relevant curriculum in Nigeria

Communal and Cultural Ways of Being	*Ethics and a Culturally Relevant Curriculum*	*Ethnicity and a Culturally Relevant Curriculum*
1 Amadasun and Gray (2023)	1 Amadasun and Gray (2023)	1 Akintayo et al. (2017)
2 Anugwom (2011)	2 Anazonwu (2019)	2 Ayangunna (2010)
3 Ebimgbo et al. (2019, 2021)	3 Archibong et al. (2017)	3 Olaore and Drolet (2016)
4 Ekoh et al. (2020)	4 Ekoh and Agbawodikeizu (2023)	4 Tangban et al. (2020)
5 Ngwu et al. (2018)	5 Emma-Echiegu et al. (2014)	5 Tanyi et al. (2021)
6 Nnama-Okechukwu et al. (2022)	6 Ezeokoli et al. (2020)	6 Ugiagbe (2015)
7 Olaleye (2013)	7 George and Ekoh (2020)	
8 Ramsey-Soroghaye (2021)	8 Isangha et al. (2020)	
9 Ugiagbe (2015)	9 Jidong et al. (2021, 2022)	
10 Ugiagbe and Ugiagbe (2014)	10 Jungari (2016)	
	11 Levy et al. (2022)	
	12 Nnama-Okechukwu and McLaughlin (2022)	
	13 Nwatu et al. (2020)	
	14 Ojua et al. (2013)	
	15 Okoye et al. (2014)	
	16 Secker (2013)	
	17 Ugiagbe (2015)	
	18 Uzuegbu (2010)	

Findings

Below we discuss the findings from the literature review and focus group, across the three main themes, using quotes from the focus group on issues associated with developing a culturally relevant curriculum in Nigeria.

Communal and Cultural Ways of Being

The volume and breadth of literature in this study (n=308) challenges the prevailing narrative that there is little published indigenous literature on Nigerian social work. This body of literature is responsive to local issues and problems, addresses the incompatibility of Western casework and therapeutic approaches, and shows social work academics' attempts to adapt to the collective cultural traditions of local ethnic groups. This literature forms the building blocks to start to correct 'the shortcomings and inadequacies of Western social work theories and practices in addressing Nigerian social problems' (Ugiagbe, 2015, p. 790). In a recent paper by Amadasun and Gray (2023), the authors highlighted the need for quality, locally relevant social work education in Nigeria for the professional growth of social workers, and the profession's fight for acceptance and recognition, noting this rested crucially on linkages to local families and communities. The quality and applicability of the education and training social workers receive at the beginning and throughout their professional careers has a significant impact on their responsiveness to and efficacy in local communities. As communicated in the focus group, things have moved on over recent years:

> [We need a] culturally relevant curriculum ... to preserve culture, ethnicity, and language. There has been a lot of improvement since own undergraduate studies, which were all Western focused, and we learnt to see this as irrelevant.

Ugiagbe (2015) finds 'good and benevolent practices and tenets of ... local culture' (p. 792) as cultural assets. For him, social work was context bound, by which he meant, it was rooted in culture. Reflecting a static view of culture, which looks back to traditional practices, Nnama-Okechukwua et al. (2022) argue cultural relevance meant staying true to the 'cultural heritage and histories of peoples that define who they are and what the social world means to them' (p. 4). Thus, a culturally relevant curriculum aims to teach students about people's culture, while intervention involves a narrative approach to capture clients' stories from their perspective. Also reflecting a static view of culture, Olaleye (2013) highlights that these traditional stories were the precursors to social work, referring to indigenous helping and support systems prior to colonisation and the introduction of social work. Many authors alluded to precolonial indigenous practices and support systems. For example, Ramsey-Soroghaye (2021) highlights the communalism of precolonial Nigerians, referring to their communal living and collective action as engagement in community development long before the introduction of modernising development. A focus group participant identified their responsibility in driving change: 'This is about being the custodians of knowledge of social work'.

Some authors explored cultural issues surrounding ageing and cultural understandings of dementia (Ekoh et al., 2020), widowhood (Anugwom, 2011), and gender- and culture-based support (Ebimgbo et al., 2019, 2021). Ngwu et al. (2018) examined indigenous age-grade systems, contending that people of the various age groups were a genuine instrument for transforming rural communities because of their shared culture and common goals and familiarity with, and loyalty to, their local communities. Unlike outside 'developers', communities trusted them. Thus, it made sense to empower young people and provide them with the requisite tools and technological know-how. The focus group participants recognised the need to understand and teach culturally relevant ways of doing, seeing, and understanding social work with different groups of people:

> We need [a] culturally relevant curriculum. In the West, things are very different, with old people going into old age homes – here it is taboo. Adoption is very alien in Nigeria, the more we develop a culturally relevant curriculum that suits our practices the better.

Acknowledging the decline of informal supports, especially within urban areas, Ugiagbe and Ugiagbe (2014) contend that formal legal recognition and empowerment of the extended family would lessen poverty significantly, ensure longevity, and spark grassroots development, all of which had eluded Nigeria since independence.

While most authors emphasised the positive aspects of culture, schisms are appearing in the literature, with critiques of traditional and indigenous cultural practices juxtaposed against global social work values. As indigenisation leans towards conservative practices aimed at returning to and maintaining age-old cultural customs, Ugiagbe (2015) highlights how this might create challenges for social workers, who saw themselves as agents of social change. These tensions, along with ethical dilemmas, are core to discourses on creating a culturally relevant curriculum.

Ethics and a Culturally Relevant Curriculum

A narrative threaded through many of the papers related to questions over maintaining international ethical standards, especially when indigenous norms and practices contradicted human rights and social justice values. Several studies recognised these ethical challenges in social work education (George and Ekoh, 2020; Levy et al., 2022; Nnama-Okechukwu and McLaughlin, 2022; Ugiagbe, 2015). Ekoh and Agbawodikeizu (2023) note the dearth of literature on social work educators' views on, and experiences of, ethical challenges arising from teaching universal social work principles and values in contexts steeped in cultural beliefs, traditions, and legislation flowing from these practices. For example, Nigeria's *Same Sex Marriage (Prohibition) Act* (Federal Republic of Nigeria (FRN), 2013) sustained cultural and ethnoreligious beliefs that construed homosexuality as a disease, and criminalised homosexual 'lifestyles'. George and Ekoh (2020) report on social workers' reticence to work with lesbian, gay, and bisexual clients, influenced, among other things, by national policies such as the 2013 Act. Their study showed that sociocultural and political constraints hindered social workers' interventions with disadvantaged social groups. Of importance to this discussion is the way in which prevailing sociocultural and religious attitudes might affect social work educators' willingness to teach students about contentious issues. These included working with lesbian, gay, and bisexual clients; abortion; and confronting gender issues and discriminatory religious and cultural attitudes that sustained gender-based violence and practices that violated girls' and women's rights. Examples were female genital mutilation (Gray and Amadasun, 2023a; Uzuegbu, 2010; Jungari, 2016); marriage practices causing vesical-vaginal fistula (VVF), especially in Northern Nigeria (Emma-Echiegu et al., 2014; Okoye et al., 2014); and child abuse (Uzuegbu, 2010).

Anazonwu (2019) examines sociocultural factors associated with perceptions of child abuse noting the adverse effects on children of culturally accepted ideologies about childrearing and child punishment and correction, such as withholding food that effectively contravened the Child

Rights Act (National Human Rights Commission (NHRC), 2003. She found that cultural beliefs, values, and traditions influenced women's perceptions of child abuse. Uzuegbu (2010) highlights early marriage, witchcraft, and female genital mutilation. Several authors highlighted cultural beliefs about spiritual causes of mental illness, its link to witchcraft, and harmful practices like exorcism and child stigmatisation (Archibong et al., 2017; Isangha et al., 2020; Nwatu et al., 2020; Secker, 2013). Most damaging was the belief that individual wrongdoing had angered the spirits and mental illness (and disability) was a consequent form of punishment, hence, the related stigma and tendency to consult traditional healers rather than seek orthodox medical care (Ezeokoli et al., 2020; Jidong et al., 2021, 2022; Ojua et al., 2013). One focus group participant noted:

> We need to think ahead [as] to how to convey this new knowledge to students, consider cultural practices that can be harmful and present ethical dilemmas to students. Need to build frameworks that can guide ways to address these potentially harmful practices. Where cultural context can be harmful, guidance should be the same across the universities. Examples presented around kidnaping, child abduction and forced marriage – need skills to manage these.

Ugiagbe (2015) has called for the investigation and discontinuation of harmful 'cultural practices like male hegemony and the treating of women as subservient members of society, the widowhood rites and disempowerment of women, children and youths' (p. 797). He also advised social workers to avoid controversial issues and culturally unacceptable practices like same-sex marriage and called for the 'selective assimilation of Western ideals of social work' (p. 797).

Ethnicity and a Culturally Relevant Curriculum

A third key theme on a culturally relevant curriculum emerging from the literature review and focus group centred on ethnicity. Advocating for culturally rooted social work, Akintayo et al. (2017) note that cultural diversity and a lack of governance in Nigeria hindered social work, and affected its ability to transfer local knowledge. Tangban et al. (2020) conceive the idea of ethnicity as an identity signifier conveying the complexity of cultural relevance. They highlighted that ethnicity signified belonging to a social group sharing 'a common language, culture, belief and historical setbacks' (p. 218). This pertained especially when ethnic loyalties led to conflicts over resource and revenue allocations, perceived as disadvantageous to a particular ethnic tribe or region. Within the discourse on cultural and ethnic diversity, and responding to unique differences, longstanding ethnic divisions meant social workers could not ignore tribalism and ethnocentrism, and other ideologies that went against the 'virtue of oneness and social solidarity' (Tangban et al., 2020, p. 796) undergirding African cultural traditions. Ethnocentrism promoted in-group solidarity and this had the potential to increase division and promote conflict (Tanyi et al., 2021).

These ethnic allegiances were further complicated when tied to religious beliefs and adherence. Rather than encourage a sense of national identity, culturalism and ethnocentrism cemented difference. Thus, Tangban et al. (2020) highlight the need for scholarship to examine the extent to which ethnic and religious patterns in Nigerian politics were a product of cultural diversity, the struggle for spoils, and the cause and consequence of political conflict. The cultural competence discourse came under heavy criticism for its claims that learning about people's particular cultural practices and beliefs was all culturally sensitive practice required (e.g., Olaore and Drolet 2016; Ugiagbe, 2015). Rather, cultural relevance is a political attitude, and federalism has led to a war for resources in Nigeria, due to its regionalism and statism. States are now free to choose whether to domesticate significant legislations, like the Child Rights Act (NHRC, 2003; Ayangunna, 2010). Furthermore authors highlighted that cultural relevance could promote ideologies of culturalism and ethnocentrism that produced 'a strong orientation towards the norms, values, history and beliefs of a particular [cultural or] ethnic group' (Pierson and Thomas, 2011, in Tangban et al., 2020, p. 219), leading in ethnocentric societies, to the interests of one group superseding those of other ethnic groups. Focus group participants understood this:

> A culturally relevant curriculum should align with social work values; if teaching social work in the community, they [should] know the values of their community. Nigeria isn't one culture.
>
> Values of privacy need to be understood; if social work is involved in a village, the whole village would know about the issue, [social workers] can't use Western approach to confidentiality. Students need to know what to do on the ground. We really need a culturally relevant curriculum in Africa.
>
> The current curriculum isn't culturally relevant. I've been reflecting on my teaching. Sometimes I've tried to domesticate, using local examples. At the same time as helping the students to understand, if we give local examples ... what they're understanding [is], it is 'ours' and to make use of it.

Against this backdrop, Tangban et al. (2020) note that indigenous (or culturally relevant) social workers require knowledge and understanding of broader power dynamics, since they strove to promote unity, progress, and peaceful co-existence to advance an egalitarian society (Tangban et al., 2020). Authentic indigenous social workers have direct experience of, or are culturally embedded in, the community and understand and accept cultural practices.

Conclusion

Challenging the narrative that there is little published literature on Nigerian social work, this study found 308 papers on this topic. Threaded through the literature review and focus group was an understanding of cultural relevance as related to the preservation of culture, ethnicity, and language. However, developing a culturally relevant curriculum requires understanding differences between Nigerian and Western cultures. Dilemmas emerged in teaching social work values and principles that did not cohere with cultural practices, as George and Ekoh (2020) highlight in relation to same-sex marriages and working with lesbian, gay, and bisexual clients. Ugiagbe (2015) goes so far as advising social workers to avoid these clients, as engaging with them would merely alienate the Nigerian public and government. The Nigerian literature conveyed the complexities of developing a culturally relevant curriculum, despite which there were concerted attempts to theorise what this might entail, noting that this is happening in the absence of concrete practice models and case examples.

This project led to the following definition of a culturally relevant curriculum:

> A culturally relevant curriculum (CRC) in social work education comprises courses that teach students to respond to local social problems, issues, and contexts that are based on, and informed by, local social work-related literature, experiential knowledge, and a critical understanding of culture. A CRC is relevant to social work education in the Global South and Global North, and aligns with global social work values and ethics to prepare graduates to work across and within different cultures.

Moving forward to achieve change, the authors believed that educators needed to harmonise indigenous and Western knowledge in the teaching of social work (Levy et al., 2022), since both are important in addressing social work's central 'principles of social justice, human rights and respect for diversities' (Nnama-Okechukwua et al., 2022, p. 1). For Nigerian academics, a culturally relevant educational strategy would engage key stakeholders in overcoming the challenges of indigenising the social work curriculum.

Recommendations

We recommend the following to establish the literature to inform culturally relevant social work education:

1. Review indigenous social work literature in other African countries and generate more research/examples of African/Nigerian social work.
2. Develop local and culturally relevant African/Nigerian social work practice models and theories.
3. Engage in the ethical dilemmas of working with traditional cultural practices.

Notes

1. http://historicalpapers-atom.wits.ac.za/association-for-social-work-education-in-africa-aswea-2

Further Reading

George, E. O., and Ekoh, P. (2020). Social workers' perception of practice with lesbians, gays and bisexuals (LGBs) in Nigeria. *Journal of Comparative Social Work*, 15(2), 56–78.

Tanyi, P. L., Odo, C. O., Omeje, A. E., and Ugwuanyi, C. A. (2021). Ethnic agitations and threat of secession in Nigeria: What can social workers do? *Journal of Social Work in Developing Societies*, 3(2), 29–45.

Ugiagbe, E. O. (2015). Social work is context-bound: The need for indigenization of social work practice in Nigeria. *International Social Work*, 58(6), 790–801.

References

Akintayo, T., Hämäläinen, J., and Rissanen, S. (2017). Social work in diverse ethno-cultural contexts: A case study of Nigeria. *African Journal of Social Work*, 7(2), 16–24.

Amadasun, S., and Gray, M. (2023). Enhancing the relevance of social work education in Nigeria. *British Journal of Social Work*, 53(1), 534–551. https://doi.org/10.1093/bjsw/bcac144.

Anazonwu, N. P., Chukwu, N. A., Agha, A. A., Nnama-Okechukwu, C. U., Eya, O. I., Obasi-Igwe, I., and Nwadike, N. C. (2017). Environmental hazard: Industrial wastes, health implication and social worker's role in collaborating the industrial menace. *Journal of Humanities and Social Science*, 22(10), 63–67. Available at: https://www.iosrjournals.org/iosr-jhss/papers/Vol.%2022%20Issue10/Version-5/J2210056368.pdf.

Anugwom, N. K. (2011). The socio-psychological impact of widowhood on elderly women in Nigeria. *OIDA International Journal of Sustainable Development*, 2(6), 89–95.

Archibong, E. P., Enang, E., and Bassey, G. E. (2017). Witchcraft beliefs in diseases causation and health-seeking behaviour in pregnancy of women in Calabar South, Nigeria. *IOSR Journal of Humanities and Social Science (IOSR-JHSS)*, 22(6), 24–28.

Ayangunna, J. A. (2010). The child rights act and the dilemma of social workers in Nigeria. *Ibadan Journal of Educational Studies*, 7, 33–42.

Dean, R. G. (2001). The myth of cross-cultural competence. *Families in Society*, 82(6), 623–630.

Ebimgbo, S. O., Chukwu, N. E., and Okoye, U. O. (2021). Gender differences in family support to older adults and implications for social work in south-east Nigeria. *Journal of Aging Studies*, 59, 100979.

Ebimgbo, S. O., Obi-Keguna, C. N., Chukwu, N. E., Onalu, C. E., Abonyi, S. E., and Okoye, U. O. (2019). Culture-based social support to older adults in Nnewi, South-East, Nigeria. *African Population Studies*, 33(2), 4891–4900. https://doi.org/10.11564/33-2-1402.

Ekoh, P. C., and Agbawodikeizu, P. U. (2023). Exploring ethical issues embedded in the call for Indigenisation of social work education in Nigeria. *Social Work Education*, 42(2), 249–262.

Ekoh, P. C., George, E., Ejimkaraonye, C., and Okoye, U. O. (2020). An appraisal of public understanding of dementia across cultures. *Journal of Social Work in Developing Societies*, 2(1), 54–67.

Emma-Echiegu, N. B., Okoye, U. O., and Odey, E. R. (2014). Knowledge of causes of VVF and discrimination suffered by patients in Ebonyi State, Nigeria: A qualitative study. *Social Work in Public Health*, 29(5), 417–427.

Ezeokoli, R. N., Adegbite, O. S., Oluwasanya, S.-S., and Banjo, O. O. (2020). Psychosocial factors influencing the wellbeing of persons living with mental illness in Abeokuta North local government area of Ogun State, Nigeria. *International Journal of Research and Scientific Innovation*, 7(8), 143–148.

Federal Republic of Nigeria (FRN). (2013). *Same Sex Marriage (Prohibition) Act*, 2013. Available at: https://www.refworld.org/pdfid/52f4d9cc4.pdf.

George, E. O., and Ekoh, P. (2020). Social workers' perception of practice with lesbians, gays and bisexuals (LGBs) in Nigeria. *Journal of Comparative Social Work*, 15(2), 56–78.

Gopalkrishnan, N. (2019). Cultural competence and beyond: Working across cultures in culturally dynamic partnerships. *The International Journal of Community and Social Development*, 1(1), 28–41.

Gray, M. (2005). Dilemmas of international social work: Paradoxical processes in indigenisation, universalism and imperialism. *International Journal of Social Welfare*, 14(2), 230–237.

Gray, M., and Amadasun, S. (2023). *Social Work, Social Development, and Social Welfare in Nigeria*. London: Routledge.

Gray, M., Kreitzer, L., and Mupedziswa, R. (2014). The enduring relevance of indigenisation in African social work: A critical reflection on ASWEA's legacy. *Ethics and Social Welfare*, 8(2), 101–116.

Hodge, D. R., and Kibirige, K. (2022). Addressing the global inequality in social work research: Challenges, opportunities, and key insights and strategies in Sub-Saharan Africa. *Social Work Research*, 46(1), 84–92.

International Association of Schools of Social Work (IASSW), International Federation of Social Workers (IFSW), and International Council on Social Welfare (ICSW). (2020). 2020 to 2030 global agenda for social work and social development framework: Co-building inclusive social transformation. Available at: https://www.iassw-aiets.org/global-agenda/.

Isangha, S. O., Olaitan, T. M., Ogar, L. E., Obasi-Igwe, I. A., Aghedo, G. U., and Iweagwu, A. O. (2020). Child witchcraft confession: Parental reaction and implication for social work practice. *Advances in Social Sciences Research Journal*, 7(12), 691–704.

Jidong, D. E., Bailey, D., Sodi, T., Gibson, L., Sawadogo, N., Ikhile, D., Musoke, D., Madhombiro, M., and Mbah, M. (2021). Nigerian cultural beliefs about mental health conditions and traditional healing: A qualitative study. *Journal of Mental Health Training, Education and Practice*, 16(4), 285–299.

Jidong, D. E., Ike, T. J., Tribe, R., Tunariu, A. D., Rohleder, P., and Mackenzie, A. (2022). Berom cultural beliefs and attitudes towards mental health problems in Nigeria: A mixed-methods study. *Mental Health, Religion and Culture*, 25(5), 504–518.

Jungari, S. B. (2016). Female genital mutilation is a violation of reproductive rights of women: Implications for health workers. *Health and Social Work*, 41(1), 25–31.

Levy, S., Gray, M., Okoye, U., and Amadasun, S. (2023). Decolonising social work through culturally relevant curricula. Paper presented at the 12th European Conference for Social Work Research (ECSWR): Social Work Research Through and Towards Human Relationships, Università Cattolica del Sacro Cuore, Milan, Italy, April 12–14.

Levy, S., Okoye, U. O., and Ingram, R. (2022). Making the 'local' visible in social work education: Insights from Nigeria and Scotland on (re)balancing and contextualising indigenous and international knowledge. *British Journal of Social Work*, 52(7), 4299–4317.

Mabvurira, V. (2016). Influence of African traditional religion and spirituality in understanding chronic illnesses and its implications for social work practice: A case of chiweshe communal lands in Zimbabwe. PhD thesis. University of Limpopo, South Africa.

Mabvurira, V., and Makhubele, J. C. (2018). Afrocentric methodology: A missing pillar in African social work research, education and training. In A. L. Shokane, J. C. Makhubele, and L. V. Blitz (eds.) *Issues around Aligning Theory, Research and Practice in Social Work Education* (Knowledge Pathing: Multi-, Inter- and Trans-Disciplining in Social Sciences Series Volume 1). Cape Town: AOSIS, 11–26.

Marsiglia, F. F., and Booth, J. M. (2015). Cultural adaptation of interventions in real practice settings. *Research on Social Work Practice*, 25(4), 423–432.

Midgley, J. (1981). *Professional Imperialism: Social Work in the Third World*. London: Heinemann.

Nadan, Y. (2017). Rethinking 'cultural competence' in international social work. *International Social Work*, 60(1), 74–83.

Nadan, Y., and Ben-Ari, A. (2013). What can we learn from rethinking 'multiculturalism' in social work education? *Social Work Education: The International Journal*, 32(8), 1089–1102.

National Human Rights Commission (NHRC). (2003). Child rights act 2003. Available at: https://www.nigeriarights.gov.ng/files/childrightact.pdf.

Ngwu, C. N., Agbo, A. A., and Onuoha, E. C. (2018). Sociodemographic and cultural factors influencing adjustment to bereavement in Umuahia, Southern Nigeria. *Journal of Loss and Trauma*, 23(8), 639–658.

Nilsen, A. C. E., Kalinganire, C., Mabeyo, Z. N., Manyama, W., Ochen, E. A., Revheim, C., and Twikirize, J. (2023). Reimagining social work education in East Africa. *Social Work Education*, 42(2), 169–184.

Nnama-Okechukwu, C. U., and McLaughlin, H. (2022). Indigenous knowledge and social work education in Nigeria: Made in Nigeria or made in the West? *Social Work Education*, 1–18. https://doi.org/10.1080/02615479.2022.2038557.

Nnama-Okechukwu, C. U., McLaughlin, H., Okoye, U., Hendricks, E., Imaan, L., Malinga, T., Wizi-Kambala, A., Ebimgbo, S., Veta, O., and Imo, N. (2022). Indigenous knowledge and social work education in Nigeria: Challenges and need for sustainable development. *International Social Work*, 1–15. https://doi.org/10.1177/00208728221098511.

Nwatu, U. L., Ebue, M. O., Iwuagwu, A. O., Ene, J. C., and Odo, C. O. (2020). Perception of witchcraft practice in Oredo local government area of Edo State, Nigeria. *Advances in Social Sciences Research Journal*, 7(12), 514–527.

Ojua, T. A., Ishor, D. G., and Ndom, P. J. (2013). African cultural practices and health implications for Nigeria rural development. *International Review of Management and Business Research*, 2(1), 176–183.

Okoye, U. O., Emma-Echiegu, N., and Tanyi, P. L. (2014). Living with vesico-vaginal fistula: Experiences of women awaiting repairs in Ebonyi State, Nigeria. *Tanzania Journal of Health Research*, 16(4), 1–9.

Olaleye, Y. L. (2013c). Indigenous cultural practices as precursors to social work education in Nigeria. *IFE PsychologIA: An International Journal*, 21(2), 106–112. Available at: https://hdl.handle.net/10520/EJC141139.

Olaore, A. Y., and Drolet, J. (2016). Indigenous knowledge, beliefs, and cultural practices for children and families in Nigeria. *Journal of Ethnic and Cultural Diversity in Social Work*, 2(3), 254–270. https://doi.org/10.1080/15313204.2016.1241973.

Olu-Olu, O. (2014). Ethnic identity and the crises of development in Nigeria. *European Scientific Journal*, 10(2), 216–229.

Osei-Hwedie, K. (1993). The challenge of social work in Africa: Starting the indigenisation process. *Journal of Social Development in Africa*, 8, 19–30.

Osei-Hwedie, K. (1995). *A Search for Legitimate Social Development Education and Practice Models for Africa*. Lewiston, NY: Edwin Mullen.

Osei-Hwedie, K. (1996a). The rationale for using indigenous knowledge in human services provision. In H. Norman, I. Snyman, and M. H. Cohen (eds.) *Indigenous Knowledge and Its Uses in Southern Africa*. Pretoria: Human Sciences Research Council, 1–12.

Osei-Hwedie, K. (1996b). The indigenisation of social work education and practice in South Africa: The dilemma of theory and method. *Social Work/Maatskaplike Werk*, 32, 215–225.

Patel, L. (2005). Social development and curriculum renewal in an African context. *Social Worker/Researcher-Practitioner*, 17, 363–377.

Patel, L., and Hochfeld, T. (2012). Developmental social work in South Africa: Translating policy into practice. *International Social Work*, 56(5), 690–704.

Pawar, M. (2015). Action research on social work knowledge creation and dissemination from the global south. *British Journal of Social Work*, 45(4), 1357–1364.

Ragab, I. (1990). How social work can take root in developing countries. *Social Development Issues*, 12, 38–51.

Ragab, I. (2017). Has social work come of age? Revisiting the authentisation debate 25 years on. In M. Gray (ed.) *Routledge Handbook of Social Work and Social Development in Africa*. London: Routledge, 33–45.

Ramsey-Soroghaye, B. N. (2021). Community development in Nigeria: History, current strategies and its future as a social work method. *People Centred: The Journal of Development Administration*, 6(4), 133–141.

Ranta-Tyrkkö, S. (2011). High time for postcolonial analysis in social work. *Nordic Social Work Research*, 1(1), 25–41.

Rankopo, M. J., and Osei-Hwedie, K. (2011). Globalization and culturally relevant social work: African perspectives on indigenization. *International Social Work*, 54(1), 137–147.

Ross, E. (2010). African spirituality, ethics and traditional healing: Implications for indigenous South African social work practice and education. *South African Journal of Bioethics and Law*, 3(1), 44–51.

Sakamoto, I. (2007). An anti-oppressive approach to cultural competence. *Canadian Social Work Review*, 24(1), 105–114.

Secker, E. (2013). Witchcraft stigmatization in Nigeria: Challenges and successes in the implementation of child rights. *International Social Work*, 56(1), 22–36.

Shawky, A. (1972). Social work education in Africa. *International Social Work*, 15(3), 3–16.

Tangban, E. E., Isokon, B. E., and Obeten, U. B. (2020). Challenges of ethnicity and social work intervention in Nigeria. *International Journal of Social Sciences and Humanities Review*, 10(3), 216–226. Available at: https://www.ijsshr.com/journal/index.php/IJSSHR/article/view/638/541.

Tanyi, P. L., Odo, C. O., Omeje, A. E., and Ugwuanyi, C. A. (2021). Ethnic agitations and threat of secession in Nigeria: What can social workers do? *Journal of Social Work in Developing Societies*, 3(2), 29–45.

Ugiagbe, E. O. (2015). Social work is context-bound: The need for indigenization of social work practice in Nigeria. *International Social Work*, 58(6), 790–801.

Ugiagbe, E. O., and Ugiagbe, I. (2014). Transcending the Eurocentric development paradigms in Nigeria: The traditional age grade in discourse. *Humanities and Social Sciences Journal of Siberian Federal University*, 8(3), 366–376.

Uzuegbu, C. N. (2010). Culture and child abuse in Nigeria. *International Journal of Research in Arts and Social Sciences*, 2, 201–206.

2
THE INFORMALITY PARADIGM IN SOCIAL WORK PRACTICE IN AFRICA

Philosophy, Continuity, and Prospects for Integration into Professional Practice

Venesio Bwambale Bhangyi, Milliam Kiconco, and Wing Hong Chui

Abstract: English

The introduction of professional social work in Africa by the colonial administration disregarded indigenous, herein, informal ways of knowing, being, and doing. The post-independence governments in Africa have also failed to expand social services to most populations, who until today depend on informal social services. As such, professional social work has lacked presence and relevance in many localities. This chapter engages with the possibilities of enhancing African social work thinking, education, and practice through utilising knowledge outside the boundaries of formal social work education and extending the frontiers of social work education to include informal learning. Through use of a qualitative systematic review methodology, the chapter advances the view that informal social work across African communities offers an alternative paradigm through which professional practice and education can be enhanced. The chapter first conceptualises informal social work, explores its pervasive continuity in Africa, and articulates its philosophical framework. Then, it visualises informal social work in practice with marginalised populations and its critiques as a paradigm. Finally, the prospects for integration of informal and professional social work are discussed. It is hoped the chapter will contribute to the decolonisation debate that seeks to place greater emphasis on building contextual indigenous knowledge for an African-oriented social work.

Introduction

In Africa, governments and other formal social sector agencies are not the largest provider of social work services (Awortwi, 2017). The majority of the poor and marginalised populations on the continent, who are often the focus of social work change and intervention efforts, have difficulties in accessing these formal agencies. Yet, professional social work is largely aligned with formal agencies. In part, this is because in many ways the profession's colonial origins and heritages associate its practice and education to what was and is formal. The existence of professional social work in Africa as a colonial imposition on the helping systems of the peoples of the continent is widely acknowledged and debated (Osei-Hwedie and Boateng, 2018; Twikirize and Spitzer, 2019). Introduced to serve colonial interests, the social work profession disregarded indigenous, herein, informal ways of doing things that had long sustained cohesion and order in African societies. Until now, informality has been adopted and continues to exist in contemporary Africa. The efforts by independent African governments to expand social services have had varying degrees of success through the public and formal approaches leaving most of Africa's population to seek redress in the informal sector. As such, professional social work has lacked presence and relevance in many localities.

This chapter explores the possibilities of enhancing African social work thinking and practice through utilising knowledge outside the boundaries of formal social work education. This is done by extending the frontiers of social work education to explore and include informal learning. As such, it advances the view that informal social work practice and education, resident in African communities, offers an alternative paradigm that can enhance, revitalise, and endear professional practice and education in local contexts. The chapter begins by offering an in-depth conceptualisation of informal social work. It then postulates the basis of the extensive continuation of informal social work in Africa. The argument of the philosophy and framework of principles that underpin informal social work are then articulated. It further offers the visualisation of informal social work in practice philosophies across client populations. In addition, it points to a possible critique of informal social work and illustrates the prospects for integration of both informal and professional social work in engendering societal change and development. In building this argument, the chapter hopes to contribute to the decolonisation debate that seeks to place greater emphasis on building contextual indigenous knowledge for an African-oriented social work.

Towards Conceptualising Informal Social Work in Africa

In most African countries, official policy and legislation categorise social services, including social welfare and social work services, as those provided by the state (Awortwi, 2017). This includes all regulated and legally registered entities, such as dispersed government agencies, private welfare agencies, non-profit, faith-based, and charitable organisations. In many African cases, however, evidence suggests that most persons who need social services are served by kin or community without ever contacting the state or other formal authority (Manful and Cudjoe, 2018; Twikirize and Spitzer, 2019, p. 245). A closer review of ten sources (publications) used in writing this chapter with the words 'informal' and or 'social work', 'social services', 'social care', or 'care' in their titles did not yield a conceptualisation of informal social work. The terms 'informal social work' or 'informal helping' are used without offering conceptual depth and clarity of what it implies. For example, Manful and Cudjoe (2018) cited Nakunya (2016), who stated that members from the extended family and other relatives perform duties that are well equipped for voluntary and philanthropic organisations.

Informal social work is therefore used in this chapter to refer to arrangements, processes, interventions, and actions that offer social work services to individuals, groups, communities, or society that would otherwise be offered by a formal professional, by an outside individual. The interventions are delivered without professionally trained social workers in a structure that is not formally registered or not organised by a legally registered agency. These interventions could otherwise be construed as consistent with the mission and values of the social work profession.

From the above conceptualisation, the following features characterise informal social work:

1. The interventions offered are compatible with the mission of the social work profession. Therefore, all informal services, interventions, or supports that do not align with the values, principles, and mission of the social work profession would not be categorised as informal social work.
2. The primary focus is to promote the wellbeing of those receiving informal social work services. The focus is on both the wellbeing in the immediate, intermediate or in the future of those receiving services. It is achieved through support in the personal, social, cultural, economic, educational, political, spiritual, environmental, and other aspects of those being supported.
3. The provider is an individual or association that is not a registered agency. This includes informal services provided by individuals or groups that could be in registered agencies but are provided outside the formal structures, procedures, and policies of such an agency.
4. The informal social work services should be within the confines of the country's legal regime and should not in any way be construed as illegal or in breach of the law.
5. The basis of knowledge for helping is often informal learning from experience, observation, cultural knowledge, or intuitive improvisation. Therefore, the helping philosophies are more often held in oral form and built through continued refinement of interventions within contextual conditions.
6. The use of these services should result in an improvement in the life conditions of those accessing them. In this regard, they are meant to meet current and or future needs that would otherwise inhibit the recipient's wellbeing.
7. In cases where the services are mentioned in a government policy document, their organisation and delivery are propagated by an informal process without direct government involvement.
8. Local resources are the basis of interventions. Such resources could be individually owned or communal trusts that promote the common good. Examples include resources in the form of materials, community assets (such as open grounds, communal buildings, or other pooled assets), community networks, local leadership, social relations, available experiences, or skill sets.
9. The interventions collectively cover a wide range of social issues. This is because they are not bound by rigid policy or legal definitions of operational practice areas. They cover any social issue where support is required and humanly possible. In this way, they have a much wider reach in African communities as they extend the boundaries of social services to cover the complexities inherent in the social conditions of living.

The Basis for the Pervasive Continuity of Informal Social Work in Africa

There are musings as to why informal social work and social services are prevalent in most parts of Africa. The reason for this tendency is found in the social-economic and political contexts of African countries. First, in many African countries, the reality is that formal social work services do not reach the majority of the populations in both rural and urban areas. This is in part attributed to the failings and inefficiencies in public provision of social work and social welfare services in many countries (Awortwi, 2017). This mass failure in state social work and or social service apparatus can be attributed to a shear lack of resources, the enormous poverty challenges, widespread bad governance, and a host of other internal challenges. In addition, most of Africa's population, especially in sub-Saharan Africa, live in distant and inaccessible rural areas. The delivery of social services for children, youth, women, and other disadvantaged groups is thus hampered due to distances, poor infrastructure connectivity, and limited government presence in remote places.

Second, the social development agenda of most post-independence governments has never yielded fruit and has failed to take services to all corners of their individual countries. Noyoo (2022) and Chikadzi (2022) attribute this failure to develop productive social services in Africa to the reliance on foreign aid and the international development actors who bring imported and foreign models to Africa not suited for the African contexts. This is because the philosophies of such development ideas are sometimes in conflict with and or contradict local values, practices, and knowledge systems. In addition, the vagaries in Africa's post-independence democratic election cycles impact development efforts before they get rooted. New manifestos with new ideas are used to win votes rather than initiate, deliver, and consolidate social development interventions.

Third, professional social work since its very beginnings was and is a foreign idea, with the colonial governments focusing on Western philosophies, and many successive schools of social work perpetuating the same philosophies. While a group of academics have, since independence, advocated for and written vigorously in pursuit of contextual, relevant, and African identity in social work, it appears it has not borne much impact in both education, research, policy, and practice (Osei-Hwedie and Boateng, 2018). This *foreignness* of social work in Africa has produced two dimensions of social work practice and education: one that is rooted in Western helping philosophies as professional social work and another that is rooted in local indigenous African helping philosophies as informal social work. To have relevance, African social work should bridge this dichotomy.

Fourth, the combined effects of the above three factors have created a long history of informal social work services that have become widely provided, accessible, known, trusted, and demanded in Africa. The provision mechanisms for informal social work services are located within Africa's communities which enables quick access through both geographical and social proximity. Those who offer the services are known by the communities and the long historical record of service has earned them the trust of community members. Practicing and schooling in these philosophies occurs naturally as people live, interact, and relate within and across communities. They are learned through accumulation of experiences, observations, and participation. In addition, they are flexible within social conditions, allowing them to cover a wide range of social issues. As such, they have become the first call of service as compared to the formal professional social work services that are bureaucratic, are located in distant government offices, and are legalistic.

The Philosophy and Framework of Informal Social Work in Africa

Utilisation of Grassroot Mechanisms

The informality paradigm in social work grounds its practice through using grassroot mechanisms that are available, accessible, plentiful, and understood by every local person. This reliance on grass-root mechanisms therefore becomes probably the best fit for implementing all-encompassing social work services within the community in the absence of state and other formal services. They build on local resources, local experiences, learnings from past local failings, and decades old practices of survival welfare as a group of people. Those who are recipients of support on one social issue are also providers of social support to others in another social issue. This means that such informal social work practices are participatory, democratic, bottom up, responsive, and evolutionary. To build professional social work on such a practice is to build on a firm foundation rooted in people's histories, survival innovations, struggles, and collective memories. These collectively build a pool of support mechanisms that cover a wide range of welfare issues. Therefore, local mechanisms are one of the most valued resources in informal social work education and practice.

Communal Mobilisation for Collective Responsibility

It is important to think of informal social work as built on communal mobilisation and collective responsibility. According to Van Wyk and Reddy (2022), this communal self-mobilisation should be viewed as a response to the shortcomings and inefficiencies of the state in providing social work services for all its people. Therefore, communities mobilise themselves for self-help in the absence of the state and formal services. In addition, they place the duty of care in their collective, in the totality of the community units and social groups. As such, they are built on the concept of collective responsibility. This implies that as a collective, everyone is responsible for sustaining the life for all in the community and helping to enact, protect, and sustain community citizenship. In the absence of the state, everyone in the community becomes the state, ensuring that everyone else survives and meets basic social wellbeing. It therefore becomes a moral, spiritual, social, and cultural duty for every person to act when it is their chance to support another community member.

Mutuality and Reciprocity

Central to informal social work is the conception of mutuality and reciprocity of the intervention framework (Kail et al., 2021; Twikirize and Spitzer, 2019). The basis of informal social work is a form of mutual aid, in which help is offered in the expectation that at another time when in need, the helper shall also receive support. This expected reciprocal support may be from the person who was helped or from another source based on the belief that the person being helped helps others or shall help others in the future. The common adage of 'you never know when and from who you need support' is the driving force of the mutual aid apparatus. Therefore, the spirit to support others is driven by both social and internal valuations. The social valuations consist of helping others to build and sustain the spirit and chain of social support during times of need within African communities. For internal valuations, the drive to help is guided by the internal satisfaction, relief, and peace of mind attained by a person or community when they have supported those that required help. This creates some form of informal social insurance within communities. An example is in times of sickness. Friends, family, and kin come and visit the sick and offer support both material and moral. These hold the hope and belief that when it is their misfortune to be sick, then the cycle is repeated in kind, offering a never-ending loop. It is important to note that because of mutuality and reciprocity, support is not necessarily directed to poor or disadvantaged members of the community but to whoever has a need that requires external assistance from the community.

Family, Kinship, and Social Relations

Informal social work is built on the pillars of family, kinship systems, and social relations to deliver social welfare (Twikirize and Spitzer, 2019). In informal social work, families are pivotal in the interventions as the providers as well as the receivers of social services. Family members look out for and support each other as a unit. Parents continue to be parents even when their children have become adults, for example through offering counsel in matters of marriage, caring for grandchildren, and offering moral support. Many of the children take care of their parents through the life course, offering help to their parents while still under parental care as part of general childhood responsibilities in a family as well as taking greater responsibility for their parent's welfare in their old age. This relationship of help has been practiced and internalised over centuries and gained spiritual dimensions. It is considered as taboo, misfortune, curse, or ill will when this responsibility is neglected. In addition, kinship is critical to informal social work through the extended family system. The uncles, aunties, brothers, and sisters are all part of the helping system. This kinship also extends to clan systems as agents of interventions, such as in times of death and grief, and settlement of land disputes. As African societies have evolved and urbanisation has caused persons to shift away from family and kinship, social relations such as friendships, workmates, schoolmates, and neighbours, have become important sources of social support. These support in numerous ways through individual troubles but also in pursuing collective developmental projects, such as savings, investments, child care, shared urban housing developments, and other forms of resource linkages.

Informed by Spirituality, Religion, and Associated Structures and Supports

Informal social work is guided by spirituality, religion, and the associated structures, interventions, and other supports. These are many times located in local contexts, communities, families, and societies as part of the informal support systems. As such, informal social work is built on an inextricable association with spirituality and religion. The belief systems in both indigenous African spirituality, Islam, Christianity, and other belief systems have been interwoven into a helping philosophy focused on care, respect, support for one another, forgiveness, shared hope, shared prosperity, and peaceful coexistence. Within communities, supporting and helping others is viewed as a divine duty. Those who help view their acts as an extension of the will of a higher power and, many times, they hope to gain spiritual rewards in their earthly lives or in their afterlife. While mainstream religious establishments are formal entities, the activities in the majority of their local, parish, and district establishments are spontaneous and informal. It is common, for example, to find members who pray in the same church to offer greater material, social, spiritual, and physical support in cases where a member or member's family suffers illness, death, or misfortune. This philosophy of social work support rooted in spirituality and religion is largely lacking in formal social work due the absence of content on spirituality and religion in formal social work education and training in many parts of Africa (Tusasiirwe et al., 2022).

Informal Social Work Actors, Associations, and Agents

It should be noted that the education and practice of informal social work is practiced in a complex web of flexible, diffused, and overlapping structures of actors, associations, and agents. As mentioned above, the family and its kinship are one of the primary agents. A further fluid institution is the 'non-family family' or other social relations comprised of friends, workmates, and neighbours. A tribe in some instances has also been mobilised as a structure, with persons belonging to the same tribal grouping in Africa viewing themselves as a tribal family (in the countries of Burundi and Rwanda, ethnicity has been de-emphasised through national policy due to the 1994 genocide). The community is a further social structure through which informal social work operates. The term 'community' here is used to refer to a geographical area or a community of interest such as savings group. Related to this are associations in which people come together for the purpose of building some intervention to change their lives and those of others. Examples include saving groups, burial societies, farmers groups, etc. Furthermore, there are also informal organisations that operate based on structured rules but are not registered by the government. Lastly, there are traditional institutions such as chiefs, clan heads, elders' forums, and mothers' groups. These belong in a wider category of traditional institutions wielding considerable traditional power but are not recognised in many countries as part of the formal traditional institutions. They continue to offer a variety of social support to individuals, families, and collective communities.

Possibilities of a Critique of Informal Social Work Knowledge

The danger of theorising in any field is that your theoretical arguments will always be debated by others. It is this intensity of scrutiny that highlights the possibility of criticism. In the first instance, the prevailing dominance of Western philosophies may offer a bedrock of critiquing the informality paradigm. In some spheres, these have become normalised and accepted as what constitutes social work theory. According to Osei-Hwedie and Boateng (2018), despite the past and current efforts for social work education and practice in Africa to develop an African orientation, it appears that many academics and professionals have accepted that what is Western is what is global, fashionable, functional, and perfect. Despite this possibility of skepticism, this chapter engages with African realities in holding that the informality paradigm offers a contextual and local knowledge system for professional social work education and practice.

There are arguments that informal social work in Africa focuses on community and social groups, which are consistent with macro and mezzo social work but may not work well with micro social work practice (Mupedziswa et al., 2019). In advancing this criticism, the argument is that informal social work is not well placed to meet individual needs. It is also argued that the personal is therefore likely to suffer further marginalisation in this process. However, it should be noted that the focus of informal social work is the collective without sidelining the individual needs. The collective is a composition of individuals, and the aim is to constantly link the individual to the collective, through which service is attained. This is the essence of the African communal life in which one person exists through others (Mugumbate and Nyanguru, 2013).

A third critique relates to the cultural knowledge that informs informal social work knowledge and practice models as being potentially harmful to sections of society, such as children, women, older persons, and other marginalised populations. Chineka and Mtetwa (2021), for example, cited gender disparities in informal savings and credit programmes in Malawi that seek to address poverty. While this is a legitimate concern, progress has been made in several communities across Africa in identifying and addressing harmful elements in informal care, support, and helping systems. In addition, the conceptualization of informal social work articulated in this chapter advances the argument that informal social work should be consistent with the mission of the social work profession and therefore address social injustices and marginalisation. Social work education and practice should therefore focus on identifying and addressing where, what, why, and by which means informal social work is contrary to the social work mission. This should be done in a critical way to avoid misrepresentation of informal social work philosophies.

Another critique of the informality paradigm is that it has not been sufficiently debated in social work education and practice in Africa. This problem we will term as *silent noise* in this chapter. *Silent noise* because there are not enough discussions on informal social work in social work literature in Africa. And *silent noise* because a lot of social work literature explores several linkages of practice in, with, or for the informal, without directly acknowledging and or realizing that informal social work is dominant on the continent (see, for example, Adanteng-Kissi et al., 2022; Dafuleya, 2018; Manful and Cudjoe, 2018; Noyoo and Boon, 2018; Twikirize and

Spitzer, 2019). This has created an invisibility problem for a paradigm that is visible and widely acknowledged. Therefore, scholars are likely to argue that this paradigm is still limited in conceptual construction.

Recommendations for Integration of Informal and Formal Social Work

Three recommendations are advanced by this chapter to support the building, expanding, and centring of informal social work in social work education, practice, and policy. It is hoped that these could make the profession gain relevance for many African people. They are:

- Research and documentation of informal social work knowledge.
- Inclusion of informal social work knowledge in educational curriculum.
- Actively and rigorously integrating informal social work into formal social work services and programmes.

The Production of Knowledge on Informal Social Work

Professional social workers in Africa should extensively produce knowledge on informal social work through mapping and documentation. Some African scholars have started the documentation of these practices (see,. for example,. Noyoo, 2021; Twikirize and Spitzer, 2019). This mapping and documentation should be particular to specific communities, societies, and even countries. This is because Africa is so vast, with differences in social, cultural, economic, political, and natural environment conditions that influence the helping systems of localities. One way is to encourage and support graduate students in social work to research and write on informal social work. Furthermore, practitioners must write critical reflections of their interactions with informal social work for distributing to, sharing with, and educating future generations. The academia and schools of social work (SSW) can initiate and execute an agenda to study informal social work. By so doing, knowledge will be generated on informal social work for wider circulation and to support the centring of such knowledge for professional social work education and training. Twikirize and Spitzer (2019, p. 2) support this view and argue that African social work knowledge should be developed first, next taught in classes, and then applied in practice.

Inclusion of Learning from Informal Social Work in Educational Curricular

Schools of social work (SSW) across continental Africa should urgently include learning from informal social work practices in their education curriculum and their practices of educating future social workers. This can be done to both fresh social work trainees in SSW and practitioners undergoing continuing professional development (CPD), in-service training or advanced studies. This form of scholarship will require a shift in thinking about a social work classroom towards an understanding of the learning environment as one in which students, educators, and the community are co-leaners and co-creators of knowledge (Tusasiirwe, 2022). This can be done in several ways. First, students can undertake their fieldwork training with informal social work providers. Second, students can be asked to analytically document an informal social work practice in their locality as part of their theory class. Third, learners can be required and supported to reflect on their personal support systems as helpers or recipients of social support and how this constitutes social work. Fourth, informal social work actors can be invited into classrooms to share their experiences as providers or recipients of social work services. And finally, practicing social workers can share with students the interfaces between their formal and informal helping and support systems in their various interventions.

Integration of Informal Knowledge and Practice Models into Formal Intervention

Informal social work knowledge systems and practice models should be actively and rigorously included in formal social work services, programmes, policies, and interventions. This should be done by both the government and other social sector actors. This may require persuasion, dialogue, political engagement, and advocacy by social work professionals to kick start and sustain this integration. One way to attain this integration could be to include informal social work practices in policy design and implementation, thereby making the resultant policy relevant to the context and benefiting from the local knowledge. This should be extended to writing the principles of informal social work philosophies informing policy and the resultant legislation that supports the policy. The South African example in which *Ubuntu* (a pan African philosophy that emphasizes social relations, connectedness, interdependence, communalism, and collective welfare interventions guided by a collection of values and practices that make people of Africa authentic human beings [Mugumbate and Chereni, 2020]) has been written in its social development agenda as the guiding factor is a case in point (Noyoo, 2021). Another option for integration is to recognise and activate informal social work actors as part of the delivery mechanisms of a formal social welfare service and programme. The Ugandan example in which child welfare social workers engage with informal actors in childcare interventions is an illustration of this potential (Bhangyi, 2022).

Conclusion

Informal social work in Africa is often contested in education and practice and with disagreements on what is and what is not formal. The resulting effect of this contestation is that informal knowledge and helping practices are largely pushed to the periphery, ignored, and absent in formal social work education and practice training. Unknowingly, however, many professional social workers in Africa engage with and in informal social work practices, sometimes as part of their professional services or as part of being members of the African community with a duty to help. Indeed, the realities of Africa dictate that for professional social work to be relevant and present in the lives of many of its people, it needs to position itself in the contextual, cultural, indigenous, and local knowledge and practice systems. These are abundantly located in the informal social work knowledge and practice systems. To attain this contextualisation, Tusasiirwe (2022) argues for a constant questioning and challenging of the current dominant knowledge and models on how to do social work. Thus, the chapter argues that African social work educators and practitioners need to assert the informal knowledge systems and practices of doing social work, which must be critically analysed and centred before any non-African models can be sought. As suggested in the recommendations above, building documented profiles of these knowledge systems, engaging students with informal social work as part of practice education, and advocacy that links and integrates informal social work into formal government policy, programmes, and service interventions are steps in the right direction. Building informal social work knowledge (for education, practice, research, and policy) and centring it creates an environment with spaces, structures, visibilities, acceptance, and applications of African epistemologies. Focusing on informal social work knowledge and practice in professional social work education settings will promote dismantling the lingering colonial legacies in social work. It will also spur an advancement of an African-oriented social work in both education and practice.

Recommendations

1. Research and document informal social work knowledge.
2. Include informal social work knowledge in educational curriculum.
3. Actively and rigorously integrate informal social work into formal social work services and programmes.

Further Reading

Noyoo, N. (ed.) (2021). *Social Welfare and Social Work in Southern Africa*. Stellenbosch: Sun Media Press.
Noyoo, N., and Boon, E. (eds.) (2018). *Indigenous Social Security Systems in Southern and West Africa*. Stellenbosch: Sun Media Press.
Twikirize, M. J., and Spitzer, H. (eds.) (2019). *Social Work Practice in Africa: Indigenous and Innovative Approaches*. Kampala: Fountain Publishers.

References

Adonteng-Kissi, B., Moyle, W., and Grealish, L. (2022). Informal care of older adults with chronic life-limiting illness in Africa: An integrative review. *International Social Work*, 65(1), 127–141. https://doi.org/10.1177/0020872819901164.
Awortwi, N. (2017). Social protection is a grassroots reality: Making the case for policy reflections on community based social protection actors and services in Africa. *Development Policy Review*, 36(S2), 897–913. https://doi.org/10.1111/dpr.12368.
Bhangyi, B. V. (2022). Towards developing ethical capacities in social work practice in Africa: Case study and critical commentary from Uganda. *International Social Work*, 1–7. https://doi.org/10.1177/00208728221136968.
Chikadzi, V. (2022). A social work and social development perspective on the need to decolonise African economies in light of the Covid-19 pandemic: Lessons for Africa. In M. C. S. Gonçalves, R. Gutwald, T. Kleibl, R. Lutz, N. Noyoo, and J. Twikirize (eds.) *The Coronavirus and Challenges to Social Development: Global Perspectives*. e-book. Springer, 389–398.
Chineka, T. S., and Mtetwa, E. (2021). Savings and credit schemes (SCSs): Towards an informal sector poverty alleviation strategy for Zimbabwe. *African Journal of Social Work*, 11(6), 403–411.
Dafuleya, G. (2018). (Non)state and (in)formal social protection in Africa: Focusing on burial societies. *International Social Work*, 61(1), 156–168. https://doi.org/10.1177/0020872815611196.
Kail, B., Pardasai, H., and Chazin, R. (2021). The better future international's family care model in Tanzania: Creating social capital as a means to empowerment in social work practice. *International Social Work*, 64(6), 975–991. https://doi.org/10.1177/0020872819884986.
Manful, E., and Cudjoe, E. (2018). Is kinship failing? Views on informal support by families in contact with social services in Ghana. *Child and Family Social Work*, 23(4), 617–624. https://doi.org/10.111/cfs.1252.
Mugumbate, R. J., and Chereni, A. (2020). Editorial. Now, the theory of Ubuntu has its space in social work. *African Journal of Social Work*, 10(1), v–xvii.
Mugumbate, R. J., and Nyanguru, A. (2013). Exploring African philosophy: The value of Ubuntu in social work. *African Journal of Social Work*, 3(1), 82–100.
Mupedziswa, R., Rankopo, M., and Mwansa, K.-L. (2019). Ubuntu as a Pan-African philosophical framework for social work in Africa. In J. M. Twikirize and H. Spitzer (eds.) *Social Work Practice in Africa: Indigenous and Innovative Approaches*. Kampala: Fountain Publishers, 21–38.
Noyoo, N. (ed.) (2021). *Social Welfare and Social Work in Southern Africa*. Stellenbosch: Sun Media Press.

Noyoo, N. (2022). Critiquing western development paradigms and theories in the age of the coronavirus (COVID-19): An African perspective. In M. C. S. Gonçalves, R. Gutwald, T. Kleibl, R. Lutz, N. Noyoo, and J. Twikirize (eds.) *The Coronavirus and Challenges to Social Development: Global perspectives*. e-book. Springer, 399–408.

Noyoo, N., and Boon, E. (eds.) (2018). *Indigenous Social Security Systems in Southern and West Africa*. Stellenbosch: Sun Media Press.

Osei-Hwedie, K., and Boateng, A. D. (2018). 'Do not worry your head': The impossibility of indigenising social work education and practice in Africa. *South African Journal of Social Work and Social Development*, 30(3). https://doi.org/10.25159/2415-5829/3978.

Tusasiirwe, S. (2022). Is it indigenisation or decolonisation of social work in Africa? A focus on Uganda. *African Journal of Social Work*, 12(1), 1–11.

Tusasiirwe, S., Nabbuma, D., and Kansiime, P. (2022). Religion and spirituality in social work in Uganda: Lessons for social work education. *Social Work Education*, 1–18. https://doi.org/10.1080/02615479.2022.2104243.

Twikirize, M. J., and Spitzer, H. (eds.) (2019). *Social Work Practice in Africa: Indigenous and Innovative Approaches*. Kampala: Fountain Publishers.

Van Wyk, D. T., and Reddy, V. (2022). Pandemic governance: Developing a politics of informality. *South African Journal of Science*, 118(5/6). https://doi.org/10.17159/sajs.2022/13163.

3
EXPLORING THE POTENTIAL OF AN ECOSOCIAL APPROACH FOR AFRICAN SOCIAL WORK EDUCATION

James Kutu Obeng and Michael Emru Tadesse

Abstract: English

As the global environmental crisis continues to threaten the wellbeing and livelihood of people in marginalised communities like those in Africa, the social work profession is urged to expand its curriculum to include natural environmental concerns. This would enable social work to understand and respond to the interactive and interdependent concerns of social, economic, political, and environmental factors. This chapter centres an ecosocial approach in African social work education to decolonise professional knowledge, promote indigenous wisdom about human-nature relatedness, and facilitate environmental sustainability in Africa. An important empirical starting point is to examine how African universities have conceptualised and operationalised the 'environment' within the social work curriculum. We reviewed the undergraduate social work curricula of 12 African universities based in Ethiopia, Ghana, Nigeria, and South Africa to determine to what extent the concepts of the ecosocial approach and its key components like ecology and the natural environment are addressed in African social work curricula. The results show that the Bachelor of Social Work (BSW) programmes/curricula of the different universities do not adequately capture the content of an ecosocial approach (or the significance of the natural environment for human wellbeing). We recommend that BSW programmes in Africa should consider a mandatory module/course in an ecosocial approach, emphasise transdisciplinarity; and use field practicum to promote an ecosocial approach.

Abstract: Amharic

የዓለም አቀፍ የአካባቢ ቀውስ በተጋላጭ ማህበረሰቦች ውስጥ ያሉ ሰዎችን ደህንነትን እና መተዳደሪያን አደጋ ላይ እየጣለ ይገኛል፡፡ ከዚህ ጋር በተያያዘ የማህበራዊ ስራ (የሶሻል ዎርክ) ሙያ የስነምህዳራዊ ስጋቶችን የሚመለከት ይዘቶችን በሥርዓተ-ትምህርቱ ውስጥ እንዲያካትት ጥሪ እየተደረገለት ይገኛል፡፡ ይህን ማድረግ የማህበራዊ ስራ ሙያው የተሳሰሩ ማህበራዊ ፣ ምጣኔሃብታዊ ፣ ፖለቲካዊ እና ስነምህዳራዊ ቀውሶችን በአግባቡ እንዲረዳና ምላሽ እንዲሰጥ ያስችለዋል ተብሎ ይታመናል፡፡ የዚህ ምዕራፍ አላማም የስነምህዳራዊ-ማህበራዊ (ኢኮ-ሶሻል) ጽንስ ሐሳብ ለአፍሪካ የማህበራዊ ስራ ትምህርት ያለውን እምቅ አቅም ለማሳየት ነው፡፡ ይህንንም ማድረጉ በአፍሪካ የማህበራዊ ስራ ሙያ ዕውቀትን ከቅኝ ግዛት ለማላቀቅ፣ የሰዉ እና ተፈጥሮ

DOI: 10.4324/9781003314349-5   37

መስተጋብርን በሚመለከት አገር በቀል እውቀትን ለማጎልበት እና ዘላቂ የሆነ የተፈጥሮ ጥበቃን ለማበረታታት ይረዳል ብለን እናምናለን። ይሁንንም አለማ ለማሳለት እንደረዳን እንደመነሻ 'የአፍሪካ የማህበራዊ ስራ ስርዓተ-ትምህርት ምን ያህል ስነምህዳርን እና ስነምህዳራዊ-ማህበራዊ ጽንስ ሐሳብን የሚመለከቱ ይዘቶችን አካቷል?' የሚል አጠቃላይ ግምገማ አካሂደናል። ይሁንንም ግምገማ ያደረግነው በአሥራ ሁለት የአፍሪካ ዩኒቨርሲቲዎች ውስጥ በሚገኙ የመጀመሪያ ዲግሪ የማህበራዊ ስራ ስርዓተ-ትምህርት መገግብት ላይ ነው። እነዚህ ዩኒቨርሲቲዎች በኢትዮጵያ፣ በጋና፣ በናይጄሪያ እና በደቡብ አፍሪካ የሚገኙ ናቸው። የግምገማው ውጤት እንደሚያሳየው በዩኒቨርሲቲዎቹ ውስጥ በሚገኙ የመጀመሪያ ዲግሪ የማህበራዊ ስራ ስርዓተ-ትምህርት መዘግብት ውስጥ ስነምህዳርን እና ስነምህዳራዊ-ማህበራዊ ጽንስ ሐሳብን የሚመለከቱ ይዘቶች በበቂ ሁኔታ አይንኙም። ከዚህ በመነሳት የሚከተሉትን ምክርሃሳቦች በአፍሪካ ለሚገኙ የመጀመሪያ ዲግሪ የማህበራዊ ስራ የትምህርት መርሃግብሮች ለመስጠት እንወዳለን። አንደኛ፣ የትምህርት መርሃግብሮቹ አስገዳጅ የሆነ ስነምህዳራዊ-ማህበራዊ ጽንስ ሐሳብን ያካተተ የማህበራዊ ስራ የትምህርት ኮርስ ወይም ሞጁል ቢቀርጹ እና ቢያስተምሩ እንላለን። ሁለተኛ፣ መርሃ ግብሮቹ ተማሪዎቻቸውን ወደ ተግባራዊ ልምምድ ሲመድቡ ስነምህዳራዊ-ማህበራዊ ጽንስ ሐሳብን ከግምት እንዲያስገቡ እንመክራለን።

Abstract: Akan

Oyene a ɛwɔ abɔdeɛ mu nneɛma a atwa yɛn ho ahyia mu de ɔhaw aba nnipa asetena mu ankanka wɔn a w'asetena mu yɛ den a wɔfiri Abibiman mu. Wei de asɛdeɛ foforɔ abrɛ adwumakuo a wɔhwɛ nnipa asetena mu nsɛm soɔ, sɛ wɔbɛ tretre wɔn ahyeɛ mu de abɔdeɛ mu nneɛma a atwa yɛn ho ahyia mu nsɛm bɛka w'adesua ne asɛdeɛ ho. Ne saa bɛboa ama adwumakuo a wɔhwɛ nnipa asetena mu nsɛm soɔ anya nteaseɛ, atumi de ntotoeɛ papa aba nnipa nkitahodie a ɛfa w'asetena mu, wɔnsikasɛm, w'amammuosɛm ho, ne abɔdeɛ mu nneɛma a atwa yɛn ho ahyia ho nsɛm mu. Krataa fa yi si no pi sɛ, adesua a ɛfa nkabom ho wɔ nnipa asetena mu ne abɔdeɛ mu nneɛma a atwa yɛn ho ahyia hia ma adwumakuo a wɔhwɛ nnipa asetena mu nsɛm soɔ wɔ Abibiman mu. Saa adesua yi bɛboa ama adwumakuo a wɔhwɛ nnipa asetena mu nsɛm soɔ atumi apaw nimdeɛ a ne fapem gyina abrɔfo-nyansa ne nkoasom soɔ, ama nimdeɛ a ɛfiri kuro mma ne nananom hɔ ɛ ɛfa nnipa ne abɔdeɛ ho abusuabɔ akɔsɔ, na aboa Abibiman anamontuo ɛde kankɔ bɛba abɔdeɛ mu nneɛma a atwa yɛn ho ahyia na atena hɔ daadaa. Ɛdikan no, na ɛbɛhia sɛ yɛhwehwɛ nwoma a sukuupɔn a wɔwɔ Abibiman mu ahyehyɛ de ama sukuufoɔ a w'ahyɛ w'adesua ase ɛfa asetena mu dwumadie mu nsɛm so. Yɛnhwehwɛmuu no kɔgyinaa sukuupɔn dummienu a wɔwɔ aman a ɛdidi soɔ yi: Ethiopia, Ghana, Nigeria, ne South Africa. Yɛhwɛɛ mpɛnpɛnsoɔ a sukuupɔn ahodoɔ no de adesua a ɛfa nkabom wɔ nnipa asetena mu nsɛm ne abɔdeɛ mu nneɛma a atwa yɛn ho ahyia mu nsɛm de aka asetena mu dwumadie nwoma mu. Nea ɛfiri nhwehwɛmu no pueɛ kyerɛ sɛ nwoma a sukuupɔn ahodoɔ no ahyehyɛ de ama sukuufoɔ a w'ahyɛ w'adesua ase ɛfa asetena mu dwumadie soɔ no ɛnni adesuadeɛ a ɛfa nkabom wɔ nnipa asetena mu nsɛm ne 'abɔdeɛ mu nneɛma a atwa yɛn ho ahyia' nsɛm so. Ne saa enti, ye krataa yi rekamfo de ama sukuupɔn a wɔwɔ Abibiman mu sɛ wɔbɛhyehyɛ nwoma afa nkabom wɔ nnipa asetena mu nsɛm ne abɔdeɛ mu nneɛma a atwa yɛn ho ahyia mu nsɛm. Afei nso ɛbɛhia sɛ sukuupɔn ahodoɔ no ne afoforɔ a wonim de wɔ abɔdeɛ mu nneɛma a atwa yɛn ho ahyia mu nsɛm ne ankorankoran a wɔn dwumadie ɛfa abɔdeɛ mu nneɛma a atwa yɛn ho ahyia mu nsɛm, ne yɛn kuro mpaninfoɔ ne nananom nyansa fa asaase so nsɛm ho nyinaa bɛka abom ahyehyɛ nwoma no de akyerɛ adesua papa yi.

Introduction

Since the industrial revolution started in the 18th century, climate change, biodiversity loss, natural disasters, environmental degradation, waste, and pollution have been increasing globally. These crises largely result from the capitalist/neoliberal system that thrives on market economy growth while externalising social and environmental costs (Raworth, 2017).

Global recognition of environmental crises has been increasing and the need for humans to live in more sustainable ways without impairing the wellbeing of all lifeforms in the present and the future has become more pronounced. Evidence shows that environmental crises disproportionately affect the poorest countries of the world, and in these countries, people with low incomes, women, children, and marginalised ethnic groups are impacted more (Dominelli, 2012; Muzingili, 2016). Similarly, in rich countries people with low incomes and those with ethnic minority backgrounds suffer the gravest effects of environmental crises (Nesmith and Smyth, 2015).

At the very least, social work is concerned with the most disadvantaged populations and communities, who face social and environmental injustices resulting from environmental crises. Therefore, social work is called upon to ameliorate these effects on lives and livelihoods (Jones, 2012). Notably, social work professionals have been involved in the evacuation and resettlement of people who suffer the effects of natural disasters like flooding, landslides, storms, and droughts in many countries around the world (Dominelli, 2012). Yet, social work has been criticised as being a pawn in a chess game for, amongst other things, contributing to the sustenance of capitalist hegemony (Boetto, 2016); being a grand colonial pacifist atoning for the colonial wrongs of the West through charity (Mtetwa and Muchacha, 2020); and being too slow to take a political stand against the destructive economic and political structures affecting sustainability. This shows that social work must do more than ameliorate the consequences of environmental crises; it should holistically pursue environmental sustainability as being interlinked with social and economic sustainability and join the global movement that seeks to steer people towards a more sustainable future (Jones, 2012).

Social work must therefore shift from its human-centeredness to an ecosocial-centred approach, to facilitate sustainability (Boetto, 2016). To do so, social work must solve its major paradox by attaining congruence among its ontological (being), epistemological (thinking), and methodological (doing) dimensions, based on holism and interdependence (Boetto, 2016).

Social work education is a medium through which an ecosocial transition can be achieved, that is, by expanding the social work curriculum to include environmental perspectives (Jones, 2012; Muzingili, 2016; Nesmith and Smyth, 2015). An ecosocial work content in social work curricula will help to shape social work professional knowledge and values (epistemology) needed to promote its identity as being interconnected with nature (ontology) and social work practice (methodology) with historically oppressed people, like those in Africa.

Africa happens to be one of the most massively affected continents when it comes to unsustainable global practices having a toll on the continent's development. The continent has historically suffered social, economic, and environmental injustices like colonisation, slavery, racism, poverty, food insecurity, war, and natural resource exploitation, and it is in urgent need of sustainability transformation. Moreover, the continent is exceptionally vulnerable to the impacts of climate change. The 2021 State of the Climate Africa report shows that Ethiopia experienced severe dry conditions and prolonged drought; Ghana experienced a short rainy season; Nigeria experienced dust storms, dry spells, and flooding that led to a cholera outbreak; and South Africa experienced rainfall deficits and rising sea levels (World Meteorological Organization (WMO), 2022). Also, the effect of climate change and human pressure on water has led to the shrinkage of Lake Chad, which borders Chad, Cameroon, Nigeria, and Niger.

Even though these environmental miseries prominently feature as key contemporary challenges jeopardising the living conditions of African people, they are sometimes overlooked in social work (Spitzer, 2019). While environmental crises in Africa do not only concern social work, social work is better positioned in terms of understanding the interactive effects of environmental crises on the livelihoods of (vulnerable) people and ways to effectively intervene in their lives. In this chapter, we discuss the need for an ecosocial work course/module in African social work education with the hope that this can improve practitioners' knowledge and skills to effectively intervene in the lives of Africans whose challenges are interlinked in environmental, social, and economic dimensions.

Self-Reflection: Connections to Ecosocial Worldview

In this section, we embrace an ecosocial worldview by recounting our lived experiences of how nature is embedded in our lives and our social work education, and how we became more mindful of our connections with nature.

Kutu: I trace my connection to the natural environment first to my ethnic identity where my clan is aligned to a totemic animal and my early childhood beginnings in a nature-abundant town in Ghana. Due to nature's propinquity to me while growing up, I remember I frequently went into nature to fetch ground water, search for food, play with friends, and engage in many other activities. I also witnessed first-hand how natural hazards like storms, flooding, and bushfires destroyed people's livelihoods. Looking back, I did not place much premium on how nature directly affected my wellbeing. Also, my social work education (bachelor's and master's degrees), received in Ghana, Portugal, Norway, and Sweden, was limited to humans and our social environment, while concerns about the natural environment were largely relegated to the background.

Tadesse: Until very recently, I had not paid enough attention to the natural environment and concepts such as the ecosocial approach. First, I was born and raised in an Ethiopian city where there was not much emphasis on the natural environment. Urbanisation and 'modernisation' were much more valued than the natural environment, especially by young people. Furthermore, even though my family sometimes raised domestic animals such as chickens and grew vegetables, I did not appreciate it. As a child, I even considered such practices backward. My university degrees and teaching experiences in sociology and social work in Ethiopia and Germany also did not help much when it came to truly understanding and appreciating the natural environment and concepts such as the ecosocial approach. My tendency as a university student and lecturer was to leave such issues to the 'professionals,' i.e., ecologists and other natural scientists.

But as 'the world has a way of guiding your steps' (Kimmerer, 2013), we had our epiphany moment for the natural environment and ecosocial work while applying for our doctoral study in the same project: Applying Sustainability Transition Research in Social Work Tackling Major Societal Challenge of Social Inclusion (ASTRA). The project applies transdisciplinary sustainability transition research in social work and underlines the interconnectivity of ecological, social, and economic drivers of (un)sustainability.

We duly acknowledge our background and positionality as Black Africans who have received social work education both in Africa and in Europe. We thus author this chapter as insiders with strong connections to our roots and not purporting to import Western concepts that may be contrary to our cherished traditions. Rather, we carefully and respectfully relate the ecosocial approach to Africa's own philosophy, such as Ubuntu, by highlighting the ways through which African traditions emphasise human-nature relationships and the need for social work education to adopt these thoughts. We pay homage and show due cognizance to our ancestors and elders who have paved the way for us, who are the custodians of our cherished traditions that enjoin us to revere nature, and who have through generations passed this knowledge onto our parents and us. Also, we appreciate the earlier works of literature by scholars, both Africans and non-Africans (Chigangaidze, 2022a; Le Grange, 2012; van Breda, 2019), who have contributed to shaping our understanding of the Ubuntu philosophy and how it relates to environmental concepts in Africa.

Ecosocial Approach and African Ubuntu Philosophy

The ecosocial approach contributes to expanding the person-in-environment perspective in social work to include the natural environment. It admonishes social work to take a holistic approach to sustainability by challenging dominant global structures like capitalism and neoliberalism that cause environmental destruction, inequalities, and injustices around the world and by combining social and ecological perspectives (Boetto, 2016; Närhi and Matthies, 2016).

The ecosocial approach is consistent with the true mission of social work in Africa, which is committed to the pursuit of social justice, human rights, and collective responsibility through indigenous knowledge (Lombard and Twikirize, 2014; Mtetwa and Muchacha, 2020). Social justice and human rights can be realised only within a healthy biophysical environment that provides our air, water, food, and living spaces (Lombard and Twikirize, 2014; Schmitz et al., 2012). Relying on case studies from Africa, Lombard and Twikirize (2014) argued that developmental social work on the continent must recognise and respond to the interconnections among social, economic, and environmental development. Social work education about human-nature embeddedness and environmental justice is critical to effecting this change (Nesmith and Smyth, 2015). More so, it is important for this education to reflect local examples and indigenous wisdom.

African social workers who seek to incorporate local and indigenous examples have often referred to the Ubuntu philosophy (van Breda, 2019). We, therefore, argue that the ecosocial approach is implicit in the Ubuntu philosophy and Africa's traditional belief systems. And, as the ecosocial approach encourages indigenous wisdom and Global South perspectives (Boetto, 2016), Ubuntu provides a good philosophical background for the realisation of an ecosocial transition in African social work education and practice. The Ubuntu philosophy has notably gained recent traction as an alternative for sustainable community development around the world. It became the first theme of the new Global Agenda for Social Work and Social Development for 2020–2030 and was one of the main values at the 2022 People's Summit for a new ecosocial world, which was co-facilitated by the International Federation of Social Workers and the United Nations Research Institute for Social Development. Ubuntu is an African philosophy themed as 'I am because we are' and expressed in different African languages and proverbs across the continent. For instance, it is represented with: 'biako ye' among Akan speakers in Ghana; 'mutunchi', 'iwa', 'agwa', and 'omwayaonyamo' in various languages in Nigeria; and proverbs such as 'ድር ቢያብር አንበሳ ያስር', which translates as 'when webs of a spider join together, they can trap a lion' in Ethiopia. Ubuntu emphasises that human beings derive our very existence from the larger and more significant interactive and reciprocal relations with other human beings, communities, nature, and the spiritual world. This imposes a collective and shared responsibility for the wellbeing of one another and nature. Ubuntu concretely expresses the ecosocial approach in social work by connecting the self, society, and nature (Le Grange, 2012) and by promoting systemic interlinkage among social, economic, and environmental sustainability (Mayaka and Truell, 2021).

Expanding African Social Work Curricula to Include Ecosocial Content

Globally, calls have been made to expand the focus of the social work profession to include environmental issues across the curriculum (Nesmith and Smyth, 2015; Rambaree, 2020). We therefore sought to examine social work curricula in Africa as one way to understand how social work education is engaging with the emerging environmental agenda (Jones, 2012). Accordingly, we examined the extent to which (to determine if) the concepts of the ecosocial approach and its key components, like ecology and natural environment, are addressed in African social work curricula. To do so, we reviewed the curricula of selected (based on convenience) Bachelor of Social Work (BSW) programmes among 12 African universities based in Ethiopia, Ghana, Nigeria, and South Africa. We conducted text searches of the curricula, course breakdowns, and course catalogues of the BSW programmes using key terms like 'ecosocial', 'ecology', and 'environment'.

We implemented two approaches to collect data: (i) retrieving curricula, course breakdown/catalogues from the official websites of the various universities and/or (ii) contacting colleagues or academic staff in the various universities for curricula and course breakdown/catalogues. In the case of Ethiopia, we reviewed the old and new harmonised curriculum used by all BSW programmes, along with reviews of another five universities: Addis Ababa University, Bahir Dar University, Mizan-Tepi University, Wollo University, and the University of Gondar. Our review was also based on the BSW curricula in the following countries and institutions: Ghana: University of Ghana and Kwame Nkrumah University of Science and Technology; Nigeria: University of Nigeria; South Africa: University of Pretoria, South African College of Applied Science (SACAP), University of South Africa (UNISA), and the University of Johannesburg. In all cases, we highlighted the main patterns we found in the search we conducted regarding the presence or absence of the key terms we were looking for, i.e., ecosocial approach, (natural) environment, and ecology. As a specific example, we used the Ethiopian case more frequently since it has a newly harmonised curriculum. Doing so helped to see if the new developments in social work education in relation to the ecosocial approach were exhibited. We also added some examples from the other countries.

The results of the review showed that the BSW programmes/curricula of the different universities are bereft of concepts such as the natural environment, ecosocial approach, and ecology. Such concepts are either absent or almost non-existent or used in other ways (as metaphors, etc.). For instance, there were no specific modules/courses teaching the ecosocial approach, environmental social work, ecological social work, or green social work. Furthermore, the term 'ecosocial' was not found in all the curricula. The term 'environment' was used in the curricula mostly to refer to the social and cultural environment as well as the built environment. There was very little mention of the natural environment. Also, the term 'ecology' was used just as a metaphor in relation to the ecological framework/perspective and systems theory to show the relationship of a client with his/her/their social environment (e.g., the person-in-environment perspective). In addition to the ecological framework, the curricula, for example in Ethiopia, focused on the biopsychosocial and spiritual model while not emphasising the natural environment. A good example, in this case, is the course 'Theories of Human Behavior and the Social Environment', which focused both on the biopsychosocial and on the spiritual model and the ecological perspective (ecology used as a metaphor). For example, a course in theories of Human Behavior and the Social Environment refers to the environment as ' systems of various sizes including groups, family, institutions, community, and society.' Thus, the lack of environmental perspectives in social work curricula corroborates our personal experiences of social work education. Similarly, other social workers in Africa have lamented the lack of education in environmental theories and approaches in social work curricula (Marlow and Van Rooyen, 2001; Muzingili, 2016).

It is also important to note that the natural environment and ecology were addressed to some extent in very few common courses that were mandatory for all first-year students irrespective of study programmes and delivered by other departments. For example, in Ethiopia, one such common course is 'Population Studies' which has a sub-section on 'Ecology and Population.' Another course named 'Global Trends' has a subsection on 'Global Environmental Issues'. However, neither course provided an ecosocial or environmental model.

Similarly, at the University of Ghana, all first-year BSW students are required to enroll in a course titled 'Science and Technology in Our Lives', which has six sub-modules that specifically address environmental concerns – 'Everyday Physics', 'Animals as Friends of Humans', 'Earth Resources', 'Geohazards', 'Food and Nutrition in Everyday Life', and 'Chemistry and Life'.

The first author recalls his experience in enrolling in one required/common course, 'Geohazards', during his BSW education, which included lessons about the causes and effects of environmental hazards. This course provided a relevant understanding of issues about the natural environment that are usually outside the traditional domain of social work education. This interdisciplinary mode of learning about the natural environment by social work students is commendable; however, the limitation is that these required/common courses hardly address the connections between social and environmental issues from a justice and/or rights-based perspective and fail to highlight the predicament of the vulnerable masses. This is why an ecosocial approach is needed to address the interconnectivity between social and environmental justice issues concerning vulnerable people.

The foregoing shows that incorporating ecosocial content in social work curricula is in its infancy in Africa. However, the lack of environmental perspectives in social work curricula is not exclusive to only Africa because social work students from other parts of the world continue to graduate into professional life without receiving education about ecosocial work (Jones, 2012; Nesmith and Smyth, 2015). For example, despite producing some of the pioneer scholars in the ecosocial approach, it is only just recently that the ecosocial approach was introduced as a university course in Finland at the University of Jyväskylä. On the other hand, previous studies have reported ecosocial content in social work education in countries like Australia (Jones, 2012), Canada (Drolet et al., 2015), Sweden (Rambaree, 2020), and the USA (Nesmith and Smyth, 2015).

In the subsequent sections, we discuss two arguments that underpin our call for introducing ecosocial content into African social work curricula: (i) ecosocial approach promotes the decolonisation and indigenisation of social work education, and (ii) ecosocial approach will enhance Africa's drive towards (environmental) sustainability. We end the section by outlining some recommendations on how social work curricula can incorporate ecosocial content.

Decolonising and Indigenising Social Work Education in Africa

In the quest for sustainability, industrialised countries have been admonished to transition from neoliberal principles like individualism, overconsumption, and constant growth and to embrace collective living (wellbeing). This makes it essential to reconsider these very neoliberal ideals upon which the social work profession was introduced into Africa. The practice of what has become social work in Africa today started before Westerners invaded African lands. From a welfarist perspective, Africans were already providing for each other's welfare needs through the family, clan system, and community during precolonial times (Shawky, 1972; Umoren, 2016). This was gradually replaced by a Western approach following the invasion of Africa by missionaries and colonialists; resulting in the establishment of professional social work around the 1960s (Spitzer, 2019; Umoren, 2016). Here it is important to note that, unlike the other countries used as cases in this chapter, Ethiopia has not been colonised. Yet, like other African countries, Ethiopia has been impacted by neocolonialism and cultural invasion perpetrated by the West.

Social work in Africa was modelled around the welfare programmes of the dominant colonial countries like Great Britain, France, and Portugal (Lombard and Twikirize, 2014; Shawky, 1972;

Umoren, 2016). The colonialists were interested in training social workers who would serve their parochial administrative interests and not necessarily the interests of the people, especially those in need and the rural dwellers. Shawky (1972) identified that social work in Africa was challenged by the wholesale importation of social welfare programmes from the West, which were originally designed to address their urban challenges that were unsuited to the local context of Africa. It seems not much has changed today as the profession remains remedialist and urbanistic in many parts of Africa (Lombard and Twikirize, 2014; Spitzer, 2019; Umoren, 2016). To develop social work education and practice that is suited to Africans, the focus must be on rediscovering indigenous wisdom, like Ubuntu, and creating a synthesis with Western theories, like the ecosocial approach, based on Afrocentric values (Nyahunda and Tirivangasi, 2021).

The ecosocial approach encourages the decolonisation of social work and shows that indigenous worldviews are rich in human-nature relatedness and environmental management. This is evident in Ubuntu and African traditional beliefs that teach us about environmental conservation and sustainability for present and future generations. Among many Africans, the natural environment is seen as a living thing possessing supernatural powers (Chigangaidze, 2022b); therefore, human activities in the environment must be guided else we face repercussions of disease, famine, drought, or even death. Africans are related to the environment, plants, and animals in sacred ways as their source of life, healing, food, water, and energy (Chigangaidze, 2022a; Le Grange, 2012; van Breda, 2019). There are several totemic animals that symbolize people's clans, and these animals are protected through taboos that prohibit their killing or destruction of their habitats (Kideghesho, 2009). Some tree species like the Okpagha and Ogriki in Nigeria, Mululwe and Mubanga in Zambia, Odum and Mahogany in Ghana, and Mvumo and Ntamanwa in Tanzania are revered as sacred trees together with the forests where they are located (Boaten, 1998; Kanene, 2016; Kideghesho, 2009; Rim-Rukeh et al., 2013). Also, water bodies are regarded as inhabiting spirits and therefore must be used sustainably (Rim-Rukeh et al., 2013). This sacred relatedness with nature among Africans promotes biodiversity and environmental sustainability. However, they have been eroded over the years due to many years of Western colonisation and capitalism, which held indigenous land management practices in contempt (Boaten, 1998; Le Grange, 2012). Unfortunately, social work education in many parts of Africa is deeply rooted in Western theories that tend to suppress indigenous wisdom. Therefore, African social work curricula must revisit African knowledge systems that emphasise human-nature relatedness to adequately prepare students for the environments of their future practice (Mtetwa and Muchacha, 2020; Spitzer, 2019). While we highlight the importance of African indigenous worldviews in an ecosocial content, we do not advocate for the wholesale importation of these ideas as some African traditional environmental methods, like the bush fallow system, may be obsolete today due to the growing population (Boaten, 1998).

Facilitating Africa's Drive towards Environmental Sustainability

Some critical questions have been raised about prioritising environmental sustainability over other pressing issues. Some people are skeptical that Western conception of sustainability is yet another form of (eco)imperialism that seeks to stunt the growth of developing countries like African ones. It is true that the economic growth of industrialised societies has been on the back of environmental degradation. For instance, even when the European Union is seen to be championing an ecosocial transition on the one hand, its main agenda remains to promote economic growth and trade (Matthies, 2016).

There have been calls for global equity; regarding who stresses the climate more, who bears the biggest brunt of the climate change consequences, and ultimately who should accept (more) responsibility for environmental sustainability (see, Gough, 2017; Raworth, 2017). Global South scholars have also outlined specific actions to be taken by the West in the form of climate and ecological reparations to tackle eco(imperialism) (Tadesse & Obeng, 2023). What now remains is a consensus that sustaining the environment automatically sustains the very foundations of lives and livelihoods and it is better not to repeat the same mistakes of other countries. Africa has a significantly large population of young people who are also primary victims of unsustainability (WMO, 2022). This reminds us that we need to start thinking about the idea of intergenerational justice. The actions we take now to bring about development should follow a sustainable path so that the wellbeing of future generations will not be endangered.

Moreover, Africa's vulnerability to climate change is highlighted in the latest WMO (2022) report. Despite contributing less stress to the global climate, natural hazards like drought, flood, and storms are common in Africa. When these hazards occur, people become displaced from their traditional homes, get afflicted with diseases, lose their lives, and farmlands and properties become destroyed, among other things. Since social workers require knowledge to be able to intervene in these situations, social work curricula in Africa must incorporate specific teachings about these environmental issues. Such knowledge would further enable social work to draw attention to the role of humans in climate change and promote humans' relatedness with nature. This is what ecosocial content will do.

Way Forward

With African social work already grappling with several challenges, including the lack of recognition in many African countries, it might seem redundant to call for an expansion of the curricula. However, incorporating ecosocial content in social work curricula could help to address some of the pressing challenges of social work in Africa, for example, by creating new employment opportunities for social work graduates and training practitioners who will help address environmental problems of vulnerable local people, thereby making the profession meaningful to local communities and increasing its visibility.

Also, incorporating ecosocial content in social work curricula will be challenging for social work educators and practitioners as some may argue that the curriculum is already full or that social workers are non-experts when it comes to environmental issues (Dominelli, 2012). However, African social work education can incorporate ecosocial content through transdisciplinary teaching and learning. That is, social work must collaborate with other academic departments that are knowledgeable in environmental perspectives as well as non-academic partners, such as organisations implementing ecosocial projects and community members like elders and chiefs who possess indigenous wisdom. This is important because environmental and social problems are complex (wicked problems) and interconnected, making it impossible to address them from the epistemic and ontological assumptions of single disciplines; either the social or the natural sciences (Nyahunda and Tirivangasi, 2021). While social work teachers, practitioners, and field instructors do not necessarily have to become environmental experts to implement ecosocial content, a decent understanding of the climate crisis, Africa's positionality in the crisis, and how social justice issues intersect with environmental justice is recommended. Thus, workshops and training can be organised for social work lecturers to enhance their knowledge of these aspects.

Another way to incorporate ecosocial content is through field practicum. A glance at the literature shows that little attention has been given to social work field practicum as a means of educating social work students about ecosocial approaches (Muzingili, 2016). Here also the principle of transdisciplinarity can be applied by expanding the focus of field practicum to address environmental justice issues and not only social justice. Social work students doing their field practicum can be placed at community projects addressing environmental, social, and economic concerns. Such ecosocial projects are increasing in Africa, for example, the Balekane Earth programme in Botswana implementing wilderness/forest-based interventions for orphaned children, and the Future Families' Plant Propagation Nursery Programme in South Africa implementing horticultural activities for vulnerable children and their families.

Conclusion

In this chapter, we have explored the potential of an ecosocial approach in African social work education. Based on reflections from our social work education and our assessment of the BSW curricula of 12 universities based in Ethiopia, Ghana, Nigeria, and South Africa, we noted that ecosocial and environmental perspectives are missing in African social work education. The absence of such perspectives hampers social work's efforts to effectively intervene in the lives of vulnerable Africans, who are the most severely affected by the environmental crises. Consistent with the Ubuntu African philosophy, we argued that an ecosocial approach will help to decolonise and indigenise social work education in Africa and facilitate Africa's drive to sustainability. Social work departments in African universities are encouraged to develop ecosocial work modules/courses for students; (i) through collaborating with other departments, such as natural sciences, economics, etc., and non-academic partners, such as elders, chiefs, etc.; and (ii) through field placement with projects that utilise ecosocial dimensions.

Recommendations

1. University departments and schools of social work must endeavour to incorporate environmental perspectives in social work education by adopting ecosocial content. The ecosocial content must reflect sustainable African indigenous environmental and social practices.
2. Social work field placements could be conducted at community-based and nature-based projects that incorporate both social and environmental concerns. For example, social cooperatives, social or care farms, school/community gardening groups, and communal labour organisations for environmental management. Social work educators responsible for field placements must collaborate with these ecosocial projects, organise workshops, and undertake training between them and students to acquaint each other with the ecosocial goals.
3. African social work education must be very focused on critiquing the structural capitalist/neoliberal market economy as a major driver of unsustainability and inequality. As an alternative, social work education must amplify examples of local/community economies.

Further Reading

Boetto, H. and Bell, K. (2015). 'Environmental sustainability in social work education: An online initiative to encourage global citizenship', *International Social Work*, 58(3), 448–462. https://doi.org/10.1177/0020872815570073.

Chigangaidze, R. K. (2023). Positioning the Natural environment in Ubuntu's Axiom 'Umuntu. Ngumuntu Ngabantu': An Ecospiritual Social Work Perspective. In Mayaka, B., Uwihangana, C., and van Breda, A. D. (eds) *The Ubuntu Practitioner: Social Work Perspectives*, 156-170, The International Federation of Social Workers.

Ersing, R. L., Ayivor, J. S., Alhassan, O., and Caruson, K. (2016). Ecological social work in a developing nation: Africa. In McKinnon, J., and Alston, M. (eds.). *Ecological social work: Towards sustainability*, 125–140, Macmillan International Higher Education.

Tadesse M. E. and Obeng J. K. (2023). An ecosocial work model for social work education in Africa. *African Journal of Social Work*, 13(2), 57-69. https://dx.doi.org/10.4314/ajsw.v13i2.2

Funding

The authors are employed in the Applying Sustainability Transition Research in Social Work Tackling Major Societal Challenge of Social Inclusion (ASTRA) project, which has received funding from the European Union's Horizon 2020 research and innovation programme under the Marie Słodowska-Curie grant agreement No. 955518. This chapter reflects the authors' views, and the European Commission is not responsible for any use that may be made of the information it contains.

References

Boetto, H., and Bell, K. (2015). Environmental sustainability in social work education: An online initiative to encourage global citizenship. *International Social Work*, 58(3), 448–462. https://doi.org/10.1177/0020872815570073.

Boaten, B. A. (1998). Traditional conservation practices: Ghana Example, *Research in Review*, 14(1), 42–51. Available at: https://journals.co.za/doi/pdf/10.10520/AJA19852007_230.

Boetto, H. (2016). A transformative eco-social model: Challenging modernist assumptions in social work, *British Journal of Social Work*, 47(1), 48–67. https://doi.org/10.1093/bjsw/bcw149.

Chigangaidze, R. K. (2022a). Environmental social work through the African philosophy of Ubuntu: A conceptual analysis. *International Social Work*. https://doi.org/10.1177/00208728211073382.

Chigangaidze, R. K. (2022b). The environment has rights: Eco-spiritual social work through Ubuntu philosophy and Pachamama: A commentary. *International Social Work*. https://doi.org/10.1177/00208728211056367.

Dominelli, L. (2012). Social work education for disaster relief work. In M. Gray, J. Coates, and T. Hetherington (eds.) *Environmental Social Work*. Taylor and Francis Group, 280–297.

Drolet, J., Wu, H., Taylor, M., and Dennehy, A. (2015). Social work and sustainable social development: Teaching and learning strategies for 'green social work' curriculum. *Social Work Education*, 34(5), 528–543. https://doi.org/10.1080/02615479.2015.1065808.

Gough, I. (2017). *Heat, Greed and Human Need: Climate Change, Capitalism and Sustainable Wellbeing*. Edward Elgar Publishing, 86–103.

Jones, P. F. (2012). Transforming the curriculum: Social work education and ecological consciousness. In M. Gray, J. Coates, and T. Hetherington (eds.) *Environmental Social Work*. Taylor and Francis Group, 213–230.

Kanene, K. M. (2016). Indigenous practices of environmental sustainability in the Tonga community of southern Zambia. *Jàmbá: Journal of Disaster Risk Studies*, 8(1), 7. https://doi.org/10.4102/jamba.v8i1.331.

Kideghesho, J. R. (2009). The potentials of traditional African cultural practices in mitigating overexploitation of wildlife species and habitat loss: Experience of Tanzania. *International Journal of Biodiversity Science and Management*, 5(2), 83–94. https://doi.org/10.1080/17451590903065579.

Kimmerer, R. (2013). *Braiding Sweetgrass: Indigenous Wisdom, Scientific Knowledge and the Teachings of Plants*. Milkweed Editions.

Le Grange, L. (2012). Ubuntu, Ukama and the healing of nature, self and society. *Educational Philosophy and Theory*, 44(S2), 56–67. https://doi.org/10.1111/j.1469-5812.2011.00795.x.

Lombard, A., and Twikirize, J. M. (2014). Promoting social and economic equality: Social workers' contribution to social justice and social development in South Africa and Uganda. *International Social Work*, 57(4), 313–325. https://doi.org/10.1177/0020872814525813.

Marlow, C., and Van Rooyen, C. (2001). How green is the environment in social work?. *International Social Work*, 44(2), 241–254. https://doi.org/10.1177/002087280104400208.

Matthies, A.-L. (ed.) (2016). The conceptualization of ecosocial transition. In *The Ecosocial Transition of Societies: The Contribution of Social Work and Social Policy*. Taylor and Francis, 17–35.

Mayaka, B., and Truell, R. (2021). Ubuntu and its potential impact on the international social work profession. *International Social Work*, 64(5), 649–662. https://doi.org/10.1177/00208728211022787.

Mtetwa, E., and Muchacha, M. (2020). Social work education for social justice and poverty reduction in Africa. In S. M. Sajid, R. Baikady, C. Sheng-Li, and H. Sakaguchi (eds.) *The Palgrave Handbook of Global Social Work Education*, 237–249. https://doi.org/10.1007/978-3-030-39966-5.

Muzingili, T. (2016). Greening the profession: A missing perspective in contemporary social work practice in Zimbabwe. *African Journal of Social Work*, 6(2), 29–38. Available at: https://www.ajol.info/index.php/ajsw/article/view/150290.

Närhi, K., and Matthies, A.-L. (2016). Conceptual and historical analysis of ecological social work. In J. McKinnon and M. Alston (eds.) *Ecological Social Work*. London: Macmillan Education, 21–38. https://doi.org/10.1007/978-1-137-40136-6_2.

Nesmith, A., and Smyth, N. (2015). Environmental justice and social work education: Social workers' professional perspectives. *Social Work Education*, 34(5), 484–501. https://doi.org/10.1080/02615479.2015.1063600.

Nyahunda, L., and Tirivangasi, H. M. (2021). Interdisciplinary approach to climate change: Intersecting environmental social work and sociology in climate change interventions from an Afrocentric perspective. Handbook of climate change management. *Journal: Handbook of Climate Change Management*, 2289–2304.

Rambaree, K. (2020). Environmental social work: Implications for accelerating the implementation of sustainable development in social work curricula. *International Journal of Sustainability in Higher Education*, 21(3), 557–574. https://doi.org/10.1108/IJSHE-09-2019-0270.

Raworth, K. (2017). *Doughnut Economics: Seven Ways to Think Like a 21st-century Economist*. Chelsea Green Publishing.

Rim-Rukeh, A., Irerhievwie, G., and Agbozu, I. E. (2013). Traditional beliefs and conservation of natural resources: Evidences from selected communities in Delta State, Nigeria. *International Journal of Biodiversity and Conservation*, 5(7), 426–432. https://doi.org/10.5897/IJBC2013.0576.

Schmitz, C. L., Matyók, T., and James, C. D. (2012). Environmental sustainability: Educating social workers for interdisciplinary practice. In M. Gray, J. Coates, and T. Hetherington (eds.) *Environmental Social Work*. Taylor and Francis Group, 280–299.

Shawky, A. (1972). Social work education in Africa. *International Social Work*, 15(3), 3–16. https://doi.org/10.1177/002087287201500302.

Spitzer, H. (2019). Social work in East Africa: A *mzungu* perspective. *International Social Work*, 62(2), 567–580. https://doi.org/10.1177/0020872817742696.

Umoren, N. (2016). Social work development in Africa: Encouraging best practice, *International Journal of Scientific and Engineering Research*, 7(1), 191–203. Available at: https://www.ijser.org/researchpaper/Social-Work-Development-in-Africa--Encouraging-Best-Practice.pdf.

van Breda, A. D. (2019). Developing the notion of Ubuntu as African theory for social work practice. *Social Work*, 55(4), 439–450. Available at: http://www.scielo.org.za/pdf/sw/v55n4/07.pdf.

World Meteorological Organization (WMO). (2022). State of the climate in Africa 2021. Available at: https://library.wmo.int/doc_num.php?explnum_id=11512 [Accessed 27 May 2023].

4
AFRICAN INDIGENOUS KNOWLEDGE SYSTEMS AND THEORIES IN TEACHING SOCIAL WORK

Mmaphuti Mamaleka

Abstract: English

The teaching of the social work curriculum is dominated by Western thinking. Disregarding the African-centred approach in the practice of the discipline is currently observed, hence the emergence of a new approach, namely, African social work. This approach fights for recognition within the discipline considering that social work embraces an interdisciplinary approach. Social work practice in Africa did not recognise the African indigenous knowledge systems as part of the knowledge developed and methods of interventions in the curriculum. Cultural belief systems and practices, which are the ingredients of indigenous knowledge, are neglected. Western thinking portrays Africans as communities that did not have prior knowledge about their own affairs. This chapter argues that Africans have ways of practicing social work characterised by indigenous knowledge. Desktop research was conducted using published journal articles and book chapters relating to the topic. Findings are based on the paradigm, epistemology, and practices in an African indigenous community. Therefore, the incorporation of indigenous knowledge in the social work curriculum adds value to the practice. This will prepare social workers for practice that is socioculturally relevant and responsive to the community's needs.

Abstract: Northern Sotho

Go rutwa ga lenaneothuto la dithuto tša bodireleago go sa theilwe kudu godimo ga dikgopolo tša bodikela. Go se elwe hloko ga mekgwa ya seAfrika ge go rutwa dithuto tše, e a bonagala ke ka lebaka leo go tšwelelago mokwa wo mofsa wo o bitšwago bodirelaleago bja seAfrika. Mokgwa wo o lwela tokologo magareng ga dithuto go elwa hloko kudu bodirelaleago ka go akaretša mokgwa wa kopakopano ya dithuto. Bošomelo bja bodirelaleago go la Afrika ga se bo ele hloko peakanyo tsebo tlhago go seAfrika bjalo ka karolo ya go godiša le mekgwa ya go tsena ka gare lenaneothuto. Tshepidišo ya tumelo ya setšo le tirišo tšeo elego dinyakwa tše bohlokwa go tsebo tlhago ga di elwe hloko. Se se tšweletša maAfrika bjalo ka setšhaba seo se hlokago tsebo ya pele mabapi le ditirgalo tša ga bo bona. Kgaolo ye e nganga gore maAfrika ba na le mekgwa ya bona bošomelong bja bodirelaleago wo o hlaolwago ka tsebo ya setlogo. Mokgwanyakišišo wa teseke o dirišitšwe ka go lekola dingwalwa go tšwa dijenaleng le dikgaolo tša dipuku tšeo di nyalelanago le hlogo. Dikhumano di theilwe godimo ga parataeme, episitimolotši le ditlwaelo mo go setlogo sa setšhaba sa maAfrika. Ka go realo, go tsenywa ga tsebo tlhago ka gare ga lenaneothuto la bodirelaleago go tla godiša bohlokwa bja bošomelo. Se se ile go beakantšha badirelaleago go bošomelo bjo bo akaretšago leago-setho bja maleba le go arabana le dinyakwa tša setšhaba.

Introduction and Background

The social work curriculum is dominated mostly by Western thinking. The African-centred approach in the practice of the discipline is disregarded, hence the emergence of a new approach, namely, African social work. Nel (2005) contests that the placement and implementation of African Indigenous Knowledge Systems (AIK) in the educational system have not been given a proper place. Muchenje and Goronga (2013) concur and say that institutions of higher learning in Africa are inclined to Western knowledge and their intellectual thinking. The education systems and approaches, such as philosophies, theories, and methodologies, reproduce Western thinking (Muchenje and Goronga, 2013). Western knowledge is still anchored in the teaching of social work, which is the gap identified.

However, AIK integration into the educational curricula is crucial (Ukwuoma, 2015) to be relevant to the needs and concerns of African societies (Kaya and Seleti, 2013). The belief that African knowledge is inferior, primitive, barbaric, and unscientific (Kaya and Seleti, 2013) delays the integration of AIK into social work curricula. The same perception arose when professional social work was introduced in Africa. This portrays a deceiving picture as if there were no approaches to solving problems in Africa before the introduction of social work by Western scholars. This author is not negating Western knowledge but showing how it dominated African knowledge. It led to Africans lacking the capacity to resolve and address their own challenges. Nkondo (2012) says Westerners replaced the African systems with their Western systems, claiming that they were repetitions of practices without any theoretical explanation – forgetting that lack of knowledge and privilege to literacy contributed indirectly to the non-documentation of some of the African theories.

However, Moahi (2007) affirms that African knowledge was not documented but was orally passed from one generation to the next. Therefore, this created a gap in the literature and in practice. Hence, little AIK literature is incorporated into teaching social work. Osman (2014) indicates that the colonial powers used brutal policies and devious methods to subjugate the African people to their systems and resources. As much as the idea of African social work is pertinent, due to globalisation and transformation, the two approaches namely, Eurocentric and Afrocentric, will not be divorced but should collaborate well. In a way, the incorporation of AIK into the social work curriculum will encourage interdisciplinarity (social sciences and humanities). Osman (2014) suggests that African universities should push AIK recognition as that will assist them in articulating their concepts and claiming their space.

Objectives of the Chapter

It is observed that many African universities do not recognize AIK in their curriculum due to the assumption of its lack of scientific proof and literature. Therefore, this chapter intends to explore AIK in social work, with the aim of achieving these objectives:

- To recognise and infuse AIK into the social work curriculum.
- To identify and establish AIK intervention strategies to be used in the social work curriculum.
- To know and understand African theories to be incorporated into the social work curriculum.

Conceptualising AIK

There is a disparity in terms of defining African indigenous knowledge (Nnadozie, 2009). The challenge in defining AIK is that people are not static, due to life encounters. Sillitoe (2002) argues that various authors used different terms, such as 'traditional', 'local', 'rural people', and 'native knowledge' to define the term. AIK is defined differently but has a common theme. Authors like Owuor (2007), define AIK as a process of learning and sharing social life, histories, and identities. This includes 'shared customs, values, attitudes, beliefs, interactions, and ideological orientations' (Ngulube and Lwoga, 2007 p.118). In Emeagwali's (2014) view AIK is inclusive of strategies, practices, techniques, tools, intellectual, resources, explanations, beliefs, and values that are developed over time. Esiubo (2019) expands the definition by indicating that AIK is intricate knowledge acquired over generations by communities to guide their daily living. Based on these definitions, AIK is perceived as knowledge developed with the aim of managing day-to-day living and it came through the interaction and sharing of experiences of a particular society. As people live together, they start to develop certain practices that guide their daily conduct. This accumulated knowledge was passed orally from one generation to the next. For example, in the Bapedi community and other ethnic groups in Limpopo province, South Africa, their practice and custom, in terms of family and community conflicts were competencies of traditional leadership through the guidance of a traditional committee called *Khuduthamaga*. This committee is given the power to address such issues. These are some of the AIK developed to address their daily challenges.

The saying 'it takes a village to raise a child' was also AIK used to explain collectivism among people. The community took collective responsibility to care for and raise their children. Why, because they believe and value a morally upright member of society. These AIK were replaced by the Western mentality of individual responsibility and privacy (individualism). AIK is rich with guidance, teaching, and encouragement information.

The Impact of Colonisation and Its Western Knowledge Systems on AIK

Western knowledge, through the power of colonisation, infiltrated African countries in diverse forms and it gained momentum. Freire (1998) indicates that academically, coloniality is a process that has an epistemological, psychological, cultural, spiritual, and linguistic impact, which made the colonised lose their identity. Hence, Arowolo (2010) refers to colonisation as an imposition of foreign rules and cultures over African indigenous traditional values and beliefs. This process and imposition established total control over the indigenous people's system of life. The characteristics of colonisation as outlined by Butt (2013) are domination, cultural imposition, and exploitation.

Hovarth (1972) indicates that domination controls how people behave, what they do, and where they stay. Butt (2013) indicates that domination portrays elements of inequality and injustice of power between different international parties. Most African countries, including South Africa, experienced this form of domination, control, and oppression. The people were grouped in terms of their language, race, and colour so they could be controlled easily. The introduction of education also portrayed elements of domination as Black people were subjected to Bantu education with Western knowledge over AIK (Mkabela, 2005). Cultural imposition occurred whereby the colonisers imposed their culture, beliefs, and customs on the African people (Butt, 2013).

Cultural imposition made African people abort their cultural practices as they were made to believe they were demonic (Mkabela, 2005). Africans started to follow Christianity and no longer interacted with their ancestors and many other practices. Colonisation made it possible for the exploitation of Africans, which is the third characteristic. Noyoo (2018) explains that the colonisers exploited African people through policies, the slave trade, misappropriation of cultural property, and forcible displacement as well as plundering of their natural resources, among other things. Noyoo (2018ap.40) indicates that 'prior to Europeans' incursion into Africa, Africa's precolonial, the socio-political landscape was linked to various indigenous polities'. African people were removed from fertile land and grouped according to their ethnicity so they could be exploited.

This led to the indigenous aspect of most Black Africans being marginalised (Makgopa, 2008). Western knowledge stripped African people of their identity and replaced it with their own, which created tension between the two knowledge systems particularly in teaching. Tobin (1993) mentioned that this replacement created a dilemma for African students to implement the knowledge acquired in the realities of their lives. Western knowledge dominated African inventions as they claim that valid and correct knowledge comes from the West. Therefore, this Western knowledge taught African people abstract things that had no direct link to their daily lives. It is against this background that Africans need to be decolonised from thinking that Western knowledge is the only universal knowledge. Asante (2005) made it clear that Africans should liberate themselves from the colonisers' thoughts and practices. The educational system in African countries should regain its own values and practices, particularly in teaching social work.

Despite all that colonisation did, Western knowledge contributed immensely to the body of knowledge. However, synergy is needed between the two knowledge systems, especially in their application. Western knowledge made it possible for most African people to be part of globalisation debates. Barriers between African and Western knowledge are broken as knowledge is now shared and exchanged, which can provide a balance in how knowledge is utilised. Institutions of higher learning use Western resources that are scientifically researched and that provide a different perspective. Western knowledge has left a footprint of events as it was able to document events as they unfolded, which is a learning curve for AIK activists. Berkes et al. (2000) postulate that Western knowledge is open, systematic, objective, and analytical, advancing by building rigorously on prior achievements, which is lacking in AIK. However, the value that AIK can bring to the social work curriculum rests on advancement of interventions that address African challenges based on their context, using Africans own knowledge systems.

Integrating AIK in the Teaching of the Social Work Curriculum

Education aims at giving students quality training to unleash their potential and meaningfully contribute to society (Department of Education, 1997). Therefore, inappropriate education impacts the outcome of the training. AIK integration into the education system will enable students to link their learning with their perspectives, experiences, and customs. AIK's inclusion in the social work curriculum will provide multiple forms of knowledge and allow students to compare knowledge systems. Odorer-Hoppers (2001) argues that Africans should build on all valuable AIK and abandon the knowledge that hinders its development, advancement, and sustainability. The opportunities for AIK integration in the social work curriculum as illustrated by Kaya (2014) and Nnandozie (2009) are discussed separately in Table 4.1.

African Indigenous Knowledge Systems and Theories

Table 4.1 African Indigenous Knowledge (AIK) Types of Opportunities and Benefits in Social Work Education

AIK Opportunities (Kaya, 2014)	Student Benefits of AIK in Social Work Education
Community attitudes and values	AIK assists students to learn appropriate community attitudes and values for sustainable livelihoods. The African people have a set of beliefs, attitudes, values, and customs used to sustain their daily lives (Emeagwali, 2014). Knowledge of community values and attitudes provides students with ways and approaches to addressing people's needs. The students benefit from what the community value and that will guide their practice. Knowledge of these values directs students where to tap when providing interventions that will fit for intended purposes.
Cultural forms	Each community has its own cultural patterns. AIK (such as folklore) enables students to understand the cultural systems of the community. The students will learn about African cultural diversities, and this will make practice more meaningful. Some cultural forms are resources in the social work practice. In the past, the traditional people used folkloric systems, such as proverbs and folktales, to teach children moral behaviour (Amos, 2013). Using folkloric proverbs to teach children discipline will add to students' list of interventions in the practice to address social ills. It will enable them to conceptualise and practically engage with the theoretical knowledge acquired in the classroom. The inclusion of AIK in social work will expand its scope of practice. Societies are currently losing moral fibre because AIK-like folklore has diminished and is less practiced. The research conducted by Mamaleka (2020) shows that African communities used AIK called taboo (*'di a illa'* meaning it's prohibited) and initiation schools (*lebollo* in Sepedi) to teach children socially acceptable behaviour and it worked for years. These cultural customs addressed the challenges of African people and are relevant to social work even today.
Involvement of community knowledge holders	Engaging with knowledge sources is advantageous for learning and practice. Ngulube and Lwoga (2007, p. 118) indicate that 'People within a community have detailed knowledge of the area in which they interact and apply meaning to their experiences'. AIK incorporation in social work assists the students to have information from reliable sources. Community members, traditional leaders, and traditional healers are the source of knowledge, and their shared information, if documented, will enrich the social work curriculum. The Sepedi proverbs say (*mahlako a maswa a ema ka a matala*) meaning the young generation stands firm with the assistance of the older people, therefore the older people's knowledge has value as wise and guiding precepts. The knowledge holder will aid in students' research activities Mawere (2015) asserts that indigenous knowledge is relevant in solving day-to-day problems and it should be given attention in higher education. Indigenous people have in-depth knowledge of their communities and know what works best for them. For example, in the past poverty was not noticed because the knowledge bearers had strategies to alleviate it. There were various strategies used, such as '*letsema*' meaning a group of people working together to plough or harvest with the aim of sharing with those unable to plough the fields or who do not have fields at all. The idea here was to alleviate poverty and encourage people to work for their share. This is unlike in the current times where people are handed food parcels or any other means without contributing in any manner. The knowledge

(Continued)

Table 4.1 (Continued)

AIK Opportunities (Kaya, 2014)	Student Benefits of AIK in Social Work Education
	bearers had strategies to address poverty and hunger in the communities. As another example, in the past, there were people with specific knowhow in causing it to rain so that there was no famine on the land. Currently, this knowledge has faded. These are examples of some of the information that knowledge holders can share with students. Kaya (2014) indicates that learning from what local communities already know creates an understanding of local conditions and provides an important context for activities designed to support them. Sharing AIK within and across communities can help enhance cross-cultural understanding and promote the cultural dimension of development (Kaya, 2014). Kaya (2014) reports that AIK incorporation into the other disciplines' curricula showed students' improvement in their achievement. AIK makes it easier for students to experience multi- and trans-disciplinary knowledge and skills, especially cultural skills.
	Student Benefits of AIK in Social Work Education
AIK Opportunities (Nnandozie, 2009)	
Opportunity to recognise own identity	Nnandozie (2009) indicates that AIK provides an opportunity to recognise one's own identity. There are various belief systems in African communities that identify the person's origin. Therefore, AIK provides students an opportunity to learn and recognise their identity and history. With this opportunity, they will understand and know the community with which they work.
Harmonisation of the two bodies of knowledge (Western and African)	Nnandozie (2009) indicates that AIK integration into the social work curriculum will empower the students intellectually and psychologically and that will increase the content of academic knowledge. Currently, the social work curriculum is rooted in Western knowledge. The AIK recognition in the social work curriculum will enhance harmony between the two bodies of knowledge. The students will draw from multiple sources of knowledge and ideas in their training. It will make it easier for them to identify which one is useful and where to apply it.
A new look at the educational system	Drawing from different streams of knowledge will make the educational system look different. Connections will be easier for learning. The inclusion of African theories in the curriculum will provide a different perspective.

AIK incorporation into the social work curriculum bears numerous benefits and opportunities for both students and the discipline. As shown by various authors, other African challenges and problems need African solutions. AIK can contribute towards providing solutions that are socioculturally responsive to the needs of African societies. The core social work knowledge emphasises the recognition of sociocultural and spiritual factors in shaping human development behaviour (Council on Higher Education (CHE), 2015). AIK is relevant in the social work curriculum as the students' competencies when they complete the curriculum should include the ability to form relationships with their clients and treat them with respect and dignity. AIK inclusion in the social work curriculum will advance decolonisation and promote indigenous knowledge, which marks a move towards African social work education. Other institutions of higher learning and basic education have started to introduce AIK into their syllabus, folklore, and belief systems. The current topical issue in universities is decolonisation of the curriculum and recognition of indigenous knowledge. Some materials used in classrooms are locally produced. There are interdisciplinary approaches in research, which is a good move towards embracing AIK.

Theories That Can Promote the Application of African Social Work

Kigotho (2015) argues that the education systems in most African countries are still inclined toward colonial practices. Most of the educational curriculum in higher education, including social work, still uses Western knowledge systems in teaching, theories, interventions, and others. Smith (2002) argues that Eurocentric social theories and perspectives applications in African conditions still dominate and marginalise the views of underprivileged social groups. The domination makes the Western research models and theories being adopted and applied in African communities without contest (Kaya and Seleti, 2013). It is worth noting that African people, though much of their information was not documented, have their own African theories. This section outlines some of the African theories that can be applied to the social work curriculum. Four African theories were selected for this chapter, namely, Afrocentricity theory, Ubuntu theory, African strength theory, and African family theory.

Afrocentricity Theory

African-centred approach, Afrocentric, Afrocentricity, and Africalogy are used interchangeably by various authors (Chukwuokolo, 2009). Despite the different names, the aim is to advocate for African ideas, values, customs, and practices. Dei (2012) defines the African-centred paradigm as an important theoretical and pragmatic space for African people to interpret and critically reflect upon their experiences. Dyson and Smith Brice (2016) view Afrocentricity as a way of thinking, acting, and living for advancing social justice and human rights. Asante (2007a) indicates that Afrocentricity infers that African people should perceive themselves as agents, or subjects, rather than spectators to their historical revolution and change. The focus of Afrocentricity is on African people and their systems. Afrocentricity theory (Asante, 2005) aims at achieving the following goals:

1. To expose and actively resist white racial domination: decolonisation is one example of resistance.
2. Transforming African Americans toward their cultural centre: Africans are becoming aware of who they are; hence, they celebrate their heritage.
3. Converting African Americans to an ideology of values, spirituals, and rituals.
4. Analysing disciplines such as literature, history, linguistics, politics, religion, science, and economics from an Afrocentric perspective.

Looking at these goals the aim is to advocate for African-centredness and this theory fits well into social work. These goals assist in fighting social injustices, domination, and exploitation of Africans.

Ubuntu Theory

Ubuntu refers to 'a collection of values and practices that black people of Africa or of African origin view as making people authentic human beings' (Magumbate and Chereni, 2020 p.iv). Metz (2011, p. 536–537) asserts that Ubuntu originates from the following African idioms: *Motho ke motho ka batho babang* in Northern Sotho; or *Umuntu ngumuntu ngabantu* in Zulu and Xhosa; which loosely translated means that a person is a person through other persons. The term 'Ubuntu' supports the saying that 'no one is an island', namely, people need each other. Ubuntu simply means humanness. Broodryk (2008) describes Ubuntu as an African cultural way of expressing compassion, reciprocity, dignity, harmony, helpfulness, forgiveness, and understanding towards other people. Manda (2009) further indicates that Ubuntu is an African way of promoting social cohesion and positive human interaction. This theory is relevant to the social work curriculum as it encourages human relationships, which is one of the social work values. Ideally, Ubuntu theory is used to guide and promote African ideas and values to decolonise Africans from Western ideologies. The inclusion of Ubuntu theory in social work will enhance the students' learning of community relations and care and support of others. They will draw from these practices to address the community's needs. Many authors have written works about Ubuntu and its application to society. Disciplines like sociology, anthropology, engage with African languages and Ubuntu. The application of this theory in the curriculum can be useful. Ubuntu theory is closely related to system theory, which points to the influence of systems. This theory is applicable though is not fully followed owing to currently prevalent social ills.

African Strength Theory

The philosophy around this theory is that every person has strengths and should focus on them (Africa Social Work Network, (ASWNet). African people have strengths that can help to deal with daily challenges. However, the colonisers made it easy for African people to undermine their strengths by imposing ideas that nullified theirs. They were made to believe that they are incapable and needed someone to assist them. Poor families are issued handouts and food parcels instead of identifying their strengths to aid their challenges. For example, in the past, agriculture and family care were African strongholds. They survived on fields and livestock to sustain their families. Support and care for one another made Africans self-sufficient and self-reliant.

However, these strengths were suppressed and replaced with Western ideologies, and Africans were seen as incapable of doing anything. In an African practice, the child belongs to the community. This practice was adopted to accommodate those who do not have children. Those without children will send whomever child he or she wants without fear of being scolded by the parents. These are some of the African strengths that social work students should know and apply in practice. The core areas of social work indicate that students should demonstrate their understanding regarding every person's ability to solve their problems. Application of this theory will enable students to know their clients' strengths.

Language was another African strength. From a young age, children were taught levels of communication, which included respect. They learned how to address an older person and people of their own age. Unfortunately, the language spoken and used currently shows no difference in this regard. All these ideologies crippled the strengths that Africans had. Some of these practices were good and if restored can make a difference. People are the assets of their communities, and, if properly channelled, they can be resources. In the same breath, currently, children are congratulated if they speak fluent English. This deceives children as doing so makes them believe that speaking English makes them good and smart while forgetting their mother tongue. This is misleading and challenges their identity and originality. However, African people are slowly realising that fact; hence, there are debates in some institutions, about implementing native languages in education systems.

African Family Theory

African family theory embraces family relations, which include extended families and tribal relatives or clans (African Social Work Network (ASWNet). This theory aims at ensuring that families look after each other. There are African family theory pillars that emphasise the value of relations in families. Pillars of African family theory according to ASWNet are outlined:

- Value for marriage.
- Value for childbearing.
- Value for providing a permanent home.
- Value for bloodline and maintain race line.
- Value for extended family (tribe or clan).
- Value for strengthening the bond within the families involved in marriages.
- Value for sharing or dividing family roles.
- Value for looking after one another and not looking at individuals first.
- Value for community.
- Maintain African values.

The social work profession aims at promoting the wellbeing of families and these values will strengthen its curriculum. Families are where society is developed, therefore, functioning families will promote well societies. In the past, African families encouraged these pillars. The extended family pillar, for example, was a stronghold in African families. In her study, Mamaleka (2020) shows that African people entrusted extended families with their children's upbringing. It was rare to find a child who showed socially unacceptable behaviour as the families played a role in modeling good behaviour in children. Again, the pillar of strengthening the bond of families involved in marriages was key as well. The rates of divorce were much lower, unlike now. Families protected marriages and, if there were challenges, extended families were there to provide support and guidance. Incorporation of African theories could constitute valuable assets as their relevance will show in practice.

African Intervention Strategies to Be Incorporated in Social Work Education

Patel (2015, p.32) indicates that 'in the pre-colonial times the welfare needs of individuals were met through the wider society and communalism, cooperation, and mutual aid, and the social groups were highly developed'. The interventions commonly used in social work are still Western-based and some are not relevant to African contexts and challenges. In the past, communities had methods of solving their challenges. Umoren (2016) indicates that in Africa, the prior establishment of welfare systems and tribal and mutual aid societies were available resources.

Examples include family, relative kinship, extended families, tribal authorities, and even community groups or clans. These types of interventions are not emphasised greatly in social work education. The theory developed from these practices is little known or even unknown. Indigenous social work would go a long way to ensure that social work practices are locally relevant. Baskin and Sinclair (2017) report that much research has indicated that Western mainstream social work practice is often not helpful, and it is, in fact, damaging in some situations for indigenous individuals, families, and communities. Therefore, the social work approach for indigenous people should reflect their values (Baskin and Sinclair, 2017). Some of the intervention strategies that can be included in social work education to promote African social work are discussed together with their purpose in this section.

- Involvement of extended families in family affairs: for discipline, handling family conflicts, and marital disputes.
- Communalism, co-parenting, and collectivity: resolving community and family challenges collectively.
- Cultural practices (taboos, traditional initiation school, Ubuntu principles, and family rules): to mould people's behaviour and ensure moral uprightness in society. To promote people's identity, family values, and preservation of culture.
- Folkloric systems (folktales, proverbs, rhymes): to instill discipline, teach culture, and prevention of wrongdoing.

These interventions, if included in the social work curriculum, will confirm what Kaya and Seleti (201330) indicated that the 'integration of AIK into the higher education system could improve its relevance'. The achievement of well-balanced and effective learning requires the closure of the gap between Western knowledge and indigenous knowledge in the formal education system. Odora-Hoppers (2002) argues that the African Renaissance is necessary and Du Toit (2005) affirms that it will assist Africans to recover their identity. Grange (2007) argues that South Africa is multicultural; therefore, institutions of higher learning can excel well with incorporation of indigenous ideas. One of the principles of adult learning in educational supervision states that a social worker learns best when the learning material is relevant to learning (Kadushin and Harkness, 2002). Therefore, social work students will learn best and be motivated to learn if they can relate their learning to their current environment or background.

Conclusion

The chapter covered the conceptualisation of the AIK and the influence of Western knowledge systems through colonisation. The value of AIK and African theories in the social work curriculum were presented. A glimpse of the African interventions with their purposes was highlighted. The recommendations for African social work education were outlined for future consideration.

Recommendations

1. Policymakers should recognise and promote AIK in institutions of higher learning with clear guidelines in the curriculum design.
2. Inclusion of AIK in the Bachelor of Social Work (BSW) curriculum, local learning materials, resources, and assessment methods should relate to the practice that is locally understandable, which will lead to improved knowledge development and production.

3. Academic support and buy-in by all the relevant stakeholders for integrating AIK into social work education.

Further Reading

Chika Ezeanya-Esiobu. (2019). *Indigenous Knowledge and Education in Africa. Frontiers in African Business Research*. Springer Open.

Twikirize, J. M. and Helmut Spitzer, H. (2019). *Social Work Practice in Africa. Indigenous and Innovative Approaches*. Kampala: Fountain Publishers.

References

Africa Social Work Network (ASWNet). https://africasocialwork.net/african-theories-of-social-work.

Amos, P. M. (2013). Parenting and culture: Evidence from some African communities. In M. L. Seidl-de-Moura (Ed.), *Parenting in South American and African Contexts* . London: IntechOpen, 65–76.

Arowolo, D. (2010). The effects of Western civilization and culture on Africa. *Afro Asian Journal of Social Sciences*, 1, 2229–5313 (1 Quarter IV 2010).

Asante, M. K. (2005). Afro-centricity notes on disciplinary position. In J. L. Conyers, Jr. (Ed.), *Afrocentric Additions*. 3rd ed. New Brunswick, NJ: Transaction Publishers, 1–13.

Asante, M. K. (2007a). *An Afrocentric Manifesto*. Cambridge, MA: Polity.

Baskin, C. and Sinclair, D. (2017). *Indigenous Peoples*. DOI: 10.1093/OBO/9780195389678-0252.

Berkes, F., Johan, C. and Carl, F. (2000). Rediscovery of traditional ecological knowledge as adaptive management. *Ecological Applications*, 10(5), 1251–1262.

Broodryk, J. (2008). *Understanding South Africa: The Ubuntu Way of Living*. Pretoria, Gauteng, SA.

Butt, D. (2013). Colonialism and postcolonialism. In H. LaFollette (Ed.), *The International Encyclopaedia of Ethics*. Wiley-Blackwell.

Chukwuokolo, J. C. (2009). 'Afrocentrism or Eurocentrism...' The dilemma of African Development. Ogirisi: *A New Journal of African Studies*, 6, 24–39.

Council on Higher Education (CHE). (2015). *Higher Education Qualifications Sub-Framework Qualification Standard for Bachelor of Social Work*.

Dei, G. J. S. (2014). African indigenous proverbs and the institutional and pedagogic relevance for youth education: Lessons from Kiembu of Kenya and Igbo of Nigeria. *Journal of Education and Training*, 1(1), 48–66. ISSN 2330-9709.

Department of Education. (1997). *Quality Education for All: Overcoming Barrier to Learning and Development: A Report of the National Commission on Special Needs in Education and Training (NCSNET) and National Committee on Education Support Services (NCESS)*.

DuToit, C. W. (2005). The environmental integrity of African indigenous knowledge systems: Probing the roots of African rationality. *Indilinga-African Journal of Indigenous Knowledge Systems*, 4(1), 55–73.

Dyson, Y. D. and Smith Brice, T. (2016). Embracing the village and tribe: Critical thinking for social workers from an African-centered approach. *Journal of Social Work Education*, 52(1), 108–117.

Emeagwali, G. (2014). Intersections between Africa's indigenous knowledge systems and history. In G. Emeagwali and G. J. S. Dei (Eds.), *African Indigenous Knowledge and the Disciplines: Anti-colonial Educational Perspectives for Transformative Change*. Rotterdam: Sense Publishers, 1–17.

Esiobu, E. C. (2019). *Indigenous Knowledge and Education in Africa, Frontiers in African Business Research*. https://doi.org/10.1007/978-981-13-6635-21.

Freire, P. (1998). *Pedagogy of Freedom: Ethics, Democracy, and Civic Courage*. Lanham, MD: Rowman and Littlefield Publishers.

Grange, L. L. (2007). Integrating western and indigenous knowledge systems: The basis for effective science education in South Africa? *International Review of Education*, 53(5–6), 577–591.

Horvath, R. J. (1972). A definition of colonialism. *Current Anthropology*, 13(1), 45–57.

Kadushin, A. and Harkness, D. (2002). *Supervision in Social Work*. Columbia University Press.

Kaya, O. H. (2014). Revitalizing African indigenous ways of knowing of and knowledge production. Retrieved May 03, 2016, from http://www.e-ir.info/2014/05/26/.

Kaya, O. H. and Seleti, Y. N. (2013). African Indigenous knowledge systems and relevance of higher education in South Africa. *The International Educational Journal: Comparative Perspectives*, 12(1), 30–44.

Kigotho, W. (2015). Indigenous knowledge can help researchers solve crisis. *University World News*. Issue No 371.

Makgopa, M. A. (2008). Contesting space in folklore studies: An interdisciplinary approach. *Southern African Journal for Folklore Studies*, 18(2), 48–58.

Mamaleka, M. M. (2020). Developing guidelines for indigenous parenting practices: A case study of Makhuduthamaga municipality at Sekhukhune district, Limpopo Province, South Africa. A thesis submitted in fulfillment of the requirements for the degree Doctor of Philosophy in Social Work, Faculty of Community and Health Sciences. University of the Western Cape, Cape Town, South Africa.

Manda, D. S. (2009). Ubuntu philosophy as an African philosophy for peace. Retrieved from www.africafiles.org/article.asp, ID=20361.

Mawere, M. (2015). Indigenous knowledge and public education in sub-Saharan Africa, in Africa. *Africa Spectrum*, 50(2), 57–71.

Metz, T. (2011). Ubuntu as a moral theory and human rights in South Africa. *African Human Rights Law Journal*, 11(2), 532–559.

Mkabela, N. Q. (2005). Using the Afrocentric method in researching Indigenous African Culture. *The Qualitative Report*, 10(1), 178–189.

Moahi, K. (2007). Globalisation, knowledge-economy, and the implications for indigenous knowledge. *An International Review of Information Ethics (IRIE)*, 7, 1–30.

Muchenje, F. and Goronga, P. (2013). Education and the revitalisation of indigenous knowledge systems in Africa: A paradigm shift in curriculum content. *International Journal. Social Science and Education*, 3(4).

Mugubate, J. R. and Chereni (2020). Now, the theory of Ubuntu has its space in social work. *African Journal of Social Work*, 10(1), v–xv. Special issue on Ubuntu Social Work.

Nel, P. (2005). Indigenous knowledge: Contestation, rhetoric and space. *Indilinga: African Journal of Indigenous Knowledge Systems*, 4(1), 2–14.

Ngulube, P. and Lwoga, E. (2007). Knowledge management models and their utility to the effective management and integration of indigenous knowledge with other knowledge systems. *Indilinga African Journal of Indigenous Knowledge Systems*, 6(2), 117–131.

Nkondo, M. (2012). Indigenous African knowledge systems in a polyepistemic world: The capabilities approach and the translatability of knowledge systems. Paper presented at the Southern African Regional Colloquium on Indigenous African knowledge systems: methodologies and epistemologies for research, teaching, learning and community engagement in higher education. Howard College Campus. University of KwaZulu-Natal.

Nnadozie, I. J. (2009). The integration of indigenous knowledge systems (IKS) in the teaching of conservation of biodiversity and natural resources: a critical case study of grade 10 life sciences educators in the Pinetown district. A thesis submitted in partial fulfillment of the requirements for the degree of Master in Science Education. Faculty of Education, University of KwaZulu-Natal, Durban, South Africa.

Noyoo, N. (2018a). The evolution of social welfare policy in Southern Africa. In V. Taylor and J. Triegaart (Eds.), *The Political Economy of Social Welfare Policy in Africa. Transforming Policy through Practice*. Cape Town, South Africa: Oxford University Press, 35–56, with contributions by Noyoo R. Schenk and M. Sesoko.

Odora-Hoppers, C. A. (2002). *Indigenous Knowledge and the Integration of Knowledge Systems: Towards a Philosophy of Articulation*. Claremont: New Africa Books.

Osman, A. (2014). Indigenous knowledge in Africa: Challenges and opportunities. Retrieved December 15, 2016, from www.ufs.za/doc/libraries provider.

Owuor, J. A. (2007). Integrating African indigenous knowledge in Kenya's formal education system: The potential for sustainable development. *Journal of Contemporary Issues in Education*, 2(2), 21–37.

Patel, L. (2015). *Social Welfare and Development*. 2nd ed. Published in South Africa. Oxford: Oxford University Publishing Press.

Sillitoe, P. (2002). Participant observation to participatory development: Making anthropology work. In P. Sillitoe, A. Bicker, and J. Pottier (Eds.), *Participating in Development: Approaches to Indigenous Knowledge*. London: Routledge, 1–23.

Smith, A. (2002). Power and hierarchy of knowledge. *Geoforum*, 40(1), 230–248.

Tobin, K. (1993). Impediments to the improvement of teaching and learning practices in science classrooms in developing countries. In S. Chasin and B. Waldrip (Eds.), *Science Education in Developing Countries: From Theory to Practice. Rehovot: Department of Science Teaching*. Weizmann Institute of Science.

Ukwuoma, C. U. (2015). *Educational Development in Africa: Changing Perspectives on the Role of Indigenous Knowledge*. Palapye: Botswana International University of Science and Technology.

Umoren, N. (2016). Social work development in Africa: Encouraging best practice. *International Journal of Scientific and Engineering Research*, 7(1), 191–203.

5
TRANSLANGUAGING AND PEDAGOGIC PATHWAYS TO CULTURALLY RELEVANT SOCIAL WORK EDUCATION

Thembelihle Brenda Makhanya and Susan Levy

Abstract: English

Coloniality, which symbolises the legacy of imperialism, remains vividly visible in African education. The curriculum content, languages, and traditions remain dominantly White and Western. Such outcries were exposed in student protests in South African higher education, such as #FeesMustFall and #RhodesMustFall. Student movements have been calling for the uprooting of colonial practices in African universities and education. Social work education is not immune from such criticism since its professionalisation has been governed by the legacy of colonial structures, which created a lack of culturally relevant and inclusive education. This chapter unpacks a way forward through engaging with decolonial approaches that provide examples of ways to develop context-based social work. We present two pathways for developing culturally relevant social work education, focused on language and knowledge. Both demonstrate the role of pedagogy in decolonising and achieving change: (1) translanguaging and the use of African languages in social work education; (2) epistemic injustice, experiential knowledge, and epistemological access in social work education.

Abstract: isiZulu

Ikholoniyalithi ekhombisa ukusalela kokubuswa amanye amazwe ibonakala ngokucacile kwimfundo yase Afrika. Okuqukethwe ikharikhulamu, izilimi, usiko kuyizinsalela zokubuswa abaMhlophe kanye neNtshonalanga. Lezi zikhalo zivezwe imibhikisho yabafundi kumabanga aphakeme emfundo eningizimu Afrika ezifana no #IzimaliKufaneleZiwe Kanye ne #RhodesKufaneleIwe. Inhlangano yabafundi ibilokhu ifuna kuqedwe imikhuba yobukoloni emanyuvesi nasemfundweni yase-Afrika. Imfundo yomsebenzi wezenhlalakahle ayivikelekile ekugxekweni okunjalo ngenxa yokuthi ukuqeqeshwa kwayo kuye kwalawulwa yifa lezakhiwo zamakholoni ezadala ukuntuleka kwemfundo ehambisana namasiko nebandakanya wonke umuntu. Lesi sahluko sivula indlela eya phambili ngokuzibandakanya nezindlela ze-dikholoniyalithi ezinikeza izibonelo zezindlela zokuthuthukisa umsebenzi wezenhlalakahle osekelwe kumongo. Sethula izindlela ezimbili zokuthuthukisa imfundo yomsebenzi wezenhlalakahle ehambisana namasiko, egxile olimini nolwazi, kokubili kubonisa indima ye-phedagoji ekuqedeni ukoloni nokufezekisa ushintsho: 1) Ukuhumusha kanye nokusetshenziswa kwezilimi zase-Afrika emfundweni yezenhlalakahle; 2) Ukungabi nabulungiswa kwe-zazi lwazi, ulwazi lokuhlangenwe nakho, ukufinyelela ezifundweni zolwazi emfundweni yomsebenzi wezenhlalakahle.

Introduction

Colonialism across Africa led to the oppression and domination of Africans by Whites. The presentation of this tragic period of history in binary form: Black/White conceals the complexity and multidimensionality of colonialism, but the use of the binary Black/White does provide a powerful reminder of how colour divided, destroyed, and continues to define lives. Whilst colonial rulers have departed, the legacy of the past remains and continues to impact everyday lives (Smith and Rasool, 2020). In the context of South Africa, the journey from colonialism to independence unsettled established norms and practices around domination and oppression, but there is much work still to be done to overcome both colonialism (1652–1961) and apartheid (1948–1994). Apartheid continued to enforce a racial segregation system through legislation enacted by the National Party. In relation to education, one example of many discriminatory policies introduced by the apartheid government resulted in the Bantu Education Act 1952, which led to Africans receiving only minimal education, sustaining them as an oppressed group. In 1959, the University Education Act 45 further limited Black's access to education, should they have managed to acquire relevant qualifications, by prohibiting attendance at 'Whites' universities (South African History Online, 2018). Higher Education (HE) in South Africa was established for Whites, by the White European population, using the languages of colonialism and apartheid, along with normalising Western knowledge as the foundation of learning. This chapter looks to an alternative future through presenting two pathways, centred around pedagogical approaches, to guide social work towards decolonising and creating culturally relevant forms of teaching and learning.

- Translanguaging and the use of African languages in social work education.
- Epistemic injustice, experiential knowledge, and epistemological access in social work education.

Colonialism was achieved through Europeans ruling over 'Blacks' for the advancement of 'Whites' (Tsotsi, 2000, p. 6). Decolonisation is the 'change that colonised countries go through when they become politically independent from their former colonisers' (Oelofsen, 2015, p. 130). Decoloniality is the practice of decolonisation by critically examining dominant practices and knowledge in post-colonial societies (Ndlovu-Gatsheni, 2015) and the untangling of the production of knowledge from a perceived universality and superiority of Western knowledge and culture.

Social work in South Africa was initially a profession designed to meet the needs of the White population (Smith, 2014), and while this is no longer the reality, the rebalancing of beneficiaries of services is incomplete. It is within this historical context of racial segregation and discriminatory services and education that social work evolved in South Africa (Smith, 2008), which is antithetical to a profession based on social justice and anti-oppressive practice. While the reach and remit of the profession is no longer limited to a minority White population, social work remains largely dependent on Western knowledge and ways of doing social work. This creates challenges for developing relationships or connecting with the majority of service users and addressing local social issues.

During 2015–2016, South African universities were dominated by the #FeesMustFall student protests. The students highlighted that university education was Western and anti-Black. They called for free, decolonised higher education, based on contextually relevant curricula without colonial influences (Kreitzer, 2012; Mbembe, 2016). Social work students supported the #FeesMustFall student protests wanting to take action to address discriminatory curricula (Mamphiswana and Noyoo, 2016) that maintained colonial and apartheid systems, and, as such, failed to prepare professionals with skills to deal with the disempowered African population (Bozalek and Boughey, 2012). Smith (2008) has called for social work education to engage with the sociopolitical realities of the post-colonial and post-apartheid era and to engage more directly and more critically with inequality, oppression, and cultural hegemony. A starting point to achieve change is the decolonising of social work education, and this chapter provides examples of how to work to achieve this.

The chapter is presented in two main sections. First, we explore the history of social work in South Africa, the development of social work education, and decolonisation within the context of social work education. Second, we discuss decolonial alternatives: two pathways that can be used for culturally relevant social work curricula focused on language and knowledge.

- Translanguaging and the use of African languages in social work education.
- Epistemic injustice, experiential knowledge, and epistemological access in social work education.

Through the exploration of these two pathways, the chapter provides achievable outcomes with applications for use in other countries to progress the decolonisation and culturally relevant debate in HE and, specifically, in social work.

Evolving Social Work and Social Work Education in South Africa

South African social work education is not free from the injustices of the past since it is the very product of colonialism and apartheid (Smith, 2008). Two key developments in social work in South Africa can be traced back to the United Kingdom and the United States. Emily Hobhouse, from the United Kingdom, was the first social worker in the country. Concerned by the conditions in British concentration camps during the Boer War, Emily travelled to South Africa in 1899. Not long after, at the turn of the 20th century, South African-born Charlotte Maxeke became the first African social worker. However, Maxeke was unable to study social work in South Africa and gained her qualifications at Wilberforce University in the United States (Smith, 2014). The South Africa Department of Welfare was established in 1927 as White people's welfare to absorb trained social workers (Patel, 2005; Smith, 2014).

During apartheid, social work education and practice were characterised by discriminatory principles (Mamphiswana and Noyoo, 2016) primarily based on race. Although African poverty and developmental needs continued in South Africa, which called for the training of more social workers, the hardships of Africans and Whites were dealt with differently, with Whites' poverty being the primary focus of the state (Smith, 2014). Apartheid systems were aligned with collective responsibility being the fundamental African ideology, and they assumed that Africans should address social issues through the family and community, with the government intervening only when informal supports failed (residual approach) (Patel, 2005; Mamphiswana and Noyoo, 2016). This approach not only discriminated against Blacks, but also a focus on individualism during apartheid undermined and weakened family responsibility and kinships (Smith, 2014).

As the poverty of the African population became more visible, the next move was to train African social workers to focus on African problems (Kreitzer, 2012). The Jan Hofmeyr College was the prominent School of Social Work in Johannesburg (Smith, 2014), and it is where Winnie Madikizela Mandela trained as a social worker. However, social work training of Africans was characterised by a lack of institutional access, resources, and infrastructure. Furthermore, since the Jan Hofmeyr College encouraged political freedom for Africans and fought against the uprooting of ancient life in the name of civilisation, it posed a threat to state ideologies (Smith and Nathane, 2018), leading to its closure in 1950 (Smith, 2014). Other institutions were established, such as Stellenbosch University, that offered social work qualifications but under apartheid ideologies.

There has been no uniformity in South African universities in social work curricula (Mamphiswana and Noyoo, 2016). The South African Council of Social Service Profession is the guiding board for the social work profession in the country, and it sets requirements for social work education; however, each university develops its own curriculum (Smith and Nathane, 2018). The Council has not envisioned decolonial education; rather, the lack of uniformity leads to a failure to differentiate African education from that of other racial groups (Mamphiswana and Noyoo, 2016). Curricula have not accounted for the needs of the larger African population (Kreitzer, 2012), with content based on British and American epistemologies and pedagogies. This has used a largely clinical approach with an individual focus (Smith, 2014) and the development of therapists skilled in dealing with Western (White) social problems. As a result, the fundamental issues of Africans, such as poverty and unemployment, were not considered in social work training (Mamphiswana and Noyoo, 2016), and social work practitioners were unable to respond to challenges facing the African population. This suggests that social work education and practice were not channelled to address social injustice (Kasiram, 2009).

Across higher education, interest is growing in understanding ways to diversify and decolonise curricula (Abdi, 2006). The dominance of a colonial legacy is particularly concerning on programmes such as social work as it arrests the colonial subjects' minds and they struggle to cast out race-based inferiority and colonial idealism (Biko, 1987). The risk is that this colonial lens is carried into practice. From as far back as the 1960s, Fanon (1963) and, more recently, Bharuthram (2018), have called for identifying and introducing practical decolonial processes to deal with the legacy of colonialism and apartheid and the hegemony and perpetuation of oppressive ways of being. Recent South African studies that have explored decolonisation of social work education include Tamburro's (2013) work on the inclusion of decolonisation in social work education and practice, which found that incorporating indigenous world views in the social work curriculum will enable the effective provision of social services. In Cape Town, Le Grange (2014) examined the Africanisation of curricula. This and other work contributed to the African Schools of Social Work International Conference, 2017, in Johannesburg, with a focus on the decolonisation of social work education. A decolonisation exercise is thus necessary for the attainment of anti-oppressive practice, social inclusion, and culturally relevant social work education (Bozalek and Boughey, 2012). Students are unable to demonstrate anti-oppressive and decolonial practice if it is not part of their teaching. We now turn to explore two pedagogical pathways that can contribute to an alternative future for African social work education.

Translanguaging and the Use of African Languages in Social Work

South Africa, like other African countries, has multiple languages that are used across the country. This contrasts with the Global North, where the norm is for the use of one or two official languages. South Africa has eleven official languages. The benefits of being multilingual are numerous, including being able to view the world from different perspectives. However, as Coetzee-de Vos (2019) argues, this breadth and richness of languages is not visible in academia, where only English (a colonial product) and Afrikaans (an apartheid product) are used. This leads to first-language speakers of the other nine indigenous languages often experiencing challenges in the absence of multilingual practice in HE. The domination of English and Afrikaans in South African universities enables White students to continue to benefit from their White ancestors' unfair privileges through the silencing of indigenous languages in education. The apparent democratising of HE, in practice, continues to privilege the colonial legacy at the expense of indigenous people, with language being a barrier to effective teaching and learning for African students (Makhanya and Zibane, 2020; Makhubele et al., 2018). Ngozi (2009) points to the challenges of engagement when that emanates from one side, as it demotivates diversity.

There are multiple impacts on students' learning emanating from studying in a language that they may not be fluent in. Furthermore, within the South African context, the use of the colonial language of English is imbued with oppression, domination, and discrimination, which can increase low self-esteem and anxiety amongst indigenous students (Rubio, 2007). As Ncube (2019) argues, this can lead to Africans losing their sense of being. Students who are less confident in using English can become alienated in class engagements. Poor enunciation and elocution, and a limited English vocabulary, all become barriers to effective learning, generating fear and a feeling of incompetency among the indigenous students (Makhanya and Zibane, 2020). Such pressure can negatively impact not only the academic progress and learning of students (Makhanya, 2021; Makhubele et al., 2018), but also their practice as social workers. Such an outcome means that current social work education is failing to equip future practitioners with the basic skills of being able to effectively and confidently communicate with service users (Schenk et al., 2015).

There is a need for diverse knowledge production, and the transmission of that knowledge in different languages in social work education. The inclusion of indigenous languages in the teaching of curriculum is one marker of decolonisation that values the intellectual capacity of the African continent (Oelofsen, 2015). Language is thus a means through which to access and develop indigenous knowledge systems (IKS). This requires the incorporation, consideration, and validation of indigenous languages alongside the prevailing dominance of English. As Nilsen et al (2023) have found, while in Norway 94% of literature used in social work education is in Norwegian, close to 100% in Rwanda, Tanzania, and Uganda is in English. Maringe and Ojo (2017) call for South African universities to adopt the Global North's approach to teaching in the country's main language. There are many reasons why English as a foreign language does not offer a comprehensive vocabulary that values African knowledge systems, which has led to African's feeling inferior to the West as superior. Because of such attitudes, Lumumba (2019) has argued that the West feels obliged to impose their perspectives on Africa, and Africa deems it necessary to submit. Mignolo (2011) explains that the first step of decoloniality should be to delink the former colonies from the colonial masters, including through the development of indigenous languages in academia. Cakatha (2015) has argued that the development of indigenous languages through compatibility with English is not necessary, due to the different content and context the languages serve. Thus, African languages must be independently developed as a unique vernacular of the unique continent. The unsilencing of the voices of indigenous people has the potential to develop sustainable education in South Africa (Nyoka, 2019), as we progress towards a future of sustainable and inclusive education, African languages must be central to and valued within knowledge production. One way to achieve this is through translanguaging.

Translanguaging, as a pedagogy, refers to the use of a range of languages to enable students to fully engage, understand, and express themselves, recognising the important connections among language, culture, and communication (Coetzee-de Vos, 2019). People's knowledge of language cannot be separated from their knowledge of human relations and human social interaction, which includes the history, the context of usage, and the emotional and symbolic values of specific socially constructed languages. The language that we use to communicate inherently influences the interaction. For social work, a profession that is framed on relational working and connecting with people, to diminish the importance of this within education for preparing for practice is counterintuitive. Translanguaging in social work education, with multilingual students and lecturers using integrated communication (mixing of languages), will impact on the epistemological meaning of texts. Engagements through translations and interpretations can ensure an enhanced understanding of the content between lecturers and students during class discussions.

The University of KwaZulu Natal is already addressing this through the development of language policies that encourage multilingualism in academic engagements. Although issues of practical implementation remain a concern for other institutions, the University of KwaZulu-Natal (UKZN) Language Policy is seen as the most practical and has been successfully implemented (Seepe, 2022). UKZN has demonstrated the value and importance of student identities through the application of its Language Policy that encourages equal use of English and isiZulu in students' learning. Considering the number of indigenous languages in South Africa, isiZulu was chosen for use at UKZN for locality and regional representation since isiZulu is dominant in KwaZulu-Natal. The University is currently exploring ways to include other languages such as siSotho and Swahili (Mngadi, 2022). The use of isiZulu is also seen as a means to enhance widening access to the institution. The Language Policy was developed in 2006, revised in 2014, and in 2022–2023 it is being reviewed again (Mngadi, 2022). This iterative process of review aims to ensure relevance, inclusivity, and practical implementation. The University understands that in language we find mental strength (Seepe, 2022). Seepe (2022) views the emphasis on context-based university language policies as a decolonial approach that has relevance to universities across Africa and elsewhere across the globe.

There are three key ways that the Language Policy at UKZN is integrated into practice. First, it is compulsory for all non-Zulu speaking first-year students to take an isiZulu course in their first year. Second, the creation of the University Language Board (ULB) ensures the practical use of the two languages at the university. The ULB has led to the scientific development of isiZulu, including:

- isiZulu bank of terms/definitions
- isiZulu lexicon
- isiZulu National Corpus
- isiZulu spellchecker (Mngadi, 2022).

Third, the ULB offices support the:

- translation of teaching materials
- training of bilingual tutors
- implementation of the requirement for all Masters and PhD abstracts to be translated into isiZulu.

The UKZN Language Policy highlights the importance of language as a key aspect of inclusive and liberating education. The central aspiration of the policy is on the valuing of the African-invested mode of knowledge production for sustainable education (Makhanya, 2021). Through the policy, UKZN is demonstrating positive progress in using pedagogy to transform and decolonise.

Translanguaging, the prioritising and valuing of indigenous languages, is one approach to decolonise social work and leads to graduates who have invested in the languages of the people they will be working with in practice. We now move to our second pathway for decolonising social work education, and the focus shifts from language to knowledge and covers epistemic injustice and experiential knowledge.

Epistemic Injustice and Experiential Knowledge and Epistemological Access in Social Work Education

The 1997 White Paper on Social Welfare states that social workers should work on enhancing social integration by focusing on people's social context in South African communities. Since a brutal history influences the context of the country, the application of the tenets of the 1997 White Paper suggests that social work graduates are expected to embark on non-oppressive practices to redress the injustices of the past (Makhanya, 2022). To achieve this would require social work education curricula to provide a foundation to work within this context. However, as Maringe and Ojo (2017) have argued, African universities offer local degrees, but there is a precariousness to the local content and epistemologies presented; meaning Western theory and practices still prevail.

Western perspectives in African academia can overlook the challenges facing indigenous African communities. Social workers have a range of theories, approaches, and models designed to empower, address social injustice, and work at a relational level with service users within their environments (Schenk et al., 2015). When these approaches do not speak to the real experiences of African people and misrepresent the African population, questions must be raised as to whether social work education is preparing future practitioners to fulfil their mandate.

Connell (2007) and Dladla (2017) have both argued that the African continent is globally viewed as not having an African philosophy; as a result, African universities rely on Western theory and knowledge. Matsiqhi (2019) has criticised this notion, arguing that it is the preservation of Western domination as a master narrative in education, which suppresses other perspectives. The Western notion of education imposed on African students hinders self-awareness, understanding, and critical engagement with the impact of colonialism in post-colonial South Africa (Makhanya, 2022). We call for the inclusion of African philosophies and theory as alternatives in knowledge production (Mignolo, 2011) and for the development of social work curricula that are responsive to the social needs of African indigenous communities (Tamburro, 2013; Makhanya, 2021).

Despite the purpose of social work education being to equip students with the basic knowledge, values, and skills required to critically engage with oppression in contemporary South Africa (Smith and Nathane, 2018), the content of modules too frequently remains detached from the South African context. The dominance of Western knowledge increases confusion in social work practice with African communities. Students need to engage with South African literature to understand anti-oppressive ethics and values in social work within contemporary South Africa. There is a need to 'develop teaching material for African social work in the classroom, based on local and regional case studies, to develop African curriculum content' (Gray et al., 2014, p.112). This requires the centring of African perspectives in social work education, not the complete exclusion of Western literature in teaching and learning, but rather a call for culturally relevant social work education and practice (Kreitzer, 2012) through the inclusion of different philosophies and epistemologies (Mignolo, 2011).

Teaching philosophies play a fundamental role in students' epistemological access to different knowledges and understandings. Lange (2017) argues that decoloniality of access is incomplete without epistemological access. This means that more than encouraging equal participation, learner-centred approaches are about engaging students with what they already know. Similarly, Duron and Giardina (2018) emphasise the importance of teaching philosophies that increase the engagement of students during academic discussions by integrating their previous, experiential knowledge into their learning. Such teaching styles are regarded as enhancing understanding and academic inclusion. Teaching philosophies are fundamental if they recognise students not as passive objects but as active contributors who come with experiences that can be integrated into knowledge development (Lange, 2017; Duron and Giardina, 2018). Field practicum and associated context-specific modules provide students with the opportunity to observe and apply what they have learnt. In addition, an academic that speaks to the realities of African people allows for effective service delivery during practice. That is a bottom-up practice approach (Gray et al., 2013) influenced by the experiences of people to be served. This is why Esau and Keet (2014) value education that cultivates critical responsiveness during practice.

A pathway into decolonialising education, and challenging a legacy of epistemic injustice (Fricker, 2007), is the inclusion of experiential knowledge in the formulation and delivery of curriculum. Bringing to the fore diverse perspectives and voices can broaden the lens of focus to be inclusive of the lived experiences and experiential knowledge of students, service users, practitioners, and indigenous communities. Civil society, traditional leaders, religious organisations, pastors, and other community leaders can and should be contributing to the co-production of knowledge and curriculum. Across Europe, the integration of experiential knowledge of service users in social work education is well established (Cabiati and Levy, 2021). However, in South Africa, work in this area is at an embryonic stage, with limited conceptualisation of partnership work and the co-production of knowledge. Instead, students are immersed in the philosophies of Western societies that create alienation and division between African scholars and African communities (Makhanya, 2021). The limited connection between lived experiences and students' learning can infringe on social work education and practice, and can demoralise students' motivation to continue into being registered as professional social workers (Gray and Lombard, 2008). South Africa can learn from good practice elsewhere to develop an African model for integrating lived experiences of African people, as experiential knowledge, into social work education. Raniga and Seepamore (2017) and Bobo and Akhurst (2019) have argued for the value of community engagement in decolonising university curricula. Baron (2018) also calls for curriculum to be co-constructed with students and the local community, for wider participation in knowledge generation.

There is a need for South African universities to challenge teaching and learning methods for relevance and applicability. Nakata et al. (2012) propose that students in lecture venues must engage with more sophisticated theoretical dilemmas, understand the conceptual limits of their thinking, and be able to critically engage propositions within their own experiences. Bozalek (2011) also suggests the importance of engagement opportunities with South African students to develop alternative learning and knowledge through participatory learning and action. Thus, a decolonised education should prioritise 'emancipatory and liberating pedagogies' (Maringe and Ojo, 2017, p. 36) and an 'epistemic revolution' of social work curriculum (Mathebane and Sekuda, 2018, p. 1).

Conclusion

As South Africa celebrates twenty-eight years of democracy, most of its citizens' lives are still characterised by injustices of the past, and they continue to experience and witness colonial legacies. The reminders and experiences of coloniality are everywhere. They are visible in university buildings, in how power and privileges are organised, in the curriculum, and in the dominant culture and language of teaching and learning. This translates into marginalisation and exclusion being embedded in social work education and practice; and a need for a deeper exploration of how history influences students' experiences, including social work, which is itself a product of the brutal historical context of colonialism and apartheid (Tjabane, 2012; Smith and Nathane, 2018). A Western curriculum alienates African cultures and interests and jeopardises practice in social work. This chapter has set out two pedagogical pathways to decolonise social work education and make changes in how and what is taught through

1. Translanguaging and the use of African languages in social work education.
2. Epistemic injustice, experiential knowledge, and epistemological access in social work education.

The lack of African indigenous languages, and an African-centred curriculum that is applicable to African communities, suggests that the legacy of colonial education creates distance between social work graduates and the African people they will support. If the status quo is not challenged, education and the university space will continue to perpetuate an inferiority complex among African students through the idealism of White and Western superiority. This portrays the university's intellectual landscape as the harbour of Western ideas, knowledge, and colonial languages at the expense of diverse perspectives reflecting the different populations to be served by academia and social work.

This chapter considers the transformation in social work not only to mean high enrolment of African students and funding support, although these aspects are critically important. The focus should also be on epistemological access for contextual, relevant curriculum. There is a need for teaching and learning methods that are sensitive to African ideas, cultures, knowledge, and diverse identities. Despite the transformative policies that allow for the inclusion of all students in the new democratic dispensation of HE, African students still suffer from academic exclusion in South African universities. Western languages and literature remain as powerful tools of coloniality. Social work is both a practice-based profession and an academic discipline (IFSW and IASSW, 2014), it is influenced by the socioeconomic and political dynamics of a given society (Smith, 2014; Schenk et al., 2015), and it should be embracing and learning from contextualised languages and experiential knowledge to address historical epistemic injustice.

Recommendations

The following pedagogical approaches are recommended for decolonising and developing culturally relevant social work education:

1. Translanguaging and the Use of African Languages in Social Work: teaching and assessing in a local language is recommended and can support developing students' confidence, identity, address marginalisation, and prepare students for contextualised practice.
2. Epistemic Injustice and Experiential Knowledge: the lived experiences of service users, students, practitioners, and local communities should be valued and integrated as forms of knowledge for decolonising and indigenising social work education.
3. Context and Epistemological Access in Social Work Education: African indigenous knowledge should be produced to generate new theoretical understandings to underpin African social work education.

Funding

This work is based on research supported by the National Institute for the Humanities and Social Sciences, South Africa.

Further Reading

Baron, P.R. (2018). Ethical Inclusive Curricula Design: Conversational Teaching and Learning. *South African Journal of Higher Education* 32(6), 326–350, https://doi.org/10.20853/32-6-2987.

Makhanya, T.B. and Zibane, S. (2020). Students' Voices on How Indigenous Languages Are Disfavoured in South African Higher Education. *Language Matters*, https://doi.org/10.1080/10228195.2020.1711533.

Raniga, T. and Seepamore, B. (2017). Critical Reflexivity beyond the Classroom: Social Work Students' Perspectives of Communities in KwaZulu-Natal. *Southern African Journal of Social Work and Social Development* 29(1), 34–48, https://doi.org/10.25159/2415-5829/1913.

References

Abdi, A.A. (2006). *Eurocentric Discourses and African Philosophies and Epistemologies of Education: Counter-hegemonic Analyses and Responses*. Edmonton, Canada: University of Alberta.

Baron, P.R. (2018). Ethical Inclusive Curricula Design: Conversational Teaching and Learning. *South African Journal of Higher Education* 32(6), 326–350, https://doi.org/10.20853/32-6-2987.

Bharuthram, S. (2018). Attending to the Affective: Exploring First Year Students' Emotional Experiences at University. *South African Journal of Higher Education* 32(2), 27–42, https://doi.org/10.20853/32-2-2113.

Biko, S. (1987). *I Write What I Like*. Oxford: ProQuest LLC.

Bobo, B. and Akhurst, J. (2019). Most Importantly, It's Like the Partner Takes More Interest in Us: Using Ubuntu as a Fundamental Ethic of Community Engagement (CE) Partnerships at Rhodes University. *Alternation Special Edition* 27, 88–110, http://doi.org/10.29086/2519-5476/2019/sp27a4.

Bozalek, V. (2011). Acknowledging Privilege through Encounters with Difference: Participatory Learning and Action Techniques for Decolonising Methodologies in Southern Contexts. *International Journal of Social Research Methodology* 14(6), 469–484, https://doi.org/10.1080/13645579.2011.611383.

Bozalek, V. and Boughey, C. (2012). (Mis)framing Higher Education in South Africa. *Social Policy and Administration* 46(6), 688–703, https://doi.org/10.1111/j.1467-9515.2012.00863.x.

Cabiati, E. and Levy, S. (2021) 'Inspiring Conversations': A Comparative Analysis of the involvement of Experts By Experience in Italian and Scottish Social Work Education. *British Journal of Social Work* 51(2), 487–504, doi.org/10.1093/bjsw/bcaa163.

Cakatha, Z. (2015). *In Search of the Absent Voice: The Status of Indigenous Languages in Post-apartheid South Africa*. Unpublished thesis (Ph.D.). University of South Africa.

Coetzee-de Vos, G. (2019). Reflections on Language Transformation at Nelson Mandela University. *Language Matters* 50(2), 1–19, https://doi.org/10.1080/10228195.2018.1524923.

Connell, R. (2007). *Southern Theory: The Global Dynamics of Knowledge in Social Science. Unwin*. Polity Press.

Dladla, N. (2017). Finding Me S03 EP74. Online Available: https://www.youtube.com/watch?v=HtbpnrBquzs. [Accessed 19 May 2020].

Duron, J.F. and Giardina, T.D. (2018). Teaching Philosophies and Practices in Social Work Education: Do the Core Competencies Influence Our Consciousness? *Social Work Education* 37(5), 603–616, https://doi.org/10.1080/02615479.2018.1450371.

Esau, M. and Keet, A. (2014). Reflective Social Work Education in Support of Socially Just Social Work Practice: The Experience of Social Work Students at a University in South Africa. *Social Work/Maatskaplike Werk* 50(4), 455–467, https://doi.org/10.15270/50-4-384.

Fanon, F. (1963). *The Wretched of the Earth*. New York: Grove Press.

Fricker, M. (2007). *Epistemic Injustice: Power and Ethics of Knowing*. New York: Oxford University Press.

Gray, M., Coates, J., Bird, Y. and Hetherington, T. (eds) (2013). *Decolonizing Social Work*. Buffalo: Ashgate.

Gray, M., Kreitzer, L. and Mupedziswa, R. (2014). The Enduring Relevance of Indigenisation in African Social Work: A Critical Reflection on ASWEA's Legacy. *Ethics and Social Welfare* 8(2), 101–116, http://doi.org/10.1080/17496535.2014.895397.

Gray, M. and Lombard, A. (2008). The Post-1994 Transformation of Social Work in South Africa. *International Journal of Social Welfare* 17(2), 132–145, https://doi.org/10.1111/j.1468-2397.2007.00545.x.

International Federation of Social Workers and International Association of Schools of Social Workers (2014). Global Definition of Social Work. Online Available: https://www.ifsw.org/what-is-social-work/global-definition-of-social-work/ [Accessed 24 March 2023].

Kasiram, M. (2009). The Emigration of South African Social Workers: Using Social Work Education to Address Gaps in Provision. *Social Work Education: The International Journal* 28(6), 646–654, https://doi.org/10.1080/02615470903027363.

Kreitzer, L. (2012). *Social Work in Africa: Exploring Culturally Relevant Education and Practice in Ghana. Galgary*. University of Calgary Press.

Lange, L. (2017). 20 Years of Higher Education Curriculum Policy in South Africa. *Journal of Education* 68, 32–68.

Le Grange, L. (2014). Currere's Active Force and the Africanisation of the University Curriculum. *South African Journal of Higher Education* 28(4), 1283–1294.

Lumumba, P.L. (2019). Time for Africa to Define for Herself What Democracy Means. Online Available: https://www.youtube.com/watch?v=VEnixCXo9pkandt=902s [Accessed 19 May 2020].

Makhanya, T.B. (2021). The Phenomenology of Colonialism: Exploring Perspectives of Social Work Graduates in the African University. *Critical Studies in Teaching and Learning* 9(1), 38–57, https://doi.org/10.14426/cristal.v9i1.279.

Makhanya, T.B. (2022). Azibuyele Emasisweni: Exploring the Discourse of Ubuntu Philosophy in Social Work Education and Practice. *African Journal of Social Work* 12(6), 1–8.

Makhanya, T.B. and Zibane, S. (2020). Students' Voices on How Indigenous Languages Are Disfavoured in South African Higher Education. *Language Matters*, https://doi.org/10.1080/10228195.2020.1711533.

Makhubele, J.C., Mabvurira, V. and Matlakala, F.K. (2018). Exploring Language as an Impediment to or a Resource for the Indigenisation of Social Work Education. *South African Journal of Social Work and Social Development* 30(1), 1–20, https://doi.org/10.25159/2415-5829/2973.

Mamphiswana, D. and Noyoo, N. (2016). Social Work Education in a Changing Socio-political and Economic Dispensation Perspectives from South Africa. *International Social Work* 43(1), 21–32.

Maringe, F. and Ojo, E. (2017). Sustainable Transformation in a Rapidly Globalizing and Decolonising World in Sustainable Transformation. In *African Higher Education*, Maringe, F. and Ojo, E. (eds.). Rotterdam: Sense Publishers, 25–39

Mathebane, M. S. and Sekuda, J. (2018). Decolonising the Curriculum That Underpins Social Work Education in South Africa. *Southern African Journal of Social Work and Social Development* 30(1), 19, https://doi.org/10.25159/2415-5829/2360.

Matsiqhi, A. (2019). Discussion. Stories Making Headlines for the Week with Aubrey Matshiqi. Online Available: https://www.youtube.com/watch?v=bXqU-rmJlmAandt=25s. [Accessed 14 May 2020].

Mbembe, A.J. (2016). Decolonizing the University: New Directions. *Arts and Humanities in Higher Education* 15(1), 29–45.

Mignolo, W.D. (2011). Geopolitics of Sensing and Knowing: On (De)Coloniality, Border Thinking and Epistemic Disobedience. *Postcolonial Studies* 14(3), 273–283.

Mngadi, K. (2022). *An Overview of the University of KwaZulu-Natal Language Policy and Plan Now and beyond Review [Symposium Paper]. Celebrating 15 Years of the Language Policy of the University of KwaZulu-Natal Colloquium*. Durban: RSA, February 23.

Nakata, N.M., Nakata,V., Keech, S. and Bolt, R. (2012). Decolonial Goals and Pedagogies for Indigenous Studies. *Decolonization: Indigeneity, Education and Society* 1(1), 120–140.

Ncube, M. (2019). On the Power of Language. *Mail and Guardian*, August 23, 2019. Online Available: https://mg.co.za/article/2019-08-23-00-on-the-power-of-language/ [Accessed 14 July 2020].

Ndlovu-Gatsheni, S.J. (2015). Decoloniality as the Future of Africa. *History Compass* 13(10), 485–496.

Ngozi, A.C. (2009). The Dangers of a Single Story: Paper presented at TED Talks Conference. Nigeria, October 7.

Nilsen, A.C., Kalinganire, C., Mabeyo, Z.M., Manyama, W., Ochen, E.A. and Revheim, C., and Nyoka, B. (2019). *Voices of Liberation: Achie Mafeje*. Cape Town: HSRC Press.

Oelofsen, R. (2015). Decolonisation of the African Mind and Intellectual Landscape. *Pronimon* 16(2), 130–146.

Patel, L. (2005). *Social Welfare and Social Development in South Africa*. Oxford.

Raniga, T. and Seepamore, B. (2017). Critical Reflexivity beyond the Classroom: Social Work Students' Perspectives of Communities in KwaZulu-Natal. *Southern African Journal of Social Work and Social Development* 29(1), 34–48, https://doi.org/10.25159/2415-5829/1913.

Rubio, F. (2007). *Self-Esteem and Foreign Language Learning*. Angerton Gardens, Newcastle: Cambridge Scholars Publishing.

Schenk, R., Mbedzi, P., Qalinge, Schultz, P., Sekudu, J. and Sesoko, M. (2015). *Introduction to Social Work in the South African Context*. Cape Town: Oxford University Press.

Seepe, S. (2022). *Keynote Address [Symposium Paper]. Celebrating 15 Years of the Language Policy of the University of KwaZulu-Natal Colloquium*. Durban: RSA, February 23.

Smith, L. (2008). South African Social Work Education: Critical Imperatives for Social Change in the Post-apartheid and Post-colonial Context. *International Social Work* 51(3), 371–383.

Smith, L. (2014). Historiography of South African Social Work: Challenging Dominant Discourses. *Social Work/Maatskaplike Werk* 50(3), 305–331.

Smith, L. and Nathane, M. (2018). #NotDomestication #NotIndigenisation: Decoloniality in Social Work Education. *Southern African Journal of Social Work and Social Development* 30(1), 1–18, https://doi.org/10.25159/2415-5829/2400.

Smith, L. and Rasool, S. (2020). Deep Transformation toward Decoloniality in Social Work: Themes for Change in a Social Work Higher Education Program. *Journal of Progressive Human Services* 31(2), 144–146.

South Africa Department of Welfare. (1997). *White Paper: Principles, Guidelines, Recommendations, Proposed Policies and Programmes for Developmental Social Welfare in South Africa*. Pretoria: Department of Welfare.

South African History Online (2018). Towards a People's History. Online Available: Http://Www.Sahistory.Org.Za/People/Winnie-Madikizela-Mandela [Accessed 05 April 2018].

Tamburro, A. (2013). Including Decolonization in Social Work Education and Practice. *Journal of Indigenous Social Development* 2(1), 1–16.

Tjabane, M. (2012). *Education Policy and Social Justice in Higher Education: A South African Case Study*. Unpublished thesis. (Ph.D.). University of Pretoria.

Tsotsi, W.M. (2000). *From Chattel to Wage Slavery*. Durban: W.M. Tsotsi.

6
FAITH AND SPIRITUALITY IN SOCIAL WORK EDUCATION AND PRACTICE IN ETHIOPIA

Ashenafi Hagos Baynesagn, Tasse Abye, and Emebet Mulugeta

Abstract: English

In Ethiopia, before 1974, religion and government were considered the same; from 1974 to 1991 the socialist government emphasised secularism, and, from 1991 onwards, the government declared 'religious freedom'. Almost all Ethiopians belong to a religion; hence, in identity formation, religion is one of the primary identities of Ethiopia. Social work education and practice in Ethiopia need to consider the reality on the ground and integrate faith and spirituality into social work. This chapter examines how faith and spirituality are being accommodated in social work education and service provision by drawing on findings from a recent study. Data were collected through a survey completed by 144 graduate social workers and 12 interviews with social work educators and service providers in Ethiopia. The findings indicate that faith and spirituality are incorporated into social work education at the undergraduate and postgraduate levels. In social work practice, whilst many social workers integrate faith and spirituality, some organisations found it challenging to utilise faith and spirituality in their services. The chapter concludes by highlighting areas for further improvement in social work education and service provision.

Abstract: Amharic

ኢትዮጵያ ውስጥ ከ1966 ዓ.ም. አብዮት በፊት ሐይማኖትና መንግሥት እንደ አንድ ይቆጠሩ ነበር። ከ1966-1983 ዓ.ም የሶሻሊስት መንግስት ሴኩላሪዝምን አፅንዖት ሰጥቶ የነበረ ቢሆንም ከ1983ዓ.ም ጀምሮ መንግስት 'የሐይማኖት ነፃነት' አውጇል። ሁሉም ኢትዮጵያውያን ማለት ይቻላል የሐይማኖት ተከታዮች ናቸው። ስለዚህም በማንነት ምስረታ ሐይማኖት በመጀመሪያዎቹ ተርታ ከሚጠቀሱት የኢትዮጵያውያን ማንነቶች አንዱ ነው። በኢትዮጵያ ያለው የሶሻል ወርክ ትምህርት እና አገልግሎት መሬት ላይ ያለውን እውነታ በማጤን እምነት እና መንፈሳዊነትን ከሶሻል ወርክ ጋር ማቀናጀት ይኖርበታል። ይህ ምዕራፍ እምነት እና መንፈሳዊነት እንዴት በሶሻል ወርክ ትምህርት እና የአገልግሎት አቅርቦት ውስጥ እየተስተናገዱ እንደሆነ በቅርብ ጊዜ የተደረገ የጥናት ግኝቶችን በመመርከዝ ይተነትናል። መረጃ የተሰበሰበው በኢትዮጵያ ውስጥ በናሙና የዳሰሳ ጥናት ከተካተቱ 144 የሶሻል ወርክ ምሩቃን እና ከ 12 ከሶሻል ወርክ መምህራን እና አገልግሎት ሰጪዎች ጋር በተደረጉ ቃለ-መጠይቆች ነው። የጥናቱ ግኝቶች እንደሚያመለክቱት እምነት እና መንፈሳዊነት በመጀመሪያ እና በድህረ ምረቃ ደረጃዎች በሶሻል ወርክ ትምህርት ውስጥ ተካተው እንደሚገኙ ያመለክታል፡ ፡ በሶሻል ወርክ አገልግሎት ውስጥ፣ ብዙ የሶሻል ወርክ ባለሙያዎች እምነት እና መንፈሳዊነትን ሲያሀዱ፣ አንዳንድ ድርጅቶች እምነት እና መንፈሳዊነትን በአገልግሎታቸው ለመጠቀም ፈታኝ ሆኖ አግኝተውታል። በሶሻል ወርክ ትምህርት እና አገልግሎት አሰጣጥ ላይ ተጨማሪ መሻሻል ያለባቸውን ቦታዎች በማሳለጥ ይህ ምዕራፉ ይጠናቀቃል።

Introduction

Current literature in social work indicates a considerable inclination to accommodate and use faith and spirituality in social work education and practice (Adedoyin et al., 2021; Ebimgbo et al., 2017). Even if there are some differences in implementation, the need for integrating spirituality and faith in social work is immense (Adedoyin et al., 2021). Given that most Africans are predominantly religious, the value of integrating it with social work education and practice will bring significant change concerning how social work education is approached in teaching, research, and practice. Cognizant of this, Agbawodikeizu et al. (2022) conclude, based on their study in Nigeria, that enhancing the connections among spirituality, religion, and social work will better equip upcoming professionals to work with the social justice values of social work and be culturally sensitive. The integration includes how clients are understood, the role faith and spirituality play in the lives of clients, and how services are rendered and made accessible to different groups of clients. In Ethiopia, the second-most populous country in Africa, most people (99%) belong to a religion. Orthodox Christians and Muslims are the dominant religions in the country. Hence, integrating faith and spirituality might help social work students consider the role of faith and spirituality in the overall wellbeing of individuals, families, and communities and in assisting social work practitioners to provide clients with better social work services (Gilligan and Furness, 2006).

Elements of faith and spirituality have been integrated into Ethiopia's social work education curriculum. Social work students are also encouraged in core modules to understand their spirituality and faith, and how these play a role in social work practice at the micro-, mezzo-, or macro-level interventions. Moreover, universities in Ethiopia have a long tradition of helping students practice their religion and spirituality without violating the rights of others. Often the students' cafeteria adjusts meal times during Ramadan and the Orthodox Christian fasting seasons. They also provide fasting meals during fasting days and seasons. On Fridays, class ends at 11:30 am and starts at 1:30 pm to accommodate prayer time for followers of Islam, while, on other days, morning classes end at noon. This has also become a practice in all government offices in the country. This indicates how the government also emphasises spirituality and faith, considering the society's fabric. These practices are considered to be a good foundation for social work programmes in the country to accommodate religion and spirituality in their programmes since the opening of the School of Social Work at Addis Ababa University in September 2004. This study investigates how faith, spirituality, and social work are integrated and utilised in Ethiopia's social work education and practice. The coming sections cover a literature review on faith and spirituality, social work in Ethiopia, the method used to develop this chapter, and findings discussed before recommendations are presented.

Faith, Spirituality, and Social Work

Faith is defined as having a strong belief and trust in religious doctrines. Besides, faith is having loyalty to God because of spiritual conviction (Gale et al., 2022). Globally there are different faiths. In most African countries, people belong to different religions according to their faith. At the national level, governments often discuss church and state being separated; in practice, they are not. According to the history of many countries, religion has been highly involved in politics and vice versa. In many countries, faith is central to politics and individuals' identity formation (Knitter, 2010).

Spirituality refers to one's religious practices, beliefs, and sense of meaning and purpose in life (Gale et al., 2022). However, others claim religion and spirituality should not be connected since it is possible to be spiritual without being religious (Carey, 2018). Compared to faith, conceptualising spirituality is more complicated. According to Ozmete et al. (2022, p.8), 'The uncertainty about how to conceptualise and measure the concept of spirituality has limited research on this subject.'

In the early stage of the development of the social work profession, secularism was the dominant orientation rather than accommodating faith and spirituality (Sheridan and Hemert, 1999). Secularism is the political tenet of Western culture, where religion plays no significant role (Lehmann, 2013). This was in relation to not only social work but also other academic disciplines; until today, faith and spirituality have been avoided, based on universities stating they are secular places. However, integrating faith and spirituality in social work pedagogy is not a choice but rather a must since it can help to obtain a holistic understanding of the client and identify the best ways of service delivery (Adedoyin et al., 2021). In the case of social work service provision, incorporating faith and spirituality becomes necessary since faith and spirituality are integral to human lives (Ebimgbo et al., 2017), helping to give meaning and purpose to life.

If clients and social workers consider their faith and spiritual beliefs vital, social workers should be mindful of that (Philip and Sheila, 2006). Since spiritual sensitivity is essential in social work service provision, many social workers have started integrating it into their service provision (Ebimgbo et al., 2017). Understanding clients' faith and spirituality help them understand their problems (Darrell and Rich, 2017).

In the Ethiopian context, services that do not consider the role of spirituality and faith are futile exercises. This was highly exhibited when HIV/AIDs was considered a health issue. Government, in general, and health institutions, in particular, were challenged since the health model only considered the physical wellbeing of individuals and families, neglecting the spiritual life. This approach became challenging when people tested positive and needed to be on antiretroviral therapy (ART). Adherence to the therapy was challenging since many believed it was not aligned with their spirituality and faith. The assessment then only focused on people's biological/physical health and psychological and social needs, neglecting the spiritual aspect of their life. Only after the approach was changed to accommodate spirituality and faith was progress in adhering to ART made (Hussen et al., 2014). This is an indication of the importance of the use of biopsychosocial and spiritual assessment in social work intervention. Social workers look at psychological or physical needs and assess how the client's faith and environment interact to affect their overall sense of wellbeing (Gale et al., 2022). As the name suggests, a biopsychosocial-spiritual examination assesses the client in four areas: biological, psychological, social, and spiritual. Nevertheless, this by no means implies that spirituality and faith alone can make a difference; rather, it indicates that it is one major component in social work.

Social workers are expected to do the biopsychosocial-spiritual assessment with every client. Biopsychosocial-spiritual assessment is a holistic approach to understanding the client's experiences, including physical and mental health (Gale et al., 2022). This indicates that spirituality is integral to social workers' practice (Darrell and Rich, 2017) since faith and spirituality are also considered one aspect of the wellbeing of an individual. Understanding their faith or spirituality is crucial to have a holistic understanding of human lives. Spiritual sensitivity is vital so that social workers can develop in service provision (Ebimgbo et al., 2017). Culturally competent practice accommodates different faith and spiritual beliefs (Gilligan and Furness, 2006). Hence, it is paramount to educate social work students on the importance of faith and spirituality and to make them aware of their faith and spirituality since it will impact their practice as social workers, from assessing clients to planning and implementing an intervention plan with a client.

Faith and Spirituality in Ethiopia

In Ethiopia, during the emperors' period (before 1974), there was no distinction between the government and the Orthodox Christian religion (Borruso, 2013). The military government came to power in 1974, declared socialism, and tried to make the country secular, denouncing all religions (Debele, 2017). Religious freedom was declared when the military government was replaced with the Ethiopian People's Revolutionary Democracy Front (EPRDF) in 1991, and competition among different religious groups emerged (Karbo, 2013). As per the Ethiopian constitution, state and religion are separated and dictate religious freedom. Religious competition exists in different parts of the country (Marcus, 2008). However, religious leaders played a significant role in handling and mediating conflict and facilitating peacebuilding (Karbo, 2013). According to Debele (2017), religious groups are often used to express disagreement with the government.

Faith and spirituality are major elements in identity formation in Ethiopia (Karbo, 2013). Among Ethiopians, many people are either Orthodox Christian or Muslim. Using religion to work with Ethiopians is considered adequate. An intervention that does not consider the faith of an individual or a family will significantly impact the process and outcome of any social work intervention. According to Hammern et al. (2015), quality of life is positively associated with religiousness/spirituality.

Social Work in Ethiopia

Social work education started in Ethiopia in 1959 as part of efforts to train professionals who could implement government policies and programmes (Baynesagn et al., 2021). It started as a two-year diploma level course and later became a bachelor's programme. The School of Social Work was founded in Addis Ababa, Ethiopia, in 1959; after 15 years, it was closed in 1974 when all the curricula were updated to reflect the socialist doctrine (Tesfaye, 1987). There was no single social work programme in the country for 30 years (1974–2004). During those times, graduates from sociology, psychology, nursing, and other business and agriculture graduates assumed social work positions. Some social work courses were offered in sociology programmes, under the name applied sociology, and later sociology and social administration (Baynesagn, 2020). Hence, sociology graduates were considered replacements for social workers.

In September 2004, social work education was reestablished at Addis Ababa University with a Masters in Social Work (MSW) programme. The MSW programme led to training of a cadre of social workers who could train other social workers. Reestablishing the profession constituted a massive step in laying the foundation for the country's current social work practices and educational programmes. Currently, social work education is offered in 12 universities and colleges. However, the number of graduates does not meet the demand for social workers (Baynesagn et al., 2021). Currently, social work positions in Ethiopia are filled by professionals and non-professionals. When organisations announce social work vacancies, they indicate they are looking for people who graduated from social work and related fields. Still, sociology and other social sciences graduates believe they can substitute as social workers. In Ethiopia, no independent professional groups or regulatory bodies regulate the provision of social work services and education (Northcut et al., 2021).

Study Methods and Participants

To understand the role of faith and spirituality in social work education and practice in Ethiopia, this study utilised a mixed methods approach. Interviews, surveys, and document reviews were used to understand how faith and spirituality are accommodated in the social work curriculum and how social work graduates use faith and spirituality in their service provision. The School of Social Work at Addis Ababa University is the pioneer in establishing and reestablishing social work programmes in Ethiopia. The School of Social Work developed the current BSW curriculum in Ethiopia, which all universities in Ethiopia use. Most of the social work programmes that operate in other Ethiopian colleges and universities are handled by graduates from Addis Ababa University.

Six universities' BSW and MSW curricula were reviewed as part of the document review to understand their content. Moreover, 12 academic staff members and service providers were interviewed. One hundred forty-four randomly selected graduates from the list of graduates from Ethiopian university registrars since 2006 participated in the survey to understand how they use faith and spirituality in their social work service provision. An ethics committee at Addis Ababa, University School of Social Work, approved conducting this study. All participants provided their consent to participate in the study. Participants in the in-depth interviews are referred to as IDI in this chapter. Data from the interview, document review, and survey were triangulated.

Among the survey participants, 71% were males, while 29% were females. This reflects our graduates' gender composition in Ethiopia, where most social work students and graduates are males. However, as compared to other social science programmes, the number of female students is higher, and the percentage is increasing. In the 2021 and 2022 academic years, the percentage of newly admitted BSW female students was 49% and 54%, respectively. Since social work education was reopened in 2004, most available graduates who are engaged in social work service delivery are young. More than half of the respondents, 52.1%, are working in a non-governmental organisation, while 20.8% are in government and United Nations/International Organizations (UN/IO), and the rest, 6.3%, are in other organisations. Among the factors that create the demand is employment opportunities in non-governmental organisations, including UN/IOs, that pay better than government organisations. Many candidates are attracted to social work education because of a job opportunity. It was also found that most of the applicants and, hence, graduates from the MSW programme were working as 'social workers' in different organisations before joining the programme, either with social work degrees or in other related disciplines such as psychology and sociology. It is also becoming a trend in the undergraduate programme to accept many social work students compared to other social sciences. The number of newly admitted students in other social science programmes in Ethiopia is declining. However, the School of Social Work still has many new students each year.

When we look at the religion of the survey participants, 58.3% were Orthodox Christian, 18.8% Protestant, 14.6% Muslim, 2.1% Catholic Christian, and 6.3% others. In Ethiopia, religion is one of the significant identities. When people introduce themselves to others, it is common to ask for their religion, assuming that everybody has a religion. Among the respondents, the majority (81.3%) considered themselves religious. As indicated above, all respondents belonged to a religion, so it is no surprise that the majority considered themselves religious. Moreover, 93.7% indicated that they fear God/Allah. It was also visible from the interviews that social workers, especially those working directly with individuals and families, considered their religion while providing social work services. A social worker in the First Federal Instance Court stated his experience working with children and their families as follows:

> I considered the religion of my clients and my own belief when working with my clients. I use religion as a guide in my social work practice. I believe the social work ethical prin-

ciples align with almost all religions I know of. Hence I always ask myself, 'Is this what God wants? Or is this something against my religion? It is particularly challenging when I am doing a child custody assessment, and one of the parents is from 'another' religion from my own. I find it difficult to consider the 'other' religion as a religion. After doing a bio-psychosocial and spiritual assessment, I always aim to decide who the best parent is and what is best for the child regardless of my own faith.

Senior Court Social Worker, IDI-2
Social Work Educator, IDI-5

The respondent is aware that, as a social worker, he must be respectful of and open-minded to others' religious beliefs. He therefore stated that he always makes an effort to avoid discriminatory service provisions. Other social workers also felt that the religion they are familiar with and follow is better than the other religion. Though they know that they should also be open-minded about their spirituality and faith, they tended to be biased towards the religion and faith they know. Social workers typically bring such situations to their weekly supervision meetings with a senior social worker because of their dilemmas. This shows that social workers think critically about their work and seek out the opinions of other social workers in order to ensure they deliver services that are in their client's best interests rather than being swayed by their own beliefs or those of their clients.

It is visible from the responses that all social workers felt that they belong to a religion and indicated that they feared God. They also indicated that they take their religion seriously, as well as their clients. However, in practice, they feel that the religion they know and belong to seems better, which could be the basis for bias. This indicates that spirituality and faith are interwoven in the lives of social workers and their clients. However, this does not imply that they are ignorant of their bias, which is an ideal place to start. They learn to respect their client's spirituality and faith in their education. As a result, some social workers struggle with it, think about it, and make improvements. With this knowledge, the social work curriculum in Ethiopia considers faith and spirituality as a topic of discussion.

Faith and Spirituality in Social Work Education

Looking into the social work curriculum in Ethiopia, faith and spirituality are treated in the courses Social Work Practice II, Case Management, Gender Studies, Diversity, Psychiatric Social Work, and Counseling. These courses treat faith and spirituality as a unit or sub-section. These units and sections discuss faith and spirituality in general without picking the predominant ones in Ethiopia. In the MSW programme, Integrated Social Work Methods is the course where faith and spirituality are addressed. The course addresses the use of faith and spirituality while applying ethical principles, doing a holistic assessment – where one aspect is spiritual assessment, and also planning an intervention. The instructors also believed that using spirituality in carrying out an intervention helps clients. It gives clients the strength to stick to the plan and achieve success without losing hope. According to the gender studies course instructor (Social Work Educator, IDI-4), 'As you know, this is a sensitive issue here in Ethiopia. I always discuss the value of utilising faith and spirituality in social work. However, I do not discuss Orthodox, Muslim, or Protestant ideologies in the classroom. The concept of spirituality is part of individuals' self-identity as gender is in the Ethiopian context'. The interviews indicated that discussing faith and spirituality in the classroom paved the way for addressing and clarifying some assumptions about faith and spirituality. In some cases, faith and spirituality are used as a disguise for the already existing gender disparities. For instance, the majority typically accepts the prevalent practice of treating women and girls as less important than men and boys, claiming that this is reflected in many religious rituals. People claim, for instance, that the absence of female priests in the Orthodox Church signifies the inferior status of women to men. The fact that all religious authorities in Ethiopia are men lends credence to the earlier claim. This can be easily construed to mean that men are wiser than women and should thus be heard.

Social work educators who participated in this study believe that it is an excellent opportunity for social work educators that the curriculum incorporates faith and spirituality. However, since this topic is sensitive, the course instructors should be careful not to offend specific faith followers in their discussions. Often it is difficult to comment on a religion outside of their own or a religious person in the classroom. Everybody wants their religion to be appreciated. Therefore, in service provision in social work education, the course instructors should be mindful of students' faith/spirituality.

In specific courses like counselling, students are taught about the value of using religious leaders in social work and how faith and spirituality can be used in counselling. According to the counselling course instructor:

> I always enjoy it when I discuss the role of religious leaders in the classroom. Religious leaders' power in individual, family, and community life is significant in Ethiopia. Often they are the ones who engage in traditional mediation and guidance. Many students, including shy ones, often participate in sharing what they know. It is clear that since students are part of the community and the reflection of the wider society, it is visible to see that faith and spirituality are something that they can easily relate to.

Among the survey participants, 83.3% indicated that what they had learned about faith and spirituality in their social work programme helped them while working with clients. Among females, 85.7%, and, among males 82.4%, indicated that what they learned helped them work with clients sensitively. The interviews also revealed that since almost all clients belong to a certain religion, it was always a good start to creating rapport between the social worker and the client. It also indicated to the clients that what social workers are doing is not entirely different from what they know. One interviewee stated the following.

> While working with clients, religion is also a good starting point, especially if we are of the same religion, to create a smooth relationship. Many clients usually assume that the so-called professionals do not have a religion or might suggest something that is not acceptable to their religion. However, the moment the client understands that religion is part of the assessment and the intervention, they feel comfortable and more willing to work with the social worker.
>
> *Senior Social Worker, IDI-1*

However, only 45.9% of the respondents indicated that what they have learned about faith and spirituality can be applied to the organisations where they work. Among females, 35.5%, and, among males, 50.0%, of what they have learnt can be applied in their respective organisations. Unlike the BSW graduates, 33.3%, and MSW, 73.3%, indicated that what they have learned can be applied in their respective organisations. The applicability often relies on the rules and regulations of specific organisations. For example, in most cases, faith-based organisations allow social workers to use faith and spirituality in their intervention.

Nevertheless, since most government, non-government, and UN/IOs are non-faith-based organisations, social workers might find it challenging to apply it. But during the interviews, it was indicated that even if their organisation does not encourage the use of faith and spirituality, social workers apply faith and spirituality in their assessment and intervention. The interviewees also indicated that since faith and religion are part of the fabric of the community, it is difficult altogether to leave out faith and spirituality in social work practice. One interviewee pointed out the following.

> People belong to one or the other religious group. Whether you are working for a faith-based or non-faith-based organisation, it is difficult not to talk about faith and spirituality. Moreover, even if the social worker refrains from talking about it, clients usually talk about their faith and religion and how it helped them cope with life. So I do not think it is possible not to talk about faith with clients in the Ethiopian context because faith/spirituality is the pillar of our society.
>
> *Social Work Service Provider, IDI-1*

Considering the challenges of using faith and spirituality in social work, 60.5% of the respondents indicated that social work service provision should not consider religion for service admission. From the interview, it was indicated that social work graduates suggest that social work service provision be open to any religions not because they feel that faith and religion do not contribute to the overall service provision but to be able to accommodate all individuals with a different faith. An interviewee indicated her concern as follows.

> There are faith-based organisations who are providing social work services. These organisations use the person's faith or religion as a criterion of admission to benefit from the service. It is my opinion that it is not fair. There are even some clients who are forced to change their religion in order to benefit from the service. Hence, I suggest the service be open to people from different religions.
>
> *Social Work Service Provider, IDI-10*

Faith and spirituality are an integral part of the life of Ethiopians; it is challenging not to talk about it. Faith and spirituality are also among the four domains of assessment and, hence, cannot be ignored. Whether organisations or social workers address faith and spirituality in their social work practice directly or indirectly, it was clear that clients talk about their faith. But it was also clear from the responses that social workers do not always agree with the selection criteria of some faith-based organisations since they use religion to favour clients from one religion and discriminate against others. Regardless of the social worker's religion or the type of organisation the social worker works in, it is clear that spirituality and faith play an essential role in the social worker's or client's personal life or professional relationship.

Faith and Spirituality in Social Work Practice

Among the respondents, 45.9% indicated they use faith/spirituality in all aspects of their life, including with their clients. Social workers are expected to be mindful of their clients' faith/spirituality while providing service. On the contrary, in some cases, social workers dictate their faith/spirituality to clients to show the values and benefits of their religion. Often they do this when their faith/spirituality is similar to their clients to create a relationship.

Among the participants, 54.2% of the respondents use their faith and spirituality in their personal life but not in the work environment with clients. This group of respondents did not bring their faith/spirituality to the discussion. Nevertheless, this does not mean they will not be mindful of the faith/spirituality of their clients. Moreover, 83.3% of the respondents had no difficulty working with clients with faith/spirituality that is different from their own. Among the respondents, 70.8% indicated that they often do not care about their clients' faith/spirituality. Instead, they focus on the client's problems or strengths. If the clients indicate their faith/spirituality is their strength, they have indicated they will consider that and work accordingly.

As the respondents mentioned, in most cases, clients are comfortable when their social worker shares a similar faith/spirituality. Especially when the faith/spirituality of the clients and the social workers are competing, it makes the service provision challenging. The social worker's clients believe that they would presume they did not share their beliefs if they were from a different religion. As a result, when social workers sense this kind of unease on the part of their clients, they typically recommend them to a social worker who practices a similar religion. To guarantee the client's comfort, this is done. For the intervention to be effective and long lasting, the clients must feel at ease talking to the social worker.

Among the respondents, 58.3% indicated that they use faith/spirituality when communicating about social work ethics with their clients. They believe associating ethical issues with the clients' faith/spirituality is helpful for the clients to understand them better. As one social work educator indicated, 'The ethical principles of social work: respect, trust, acknowledging a person's intrinsic value and dignity, and others, are present in many of Ethiopia's religions and spiritual traditions. It might be ideal to apply that when working with clients' (Social Work Educator, IDI-9).

Rapport building is one of the essential elements in social work service provision. During this stage, 39.6% of the respondents indicated using faith/spirituality. At this stage, clients could be shy in opening up. It would be wise to start with something they are familiar with and comfortable with. Letting them speak about their faith/spirituality could be good if they are comfortable. However, faith/spirituality is personal for others, and they might not be interested in such a discussion. As per the respondents, it is preferable to follow the lead of the clients when it comes to faith/spirituality.

During the assessment stage of service provision, 40.0% of the respondents indicated that they also assessed the respondents' faith/spirituality. Social workers evaluate the client's spiritual life regardless of the organisational protocol. Since the assessment stage is the cornerstone, social work service providers conduct a comprehensive evaluation that considers religion and spirituality. The assessment aims to comprehend the client holistically and pinpoint his or her strengths, challenges, and advantages rather than favour or discriminate against the client. Additionally, this aids in the intervention's design, implementation guidance, and maintenance of the client's progress.

It was also clear from the interview with social work practitioners that using faith and spirituality in the intervention process is very fruitful. It motivates clients to continue with the intervention, even if there are ups and downs. Social work practitioners also indicated that integrating faith in the intervention helps clients sustain the change after the termination of the service. It helps clients to try persistently without losing hope. Interviewees also indicated that it is their faith that keeps service users strong and motivated to continue to maintain the progress they have made. In Ethiopia, there is no proper follow-up and monitoring of clients' progress once the service is terminated due both to the lack of social workers and to limited resources available. Hence, using their faith to progress in life and cope with the challenges they may face is of paramount importance.

Discussion and Conclusion

Faith and spirituality are part of the social work curriculum in core modules at the BSW and MSW levels. This was found to be an essential step in helping social workers to do a biopsychosocial-spiritual assessment. It is also in line with Ethiopia's reality that faith and spirituality shall be integral to social work service provision and play crucial roles in people's lives. For most social workers who participated in this study, what they learned in the classroom helped them in social work practice. It can be considered that what is in the curriculum regarding faith and spirituality contributes to service provision. However, regarding applicability, most MSW graduates (73%), but only 33% of the BSW graduates believed that what they have learned can be applied. It could indicate that more effort is needed in BSW education than in MSW.

Some organisations consider themselves secular, while others try to accommodate faith and spirituality. Due to their challenges, most social workers believe that social work service provision should be open to people from any religion. Accommodating faith and spirituality does not come overnight (Sheridan and Hemert, 1999); instead, it takes time. Accommodating faith and spirituality in social work is a process (Adedoyin et al., 2021). Ethiopia's social work education and service provision seem to be in the right direction. Since most (99%) Ethiopians belong to a religion and consider faith and spirituality as part of their identity, as indicated by Knitter (2010), accommodating faith and spirituality in social work in Ethiopia can help a lot.

Social workers, like others, reflect the society they live in. One such reflection is demonstrated in the finding that 58.3% of the respondents believed that their faith/spirituality was the best. Accepting other religions and forms of spirituality is a constant struggle for this group of social workers. They are mindful that this is the wrong attitude and work to change it daily. However, 91.6% do not try convincing others to follow their religion, differentiating them from others. The vast majority of social workers who participated in this study accepted clients with a faith/spirituality different from their own without any negative attitude. Moreover, they had no difficulty working with clients, even if they considered their faith and spirituality acceptable for them.

Even if integrating faith and spirituality in social work education and service provision is appreciated, it does not mean it should be a criterion for admission. Social work service provision based on the faith and spirituality of the person was denounced by the majority of social workers who participated in this study because of the fear of discrimination. They think accepting or refusing a service user based on their religion is discriminatory and unconstitutional. It is not favouritism or discrimination to incorporate faith and spirituality into social work education and to employ it in service delivery. It means appreciating and using the service user's faith and spirituality to help in the care, planning, and implementation of the plan as well as for the sustainability of the change made by the service user. However, most social workers see the value of faith and spirituality in their service provision, even if some were not allowed by their respective organisations. But it should also be considered that most organisations do not allow social workers to use religion and faith to interfere in protecting service users from discrimination based on their religion, faith, or spirituality.

Participants indicated that faith and spirituality are essential in communicating ethical standards with clients. For instance, all religions uphold the essential ethical precepts of social work, such as believing in the inherent value and dignity of every human being, treating every individual with kindness and respect, and refraining from discriminating against people based on their differences. Social workers use this to explain the moral standards they uphold when interacting with clients. A reasonable number of social workers use faith and spirituality in social work processes, especially in the engagement and assessment stage. Since these stages constitute foundations for other social work processes, what they have at these stages is often utilised later. It was also found to be important to sustain improvement in the lives of service users. In a country like Ethiopia, where there are few social workers, following up on clients' progress is difficult after the service is terminated. Hence, the clients' faith is an important aspect that motivates them to sustain the change that they have made during the social work intervention. Integrating faith and spirituality in social work service provision and in ethical consideration can be considered essential elements in the process of faith and spirituality with social work service provision.

Recommendations

1. Social work education curricula should rethink the form of education concerning integrating faith and spirituality in social work practice, incorporating creative ways to include faith and spirituality in the social work process without discrimination or judgement. Social work students should be equipped with the skills to differentiate between individual religion and faith and social workers' professional self, and they should be given space to reflect on existing biases and ways of handling conflicting views and attitudes.
2. Social workers must educate service providers and organisations that profess to be 'secular' about the benefits and contributions of faith and spirituality to individuals, families, and communities.
3. Research with social workers needs to be carried out in areas of faith and spirituality and the role of religion, faith, and spirituality in the daily lives of people in the Ethiopian context. This will help enrich the social work curriculum and develop evidence-based social work practice.

Further Reading

Agbawodikeizu, P.U., Levy, S., Ekoh, P.C., Chukwu, N.E., and Okoye, U.O. (2022). Religion and spirituality as a core module in social work education in Nigeria: Perspectives of social work educators. *Journal of Religion and Spirituality in Social Work: Social Thought*, *41*(4), 333–350. https://doi.org/10.1080/15426432.2022.2089316.

Adedoyin, C., Moore, S., Copeland, R., and Folaranmi, O. (2021). Integration of faith and spirituality in social work education: A systematic review of evidence in the last 35 years (1985–2020). *Social Work and Christianity*, *48*(3), 288–307. https://doi.org/10.34043/swc.v48i3.233.

Ebimgbo, S., Agwu, P., and Okoye, U. (2017). Spirituality and religion in social work. In *Social Work in Nigeria: Book of Readings* (pp. 93–103). Nsukka: University of Nigeria Press Ltd.

Hamren, K., Chungkham, H.S., and Hyde, M. (2015). Religion, spirituality, social support and quality of life: Measurement and predictors amongst older Ethiopians living in Addis Ababa. *Aging and Mental Health*, *19*(7), 610–621.

Ozmete, E., Gok, F.A., and Pak, M. (2022). Spirituality in social work practice with young college students: A validation study. *Research on Social Work Practice*. https://doi.org/10.1177/10497315221118851

References

Adedoyin, C., Moore, S., Copeland, R., and Folaranmi, O. (2021). Integration of faith and spirituality in social work education: A systematic review of evidence in the last 35 years (1985–2020). *Social Work and Christianity*, *48*(3), 288–307. https://doi.org/10.34043/swc.v48i3.233

Agbawodikeizu, P.U., Levy, S., Ekoh, P.C., Chukwu, N.E., and Okoye, U.O. (2022). Religion and spirituality as a core module in social work education in Nigeria: Perspectives of social work educators. *Journal of Religion and Spirituality in Social Work: Social Thought*, *41*(4), 333–350. https://doi.org/10.1080/15426432.2022.2089316.

Baynesagn, A.H. (2020). Being visible in the policy process: The experience of the School of Social Work at Addis Ababa University. *The British Journal of Social Work*, *50*(8), 2389–2404. https://doi.org/10.1093/bjsw/bcaa188.

Baynesagn, A.H., Abye, T., Mulugeta, E., and Berhanu, Z. (2021). Strengthened by Challenges: The path of the social work education in Ethiopia. *Social Work Education*, *40*(1), 95–110. https://doi.org/10.1080/02615479.2020.1858044.

Borruso, P. (2013). Politics and religion in Haile Selassie's Ethiopia: Apogee and crisis of a confessional African State (1916–1974). *International Journal of Ethiopian Studies*, *7*(1 and 2), 101–124. https://www.jstor.org/stable/26586233.

Carey, J. (2018). Spiritual, but not religious? On the nature of spirituality and its relation to religion. *International Journal for Philosophy of Religion*, *83*(3), 261–269. 10.1007/s11153-017-9648-8.

Darrell, L., and Rich, T. (2017). Faith and field: The ethical inclusion of spirituality within the pedagogy of social work. *Field Educator*, *7*(1), 17–157.

Debele, S.B. (2017). Religion and politics in post-1991 Ethiopia: Making sense of Bryan S. Turner's 'Managing Religions. *Religion, State and Society*, *46*(1), 26–42. https://doi.org/10.1080/09637494.2017.1348016.

Ebimgbo, S., Agwu, P., and Okoye, U. (2017). Spirituality and religion in social work. In *Social Work in Nigeria: Book of Readings* (pp. 93–103). Nsukka: University of Nigeria Press Ltd.

Gale, L., Therivel, J., and Richman, S. (2022). *Biopsychosocial-Spiritual Assessment: An Overview*. Glendale, CA: Cinahi Information Systems, 1509 Wilson Terrace, Glendale, CA 91206.

Gilligan, P., and Furness, S. (2006). The role of religion and spirituality in social work practice: Views and experiences of social workers and students. *British Journal of Social Work*, *36*(4), 617–637.

Hamren, K., Chungkham, H.S., and Hyde, M. (2015). Religion, spirituality, social support and quality of life: Measurement and predictors amongst older Ethiopians living in Addis Ababa. *Aging and Mental Health*, *19*(7), 610–621.

Hussen, S.A., Tsegaye, M., Argaw, M.G., Andes, K., Gilliard, D., and del Rio, C. (2014). Spirituality, social capital, and service: Factors promoting resilience among Expert Patients living with HIV in Ethiopia. *Global Public Health*, *9*(3), 286–298. https://doi.org/10.1080/17441692.2014.880501.

Karabo, T. (2013). Religion and social cohesion in Ethiopia. *International Journal of Peace and Development Studies*, *4*(3), 43–52. https://doi.org/10.5897/IJPDS 2013.0164.

Knitter, P.F. (2010). Social work and religious diversity: Problems and possibilities. *Journal of Religion and Spirituality in Social Work: Social Thought*, *29*(3), 256–270. https://doi.org/10.1080/15426432.2010.495632.

Lehmann, D. (2013). Religion as heritage, religion as belief: Shifting frontiers of secularism in Europe, the USA and Brazil. *International Sociology*, *28*(6), 645–662. https://doi.org/10.1177/0268580913503894.

Marcus, C. (2008). Sacred time, civic calendar: Religious plurality and the centrality of religion in Ethiopian society. *International Journal of Ethiopian Studies*, *3*(2), 143–175. http://www.jstor.org/stable/27828896.

Northcut, T.B., Getachew, A., Kebede, E., Zenbe, K., and Abebe, A. (2021). Clinical social work in Ethiopia: A field study in Gondar. *Clinical Social Work Journal*, *49*(3), 312–324. https://doi.org/10.1007/s10615-020-00757-w.

Ozmete, E., Gok, F.A., and Pak, M. (2022). Spirituality in social work practice with young college students: A validation study. *Research on Social Work Practice*. https://doi.org/10.1177/10497315221118851

Sheridan, M.J., and Hemert, K.A. (1999). The role of religion and spirituality in social work education and practice: A survey of student views and experiences. *Journal of Social Work Education*, *35*(1), 125–141. http://www.jstor.org/stable/23043449.

Tesfaye, A. (1987). Social welfare programmes and social work education in Ethiopia. Addis Ababa University, Ethiopia. *The Indian Journal of Social Work*, *47*(4), 363–377.

7
FAITH AND SPIRITUALITY IN SOCIAL WORK EDUCATION AND PRACTICE IN NIGERIA

Oghenechoja Dennis Veta

Abstract: English

This chapter examines the curriculum contents of faith and spirituality in the departments of social work at the University of Nigeria, Nsukka, and University of Ilorin, Nigeria, among others. The introductory section discusses Nigerian people and religious beliefs and practices. The paper also covers the meaning of faith and spirituality and the functions of social work in relation to the roles of faith and spirituality in social work education and practice in Nigeria. The importance of the integration of faith and spirituality into social work education and practice in Nigeria, and the challenges facing the integration of faith and spirituality into social work education and practice, are discussed. This chapter also makes some recommendations to mitigate the challenges facing the integration of faith and spirituality into social work education and practice. They include the need for student social workers to adequately acquire the needed social work knowledge, skills, and values in the application of faith and spirituality, if required, in the intervention process. Courses on faith and spirituality in social work curricula should be made compulsory by social work departments for all student social workers across all Nigerian tertiary institutions.

Abstract: Urhobo

Ebere robe nana fuerobo risegbuyota ve egbarerhi vwe evu riwhovwin ride re ebe yono ri hevu re Nsukka, Ilorin, ve efa vwe evu re Nijiria. Ebere redjephia na, ota vwo kpahe iruaru riwho re Nijiria vobo rayen segbuyota viruorayen eje. Obere robe nana je ta kpahen otor risegbuyota, iruo egbarerhi vobo rayen hephan vwo ma re arhuere vwe evu re Nijiria. Ebere ro be nana ta kpahe oboro fori ne avwe isebguyota ve egbarerhi vwo ba yono, je vwo whian vwe vu re Nijiria, kugbe obeben ro she kpahen evwobaruo royen. Ebere ro be nana je ta ne evwo phi kparobor vwe evu re bebe na, emo ri sukuru ri yone arhuere na we vwe erierien, ena, ve uruemuesiri vwo kpahe obo ra vwe isegbuyota ve egbaerhi vwo wian, sie obo reguonukecha ya no vwe evu re idjere rukecha rayen. Ofori ne akon ruyono rarhuare vwiwhovwin ride re Nijiria eje, vwe uyono risegbuyota ve egbarerhi ke emo risukuru ri yone arhuere eje.

Introduction

Nigeria is an African nation with a population of 218,541,212 million (World Population Review, 2022), it is a multiethnic and multilingual country that comprises 371 ethnic nationalities. Hausa, Yoruba, and Ibo are classified as major ethnic groups with reference to their dense populations, while the others, such as Urhobo, Isoko, Izon, Ibibio, Andoni, Ikwerre, Anioma, Epie, Idoma, Itsekiri, Bini, Esan, Idoma, Gwari amongst others, are seen as minority ethnic groups because of their sparse populations. However, no ethnic group is superior to the other; this is because each ethnic group has its cherished cultural heritage, which, in extension, includes religious beliefs and practices. Cultural heritage is a unique symbol of identity and each has equal ranking irrespective of demographic measures. In other words, Nigeria is multilingual, multicultural, and complex in cultural diversity, and each of the ethnic groups and its culture is to be reckoned with at the micro level of social work education and practice.

There are three major religions in Nigeria, namely Christianity, Islam, and African Traditional Religion (ATR), and Nigerians are deeply embedded in one of these religions. In this vein, Owumi et al. (2013) argue that religious beliefs and practices dominate the social lives of most people in Nigeria. They further reveal that 50.4% of Nigerians practice Islam; 48.2% practice Christianity; and the remaining 1.4% are Traditional African Worshippers (Owumi et al., 2013). African Traditional Religion was widely practiced in pre-colonial Nigerian society before the advent of Christianity and Islam in the colonial era (Ngbeaa and Achunike, 2014). In other words, from time immemorial, Nigerians have been deeply involved in religious beliefs and practices, which tend to shape their lifestyles to the extent that virtually all aspects of their lives, be it physical, social, economic, political, or cultural, are committed, through faith and spirituality, to God or Gods or the Cosmos for succour, and directives.

In Nigeria, religious beliefs, identities, and practices are very public social markers and animate everyday behaviours and interactions (Pinter et al., 2016). Moreover, the beliefs and religious practices of Nigerians widely influence the choices or decisions made on whether to seek and/or accept any form of help or services be it social, financial, medical, or otherwise. Religion, therefore, is often an important part of the cultural fabric of communities and, as such, can influence decision-making, ideologies, and moral and ethical behaviours (Pinter et al., 2016), particularly in Nigeria where religion is part of the warp and weft that have shaped the sociopolitical structure (Vaughan, 2016). This could be one of the reasons for which Pinter et al. (2016) opined that in interactions ranging from social events to workplace meetings, the demonstration of a belief in a divine being that determines fortunes and outcomes as well as apportioning rewards and punishments is highly visible across Nigeria. Thus, due to Nigerian peoples' religiosity, beliefs, and practices, religious leaders to a great extent dictate and or influence decisions, actions, and inactions in almost every aspect of adherents' life situations.

The Meaning of Faith and Spirituality

There are no universally accepted definitions of faith and spirituality. Faith emanates from spirituality in the sense that once one's sense of existence and connectedness to the supernatural is established, then comes faith, which is a tenacious adherence to a particular belief(s), and trust in such supernatural or supreme power(s) to various degrees amongst individuals, groups, or communities. Faith refers to a belief and trust in a higher power and it is an integral aspect of spirituality and religion (Williams and Smolak, 2007). For Barsky et al. (2015), faith is a transaction, communication, and actionable belief in the realm of the spirit or higher power that encompasses a person's belief in the spiritual and religious realms or entities (Christson et al.,

2021). Faith is personal and it has different meanings for different individuals (Seitz, 2014). Thus, faith can influence individuals to a varied level of decision-making in relation to their lifestyles as to whether to access and/or utilise required social services from service providers or a helping profession.

On the other hand, spirituality is centred on steady connections between a person, others, and the supernatural. Spirituality is a relationship between humans in the temporal sphere and in realities that exist in perpetual continuity for the service, or good, of mankind in the terrestrial (Barker, 2013; Barsky et al., 2015). Similarly, spirituality refers to the human desire for transcendence, introspection, interconnectedness, and the quest for meaning in life (King and Boyatzis, 2015). In other words, spirituality is a conscious search by the individual for a satisfactory close connection between the spiritual realm and the physical environment for the achievement of one's life aspirations. Thus, purpose, morality, transcendence, wellbeing, and profound relationships with themselves, and others, lead to the ultimate reality in life (Canda and Furman, 2010).

Spirituality is a key dimension of self-understanding and is part of relationships, of social engagement, of an understanding of meaning and purpose in life, and of an overall sense of happiness and joy (Kavar, 2015). It is a more general, unstructured, personalised, and naturally occurring phenomenon, where a person seeks closeness and/or connectedness between himself or herself and a higher power or purpose (Joseph et al., 2017). Therefore, faith and spirituality could have a great influence on how people live, experience, and decide on causes and how to attain their life aspirations, what they need, and how to seek help from the helping profession – social work.

From the foregoing, it could be argued that faith and spirituality enable individuals to endure suffering and assist them to find meaning and purpose in challenging times, which can ultimately turn into a transcendent experience and bring personal growth (Asgeirsdottir et al., 2013; Lalani et al., 2019). In Nigeria, members of each of the religious groups sometimes make efforts to convert others to their belief system in an attempt to dominate the others mainly for socioeconomic and political gains. This practice undermines the fact that the experience of faith and spirituality cuts across all belief systems, and practices in reflecting on what one understands by meaningful and fulfilled reason for being human. Therefore, social work education and practice do not need an attempt to proselytise in the process of building a helping relationship. In line with this, Harris and Yancey (2017) argued that human beings have been endowed with the faculty of choice, which must not be denied them except by due process of law, or where their actions or threatened actions are demonstrably gravely harmful to others or are self-destructive, or where they voluntarily surrender this right for a prescribed purpose. Ethically, proselytising in the process of building a helping relationship is an oppressive practice that should not be countenanced in social work education and practice in Nigeria. The Social Work Code of Ethics requires social work professionals and social work students to operate within the values of the profession by working with clients of any denomination or faith and spiritual background while taking cognisance of personal beliefs and values (National Association of Social Workers [NASW], 2008).

Furthermore, the principles of acceptance, self-determination, and community determination have to be prioritised in the helping relationship or process, reflecting on the faith and spirituality of oneself (service provider) and the client's faith and spirituality. Community determination is the acceptance of a community's right to benefit from development projects irrespective of its religious belief and practices, accepting it as it is, and beginning intervention plans from its prioritised needs, in the case of social work practice with communities. This competency is very much required for a fulfilled social work education and practices in Nigeria due to its multiculture, multiple faiths, and spiritual diversity.

Faith and Spirituality in the Curriculum Contents of the Departments of Social Work in Nigeria

The integration and pedagogy of religion and spirituality have been parts of social work programmes in some Nigerian universities, such as the University of Nigeria, Nsukka (Department of Social Work, 2017). Similarly, spirituality and social work have been integrated into the social work curriculum of the University of Ilorin, Nigeria, as compulsory courses (Department of Social Work, 2019) as well as in the curriculum of Ebonyi State University, Abakaliki (Department of Psychology and Sociological Studies, 2020).

However, most of the Nigerian universities running social work programmes have yet to make courses on religion and spirituality compulsory or non-compulsory in their curricula. For instance, the Department of Social Work, University of Benin, Benin City, has yet to integrate religion and spirituality into its curriculum (Department of Social Work, 2018). Similarly, the University of Calabar, Calabar, has not included religion and spirituality in its social work curriculum; rather, the student social workers are made to take courses on religion from the Department of Religion (Department of Social Work, 2020). This does not mean that religion as a discipline has nothing meaningful to contribute to the social work profession. The courses may not be taught to reflect social work pedagogy and practice to develop the needed competence in the student social workers to respond adequately to clients who express faith and spirituality in the intervention process to attain holistic outcomes. This is because the educators in the Department of Religion may not have acquired the skills and knowledge needed in the social work profession as it relates to faith and spirituality.

The Importance of Faith and Spirituality in Social Work Education and Practice in Nigeria

Social work plays vital roles in areas of bereavement, end-of-life care, substance use, migration, refugees, health, and reintegration. These areas of social work practice, as Crisp and Dinham (2019) argue, are commonly associated with religion and spirituality, making the role of faith and spirituality a very important one in social work education and practice in Nigeria. Moreover, most Nigerians adhere strongly to faith and spirituality to avert or struggle through difficulties in life. Ebimgbo et al. (2017) argue that when Nigerians are confronted with trauma, illness, loss or bereavement, substance abuse, violence in the home or workplace, unemployment, and other social problems they seek solace in spiritual and religious activities as support systems. Thus, social work professionals dealing with clients affected by these life circumstances need to integrate faith and spirituality into their assessment and intervention (Ebimgbo et al., 2017).

Faith and spirituality influence to a great extent the person in the environment, and the person and environment. Hence, they have essential roles to play in understanding what life ought to be, in how decisions are made and implemented, and in utilising outcomes of a helping profession, particularly social work. In the view of Tsebee and Toyin (2017), religion is a good instrument for the development of society – it can bind people together, feed their spiritual needs, destroy superstitions, and make the mind receptive to ideas. Religion is a very emotive issue that touches on all aspects of our life – good versus evil, struggle to admit hardship, reconciliation, and forgiveness, success against all odds in communities, and families, hence the need to give it a new pivotal place and packaging (Tsebee and Toyin, 2017), particularly in social work education and practice in Nigeria. Therefore, faith and spirituality play vital roles in promoting and sustaining peaceful and harmonious relationships among peoples and communities and engendering a spirit of hard work and honesty for the development of human society (Utensati, 2020).

In Nigeria, the affiliation of individuals to different religions also makes possible exposure to religious beliefs or practices that could shape their health decision-making, health behaviour, and health-seeking behaviour (Padela and Curlin, 2013; Rumun, 2014), and their efforts to seek help, acceptance, and utilisation of interventions provided by such helping professions, including social work. Considering the role and influence faith and spirituality have on the lifestyle of Nigerians, Odion (2022) opines that faith and spirituality are two vital components that help to bridge the gap between sociopolitical realities and economic life, and, as such, due to inequalities in economic distribution, most Nigerians have learnt to rely on their faith for their daily sustenance. Social work educators and practitioners in Nigeria do not live in a vacuum, they are humans who are also adherents of one religion or another in a social environment, and, as such, they find faith and spirituality as veritable tools to overcome the problems of life and occupational stressors. In this perspective, faith and spirituality are coping mechanisms against occupational stress and burnout in the helping professions (Chirico and Magnavita, 2019).

Faith and spirituality have a way of succoring the pains and suffering of the sick and the needy as they contribute to the rapid healing process, and they can be very protective against emotional, physical, and mental ailments. In Nigeria, religion is a source of comfort in a time of sickness, a coping mechanism in times of need, and a means of social support (Fadeyi and Oduwole, 2016; Owumi et al., 2013; Rumun, 2014). In most cases, faith and spirituality are exercised by praying, meditating, reading spiritual texts, and placing fervent hope in God. Thus, in Nigerian contexts, where faith and spirituality are held tenaciously, when these exercises, prayers, meditations, reading of spiritual texts, and fervent hope placed in God or gods are recommended or applied by social workers to the intervention process of clients who express faith and spirituality, their coping capacity can be heightened or strengthened. In addition, religious organisations also play a vital role in Nigeria by providing social services, counseling, financial support, and the means for social mobility to adherents (Hoffmann and Patel, 2021). Considering the level of religious beliefs, practices, and their importance, as brought to the fore, faith and spirituality are essential for a successful education and holistic interventions in social work practice in Nigeria. Therefore, it it is essential to integrate faith and spirituality into social work education and practice in Nigeria.

There are two major rationales for the integration of faith and spirituality into social work education and practice. The first rationale is that faith and spiritual beliefs and practices are part of multicultural diversity. Second, human existence is beyond the biopsychosocial framework that can be used to understand human behaviour (Hutchinson, 2013). The integration of faith and spirituality into social work education and practice can be seen as the way students and practitioners know and understand their own understanding of the world to better understand clients (Olson, 2014). That is, student social workers and practitioners are expected to have a knowledge of the 'self' in this case regarding their own religious beliefs and practices before they can thoroughly interpret and understand the influence of religious beliefs and practices on client(s).

The inclusion of faith and spirituality into social work education and practice is a valuable resource for Nigeria. In this same vein, Mabvurira and Nyanguru (2013) argue that spiritual sensitivity fosters an ethic of mutual benefit and social justice rather than selfish gain, as the science of social work alone may not be sufficient to address the multiple dimensions of the individual mind, body, and soul conceptions (Mabvurira and Nyanguru, 2013). Therefore, social work knowledge of human functioning has strong spiritual underpinnings, making it of utmost importance in our diverse world to find common ground in all human interactions (Hutchinson, 2013). In line with the foregoing and the increasing awareness of the integration of faith and spirituality in the social work literature, there is a need to integrate faith and spirituality into social work education and practice in Nigeria.

In sum, the importance of integrating faith and spirituality into social work education and practice in Nigeria includes enhancing an effective holistic helping process and attaining the existing positive correlation among spirituality, health, and wellbeing (Koenig, 1997) of service users generally, particularly Nigerians.

Challenges Facing Integration of Faith and Spirituality into Social Work Education and Practice in Nigeria

The social work profession is primarily faced with the challenge of maintaining a professional status in African nations, particularly in Nigeria. Similarly, the integration of faith and spirituality into social work education and practice in Nigeria is faced with several challenges. One of these challenges is the possibility that some educators, student social workers, and practitioners will impose their beliefs on the people with whom they are working, both beneficiaries and colleagues (Asher, 2001). In other words, in Nigeria where three religions exist competitively, most importantly between Islam and Christianity, and where both sometimes find it difficult to accommodate African Traditional Religion (ATR), service providers may be tempted to proselytise their faith and spirituality or convictions on their colleagues and service users. Thereby making the interventions available to people who are willing to practice a particular faith and spirituality instead of focusing generally on the target population. The imposition of one's faith and spirituality on clients, however well intended, violates a client's right to self-determination (Reamer, 2013). Converting service users and colleagues to the faith and spirituality of service providers violates social work ethics and anti-oppressive practice. In other words, ethical codes of the social work profession propagate social justice based on the principle of acceptance of the people they serve irrespective of their socioeconomic and political status. This competency has not been achieved in Nigeria.

Inquiring into the faith and spirituality of a client is expected to be carried out in a competent manner with the capability to exhibit spiritual sensitivity. This could be done by experience and/or training in this area. Presently, faith and spirituality are yet to be made compulsory courses in most social work curricula across Nigerian universities offering social work education, thereby exposing few students to theories and applications of faith and spirituality during fieldwork practice and after graduation.

The integration of faith and spirituality into social work education and practice is not widely seen as a professional discourse. Faith and spirituality are seen as lacking a relationship with professional education and practice, especially in the helping profession, and, as such, they are not regarded as necessary in social development agencies. This is because the phenomenon of faith and spirituality lacks professional understanding regarding practice and research implications, and helping professionals rarely discuss the concepts with their clients/patients (Barreto de Oliveira and Menezes de Oliva, 2018; Tate, 2011).

The ambivalence of faith and spirituality is another challenge facing the integration of faith and spirituality into social work education and practice in Nigeria. Faith and spirituality can be agents of peace and of destabilisation, inclusion, and exclusion (Ezeanya et al., 2022). Faith adherents can be resistant to totalitarianism and, on the other hand, they can be totalitarians, they can also be inclusive in terms of tolerance and become exclusive in terms of becoming hostile to non-adherents or followers. They can be prone to use political interests to abuse political processes and, on the other hand, they can checkmate abuse of political processes.

In spite of the challenges discussed in this chapter, the integration of faith and spirituality into social work education and practice in Nigeria is vital. However, there is limited attention to curriculum content development and inadequate pedagogical models on how to incorporate spirituality into the social work curriculum (Seitz, 2014). This necessitates a quest for social work curriculum development or review to reflect Nigerian contexts on faith and spirituality and the need for the development of evidence-based models to work out adequate assessments and interventions, taking cognisance of clients' expressed faith and spirituality in all engagements.

Ways of Integrating Faith and Spirituality into Social Work Education and Practice in Nigeria

The responsibility for integrating faith and spirituality into social work falls on schools to prepare new professionals for ethical work with faith and spiritual diversity in practice (Oxhandler and Pargament, 2014). Some social work educators suggest that social work students should learn about clients' experiences of religion, but they should not be studying religion per se (Williams and Smolak, 2007). This suggestion calls for a total commitment and conscious attitude towards the integration of faith and spirituality into social work education and practice in Nigeria. In line with this observation, this chapter suggests that the following ideas could be utilised for the effective integration of faith and spirituality into social work education and practice in Nigeria and Africa:

1. Making religion and spirituality in social work education compulsory courses in all Nigerian tertiary institutions that are running social work programmes.
2. Accept the tenets, beliefs, and practices of clients and be tolerant of clients who are adherents of other religions, that is, remain focused on the general wellbeing of the clients irrespective of their faith and spirituality.
3. Counsel the clients to help themselves out of destructive religious beliefs and practices. This is to ensure that religious beliefs and practices do not stand as barriers to the accessibility of social services while ensuring that the service providers do not pose barriers to service users by the tenets of their faith and spirituality.
4. Collaboration between the three religions in Nigeria. Religious leaders could be invited by social work departments to give talks on areas of their beliefs and practices that are not very clear to social work educators and student social workers in the course of the educational programmes.
5. Social workers should be willing to apply faith and spiritual exercises, such as prayers, reading of scriptures, and meditations, at the request of clients in the course of interventions, and refer them to their spiritual leaders, if need be, without allowing a particular faith and spirituality to prevail over another.
6. Social workers should always accept the client as he/she is and start the assessment, and intervention process irrespective of where his/her faith and spirituality are based.
7. Social workers should provide accepted conceptualisations of faith and spirituality and articulate areas of difference(s) and relationship(s) between these concepts in relation to Christianity, Islam, and African Traditional Religion (ATR).
8. Social workers should build a relationship that brings the presence of faith and spirituality to bear, develop and include methods of assessing the faith and spirituality of clients in social work curricula, and teach how to ask about the role of faith and spirituality in the client's life by using open-ended questions.
9. Social work researchers should foster research and publications on faith and spiritual matters and make the outcomes accessible to social work educators, students, and practitioners.

10. Social workers should develop skills and knowledge to respond competently and ethically to the diverse spiritual and religious perspectives of the client(s).

Conclusion

In conclusion, this chapter has examined faith and spirituality in social work education and practice in Nigeria. Nigeria is an African nation with a population of 218,541,212 million, and it is a multi-ethnic and multilingual country that comprises 371 ethnic nationalities. None of the ethnic groups is superior to the other, this is because each ethnic group has its own cherished cultural heritage. Cultural heritage is a unique symbol of identity, and each possesses equal ranking irrespective of demographic measures. The chapter reveals that faith and spirituality have no universally accepted definitions. Faith is personal and it has different meanings for different individuals. Thus, it can influence individuals to a varied level of decision-making in relation to their lifestyles as to whether to access and or utilise required social services from a helping profession. On the other hand, spirituality is a conscious search by the individual for a satisfactory, close connection between the spiritual realm and the physical environment for the achievement of one's life aspirations. Thus, it is a key dimension of self-understanding and is part of relationships, social engagement, an understanding of meaning and purpose in life, and in providing an overall sense of happiness and joy.

On faith and spirituality in the curriculum contents of the departments of social work in Nigeria, the chapter reveals that the pedagogy of religion and spirituality has been integrated into parts of social work programmes in some Nigerian universities, while others have yet to adopt religion and spirituality as compulsory or non-compulsory courses. This chapter also reveals the importance of faith and spirituality in social work education and practice in Nigeria due to the vital roles these play in areas of bereavement, end-of-life care, substance use, migration, refugees, health, and reintegration. Challenges facing the integration of faith and spirituality into social work education and practice in Nigeria include service providers being tempted to proselytise their faith and spirituality among their colleagues and service users, inadequate professional competency among students in the area of faith and spirituality that are not widely seen as a professional discourse, and ambivalence of faith and spirituality in the society.

Finally, ways of integrating faith and spirituality into social work education and practice in Nigeria are suggested. These include, among others, making religion and spirituality in social work education compulsory courses in all Nigerian tertiary institutions, accepting clients who are adherents of other religions, counseling the clients to help themselves out of destructive religious beliefs and practices, applying faith and spiritual exercises, providing accepted conceptualisations of faith and spirituality, developing and including methods of assessing the faith and spirituality of clients in social work curricula, teaching how to ask about the role of faith and spirituality in the client's life, fostering research and publications on faith and spiritual matters and making the outcomes assessable, and developing skills and knowledge to respond competently and ethically to the diverse spiritual and religious perspectives of the client(s).

Recommendations

1. There is a need for student social workers to adequately acquire the needed social work knowledge, skills, and values in the application of faith and spirituality from social work educators to enable them to respond positively to clients who express a devotion to faith and spirituality in the intervention process, irrespective of their religious affiliations and that of the service users.

2. There is a need for departments of social work to make courses on faith and spirituality in social work curricula compulsory for all student social workers across all Nigerian tertiary institutions.
3. Social work educators should explore integrating faith and spirituality into social work education and practice in Nigeria, and harmful religious beliefs and practices should be discouraged.

Further Reading

Canda, E. R., and Furman, L. D. (2010). *Spiritual Diversity in Social Work Practice: The Heart of Helping* (2nd ed.). New York, NY: Oxford University Press.
Okoye, U., Chukwu, N., and Agwu, P. (Eds.). (2017). *Social Work in Nigeria: Book of Readings*. Nsukka: University of Nigeria Press Ltd.
Vaughan, O. (2016). *Religion and the Making of Nigeria*. Durham: Duke University Press.

References

Asgeirsdottir, G. H., Sigurbjörnsson, E., Traustadotti, R., Sigurdardottir, V., Gunnarsdottir, S., and Kelly, E. (2013). To cherish each day as it comes: A qualitative study of spirituality among persons receiving palliative care. *Supportive Care in Cancer*, 21(5), 1445–1451.
Asher, M. (2001). Spirituality and religion in social work practice. *Social Work Today*, 1(7), 1–5. http//.www.gatherthepeople.org/.
Barker, S. L. (2013). A qualitative examination of the experiences of Christian students in social work educational programs. *Social Work and Christianity*, 40(1), 3–22.
Barreto de Oliveira, A. L., and Menezes de Oliva, T. M. (2018). The meaning of religion/religiosity for the elderly. *Revista Brasileira de Enfermagem*, 71, 770–776.
Barsky, A., Sherman, D., and Anderson, E. (2015). Social work educators' perceptions of faith- based BSW programs: Ethical inspiration and conflicts. *Journal of Social Work Values and Ethics*, 12(1), 77–87.
Canda, E. R., and Furman, L. D. (2010). *Spiritual Diversity in Social Work Practice: The Heart of Helping* (2nd ed.). New York, NY: Oxford University Press.
Chirico, F., and Magnavita, N. (2019). The spiritual dimension of health for more spirituality at workplace. *Indian Journal of Occupational and Environmental Medicine*, 23(2), 99. https://www.ijoem.com/text.asp?2019/23/2/99/267756.
Christson, A., Adedoyin, A., Sharon, E. M., Copeland, R., and Folaranmi, O. O. (2021). Integration of faith and spirituality in social work education: A systematic review of evidence in the last 35 years (1985–2020). *Social Work and Christianity*, 48(3), 288–307. https://doi.org/10.34043/swc.48i3.233.
Crisp, B. R., and Dinham, A. (2019). Are the profession's education standards promoting the religious literacy required for twenty-first-century social work practice? *British Journal of Social Work*, 49(6), 1544–1562. https://doi.org/10.1093/bjsw/bcz050.
Department of Psychology and Sociological Studies (2020). *Handbook for BSc Social Work Programme*. Abakaliki: Enboyi State University Printing Press.
Department of Social Work (2017). *Social Work Curriculum*. Nsukka: University of Nigeria Printing Press.
Department of Social Work (2018). *Social Work Curriculum*. Benin City: University of Benin Printing Press.
Department of Social Work (2019). *Handbook for Students of Social Work 2020–2024 Academic Sessions*. Ilorin: University of Ilorin Printing Press.
Department of Social Work (2020). *Social Work Curriculum* (4th ed.). Calabar: University of Calabar Printing Press.
Ebimgbo, S., Agwu, P., and Okoye, U. (2017). Spirituality and religion in social work. In U. Okoye, N. Chukwu, and P. Agwu (Eds.), *Social Work in Nigeria: Book of Readings* (pp. 93–103). Nsukka: University of Nigeria Press Ltd.
Ezeanya, O. C. P., Ajah, B. O., Ibenwa, C. N., Onuorah, C. P., and Eze, U. A. (2022). A critical analysis of the impact of religion on the Nigerian struggle for nationhood. *HTS Teologiese Studies/Theological Studies*, 78(4), a7225. https://doi.org/10.4102/hts. v78i4.7225.
Fadeyi, A. O., and Oduwole, T. A. (2016). Effects of religion on reproductive health issues in Nigeria. *International Journal of Innovative Healthcare Research*, 4(1), 17–33.

Harris, H. W., and Yancey, G. I. (2017). Values, dissonance, and rainbows: Practice tips for Christian social workers in a polarized world. *Social Work and Christianity: An International Journal*, *44*, 123–142.

Hoffmann, L. K., and Patel, R. N. (2021). *Collective Action on Corruption in Nigeria: The Role of Religion*. London: Royal Institute of International Affairs. https://www.chathamhouse.org › default › files.

Hutchinson, E. D. (2013). *Essentials of Human Behavior: Integrating Person, Environment, and the Life Course*. Los Angeles, CA: Sage Publications.

Joseph, R. P., Ainsworth, B. E., Mathis, L., Hooker, S. P., and Keller, C. (2017). Incorporating religion and spirituality into the design of community-based physical activity programs for African American women: A qualitative inquiry. *BMC Research Notes*. https://doi.org/ 10.1186/s13104-017-2830-3.

Kavar, L. F. (2015). Spirituality and the sense of self: An inductive analysis. *The Qualitative Report*, *20*(5), 697–711. https://doi.org/10.46743/2160-3715/2015.2144.

King, P. E., and Boyatzis, C. (2015). Religious and spiritual development. In M. E. Lamb and R. M. Lerner (Eds.), *Handbook of Child Psychology and Developmental Science: Socioemotional Processes*, (pp. 975–1021). Hoboken, NJ: John Wiley and Sons.

Koenig, H. G. (1997). *Is Religion Good for Youth Health? The Effects of Religion on Physical and Mental Health*. Binghamton, NY: Haworth Pastoral Press.

Lalani, M., Fernandes, J., Fradgley, R., Ogunsola, C., and Marshall, M. (2019). Transforming community nursing services in the UK: Lessons from a participatory evaluation of the implementation of a new community nursing model in East London based on the principles of the Dutch Buurtzorg model. *BMC Health Services Research*, *19*(1), 945. https://doi.org/10.1186/s12913-019-4804-8.

Mabvurira, V., and Nyanguru, A. (2013). Spiritually sensitive social work: A missing link in Zimbabwe. *African Journal of Social Work*, *3*(1), 65–81.

National Association of Social Workers (2008). Code of ethics. http://www.nasw.org/.

Ngbeaa, G. T., and Achunike, H. C. (2014). Religion: Past and present in Nigeria. *International Journal of Sciences: Basic and Applied Research (IJSBAR)*, *17*(2), 156–174.

Odion, O. E. (2022). A global perspective on the role of faith and spirituality in a post-COVID-19 national and community recovery: The Nigeria case of the pandemic. *European Scientific Journal (ESJ)*, *18*(16), 43–66. https://doi.org/10.19044/esj.2022.v18n16p43.

Olson, E. (2014). Faith in the classroom: The ethical implications of teaching adolescent development of faith and spirituality in a human behavior and the social environment course. In *NACSW Convention Proceedings* (pp. 1–20).

Owumi, B., Raji, S. O., and Aliyu, T. K. (2013). Religious beliefs and the utilization of traditional medicine among members of pentecostal churches in Emurin, Ogun State, Nigeria. *African Journal of Social Sciences*, *3*(4), 23–34.

Oxhandler, H. K., and Pargament, K. I. (2014). Social work practitioners' integration of clients' religion and spirituality in practice: A literature review. *Social Work*, *59*(3), 271–279.

Padela, A. I., and Curlin, F. A. (2013). Religion and disparities: Considering the influences of Islam on the health of American Muslims. *Journal of Religion and Health*. https://doi.org/ 10.1007/s10943-012-9620-y.

Pinter, B., Hakim, M., Seidman, D. S., Kubba, A., Kishen, M., and Di Carlo, C. (2016). Religion and family planning. *European Journal of Contraception and Reproductive Health Care*, *21*(6), 486–495.

Reamer, F. G. (2013). Distance and online social work education: Novel ethical challenges. *Journal of Teaching in Social Work*, *33*(4–5), 369–384. https://doi.org/10.1080/08841233.2013.828669.

Rumun, A. J. (2014). Influence of religious beliefs on the healthcare practices. *International Journal of Education and Research*, *2*(4), 37–48.

Seitz, C. R., Jr. (2014). Utilizing a spiritual disciplines framework for faith integration in social work: A competency-based model. *Social Work and Christianity*, *41*(4), 334–354.

Tate, J. D. (2011). The role of spirituality in the breast cancer experiences of African American women. *Journal of Holistic Nursing*, *29*(4), 249–255.

Tsebee, A. K., and Toyin, O. (2017). Comparative analysis of religion reporting in Nigeria and selected countries of the world. *Mgbakoigba, Journal of African Studies*, *7*(1), 101–109.

Utensati, A. A. (2020). The use and abuse of religion: Implications in Nigerian society. *Ilorin Journal of Religious Studies, (IJOURELS)*, *10*(1), 65–75.

Vaughan, O. (2016). *Religion and the Making of Nigeria*. Durham: Duke University Press.

Williams, M., and Smolak, A. (2007). Integrating faith matters in social work education. *Journal of Religion and Spirituality in Social Work*, *26*(3), 25–44.

World Population Review (2022). Nigeria population 2022 (Live). https://worldpopulationreview.com/countries/nigeria-population.

8
SOCIAL WORK AND PASTORAL COUNSELLING IN SOUTH AFRICA
Inter-sectoral Partnership

Selelo Frank Rapholo and Zibonele France Zimba

Abstract: English

This chapter provides a critical analysis of inter-sectoral partnership of social work and pastoral counselling in South Africa through extensive integrative literature review and authors' personal experiences as both Christians and social workers. Social workers and spiritual leaders are both essential workers to support the needs of clients within communities. Literature shows that social workers are trained to deliver a variety of social support services to diverse populations, including religious populations. However, there are quite a few studies in South Africa that have rigorously focused on the relationship between social work education and pastoral counselling in African Christianity. The social work curriculum within the training institutions in South Africa should include Christianity wherein social work students would be taught about the importance of pastoral counselling. The authors recommend that during counselling with clients who come from a Christian background, social workers should seek pastoral services.

Introduction

South Africa and other African countries are confronted by a number of social problems that require collaborative intervention by multi-disciplinary teams, such as social workers, psychologists, and spiritual/religious leaders just to mention a few. In South Africa, clients who come from a Christian background, particularly Pentecostal Christians, prefer to also consult with their pastors when they go through adversity or hardships. This is confirmed by Mauda (2022), who conducted a study on the perception and treatment of mental illness by selected Pentecostal pastors in Polokwane that people with mental illness preferably call their faith healers or religious/spiritual leaders (who are pastors in the context of this chapter) when experiencing mental health problems. Mauda argues that pastors are more accessible, share the same religious/spiritual beliefs about mental illness with their congregants, and often provide religious/spiritual solutions to those who consult with them. Pentecostals are Christians who believe that worship is a full-body (participatory) engagement with God (Wolfgang, 2020). These Christians also believe in full-body prayer sessions led by their spiritual leaders (pastors) as a powerful mechanism to cope with adversities/

hardships. During counselling, some clients – especially Pentecostals – cite full-body prayer sessions led by their spiritual leaders (pastors) as a powerful mechanism to cope with adversities/hardships. This notion is supported by some scholars who claim that clients often cite prayer as one of the strategies they use to cope with their life challenges (Dykes and Carelse, 2019). The authors in this chapter argue that pastors are rarely involved as partners during social work counselling with clients who come from a Christian background. Religious or spiritual beliefs and values are very crucial in many African clients seeking social work intervention. These values and beliefs of African clients and families influence resilience during their hardships and shape their choices during social work counselling. However, there is less literature in South Africa on spirituality and religion – and its relevance to social work practice. The Western-based intervention methods that exclude the domain of Christian spirituality continue to dominate the practice of social work in Africa. In this chapter, the authors used the wider African literature.

Social work and spirituality are complementary (Wolfgang, 2020). There is an intersection between pastoral support and clinical social work in addressing social problems that clients face. Social workers are trained and poised to deliver a variety of social and supportive services to clients from diverse populations, including Christians. Social workers are often confronted with various biopsychosocial challenges that clients, including Christians, face.

Christianity in South Africa

Several studies show that South Africa upholds Christian values and beliefs (Bhagwan, 2010; Ross and Deverell, 2010; Mauda, 2022). Christianity emphasises the fatherhood of God and that every human being is a child of God. Christians believe that Jesus Christ was the only son of God who was conceived through the power of the Holy Ghost and was given birth by a virgin Mary according to the biblical book of Matthew 1:18. Christians believe that Jesus Christ was crucified and died at the cross of Calvary and was buried and resurrected on the third day and 40 days after his resurrection he ascended to heaven to be with God. Christians believe that Jesus Christ lives to help them with their life challenges. Mauda (2022) avers that many South Africans are Christians. Some of these Christians belong to the African Independent Churches (AICs), such as Zionists and Apostolic Christian Churches. It is crucial to also note that there is another group of Christians called Pentecostals that is currently increasing worldwide and in South Africa – these are the Classical and the New Charismatics churches/ministries. Christians are taught human values in the church that is led by a pastor. These values according to Luthar et al. (2015) are useful for the resilience of the Christians as follows:

- maintaining a good relationship with close family members, friends, and others.
- not regarding crises and stressful events as unbearable problems.
- accepting circumstances that cannot be changed.
- developing realistic goals and moving towards them.
- taking decisive action in adverse situations.
- looking for opportunities of self-discovery after a struggle with loss.
- developing self-confidence.
- keeping a long-term perspective and considering stressful events in a broader context.
- maintaining a hopeful outlook, expecting good things, and visualising what is wished for.
- taking care of your mind and body by exercising regularly and paying attention to your own needs and feelings.

When people face difficulties in accessing services and resources that are sometimes provided by the government (South African government in the context of this chapter), they consult with pastors (Burns and Tomilta, 2015), who the authors argue should work collaboratively with social workers during counselling. It is crucial that social workers understand the spiritual needs of clients as this will help them to refer such clients to pastors whenever a need arises. Ross and Deverell (2010) support this notion by stating that health professionals need to be aware of the impact of Christianity during counselling. The practice of people consulting with pastors is not new, not only in South Africa but also in Africa at large. In a study on the perception and treatment of mental illness by Pentecostal pastors in South Africa, Mauda (2022) maintains that when people experience various diseases, they consult with pastors for their resilience. Dykes and Carelse (2019) concur with this notion in that, often when asked how they have managed to cope with their challenges, some clients cite prayer led by their pastors as the internal resources and coping measures they draw on. Pastors generally serve as resources to address the needs of their congregants where they feel misunderstood, being misdiagnosed, and falsely labelled (Masola, 2019). Equally, social workers serve as resources to mitigate the needs of clients who come from diverse populations, including Christians (Sytner, 2018). Thus, the intersection between social work and pastoral counselling cannot be ignored. This validates findings by Bhagwan (2010) who established that the South African university students who come from Christian backgrounds have some strong beliefs that spiritual intervention plays an enormous role in their personal lives.

There is an exponential literature that enriches the salience of spirituality in social work practice (Al-Krenawi and Graham, 2000; Sahlein, 2002; Holloway, 2006), but very little has been explored on Christianity (that is where pastoral counselling in the context of this chapter features). Social workers do not always have direct access to populations that maintain a more private community, such as Christians; hence, their interaction with spiritual leaders in addressing social problems is of paramount importance. South Africa is a pluralistic society that is idiosyncratically multicultural in nature. Hence, it is important that social workers incorporate the culture and spiritual and/or religious beliefs of the indigenous people in their practices.

Social Work Assessment

Social work practice in South Africa currently embraces multiculturalism. Social scientists argue that social work knowledge should be broadened to include knowledge and wisdoms from different cultures (Furman, 2005), including a Christian culture. Social work in its history neglected spirituality and religion in social work practice (Zastrow, 2009). According to Zastrow, a possible reason for this quandary was that spirituality and religion only focused on heavenly concerns whilst social work stressed earthly concerns. The authors argue that spiritual and religious practices in South Africa influence clients' decision-making. Therefore, spirituality should be part of the assessment of clients' lives during social workers' first contact with clients. Social workers during the initial stage must screen clients' religious affiliation to acquire knowledge about their religion and/or Christianity. In the same breath, social workers should possess knowledge of pastors from diverse religions as they shall help them refer clients to the relevant pastor whenever a need arises. However, it should also be noted that even if clients do not self-identify themselves as religious affiliates, that does not necessarily mean they do not have religious concerns (Collin, 2012). Social workers need an intensive training in spirituality and religion to be able to conduct effective assessment with clients. The religious competency can assist in demonstrating an awareness of genesis of problems from a religious point of view. Dykes and Carelse (2019) maintain that spirituality plays a significant role in human existence. Thus, it should not be neglected during assessment. This involves asking a set of questions to determine if the client is experiencing a spiritual crisis. Furthermore, understanding a client's religious crisis may be vital to understand its possible influence in the reception of counselling services. Nickles (2011) proposes that understanding the role of religion and spirituality in counselling is essential towards reaching the goals of counselling.

Clients who come from a Pentecostal background (those who believe in the power of the holy spirit) are very sensitive to some practices. Thus, if not screened thoroughly during social work counselling, the entire therapeutic process may be compromised and leave such clients suffering from their hardships of life. Pentecostals are taught to exercise faith for their breakthrough and to pray without ceasing according to 1 Thessalonians 5:17 rather than seeking help from a secular source during difficult times (Bjorck and Trice, 2006). As such, Pentecostals and their pastors hold the beliefs that cause them to underutilise some services, such as social work services. Hence, it is important that social workers conduct a thorough screening, and, in case they find such kind of clients, then refer such clients to the relevant pastor. In some instances, social workers may need to make an immediate referral to a certified chaplain or spiritual care professional (who is a pastor in the context of this chapter), especially when social workers are not trained in spirituality or when clients have specific religious concerns that are out of the scope of social work practice.

Social Work Education

This chapter is written at the right time wherein South Africa has joined a movement for the decolonisation of the curriculum. In 2015, students across higher education institutions in South Africa reached a tipping point regarding the continued colonisation of higher education. This manifested mostly in the #FeesMustFall movement wherein, amongst others, students demanded an education that is rooted in Africa that would address the post-colonial era in which we now live, study, and work. Social work is one of the disciplines in higher education that heeded this call and started to collectively work towards the decolonisation of the Bachelor of Social Work (BSW) programmes. The Association of South African Higher Education Institutions (ASASWEI) organised regional dialogues with social work academics in 2016 and in 2017 in this regard. The association in partnership with the Department of Social Development (DSD) and Association of Schools of Social Work in Africa (ASSWA) organised an international conference on decolonial social work education and practice. Whilst the decolonisation of social work education and practice is still a work in progress in South Africa, the writers argue that very little has been explored on Christianity in addressing social ills that the social workers are confronted with. Thus, it is very crucial for social workers and pastors to collaborate their services in the form of referral for clients who needs spiritual intervention.

Social work education should prepare social work students with skills that will help them to meet the needs of clients who are grappling with their spiritual or religious beliefs. Several studies show that some clients draw their coping mechanisms from their spiritual beliefs (Dykes and Carelse, 2019). For instance, clients who come from a Christian background usually cite prayer and fasting that is led by their pastors for their breakthrough from the challenges of life. Dreyer (2015) asserts that one's relationship with God contributes towards people's resilience during times of adversity. Thus, during social work counselling, it is imperative that after the assessment during the first contact with clients, social workers refer clients to pastors for a spiritual intervention but that should be through the consent of the concerned client. The profession of social work in South Africa currently accentuates the holistic nature of social work, thus focusing on a thorough biopsychosocial as well as spiritual assessment of clients and their families.

South Africa is a multicultural society (Ross and Deverell, 2016) with a vast number of beliefs and values. Dykes and Carelse (2019) maintain that with the many cultures and ethnic identities according to which people enact their lives, South Africa practices spirituality and religion in many ways, for example formal/charismatic church, worshipping of ancestors and in synagogues. Canda (1989), who founded the field of spirituality in social work, argues that social workers ought to be knowledgeable and ready to assist clients, including those who come from a Christian background, in the full range of their needs without exclusion (Canda, 1989). Thus, there is a need for effective and commensurate training of social workers to be able to incorporate pastoral intervention during counselling. Social workers often are reported to be unequipped to address and discuss faith-based concerns (Bauer-Wu, 2007); hence they are unable to bring in pastors during counselling sessions with clients. This gap should be closed right from BSW training at higher education institutions wherein a social work curriculum should have course content that would expose students to the tenets of major religions in Africa, such as Christianity. This would lead an intersection of social workers and pastors during counselling to be effective. Hutchison (2013) states that if social workers are equipped with knowledge and skills in these areas, they will be able to effectively work with diverse client groups, including clients who are rooted in spirituality and religion. Considering that South Africa is a Christian country, the writers argue that there is a very strong need for social work education to include training in spiritual and religious perspectives. It is also pertinent for the institutions that offer theological training to consider lay counseling courses for pastors who did not receive any pastoral training so as to provide them with foundational knowledge of and skills in counselling as this is useful during social work intervention with clients from a Christian background.

Roles of Pastors in Social Work Counselling

The church has been serving and continues to play a very pivotal role for its members (Leavey et al., 2016), who also happen to seek social work intervention. Many people in South Africa, even those who are not Christians, seek the support of pastors when they face life challenges. Pastors play a very important role in providing both spiritual and social support to the people of South Africa; hence, the writers argue that they have an intersectional relationship with social workers in addressing the needs of clients. Below are the roles of pastors during counselling:

Teachers of the Word of God and Praying

When going through adversity, Christians and non-Christians in South Africa often consult with pastors for a prayer before they can see professionals. This is supported by Grossklaus (2015), who states that church members often go and see their minister first, and, depending on their problems, they can either help or refer them for professional intervention. Thus, there is an interactional relationship that social workers and pastors should strengthen during the helping process of clients. For example, where there is a suspicion of demonic spirit amongst clients during social work counselling, the pastor should be brought in. Some clients in South Africa believe in the power of prayer for their resilience; however, such should be done with the consent of a client in question. Park (2015) states that prayer amongst the many spiritual and religious practices in South Africa appears to the most dominant form of spiritual or religious intervention. In addition to prayer, pastors also quote scriptures during their counselling sessions that lead to confessions, repentance, and faith healing (Young et al., 2003). The authors argue that there are not enough studies in South Africa that have explored the efficacy of prayer as a form of resilience for Christians, particularly when they go through adversity. It is therefore crucial that social workers receive an intense training in Christian religion.

Biblical Counselors

Pastors are extensively involved in counselling services (Murambidzi, 2016; Mauda, 2022). Thus, there is a need for social workers and pastors to collaborate their services in meeting the needs of clients. In a study conducted by Murambidzi (2016), most participants expressed that the church, through the pastors, has a crucial role in offering counselling and crisis support services to people experiencing various life problems. This clearly indicates that Christianity cannot be ignored during social work education and practice. The same was uncovered in a study that was conducted by Asamoah et al. (2014) wherein the participants indicated that pastors offered them counselling and social support, although it was not formal as a professional counselling, and that they were helped. This calls for an immense training of pastors as counsellors to work jointly with social workers during counselling sessions, particularly with Christian clients. If their roles can be cleared and understood by social workers who also see their congregants, the two parties will be able to work harmoniously for the benefit of the affected clients.

Sources of Referral

As already indicated in this chapter, people when they go through life challenging situations, they often tend to consult with their pastors. Mabitsela (2003) states that although pastors play a very significant role in the society, they do not have adequate training to address some problems. In such instances, pastors refer their congregants and the individuals whom they see to the experts for further assistance. In a study conducted by Frontus (2015), most pastors have highlighted that it is their pastoral obligation to refer their congregants to the professionals for help in case the counselling sessions go beyond their scope of practice. Therefore, social workers need to establish a very strong relationship with pastors in addressing the social problems of their clients.

Social Support Systems

Pastors serve as carers of the people. They provide social support by meeting the basic needs of their congregants and the surrounding communities. In a study by Asamoah et al. (2014) it was found that pastors provide emotional care through hospital visitation and sometimes with members of the church to patients who are suffering from mental health issues. The church is the foundation for psychosocial and emotional care and support to people who are suffering from social problems. Mauda (2022) maintains that pastors are trusted, are more accessible, and maintain close relations with those they minister to by means of follow up. In a study by Murambidzi (2016) it was established that some pastors in their churches have established various departments, such as hospitality and welfare ministry, that are focused on ensuring that the basic needs of congregants and communities are met. Some churches have close working relationships with the families within the communities. The church also creates an environment where its members feel a sense of belonging and share spiritual and religious values. In addition to this, Mabitsela (2003) has also found that through the church leadership and the pastor, some churches have life skills programmes that are useful in empowering the community by disseminating such information through workshops, conferences, and preaching services.

Educators

Most churches in South Africa serve as sites wherein congregants and community members participate in education for the prevention of some problems, a practical example is health education where pastors are involved. In a study conducted by Asamoah et al. (2014) some pastors reported that they participate in mental health education in collaboration with social workers and psychologists. Pastors appear to be creative in the environment of the church setting for programmes useful for life enhancement to run. Thus, there is a serious need for social workers and pastors to collaborate their services for the benefits of the affected individuals, families, and communities. Contrary to this, pastors also offer biblical tutorials for the growth of the congregants' faith, particularly when they have lost hope due to the problems they encounter. This helps the congregants to bounce back from such adversities. The more conservative members of religious/spiritual groups who rely more on God and ministers/pastors during their time of distress see pastoral education as eminent for their resilience. Thus, social workers and pastors should work collaboratively when rolling out certain educational programmes to the communities.

Conclusion

Literature confirms that there is an intersectional relationship between pastoral and social work counselling. South Africa is found to be a Christian country and, as such, a collaboration between pastors and social workers cannot be ignored. Although the issue of spirituality and religion in Africa generally has been explored, there is still a gap in terms of Christianity as one of the religions that is practiced in Africa and its role in addressing the needs of people. Christianity has been playing a very significant role in meeting the needs of congregants and communities and very little is written in relation to such a contribution. It is therefore imperative that during counselling social workers work closely with pastors who are coming from a Christian religion. Christians who happen to be social work clients are extensively taught values and strategies in church that they can use for their resilience and, as such, social workers should be knowledgeable of such. It would be very appropriate that an intersectional programme for social work curriculum and practice and pastors be designed wherein the role and each of these parties be clearly designed.

Recommendations

1. Social workers and pastors should work together during the client helping process, and they should not be limited to Christian clients only but to every client they meet.
2. It is crucial that social workers screen clients' spirituality during the first or initial session of counselling.
3. Based on the role of Christianity in Africa, integrating Christian values and social work values in social work curriculum should be in training social workers who will be responsive to African issues.

Further Reading

Sytner, A. (2018). Social work and pastoral counselling: Empowering each other. *Journal of Religion and Spirituality in Social Work: Social Thought*, 37(2), 202–219.

References

Al-Krenawi, A., and Graham, J. R. (2000). Culturally sensitive social work practice with Arab clients in mental health settings. *Health and Social Work*, 25(1), 9–22.

Asamoah, M. K., Osafo, J., and Agyapong, I. (2014). The Role of Pentecostal pastors in mental health-care delivery in Ghana. *Mental Health, Religion and Culture*, 17(6), 601–614. DOI: 10.1080/13674676.2013.871628.

Bauer-Wu, S., Barrett, R., and Yeager, K. (2007). Spiritual perspectives and practices at the end-of-live. A review of the major religions and applications to palliative care. *Indian Journal of Palliative Care*, 13(2), 53–58. DOI: 10.4103/0973-1075.38900.

Bhagwan, R. (2010). Spirituality in social work: A survey of students at South African universities. *Social Work Education*, 29(2), 188–204.

Bjorck, J. P., and Trice, P. D. (2006). Pentecostal perspectives on causes and cures of depression. *Professional Psychology: Research and Practice*, 37(3), 283–294. DOI: 10.1037/0735-7028.37.3.283.

Burns, J. K., and Tomita, A. (2015). Traditional and religious healers in the pathway to care for people with mental disorders in Africa: A systematic review and meta analysis. *Social Psychiatry and Psychiatric Epidemiology*, 50(6), 867–877. DOI: 10.1007/s00127-014-0989-7.

Canda, E. R. (1989). Religious content in social work education: A comparative approach. *Journal of Social Work Education*, 36–45. DOI: 10.1080/10437797.1989.10671268.

Collin, M. (2012). The search for a higher power among terminally ill people with no previous religion or belief. *International Journal of Palliative Nursing*, 18(8), 384–389.

Dreyer, Y. (2015). Community resilience and spirituality: Keys to hope for a post-apartheid South Africa. *Pastoral Psychology*, 64(5), 651–662.

Dykes, G., and Carelse, S. (2019). Spirituality. In Adrian Van Breda and Johannah Sekudu (eds.), *Theories for Decolonial Social Work Practice in South Africa*. Oxford: Oxford University Press, 222–242.

Frontus, M. K. (2015). Clergy's perceptions of their role in mental health service delivery: A Qualitative examination (Publication No 0054D 12523) [Doctoral Thesis, Columbia University]. https://academic-commons.columbia.edu/doi/10.7916/D8VH5MSMia.edu.

Furman, L. D., Benson, P. W., Canda, E. R., and Grimwood, C. (2005). A comparative international analysis of religion and spirituality in social work: A survey of UK and US social workers. *Social Work Education*, 24(8), 813–839.

Grossklaus, M. (2015). Free Church Pastors in Germany – Perceptions of spirit possession and mental Illness (Publication No. 10500/55685) [Doctoral Thesis, University of South Africa]. http://uir.unisa.ac.za/handle/10500/22658.

Holloway, M. (2006). Death the great leveller? Towards a transcultural spirituality of dying and bereavement. *Journal of Clinical Nursing*, 15(7), 833–839.

Hutchison, E. D. (2013). *Essentials of Human Behavior: Integrating Person, Environment, and the Life Course*. Thousand Oaks, CA: Sage.

Leavey, G., Lowenthal, K., and King, M. (2016). Locating the social origins of mental Illness: The explanatory models of mental illness among pastors from different ethnic and faith backgrounds. *Journal of Religion and Health*, 55(5), 1607–1622. DOI: 10.1007/s10943-016-0191-1.

Luthar, S. S., Crossman, E. J., and Small, P. J. (2015). Resilience and adversity. In R. M. Learner, M. H. Bornstein, and T. Leventhal (eds.), *Handbook of Child Psychology and Developmental Science*. New York: Wiley.

Mabitsela, L. (2003). Exploratory study of psychological distress as understood by Pentecostal pastors (Publication No.2263/30114) [Masters dissertation, University of Pretoria]. https://repository.up.ac.za/bitstream/handle/2263/30114/Complete.pdf?sequence=10.

Masola, N. J., Sigida, S. T., and Khorommbi, E. M. (2019). Spiritual diagnostic criteria in an African setting: The case of Baruti in Limpopo Province, South Africa. *Theologia Viatorum*, 43(1), 1–5.

Mauda, L. T. (2022). The perception and treatment of mental illness by selected Pentecostal pastors in Polokwane: Towards an intervention [Doctoral dissertation, University of Limpopo]. THE PERCEPTION AND TREATMENT OF MENTAL ILLNESS BY... - Google Scholar.

Murambidzi, I. (2016). Conceptualisation of mental illness among Christian clergy in Harare, Zimbabwe (Publication No.11427/23421) [Masters dissertation, University of Cape Town]. https://open.uct.ac.za/bitstream/handle/11427/23421/thesis_hsf.

Nickles, T. (2011). *The Role of Religion and Spirituality in Counseling*. Unpublished Bachelor of Science Degree in Psychology Senior Research Project. California Polytechnic State University.

Park, J. C. (2015). Do Clergy in Hidalgo County, Texas Serve as a Bridge or Barrier to Mental Health Services? (Publication No 2581) [Doctoral thesis, Loma Linda University. Coalition Members]. Hidalgo County, TX: Official Website.

Ross, E., and Deverell, A. (2010). *Health, Illness and Disability: Psychosocial Approaches*. Pretoria: Van Schaik Publishers.

Sahlein, J. (2002). When religion enters the dialogue: A guide for practitioners. *Clinical Social Work Journal*, 30(4), 381–401.

Sytner, A. (2018). Social work and pastoral counselling: Empowering each other. *Journal of Religion and Spirituality in Social Work: Social Thought*, 37(2), 202–219.

Wolfgang, V. (2020). *The Routledge Handbook of Pentecostal Theology*. Abingdon: Routledge.

Young, J. L., Griffith, E. E., and Williams, D. R. (2003). The integral role of pastoral counselling by African-American clergy in community mental health. *Psychiatric Services*, 54(5), 688–692. DOI: 10.1176/appi.ps.54.5.68.

Zastrow, C. (2009). *The Practice of Social Work: A Comprehensive Worktext*. Belmont, CA: Cengage Learning.

PART 2

Social Work Education
Evolution across Contexts

9
EXPLORING THE CHALLENGES OF CHILD PROTECTION IN NIGERIA

Abiodun Blessing Osaiyuwu

Abstract: English

Child protection is a major element in the practice of social work that covers both family-based care and institutional care. Family welfare institutions encounter many challenges when dealing with child protection services in Nigeria. These include, inter alia, a shortage of competent and/or experienced professional social workers; matters of child rights violations and weak implementation of laws prohibiting the abuse and exploitation of children. Social workers' core responsibilities within the context of children's welfare include responding to cases of child abuse and neglect, removing children from dangerous home settings that are not compliant with regulatory standards, and working with children and their families. For social workers to meet with these multi-tasks, support is needed from the government to address the child protection challenges encountered during practice. Additionally, there is a need for social work education to be focused on understanding cultural sensitivity, child development, and child rights with knowledge of child protection laws and policies. Strengthening the legal framework and ensuring that laws are enforced through the application of social work education will help to protect children from abuse, neglect, and exploitation. Secondary data are utilised in exploring these child protection challenges encountered by social workers.

Introduction

Children are considered vulnerable because of the circumstances surrounding their birth or the immediate environment in which they live. They are more likely to experience abuse or be deprived of care and protection for basic requirements, making them less privileged than their peers (Federal Ministry of Women Affairs and Social Development [FMWASD], 2008). Vulnerable children, inter alia, include children who require alternative family care, abused, or neglected children, children with disability, children impacted by armed conflict, and children who need to be legally protected (FMWASD, 2008). When parents are unable to fulfil their parental responsibilities, the alternative care system has been highlighted to provide care and assistance for vulnerable children (Williamson and Greenberg, 2010).

Despite mandatory legislation intended to improve children's conditions, the Global Fund for Children (2007) reports that children in West Africa are currently more likely to be raped, trafficked, beaten, or abused and less likely to attend school, receive proper healthcare, and/or be malnourished than their Western counterparts. The abuse includes neglecting physically challenged children, child trafficking, child marriage, and child sexual abuse. Child abuse is an enduring social issue that needs the urgent attention of the national governments in every country. In Nigeria for example, numerous reasons sighted for child abuse and neglect include poverty, illiteracy, and unemployment/underemployment. Sossou and Yogtiba (2009) explain that the psycho-social development of children is endangered due to lack of governmental commitment to resource allocation, law enforcement, and the non-creation of comprehensive children and family welfare programmes to protect children. Despite the rich and abundant natural and human resources in Nigeria, a lot of poverty remains in the country. Poverty, unemployment, and underdevelopment are widespread while violence against children is becoming a very severe social issue that requires immediate attention and expert action (Sossou and Yogtiba, 2009). Sexual assault, child marriage, child labour, and other forms of child violence against children are all violations of human rights and societal injustices that cut across all socioeconomic classes and cultural origins. It is apparent that the psychological, physical, and emotional strains children endure because of denial or lack of opportunity for sufficient nutrition, education, good health, and protection cannot be overemphasised, notwithstanding the various cultural definitions of child abuse. Social work education can help social workers in developing the knowledge and skills to understand child protection, child abuse, and child neglect.

The Concept of Child Protection, Child Abuse, and Child Neglect

Child protection is the protection of children against child abuse or child neglect. The United Nations Children's Fund (2017) states that child protection is any action aimed at preventing, protecting, and responding to violence, exploitation, and abuse against children. Abuse could be physical, which includes neglect, emotional, psychological, financial, and sexual. Abuse or neglect need not take place before action is taken. Action is necessary for protection processes, such as risk assessment for children who are endangered. Child protection frameworks include laws and policies that provide specific rights to children and services that support protection of children in the community.

Despite the support of the Sustainable Development Goals (SDGs) and the United Nations Convention on the Rights of the Child (UNCRC), there is minimal action in providing necessary and effective professional, educational, and psycho-social assistance for Nigerian children. According to Article 19 of the Convention, children must be protected from all kinds of harms. The majority of the victims of various abuses, undergo behavioural, emotional, and psychological trauma, necessitating expert medical, therapeutic, and culturally relevant interventions. However, there is a shortage and/or lack of these services due to limited funding and a lack of organised social programmes for child welfare interventions. To coordinate and have control over matters relating to children's rights, family welfare, and governmental accountability, in 1986, Nigeria founded the African Network on Prevention and Protection against Child Abuse and Neglect (ANPPCAN).

In the fight against child abuse and neglect in West Africa, professional social workers have always played key roles. Even when all the factors hindering the protection of children are addressed without having professional social workers with the knowledge and skills on the ground to adequately utilise the available resources and implement policies, children will not be properly protected against various types of abuse (Wilkinson and Bowyer, 2017). According to Lachman, Poblete, Ebigbo, Nyandiya-Bundy, Bundy, Killian and Doek (2002), it is essential to consider ingrained cultural norms that act as barriers to the implementation and enforcement of universal objectives like girls' protection from sexual abuse. African governments are charged with ratifying international agreements without actually implementing any programmes or plans that would result from them. For instance, the Department of Social Welfare, which is in charge of child protection in Nigeria, receives insufficient budgetary allocation for the implementation of this policy. Additionally, no funding is set aside for research that would analyse the problems, occurrences, and prevalence of the many forms of child abuse, neglect, and exploitation that Nigerian children experience (UNICEF, 2006).

Nigeria was one of the first nations to ratify the UNCRC in 1991, but it took until 2003 for the legislature to establish the first complete Children's Act. One of the pressure groups that pushed for the eventual passage of this law was the Nigerian Chapter of the ANPPCAN, an organisation tasked with minimising the effects of child abuse and neglect. However, the institutional framework in charge of delivering these social services is understaffed and underfunded. Research, according to Ike and Twumasi-Ankrah (1999), is the key to public education, which, in turn, is the key to prevention of child abuse and neglect. In order to find long-lasting and sustainable solutions to child maltreatment and abuse, it is necessary to create multidisciplinary national and regional scientific databases on the incidence, prevalence, dimensions, and effects of all types of child abuse and neglect. This is because there are numerous contributing factors to this issue. The culture of silence, the failure to recognise the problems as social problems, and the unreliable/inadequate records from law enforcement authorities have all been named as obstacles (Nwokolu-Nte and Onyige, 2020). To offer scientific baseline data on the issues in West Africa, it has been stressed that academic institutions, medical and social work experts, nurses, psychologists, and sociologists must all engage in various forms of epidemiological research that incorporates African environmental knowledge and practices into the curriculum that promote sustainable development (Briant, 2009). The creation of an integrated strategy framework, known as the New Partnership for Africa's Development (NEPAD), aims to address the current difficulties and societal problems facing the continent.

Problems, such as physical, behavioural, or social issues, arise while evaluating the circumstances and the susceptibility of young children because of their size and fragility, which prevents them from defending themselves (Daniel, 2010; Chaudhary et al., 2014). Children sometimes are unable to completely understand their own vulnerability, which increases the risk of them being endangered (Ayodele and Olubayo-Fatiregun, 2014). Cisneros Neumann (2009) contend that children in vulnerable situations are capable of participating in problem-solving and understanding their settings if given the chance. Attending to children's physical, psychological, and emotional needs through social work education will help to build good, physical, mental, and spiritual health, which will help the children grow to become brighter and responsible adults that contribute to the society (Bhanje and Halli, 2012). Adults must adopt safe behaviours to reduce the likelihood that children will experience harm. This can be achieved by equipping social workers with the necessary knowledge and skills to protect children from various forms of abuse and neglect involving collective responsibility within a traditional African society.

Child Protection in the Traditional African Society

Every nation in the world today has some type of social welfare programme in place, created by the government to meet the social and economic needs of its population. Several non-governmental organisations, religious organisations, and the government have been offering social welfare services to those with social issues. Traditional African civilisations had their own ways of ensuring social cohesiveness through the provision of social welfare services to those in need before the arrival of the colonialists (Sossou and Yogtiba, 2009). The extended family was used in carrying out these social welfare projects. The communalism idea serves as the foundation for the family and clan's social assistance system. In the foundation of the traditional African society, there is a sense of belonging within the community (Sossou and Yogtiba, 2009). However, the impact of Western civilisation is eroding the African social welfare system for families and the sense of community through a rise in individualism (Arolowo, 2010; Sibani, 2018). The importance they placed on the family and its values sets most traditional Africans apart from other people on the globe.

Some modern Western civilisations place little value on the extended family, while the nuclear family structure is more favoured. Emphasis is placed more on the assistance provided by the government and society than by the family. Traditional Africans, on the other hand, rely more on considering the wellbeing of people in need within the extended family. Despite cultural changes, many African communities still place strong emphasis on the family. It influences everyone's daily experiences in the neighbourhood. Traditional Africans had their own methods for delivering social welfare services to individuals in need before the current paradigm of social welfare services being provided to citizens by the government came into existence (Sossou and Yogtiba, 2009). Services for social welfare were provided by the family and, indirectly, the clan. It is crucial to remember that the majority of traditional Africans did not manage social issues the way people do today (Duke and John, 2019). The extended family is a long-established institution that offers its members a sophisticated social security system; economic support to meet their basic needs for food, shelter, and clothing; and a large circle of relatives to whom they can turn in times of crisis, unemployment, sickness, poverty, old age, and bereavement (Mokomane, 2012). Scholars and researchers have praised the effectiveness of the traditional African family and clan and the social services that are provided. This is because the family social welfare system is a grassroots programme involving direct contact with people (Duke and John, 2012).

Recognising and Prioritising the Role of the Family

The state's major responsibility is to promote parental care and prevent unnecessary separation of children. If children are unavoidably separated from their parents or family, it is the responsibility of the state to facilitate the reintegration of the children with their parents/family appropriately. Families play a crucial role in the physical, social, and emotional development of the growing child. Families are also able to promote good health and reduce intergenerational poverty through the support of the state (Desmond, Watt, Saha, Huang and Lu, 2020). When the vital roles of parents are considered, services delivered to children will be most effective. Moreover, it is the responsibility of the government to protect children who are without parental care and ensure that the children get high-quality and appropriate alternative care. Comprehensive systems for the welfare and protection of children were also required to be supported in order to address the complex needs of children at risk of, or in, alternative care (Desmond et al., 2020). It has been emphasised that registration and licensing should be made compulsory and be put in place for all formal care institutions (Jones, Presler-Marshall, Cooke and Akinrimisi, 2012). Desmond et al. (2020), espouse that it is the responsibility of the states to strengthen community-based, national, and international systems for child protection that can assess and meet the needs of vulnerable children as policies were required to be implemented while children in the care of their parents or adults are protected.

Scholars have argued that states should be able to recognise that funding institutions can intensify unnecessary family–child separation and institutionalisation. It is expected that states allocate human and financial resources for the welfare services of the child and family (Browne, Hamilton-

Giachritsis, Johnson and Ostergren, 2006; Desmond et al., 2020). They advise that states should provide resources and funds for training the social service workforce. Desmond et al (2020) opine that it is essential that mechanisms for the participation of children in the planning and implementation of policies and services be strengthened while competent monitoring mechanism are established.

It is estimated that between five to six million children (aged 0–18 years) globally live in institutions rather than family-based care settings (Desmond et al., 2020). Global agencies and organisations have been advised to jointly work to progressively eliminate institutional care and promote family-based care. It is emphasised that community-based and family-based programmes are efficiently economical and able to promote long-term development of human capital while states are responsible for promoting parental care, preventing unnecessary child separation, and facilitating reintegration where appropriate (Desmond, et al., 2020). Families have a crucial role in physical, social, and emotional development, health, and intergenerational poverty reduction. Services delivered to children are most effective when they consider the vital role of the family. Comprehensive systems for the welfare and protection of children should be supported to address the complex needs of children at risk of, or in, alternative care.

Child Protection in Nigeria

Every child has the right to protection from any harm and the right not to be coerced into doing anything against their will. According to Britain's Children's Act of 1989, a child must be protected from any severe injury, which is described as 'the abuse or the detriment to health or development' (Section 31:9b). The idea of 'serious harm' is introduced in the Act as the 'boundary that warrants forced involvement into family life to protect the child's safety and wellbeing'. While the idea of serious harm or significant harm is not indicated in the Nigerian context, the emphasis is on the child's best interests in regard to their overall wellbeing (CRA, 2003). Nigerian children are vulnerable to a number of economic and social factors. These include environmental degradation; domestic violence and family fragmentation; broader societal violence and conflict; social exclusion and discrimination; harmful traditional practices based on cultural values; orphanhood and loss of family are all issues for different reasons (Jones et al., 2012).

The Child Protection Sub-Sector (CPSS) established in northeastern Nigeria in 2017 recognised that the Nigerian government has the primary responsibilities for the protection of Nigerian children through which child protection is coordinated in emergency response in northeastern Nigeria, which includes Adamawa, Borno, and Yobe. The CPSS has yet to be introduced to other states in the country. The objective of the CPSS is ensuring that the child protection services for children, including adolescents and caregivers who has been mostly affected by humanitarian crisis are being reflective and inclusive in their response and efficient and effective in the intervention process. The CPSS is under the FMWASD and supported by the United Nations Children's Fund (UNICEF). It is operationally coordinated and managed from Maiduguri, Borno State, with Working Groups in FCT Abuja, Adamawa, and Yobe. The relevant government ministries, agencies, national non-governmental organisations (NNGOs), international non-governmental organisations (INGOs), United Nations (UN) agencies, and other actors relevant to child protection technicality and operations are brought together by the CPSS.

Child Protection Policy in Nigeria

Globally, three major factors affect child protection. These are poverty, HIV/AIDs infection, and war (Lachman, et al., 2002). Both financial and psychological poverty affect the prevention process that may affect child protection programmes. Most research in Africa is targeted at the documentation of the incidence and the prevalence of child protection, while undermining the evaluation of programmes, risk assessments, and interventions. Factors that have affected the dearth in research include the lack of resources and the lack of trained researchers (Lachman, et al., 2002).

The mandate for promoting, protecting, investigating, and monitoring human rights violations as well as receiving and treating complaints from citizens, especially children, about the violation of their rights is held by the National Human Rights Commission of Nigeria, which was established by Decree No. 22 of 1915. Nigeria has 36 states with a Federal Capital Territory in Abuja. Each of the states has the responsibility of signing into law the child protection policy so it can be implemented. The Lagos state government signed the policy into law in 2016 and the policy provides structure and states clear processes that can be used for the protection of children who are victims of sexual abuse within children's institutions, such as their schools and homes (Aliogo, 2020). The key issues that this policy seeks to achieve, including working in collaboration with child rights, is to protect the rights of the child. It also seeks to ensure that government puts in place referrals with the people in understanding what the rules and responsibilities are. Since Nigeria ratified the UNCRC, the African Charter on the Rights and Welfare of the Child (ACRWC), and other relevant international instruments, there has been various legislative and institutional measures at the federal and state levels established by the Nigerian government that are aimed at addressing various forms of violence against children. Some of the enacted legislation includes:

- The Child's Rights Act (CRA) 2003.
- National Policy and Plan of Action on Elimination of Female Genital Mutilation in Nigeria (2002).
- Trafficking in Persons, (Prohibition) Law Enforcement and Administration Act 2003.
- Ebonyi State Law No. 010 (2001) on the Abolition of Harmful Traditional Practices against Children and Women.
- Edo State Female Genital Mutilation, Prohibition Law 2002.
- Bauchi State Hawking by Children, Prohibition Edict of 1985 CAP 58.
- Cross River State Girl Child Marriages and Female Circumcision, Prohibition Law 2000.
- The Sharia Penal Codes of Zamfara, Kano, Kebbi, Kaduna, and Sokoto States protect children against physical and psychological violence.

While there are provisions prohibiting all aspects of child abuse, child neglect, and violence against children in the CRA (2003), with the Act also providing counselling and rehabilitation of children as well as the prosecution of the perpetrators of violence against children, there are no comprehensive policies on violence against children. Save the Children (2002) reports that it is essential that all children in Nigeria be protected from violence and harm, and it works especially to protect orphans, vulnerable children, and children affected by conflicts. The report explained that the organisation operates programmes from the community up to the national level to promote children's rights and protection. Focus areas include preventing early child marriage, ending violence against children, and meeting the needs of orphans and vulnerable children. Through these humanitarian responses, psycho-social support in child-friendly spaces and services are provided for unaccompanied and/or separated children (Save the Children, 2002). These children are often placed within family-based or institutional care.

Family-Based Care and Institutional Care

In most African countries, including Nigeria, the extended family system is the primary source of care that provides a social safety net to meet the people's basic needs (Korang-Okrah et al., 2019). Africans provided remedies to the social, economic, and other existential issues that were present in their communities through the traditional family and clan structures. The victims' level of living was not highlighted by the services provided; rather, they regulated the social problems (Duke and John, 2019). In sub-Saharan Africa (SSA), including Nigeria, the extended family has historically served as the cornerstone of society's sustenance by providing its members with financial, social, emotional, and caregiving assistance during challenging times. The demographic and socioeconomic changes that have persisted in the area over time, however, have had an impact on this institution. The changes have led to diminished family support for home duties and caregiving tasks as well as economic fragility and crippling poverty that characterise family conditions. Mokomane and Rochat (2012) expound that more extensive social protection policies and programmes need to be developed and implemented in SSA to lessen the effects of the changes on families and their members. Brown et al. (2006) reports that few children do not live with their parents either because they have lost their biological parents, they have been abandoned by their parents, or their parents are unable to give adequate care to the children due to not having the means to care for them appropriately.

Child protection is one of the key elements of social work practices, which includes both family and institutional care. In family-based care, social workers support the network and observe the care of children with their birth parents. This includes care by relatives. Family-based care refers to caregiving by extended family or foster, kafalah (the practice of guardianship of orphaned children in Islam), or adoptive family, preferably in close physical proximity to the biological family to facilitate the continued contact of children with significant others in their life, when this is in their best interest. The Rights of Children recognises that children should grow up in a family environment in order to have a well-balanced development of their personality and potentials. The rights also urge member states that have adopted the UNCRC, which includes Nigeria, to take actions to progressively replace institutionalisation with quality alternative care and redirect resources to family and community-based services (Browne, 2006).

In Nigeria, family-based care with extended family or unrelated households are the most common form of care, and these are mostly unregulated and undocumented, and most children in this form of care are vulnerable and at high risk of abuse and exploitation, including being denied access to education (Nnama-Okechukwu and Okoye, 2019; Connelly and Ikpaahindi, 2016). Institutional care homes are also available across the country, and these include orphanage homes, motherless babies' homes, sheltered homes, children's reception centres (CRC), and other non-family-based homes (Connelly and Ikpaahindi, 2016). Connelly and Ikpaahindi (2016) explain that non-governmental organisations, such as religious bodies, international organisations, and philanthropists, are responsible for running residential homes for children, providing care, support, and protection.

The design of institutional childcare allowances as part of child welfare provision for parents or children without relative care is the basis of all philanthropy and development. The institutionally based care provides care for children whose parents are not capable of caring for them, due to social and/or economic factors, and children whose parents are deceased. Institutional care is seen as the ultimate insurance choice for children, despite the apparent negative consequences for them. Children's health and wellbeing are dependent on the safety and quality of their environment at home, school, and the community where they live. This should also be an environment that protects children from diverse types of abuse that includes violence, economic/

sexual exploitation, and neglect (Elegbeleye, 2013). Research has shown that placement is critical in the overall outcome of vulnerable children as institutional care has a negative impact on such children and this can be determined by assessing the quality of life of each child (Ishaya, 2016).

Challenges of Family Welfare Institutions

There are significant limitations on government responses to the protection of vulnerable children. This has led to the involvement of non-governmental organisations (NGO) and international non-governmental organisations (INGO). International agencies, such as the International Labour Organization (ILO) and UNICEF, have been playing vital roles in the fight against child labour and child abuse in Nigeria. They have done so in partnership with government and national NGOs, which include work in rescuing children, running shelters, vocational training, and sensitisation and mobilisation of communities (Jones et al., 2012).

The Nigerian government after independence in 1960 established projects that included the creation of welfare centres in Lagos, Calabar, Enugu, Port Harcourt, and Warri. The government also established various programmes that included the National Council of Social Work (1969), the Federal Ministry of Social Development, Youth and Sports (1975), and social work professional bodies, with the incorporation of social work as an academic discipline in Nigerian tertiary institutions (Obeten, Onyenemerem and Mbah, 2020). Although these projects and programmes have the potential to help, the social work curricula are based on Western knowledge and pedagogies (Obeten, 2020). It has been emphasised that social work education and practice in Nigeria still grapple with different challenges as the profession is not recognised by the populace. Obeten (2020) expounds that out of the over 170 tertiary institutions currently established in Nigeria, only 17 of these institutions run social work programmes. These universities include the University of Nigeria, University of Lafia, University of Calabar, University of Lagos, University of Ibadan, University of Benin, and the Federal School of Social Work, Enugu. This has made non-professionals, who lack a fundamental knowledge of the social work profession, to be involved with individuals, families, and communities with different challenges.

Sossou and Yogtiba (2008) expound on children's psycho-social development. They stated that the sub-psycho-social regions of children's growth has been jeopardised by the apparent lack of governmental commitment to resource allocation, law enforcement, and the creation of comprehensive children and family welfare programmes. Although violence against children has been ongoing for a long time, it has currently become a social problem that needs attention and professional intervention from the Nigerian government (Sossou Yogtiba, 2008). Traditionally, police officers have collaborated with social workers to provide social services as part of their duties and responsibilities. A significant portion of community policing involves collaboration between police departments and skilled social workers in preventing and intervening in the social problems and other issues that can affect the peace and safety of the community and its citizens. These social problems can extensively be addressed through the knowledge and understanding of social workers about the challenges facing social workers.

Challenges of Social Work in Nigeria

Social work, compared to other helping professions like medicine, psychiatry, and nursing, is a relatively young profession. Despite its recent development, social work is globally a rapidly growing field. The profession's phenomenal growth and development throughout the world is a clear indication of its contribution to the alleviation of social problems. However, in Nigeria challenges in social work have slowed the development and the practice of the profession. Ngwu (2014) observes that the Federal Ministry of Social Development, Youth and Sports has been making efforts since 1975 to promote social work education and practice in Nigeria. In 1976, the ministry, in its first attempt, gathered social work educators from various institutions where social work was being taught to examine and propose solutions to the challenges of social work education in Nigeria. Ngwu (2014) argues that, despite the frantic efforts of the ministry and the Nigeria Association of Social Workers/Educators, there have been many factors militating against social work education and practice in the country. This includes the lack of awareness/sensitisation of the public about the profession. Obeten et al. (2020) stress the need for the public to be enlightened and acknowledge the relevance of social work in nation-building.

Social work education entails professional training that emphasises and places importance on practice. Therefore, the determination of who goes into the programme and who graduates out of it should be the responsibility of the social work professionals. Lack of funding for social work agencies and insufficient allocations of budget funds for social services departments lead to a scarcity of financial resources, resulting in inadequate office facilities and supplies, which can cause highly problematic recordkeeping and confidentiality. Fund shortage also means inadequate transport and communication facilities, which influence inefficiency in home visits, especially for clients residing in rural areas. Social work is one of the most overworked, underpaid, underrecognised, and stressful professions. The Nigerian government's poor recognition of the profession reflects in the poor allocation of funds to the sector (Alamu, 2022). However, the recent signing of the National Council for Social Work [Establishment] Bill 2022 into law formally legalises social work practice in Nigeria. Social workers face a lot of challenges, including overwhelming caseloads and poor working conditions (Obeten et al., 2020), resulting in many Nigerian social workers, especially those in medical settings, finding it difficult to manage work-related stress, causing frustration and reducing efficiency.

The lack of social work learning/research materials affects social work education and practice in Nigeria. Most of the relevant books and journals are foreign based and deal with problems, policies, and strategies that are alien to students with African backgrounds (Ngwu, 2014). This makes the learning and teaching of social work education difficult in Nigeria. The involvement of non-professionals in the teaching of all the core social work courses in Nigerian tertiary institutions is one of the predominant challenges associated with social work education and practice in Nigeria (Alamu, 2022). This should be discouraged as they do not have the fundamental knowledge of the social work profession and may not impart adequate knowledge to the students (Ngwu, 2014).

Conclusion

Child protection is a critical issue in Nigeria with several challenges that should be addressed. It is imperative that Nigerian social workers' duties and responsibilities be outlined and that policies that do not promote the social work ethics and values be discouraged through teaching and learning in social work education. Moreover, the lack of recognition of the social work profession in Nigeria due to a weak registration system has also contributed to the profession being relegated to the background while other professions, such as medicine, nursing, and the police, take on the roles/duties of a social worker in child protection. It is therefore important that the social work registration system be strengthened.

Recommendations

1. There is a need for accreditation with continued professional development both in learning and in practice.
2. There is a need for awareness of and education about child protection among parents, caregivers, and children on the importance of child protection and the risk associated with child abuse.
3. There is a need for social work education to include case studies and examples from African countries and communities as this will help students understand the unique challenges faced by African families and communities and develop culturally appropriate interventions.

Further Reading

Folami, O. M. (2011). Criminal Exploitation of Children in Contemporary Nigeria. *Social Work Review*, 2(20), 39–49.

Jones, N., Presler-Marshall, E., Cooke, N. and Akinrimisi, B. (2012). *Promoting Synergies between Child Protection and Social Protection in Nigeria*. Centre for Women's Health and Information. Overseas Development Institute. Report to UNICEF. Available at http://bit.ly/social-protection-nigeria.

References

Alamu, O. I. (2022). Challenges of Social Work in Nigeria: A Policy Agenda. *African Journal of Social Work*, 11(3), 116–122.

Aliogo, U. (2020). Nigeria: Domesticating, Enforcing Child Protection Policy in Schools. *This Newspaper*, 25 September 2020.

Arolowo, D. (2010). The Effect of Western Civilisation and Culture on Africa. *Afro Asian Journal of Social Sciences*, 1(1) Quarter, I. V. (2010). ISSN, 2229–5313.

Ayodele, R. B. and Olubayo-Fatiregun, A. A. (2014). Accidental Injuries among Juvenile Hawkers: Clog in the Wheel of Sustainable Socio-Economic Development of a Nation. *Asian Journal of Humanities and Social Studies*, 2(2), 19–30.

Bhanje, S. and Halli, A. (2012). Child Rights in Perspective of Their Development. *Asia Pacific Journal of Management & Entrepreneurship Research*.

Briant, M. (2009). Research Situation Analysis on Orphans and Other Vulnerable Children, Country Brief. *Boston University Centre for Global Health and Development*. Available at https://hdl.handle.net/2144/26992.

Browne, K. D., Hamilton-Giachritsis, C., Johnson, R. and Ostergren, M. (2006). Overuse of Institutional Care for Children in Europe. *BMJ*, 332(7539), 485–487. Available at: https://doi.org/10.1136/bmj.332.7539.485.

Chaudhary, P., Vasabhai, A. A. and Bhagyalaxmi, A. (2014). A Study to Assess and Measure the Breaches in the Child Rights. *Cabidigitallibrary.org*.

Cisneros, A. and Neumann, M. (2009). Finding the Voices of Children and Youth in Street Situations in Rio de Janeiro. *Childhood Today*, 3(2). http://www.childhoodstoday.org/article.php?id=42.

Connelly, G. and Ikpaahindi, S. (2016). Alternative Childcare and Deinstitutionalization: A Case Study of Nigeria. Available at www.celesis.org.

Daniel, B. (2010). Concepts of Adversity, Risk, Vulnerability and Resilience: A Discussion in the Context of the 'Child Protection System'. *Social Policy and Society*, 9(2), pp. 231–241.

Desmond, C., Watt, K., Saha, A., Huang, J. and Lu, C. (2020). Prevalence and Number of Children Living in Institutional Care: Global, Regional, and country's Estimates. *The Lancet Child & Adolescent Health*, 4(5), 370–377.

Diriwari, W. O. (2016). Efficacy of the Legal Frameworks for Child Protection in Nigeria. A thesis submitted for the degree of Doctor of Philosophy by Wilson Ola Diriwari. Department of Politics, History and the Brunel Law School. Brunel University, London.

Duke, E. O. and John, E. O. (2019). A Critical Evaluation of Traditional African Family System and Contemporary Social Welfare. *Nduñòde*, 15(1), 229–236.

Elegbeleye, A. O. (2013). Evaluation of Support Facilities for Institutionalized Orphans in Nigeria. *International Journal of Current Research*, 5(5), 1049–1053.

Farris-Manning, C. and Zandstra, M. (2003). *Children in Care in Canada. A Summary of Current Issues and Trends with Recommendations for Future Research*. Child Welfare League of Canada (CWLC).

Federal Ministry of Women Affairs and Social Development. [Nigeria] (2008). *Key Findings from the Situation Assessment and Analysis on OVC in Nigeria, 2008*. Nigeria: Federal Ministry of Women Affairs and Social Development.

Folami, O. M. (2011). Criminal Exploitation of Children in Contemporary Nigeria. *Social Work Review*, 2(20), 39–49.

Ishaya, A. I., Okolo, S. and Ayuba, Z. (2016). Comparison of the Quality of Life of Vulnerable Children Resident in Household and Those Resident in Institution in Jos Nigeria. *British Journal of Medicine & Medical Research*, 16(8), 1–10.

Joebarth, A. (2014). Children's Rights and Human Trafficking and Responsible Parenthood in West African Country Nigeria. *Journal of Arts and Humanities*, 3(5), 81–88. Available at: https://doi.org/10.18533/journal.v3i5.457.

Jones, N., Presler-Marshall, E., Cooke, N. and Akinrimisi, B. (2012). *Promoting Synergies between Child Protection and Social Protection in Nigeria*. Centre for Women's Health and Information. Overseas Development Institute. Report to UNICEF. Available at http://bit.ly/social-protection-nigeria.

Lachman, P., Poblete, X., Ebigbo, P. O., Nyandiya-Bundy, S., Bundy, R. P., Killian, B. and Doek, J. (2002). Challenges Facing Child Protection. *Child Abuse and Neglect*, 26(6–7), 587–617.

Mokomane, Z. (2012). Social Protection as a Mechanism for Family Protection in Sub-Saharan Africa. *International Journal of Social Welfare*, 22, 248–259.

Mokomane, Z. and Rochat, T. J. (2012). Adoption in South Africa: Trends and Patterns in Social Work Practice. *Child and Family Social Work*, 17(3), 347–358.

Nnama-Okechukwu, C. U. and Okoye, U. O. (2019). Rethinking Institutional Care Using Family-Based Alternative Child Care System for Orphans and Vulnerable Children in Nigeria. *Journal of Social Work in Developing Societies*, 39, 1(3), 39–57.

Nnama-Okechukwu, C. U., Anazonwu, N. P. and Okoye, U. O. (2018). Vulnerable Children, Alternative Care System and Placement Decision in Nigeria: In Who's Best Interests. *African Population Studies*, 32(2), 1–13.

Nwokolu-Nte, M. S. and Onyige, C. D. (2020). Family Welfare: Implications for Child Development in Nigeria. *American Scientific Research Journal for Engineering, Technology, and Sciences*, 67(1), 144–154.

Obeten, U. B., Onyenemerem, N. P. and Mbah, F. (2020). The Challenges of Social Work Practice in Nigeria and Its Implication on National Development. *International Journal of Research in Arts and Social Sciences*, 13(1), 82–89.

Sinani, C. M. (2018). Impact of Western Culture on Traditional African Society: Problems and Prospects. *International Journal of Religion and Human Relations*, 10(1), 56–72.

Sossou, M. A. and Yogtiba, J. A. (2008). Abuse of Children in West Africa: Implications for Social Work Education and Practice. *British Journal of Social Work*, 39(7), 1218–1234.

Wilkinson, J. and Bowyer, S. (2017). *The Impacts of Abuse and Neglect on Children; and Comparison of Different Placement Options: Evidence Review: Research in Practice*. Department for Education.

10
SOCIAL WORK EDUCATION
Opportunities and Challenges in Tanzania, East Africa

Johnas A. Buhori

Abstract: English

This chapter presents a historical overview of social work education in the East Africa region while giving special attention to Tanzania before and after the period of the 1960s. The origin of social work education can be traced from various sources, where it is largely agreed to have been brought by colonialists as one of the means to extend their superiority over African notions of wisdom and knowledge of humanness. As a result, social work education and training replaced African models of living and helping each other. Further, the chapter recognises that social work education is relatively new and still invisible in most of East Africa and, ultimately, in Tanzania. Consequently, the chapter employs narrative methods to inform the findings and discuss the history of social work education and training in East Africa, particularly in Tanzania. Additionally, drawing on various literary sources in the region and Africa, the chapter further identifies numerous opportunities offered by social work education and training. Besides this, the chapter recognises social work education and training challenges. With these in mind, the chapter proposes recommendations to guide transformation and move forward with social work education and training relevant to East Africa, particularly Tanzania.

Abstract: Kiswahili

Sura hii ya elimu ya kazi za kijamii, fursa, na changamoto inawasilisha muhtasari wa kihistoria wa elimu ya kazi za kijamii na mafunzo katika ukanda wa Afrika Mashariki huku ikitoa kipaumbele maalum kwa Tanzania kabla na baada ya kipindi cha miaka ya 1960. Asili ya elimu ya kazi za kijamii inaweza kufuatiliwa kutoka vyanzo mbalimbali, ambapo kwa kiasi kikubwa inakubalika kuwa imeletwa na wakoloni kama ilivyo kwa nchi nyingine, huku wakiamini kuwa elimu na mafunzo yao yalikuwa bora kuliko ya Mwafirka. Matokeo yake, elimu na mafunzo ya kazi za ustawi wa jamii yaliyoletwa na wakoloni, yalichukua nafasi ya mifano ya Kiafrika ya kuishi na kusaidiana. Zaidi ya hayo, sura inatambua kuwa elimu ya kazi za kijamii bado ni mpya na haionekani katika sehemu kubwa ya Afrika Mashariki na hata nchini Tanzania. Kwa hiyo, sura imetumia mbinu za simulizi kupata taarifa na kujadili historia ya elimu na mafunzo ya kazi za kijamii katika Afrika Mashariki, hasa nchini Tanzania. Aidha, kwa kutumia fasihi mbalimbali katika kanda na Afrika, sura hii imebainisha zaidi fursa mbalimbali zinazotolewa na elimu na mafunzo ya kazi za kijamii. Mbali na hayo, sura hii imetambua elimu ya kazi za kijamii na changamoto za mafunzo. Kwa kuzingatia hayo, sura inapendekeza kusonga mbele na elimu ya kazi za kijamii na mafunzo yanayotokana na maarifa na ya Afrika Mashariki, hasa Tanzania.

The Historical Perspective of Social Work Education and Training in Tanzania

The history of social work education and training in Tanzania is presented in two parts: Social Work Education and Training in Tanzania during the Colonial Era; and Social Work Education in the Post-Independence Period. The chapter provides a historical background to social work education in Tanzania from the colonial era to the present while highlighting the opportunities and challenges facing the profession in the country.

Social Work Education and Training in Tanzania during the Colonial Era

The Tanzanian history of social work education and training cannot be separated from the industrial revolution in the 19th century. According to Manyama (2019a), it inevitably forced colonial masters to search for cheap labour and raw materials, and Africa was one place to cater to such needs. The colonials opened large farms and mines to obtain raw materials; on the other hand, these investments demanded cheap labourers (United Republic of Tanzania, 2011). The colonials introduced a head tax to maintain a cheap labour supply without considering its impact on the family's welfare. Since the labourers were supposed to work for longer hours while producing less food for the family, this treatment by colonials led to socioeconomic challenges such as family dysfunction, divorce, prostitution, theft, street children, and alcohol abuse, to list but a few. In response to the identified constraints, the British colonial government introduced probation services; it intended to maintain social order (Manyama, 2019b).

The effectiveness and efficiency of social orders were intended to identify all the lawbreakers punished in a way that led to profit maximisation for the colonial government. The common practice utilised to maintain order was community correctional services (United Republic of Tanzania, 2011). The lawbreakers were assigned specific tasks under supervision while saving their economics' interest (Spitzer, 2019). However, the approach of community services ignored the aspiration of African families; it proved more beneficial to the colonial government. Although, in the eyes of colonialists, the community services reduced congestion and the operation, it forced Africans to spend more time on allocated work than on working to meet the welfare of their families.

Despite knowledge of social welfare among the colonial administrators on the benefits of social workers to address the socioeconomic challenges, they did not invest in social work education and training. However, the emerging social problems due to urbanisation forced the colonial government to enact numerous laws. Enacted laws included the Probation of Offenders Ordinance of 1947, the Maintenance Order of 1949, and the Affiliation Ordinance of 1955. It further built homes for older people and centres for people with leprosy in various locations in Tanzania (United Republic of Tanzania, 2011). However, these laws were enacted while ignoring social work education and training investment. Generally, the colonial government invested in a few elites by imparting secretarial skills that could support the colonial administration (Spitzer, 2019).

Social Work Education and Training in Tanzania – The Post-Independence Period 1961–2020

Even though the colonial government had invested less in social welfare, the formulation of various social laws, as highlighted above, showed the need for social work education and training (Manyama, 2019a). Therefore, it created gaps with the enactment of the laws that obligated the government after independence to invest in social work education and training to get trained social workers to implement the rulings and provide social welfare services accordingly. Owing to this reality, Mabeyo (2014) notes that Tanzania launched the first social work programme in 1973 at the Institute of Social Work, based in the city of Dar es Salaam.

Not only did the colonial governments show less interest in and prioritisation of social welfare services, but also this attitude was retained by African governments after independence, which showed less interest in professionalising both social work training and practice in their countries (Manyama, 2019a). For instance, Tanzania's first social work programme was born on hired premises in Dar es Salaam (Manyama, 2019b). The generous funds of Canadians supported the initiative to establish social work education and training. They developed the curriculum, taught it, and provided the teaching tools that were used for over a decade.

Despite the support and collaboration from the Canadians, social work education in Tanzania, particularly at the Institute of Social Work, did not utilise the readily available opportunities to advance social work education and training (Association of Schools of Social Work in Tanzania, 2021). The Institute continued offering social work certificates and ordinary diplomas until 1977 when it launched an advanced social work diploma. For all this time, the Institute remained the sole training and education provider for social work education (Manyama, 2019a). Aside from the support received from the Canadians in terms of human resources and finances, the Institute could not develop bachelor's and master's programmes. On the same note, social work education and training in Tanzania had to wait for more than twenty years before the Institute launched a bachelor's programme in 2006 (Association of Schools of Social Work in Tanzania, 2020).

Due to dependence on the resources of Canadians in terms of manpower and finances, the Institute could not develop a master's programme. Not having social workers at an advanced level had a negative impact on social work education and practice (Association of Schools of Social Work, 2020). Some social workers who aspired to advance academically had to pursue a non-social work programme at the master's level; for the few who could afford to meet the cost, they travelled to Zambia and Britain (Mabeyo, 2014). Seeing the knowledge gap, the Open University of Tanzania, launched the first masters degree in social work in 2009. The efforts and initiative to establish a social work programme at this level were supported not only with funds but also with the technical support of the American people. The Institute of Social Workers had to wait until 2014 when it launched its own masters. This achievement deserves to be cherished around social work education and training in Tanzania. The launch of the master's degree programme at the Open University opened the learning doors for social work education and training in Tanzania (Association of Schools of Social Work, 2021). It allowed young social work educators who could not afford to pay the cost of studying outside of Tanzania to meet their desire to earn a qualification at the advanced level. The Institute of Social Work, the University of Dar es Salaam, and the Open University of Tanzania are the only public schools that offer social work education and training in Tanzania and are based in the city of Dar es Salaam, which is the focus of this study. In a nutshell, it can be argued that social work education and training in Tanzania is still influenced by the content not only from Canada but also from the United States of America.

Commenting on the development of social work education and training in Tanzania, the Association of Schools of Social Work in Tanzania (ASSWOT, 2021) revealed that despite the University of Dar es Salaam being the old hub of education in Tanzania, social work education was never given an opportunity of being taught. All other disciplines, such as sociology and development studies, were prioritised at the expense of social work. It was not until 2015 that the social work bachelor's programme was launched. The programme started with only three employees, while others were part-time lecturers from other social work schools. Further, the University of Dar es Salaam has still not launched a master's programme for social work.

Additionally, the ASSWOT (2020) of other schools based in Dar es Salaam offering social work education and training are Hubert Kairuku Memorial University (HKMU) and Kampala International University (KIU), both are private entities. The HKMU was established in 1997, while social work education and training in the bachelor's programme were launched in 2014. Further, KIU was established in 2009, and the same year social work education and training were founded, with a lot of content drawn from Uganda's programmes. To ensure that the content reflected Tanzanian context, the Association of Schools of Social Work in Tanzania (ASSWOT) had to work collaboratively with the Tanzania Commission for Universities to make the curriculum reflect local conditions. The summary of social work education and training is presented below. Table 10.1 indicates the social work training institutions based in Dar es Salaam, the time when each university started, and when social work programmes at the bachelor's and master's levels were launched (ASSWOT, 2021).

Opportunities for Social Work Education in Tanzania

The following are identified opportunities for social work education and training in Tanzania.

Number of Universities in the Region

It is important to understand, as Manyama (2019a) reveals, that Tanzania is still challenged by deep-rooted socioeconomic constraints, which include poverty, injustice, high prevalence of HIV/AIDS infection, drug use and substance abuse, prostitution, child violence and abuse, and increased matrimonial conflicts, to list but a few, which demands the presence of social workers (Mabeyo, 2014). However, the available social work universities have no capacity to produce enough social workers to lead the process of transformation among the needy, vulnerable, and marginalised populations (ASSWOT, 2020). The limited number of social work universities in the region presents a significant constraint on the need to have qualified trainers in various schools of social work in the country. In the case of Tanzania, with a population of more than 50 million, it depends on only eight universities that have social work education courses, with more than 50 universities in the country (ASSWOT, 2021).

Fostering Indigenous Knowledge through Research

Highlighting measures that social work educators must take to overcome the dependence on Western social work literature, Baynesagn et al. (2021) note that the true liberation of Africans has to begin with having their own locally produced social work literature, which has the content and carries the aspirations of Africans. This offers the opportunity for all social work educators

Table 10.1 Development of Social Work Education and Training in Tanzania

	Social Work School	*School Est.*	*BSW Est.*	*MSW Est.*
1	University of Dar es Salaam	1970	2015	None
2	Institute of Social Work	1973	2006	2014
3	The Open University of Tanzania	1992	2008	2008
4	Hubert Kairuki Memorial University	1997	2014	2014
5	Kampala International University	2009	2009	None

Source: Association of Schools of Social Work Report, 2021

to begin researching the appropriate techniques and methods that can be adopted to inform social work education. By conducting research, it can generate Tanzanian knowledge, and harnessed evidence appropriate and relevant for the indigenous people can be documented and shared widely with social work educators.

As pointed out by Mabeyo et al. (2019), there is a very useful model in Tanzania. When used it can be very effective in addressing individual, family, and community socioeconomic problems. One such well-known model, commonly practiced in the Kilimanjaro region, northern Tanzania, is known as Msaragambo. This model normally sets a platform for elders to meet in the evening. During the meeting, the social-economic challenges confronting the community are identified and a solution is anonymously proposed for implementation. The elders must lead the process by revisiting the history of when a similar problem was tabled; this is done to assess the credibility of the intervention used. In case of a new emerging challenge, the slogan that is popularly followed is known as *the voice of elders is the voice of God*. They gather different opinions and views from each other and come up with advantages and disadvantages of each of the proposed interventions. From this understanding, for instance, the Msaragambo model has been very effective in resolving not only family disputes but also land conflicts.

Additionally, Mabeyo et al. (2019) note that the Msaragambo model is drawn from indigenous knowledge. It is acceptable and credible in managing natural resources such as water. The water source is treated as community property, no community member is allowed to make personal use of the water bodies. This approach has helped the region not to experience any shortage of water, even though the water passages are just locally dug waterways. Further, the model is useful in maintaining peace and reducing matrimonial conflicts and infidelity, as with it, no child is considered an illegitimate child among Changa tribesmen. Moreover, the utilisation of this model has fuelled the development of the region. The elders use it to mobilise community members to actively participate in community development activities, such as the construction of community infrastructure, including roads, waterways, and schools.

Despite the evident socioeconomic changes globally that have negatively affected the family and community involvement in child rearing, Mabeyo and Kiwelu (2019) note that the model of seeing a child as belonging to the community is still useful and deserves to be cherished for the protection and welfare of children. The equality among children at the family level has helped to reduce the need for orphanages in Tanzania. The model of oneness among the community members has helped to resolve problems while providing protection for children and treating them equally. An elderly person who was allowed to punish a child that has committed a mistake. With this model, children not only have the right to be protected but also they have a responsibility to observe respect for their elders and all community members.

Acquiring Competences for Social Work Curricular Development

Social work education and training in Africa have evolved and developed from the influence of colonial masters or other Westerners (Mwansa, 2010). The influence of Western social work education, which took less consideration of African aspirations and indigenous knowledge, was made superior to local beliefs and made relevant to the context of Africa (Wairire, 2014). However, this approach has failed to address the social-economic challenges confronting Africans in general; the problems of Africans demand their own indigenous knowledge to inform effective interventions and proposed solutions (Mupedziswa and Sinkamba, 2014). While suggesting a solution to the current social work education and training based on Western models, Mupedziswa (2001) notes that there is nothing wrong in adopting their content; however, upon careful research into relevant

African knowledge and aspirations, these have to be included in the curriculum to inform social work interventions.

Moreover, in the context of Tanzania, Manyama (2019a) and Mabeyo (2014) have noted the influence of Canadian social work educators who supported the inception and development of social work in Tanzania. Due to their power, social work curriculum development largely has continued to inherit Canadian social work education. However, this is an opportunity for social work educators and trainers in Tanzania to use available local resources, including finances, to develop their own curriculum, which considers significant, priority issues that matter for the nation. Investment in human resources has to be done while considering trainers and educators with commitments so that, after acquiring the said competencies, they can make good use of them. This investment should be spearheaded by social work professional organisations such as the Association of Schools of Social Work in Tanzania (ASSWOT), the Tanzania Social Workers Association (TASWO), and the government of Tanzania.

Employment Opportunities for Social Work Educators

Africa is still confronted with structural challenges, poverty, unemployment, and exploitation; these challenges cannot be dealt with and addressed using a single intervention (Mabeyo, 2014; Kaseke, 2001). Apart from using direct or indirect interventions, the identified challenges may demand a consolidated or multi-intervention approach drawing on both indigenous knowledge and Western theories (Kaseke, 2001; Resnick, 1995; Midgeley and Toors, 1992). Approaches and interventions that have to be researched to establish their relevancy and applicability can be considered as an opportunity for employment opportunity.

Few universities in Africa offer social work education, which results in a limited number of qualified social work educators. To deal with this shortage, many of these universities recruit part-time educators, who are mostly not qualified due to the low wages set for remuneration (Mupedziswa 2001). This is the reality in many universities in Tanzania; for instance, as the ASSWOT Report (2021) indicates, the University of Dar es Salaam has only three employees to run the social work programme while others are part-time instructors. Due to little awareness and less priority given by decision makers to social work education, it takes time to train enough qualified educators. However, this can be dealt with by considering bringing on board faculty members from other fields, such as health, development studies, psychology, and law. These disciplines offer courses that are central to social work education. Some of the courses such as health, development studies, and psychology using evidence-based practices, have adopted some indigenous knowledge during their interventions. For instance, the village community bank has helped women and poor families to reduce the severity of poverty and household levels; the use of local herbs as first aid to slow down snake poison.

Indicating unexplored opportunities for employment among social workers and educators, Spitzer and Twikirize (2014b) reveal that, due to limited knowledge of social work education and practice, many employees, such as social welfare organisations and non-government organisations, in most cases prefer to employ graduates from sociology or counselling and guidance for social work-related jobs. It is, therefore, the role of social work educators to advocate and educate employees on the skills needed to hire a social worker in relation to other preferred fields. By doing this, social workers can be employed and occupy positions that were wrongly taken by other fields.

Considering the population of the East Africa region and the emerging regional socioeconomic challenges, social workers are in high demand. However, Spitzer et al. (2014b) note that the area has no single university offering a PhD programme, which creates an opportunity for knowledge and awareness of social work education. Further, the introduction of a PhD programme in the region can create employment opportunities for social work educators and young researchers. Hence, social work educators must capitalise on the available options.

It is also important to note, as Spitzer Twikirize (2014b) point out, that there is an increasing amount of locally based literature on social work education and training in Africa in general. However, Mupedziswa (2001) s that, due to limited resources needed for publication, much of this literature is not published despite the knowledge and value it has. Further, Spitzer and Twikirize (2014b) and Mupedziswa (2001) opine that publishing should be seen as an opportunity among social work educators. They must organise themselves, where possible, and establish small firms that can charge reasonable prices for any social work literature that needs to be published or printed.

Challenges Facing Social Work Education and Training in Tanzania

This section covers the challenges facing social work in Africa while giving specific attention to East Africa and Tanzania in particular. Several references have been utilised to identify the challenges, for instance, Ajuwon (2022), Association of Schools of Social Work in Tanzania Reports (2017 2021 2020), Spitzer (2019), Twikirize and Spitzer (2019), Manyama (2019b), United Republic of Tanzania (2019), Mupedziswa and Sinkamba (2014), Mabeyo, 2014, Kreitzer (2012), and Sewpaul and Lombard (2004), to list but a few. More details are presented below.

The Existence of Social Work Education and Practice without a Regulatory Organ

This is an issue of concern as in Africa generally it is only in Ghana, South Africa, Zimbabwe, and, recently, Nigeria where social work education and practice are regulated by a council (Kreitzer, 2012); Mupedziswa and Sinkamba (2014); and Ajuwon, (2022). A remarkable recognition of social work education has been noted recently in Nigeria, where His Excellency President Buhari allowed the social worker's bill to be presented before the Parliament (Ajuwon, 2022). These developments and recognition of social work education in the listed countries are contrary to conditions in East Africa, as observed by Spitzer (2019), who notes that in all countries in the region, namely, Burundi, Rwanda, Uganda, Kenya, and Tanzania, social work education is not yet regulated by government authorities; rather, it is the purview of the National Association for Social Workers in each country. These national associations, however, cannot regulate professional practices, as Twikirize et al. (2014) observe. It is for this reason; therefore, that the term 'social work' is not protected as it is often abused or allows any social service provider to be called so. Additionally, social work education, in the context of East Africa and Tanzania in particular, is confronted with a lack of regulatory organs, which ultimately can lead to a violation of the rights of service recipients as there is no regulatory mechanism to protect the rights of service providers and service beneficiaries.

Little Recognition of Social Workers by the Government and Others

Social work education and practice have continued to experience little recognition among other fields of human service. This is exacerbated by the recognition of other disciplines to provide social welfare services (Spitzer, 2019). For instance, in Tanzania, the government under the scheme of services provides an open space for any person categorised as social welfare to compete with social workers for any available employment opportunity (URT, 2019). It is these practices that are enforced by the social welfare scheme of services that perpetuate the recognition and visibility of social work education and practice in Tanzania. Adding on, ASSWOT Report (2021) notes that allowing just any social scientists to provide social welfare services compromises the quality of services provided to vulnerable groups, as it is difficult to set standards as to the quality of services to be provided as the open space gives a mandate to the wider workforce to use their own intervention as per their trained field. Due to the open space approach in Tanzania, when it comes to social work education and practice social work training is not given the recognition that is granted to other fields of study.

Social Work Education Housed under Other Departments

Consequently, social work education is still one of the new programmes in many universities in East Africa. Due to increasing awareness of the impact it has on people in the region, many universities have introduced social work education (Manyama, 2019b). Despite the good intention of establishing a program, very few universities have qualified social work educators and relevant literature to impart the required knowledge while applying social work-related scenarios or cases (Spitzer, 2019). As Sewpaul and Lombard (2004) note, social work education is often housed in other departments while department members other than social work educators are employed to teach social work education. In the context of Tanzania, this is the reality as in many universities, social work is still housed under the Department of Sociology and Anthropology; headed by one of the department members who does not possess social work training. In most cases, social work is taught by department members with a background in sociology, anthropology, or community development. This approach at the universities has trickled down to the policymaker, at the ministry and department levels, where social work education and practice is treated as any other social sciences discipline.

The Scheme of Service and Workers' Development

In the context of Tanzania, all matters related to recruitment, retention, and development of public servants are under the Ministry of State, housed in the President's Office for Public Service Management and Good Governance. The ministry, using the scheme of service and workers development, has categories of social work practitioners under the social welfare workforce. The social welfare categorisation includes Social Work, Sociology, Anthropology, Social Policy, Child Protection, Early Childhood Development, Divinity, and Psychology to list but a few (URT, 2019). This approach of treating social work education and practice just like other fields imposes challenges on the visibility of social work education in Tanzania. Due to this treatment of the government of Tanzania, Spitzer (2019) reveals that social work practice in Tanzania can be carried out by anyone, including a layperson. Challenges such as this water down not only the quality of social work education but also the delivery of social work services as the ethical considerations during service delivery are hardly observed.

Social Work Field Practicum

Commenting on the significance of field practice in the context of social work education, its significance cannot be overemphasised as it contributes equally to classroom-based teaching and assessment. However, as Wairire (2014) notes that, due to curriculum structure, administration, governance of resources, lack of standardisation, and poor quality control, social work education has not managed to help students put the acquired knowledge and skills into practice. The field practice is encumbered with such constraints, which exposes social work education to vulnerability. In the context of Tanzania, as reported by the ASSWOT (2017), where ASSWOT, with the support of the American Health Alliance (AIHA), developed a minimum standard for field practice at certificate, diploma, bachelor's, and master's degree levels, respectively, they are not used accordingly. AIHA was an American-based organisation that had a role in strengthening the social welfare structure in Tanzania. Further, the organisation supported the government in developing social welfare policies, procedures, and guidelines. It is on this basis that the existing gap in social work education was supported and addressed. In some cases, universities have developed their own logbooks, which are used across all social sciences courses, and social work students are obliged to use the same logbook just like others.

Poor Working Environment among Social Workers

The African Child Policy Forum (2016) points out that for any profession to have young people who aspire later to advance their education, depends on the existing working environment among its graduates or employees. Social workers in Tanzania are among other employees who have a poor working environment as they lack basic working facilities, such as furniture, stationery, lockable shelves, and a private room to conduct counselling for their clients. Under these conditions, young people considering choices of career find it hard to consider social work education at the tertiary level. Faced with these challenges, only the most determined succeed, while some are not informed of the challenges ahead of them.

Conflicts of Interest between Social Workers and Community Development Officers

The African Child Policy Forum (2016) notes that community development officers have offices at ward levels all over Tanzania, while social welfare officers, where social workers fall, have their offices at district levels. Hence, most social welfare tasks at ward levels are executed by the community development office since they are the only ones available at these levels. Regardless of the way they carry out their work around individual or group work, there is no social welfare office to do it otherwise. Further, it is worth noting that several programmes that deal with women and children have recognised that either social welfare or community development officers coordinate such activities, which to a large extent are supported by donors. There are no conflicts between these programmes when there are no donors supporting them. The problem arises when there is a donor providing incentives. Most of the time, it leads to constant conflicts between them. Though the Child Law of 2009 recognises that social welfare officers execute all matters affecting children, the Department of Community Development uses its power to suppress the social work training and guidelines in the country as the results affect social welfare workers who are the custodians of child welfare in the country. The identified challenge of this conflict of interest has contributed to a large extent to denying social work education and training its visibility, which could serve to attract the younger generation as it does for other disciplines.

Frequent Transfer of Social Welfare Services from One Ministry to Another

Manyama (2019b) opines that there is still a problem of political will in realising the contribution of social work education in addressing available social problems. The government has not yet recognised that existing social problems can be dealt with by social workers (United Republic of Tanzania, 2019). Instead, social welfare services have never been concentrated in one ministry, as it is constantly transferred from one ministry to another. For instance, it has been transferred to more than ten ministries; and it is currently hidden within the Ministry of Community Development, Gender and Special Groups, where the phrase 'social welfare service' is not indicated in the name of the ministry (United Republic of Tanzania, 2011). With this shortcoming, it is not easy for the same ministry to advance the promulgation of the regulatory organ or law to oversee the social welfare service. Given this scenario, it is obvious that such efforts are in vain and prove unsuccessful. Despite the identified challenges, socialworkers still strive to provide quality social welfare services to vulnerable and marginalised individuals.

Social Work Organisations in Tanzania

The establishment of social work organisations to oversee the development of social work education, including the establishment of the programme at each university, development of social work curriculum, recruitment of social work educators, and coordination and supervision of field practice, are important and have to be treated very seriously to ensure the quality of social work education in any country in East Africa (Twikirize and Spitzer, 2019). However, Spitzer and Twikirize (2014b) note that all countries in the region have such organisations to oversee the education and training of social workers. In a few cases, where these organisations of social work educators exist, they have no teeth to make them effective (Twikirize, 2014b). In Tanzania, for instance, with the funds provided by American donors, a programme called Tanzania Emerging Schools of Social Work Education Programme (TESWEP) was established, which to a large extent helped to develop social work competencies and sponsored at least ten faculty members to undertake social work training at master's degree level at the Open University of Tanzania in 2014. Despite the financial support in paying tuition fees and funding supplies, some faculty members have not completed their studies and still teach social work education (ASSWOT, 2017). In a context where the available social organisation has no power to sanction or regulate its members, it creates a vacuum for malpractice to take place, among other effects.

Additionally, ASSWOT (2017) reveals that efforts were made to move from an educational programme of TESWEP that had no mandate to make decisions as it was operating under the Tanzania Association of Social Workers (TASWO). In 2016, the Association of Schools of Social Work in Tanzania (ASSWOT) was registered under the Ministry of Home Affairs. Its primary objective is to uphold accountability in all universities/training institutions offering social work and, while not lessening the international standard, to draw on indigenous knowledge to inform Tanzanian social work.

Conclusion

The chapter has shown that social work education and training in East Africa, as in other parts of Africa, were brought by colonialists. Their intentions were to use education to suppress the indigenous knowledge of Africans, which they considered constituted a threat to them. The weaknesses and shortcomings of Western social work education, which is focused on curative and remedial approaches, need to be replaced with African regional relevant and appropriate knowledge of social work.

Further, the development of social work curricula in East Africa has been highly influenced by colonialists such as the British and French. In Tanzania, the Canadians strongly influenced the curriculum with a focus that was appropriate to them. It is therefore time for social work educators to strive to adopt what is relevant for the country in replacing Western dominante thinking. Further, the development of new curricula should consider the available research on models and indigenous knowledge that is relevant to African conditions.

Recommendations

1. The Tanzania Commission for Universities in collaboration with the Association of Schools of Social Work in Tanzania (ASSWOT) and the Tanzania Social Workers Organisation (TASW) must make sure all educators and trainers in social work education have relevant qualifications.
2. Social work education has to be supported in all universities in Tanzania by having a flagged department.
3. The government of Tanzania must show the political will to support the recognition of social work education by allowing the promulgation of the regulatory organ.

Further Reading

Mabeyo, Z.M. (2014). The Development of Social Work Education and Practice in Tanzania. In H. Spitzer, J.M. Twikirize, and G.G. Wairire (eds.) *Professional Social Work in East Africa: Towards Social Development, Poverty Reduction and Gender Equality*, 121–135. Kampala, Uganda: Fountain.

Manyama, W. (2019b). *Social Work, Social Policy Process and Practice: Tanzania's Perspective*. Dar es Salaam – Tanzania: The Institute of Social Work.

Spitzer, H. (2019). Social Work in East Africa: A Mzungu Perspective. *International Social Work*, 62(2), 567–580. DOI: 10.1177/0020872817742696.

Twikirize, J.M. (2014a). Indigenisation of Social Work in Africa: Debates, Prospects, and Challenges. In H. Spitzer, J.M. Twikirize, and G.G. Wairire (eds.) *Professional Social Work in East Africa: Towards Social Development, Poverty Reduction and Gender Equality*, 75–90. Kampala, Uganda: Fountain.

References

Ajuwon, T. (2022). Group Hails Buhari over Assent to Social Workers' Bill. Online. Available from https://gazettengr.com/group-hails-buhari-over-assent-to-social-workers-bill/ [accessed 26 March 2023].

Association of Schools of Social Work in Tanzania (ASSWOT) (2017). *Social Work Education, Progress and Challenge: Annual Report*. Dar es Salaam – Tanzania: Association of Schools of Social Work in Tanzania (ASSWOT).

Association of Schools of Social Work in Tanzania (ASSWOT) (2020). *Social Work Education, Progress and Challenge: Annual Report*. Dar es Salaam – Tanzania: Association of Schools of Social Work in Tanzania (ASSWOT).

Association of Schools of Social Work in Tanzania (ASSWOT) (2021). *Social Work Education, Progress and Challenge: Annual Report*. Dar es Salaam – Tanzania: Association of Schools of Social Work in Tanzania (ASSWOT).

Kreitzer, L. (2012). *Social Work in Africa: Exploring Culturally Relevant Education and Practice in Ghana*. The University of Calgary Press. PRISM: University of Calgary's Digital Repository.

Mabeyo, Z.M. and Kiwelu, A. (2019). Indigenous and Innovative Models of Problem Solving in Tanzania: Strengths and Obstacles for Their Adoption. In J.M. Twikirize and H. Spitzer (eds.) *Social Work Practice in Africa: Indigenous and Innovative Approaches*, 95–110. Fountain Publishers. https://doi.org/10.2307/j.ctv2tp73vt.12.

Mabeyo, Z.M., Mvungi, A.K. and Manyama, W. (2019). Community Organising in Tanzania: Learning from the Msaragambo Model in Kilimanjaro Region. In J.M. Twikirize and H. Spitzer (eds.) *Social Work Practice in Africa: Indigenous and Innovative Approaches*. Kampala: Fountain Publishers.

Manyama, W. (2019a). *Social Welfare Services, Political Ideologies and Economic Development in Tanzania: Past, Present and Future*. Dar es Salaam – Tanzania: The Institute of Social Work.

Manyama, W. (2019b). *Social Work, Social Policy Process and Practice: Tanzania's Perspective*. Dar es Salaam – Tanzania: The Institute of Social Work.

Mwansa, L.K.J. (2010). Challenges Facing Social Work Education in Africa. *International Social Work*, 53(1), 129–136.

Mupedziswa, R. (2001). The Quest for Relevance towards a Conceptual Model of Development Social Work Education and Training in Africa. *International Social Work*, 44(3), 285–300.

Mupedziswa, R. and Sinkamba, R.P. (2014). *Social Work Education and Training in Southern and East Africa: Yesterday, Today and Tomorrow*. Routledge Handbooks.

Sewpaul, V. and Lombard, A. (2004). Social Work Education, Training, and Standards in Africa. *Social Work Education*, 23(5), 537–554.

Spitzer, H. (2019). Social Work in East Africa: A Mzungu Perspective. *International Social Work*, 62(2), 567–580.

Spitzer, H. and Twikirize, J.M. (2014b). Breaking New Grounds: Conceptual and Methodological Framework of a Regional Research Project. In H. Spitzer, J.M. Twikirize, and G.G. Wairire (eds.) *Professional Social Work in East Africa: Towards Social Development, Poverty Reduction and Gender Equality*, 175–188. Kampala, Uganda: Fountain.

Resnick, R.S. (1995). South America. In T.D. Watts, D. Elliot, and N.S. Mayadas (eds.) *Handbook of Social Work Education*
, 65–85. Westpoint, CT: Greenwood.

Twikirize, J.M. (2014b). Social Work Education and Practice in Uganda: A Historical Perspective. In H. Spitzer, J.M. Twikirize, and G.G. Wairire (eds.) *Professional Social Work in East Africa: Towards Social Development, Poverty Reduction and Gender Equality*, 136–148. Kampala, Uganda: Fountain.

Twikirize, J.M. and Spitzer, H. (2019). Indigenous and Innovative Social Work Practice: Evidence from East Africa. In J. M. Spitzer (ed.) *Social Work Practice in Africa Indigenous and Innovative Approaches*, 1–19. Kampala: Fountain Publishers.

Twikirize, J.M., Spitzer, H., Wairire, G.G., Mabeyo, Z.M. and Rutikanga, C. (2014). Professional Social Work in East Africa: Empirical Evidence. In H. Spitzer, J.M. Twikirize, and G.G. Wairire (eds.) *Professional Social Work in East Africa: Towards Social Development, Poverty Reduction and Gender Equality*
, 189–216. Kampala, Uganda: Fountain.

The African Child Policy Forum (2016). *Implementing Child Rights in Tanzania: What Is Working Well, What Is Not? Background Paper to the African Report on Child Wellbeing 2016*. Addis Ababa: The African Child Policy Forum (ACPF). Online. Available from https://www.africanchild.report/images/Implementing-Child- Rights-in-Tanzania-final-13-10-16.pdf [accessed 26 April 2022].

United Republic of Tanzania (URT) (2011). *Hali ya Afya na Ustawi wa Jamii katika Miaka ya Uhuru (1961–2011)*. Dar es Salam: Ministry of Health. Jambo Concepts Tanzania Limited.

United Republic of Tanzania (URT) (2019). *The Scheme of Service and Development of Social Welfare Officers in Tanzania*. Ministry of State in the President's Office for Public Services Management and Good Governance.

Wairire, G. (2014). The State of Social Work Education and Practice in Kenya. In H. Spitzer, J. Twikirize, and G. Wairire (eds.) *Professional Social Work in East Africa: Towards Social Development, Poverty Reduction and Gender Equality*, 93–107. Kampala: Fountain Publishers.

11
ADVANCING SOCIAL WORK EDUCATION USING ONLINE LEARNING IN SOUTH AFRICA

Challenges and Prospects

Ntandoyenkosi Maphosa and Mziwandile Sobantu

Abstract: English

The impact of COVID-19 on higher education institutions has been unprecedented. For the first time in the history of social work education in South Africa, some institutions had to teach social work using online platforms during the COVID-19 lockdowns. In this chapter, the authors used secondary literature and shared their experiences as social work educators at a higher education institution in Johannesburg, South Africa. This chapter is aimed at discussing how this institution adapted to online learning space in response to the teaching and learning challenges occasioned by the COVID-19 pandemic. It is germane to note that the responses of South African higher education institutions to COVID-19 were varied and limited in some ways, owing to the social and economic circumstances pertaining in Africa and in South Africa. The institutions assumed the additional responsibility of ensuring participation, inclusion, and fair treatment of their students during online teaching and learning sessions. This was in line with the profession's principle of social justice, which the authors also used as a theoretical framework for this chapter. In conclusion, the authors provide recommendations on how higher education institutions could improve their adaptability to eventualities such as COVID-19.

Introduction

Almost all South African higher education institutions (HEIs) offer traditional teaching and learning through contact classes. With the advancement of technology and the Fourth Industrial Revolution (4IR), several HEIs had been gravitating towards blended learning, which involved combining traditional and virtual approaches to learning and teaching, even before the advent of the Coronavirus (COVID-19). With the emergence of COVID-19 in March 2020, these institutions were forced to abruptly adopt online learning methods because of the pandemic and accompanying lockdowns that were aimed at containing the spread of the disease (Ogunode et al., 2021). The COVID-19 pandemic and the subsequent lockdown restrictions had a huge impact on the global higher education sector, and social work education was not exempt (Lischer et al., 2021). Social work education providers had to adapt to using online learning platforms quickly, although these are very complex to implement, particularly for internship programmes that include classes, fieldwork practicums and supervision (McFadden et al., 2020; Tanga et al., 2020). The social work curriculum followed at the institution of focus in this chapter comprises well-structured building blocks that are not easily implementable through distance and online learning; therefore, the transition to online learning posed numerous challenges to both staff and students (Lischer et al., 2021). McLaughlin et al. (2020) liken the sudden unprecedented shift to online learning to a tsunami because of its widespread, sudden, and severe global impact on teaching and learning. In their response, most social work education institutions (including the one at which the authors are based in Johannesburg, South Africa) and educators were reactive in providing educational and support services to students within a very short time. This support was often inadequate and less coordinated at many institutions, as indicated by Tanga et al. (2020).

Using the social justice perspective, this chapter explores how ready and adaptable was social work education to the demands of online learning during COVID-19 in South Africa. Secondary data (literature on COVID-19 and social work education), as well as the experiences of the authors as social work educators at a HEI in South Africa, were used. The chapter first provides a brief background to social work education and practice in South Africa, and Africa more generally, and acknowledges the challenges that arose for social work education because of COVID-19. It should be borne in mind that South Africa is a developing nation that has been contending with high rates of inequality and poverty, which have impacted the preparedness of this institution and others in the country to fully embrace online learning and advance social work education under circumstances such as the COVID-19 pandemic. Next, social justice is discussed as a theoretical lens that is employed in this chapter. The various challenges that arose from COVID-19 are also discussed as well as the support mechanisms that were extended to students particularly by this institution of focus. The chapter ends by discussing the lessons that were learnt and by providing recommendations and conclusions.

Social Work Education in South Africa

The history of social work education in Africa can be traced back to the 1960s. This is the time when several countries on the continent were implementing decolonisation. Social work education and practice were mostly facilitated by European missionaries, and they largely buttressed colonial apartheid interests in South Africa (Mamphiswana and Noyoo, 2000). The social work curricula in the first social work training institutions established in Africa were framed like those at European universities. For example, social work students at the Higher Education Institute of Social Work in Cairo (established in 1940) were taught by academics and staff from the United States of America and the United Kingdom (Hamido, 2003 in Veta and McLaughlin, 2022). Thus, Western epistemologies were embedded in these curricula and influenced practice that was not expected to tackle social problems, but rather just to 'remedy [those] social problems that would obstruct their administration's wealth creation' in Lesotho (Veta and McLaughlin, 2022, p.3). Social work education institutions in South Africa have existed since the 1930s, according to Gray and Mazibuko (2002), with the professional practice dating back to the 1920s (in response to white poverty) (Drower, 2002).

The post-colonial and apartheid socioeconomic challenges are numerous and require transformed social work education that will equip graduates to address these problems adequately, in line with the nation-building and social development agendas in the case of South Africa. Social work is a practice-based profession and an academic discipline that promotes social change and development, social cohesion, and the empowerment of people and communities.

Principles of social justice, human rights, collective responsibility, and respect for diversity are central to social work. Underpinned by the theories of social work, social sciences, humanities, and indigenous knowledge, 'social work engages people and structures to address life challenges and enhance wellbeing' (International Association of Schools of Social Work [IASSW], 2014, p. 2). The global definition of social work explains the mandate of the profession as one of helping, with a focus on social justice and addressing the needs, particularly of the vulnerable populations in various communities. Relevant context-based approaches are employed to make social work interventions dynamic, relevant, and thus responsive to local cultures and challenges (Turton and Schmid, 2020). South Africa embraces the developmental social welfare approach to providing social welfare services. As articulated in Patel (2015, p. 127), this approach involves employing appropriate skills and values to enhance the wellbeing of individuals, families, and groups. It is meant to respond to the country's unique history of colonialisation and apartheid, which violated human rights and deepened racial inequality and poverty. Therefore, social workers are required to practice developmental social work by drawing on a range of theories to assess, intervene, and continuously evaluate the services that are rendered to clients. These theories stress the interconnectedness and the complexity of human problems, life situations, and social conditions (Patel, 2015).

Compared to some other countries in Africa, social work practice and education in South Africa enjoy high recognition as a profession, and formalised statutory bodies and policies are enacted to support the profession. According to the South African Council for Social Services Professions (SACSSP, 2023), South Africa has 16 universities and two colleges that offer social work training. The University of Johannesburg and the University of the Witwatersrand are but two of these, both located in Johannesburg. In addition to having an urban location, these two institutions enjoy better infrastructure and financial wherewithal because of their historical privilege as historically White universities (HWUs) compared to the historically Black universities (HBUs), which were also referred to as 'bush' or 'rural' universities (Mamphiswana and Noyoo, 2000). The authors are based in the social work department at one of the two universities.

Social work education in South Africa is framed towards providing social workers with the relevant skills and knowledge they require to address historical social and economic injustice (Mamphiswana and Noyoo, 2000). Social work students are prepared for practice through fieldwork practicums or internship placements at agencies where they could work with actual clients and practice all the methods of social work before they qualify as social workers (Zvomuya, 2021). The core of social work training in a four-year programme includes field placements, theory, and a minor research component for final year students.

Social work education needs to mirror an inclusive developmental social welfare system that promises to cater to all citizens in a democratic way, particularly in South Africa, given its previously racialised welfare system (Mamphiswana and Noyoo, 2000). SACSSP regulates, conducts quality checks, and exercises general authority on all matters relating to social work education and training in the country (SACSSP, 2022). It also benchmarks these standards against international expectations for social work education and training. Thus, social work education institutions are required to be meticulous in providing training to social workers who will render services effectively locally or internationally after graduation. Countries in the Global South face serious structural challenges related to poverty, unemployment, and inequality, which perpetuate gender-based violence (GBV) and other related social ills and crimes. Thus, social workers and the profession in these contexts are more often challenged to demonstrate and validate their relevance in the face of these complex interrelated problems (Gray and Mazibuko, 2002). This became more evident during the COVID-19 pandemic when both social work education and practice had to contend with unprecedented problems, such as gender-based violence (GBV), child abuse, loss of income, and related psychosocial stressors.

All HEIs that offer the Bachelor of Social Work (BSW) qualification in South Africa have internship programmes. Field placements are a central component because students interact with clients under the supervision of a qualified social worker. Herein, they are expected to integrate values, skills, methods, and theoretical knowledge learnt in the classroom into their social work practice. More importantly, the students appreciate, and practice ethics and techniques learnt from theory and internship classes. Due to the lockdowns during COVID-19, multiple adjustments were implemented by educators involved in internship programmes at this institution of focus, such as block placements instead of year-long placements. Thus, students went to their field placements only when lockdown levels were less restrictive. Community work practicums were extremely difficult because of the related community processes, most of which involved tasks undertaken by various task teams over a much longer time. While universities managed to negotiate the lockdowns to various extents, some internship programmes at this institution were even extended to the following year to allow students to make up for time lost during the COVID-19 lockdowns.

The upside of this was that social work educators were forced to be creative and innovative in their teaching methods, whilst still meeting the minimum university and professional expectations and standards (McLaughlin et al., 2020). Placement hours were reduced slightly but were still aligned with international standards. This modification made it possible for most students to meet the requirements, despite the challenges experienced at the beginning of their placement blocks. To support educational institutions, SACSSP provided standards to assess or conduct simulated learning for group and community work (SACSSP, 2020). It also became apparent that the Council and other support institutions had not anticipated data protection issues and other ethical problems associated with online teaching (Csoba and Diebel, 2020). The authors agree with Zvomuya (2021) that whilst the delivery of theory content can be done online, fieldwork using virtual platforms remains a challenge in the Global South. The same applies to conducting role-play simulations for both casework and group work. Ensuring that no one is left behind in higher education calls for a social justice framework to be adopted by all stakeholders in the higher education sector. Issues of access, participation, inclusion, fair treatment, human dignity, and human rights are central to ensuring that higher education gives students meaningful learning experiences.

Social Justice in Higher Education as a Theoretical Lens during COVID-19

This chapter is underpinned by a social justice lens for various reasons. There is no doubt that the pandemic resulted in a serious challenge to social work students from poor families being able to participate in remote teaching and online learning. It is beyond the scope of this chapter to discuss the different strands of thought and the many definitions of social justice, therefore Sturman's (1997, p. 1) understanding of social justice as advancing equal opportunities that emphasises equity was adopted. Rawls (1999 cited in Nelson et al., 2009, p.4) describes it as a 'rearrangement of social and economic goods ... guided by considerations of opportunity and ... differences ... from individual circumstances'. Access to higher education in South Africa occupies a central position in the discourse on democracy, redistribution, social justice, and nation-building. Nkala and Sobantu (2021) point out that access, and more importantly epistemological participation in higher education, is the real barometer for social and economic transformation of South African society post-1994. South Africa is racially unequal and student participation in higher education is more than a freedom and right: it improves opportunities for capital development opportunities for students from poor families (Nkala and Sobantu, 2021), i.e., in essence, rearranging social and economic good, as envisioned by Rawls (1999 cited in Nelson et al., 2009).

Social work is synonymous with social justice and social work education should therefore model access, equity, non-discrimination, and empathy by educators. The International Federation of Social Work (IFSW) (2014) emphasises that the 'principles of social justice, human rights, collective responsibility…as central to social work' are central to the profession. Having said that, it is easy to understand why the COVID-19 measures had ramifications of a violation of human rights for many poor social work students who were improving their life circumstances through education. High rates of poverty amongst students are a microcosm of their communities of origin, as most of the members rely on community services rendered by the social work students doing fieldwork practicums. Sadly, the lockdowns undermined the gains that had arguably been made by the government since 1994 to tackle a labyrinth of social ills, such as poverty, sexual abuse, and GBV through social work education. Thus, the adoption of online learning by the social work education department saved the BSW programme and instilled hope that the students could continue to participate in the teaching and learning programme, notwithstanding the challenges encountered during its adoption.

Adapting to Challenges Posed by COVID-19

In the Global North, online learning, and more particularly, blended learning, had been explored and used prior to COVID-19. It is therefore reasonable to assume that social work education institutions in these countries transitioned more easily to a full-time online teaching and learning process. On the contrary, HEIs in the Global South contended with limited human and technical resources and skills to implement online learning on a full-time basis and apply relevant pedagogies. However, most social work education institutions in South Africa (including the one at which the authors are based) must be commended for swiftly adapting to digital platforms and providing support, e.g. electronic devices such as laptops, phones, and data for connectivity. The historically disadvantaged HEIs, also referred to as HBUs, are mostly located in rural areas and cater mainly to Black students in the country. They faced serious challenges with adopting an online learning methodology for the social work curriculum (Vijayan, 2021). In addition, the lack of devices available to students and academics and poor connectivity in rural areas had a severe impact on students participating in the digital learning offerings (Kajiita et al., 2020; Tanga et al., 2020). It became very clear that a distinctive set of skills and abilities in academic staff and support is key to a successful implementation of online learning (Lischer et al., 2021). Unfortunately, most academics and students lack these skills, which makes teaching and learning difficult (Tanga et al., 2020).

The numerous challenges encountered by HEIs in responding to COVID-19 should be understood in the context of the social and economic circumstances of the Global South, including in South Africa (Azman et al., 2020). For example, South Africa has had to contend with a very high unemployment rate since 1994 and, thus, with very slow growth, which deepens inequality and poverty (Statistics South Africa, 2022). Social work educators at this Johannesburg-based institution were forced to teach students remotely, which required reliable gadgets such as a laptop, access to a stable internet connection, and a conducive home environment that supports learning. Even when provided with gadgets and Internet connectivity (mostly by the HEIs), many students lived in very poor housing conditions and neighbourhoods plagued by crime and violence; therefore, a few performed poorly because of the adverse impact of these learning environments on the learning process.

Similarly, social work education in other African countries faced similar complications because of COVID-19. Zvomuya (2021) states that in Zimbabwe, student fieldwork, research and social work practice relied on digital mediums for learning, counselling sessions, follow-ups, and linkages. In a multi-country study on the impact of COVID-19 on social work education in the United States of America, McFadden et al. (2020) indicated that institutions had no choice but to adapt to online learning to save their programmes while ensuring inclusion in the process. Ogunode et al. (2021) posit that, in Nigeria, the adoption of online learning rescued social work education from collapse due to the pandemic. It is highly likely that some institutions will continue to use some online learning innovations that they used during the pandemic. In a way, the pandemic stretched social work education in unprecedented ways and prepared it for other eventualities that may arise in the future.

The impact of Covid-19 on social work education was widespread, but obviously, some areas were more affected than others. In South Africa, student internship placements, face-to-face consultations, supervision, and other aspects of the programme were adversely impacted, with most agencies offering student placements being closed, in line with the COVID-19 regulations. The section below discusses how this university situated in Johannesburg, South Africa, was innovative regarding aspects of social work education, including in terms of theory classes, the final year research project, and assessments, in order to mitigate the serious challenges posed by the pandemic.

Theory Classes

Theory classes at this institution comprised synchronous and/or asynchronous learning, as some students were not able to participate in virtual classes because of connectivity challenges. Thus, academics were implored to arrange make-up sessions for students who missed the main classes. Adedoyin and Soykan (2020) commend asynchronous and synchronous online classes, but they warn that instructors, organisations, and institutions must have a comprehensive understanding of the associated benefits and limitations. They recommend training academics regarding the implementation and benefits of these types of virtual classes. In addition to these classes, academics made learning material available via online platforms such as Blackboard and via WhatsApp and emails, which made it easier for social work students to download the work for self-study. Opportunities for engagement and consultation were provided using the online platforms.

To ensure that all students participated (synchronously and/or asynchronously), HEIs provided gadgets and data for all enrolled students, including those on the BSW programme. There were minimal delays in the procurement process, but these disadvantaged the students who relied on institutional support. In these instances, some lecturers in the institution printed out learning material and posted it to the affected students, the majority of whom were from rural areas. One Head of Department in the institution of focus sourced gadgets and data, and sent these to students in his department using personal funds. Also worth mentioning is that he played an immense role in inducting staff to online learning, for example, different low-data platforms, how to save data, downloading and saving videos at low data, and preparing 'voice-over' Power Point presentations. This demonstrated his commitment to social work values such as Ubuntu. Through these measures, international students from neighbouring countries (such as eSwatini), who did not benefit from the data assistance available only in South Africa, were included in the learning process, which enabled them to continue their studies, despite the COVID-19 restrictions and challenges. Vijayan (2021) states that educators went to extraordinary lengths to ensure that quality content could be delivered in an effective way in order to ensure that learning outcomes were met. This came at a personal cost for some social work educators.

Students indicated that they faced multiple problems while learning from their homes. Due to the legacy of apartheid separating urban and spatial development, most poor families live in precarious living arrangements. For example, more than seven million South Africans live in informal settlements, some of which are overcrowded, and they do not have water, sanitation, or electricity (Nyashanu et al., 2020; Sobantu, 2019; Sobantu and Nel, 2019). Some of the formal housing structures are very small, thus making it very difficult for students to participate in classes or study, due to overcrowding (Sobantu et al., 2019). In terms of the effect of COVID-19 on social work education, Kajiita et al. (2020) found that students from rural institutions were severely affected by adverse home circumstances, such as poor connectivity, lack of electricity, and devices that did not support online learning. Several academics at these institutions were also affected by similar challenges.

Some students complained that they were overwhelmed by family responsibilities and chores, such as cooking and caring for their siblings, and therefore they had very little time or none to study and attend classes. Their families provided little or no support, which made the learning process quite challenging and frustrating for the students. Students from the Netherlands faced similar issues, as revealed by a study done by De Jonge et al. (2020), many students were confronted with a substantial loss of their usual supportive networks and their daily routines because they had to study from home. This caused great frustration in terms of social work learning and teaching for both academics and students. The impact of housing on education was discussed by Sobantu (2019), who argued that social workers need to understand housing as more than just bricks and mortar and, instead, as a right that undergirds all social and economic relations.

Final Year Research Projects

At this institution, all BSW students are required to undertake fieldwork research as they complete their studies and write a report that introduces them to the research process (Zvomuya, 2021). Normally, the students conduct face-to-face interviews as part of the data collection process. However, during the pandemic, virtual tools (mainly WhatsApp) were used as an alternative because of the lockdown restrictions. Using these tools proved a challenge because of the cost of data and the devices, which many students could not afford. An additional difficulty for many social work students was that it was the first time they were conducting research using online platforms, and they had no experience or skill to do so. Most students indicated that it was a challenge for them to apply the data collection and interviewing skills they had learnt in the theory classes. Micro skills such as probing, observing non-verbal behaviour, empathy, and values such as confidentiality are difficult to apply when doing online interviews. It requires experienced social work researchers. Some HEIs had to postpone the student research elements until the lockdown restrictions were eased. When this happened, some universities in the country organised transport and accompanied students to their research sites (mostly schools) where they were to interview learners. The students appreciated this coordinated support, which gave them an opportunity to practice the appropriate skills, values, and ethics during the interviews.

Assessment Opportunities

Traditionally, HEIs and social work departments include various types of assessment in a programme, such as online tests, assignments, peer presentations, portfolios, and oral and written examinations. Adedoyin and Soykan (2020) posit that assessments are common after instructional delivery, with the instructors ascertaining if the instructional objectives were achieved. These assessments include tests, quizzes, and examinations. With the onset of the COVID-19 pandemic and the associated restrictions, creative and non-contact ways of assessing had to be used. Vijayan (2021) states that the assessments and evaluation of learning outcomes raised several difficulties during COVID-19, and designing and developing effective online evaluation mechanisms became an urgent priority. Prior to COVID-19, one university in Johannesburg required internship students at all levels to submit a hard copy file (portfolios of evidence (PoE)) on all fieldwork conducted. However, submitting this file became very difficult during the pandemic. Therefore, all internship coordinators at all levels were urgently required to design an e-portfolio for students to complete and submit online via email or Google Drive. Students appreciated this initiative because it saved the cost of printing and provided the convenience of submitting online from their residence.

Assignments became the most popular mode of assessment, as sit-in online tests could not be done due to the lockdowns. In addition, in 2020, most universities lacked the capacity to invigilate online tests written by students in their residences. The integrity of the assessments faced a huge threat from the possibility of students sharing answers via WhatsApp or email. It is exciting to note that invigilation apps for online tests and exams have been developed to monitor students and eliminate the chance of cheating in an online test (Du Plessis and Van der Westhuizen, 2022). The authors are aware of the complexity of these apps, for example, overloading students' cognitive engagement because of writing the exam while constantly checking that they are logged onto the apps (Cramp et al., 2019). Most institutions replaced sit-in examinations with assignment examinations, where they were required to apply theory and critical thinking in their responses. Jacobs (2022) posits that these types of examinations provide students with an opportunity to fully apply their minds to real-life contexts, instead of merely regurgitating content learnt in class in their examinations. Challenges with this adaptation included students being unhappy about one method of assessment being used, given that they were used to various methods being used to increase their chance of passing a module. However, with the development of invigilation apps, online assessments are possible once again, but without requiring students to all sit in one venue. There are contradicting reports on how students performed during this period compared to regular assessments (Vijayan, 2021), but at the authors' institution, success rates improved compared to pre-COVID-19 sit-in exams.

Student Support

Providing support to students at all universities is key to a successful learning process. As Tanga et al. (2020) argue: 'for online learning to be successful, there is a need for institutions to invest in a total ecosystem of learner needs and support and this takes time to identify and put into place'. The institution where the authors are based provided a lot of support to students doing the internship, as well as in the theory classes during the pandemic. For example, as part of its ongoing support, the university hires department-based tutors to provide academic support, whilst psychological counselling services and writing centres are also made available to the students. Unfortunately, many students did not use some of these support mechanisms during the lockdowns because some services are more effective when conducted face to face. Virtual tutor support was made available, but given the connectivity issues, most students failed to attend the virtual sessions. The students required a lot of psychosocial and academic support because of the multiple stressors that they had to contend with because of COVID-19. This institution provided a toll-free number for students to access a 24-hour counselling service, if the need arose. Lecturers, facilitators, and supervisors were the only form of reliable academic support available to students. With no writing centres available to assist students with improving their writing skills, social work students had to cope on their own.

Lessons Learnt

While there are several success stories in terms of this institution's response to COVID-19, there are also several important areas to note and target for improvement. The pandemic period clearly highlighted the digital divide that is perpetuating inequality in South Africa. Access to even basic and reliable Internet access has been found wanting in most South African communities; therefore, the government, in partnership with private entities, should address this by providing technological infrastructure if social work students and academics in HEIs are to fully embrace 4IR in advancing social work education. The authors concur with Zvomuya's (2021) study in Zimbabwe that recommended that social work education providers in the Global South invest in developing technical skills of students and staff and in technological infrastructure. Some educators and students had not been exposed to many of the pedagogies used, such as online and distance learning, and many had to navigate a steep learning curve to deliver and receive content (Shulman, 2005; Vijayan, 2021). This necessitates compulsory information and communications technology (ICT) training for university students in their first year of study, as well as for academics.

Lischer et al. (2021) state that digitisation is playing an increasingly important role in all areas of work, and it is a positive development that the pandemic led to an increase in digital literacy among both staff and students. Thus, digital literacy is no longer a 'nice to have', but rather an indispensable competence for both staff and students. However, given that core teachings require fieldwork placement, online and distance learning is not necessarily the best option for social work education. While there is evidence that theory and other aspects of the programme can be delivered online, practicums are a serious challenge. As much as 4IR advanced social work education during the COVID-19 pandemic, there does not appear to be an urgent need to completely review and overhaul the current social work education and training offerings at higher education institutions in South Africa. What is recommended, however, is that social work educators should be prepared to include uncertainty in curriculum development and pedagogical approaches, as highlighted by Afrouz (2021). COVID-19 taught us that, in social work education, when there is immediate uncertainty, there is no clear map to follow, so rather than wait for definitive direction, we may need to embrace changes quickly and later revise what is done, if necessary.

Conclusion

The pandemic came as a surprise to academia and all the other facets of society, and it will not be the last in the history of humankind. Despite the disruptions that the pandemic and the hitherto lockdowns posed on the internship programme, it is important for social work education to be versatile in embracing technology and 4IR in its curricula. With the success of the social work programmes that were conducted during COVID-19, both students and academics should be commended for their resilience and hard work. The notion that personal interpersonal communication and human relationship development cannot be developed through remote and online learning may not be entirely true. What is evident is the value of both face-to-face and interactive 4IR technology employed on a complimentary basis.

Recommendations

1. There is a huge need for social work classrooms to step up to using interactive 4IR technology even after COVID-19 restrictions to encourage students to develop human interaction and social relationships and facilitate online learning.
2. There is an urgent need for social work education institutions to enhance the capacity of staff with technical skills that are required for online learning.
3. In planning for every internship programme, careful considerations for 4IR should be integrated, with students constantly encouraged and reminded to be versatile and ready to switch to remote and online learning at any time during their programme.

Further Reading

Gurajena, C., Mbunge, E. and Fashoto, G. (2021). Teaching and learning in the new normal: Opportunities and challenges of distance learning amid COVID-19 pandemic. Available at https://papers.ssrn.com/sol3/papers.cfm?abstract_id=3765509. Accessed on 30 May 2023.

McNutt, J.G. (ed.) (2018). *Technology, Activism, and Social Justice in a Digital Age*. Oxford University Press.

Paschal, M.J. and Mkulu, D.G. (2020). Online classes during COVID-19 pandemic in higher learning institutions in Africa. *Global Research in Higher Education*, 3(3), 1–21.

References

Adedoyin, O.B. and Soykan, E. (2020). Covid-19 pandemic and online learning: The challenges and opportunities. *Interactive Learning Environments*, 1–13.

Afrouz, R. (2021). Approaching uncertainty in social work education, a lesson from COVID-19 pandemic. *Qualitative Social Work*, 20(1–2), 561–567.

Azman, A., Singh, P.S.J., Parker, J. and Crabtree, S. (2020). Addressing competency requirements of social work students during the COVID-19 pandemic in Malaysia. *Social Work Education*, 39(8), 1058–1065.

Cramp, J., Medlin, J.F., Lake, P. and Sharp, C. (2019). Lessons learned from implementing remotely invigilated online exams. *Journal of University Teaching and Learning Practice*, 16(10), 1–20.

Csoba, J. and Diebel, A. (2020). Worldwide closed! Social worker field practice during the 'lockdown' period. *Social Work Education*, 39(8), 1094–1106.

De Jonge, E., Kloppenburg, R. and Hendriks, P. (2020). The impact of the COVID-19 pandemic on social work education and practice in the Netherlands. *Social Work Education*, 39(8), 1027–1036.

Drower, S.J. (2002). Conceptualizing social work in changed South Africa. *International Social Work*, 45(1), 7–20.

Du Plessis, E. and Van der Westhuizen, G. (2022). Building academic integrity through online assessment apps. *Education and New Developments*, 49–53.

Gray, M. and Mazibuko, F. (2002). Social work in South Africa at the dawn of the new millennium. *International Journal of Social Welfare*, 11(3), 191–200.

IFSW (2014). Global definition of social work. Available at: https://www.ifsw.org/what-is-social-work/global-definition-of-social-work/. Accessed on 1 July 2022.

Jacobs, A.D. (2020). Utilizing take-home examinations in upper-level analytical lecture courses in the wake of the COVID-19 pandemic. *Journal of Chemical Education*, 98(2), 689–693.

Kajiita, R.M., Nomngcoyiya, T. and Kang'ethe, S.M. (2020). The 'revolution' on teaching and learning: Implications of Covid-19 on social work education in institutions of higher learning in Africa. *African Journal of Social Work*, 10(3), 25–33.

Lischer, S., Caviezel Schmitz, S., Krüger, P., Safi, N. and Dickson, C. (2021). Distance education in social work during the COVID-19 pandemic: Changes and challenges. In *Frontiers in Education*. Frontiers Media SA.

Mamphiswana, D. and Noyoo, N. (2000). Social work education in a changing socio-political and economic dispensation: Perspectives from South Africa. *International Social Work*, 43(1), 21–32.

McFadden, P., Russ, E., Blakeman, P., Kirwin, G., Anand, J., Lähteinen, S., Baugerud, G.A. and Tham, P. (2020). COVID-19 impact on social work admissions and education in seven international universities. *Social Work Education*, 39(8), 154–1163.

McLaughlin, H., Scholar, H. and Heater, B. (2020). Social work education in a global pandemic: Strategies, reflections, and challenges. *Social Work Education*, 39(8), 975–982.

Nelson, K., Creagh, T. and Clarke, J. (2009). *Literature and Analysis: Development of a Set of Social Justice Principles*. Queensland: Queensland University of Technology.

Nkala, N.Z. and Sobantu, M. (2021). Writing centres and social justice in higher education: Students' voices in a higher education institution in Johannesburg, South Africa. *African Journal of Social Work*, 11(2), 67–75.

Noyoo, N. (2003). *Social Welfare Policy, Social Work Practice and Professional Education in a Transforming Society* (PhD dissertation). University of the Witwatersrand, Johannesburg.

Nyashanu, M., Simbanegavi, P. and Gibson, L. (2020). Exploring the impact of COVID-19 pandemic lockdown on informal settlements in Tshwane Gauteng Province, South Africa. *Global Public Health: An International Journal for Research. Policy and Practice*, 15(10), 1443–1453.

Ogunode, N.J., Ndubuisi, A.G. and Terfa, A.C. (2021). Impact of the Covid-19 pandemic on Nigerian educational institutions. *Electronic Research Journal of Engineering, Computer and Applied Sciences*, 3, 10–20.

Patel, L. (2015). *Social Welfare and Social Development*. Cape Town: Oxford University Press.

Rawls, J. (1971). *A Theory of justice*. Oxford: Oxford University Press.

SACSSP (2020). *General Notice. 6 of 2020 (15 April 2020): Interim Guidelines on Use of e-Social Work*. Pretoria: SACSSP.

SACSSP (2022). South African council for social service professions. Available at: https://nationalgovernment.co.za/units/view/164/south-african-council-for-social-service-professions-sacssp. Accessed on 30 June 2022.

SACSSP (2023). Education. *Training and Development*. Available at: https://www.sacssp.co.za/education-training-and-development/. Accessed on 3 March 2023.

Shulman, L.S. (2005). Signature pedagogies in the professions. *Journal of the American Academy of Arts & Sciences*, 134(3), 52–59.

Sobantu, M. (2019). *A Model for Enhancing Voluntary Housing within a Social Development Approach in South Africa* (Doctoral thesis). University of Johannesburg, Johannesburg, South Africa.

Sobantu, M. and Nel, H. (2019). Voluntary housing delivery: The contribution of partnerships to the success of a community-based organisation (WASSUP) in Diepsloot low-income community, Johannesburg, South Africa. *Matskaaplike Werk/Social Work*, 55(3), 284–300.

Sobantu, M., Zulu, N. and Maphosa, N. (2019). Housing as a basic human right: A reflection on South Africa. *Southern African Journal of Social Work and Social Development*, 31(1), 1–18.

Stats, S.A. (2022). Statistical release P0341 victims of crime: Governance, Public Safety, and Justice Survey GPSJS 2021/22. *Stats SA*. Available at: https://www.statssa.gov.za/publications/P0341/P03412022.pdf Accessed on 16 March 2023.

Sturman, A. (1997). *Social Justice in Education*. Melbourne: The Australian Council of Educational Research.

Tanga, P., Ndhlovu, G.N. and Tanga, M. (2020). Emergency remote teaching and learning during COVID-19: A recipe for disaster for social work education in the Eastern Cape of South Africa? *African Journal of Social Work*, 10(3), 17–24.

Turton, Y. and Schmid, J. (2020). Transforming social work: Contextualised social work education in South Africa. *Social Work*, 56(4), 367–382.

Veta, O.D. and McLaughlin, H. (2022). Social work education and practice in Africa: The problems and prospects. *Social Work Education*, 1–12.

Vijayan, R. (2021). Teaching and learning during the COVID-19 pandemic: A topic modeling study. *Education Sciences*, 11(347), 2–15.

Zvomuya, W. (2021). The impact of COVID-19 pandemic on social work education and practice. *African Journal of Social Work*, 11(4), 189–200.

12
INSURMOUNTABLE BARRIERS TO SOCIAL WORK EDUCATION

Experiences of Online Learning from Rural South Africa

Eleanor A Hendricks and Richard Ingram

Abstract: English

Whilst this chapter has its roots in an evaluation of the pivot towards online modes of delivery in social work education due to the COVID-19 pandemic, it engages in wider issues relating to the universalist assumptions underpinning a global acceptance that online learning was an appropriate response. Staff and students from two universities in South Africa engaged in a research project with a dual-method approach involving a questionnaire and thematically focused interviews. Findings reveal the profound challenges experienced by staff and students relating to lack of equipment, Internet access, inconsistent power supplies, and financial constraints. This chapter highlights and explores issues relating to equity of access, student experience, staff skill levels, the marketisation of education, and the imposition of solutions that may not meet the needs of the key stakeholders involved specifically driven by the Global North and applied across the Global South. The chapter concludes with a proposed lens with which to understand and determine future thinking around modes of delivery of social work education for diverse staff and student populations.

Introduction

The COVID-19 pandemic that gripped the world in March 2020 is still having an impact on the lives of people across the globe as this chapter is being written in 2022. The legacy of enforced changes to the way people live their lives is still uncertain in terms of their longevity and ongoing presence. The world of higher education was no different, with universities across the globe looking towards pivoting to online delivery of educational programmes and online-based ways of communicating with each other as individuals and organisations. It would be tempting to view this unexpected and enforced transition as one that was universally applied and experienced.

However, it serves as the catalyst for this chapter in that it allows us to consider the following issues:

- The extent to which the Global North and the Global South shared the same experience of the transition to online learning.
- The nature and complexity of the experience of online learning in the Global South using South Africa and social work education as the exemplar.
- Consideration of the findings of a small research project in South Africa that highlight the dimensions of experience for staff and students in terms of their experience of online learning in a social work education context.
- Identification of key themes that allow us to view online learning through a lens that allows for cultural and contextual differences globally to be understood and recognised.

The emergence of COVID-19 led to a paradigm shift from the traditional face-to-face teaching and learning to online teaching and learning in higher education institutions globally. This paradigm shift required 1.5 billion students and 63 million educators (World Bank, 2020a; United Nations Education Scientific and Cultural Organization (UNESCO, 2020) to modify their face-to-face academic practices, wherever possible. The modification resulted in academics facing enormous challenges of acquiring and implementing the IT skills required for teaching; and students on the other hand, were required to rise to the challenge of a new method of learning. So, can we be confident that such a global challenge had a shared effective global solution? Statistics provided by the World Bank (2020b) highlight that approximately 84% of the citizens of member states of the European Union and 66% in Latin America had access to the Internet in 2018. In the United States of America (USA), the same report revealed that more than 90% of the citizens had access to the Internet. In contrast, the World Bank stated that in countries from the Global South, such as South Africa, only 18% of the citizens had access to the Internet in 2018. These data, whilst approximate, provide this chapter with a crucial foundation stone, namely, the significant differences in terms of context and capacity in African social work education. The staggering statistics highlighted above reveal the disparity across geographies and the differing challenges and experiences that arise as a consequence.

Moreover, a review of the literature on the proliferation of online learning revealed that the adoption and implementation of online teaching and learning systems in the Global South, such as in South Africa, are lagging because of cultural, economic, political, and technological issues. Nonetheless, though online teaching and learning in the Global South is not new, a very limited number of studies have investigated the challenges of online teaching and learning especially from a student perspective. Successful understanding of online teaching and learning requires an in-depth investigation of the challenges from both academics and students and provides recommendations to motivate more active engagement from both academics and students with these systems. This study and chapter therefore will investigate and explore the online education challenges faced by social work academics and students in two South African universities. Investigating the online education challenges faced by social work academics and students will provide a multi-faceted perspective on the challenges faced in the use of online teaching and learning.

Setting the Scene – Education, Online Technology, and Access

Education is highlighted by UNESCO (2020) as one of the fundamental factors that is used to alleviate poverty and drive economic growth in the Global South. This is underpinned by a belief that access to education can provide individuals and communities with the knowledge and skills to positively impact growth and development at an individual, societal, and international level. It is of course counter-balanced by an acknowledgement that access, applicability, and quality of education are not equitable and fixed commodities but ones that are often as unequal as the economic disparities that exist between different parts of the globe (Sekonyela, 2021). Furthermore, the link between education, positive outcomes and change is to be viewed with caution as structural, political, and cultural factors will still compromise and shape opportunities and lived experiences (Yende, 2021). It is this critical lens that underpins this chapter and the focus on South Africa as the location of our inquiry and discussion is pertinent in terms of the messages it may hold for the country and the Global South more generally. For example, within South Africa there are significant issues relating to access and resourcing of education at all levels that mirror existing inequalities within society (Yuhan and Kim, 2014).

The delivery of education using Information Communication Technologies (ICT) as a tool and vehicle for teaching and learning is often cited as a source of huge potential for higher education institutions struggling to meet the growing demand for higher education within a context of limited resources in terms of academic staff and accommodation (Yuan and Kim, 2014). This is very much true of the South African context. As a result, a significant number of higher education institutions have realised the importance of delivering higher education and training by means of online teaching and learning or a hybrid of on-campus and online delivery, to improve the efficiency, cost, and quality of teaching and learning and appreciate the high demand for higher education.

The use of ICT to support and enhance teaching and learning is founded in human capital theory, which acknowledges and suggests that academics and students can acquire and advance knowledge through cognitive processes that are complex and implicit in an education system (Bucciarelli et al., 2010). This implies that the incorporation of online teaching and learning practice in the higher education system benefits both academics and students, irrespective of the challenges both parties encounter in the learning process. Thus, online teaching and learning have become an essential means through which higher education institutions do acquire, manage, and disseminate knowledge. Despite the success and potential of online teaching and learning noted above, there are notes of caution that academics and students still face significant challenges when engaging in online teaching and learning practice, especially in the Global South (Sun and Chen, 2016; Jung and Lee 2018). The challenges can be illustrated in data that show much higher dropout rates of students than in traditional classroom face-to-face teaching and learning (Jung and Lee, 2018).

It is beyond the scope of this chapter to cover the enormous body of literature that reveals the best practices and pitfalls associated with education in the online sphere. It is worth noting that there are recurrent themes, such as the opportunities afforded by online learning in terms of student's networking and the importance of a shared goal, purpose, and identity (Boling et al., 2012). This is especially crucial within social work education, where all students are engaged in learning underpinned by a shared value base and an engagement with a knowledge base that seeks to establish a robust professional identity.

Methodology

We sought to explore the experiences of social work staff and students at two South African universities that deliver social work education programmes and undertook the pivot and transition to online learning. Both institutions are public universities: one based in the Eastern Cape and one based in Limpopo Province in South Africa. These institutions were selected due to their shift to online learning being an almost entirely new activity. The academic staff and the third-year social work students were both involved in the same programmes of study, which provided a multidimensional case study. 'An exploratory case study simply means that the exploration and description of the case occur through detailed and in-depth methods from multiple sources that are rich in context' (Denzin and Lincoln, 2012, p. 54). A qualitative approach provided us with a chance to study and understand the diverse social and cultural contexts in which these social work academics and students were located. The data were collected through semi-structured interviews that allowed for depth and breadth of response bespoke to an individual's experiences and viewpoint of online learning in social work education (Denzin and Lincoln, 2012).

The study sample consisted of 20 participants: ten students and ten academics. The ten staff members consisted of four males and six females, from the ten staff members, four held PhD qualifications and six Masters, the racial composition of the staff members were diverse, two were White, two were Colored, and six were African/Black, five of the staff members were from the University of Limpopo (UL) and five from the University of Fort Hare (UFH). The ten students who participated in the study consisted of four males and six females, all were third-year social work students (five from UL and five from UFH), two students were White, one Colored, one Indian, and six African/Black.

The inclusion criteria that were used to select participants stipulated that participants needed to have had experience with online teaching and learning during the COVID-19 pandemic. The participants were identified by one researcher as staff were from the social work department in both universities and shared their frustrations of online teaching during meetings. The students were selected through snowball sampling information about the study that was shared in various WhatsApp groups on both campuses with third-year social work students and ten student participants, who arrived on the scheduled day of interviews. The rich data that emerged from these interviews lent themselves to a thematic analysis that allowed us to identify shared and divergent viewpoints across the interviews and populations (Rubin and Rubin, 2012). We have developed these into five distinct themes, which we will explore in the remainder of the chapter:

- Financial implications.
- Rural/urban divide.
- Lack of adequate training.
- Academic misconduct and plagiarism.
- Implications for fieldwork and tutorial leaning.

Online Learning in Social Work Education: Opportunities, Obstacles, and Inequalities

As noted earlier in this chapter, there are multiple dimensions to the incorporation of online learning in social work education in South Africa and the Global South more generally that highlight the limitations in viewing online learning as a universal solution or panacea. Rather, we will identify structural, economic, and societal factors that create a less even and predictable educational environment. We provide contextual commentary that will be illuminated further by the vivid contributions of academics and students from the study.

Financial Implications

To fully understand the challenges that are connected to the proliferation of online approaches to education it is important to explore the financial profile of students in higher education in South Africa. In South Africa most students from disadvantaged backgrounds rely on the National Student Financial Aid Scheme (NSFAS) established in 1999 to fund their studies. This is a substantial scheme that reflects a commitment to widening access to South African higher education and underlines the degree of financial hardship experienced by significant portions of the population. This scheme diverges from many other schemes offered by countries globally in that it is not a loan and does not require repayment following completion of studies (Yende, 2021).

Sokhweba et al. (2021) note that this scheme has led to the inclusion and diversification of the higher education sector in South Africa with much greater access to education for those from a financially poor background. To put this in some context, in 2020 there were 543,268 applications to NSFAS of which 393,607 were approved. In addition to this hugely significant number of assisted students, it is important to recognise also that this has disproportionately benefitted Black students in South Africa who submitted over 500,000 of the applications. This not only reflects the issues of poverty among many Black communities, but also underlines a significant commitment to widening inclusion and access to education for this population.

This contextual background is important as it may suggest a 'levelling up' of the experience of education in South Africa. Whilst this is true to an extent it does not remove the wider inequalities that may exist between different groups of students, and these have been illuminated by the widening use of online approaches.

The following quotes from students were typical and highlight that access goes beyond simply entry to university but has online implications too.

Social Work Student 1 – *Data was also a major problem because it is expensive and I wasn't getting any free data from the university for a few months. Thus, I submitted most of my work late, I was at the verge of deregistering because I saw no point of studying at all. Unfortunately, I have no success story as to using the online way of learning.*

Social Work Student 2 – *Some students did not attend all online classes and they did miss classes and failed modules due to network connectivity and the issue of data. So online learning was not effective at all but it works for students who are financially stable and have parents or guardian to assist.*

These quotes highlight that financial difficulties went hand in hand with the unanticipated need for data to access classes and eLearning resources, these challenges are exacerbated when one also considers access to equipment such as laptops and mobile phones.

Social Work Student 10 – *It is hard to progress on studies at times when you have to worry about where your next meal will come from. The financial constraints amongst university students is real we struggle because many students use NSFAS money to support our families and home which leaves us with little or nothing.*

Social Work Staff 9 – *The NSFAS funding scheme only starts paying in April each year so for the first three months students we will be left destitute with no equipment for learning and worse no food. Many students drop out within this time period as the financial burden and academic stress is too great.*

The aforementioned NSFAS funding scheme is undoubtedly of benefit to students and reflects a commitment to inclusion and widening access. The precarious nature of such assistance is laid bare here in that social work students may have access to education through such funding, but the funding is not sufficient to cope with additional and crucial costs that online learning may give rise to. The profundity of such financial constraints can be seen in the stark choices around being able to access food and support family members. These examples underline the complexities of introducing a reliance on online provision within the South African context.

Rural/Urban Divide: A Digital Divide

There has been a long history of underequipped infrastructure, financial challenges, and incoherent curriculum development (Dube, 2020) in South Africa. These challenges and inequities are brought into sharp focus when the resources and flexibility required to pivot to online learning occurs. Although imperfect as an exact binary comparison, socioeconomic inequalities can commonly be viewed through the lens of a rural/urban divide, with rural communities experiencing greater levels of poverty and lack of infrastructure (Czerniewicz and Rother, 2018). Thus, it is imperative that an 'equity and social justice lens be used to examine the way in which online instruction is delivered in South African higher education institutions' (Dube, 2020, p. 136). Online learning in social work education can be viewed as an opportunity to recognise and address the challenges faced by students from rural areas.

Students from poor backgrounds experienced major challenges accessing technology during the COVID-19 pandemic when they had to attend online classes from their homes in rural areas (Dube, 2020). In South Africa there are various challenges students from rural areas encounter when attempting to access online classes from home, these challenges include loadshedding (power outages across the country), poor to no connectivity in rural areas, no electricity in some villages, limited to no funds to purchase data, and unequal ownership of digital devices such as tablets, smartphones or laptops to attend online classes. Further issues that hinder online learning are limited computer literacy skills and minimal training in computer literacy skills at tertiary level. This collision of issues that relate to individual and community-level poverty and infrastructure create a perfect storm for social work students learning within an online sphere.

Social Work Student 3 – *Some students experienced issues of network connectivity because of the areas that they located geographically, also the issue of data it really cost, as some of student are coming from poor family. Other students at their homes have no proper places to study, and the other issue of parents who did not understand the student when it was time to study, they just give house chores to a student every day and we end up losing focus as students.*

The quote illustrates the frustrations and challenges of social work students when they are confronted with the economic and infrastructural inequalities in rural communities. This shows that there is an interplay and relationship between the financial issue raised in the previous section and the impact of a rural/urban divide. The challenges of online learning raise significant concerns about student access because numerous students who are reliant on financial schemes (such as the aforementioned NSFAS) or student loans have limited to no access to wireless networks at home and may not have sole access to required devices (Czerniewicz and Rother, 2018). The digital divide as described above reflects and illustrates the inequalities that are present across South Africa and highlight how these can be exacerbated due to the economic underpinnings of online technology and access. Preceding research exploring 'inequities arising from the emergence of digital technologies has incorporated socioeconomic factors, especially gender, age, race, educational level, income, and habitat' (Hidalgo et al., 2020:119754). Soomro et al. (2020, p. 1) suggest the 'digital divide centers on access to various dimensions of information and communication technology (ICT) including physical access, motivation, skills, and actual usage of digital technologies'. The infrastructural challenges are twofold. On a national level, there may be limited Internet coverage due to lack of investment, and, at an individual level, there may be limited access to devices and support services (Abdulmajeed et al., 2020).

It is important to note that these challenges impact staff and students alike, and, as such, they create issues for both the delivery and the receipt of online learning (Gómez-Ciriano, 2020). Whilst the financial context here is not specific to social work students and reflects a wider issue in higher education and the Global South more generally, the pedagogical orientation of social work and the desired learning outcomes add another layer of complexity to this digital divide. Social work is a practice-based profession that requires the development of interpersonal skills. Such approaches as role-playing and practicum can be modified to exist online, but if this is not predictable and accessible then a cornerstone of social work education is missing altogether. This makes this pedagogical compromise even less effective as in-person skills work is the preferred and most effective way of delivering these aspects of social work education. Furthermore, students are required to undertake fieldwork in the community as part of the curriculum, which was deemed another impossible task during COVID-19 (Dube, 2020). Any consideration of online practicum opportunities faces the same digital divide with the addition of further constraints in terms of community capacity to engage online. Thus, online learning is not an ideal fit for practicum professions like social work where practical experience forms a major part of the curriculum to produce competent graduates.

Lack of Adequate Training

The use of online learning platforms in higher education in sub-Saharan African countries has steadily increased over the last few years. The merits of online learning are well documented and persuasive. Online learning can improve the enthusiasm and active engagement of students in the virtual classes (Mpungose, 2020). Online learning ought to proliferate access to education through flexible and cost-effective methods. Simply put, reducing the need for travel, relocation, and expensive buildings. However, it is a misnomer to think that online learning is a shortcut or a simpler option. Considerable work is necessary by academic staff in their respective institutions in terms of translating learning objectives, content, methods, evaluations, and assessment of the knowledge acquisition throughout the virtual learning processes (Dube, 2020). Thus, the execution, practice, management, and sustainability of eLearning methods to teaching and learning in institutions of higher education mainly depend on academic staff. There have been multiple studies conducted on the experience of students about online learning (Arthur-Nyarko and Kariuki, 2019). The findings of some studies revealed knowledge gaps amongst academic staff on navigating their way through online learning platforms in South African previously disadvantaged/ Black universities

Social Work Staff 1 – *The training sessions for learning management systems were taught online. This was challenging because one is alone in his/her corner trying to understand foreign interventions and there is no one able to assist as all academic staff were unfamiliar with e-learning. Thankfully some of the colleagues managed to navigate their way through Blackboard and assist the rest of us in the department.*

Social Work Student 1 – *Online learning affected me tremendously and negatively because I felt like a failure. Not knowing how to engage in a class session with everyone else was very stressful.*

The views of the academic underline individually held fears and anxieties when confronted with the complexities of online teaching delivery. The use of the term 'foreign interventions' also evokes the sense of a pedagogy that is imposed from outside and is not necessarily cognisant of local realities. This emphasises that online learning may not be, or at least feel like, a universal solution to a learning challenge. The sense of challenge had a clear impact on student learning and wellbeing. Such reactions must be considered when working with social work students who need to be able to engage in classes not only to attain the required professional knowledge, but also to model and develop the interpersonal skills that are inherent in the profession.

Plagiarism

Anney and Mosha (2015) report that student plagiarism in South Africa is a major issue and the rise of online learning and the use of the Internet more generally exacerbates the issue and complicates its identification. The assessment of online exams is difficult to 'police' in that students can access and use external sources to help them in their answers and can share ideas with each other. The example below not only illustrates this, but also brings into view an additional ethical issue for social work students in that honesty and trustworthiness are the cornerstones of the value base of the profession.

Social Work Student 2 – *The other online technology that was used for teaching and learning was the use of cell phones whereby learners will share documents then write a test answering the document while reading shared documents.*

One key issue is that most lecturers complain about plagiarism, but they do not enforce the use of plagiarism checks for their students work from an early stage, such as the first year of study. Commonly the reasoning behind not introducing plagiarism checks at the commencement of studies is because lecturers are of the view that plagiarism checks are more applicable to student research in the final year of study than for general assignments (Nwosu and Chukwuere, 2020). The ethical and values base of social work is promoted and adhered to from the start of a social work programme rather than one that develops over time. This places social work education in an ethical dilemma compared to other academic programmes as issues of plagiarism have importance at all levels of study. The educational environment and workload are often not conducive to the application of plagiarism checks as it is perceived to create more work for lecturers; hence, many lecturers complain about plagiarism but opt not to apply the use of plagiarism checks (Nwosu and Chukwuere, 2020). This has significant implications for social work education and is an important challenge and issue to surfaced as the proliferation of online learning and assessment emerges. The quote below shows how the issue is 'felt' by social work staff, and the implications it has for the staff/student relationship.

Social Work Staff 3 – *I have started reporting cases of plagiarism to the faculty of humanities to deal with students because it became exhausting to constantly warn students about plagiarising.*

In social work education, the need to be able to accurately assess student knowledge and skill acquisition is central to the trust that the public can have of the profession. There are elements, such as practicum, that commonly exist outside the online sphere. However, the use of long essays as a means of assessment is common in that they allow for reflection and criticality to emerge and be visible. This type of assessment is vulnerable to inappropriate use of textual online sources and indeed the proliferation of essay writing websites. This will be a challenge for social work education globally but is exacerbated in contexts where skills and accessibility are patchy and inconsistent.

Implications for Fieldwork and Integration of Knowledge

The South African Council for Social Service Professions (SACSSP, 2020) established minimal norms and standards for social work education and training in South African universities to uphold quality education of the Bachelor of Social Work (BSW) programmes. The SACSSP standards aim at ensuring that the BSW programme presented at South African universities produces knowledgeable graduates who understand and effectively implement the ethics and values of the profession. These foundations are familiar with accredited programmes across the globe, and, at their core, they require students to gain a broad range of knowledge and skills that are then developed and used in practice contexts. This essential application of knowledge is underpinned by the need to ensure that students can access suitable learning opportunities to give confidence to universities, service providers, and service users that practice is informed and infused with appropriate knowledge and values (Smith and Rasool, 2020). The incorporation of online approaches (as we have seen) compromises the ability to track engagement, assess knowledge, and facilitate access.

In the context of the inconsistent access, technical difficulties and limited training, the online sphere can also reduce the opportunities for scaffolded learning of skills in the classroom using techniques such as role-playing and simulated practice contexts (Smith and Rasool, 2020). If we accept that social work is a relationship-based endeavor (Ingram, 2015) that relies upon the purposeful and effective interpersonal interactions between social workers and service users, then we can see the pitfalls that await a social work programme that risks the reduction of such skills development. Motaung and Makombe (2021, p. 110)

'identified three challenges of online learning, namely

(i) the tendency for tutors to lecture instead of probing students to think critically,
(ii) not allowing students sufficient time to reflect on what was learned, and
(iii) the general tendency among students to read posts without replying (lurking)'.

This tendency to passivity and reduced criticality is also a concern even if students are engaged and able to access their learning in a timely manner. The first-hand experience that students gained from practice placements prior to lockdown that sought to improve and reinforce professional ethics, principles, and knowledge became restricted as personal contact was limited to non-existent. This context was temporary, but the continuance of online learning may perpetuate these concerns and issues (Sekonyela, 2021). The driver behind the research project that underpins this chapter was the unplanned response to the COVID-19 pandemic. The views and experiences explored above emerge from this context, but they also have provided an opportunity to consider the multifaceted challenges involved in online learning in the Global South and specifically within the pedagogical and professional context of social work education. Subsequent to this study, the selected universities have reviewed the potential for continuing with elements of online learning and have decided to return to a campus-based in-person mode of delivery. This academic decision is underpinned by the factors explored in this chapter: the digital divide caused by financial inequalities; the value placed on in-person modes of teaching delivery and practice pedagogies; the rise in issues of plagiarism and academic performance; and the need to ensure that students attain and can apply a robust body of knowledge in keeping with the social work profession.

Conclusion

This chapter articulates a lens that recognises the need to consider social work education issues within the context of prevailing social and economic conditions as well as historical and current disparities in terms of power, imperialism, and assumed universalism of solutions and developments. The exceptional circumstances of the COVID-19 pandemic prompted the need for seeking alternative ways of delivering education, and online learning became the default response globally. This chapter highlights that, once enacted, the effectiveness and experience of using online learning diverges in differing contexts, and many of the issues raised here are indicative of the context of the Global South. Additionally, there are messages here for social work education globally to consider the specific needs and aspirations for the profession and the impact online learning may have on equipping the next generation of practitioners with the requisite knowledge, skills, and values and to reflect upon and protect the pedagogical approaches that most richly deliver on the needs of the profession.

Recommendations

1. Universities should embed plagiarism checking tools into Blackboard to manage plagiarism.
2. Service providers should be engaged by university management to upgrade fibres and cables closer to rural university campuses to improve connectivity.
3. As a means of embracing the fourth industrial revolution, regular training on eLearning should be provided to staff and students across South Africa to reach the same level of competency as the Global North.

Further Reading

Banks, S., Cai, T., De Jonge, E., Shears, J., Shum, M., Sobočan, A. M., Strom, K., Truell, R., Úriz, M. J., and Weinberg, M. (2020). Practising ethically during COVID-19: Social work challenges and responses. *International Social Work*, *63*(5), 569–583.

Pete, J., and Soko, J. (2020). Preparedness for online learning in the context of Covid-19 in selected Sub-Saharan African countries. *Asian Journal of Distance Education*, *15*(2), 37–47.

Zimba, Z. F., Khosa, P., and Pillay, R. (2021). Using blended learning in South African social work education to facilitate student engagement. *Social Work Education*, *40*(2), 263–278.

References

Abdulmajeed, K., Joyner, D. A., and McManus, C. (2020). Challenges of online learning in Nigeria. Proceedings of the Seventh ACM Conference on Learning@ Scale, 417–420.

Anney, V. N., and Mosha, M. A. (2015). Student's plagiarisms in higher learning institutions in the era of improved Internet access: Case study of developing countries. *Journal of Education and Practice*, *6*(13), 203–216.

Arthur-Nyarko, E., and Kariuki, M. G. (2019). Learner access to resources for elearning and preference for eLearning delivery mode in distance education programmes in Ghana. *International Journal of Educational Technology*, *6*(2), 1–8.

Boling, E. C., Hough, M., Krinsky, H., Saleem, H., and Stevens, M. (2012). Cutting the distance in distance education: Perspectives on what promotes online learning experiences. *Internet and Higher Education*, *15*(2), 118–126.

Bucciarelli, E., Muratore, F., and Odoardi, I. (2010). Consolidation processes of human capital in modern economic growth dynamics: An estimate based on the role of European corporate e-learning activities. In H. Keser, Z. Ozcinar, and S. Kanbul (Eds.), *World Conference on Learning, Teaching and Administration Papers* (Vol. 9). Amsterdam: Elsevier Science Bv.

Czerniewicz, L., and Rother, K. (2018). Institutional educational technology policy and strategy documents: An inequality gaze. *Research in Comparative and International Education*, *13*(1), 27–45.

Denzin, N. K., and Lincoln, Y.S. (2012). *Strategies of Qualitative Research*. Thousand Oaks: Sage.

Dube, B. (2020). Rural online learning in the context of COVID 19 in South Africa: Evoking an inclusive education approach. *REMIE: Multidisciplinary Journal of Educational Research*, *10*(2), 135–157.

Gómez-Ciriano, E. J. (2020). Making virtue of necessity. Experiences and lessons from Spain during Covid-19. *Social Work Education*, *39*(8), 1002–1009.

Hidalgo, A., Gabaly, S., Morales-Alonso, G., and Urueña, A. (2020). The digital divide in light of sustainable development: An approach through advanced machine learning techniques. *Technological Forecasting and Social Change*, *150*.

Ingram, R. (2015). *Understanding Emotions in Social Work: Theory, Practice and Reflection*. London: McGraw Hill.

Jung, Y., and Lee, J. (2018). Learning engagement and persistence in massive open online courses (MOOCS). *Computers and Education*, *12*(2), 9–22.

Motaung, L. B., and Makombe, R. (2021). Tutor experiences of online tutoring as a basis for the development of a focused tutor-training programme. *The Independent Journal of Teaching and Learning*, *16*(2), 101–117.

Mpungose, C. B. (2020). Emergent transition from face-to-face to online learning in a South African University in the context of the coronavirus pandemic. *Humanities and Social Sciences Communications*, *7*(1), 1–9.

Nwosu, L. I., and Chukwuere, J. E. (2020). The attitude of students towards plagiarism in online learning: A narrative literature review. *Gender and Behaviour*, *18*(1), 14675–14688.

Rubin, H. J., and Rubin, I. S. (2012). *Qualitative Interviewing: The Art of Hearing Data*. 3rd ed. Los Angeles: Sage.

Sekonyela, L. (2021). Student challenges with the university access programme in South Africa. *Journal of Ethnic and Cultural Studies*, *8*(1), 239–270.

Smith, L., and Rasool, S. (2020). Deep transformation toward decoloniality in social work: Themes for change in a social work higher education programme. *Journal of Progressive Human Services*, *31*(2), 144–164.

Sokhweba, X., Obokoh, L., Abiola, B., and Oji, C. C. (2021). The effect of national student financial aid scheme on Student's access to tertiary education in a selected university in the Western Cape. Reshaping Sustainable Development Goals Implementation in the World: Proceeding of 7th International Conference on Business and Management Dynamics, 200–211. https://doi.org/10.9734/bpi/mono/978-93-5547-236-6/CH15.

Soomro, K. A., Kale, U., Curtis, R., Akcaoglu, M., and Bernstein, M. (2020). Digital divide among higher education faculty. *International Journal of Educational Technology in Higher Education*, *17*(1), 1–16.

South African Council for Social Service Professions. (2020). Guidance for social service professionals and their employers on sustained and professional practice during the national state of disaster: COVID-19 pandemic. Notice 2 of 2020. www.sacssp.co.za/2020/GENERAL%20NOTICE%20%202%20OF%202020%20-COVID-19%20AND%20SSPs%2027%20March%202020.pdf.

Sun, A., and Chen, X. (2016). Online education and its effective practice: A research review. *Journal of Information Technology Education: Research*, *15*, 157–190.

United Nations Education Scientific and Cultural Organisation (UNESCO). (2020). COVID-19 educational disruption and response. https://en.unesco.org/covid19/educationresponse.

World Bank. (2020a). Individuals using the internet (% of population) data. https://data.worldbank.org/indicator/IT.NET.USER.ZS?name_desc=false.

World Bank. (2020b). World Bank education and COVID-19. https://www.worldbank.org/en/data/interactive/2020/03/24/world-bank-education-and-covid-19.

Yende, S. J. (2021). Funding opportunities and challenges: A case of South African institutions of higher learning. *Journal of Public Administration*, *56*(1), 70–79.

Yuan, J., and Kim, C. (2014). Guidelines for facilitating the development of learning communities in online courses. *Journal of Computer Assisted Learning*, *30*(3), 220–232.

13
SOCIAL WORKER ROLE-TAKING DURING COMMUNICABLE DISEASE OUTBREAKS IN SOUTH AFRICA

The Need for Disaster Management Training

Christo Heunis, Mariëtte Joubert, and Alice Ncube

Abstract: English

From being a voluntary job caring for the poor in late-19th-century Europe and North America, social work has become an occupation and, of late, a profession. Professional social work demands operating within a multi-stakeholder system, rendering psychosocial services to vulnerable populations in a coordinated manner. The South African Council for Social Service Professions (SACSSP) directs that social workers are ethically obliged to assist during public emergencies. However, these professionals mostly lack knowledge on how to render adequate mental health services to vulnerable groups and frontline responders during communicable disease disasters. Declared a disaster globally and nationally, the COVID-19 pandemic is a poignant case example. Although the social work curriculum in South Africa includes training on primary social work methods, no local university offers under- or post-graduate training in disaster management or communicable disease disaster management specifically. This chapter attempts to integrate knowledge from the disaster management and social work disciplines to highlight the gaps among legislation, policies, guidelines, training, and practice. The chapter advocates for changes to the social work curriculum to include disaster mental health training. It also provides a checklist for minimum competencies and value standards for social work services during communicable disease disasters.

Abstract: isiZulu

Ngesikhathi esedlule sezigidi zeminyaka angamashumi ayisishiyagalolunye (19th century), emazweni anjenge Europe ne North America, umsebenzi wabezenhlalakahle waqala ngokuba abantu bazinikele ukwenza umsebenzi wokunakekelwa kwabantu abahluphekayo ngaphandle kokuthola inzuzo. Manje, lomsebenzi usungumsebenzi wobuchwepheshe.

Ubuchwepheshe kwezehlalakahle kudinga ukusebenzisana kwabantu abaningi kanye nayoyonke imikhakha ekhona ukuze kulethwe izinzisa zokululeka abantu ngokwenqondo.

Umkhandlu wase Ningizimu Afrika obhekene nezenhlalakahle (South African Council for Social Service Professions) ikubona kubalulekile ukuthi abezenhlalakahle basize umphakathi uma kunezimo eziphuthumayo. Kodwa, ucwaningo luveza ukuthi abezehlalakahle abanalo ulwazi olwanele lokusiza umphakathi ozithola uhlaselwe izinhlekelele kanye nalabo abawulethela usizo, ikakhulukazi labo abasebenza ngezifo ezithathelanayo. Isifo seCOVID-19 (esabayinhlekelele eNingizimu Afrika nasemhlabeni wonke) siyisibonelo esihle esaveza ukuthi ulwazi ngezinhlekelele luyadingeka kwabezenhlalakahle.

Amanyuvesi aseNingizimu Africa afundisa abezenhlalakahle, mazifundisi izifundo zolwazi ngezinhlenkelele kanye nezifundo ezimayelana nezifo ezithathelanayo. Afundisa kuphela ngolwazi lokusebenza ngomphakathi.

Lesisahluko sizama ukuhlanganisa ulwazi lomsebenzi wabezenhlalakahle kanye no lwazi ngo kusebenza ngezinhlekelele. Lokhu kwenziwa ngokucwangingisisa imithetho yase Ningizimu AfriKa, ulwazi olukhona, imihlahlandlela kanye nendlela yokusebenza.

Lesisahluko siphide sikhuthaze ukubaluleka kokufundisa abezenhlalakahle ngokusebenza ngezinhlekelele ikakhulukazi ukusiza umphakathi ngokwelapha ngokwengqondo bese sikhombisa indlela yokwenza ezosiza abazenhlalakahle ibakhombise okufanele bakwenze uma bebhekene nezimo zezinhlekelele.

Introduction

The social work profession plays a critical role in the social care trajectory of individuals in times of need and social vulnerability. Social workers deal with people's 'hearts' as much as their minds. They can have a 'make or break' influence on vulnerable people's responses to a communicable disease disaster. While social work curricula focus on teaching students generic social work skills, it is also important for social workers to understand disaster management legislation, frameworks, policies, guidelines, and resources, as well as their application in practice. This will enable them to more effectively and efficiently perform their roles in multidisciplinary frontline responder teams during man-made and natural disasters.

Because social workers are not always aware of international and national requirements and guidelines, they may fail vulnerable communities during disasters. Just as they are more susceptible to the impacts of disasters, vulnerable groups are more prone to discrimination and stigma, further decreasing their mental health and psychosocial wellbeing during these events. Besides the need to be knowledgeable about universal social work and disaster management principles (such as human rights, social justice, and empowerment/resilience), social work students also need practical training on how to effectively fulfil their roles in multidisciplinary disaster management teams as professional frontline responders during disasters.

As articulated below, another challenge is to indigenise and attune social work services and the social work training curriculum to African conditions and cultures:

"The current system has been transplanted from elsewhere, with alien traditions and cultural forms. It needs to be reconstructed, not only to fit the social structures and cultural environments in Africa, but also to serve African needs and aspirations," (Qalinge and van Breda, 2018, p. 1).

"For years, social work has been taught and practised based on Western and Northern theories … As a result, there is a need to focus on developing a local theory that will be responsive to the needs of local clients. [It would] be beneficial to the profession and to indigenous communities if all practitioners could commit to this call." (Sekudu, 2019, p. 280)

This chapter explores role-taking by South African social workers to assist vulnerable populations during communicable disease disasters, such as the COVID-19 pandemic. Global, continental, and South African disaster management policies are elucidated. Case study 1 reports on research conducted among qualified social workers practicing in the Mangaung Metropolitan Municipality in the Free State province of South Africa to establish if they rendered adequate psychosocial services to vulnerable groups during this communicable disease disaster. The case argues for including disaster management competency areas in under- and post-graduate social work training curricula. Case study 2 draws attention to the need for social worker support of frontline responders, i.e. public and private sector nurses who experienced high levels of post-traumatic stress disorder (PTSD) during the COVID-19 pandemic in the Free State. Finally, the chapter provides a checklist of guidelines and standards for minimum competencies and value standards for social work during communicable disease disasters specifically.

The Social Work Landscape in South Africa

The social work landscape in South Africa is marked by continuing and widening inequality and poverty. This is most vividly illustrated by the country's GINI index, which, at 0.63, was the highest of any country in the world in 2014 (World Bank, 2022a). In 2020, approximately 30.3 million people (56%) lived in poverty as measured at the national upper poverty line at 992 South African Rand (World Bank, 2022b).

Originating in the apartheid era, South Africa's social security system sought to create a welfare system exclusively for white citizens. Since 1994, the democratic state's relief services have thus been focused on providing social grants for all population groups, especially those that were previously disadvantaged. Roughly one-third of the population are beneficiaries of social grants for older persons, people with disabilities, and children (Patel et al., 2023). According to these authors, the expansive temporary Social Relief of Distress (SRD) grant introduced for unemployed adults by the government in 2020 in response to the COVID-19 pandemic implied that almost half of the nation's population received social assistance in the form of an 'unconditional' monthly cash transfer. In 2022, the social grant investment accounted for 99.6% of the Department of Social Development's (DSD) entire budget allocation (DSD, 2022). It could, however, be argued that the pervasive lack of psychosocial and mental health services to vulnerable populations in South Africa is a result of the DSD's budget being overly directed towards (relief) grants rather than (relief) services.

In a country with a long history of colonial and apartheid-induced inequality and inequity in social and healthcare generally, the social work landscape in South Africa also includes the dire need to provide social work support to individuals and vulnerable groups amidst a rising 'quadruple burden of disease'. Even before COVID-19, the country experienced four 'colliding epidemics,' namely (1) human immunodeficiency virus (HIV) and tuberculosis (TB), (2) chronic illness and mental health, (3) injury and violence, and (4) maternal, neonatal, and child mortality, all with substantial adverse effects on the health and wellbeing of the population (Samodien et al., 2021; Achoki et al., 2022). South Africa's healthcare system broadly reflects structural challenges also faced by other southern African countries with similar disease burdens, lack of systemic infrastructure and cohesiveness, and pervasive social inequalities.

Defining 'Disaster'

Social researchers often emphasise 'social disruption' as a disaster's key defining feature or essential dimension. According to the United Nations (UN, 2016, p. 13), a 'disaster' is:

> A serious disruption of the functioning of a community or a society at any scale due to hazardous events interacting with conditions of exposure, vulnerability and capacity, leading to one or more of the following: human, material, economic and environmental losses and impacts.

South Africa's Disaster Management Act, No. 57 of 2002 (Chapter 1) defined a disaster as:

> a progressive or sudden, widespread or localised natural or human-caused occurrence which causes or threatens to cause death, injury or disease, damage to property, infrastructure or the environment, or significant disruption of the life of a community.

Adverse events such as disasters are interpreted through a system of meaning provided by culture. Historically, research into societies' responses to disasters focused on communities' resilience when facing adversity. However, since the 1980s, many scholars have questioned the earlier optimistic accounts. They have contended that disasters cause deep-seated long-term damage to communities. The new 'vulnerability paradigm' signalled a shift from an expectation of resilience to one of vulnerability.

Communicable Disease Disasters in Africa and South Africa

The detrimental effects of natural disasters have been documented since the start of recorded history around the fourth millennium before the common era. The damage and casualties caused by natural disasters significantly increased when humans began to inhabit built-up settlements. Africa is no exception; a study of regional humanitarian consequences of natural disasters between 1980 and 2004 showed that 2.61 per 100,000 population died during 861 natural disasters in this region (Strömberg, 2007, p. 203). Over the same period, other world regions reported substantially lower per capita death ratios resulting from natural disasters.

The period between 1500 and 1700 when several indigenous societies in North and South America, Africa, Australia, and Oceania were exposed to many Western epidemic diseases has been called 'the unification of the globe by disease' (Ladurie cited in Huber, 2006, p. 453). In the 'Cape of Good Hope' in South Africa, the indigenous population, the Khoikhoi, were particularly hard struck by smallpox. Smallpox epidemics that remained endemic in southern Africa for another century struck the Cape in 1713, 1755, and 1767, 'and so decimated the Khoikhoi that the very names of some hordes were forgotten' (Ross, 1977, p. 416).

The Spanish influenza outbreak in 1918–1919 was one of the worst natural disasters in African history. Of all six continents, Africa, particularly sub-Saharan Africa, suffered the highest mortality rate in the pandemic, decimating about 2% of the continent's population in just six months (Phillips, 2015). In South Africa, the total death count was between 250,000 and 300,000 out of a population of about 6.1 million in 1918 (Katzenellenbogen, 1988, p. 362). This country experienced altogether 150 years of European colonisation. The racial segregation in healthcare that first emerged during Dutch and English colonisation intensified under apartheid (or white Afrikaner) rule in the latter half of the 20th century. Described as the country's first national public health measure, the Public Health Act No. 36 of 1919 was a reaction to the influenza pandemic. The Act established a fragmented healthcare system with three tiers, namely national, provincial, and municipal/local, which, with some modifications, persisted into the apartheid and post-apartheid.

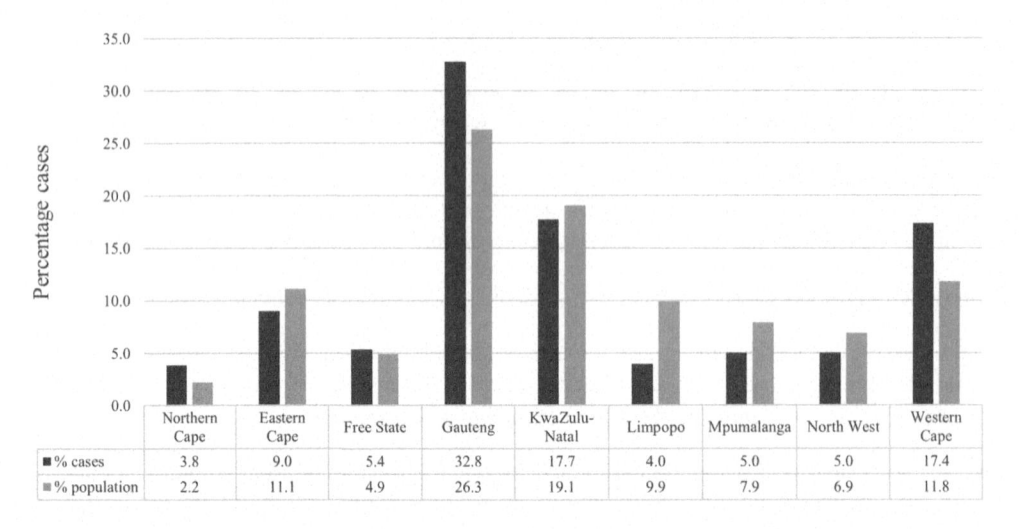

	Northern Cape	Eastern Cape	Free State	Gauteng	KwaZulu-Natal	Limpopo	Mpumalanga	North West	Western Cape
% cases	3.8	9.0	5.4	32.8	17.7	4.0	5.0	5.0	17.4
% population	2.2	11.1	4.9	26.3	19.1	9.9	7.9	6.9	11.8

Figure 13.1 Cumulative COVID-19 cases by province, 7 July 2022

Sources: National Institute of Communicable Diseases (2022); Statistics South Africa (2021).

The first COVID-19 case was confirmed in South Africa on 5 March 2020. By 31 August 2022, the cumulative number of cases had reached 4,011,937 (National Institute of Communicable Diseases, 2022). Figure 13.1 depicts the unequal distribution of cases across the country's nine provinces. Three mostly urban provinces, Gauteng, KwaZulu-Natal, and the Western Cape, represented the epicentres of the communicable disease disaster. These provinces' metropolitan areas are the major industrial hubs, destinations for local travel, as well as the major ports of entry for foreign visitors to the country. Simultaneously some more rural provinces, such as Limpopo, Mpumalanga, North West, and the Eastern Cape, recorded COVID-19 incidences far exceeding their proportions of the population.

The Sustainable Development Goals (SDGs) report of 2021 highlighted vast international inequities in COVID-19 vaccine distribution (UN, 2021, p. 3). As of 17 June 2021, around 68 vaccines were administered for every 100 people in Europe and Northern America, while fewer than two in every 100 people in sub-Saharan Africa were vaccinated. Therefore, there is a need for social workers to advocate for and convince African people of the need to undergo vaccination.

Global Agendas for Social Work and Frameworks for Disaster Risk Reduction

The Global Agenda for Social Work and Social Development was launched by three global bodies of social work, namely (1) the International Association of Schools of Social Work (IASSW), (2) the International Council on Social Welfare (ICSW), and (3) the International Federation of Social Workers (IFSW) during the 2010 Joint World Conference on Social Work and Social Development in Hong Kong (IASSW et al., 2020). The four pillars of the Global Agenda are to (1) promote social and economic equality, (2) advance the dignity and worth of people, (3) foster community and environmental sustainability, and (4) strengthen recognition of the importance of human relationships (IASSW et al., 2020).

Gaps between the social work profession's global and national agendas and their implementation have been criticised in African countries such as Zimbabwe, Ethiopia, Malawi, Ghana, and

Botswana. South Africa is no exception; in this country appropriate role-taking and plan enactment by social workers is continually frustrated by serious policy-implementation gaps in social work, generally, and in social work disaster mental health services, in particular.

Social Work in Africa

Globally, the social work profession first emerged in Europe and North America in the late 19th century. In Africa, social work was introduced by colonial administrators, missionaries, and industrialists with little concern for indigenous peoples' wellbeing. Professional social work in Africa was not widely accepted until the 1960s, when many nations gained independence. With many African countries now training their own social workers, it has since become a more widely recognised profession.

However, tribal and mutual assistance societies have existed in Africa for a long time. Before the creation of a legislative welfare system, individuals relied on family or kin, cultural structures, and/or religion. The African extended family is a prime example of a consistently operating social welfare system.

Social Work in South Africa

South Africa was the first country in Africa to begin social work education and training in the 1920s. As in the West generally, the social work profession was born out of a concern for 'white poverty' and was predominantly a 'white profession'. Initially, a 'residual approach' was followed, meaning that state welfare would be introduced if the economy and family systems failed people. In the post-apartheid era, South Africa's social services have moved towards following a 'social development approach'.

The social development approach is in line with the Global Agenda for Social Work and Social Development (IASSW et al., 2020), the Sendai Framework for Disaster Risk Reduction 2015–2030 (SFDRR) (UN, 2015a), the SDGs (UN, 2015b), Agenda 2063 (African Union [AU] Commission, 2015) and Southern African Development Community (SADC) protocols (2020) that motivate community-based, non-discriminatory, and unifying practices to prevent and mitigate the effects of disasters and build communities' resilience. However, as shown in Case study 1, research in a metropolitan setting in South Africa showed that only about half of the social workers rendered services to vulnerable population groups during the first three COVID-19 'lockdown' stages.

Case Study 1: Social Work Services to Vulnerable Populations in Mangaung Metropolitan Municipality, Free State, South Africa

A quantitative study was conducted to establish whether social workers in the urban area of Mangaung Metropolitan Municipality were able to render adequate resilience-focused interventions to vulnerable groups to optimise their mental health and psychosocial wellbeing during the COVID-19 pandemic from 27 March until 30 September 2020. Data were collected among 159 social workers using a voluntary and anonymous online self-administered questionnaire. The results showed that only a small minority of participants had received disaster management training before 2020 (17.6%, n=28). Some participants (13.8%, n=22) indicated they received disaster management training after the commencement of the COVID-19 outbreak. However, the majority (68.6%, n=109) of social workers stated that they had not received any disaster management training.

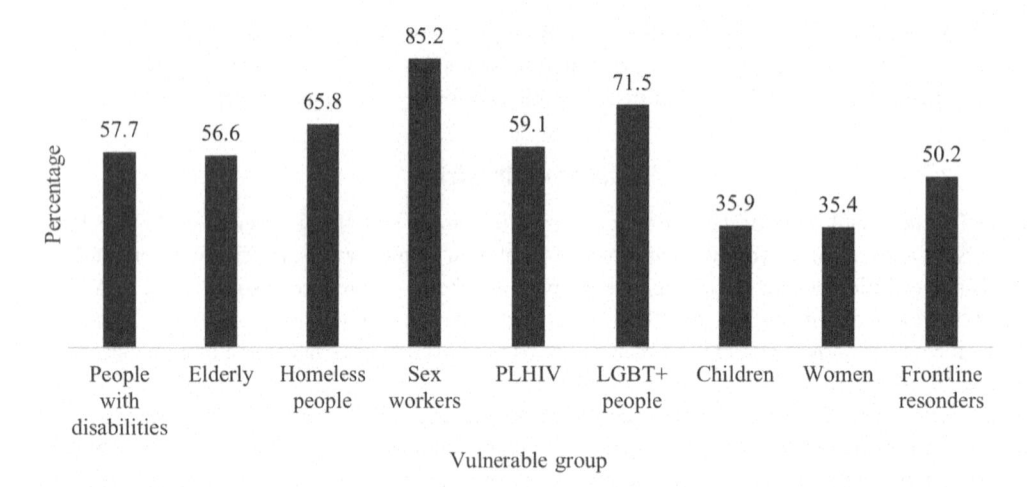

Figure 13.2 Social workers indicating non-delivery of services to vulnerable groups in MMM during COVID-19

Figure 13.2 shows that during COVID-19 more than one-third of social workers did not provide services to children (36%) and women (35%); half did not provide services to frontline responders (50%); and the majority did not provide services to people with disabilities (58%), the elderly (57%), homeless people (66%), sex workers (85%), PLHIV (59%), and LGBT+ people (72%).

Case Study 1 found that social workers did not effectively support health professionals during the COVID-19 outbreak. This is concerning because, as shown in Case Study 2, high levels of PTSD occurred among both public and private sector nurses during the second wave (5 December 2020 to 3 March 2021) of COVID-19 in the Free State province.

Case Study 2: Post-traumatic Stress among Nurses during the Second Wave of the COVID-19 Pandemic in the Free State Province, South Africa

Prior to the 2019 novel coronavirus (COVID-19) outbreak, the South African healthcare system was already under severe strain due to lack of human resources, poor governance and management, and an unequal distribution of resources between the provinces, on the one hand, and the public and private healthcare sectors, on the other hand. At the center of these challenges were primary healthcare (PHC) nurses, the 'backbone of the healthcare system,' and the first point of call for most healthcare users in the country. This research investigated the incidence of PTSD among 286 public and private sector nurses during the second wave (5 December 2020 to 3 March 2021) of COVID-19 in the Free State province. Overall, the nurses had a mean score of 31.5 (SD 20.586) on the Impact of Events Scale-Revised (IES-R). As shown in Figure 13.3, 44.4% of the nurses scored above 32 on the IES-R, which is indicative of high levels of PTSD, with 38.8% of the nurses experiencing severe PTSD.

Unpreparedness and inexpertness to manage COVID-19 patients, poorer health, and avoidant coping strategies were associated with PTSD. Emotional, psychological, and debriefing intervention sessions that focus on positive coping strategies to actively address stress; positive and open communication between managers and their subordinates; psychological support; referral for more intensive psychotherapy where necessary; regular debriefing sessions where nurses can share their experiences; positive messaging from the provincial and national health departments; and an uninterrupted supply of quality personal protective equipment (PPE) were recommended.

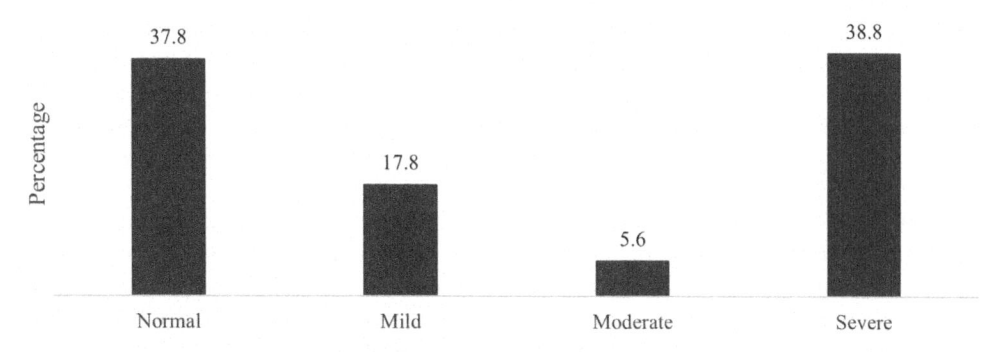

Figure 13.3 Levels of post-traumatic stress

Case Study 2 suggests that social workers may not be trained and capacitated to provide mental health services to frontline responders, including the crucial healthcare workers at the coalface of the pandemic. This belies the importance of a multi-agency or whole-system response where the social work profession efficiently and effectively supports and cares for their health sector counterparts.

Africa's Policy Framework for Disaster Risk Management

The African Union's (AU) Africa Regional Strategy for Disaster Risk Reduction (ARSDRR) was adopted in 2004 (AU, 2004). A Programme of Action (POA) for implementing the SFDRR 2015-2030 was launched to align the ARSDRR with the SFDRR (AU, 2017). The POA promotes a multi-disciplinary approach focused on the importance of indigenous knowledge and community participation to build resilience, reduce poverty, and increase sustainable development (AU, 2017). However, the POA, the Guide for Integrated Planning (SADC, 2020), and Agenda 2063 (AU Commission, 2015) do not explicitly refer to mental health or psychosocial services and thus do not recognise the vital role that mental health professionals, including social workers, can play in assisting vulnerable populations to improve their psychosocial and mental welbeing during disasters. To build community resilience that draws knowledge from indigenous, culturally appropriate community engagement, the importance of trusting relationships and psychosocial interventions must be highlighted and included in disaster management frameworks, as well as social work training curricula.

South Africa's Policy Framework for Disaster Risk Management

Dramatic, complex, and interrelated sociopolitical, economic, and environmental disruptions brought about by various natural and man-made disasters informed the continuous revision of civil protection or disaster management frameworks and legislation in South Africa. In 1998, the first Green Paper and, in 1999, the first White Paper on Disaster Management were issued by the Department of Justice and Constitutional Development (DoJ&CD). The White Paper advocated for improved ability to reduce disaster risk. The Disaster Management Act No. 57 of 2002 prompted continued discussions with relevant stakeholders to facilitate consensual understanding of the concept of 'disaster'. The Department of Provincial and Local Government's (DPLG) National Disaster Management Framework 2005 (NDMF) was a strategy to align South Africa's disaster management legislation with international best practices in the field.

While not explicitly referring to 'disasters', the SACSSP's Policy Guidelines for Course of Conduct, Code of Ethics and the Rules for Social Workers stated that social workers are ethically obliged to provide appropriate professional services during 'public emergencies' (2004, p. 42). In the social work perspective, emergency management implies the coordination of the disaster social services delivery system to ensure resources are redistributed to benefit vulnerable populations most heavily impacted by disasters.

The NDMF (RSA, 2005) is the legal instrument to address the need for consistency across multiple interest groups by providing a coherent, transparent, and inclusive policy on disaster management appropriate for the country as a whole. The Framework emphasised measures that reduce the vulnerability of 'disaster-prone areas, communities and households' and advocated for a 'multi-state organ' approach to plan and operate in the disaster risk response through implementing policy and legislation (RSA, 2005, p. 15).

No reference to mental health or psychosocial services per se was made in the Disaster Management Amendment Act No. 57 of 2015. The role of social workers in mitigating mental health challenges during disasters is thus negated in this legislation, which does not explicitly recognise social workers as frontline responders to disasters.

A further policy gap is that not a single South African university's social work curriculum currently includes training in disaster management to equip students with resilience-building skills and coping mechanisms to help sustain and improve vulnerable groups' emotional wellbeing during and after disasters. There is thus an urgent need to include disaster social work in under- and post-graduate curricula, including attention to disaster social work–related policies, legislation, and, importantly, practice guidelines. It is also necessary to develop Afrocentric social work practices attuned to local cultural understandings of (communicable disease) disasters and how to mitigate their effects. The aforesaid wide non-uptake of COVID-19 vaccination in African populations attests to the need to address 'cultural' challenges during communicable disease disasters.

Social Work and Disaster Management Responses to COVID-19 in Africa

The COVID-19 pandemic has again drawn attention to the contentions and inadequacies of social work in Africa:

> Pointedly, social work is challenged in Africa, given the profession's colonial heritage in which the casework model has long been the hallmark of and gold standard for education and practice (Amadasun, 2021, p. 246).

Social work is a human rights profession and assumes that human rights are embedded in social work practice and education. However, in Africa, where human rights violations are rife, with severe implications for social work practice and education, thus far, a human rights focus on social work education has not yet received sufficient attention. Social work educators in Africa should take up the challenge of adopting and integrating a pedagogy to expedite the infusion of human rights values in the social work curriculum.

Guidelines and Standards for Minimum Competencies and Value Standards for Social Work during Communicable Disease Disasters

Derived from literature, legislation, and the case study results, the below suggested checklist (Table 13.1) indicates minimum competencies and value standards for social work during communicable disease disasters.

Table 13.1 Checklist for Minimum Competencies and Value Standards for Social Work during Communicable Disease Disasters

---

As a social worker:
- I am well informed about current international guiding frameworks and my own country's directives for disaster management, mental health, and social work.
- I know my designated community well enough to render appropriate services that community members will want to access.
- I know:
1. the main community roleplayers/leaders; and
2. the communities' values, traditions, cultural practices, strengths, and resources.
- I recognise that my community situation analysis should include:
1. the social determinants of the communicable disease outbreak;
2. risk factors making the community vulnerable to the disease;
3. disease protective factors, such as personal protective equipment;
4. communicable disease control strengths; and
5. resources to mitigate the severity and enhance communities' resilience to withstand and 'build back better' after disasters.
- I adopt an Afrocentric intervention approach focusing on preventing and mitigating communicable disease disasters during the pre-disaster phase.
- During the communicable disease disaster, my interventions are aimed at immediate psychosocial assistance to vulnerable groups, including frontline healthcare workers.
- Post-disaster, my interventions relate to 'building back better' (i.e., increasing clients' coping skills, rendering trauma counselling, and endeavouring to optimise clients' emotional wellbeing) during future disease outbreaks.
- I value feedback from communicable disease control stakeholders, roleplayers, and clients and try to incorporate their suggestions in the subsequent interventions.
- My communicable disease control interventions are relevant and timely and consider clients' needs.
- I recognise the importance of a well-coordinated and complementary multisector and multidisciplinary frontline team to provide the best possible communicable disease control interventions.
- I endeavour to enhance communicable disease vulnerable groups' (including healthcare professionals) physical and emotional safety, dignity and rights, and resilience.
- I advocate on all system levels for just and fair systems that promote my clients' rights and access to mental health and psychosocial resources during communicable disease disasters.
- I ensure that my clients can access the correct information regarding communicable diseases.
- I help my clients to timeously access prevention services and, if needed, treatment for communicable diseases at their nearest healthcare facility.
- I provide impartial psychosocial assistance according to disproportional needs during communicable disease outbreaks.
- I attempt to strengthen Afrocentric resources and capacities during communicable disease outbreaks.
- I advocate for the provision of adequate resources and psychosocial support for social workers to provide suitable mental health services during communicable disease outbreaks.
- I advocate, promote, and facilitate the destigmatisation of communicable diseases, mental health illnesses, and access to social and health services.

Sources: Core Humanitarian Standard (CHS, 2015); UN (2015a 2015b); Sphere Association (2018); Inter-Agency Standing Committee (2021)

Conclusion

As part of multidisciplinary teams, social workers can provide valuable holistic mental health and psychosocial assistance to vulnerable groups, including frontline healthcare workers, thereby strengthening their resilience and mental health wellbeing during and after disasters. This chapter provides a synthesis of available international and national social work disaster mental health policies and guidelines. This information may aid curriculum developers and instructional designers in planning under- and post-graduate training programmes for social workers. In so doing, social workers can be empowered and capacitated to fulfil their profession's crucial role in a multidisciplinary team approach to communicable disease disasters that utilises all available state organs and apparatuses efficiently and effectively.

As evidenced by the inequitable effects of the COVID-19 pandemic in South Africa and Africa at large, culturally appropriate or Afrocentric social work provision will facilitate prompt and sustainable responses among socially vulnerable communities disproportionally affected by communicable disease disasters. The inclusion of communicable disease disaster management in under- and postgraduate social work curricula will further the national and continental drive towards achieving the Global Agenda for Social Work and Social Development, the SFDRR, the SDGs, Agenda 2063, and the SADC protocols.

Recommendations

The following recommendations are made for improved South African and African social work education and culturally relevant curricula:

1. Include Afrocentric communicable disease-specific disaster social work mental health training into under- and post-graduate social work training curricula.
2. Develop and present short courses or continued professional development in communicable disease disaster social work mental health for qualified social workers.
3. Advocate for the inclusion of social workers in multidisciplinary communicable disease frontline teams.

Further Reading

Africa Union (2017). Programme of action for the implementation of the Sendai framework for disaster risk reduction 2015–2030 in Africa. Available at: https://www.unisdr.org/files/49455_poaforsendaiimplementationinafrica.pdf (Accessed: 20 May 2023).

United Nations (2015). Framework for Disaster Risk Reduction 2015–2030. Available at: https://www.preventionweb.net/files/43291_sendaiframeworkfordrren.pdf (Accessed: 20 May 2023).

References

Achoki, T., Sartorius, B., Watkins, D., Glenn, S.D., Kengne, A.P., Oni, T., Wiysonge, C.S., Walker, A., et al (2022). Health trends, inequalities and opportunities in South Africa's provinces, 1990–2019: findings from the global burden of disease 2019 study. *Journal of Epidemiology and Community Health*, 76(5), 471–481. doi: 10.1136/jech-2021-217480.

African Union (2004). Disaster risk reduction for sustainable development in Africa. Africa regional strategy for disaster risk reduction. July 2004. Available at: https://www.undrr.org/publication/africa-regional-strategy-disaster-risk-reduction (Accessed: 5 June 2023).

African Union (2017). Programme of Action for the Implementation of the Sendai Framework for Disaster Risk Reduction 2015–2030 in Africa. Available at: https://www.unisdr.org/files/49455_poaforsendaiimplementationinafrica.pdf (Accessed: 19 May 2023).

African Union Commission (2015). Agenda 2063: The Africa we want. Available at: https://au.int/en/agenda2063/overview (Accessed: 19 May 2023).

Amadasun, S. (2021). COVID-19 pandemic in Africa: What lessons for social work education and practice? *International Social Work*, 64(2), 246–250. doi: 10.1177/0020872820949620.

Core Humanitarian Standard Alliance (2015). *CHS Guidance Notes and Indicators*. 2nd edn. Available at: https://d1h79zlghft2zs.cloudfront.net/uploads/2020/09/CHS_GNI_2018.pdf (Accessed: 19 May 2023).

Department of Justice and Constitutional Development (1999). White Paper on Disaster Management. Available at: https://www.gov.za/documents/disaster-management-white-paper (Accessed: 19 May 2023).

Department of Provincial and Local Government (2005). SA National Disaster Management Framework, 2005. Available at: https://www.westerncape.gov.za/text/2013/July/sa-national-disaster-man-framework-2005.pdf (Accessed: 19 May 2023).

Department of Social Development (2022). Minister Lindiwe Zulu: Social development dept budget vote 2022/3. Available at: https://www.gov.za/speeches/minister-lindiwe-zulu-social-development%C2%A0dept-budget-vote-202223-13-may-2022-0000 (Accessed: 20 May 2023).

Dikoko, V. and Patel, L. (2023). *Social Grants and Livelihoods. An Analysis of NIDS Waves 1 and 5 (2008 and 2017) and NIDS-CRAM Wave 1 and Wave 5 (2020 and 2021)*. Johannesburg: University of Johannesburg.

Disaster Management Act, No. 57 of 2002. *Government Gazette*. 5 January 2003. Cape Town.

Disaster Management Amendment act, No. 16 of 2015. *Government Gazette*. 15 December 2015. Cape Town.

Engelbrecht, M.C., Heunis, J.C. and Kigozi, N.G. (2021). Post-traumatic stress and coping strategies of South African nurses during the second wave of the COVID-19 pandemic. *International Journal of Environmental Research and Public Health*, 18(15), 7919. doi: 10.3390/ijerph18157919.

Huber, V. (2006). The unification of the globe by disease? The International Sanitary Conferences on Cholera, 1851-1894. *The Historical Journal*, 49(2), 453–476. doi: 10.1017/S0018246X06005280.

Inter-Agency Standing Committee (2021). *Technical Note. Linking Disaster Risk Reduction (DRR) and Mental Health and Psychosocial Support (MHPSS): Practical Tools, Approaches and Case Studies*. Geneva: IASC.

International Association of Schools of Social Work, International Council on Social Welfare and International Federation of Social Workers (2020). *Global Agenda for Social Work and Social Development: Fourth Report. Strengthening Recognition of the Importance of Human Relationships*. Rheinfelden: IFSW.

Joubert, M., Heunis, C., Ncube, A. and Szarzynski, J. (2021). Delivery of disaster social work services to increase the resilience of vulnerable groups during COVID-19 in Mangaung metropolitan municipality. 9th Annual Free State Health Research Day on Health, Disease Management and Health Systems in COVID-19 Times, 4 November. Free State Department of Health and University of the Free State, Bloemfontein.

Katzenellenbogen, J. (1988). The 1918 influenza epidemic in Mamre. *South African Medical Journal*, 74(7), 362–364.

Miner, C.A., Timothy, C.G., Mashige, K.P., Osuagwu, U.L., Envuladu, E.A., Amiebenomo, O.M., Ovenseri-Ogbomo, G., Charwe, D.D. et al. (2023). Acceptance of COVID-19 vaccine among sub-Saharan Africans (SSA): A comparative study of residents and diasporan dwellers. *BMC Public Health*, 23(1), 191. https://doi.org/10.1186/s12889-023-15116-w.

National Institute for Communicable Diseases (2022). National COVID-19 situation summary. Available at: https://www.nicd.ac.za/diseases-a-z-index/disease-index-covid-19/surveillance-reports/national-covid-19-daily-report/ (Accessed: 19 May 2023).

Patel, L., Dikoko, V. and Archer, J. (2023). *Research Brief. Social Grants, Livelihoods and Poverty Responses of Social Grant Beneficiaries in South Africa*. Johannesburg: Centre for Social Development in Africa, University of Johannesburg.

Phillips, H. (2015). Influenza pandemic (Africa). In Daniel, U. et al. (eds.) *International Encyclopedia of the First World War*. Available at: https://encyclopedia.1914-1918-online.net/article/influenza_pandemic_africa (Accessed: 20 May 2023).

Public Health Act No. 36 of 1919 (1919). *Union Gazette Extraordinary*. Cape Town: Prime Minister's Department, June 24.

Qalinge, L. and van Breda, A. (2018). Editorial: Decolonising social work education in South Africa. *Southern African Journal of Social Work and Social Development*, 30(1), 1–4. https://doi.org/10.25159/2415-5829/4192.

Ross, R. (1977). Smallpox at the cape of good hope in the eighteenth century. *African Historical Demography*, 416–428. Available at: https://scholarlypublications.universiteitleiden.nl/handle/1887/4200 (Accessed: 20 May 2023).

Samodien, E., Abrahams, Y., Muller, C., Louw, J. and Chellan, N. (2021). Non-communicable diseases – A catastrophe for South Africa. *South African Journal of Science*, 117(5/6), 8638. https://doi.org/10.17159/sajs.2021/8638.

Sekudu, J. (2019). Mapping the way forward in decolonising social work theory in South Africa. In van Breda, A. and Sekudu, J. (eds.) *Theories for Decolonial Social Work Practice in South Africa*. Cape Town: Oxford University Press Southern Africa, pp. 280–286.

South African Council for Social Service Professions (2004). *Policy Guidelines for Course of Conduct. Code of Ethics and the Rules for Social Workers*. Rivonia: SACSSP.

Southern African Development Community (2020). *SADC Regional Indicative Strategic Development Plan (RISDP) 2020–2030*. Gaborone: SADC.

Sphere Association (2018). *The Sphere Handbook: Humanitarian Charter and Minimum Standards in Humanitarian Response*. 4th ed. Geneva: Shortrun Press.

Statistics South Africa (2021). Mid-year population estimates 2021. Available at: https://www.statssa.gov.za/publications/P0302/P03022021.pdf (Accessed: 19 May 2023).

Strömberg, D. (2007). Natural disasters, economic development, and humanitarian aid. *Journal of Economic Perspectives*, 21(3), 199–222. Available at: https://www.aeaweb.org/articles?id=10.1257/jep.21.3.199 (Accessed: 20 May 2023).

United Nations (2015a). Sendai framework for disaster risk reduction 2015–2030. Available at: https://www.preventionweb.net/files/43291_sendaiframeworkfordrren.pdf (Accessed: 19 May 2023).

United Nations (2015b). Sustainable Development Goals. Available at: https://sustainabledevelopment.un.org/?menu=1300 (Accessed: 19 May 2023).

United Nations (2016). Report of the open-ended intergovernmental expert working group on indicators and terminology relating to disaster risk reduction. Available at: (Accessed: 21 May 2023).

United Nations (2021a). *The Sustainable Development Goals Report*. New York: UN.

World Bank (2022a). GINI-index South Africa. Available at: https://data.worldbank.org/indicator/SI.POV.GINI?locations=ZA (Accessed: 19 May 2023).

World Bank (2022b). Poverty & equity brief. Sub-Saharan Africa. South Africa. April 2020. Available at: https://www.worldbank.org/en/topic/poverty/publication/poverty-and-equity-briefs (Accessed: 19 May 2023).

14
CYBER COUNSELLING COMPETENCIES
Implications for Curriculum Development and Training of Social Work Practitioners

Cecilia Tutu-Danquah and Lawrence Murphy

Abstract: English

In 2010, at the global campaign level in Hong Kong, the International Federation of Social Workers (IFSW) and the International Association of Schools of Social Work (IASSW) initiated a global agenda to promote social equalities, mental health, and other key issues. In Ghana, some social workers provide basic in-person counselling services in their community of work and make referrals to counselling psychologists when applicable. Unfortunately, the social distancing protocols of COVID-19 restricted the in-person sessions. In view of this, many practitioners transitioned to cyber counselling. Unfortunately, there is little or no empirical data on practitioners' competencies in cyber counselling. This chapter reviews findings of our study, which investigated participants' competencies in cyber counselling as the basis to develop a curriculum for training. The findings reveal high (94%) personal use of technologies but very low (27.6%) use of its application in cyber counselling. Building on the findings, this chapter provides a curriculum framework for social work practitioners to acquire competent skills for cyber counselling. We also review an ongoing collaboration between the authors in Ghana and Canada that seeks to introduce technological and professional competencies in cyber counselling to social work students and organise continuous professional development programmes for all social workers.

Introduction

In 2014, a global definition for social work was approved by the International Federation of Social Workers (IFSW) and the International Association of Schools of Social Work (IASSW) during their general meeting and general assembly, respectively. They approved that social work must be defined as a practice-based profession and an academic discipline that promotes social change and development, social cohesion, and the empowerment and liberation of people. Principles of social justice, human rights, collective responsibility, and respect for diversities are central to social work. Underpinned by theories of social work, social sciences, humanities, and indigenous knowledges, social work engages people and structures to address life challenges and enhance wellbeing.

This definition brought into the limelight the issue of mental help in social work. It was therefore not a surprise when IFSW and IASSW pronounced mental health as a priority for global development (IFSW, 2014). In Hong Kong, at the global campaign level, these organisations jointly initiated a global agenda to support the United Nations (UN) Sustainable Development Goals (SDGs). This, they sought to do by:

- promoting social and economic equalities.
- ensuring the dignity and worth of the persons.
- promoting sustainable communities and environmentally sensitive development.
- promoting well-being through sustainable human relationships.
- ensuring an appropriate environment for practice and education.

The agenda of IFSW and IASSW towards the SDGs propelled social work educators to focus on the provision of mental health education for all social work practitioners. The authors of this chapter believe that, in a broader sense, social work education and practices prepare social work professionals to provide direct counselling services to help individuals and families to overcome identified challenges, often around behavioural, emotional, and mental health.

In 2010, the America Counsellors' Association at their annual meeting redefined as a professional relationship that empowers diverse individuals, families, and groups to accomplish mental health, wellness, education, and career goals (Kaplan and Gladding, 2011). Similarly, Akinade (2012) defines counselling as a process of helping an individual become fully aware of themselves and the ways in which they are responding to the influences of their environment.

These definitions and others have been mentioned extensively in many studies and have also been applied by many counsellors. However, in reviewing literature and observing current professional counselling practices, the authors of this chapter define counselling as:

> an intentional and professional helping-relationship that aims at providing adequate, relevant and timely information to guide clients to make an informed decision towards the facilitation or restoration of sound mental health.

Until the emergence of the COVID-19 pandemic, the process of delivering counselling services across many countries and particularly in Ghana was predominately via in-person or face-to-face sessions. Clients met their practitioners in comforting and relaxing rooms to facilitate rapid healing. Unfortunately, the high infection rate of COVID-19 at the time led to the implementation of a set of protective behavioural protocols. These protocols were initiated to prevent further spread of the virus and alleviate the situation. Among the protocols introduced were social alterations, such as social distancing, self-isolation, and self-quarantine. These measures were strictly implemented to prevent further infection and to help health authorities to tackle the disease (Anderson et al., 2020). However, these social alterations prevented social workers from having in-person sessions with their clients. It then became necessary for social workers who provide counselling services to transition to cyber counselling modalities that have the ability to support the provision of counselling amidst social distancing.

This transition obviously needed a form of competency to help the counsellors in providing quality cyber counselling services. For instance, Beel (2021) reported that the Psychotherapy and

Counselling Federation of Australia (PACFA) responded to the pandemic by providing professional development in online counselling (PACFA, 2020a). He indicated that many face-to-face counsellors transitioned to online counselling. In addition, Békés and Aafjes-van Doorn (2020) in Indonesia found that a great majority of psychotherapists were prepared for the transition to online therapy during the COVID-19 era. In the United State of America, the International Association of Counsellors (IAC) organised cyber counselling training for approximately 3,000 counsellors (Campana, 2020). These trainings were designed to equip the counsellors with the best practices in cyber counselling.

The case in Africa, and specifically in Ghana, looks different. Even though some counsellors and social workers transitioned to providing cyber counselling services, there is little or no empirical data on their competencies in cyber counselling delivery. These social work practitioners are likely to face major challenges especially in instances where their initial academic training did not expose them to any form of cyber counselling competency skills. This propelled the authors to investigate the cyber counselling competencies possessed by social work practitioners who provide cyber counselling services and, subsequently, to find out their experiences and challenges.

This chapter therefore discusses the findings of a study that investigated the level of cyber counselling competencies among counsellors and social workers who transitioned to providing cyber counselling services, as well as their experiences and the challenges they face. The aim of this chapter is to bring to the fore the identified training needs of these practitioners in the application of cyber counselling services and then build on the findings to provide a curriculum framework for training to acquire competency skills for cyber counselling.

Cyber counselling is a branch of the cyber psychology field that involves the use and study of human experiences (i.e. cognitive, emotional, and behavioural) that are related to or affected by the use of emerging technologies (Richards and Vigan´o, 2012). Inferring from the definitions reviewed by other authors, this chapter considers cyber counselling as:

> The practice and delivery of counselling services via cyberspace where counsellor(s) and client(s) engage in therapeutic relationships through emerging and relevant internet and non-internet based communications technologies and processes.

In the definition, two key skills are established: the professional skills and the technological skills. This implies that counsellors must be skilled in face-to-face therapy as well as the skills for the application of emerging technologies that are relevant to counselling. It is not an automatic occurrence for professional counsellors to successfully transfer these skills to the cyber counselling environment.

To effectively deliver cyber counselling services, it is very important for counsellors to gain the appropriate competency skills and experience in the use of applicable communications technologies and processes within the ethical and legal framework of the counselling profession and the cyber world. This concern prompted the Canadian Counselling and Psychotherapy Association (CCPA) to include ethical codes that will guide counsellors in the use of technologies in counselling. One of the codes that is of particular interest to the provision of cyber counselling is the Standard B16 regarding computer use and counselling. This standard states that when computer applications are used as a component of counselling services, counsellors must ensure that:

(a) Client and counsellor identity is verified;
(b) The client is capable of using the computer application;
(c) The computer application is appropriate to the needs of the client;

(d) The client understands the purpose and operation of client-assisted and/or self-help computer applications; and
(e) A follow-up of client use of a computer application is provided to help with subsequent needs.

In 2020, the standard B16 was upgraded and implied in the standard H1–H7 of the ethical code of the CCPA (2020). The content of the ethical code standard H1–H7 provides guidelines for the use of electronic and other technologies in the provision of counselling. Brief descriptions of the standards H1–H7 are as follows:

H1. Technology-Based Administrative Functions

As part of the informed consent process, counsellors/therapists indicate to clients at the outset of services whether digital records will be kept. If electronic record-keeping is to be implemented, counsellors/therapists ensure that digital security measures necessary to protect client confidentiality and privacy are in place (e.g., encryption, firewall software).

H2. Permission for Technology Use

Counsellors seek informed consent prior to using Internet-based communication with clients (e.g., email, texting, and related forms of digital communication). Counsellors/therapists take necessary precautions to avoid accidental breaches of privacy or confidentiality when using Internet-based communication devices and apprise clients of associated risks.

H3. Purpose of Technology Use

Counsellors clarify under which circumstances and for which purposes technology-based-communication will be used (e.g., setting up appointments, counselling/therapy sessions, record-keeping, billing, assessment, third-party reporting) and they review their related policy as part of the informed consent process with clients.

H4. Technology-Based Service Delivery

When technology-based applications are incorporated as a component of counselling/therapy programmes and services, counsellors/therapists ensure that;

a) they have demonstrated and documented competence through appropriate and adequate education, training, and supervised experience.
b) necessary digital security measures are in place to protect client privacy and confidentiality.
c) technology applications are tailored or matched to unique client concerns and contexts.
d) research evidence supports the efficacy of the technology for the particular purpose identified.
e) decisions to implement new and emerging technologies that are not yet accompanied by a solid research foundation are based on sound clinical judgement and the rationale for their selection is documented.
f) client preparedness to use the specific technology-based application is assessed and education and training are offered as warranted.

g) informed consent is tailored to the unique features of the technology-based application being used. The counsellor/therapist to act in accordance with the CCPA Code of Ethics and Standards of Practice, and, in particular, to ensure adherence to the principles of confidentiality, informed consent, and safeguarding against harmful effects.

H5. Technology-Based Counselling Education

Counsellor/therapist educators who use technology to provide or enhance instruction in fully online or blended counselling/therapy programmes have demonstrated competency in this mode of delivery through their education, training, and/or experience.

H6. Personal Use of Technology

In their use of social media and related technology in their personal lives, counsellors/therapists monitor the style and content of their communication for ethical congruity and professionalism. They attend to privacy/security features, continue to honour client confidentiality, demonstrate respect for and valuing of all individuals, and represent themselves with integrity.

H7. Jurisdictional Issues

Counsellors/therapists who engage in the use of distance counselling/supervision, technology, and social media within their therapeutic practice understand that they may be subject to laws and regulations of both the counsellors' practicing location and the client's place of residence. Counsellors/therapists ensure that clients are aware of pertinent legal rights and limitations governing the practice of counselling across provincial/territorial lines or international boundaries.

Reflections on Standard H1-H7 of CCPA 2020

In an extensive work relationship with Lawrence Murphy, a pioneer in cyber counselling in Canada, the gaps in the cyber counselling practices in Ghana were reflected. For instance, in 2022, Murphy revealed that he had trained over 15,000 mental health professionals in Canada to instruct them on the ethics, standards, policies, and procedures for cyber counselling as spelt out in the standard H1–H7. He further explained that the training prepared most counsellors in Canada to better serve their clients in the cyber world and most of them have transitioned to online counselling. This was also confirmed by Beel (2021), who stated: 'Having reviewed the influence of the standard H1–H7 on the practise of the Canadian counsellors, our study adopted standard H1–H7 as the reference for investigating the Ghanaian counsellors' competencies in providing cyber counselling'.

Study Approach

To be able to ascertain the level of the counsellors' competencies in the delivery of cyber counselling as indicated in the standards H1–H7, the authors used a mixed-method approach with quantitative data preceding qualitative data collection. This is typical of an explanatory sequential design where qualitative information is sought from the same sample to further explain earlier findings from quantitative responses.

Study Population and Sample

The study population was 587, which included counsellors (n=227), social workers (n=200), and child development workers (n=160) who were members of the Ghana National Association of Certificated Counsellors (GNACC). Even though the study population consisted of different categories of practitioners, the study collectively referred to them as counsellors or practitioners because they were either professional members or associate members of the association depicting their skills and competencies in counselling.

At the time of the study, 327 of the study population indicated that they had engaged with clients via cyber counselling during the COVID-19 period of social distancing. The majority of the counsellors (78%) were individuals who had provided counselling services in urban Ghana, where communications technologies and other electronic devices were readily accessible to both counsellors and clients. In sampling the participants, letters were sent to all the 327 counsellors to seek their consent in participating in the study. In response, 272 of them indicated their willingness to participate in the study. This included 120 professional counsellors, 113 social workers, and 39 child development workers.

Data Administration and Analysis

A five-point Likert-scale questionnaire consisting of 35 items and a semi-structured interview guide consisting of 10 items were used to collect data from participants. The level of measure for the questionnaire items were: 1=Very Low; 2=Low; 3=Not sure; 4=High; 5=Very High.

To ensure that all ethical concerns were addressed, the study description, purpose, and possible benefits of the study were mentioned to participants. The study permitted participants to freely withdraw or leave at any time if they clearly desired. As a way of avoiding plagiarism, all ideas, writings, drawings, and other documents or intellectual property of other people were referenced indicating the authors, title of publications, year, and publishers.

Descriptive statistics (frequencies, percentages, and means) were used to analyse the research questions, and the findings were represented by tables and figures. The interview data were analysed and presented in verbatim quotations to support participants' perspectives. Figure 14.1 shows the summary of Ghanaian counsellors' cyber counselling competencies as measured against the technology-based competencies for counsellors (standard H1–H7) proposed by the CCPA, (2021).

Source: Study data (2021)

Discussion of Findings on Cyber Counselling Competencies among Practitioners

Practitioners Used Technologies for Personal Engagement Rather Than Professional Practices

The findings as shown in Figure 1 indicate that a majority of counsellors (94%, n=235) in Ghana use communications technologies for their personal use rather than for professional counselling delivery. It was further revealed in the interview responses that counsellors engaged clients on general phone call practices with practising professional ethics. Excerpts from a few participants are indicated below:

Participant 1: 'I usually place a call to my clients to make a follow up on a given assignment or reschedule of appointments. I don't consider any professional standards during the call. Actually, I am not even aware of any counselling ethics for placing a call to a client'.

Counsellors' responses on standard H1-H7

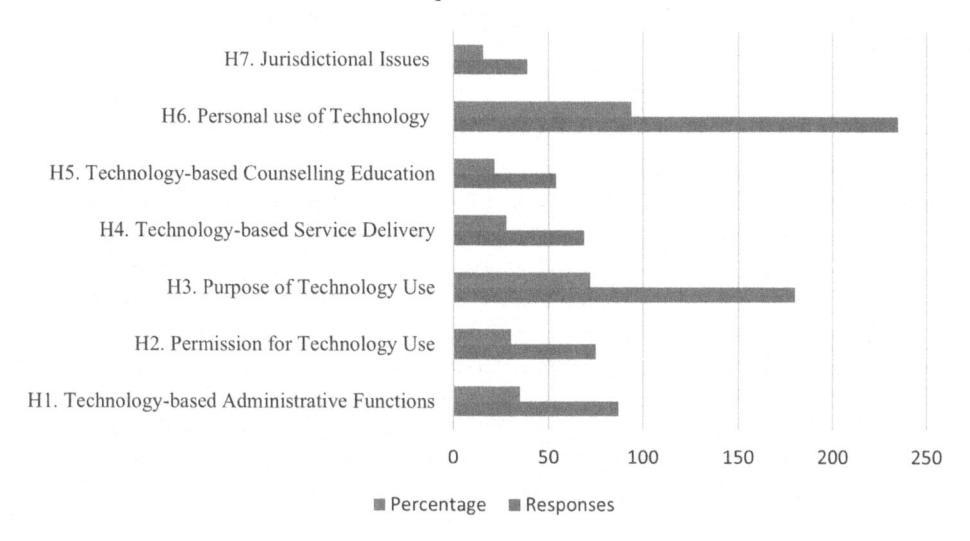

Figure 14.1 Summary of Ghanaian Counsellors' Competencies of Standard H1–H7

Participant 2: 'Oh yes, I do engage my clients via WhatsApp chat just as I do with any other person. I have not thought of having a session with clients through WhatsApp. I am not sure it will be appropriate'.

Subsequently, the findings reveal that the use of technologies for counselling services among counsellors in Ghana is, by comparison, relatively low (27.6%, n=69). To probe further into the specific professional use of technologies in counselling, we used standards H3 and H4 to raise interview items. Responses from approximately 72% (n= 180) of the counsellors show that most counsellors in Ghana use technologies to advertise their counselling services, make follow-up, and place appointments, and not necessarily for cyber counselling delivery. The popular excerpts from their responses are shown below:

An excerpt from one counsellor is: 'I use my social media handles such as Facebook and TikTok to advertise my counselling services and it has been very useful. As the views increase, I get more clients calling me for sessions'.

Another counsellor put it in this way: 'ICTs are very good because they help me to show my programmes to the world. I upload most of my programme videos on YouTube and I get more views'.

The interview results again revealed that although the counsellors use technologies to set up appointments and make fellow-ups, they are ignorant about the effective use of technologies for keeping of clients' records. One of the participants put it this way:

How can I use technologies to keep records of my counselling session, especially when my counselling notes contain confidential issues about my client? If someone gets to my computer, the person can read all this information and this will seriously be against my professional ethics and principles of confidentiality. It is better for me to keep it in my cabinet under lock and key to save myself from breaching my professional ethics.

These findings suggest the need for awareness creation and training for the counsellors on how technologies can be used for cyber counselling practices, such as safe record-keeping, assessment, and third-party reporting.

Counsellors Are Unable to Ensure Digital Security during Cyber Counselling

The items in standards H1 and H2 sought to find out if counsellors inform clients at the outset of the cyber counselling services where their digital records will be kept. It was also to find out if counsellors ensured that digital security measures necessary to protect client confidentiality and privacy, such as encryption and firewall software, were in place. The results, as shown in Figure 14.1, indicate that the majority of the counsellors (H1:65.2%) and (H2: 70%) do not know about the technology-based administrative functions and the need to seek clients' permission before engaging them in cyber counselling delivery, respectively.

The study sought to find out why such competency skills were not considered by the majority of the counsellors during cyber counselling delivery. The interview responses were analysed and the following responses were found relevant for curriculum development and training. The verbatim responses of some participants are indicated below:

> I have no idea about the concept of encryption. I see such words on my WhatsApp chat at times but I never knew it was something I needed to work with it in cyber counselling delivery. I have no idea about it.

Another participant explained that: 'I think with cyber counselling, all I needed was to call clients on phone and talk to them just as making calls to any other person. I believe in our usual calls, the service providers provide security measures so as a counsellor, it has nothing to do with me'.

A further excerpt from a participant is shown below:

When I want to send e-mail to someone, I do not need to ask permission from the person, neither will I seek permission from the person before I place a call. I am sure same concept is applied when you communicate with the client via phone call or e-mail. I actually don't need the clients' permission. They even need me more for their restoration so they will be happy to receive my call.

These responses, coupled with the quantitative results, give a clear indication that most counsellors in Ghana are ignorant about the competency skills relating to technology-based administrative functions in their delivery of cyber counselling services. They perceive cyber counselling as mere interaction with clients via technologies and not as a special professional body of practice. If this perception is not corrected through adequate training and supervision, these counsellors may do more harm than good to clients who patronise their cyber counselling services.

Counsellors Do Not Have Professional Training in Cyber Counselling

The fact that a counsellor is extremely skilled in face-to-face therapy does not guarantee successful transfer of these skills to the cyber counselling environment. Cyber counselling requires extensive training in the theories, ethics, legalities, modalities, and clinical requirements in the practice. This is why the standard H5 encourages counsellors to subject themselves to acquiring the right competency skills before practising in the cyber space. The study used four categorical items and five interview items to find out the cyber counselling competency training needs of counsellors in Ghana. The result is shown in Table 14.1 below.

Table 14.1 presents evidence that counsellors (84%, n=210) who were trained in Ghanaian institutions were not introduced to cyber counselling in their initial college training. This is an indication that counselling training institutions do not have a curriculum for cyber counselling training. Drawing information from the interview data to find out the counsellors' perceptions on why they were not trained in cyber counselling, one participant commented that:

> While in college, we were made aware that counselling sessions must always be organised in a face-to-face session so the clients can feel warmth and accepted. Aside that, we were told that face-to-face sessions allowed the counsellor to observe the non verbal clues of the client. I personally believe that counselling on phone will not allow to me see the non-verbal clues of my client too.

Another participant indicated that in Ghana speaking to an elderly person via telephone is regarded as being disrespectful.

> For instance, you cannot call your superior on phone and ask for permission to be absent yourself from work. In this regard, I believe it may be difficult for most Ghanaian youth to interact with counsellors via cyber counselling if they still have these assumptions.

The above response has brought to bear another area of concern that relates to clients' readiness to patronise cyber counselling services. This shows a clear influence of cultural or contextual beliefs and practices on the implementation of cyber counselling in Ghana. Further research would be needed to explore this particular area.

Counsellors Are Passionate about Practising Cyber Counselling

The result again reveals that few counsellors (16%, n=40) have received continuous professional development in Ghana on cyber counselling. Similarly, the result indicates that 82% (n=205) of the counsellors are passionate about practising cyber counselling; however, these passionate counsellors do not have the rudimentary skills and knowledge needed for cyber counselling practice. A follow-up through the interview session to explore why they need the cyber counselling training revealed the following sentiments from some participants:

Excerpt 1: 'After the COVID-19 pandemic, most people are comfortable using services on the cyber space. These days most people are using the virtual platforms to make counselling accessible so I need to learn it too'.

Table 14.1 Cyber Counselling Training for Counsellors

Cyber counselling training needs	Frequency	Percentage
I received cyber counselling training at the college	17	6.8
I have been trained through workshops and seminars	40	16
I applied my experience in general call ethics	198	79.2
I need professional training in cyber counselling	210	84
I need a professional standard of practice in cyber counselling	205	82

Source: Study data (2021)

Excerpt 2: 'I believe that if anything must be done, it must be done well. I will need the training to help me give out my best to the client'.

Implication for Curriculum Framework for Cyber Counselling Competency Training

The findings, conclusions, and recommendations drawn from our study revealed three major thematic areas for the development of curriculum framework for cyber counselling competency training. The thematic areas are: Knowledge Creation, Competency Acquisition, and Practice Level. These three thematic areas also reflect three modular programmes for training purposes, as shown in the framework in Figure 14.2.

Source: Study data, (2021)

Description of the Framework

Knowledge Creation Thematic Area

This thematic area seeks to educate the counsellors to acquire the fundamentals of cyber counselling. At the knowledge acquisition level, the counsellors will be introduced to:

a. General Knowledge in Cyber Counselling.
b. Theories and Practice in Cyber Counselling.
c. Ethics and Legalities in Cyber Counselling.
d. The Cyber Counselling Environment and Human Behaviour.

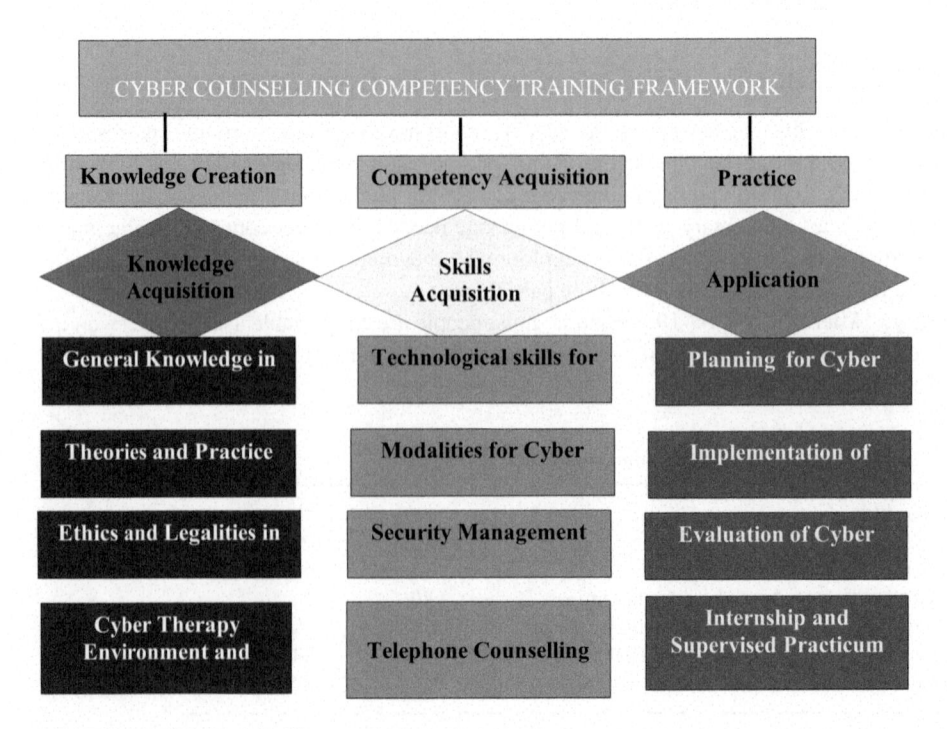

Figure 14.2 Cyber counselling competency framework

Aim and Content

The aim is to engage learners to explore the various theories that guide cyber counselling practice and also to introduce them to the fundamental principles and best practices that guide the cyber counselling process and work environment. The conceptual frameworks, theories, and principles of cyber counselling will also be emphasised. Counsellors will also be guided to explore the key benefits, challenges, and implications of professional cyber counselling services for themselves and their clients.

This thematic area will also help the counsellors to examine the conscious and unconscious motivations behind people's online presence and how they behave across different media spaces. A research-mediated approach will be adopted in understanding the nature of computer-facilitated communication between clients and counsellors and how to maximize the benefits of such sessions within specific cyber counselling contexts. The key differences between people's potential behaviour when e-communicating as opposed to when they interact in face-to-face situations, and the important implications these different behaviours have for the therapeutic process will be highlighted.

Furthermore, the counsellors will be guided to understand and uphold the unique codes of conduct appropriate to professional cyber counselling practice. In this regard, the counsellors will be equipped with the relevant legal and ethical knowledge that will guide their professional cyber counselling practice.

Competency Acquisition Thematic Area

This thematic area seeks to train the counsellors to acquire the fundamental technological skills for cyber counselling practice. At the skills acquisition level, the counsellors will be introduced to:

a. Technological Skills for Counselling.
b. Modalities for Cyber Counselling.
c. Security Management in Cyber Therapy.
d. Telephone Counselling and the Use of Mobile Technology.

Aim and Content

The aim is to provide a detailed overview of the importance of information and communications technologies (ICTs) that are applicable in the counselling process and practice. The role of existing and emerging technologies in professional counselling will be discussed in depth, along with key information literacy, digital literacy, and integration literacy skills relevant to the counselling process. The counsellors will also be guided to create a plan for sustaining their ICT literacy and technological skills during training and subsequently in their professional practice.

Again, this thematic area seeks to draw counsellors' awareness to the risks posed to clients and counsellors when adopting cyber counselling service delivery (e.g., telephone, text, email, video) and learn ways of reducing and managing such potential risks. It is expected that counsellors will develop a thorough understanding of cyber risk factors and be able to manage work with clients at risk, including providing additional support services as deemed appropriate. Furthermore, the counsellors will be guided to examine the importance of maintaining confidentiality and data security within a therapeutic cyber counselling relationship. Appropriate ways of achieving this goal will be explored, including the various ways in which clients' data can be protected.

This content area is also designed to explore the ethical, practical, and clinical fundamentals of the various modalities available for cyber counselling. In Ghana specifically, the telephone counselling modality is most prevalence so the counsellors will be thoroughly trained in telephone counselling. Attention will be paid to specific clinical considerations and impacts of being in a voice-only environment with a specific focus on issues related to the use of mobile technology. Counsellors will also look at possible scenarios for phone counselling in the future, carefully contrasting it with video, chat, and in-person counselling.

Practice Level Thematic Area

This area of the framework seeks to guide the counsellors to practice the knowledge and skills they acquire at the knowledge and skills acquisition stage. This stage deals with the application of skills, knowledge, and general experiences of the counsellor under the auspices of the counselling training institution. In this area, the counsellors will be introduced to:

a. Planning for Cyber Counselling Practice.
b. Implementation of Cyber Counselling.
c. Evaluation of Cyber Counselling Practice.
d. Internship and Supervised Practicum.

Aim and Content

This part of the framework introduces counsellors to the practical steps for planning, implementing, and evaluating cyber counselling services. At the planning stage, the counsellors will be introduced to strategies that will help them explore the clients' demographic data (e.g., age, educational background, digital literacy status) as well as clients' expectations before choosing to prescribe cyber counselling for them. To ensure successful implementation of cyber counselling delivery, counsellors will be guided to explore various ways to maintain cyber counselling service quality as well as various ways to monitor the experiences of the client during cyber counselling sessions.

Clients' satisfaction of a given product or service is a critical success factor in the sustainability of any intervention. In this regard, the counsellors will be introduced to practical ways of evaluating clients' satisfaction as well as strategies they can use to predict clients' continuous usage intention of cyber counselling services. Furthermore, this thematic area seeks to provide internship opportunities and supervised practicum sessions for the counsellors.

Conclusion

Based on the study findings, this chapter concludes that the majority of the practitioners do not have the rudimentary skills needed for the provision of cyber counselling services. They are ignorant about matters of digital security, specifically those necessary to protect client confidentiality and privacy, such as encryption and firewall software during cyber counselling delivery.

It furthers concludes that all practitioners in social work, counselling, and child development sectors need training in cyber counselling.

Recommendations

1. Social work education institutions must consider the introduction of an academic course on counselling, in general, and, specifically, in cyber counselling to prepare their students to meet the changing and challenging demands of the society in which they serve.

2. To facilitate the training process, it is recommended that trainers use the curriculum framework provided in this chapter.
3. Social work practitioners, educators, and associations should organise awareness creation programmes as well as continuous professional development programmes to enhance their practice in the area of mental health and cyber counselling.

Further Reading

Beel, N. (2021). COVID-19's nudge to modernise: An opportunity to reconsider telehealth and counselling placements. Available from: https://www.researchgate .net/publication /351307993_COVID-19%27s_ nudge _to_modernise_An _opportunity to_ reconsider _telehealth _and_ counselling _placements _pac-jaorgau202104covid-19s-nudge modernise -an-opportunity-to-reconsider-telehealth-and-counselling-_p.

Mitchell, D. L., and Murphy, L. J. (2004). E-mail rules! Organizations and individuals creating ethical excellence in telemental-health. In J. Bloom & G. Walz (Eds.), *Cybercounseling and Cyberlearning: An ENCORE*. CAPS Press and American Counseling Association.

Murphy, L. J., and Mitchell, D. L. (1998). When writing helps to heal: E-mail as therapy. *British Journal of Guidance and Counselling*, 26(1), 21–32.

Murphy, L. J., MacFadden, R. J., and Mitchell, D. L. (2008). Cybercounseling online: The development of a University-based training program for e-mail counselling. *Journal of Technology in Human Services*, 26, 447–469.

Stoll, J., Müller, J. A., and Trachsel, M. (2020). Ethical issues in online psychotherapy: A narrative review. ***Frontiers in Psychiatry***, 10, Article 993. https://doi.org/10.3389/ fpsyt.2019.00993.

References

Akinade, E. A. (2012). ***Modern Behaviour Modification, Principles and Practices***. Ibadan: Bright Way Publishers.

Anderson, R. M., Heesterbeek, H., Klinkenberg, D., and Hollingsworth, T. D. (2020). How will country-based mitigation measures influence the course of the COVID-19 epidemic? ***The Lancet***, 395(10228), 931–934.

Beel, N. (2021). COVID-19's nudge to modernise: An opportunity to reconsider telehealth and counselling placements. Available from: https://www.researchgate .net/publication /351307993_COVID-19%27s_ nudge _to_modernise_An _opportunity to_ reconsider _telehealth _and_ counselling _placements _pac-jaorgau202104covid-19s-nudge modernise -an-opportunity-to-reconsider-telehealth-and-counselling-_p [accessed on December 16 2021].

Békés, V., and Aafjes-van Doorn, K. (2020). Psychotherapists' attitudes toward online therapy during the COVID-19 pandemic. ***Journal of Psychotherapy Integration***, 30(2), 238–247. https://doi.org/10.1037/int0000214.

Canadian Counselling and Psychotherapy Association (2021). ***Standards of Practice***. 6th ed. Available from: CCPA-Standards-of-Practice-ENG-Sept-29-Web-file.pdf (ccpa-accp.ca) [accessed on December 12, 2021.

IFSW (2014). Global agenda for social work and social development. Available from: http://cdn.ifsw.org/assets/ifsw_23031-6.pdf.

Kaplan, D. M., and Gladding, S. T. (2011). A vision for the future of counselling: The 20/20 Principles for unifying and strengthening the profession. ***Journal of Counseling & Development***, 89(3), 367–372.

Marco Campana (2020). An interview with Lawrence Murphy - The future of online counselling is now, August 11. Available from: https://km4s.ca/2020/08/an-interview-with-lawrence-murphy-the-future-of -online-counselling-is-now/ [accessed on October 21, 2021].

Psychotherapy and Counselling Federation of Australia (2020a). New PACFA member only resources now. Available from: https://www.pacfa.org.au/new-pacfa-member-only-resources-now-available.

Richards, D., and Vigan´o, N. (2012). Online counselling. In Y. Zheng (Ed.), ***Encyclopaedia of Cyber Behaviour***, vol. 1, 699–713. New York, NY: IGI Global.

World Health Organization (WHO) (2020). Novel coronavirus (2019-nCoV) situation report 1, January 21, 2020. Available from: https://www.who.int/docs/ default-source/coronaviruse/situationreports/20200 121-sitrep-1-2019- ncov.pdf (accessed on 25 November 2021).

15
THE COMING OF AGE OF SOCIAL WORK EDUCATION IN ZIMBABWE

Towards Reinforcing the Developmental Social Work Agenda

Tatenda Goodman Nhapi

Abstract: English

The 1960s inception of social work training in Zimbabwe up to the present time has, over time, produced skilled and internationally recognised social work cadres who maintain receptiveness for transforming lives of the marginalised. Nevertheless, reflection and self-introspection is required as the profession is now at a crossroads as a result of various intractable socioeconomic challenges. Enduring remedial approaches originating from Global North origins are undoubtedly becoming redundant. The dominant narrative in African social work scholarship discourses is about mainstreaming developmental social work. Henceforth, this chapter interrogates the extent social work training has embraced developmental social work in the curricula. Galvanising the repertoire of social work methods of interventions in Zimbabwean social work training guarantees future social workers with creative approaches to confront pervasive challenges like failed poverty mitigation interventions. After interrogating the developmental social work approach in the Zimbabwean social work curriculum, major findings highlight the need for blending aspects of indigenous knowledge in recognising environmental social work as crucial for robust and holistic transformation of the marginalised. The chapter's methodology is secondary literature based on relying on discourse analysis of social work teaching scholarship on some of the major findings after interrogating the developmental social work approach in social work curricular in Zimbabwe. The chapter concludes by offering pathways towards robust innovations in social work teaching that can buttress the mainstreaming of developmental social work. This is in keeping with the United Nations Sustainable Development Goals (UNSDG) agenda of leaving no one behind.

Introduction

The chapter reflects on the extent to which developmental social work as an approach is embraced in social work curricula in Zimbabwe. Critical elements are underscored towards social workers' training for versatility in a curriculum that is aligned with implementing pro-poor and developmental social work interventions. A number of research papers, books, blogs, and other articles reflect an increasing focus on developmental social work. The necessity of mainstreaming a developmental social work method of interventions-oriented curriculum is urgent. According to Gray and Lombard (2022), developmental social welfare is of interest in postcolonial contexts where poverty is rife, fuelled by violent conflicts, government failures, and social and economic exclusion. As a policy strategy, the design of developmental social work is to enlist the poor's participation in development activities for 'social and economic justice, human rights, social solidarity and active citizenship' achievement (Patel, 2005, p. 73).

Pertinently, having African frontline social workers and student social workers oriented to the developmental social work approach further enriches individuals and communities' capacities for transformative change. In mainstreaming developmental social work, the core argument is that the assumptions so embedded in (largely) Western constructions of social work curriculum must be questioned. This is a necessary enterprise achievable through analytical examination, and creative reflection on curriculum transformation. A curriculum embedded with developmental social work tenets is fertile terrain for theorising dynamics of communities' structural transformation. Undeniably, multiple uncertainties, including climate chaos, food insecurity, migration flows, economic volatility, conflict, epidemic disease outbreaks, and fragile governance issues, dominate popular academic and media coverage (Cheru, 2021). The solution, so the narrative goes, is economic and governance 'reform', aiming to 'stabilize' economies and societies and so control uncertainty (Scoones, 2022).

These complex emergencies are leading to a reconfiguration of the world. As it is shown later, marginalised communities are rendered invisible and their fundamental human rights are being erased when developmental social work methods of intervention are not upheld. Being an enduring and complex global social problem, addressing poverty and its eradication must be through a variety of applied action research studies co-produced with communities for better insight into different perspectives of social, behavioural, and public health methods of interventions that social workers and other allied professionals collaboratively roll out.

Given this context, when social workers engage vulnerable, marginalised communities, such interventions cumulatively bolster livelihoods and coping capabilities. Furthermore, social workers get to broker a platform under which demands of the poor and marginalised are captured for the attention of policymakers for processes like national budget crafting. In the same vein, social workers are front-row witnesses of intensifying humanitarian crises compounding states' capacities to function and provide essential services, catalysing pre-existing tensions that can generate social unrest (International Federation of Social Workers [IFSW], International Association of Schools of Social Work [IASSW] 2022).

The following research questions are posed:

- What are the drivers and actors in Zimbabwe's developmental social work curriculum trajectory?
- What are the pathways for mainstreaming developmental social work, a pathway that delivers universal social rights and environmental justice?
- What is the extent of developmental social work in curricula in Zimbabwe?

In the first section, I ground the chapter in key concepts relevant to developmental social work. This chapter interrogates the extent to which Zimbabwean social work training has embraced developmental social work in the curricula. After this, I provide evidence of the kinds of deeper knowledge on social work that must be considered to build genuinely developmental social work–oriented curriculum. In the next section, I outline the conceptualisation of developmental social work, and the methodology, before concluding by offering insights into Zimbabwe's socioeconomic trajectory.

Conceptualising Developmental Social Work

The following section outlines the conceptual basis of developmental social work. It is worthwhile to highlight that, internationally, critiques of dominant approaches in social work have been ongoing (Turton and Schmid, 2020). In Spitzer et al.'s (2014) analysis, many countries identify developmental social work as being a theoretical model encapsulating and incorporating local helping practices. It is a pro-poor model (Rao, 2013) that acknowledges the community as the primary site of intervention (Mwansa, 2011). Through analytical lens categorising the profession by various monikers, such as 'mainstream', 'White', 'Western', 'Northern', or 'Anglophone', scholars are increasingly problematising dominant social work approaches due to its emphasis on individual experience and intervention (Weaver and Congress, 2009).

A reversal in processes of knowledge-making and understanding is required, drawing from local perspectives with often quite different framings. Knowledge being mainstreamed in many social work practice contexts is inappropriate and eclipses alternative ways of knowing, being, and doing. For example, Indigenous Knowledge Systems (IKS) significance may be looked down upon as being unscientific. This could be the case in rural development interventions implementation where sacred groves and ancestral spirits recognition may be negated as mythical and not scientific. Moreover, harmful dominant approaches perpetuating colonial perspectives, ignoring structural conditions underlining social control and advancing decontextualized individualism, have been promoted by professional imperialism. Therefore, continued social work relevance to local populations must therefore build on traditional helping strategies and use contextualized worldviews/knowledge(s) to shift the focus to parochial concerns.

Some enduring helping traditions like *nhimbe*, Income Savings and Lending (ISALs) feed into community and social development methods of interventions implemented collaboratively by social workers. These can be platforms for embedding ecosocial work aided by harnessing IKS. Rural life is hard work and Zimbabwean communities developed systems like *nhimbe*/work parties to help each other with large tasks, such as cultivating, planting, weeding, harvesting, and threshing. Through the enduring IKS of ubuntu which embraces humanness, mutual support, and solidarity as encapsulated by *nhimbe*, social workers' harnessing eco-social work for rural development outcomes can target rotational arrangements, where, for example, mutual groups engaged in rearing goats for sustainable livelihoods can be initiated by social workers who are employed by agencies implementing community development.

Importantly, analysing the concept of development is crucial. The development concept has gained traction and currency given its ability to tackle human needs and aspirations. Development is growth of a person physically or biologically, socially, psychologically, and intellectually, or the process of ensuring that a family, community, society, country, continent, or world has all the tangible and nontangible goods, infrastructure, and services required to satisfy short- to long-term needs and aspirations – the end result being development (Mugumbate et al., 2022). The IFSW's ethical statement of principles suggested that social workers should respect people's rights to self-determination, involvement, and participation in ways that empower them, while simultaneously working towards the promotion of social justice and inclusive society values (IFSW/IASSW, 2004). These are central values within a social development context.

Developmental social work methods of intervention application in contrast to the emphasis on individualised problems that the remedial model makes promote peoples' liberation and empowerment. Departure from neoliberal, colonised thought and practice and a liberation of the mind for ideas rooted in African initiative and local economies is proposed by Patel (2005). She outlines a range of strategies focused on social investments as micro-enterprises, public works programmes, human capital development (e.g., education and skills development). Another perspective is offered by Spitzer and Twikirize (2021) regarding the nexus between social work and social innovation and they insist both concepts' focus on social problems and impetus for social change all implicitly transform communities and societies.

As opined by Veta and McLaughin (2022) social work's education and practice major focus should be effects of socioeconomic and political structure on the people and vice-versa. Shifting social work education and practice from an individual-centric practice towards targeting root causes of social ills should be from 'environment and person' rather than 'person-in-environment' approach. This is whereby, outcomes identified are often located in the person, while in most cases, environmental changes or effects are specified less (Veta and McLaughlin, 2022). This influences social policy formulation towards solving ills at the macro level and advocacy for transformative social policies mitigating harmful conditions for the vulnerable.

In his analysis, Kurevakwesu (2017) asserts remedial social work practice in Africa is like installing an android application that is incompatible in an iPhone. Kurevakwesu (2017) argues that it would never work unless installed in the right phone with the requisite applications. However, effectively pursuing a social work curriculum with theories, methods, knowledge, and principles grounded on methods of interventions that achieve individuals, groups, or communities' basic needs curricula should be reflective of People with Lived Experiences (PWLE)'s (formerly referred to as service users) cultures (Veta and McLaughlin, 2022).

One critical role of social work is creating paths for excluded, marginalised, and oppressed PWLE making them central and giving them a voice in the policy process in the wider societal contexts (Sheedy, 2013; Lombard, 2021). In this regard, Mingle (2013) notes developmental social work as a process of planned social change targeting the population's well-being holistically within the context of a dynamic multifaceted development process. Resting social work training curriculum on developmental social work pivots involvement and participation complemented by direction provided by the grassroots communities is therefore vital. This is because future frontline social workers are equipped with a repertoire of developmental social work strategy tenets.

It is important to highlight that mainstreaming developmental social work collaboratively by academia and grassroots organisations is not without tensions and power imbalances. The current hegemonic order dictates that academic knowledge be the primary reference for expertise, rigour, or accuracy. For low-income communities, engaging academics may mean enduring disqualification of their knowledge. Western academic institutions, particularly, wield immense power to conceive what Musila (2017, p. 694) refers to as 'normative credibility'. This means there is a strong likelihood that some knowledge systems will remain subjugated. This is also peculiar in the social work curriculum, where courses like rural and community development may not have a flair of vitality of indigenous knowledge systems when equipping students with how to design and measure efficacy of community interventions.

On the other hand, developmental social work practices are people-centred and multidimensional, and they facilitate macro-level interventions for desired outcomes of poverty and social injustices alleviation (Gray et al., 2018). As Patel and Hochfeld (2008) observe, developmental social work indigenised social work practice, particularly in the sub-Saharan Africa context as it ensures communities partaking in the matters that concern them as a prerequisite for meaningful developmental efforts.

However, in professional and academic settings, it is disconcerting to note that most social justice discourses have been expert-led, leaving a gap regarding the absence of voices of marginalised groups. With developmental social work discourses, emphasis is on rights-based approaches, democracy and participation, income generation and micro-enterprises (Lombard, 2008). It is worthwhile to highlight that when contrasted with remedial social work models, developmental social work methods of intervention mobilise, empower, and organise local communities to influence local development, making it seen as indigenised social work practice. Importantly, the developmental social work approach values a range of ways of knowing, doing, and being, and it focuses on communal identities and collective decision-making.

Methodology

The chapter relies on a desk review of peer-reviewed articles and other reports, providing qualitative and quantitative evidence on developmental social work implementation dynamics, constraints, and contestations. In reviewing documents related to developmental social work, reliance was made on discourse analysis of scholarly journal articles produced between 2015 and 2022. The discourse analysis included published, official government documents; the International Federation of Social Workers (IFSW), the International Association of Schools of Social Work (IASSW) and United Nations (UN)/non-governmental organisational (NGO) documents/evaluation; and technical, programmatic, and funding support reports.

Socioeconomic Trajectory and Social Work Trends in Zimbabwe

The immediate family (parents and siblings), near-immediate family (*vatete* [father's sister], *sekuru* [mother's brother]), extended family or clan structures such as *sahwira* (a family friend) comprise the context of key indigenous Zimbabwean social services providers (Mugumbate and Bhohwasi, 2021). Several ways of preventing social ills and ensuring the social functionality of their families, villages, and societies at large were harnessed by Madzimbabwe (people of Zimbabwe). Pre-colonisation systems, which grew naturally, were in place for welfare provision to the vulnerable populations merged with or submerged in foreign welfare systems at the arrival of missionaries, traders, and colonialists. Colonisation of the 1890s brought turbulence, including colonial wars against imperialists, complemented by dispossession and the emergence of urban centres. Arrival of 'legless' people resulted in the establishment of urban settlements where they lived. The advent of colonialism introduced a money economy in Zimbabwe and marked the beginning of a capitalist penetration. Kaseke (1987) highlights that the money economy created amongst the indigenous population, the need to work resulting in rural-urban migration. In Kaseke's (1987) analysis, the urban economy struggled with the large rural-urban migrants, and destitution, unemployment, adjustment problems, social disorganisation, overcrowding, and lack of shelter proliferated. Furthermore, Zimbabwean social work development was closely linked to the containment of juvenile delinquency and truancy challenges (Kaseke, 1987).

According to Mugumbate and Bhohwasi (2021), most government services offered at this time were for the Whites' kith and kin and a few urban Blacks who were working for them. These services included disability support, boarding schools, old people's homes, clinics and hospitals, social welfare grant, clothes and blankets and others. The missionaries worked with the colonial government. With urban centres a proliferation of unemployment, prostitution, homelessness, and overcrowding for Black people became the socio-pathological challenges (Mugumbate and Bhohwasi, 2021). When vagrancy, delinquency, and destitution emerged amongst their children and youths, the white settlers introduced a Western value-based social welfare model. The underlying value was social control.

Kaseke (1998) notes that the 1936 Probation and School Attendance Compliance Officer programme resulted in the hiring of British probation officers by the colonial government. After the Ministries of Education, Justice, and Home Affairs mutually investigated issues related to school attendance, non-attendance, and children in conflict with the law, it was recommended that probation services be instituted (Kaseke, 1998). Employment of British native F.S. Caley as the first probation officer by the colonial government saw the introduction of probation programmes for white children in 1936 and, concurrently, education was made compulsory for white children (Kaseke, 1998).

The start of formal social work training was through the first admission of social work students for a one-year Certificate Course in Group Work in 1965 by the Jesuits missionaries' run School of Social Work. Further expansion of the School of Social Work saw the 1975 Bachelor of Social Work degree introduced (Chogugudza, 2009). Following Zimbabwe's independence in 1980, the expectation was that social workers would fully engage in social and economic development. This paradigm emphasised the need for the profession to take on board the macro-economic and wider societal factors that had led to structural inequality, endemic poverty, and social exclusion in the first place. Therefore, the social development thrust in the curriculum encompassed modules concerned with community work and 'integrated' social work methods in working on an appropriate model of social development (Hall, 2021). Hall observes the government's own Department of Social Welfare retained its 'colonial' structures, placing little emphasis on social or community development, whilst traditional areas of fostering and adoption, casework, and relief of destitution were preferred. This could have been partly on account of departmental resource limitations, but it reflects a lack of clarity from government concerning the role of social workers in a post-conflict and reconstructionist situation. In Hall's (2021) analysis, international and local voluntary organisations developed the more exciting and ground-breaking community action strategies.

The National Social Protection Policy Framework for Zimbabwe (NSPPF) was initiated in 2016. As of June 2020 the name was changed from the Department of Social Welfare to the Department of Social Development by the Government of Zimbabwe (GoZ), reflected transformation towards embracing a developmental social welfare approach in 2016. Fieldwork placements are a critical element of the curriculum and students following a four-year programme of training generally have a mandatory two blocks of fieldwork attachment of twelve and fifteen weeks, respectively. The first attachment is done in the second year, and the second and longer one is done in the final semester of the third year. However, in partial fulfilment of masters or undergraduate social work degree requirements, most students prefer to undertake fieldwork in urban settings. Furthermore, it can be argued that there is an ongoing preference by students for child protection-oriented fieldwork principally in the Department of Child Protection and Welfare Services (DCPWS). This tends to complicate social work fieldwork training, which could encompass all facets of developmental social work. The intractable socioeconomic challenges and a rejuvenated and ongoing recruitment drive of social workers by English local authorities and Australian states motivates students to prepare themselves for such eventual recruitment by doing fieldwork predominantly in child protection settings. Emigrating from Zimbabwe has become a livelihood strategy for many citizens, trained social workers included. British social work regulator, Social Work England approves of

Zimbabwean social work education and training as meeting international standards and thus validating the appropriateness and universality of this training (Social Work England, 2023).

Therefore, a practice buttressed on a broader developmental social work agenda consisting of social work teaching approaches and methods that embrace the wide spectrum of human rights, reflective practice, and critical pedagogy is crucial. This is because it would serve as an appropriate grounding for upcoming Zimbabwean social workers. Reinforcement of the social work profession's belief in the worth and dignity of all human beings and their inherent capacity for purposeful change is essential. The adoption of the developmental social work approach therefore makes people more self-conscious and aware of their rights as well as making people self-reliant (Nhapi and Dhemba, 2020). Recalibration of social work education and the education pathway to conform to multiple continental policy and strategic frameworks, including the *Agenda 2063: The Africa We Want that* outlines an African Union (AU) strategic framework for the socioeconomic transformation of Africa within 50 years are also called for.

Developmental social work appropriateness and necessity makes necessary social work education to meaningfully engage curriculum-related activities so that practitioners have clear guidelines on its operationalisation. Furthermore, it will also be necessary to provide the resources required to capacitate social workers to engage in developmental work and to ensure that social work education standards and programmes relate directly to local needs (Hochfeld et al., 2009).

The challenge facing social work education in Zimbabwe is to make it continually relevant and appropriate, particularly in terms of preparing social workers to address complex structural problems in society. Some of the arising complex structural problems include socio-pathological vices like drug abuse and negative coping mechanisms to crises like hunger, child marriages, and the destitution of older persons. In its indigenous form, social work philosophy finds much support in Zimbabwean cultural and traditional values. Yet some social work values do challenge local traditional values, e.g., the role of the disabled or those suffering mental illness, people who could sometimes be marginalised because of fear in local cultures.

Pervasive socioeconomic challenges and increasing natural climatic shocks, like the 2019 Cyclone Idai, and shocks, like the COVID-19 pandemic, inhibit social work cadres to robustly operationalise themes, concepts, and approaches learnt during training within a developmental social work–oriented social work curriculum framework. However, by incorporating a critical stance into their practice, social workers are able to question and analyse the forces in society that produce and maintain injustice, discrimination, and oppression (Sheedy, 2013). It becomes vital that the Zimbabwean institutions offering social work training continuously move towards mainstreaming a progressive and multi-pronged curricula that goes beyond the eclectic base of social work education and incorporates clinical and developmental aspects of social work as key areas of specialisation in their programmes. The noticeable strengths of social work education and training are recognition that intractable challenges posed by the majority experience are symptomatic of deep-rooted structural socioeconomic challenges and natural climatic shocks. Zimbabwe's predominantly semi-arid climate is extremely variable, with shifting rainfall patterns, droughts, and floods exacerbated by substantial environmental challenges, including land degradation, deforestation, and inadequate water quantity and quality. Climate stressors affect agriculture and food and nutrition security, disproportionately affecting women and girls.

Students should be engaged in policy development and practice, preparing them to work alongside people who plan and engage in their own development from within their lived experiences (Lombard, 2015). In Lombard's (2015) view, students have their own lived experiences, which have to be used in their teaching and learning to harness their understanding of the local and integrate it with the international. Students must be capacitated through the developmental social work-oriented curriculum for applied action research capabilities, adopting a social justice lens to examine the contextually situated processes through which marginalised and vulnerable communities are overcoming.

On that basis, Ife (2012) explains that, in critical pedagogy, knowledge is not natural, but contextualised, and that both the teacher and the student construct and reconstruct the knowledge. Enforcing a pro-developmental social work curriculum, it is worthwhile to highlight that curriculum regulation is a contested terrain. In its regulator role, the Council of Social Workers Zimbabwe (CSWZ), a product of the Social *Workers Act, 2001,* has a remit of providing oversight and playing a quality assurance role for social work undergraduate and postgraduate courses. Its mandate is to register, regulate, and enforce ethical practice for all social work professionals in Zimbabwe. Regulation in Zimbabwe is an intricate process that needs to be treated with precision and dynamism. To contextualise this, in 2021 the Ministry of Public Service, Labour and Social Welfare rescinded CSW's decision to suspend social work programmes in some universities stating it was not the CSW's prerogative to make the call. CSW had issued a statement suspending social work programmes at Women's University in Africa, Zimbabwe, the Ezekiel Guti University, and Africa University, citing limited compliance to set regulations. However, Public Service, Labour and Social Welfare Minister overturned this (The Sunday Mail, 2021).

Conclusion

This chapter has sought to discuss how embedding developmental social work methods and interventions in the curriculum can reinforce a path for enhancing the current cadre of student social workers and to spearhead developmental social work. The implications of thinking about framing narratives in embedding developmental social work research and action agendas in Zimbabwe's social work curriculum are varied. Social work in Africa is engaged in finding pathways to respond to complex, multidimensional social issues. The genesis of many of these contemporary challenges has its roots in colonialism and the legacy of colonialism. Social work education should empower students to challenge injustice rather than perpetuate the status quo (Muridzo et al., 2022). A strong social work voice is needed along with a foundation provided by the curriculum. Embedding developmental social work provides an outlook for the curriculum to examine current thinking in terms of African-oriented principles of social justice, human rights, collective responsibility, and respect for diversities in line with the African Union's Agenda 2063, Africa's development blueprint to achieve inclusive and sustainable socioeconomic development over a 50-year period. To further efforts to galvanise enhanced developmental social work, methods of interventions embedded in the curriculum fieldwork need to reflect an appreciation for placements for which developmental social work is prioritised.

Recommendations

1. Indigenous knowledge theories and inclusion of these theories enrich the Zimbabwean social work education curriculum. This is achievable by sustained African social work publication outputs. Knowledge outputs like the National Association of Social Workers Zimbabwe-hosted *African Journal of Social Work* have begun to capture and sustain the mobility, fluidity, and plurality of knowledges (Levy, 2022).
2. Problem-based learning (PBL) is worth incorporating in a developmental social work-oriented fieldwork curriculum to enrich understanding of how social work can be relevant and robust.

3. Students attain better knowledge of how vulnerable communities achieve adaptive, absorptive, and transformative capacities within the developmental social work curriculum realm through relevant case studies and field visits. Henceforth, reestablishing mandatory rural fieldwork is necessary.

Further Reading

Powers, M. C. F., et al. (2018). Environmental migration: Social work at the nexus of climate change and global migration. *Advances in Social Work*, 18(3), 1023–1040. Available from http://advancesinsocialwork.iupui.edu/index.php/advancesinsocialwork/article/view/21678/22063.

References

African Social Work Network (ASWNet) (n.d). History of social services and social work in Zimbabwe. Available from https://africasocialwork.net/zimbabwe/ [Accessed 12 March 2023].

Begum, N., & Saini, R. (2019). Decolonising the curriculum. *Political Studies Review*, 17(2), 196–201. https://doi.org/10.1177/1478929918808459.

Cheru, F. (2021). On resuscitating the aborted national project: A retrospective and prospective view (notes from my last conversation with Thandika Mkandawire) text of the inaugural Thandika Mkandawire annual memorial lecture. Presented at the 3rd Edition of the Social Policy in Africa Conference Convened Virtually from 22–24 November 2021.

Chitambara, P. (2022). New perspectives: Pro-poor lens review of budget. Available from https://www.newsday.co.zw/theindependent/opinion/article/200004444/new-perspectives-pro-poor-lens-review-of-budget [Accessed 3 March 2023].

Chogugudza, C. (2009). Social work education, training and employment in Africa: The case of Zimbabwe. *Ufahamu: A Journal of African Studies*, 35(1), 1–9.

Dhemba, J. (2012). Fieldwork in social work education and training: Issues and challenges in the case of eastern and Southern Africa. *Social Work &Society International Online Journal*, 10(1), 1–16.

Dirlik, A. (2007). Global south: Predicament and promise. *The Global South*, 1(1), 12–23.

Gray, M., & Coates, J. (2010). Indigenization and knowledge development: Extending the debate. *International Social Work*, 53(5), 613–627.

Hall,N. (2021). Commentary on publications -Building the social work profession in Africa. Available from https://www.ifsw.org/wp-content/uploads/2021/12/Nigel-Hall-Commentary-on-Publications-Building-the-Social-Work-Profession.pdf [Accessed 13 February 2023].

Hochfeld, T., Selipsky, L., Mupedziswa, R., & Chitereka, C. (2009). *Developmental Social Work Education in East and Southern Africa*. Johannesburg: Centre for Social Development in Africa, University of Johannesburg.

Ife, J. (2012). *Human Rights and Social Work. Towards Rights-Based Practice* (3rd ed). London: Cambridge University Press.

International Association of Schools of Social Work (IASSW), & the International Federation of Social Workers (IFSW) (n.d.). Positioning social work in an eco - Social world: Building new partnerships and alliances. Available from https://cdn.unrisd.org/assets/legacy-files/301-info-files/6DA84DA33D300798802587D10039B2EE/Concept%20note%20WSWD%202022.pdf.

International Federation of Social Workers, & International Association of Schools of Social Work (2004). *Ethics in Social Work, Statement of Principles*. Bern: International Federation of Social Workers, p. 1. Available online at: http://www.ifsw.org/p38000324.html.

Kaseke, E. (1987). Social work in Zimbabwe: A short country statement. ASWEA 6th Annual General Meeting. Abidjan .

Koranteng, K. (2022). Bridging the disconnect between science, policy and practice for African cities. Available at https://www.african-cities.org/crafting-sustainable-development-research-that-matters/ [Accessed 12 December 2022].

Kurevakwesu, W. (2017). The social work profession in Zimbabwe: A critical approach on the position of social work on Zimbabwe's development. *Afro Asian Journal of Social Sciences*, VIII (I Quarter), 1–19.

Levy, S., Okoye, U. O., & Ingram, R. (2022). Making the 'local' visible in social work education: Insights from Nigeria and Scotland on (Re)balancing and contextualising indigenous and international knowledge. *The British Journal of Social Work*, 52(7), 4299–4317. https://doi.org/10.1093/bjsw/bcac028.

Lombard, A. (2008). The implementation of the white paper for social welfare: A ten-year review. *The Social Work Practitioner-Researcher/Die Maatskaplikewerk Navorser-Praktisyn*, 20(2), 154–173.

Lombard, A. (2015). Global Agenda for social work and social development: A path towards sustainable social work. *Social Work/Maatskaplike Werk*, 51(4), 482–499.

Mugumbate, J. R., & Bohwasi, P. (2021). History and development of social work in Zimbabwe. In V. Mabvurira, A. Fahrudin, & E. Mtetwa (Eds.), *Professional Social Work in Zimbabwe. Past, Present and the Future* (pp. 1–28). Harare: National Association of Social Workers.

Mugumbate, J. R., Tarusikirwa, M. C., Nyoni, C., Mtetwa, E., Nyikahadzoyi, K., Dhemba, J., & Nyaruwata, L. T. (2022). People-centred development (PCD): Philosophies, key concepts and approaches to teaching, learning and practice. People centred. *The Journal of Development Administration (JDA)*, 7(1), 1–12.

Muridzo, N., Mukurazhizha, R., & Simbine, S. (2022). Social work in Zimbabwe: From social control to social change. *International Journal of Social Work Values and Ethics*, 19(2), 227–243. https://doi.org/10.55521/10-019-213.

Musila, G. (2017). Navigating epistemic disarticulations. *African Affairs*, 116/465(465), 692–704.

Mwansa, L. K. (2011). Social work education in Africa: Whence and whither? *Social Work Education*, 30(1), 4–16. https://doi.org/10.1080/02615471003753148.

Nhapi, T. G., & Dhemba, J. (2020). Embedding the developmental approach in **social work** education and practice to overcome poverty: The case of Southern Africa. *Greenwich Social Work Review*, 1(1), 11–20.

Oghenechoja, D. V., & McLaughlin, H. (2022). Social work education and practice in Africa: The problems and prospects. *Social Work Education*. https://doi.org/10.1080/02615479.2022.2029393.

Patel, L. (2005). Social development curriculum renewal in an African context. *The Social Work Practitioner-Researcher*, 17(3), 363–377.

Patel, L. (2005). *Social Welfare and Social Development*. Oxford University Press.

Patel, L., & Hochfeld, T. (2008). Indicators, barriers and strategies to accelerate the pace of change to developmental welfare in South Africa. *The Social Work Practitioner-Researcher*, 20(2), 192–211.

(2) (PDF) developmental social work in South Africa: Translating policy into practice. Available from https://www.researchgate.net/publication/258143534_Developmental_social_work_in_South_Africa_Translating_policy_into_practice [Accessed 15 July 2022].

Rambaree, K. (2020). Environmental social work Implications for accelerating the implementation of sustainable development in social work curricula. *International Journal of Sustainability in Higher Education*, 21(3), 557–574.

Rankopo, M. J., & Osei-Hwedie, K. (2011). Globalization and culturally relevant social work: An African perspective on indigenization. *International Social Work*, 54(1), 137–147. https://doi.org/10.1177/0020872810372367.

Scoones, I. (2022). A new politics of uncertainty: Towards convivial development in Africa. In C. Greiner, S. van Wolputte, & M. Bollig (Eds.), *African Futures* (pp. 101–110). Brill. http://www.jstor.org/stable/10.1163/j.ctv2kqwzjh.15.

Sheedy, M. (2013). *Core Themes in Social Work. Power, Poverty, Politics and Values*. New York, NY: Open University Press.

Social Work England. (2023). List of overseas qualifications. Available from https://www.socialworkengland.org.uk/registration/list-of-overseas-qualifications/.

Spitzer, H., Murekasenge, J., & Muchiri, S. (2014). Social work in Burundi's post-conflict society. In H. Spitzer, J. Twikirize, & G. Wairire (Eds.), *Professional Social Work in East Africa: Towards Social Development, Poverty Reduction and Gender Equality* (pp. 149–160). Kampala, Uganda: Fountain Publishers.

The Sunday Mail (2021). Minister reverses social work training ban. Available from https://www.sundaymail.co.zw/minister-reverses-social-work-training-ban.

Turton, Y., & Schmid, J. (2020). Transforming social work: Contextualised social work education in South Africa. *Social Work*, 56(4), 367–382.

UNCT (United Nations Country Team) (2014). Zimbabwe Country Analysis working document final draft. *Information*. https://ims.undg.org/.../7e40fe82fedfcf6fb92306b459a8c1bdd0d13cc9ea8e9a18cadb [Accessed 12 May 2022].

UNICEF Zimbabwe Country Programme (2022). More funding needed for the child protection sector in Zimbabwe. https://www.unicef.org/zimbabwe/press-releases/more-funding-needed-child-protection-sector-zimbabwe [Accessed 22 August 2022].

United Nations Research Institute for Social Development (UNRISD) and International Federation of Social Workers (2022). Co-building a new eco-social world: Leaving no one behind the people's global summit. 29 June to 2 July 2022 – Online.

Weaver, H., & Congress, E. (2009). Indigenous people in a landscape of risk: Teaching social work students about socially just social work responses. *Journal of Ethnic and Cultural Diversity in Social Work*, 18(1–2), 166–179. https:// doi.org/10.1080/15313200902905435.

16
SOCIAL WORK EDUCATION AND TRAINING IN FRANCOPHONE AFRICA
The Case of Cameroon

Pius T. Tanga and Gabriel A. Ekobi

Abstract: English

Social work education and training in Francophone Africa and Cameroon has been modelled by Western (French) pedagogies. The aim of this chapter is to examine social work education and training in Francophone Africa with Cameroon as a case study. Data were collected through literature and personal communication with one senior social work official and another from the Ministry of Higher Education and Scientific Research. The findings show that social work education has gone through turbulent periods of closures and reopening of training institutions. The current social work curriculum continues to reflect French ideologies and practices. Compared to the Global Standards for social work education, the curriculum falls short in some important areas and, consequently, the probability of deficiencies in some social work competencies of graduates. Some of the challenges of social work education in Cameroon include the lack of an accreditation body and a legislative framework as found in some Francophone countries. To transform social work education from French-centric to Afro-centric, we recommend that social work education in Cameroon and other Francophone countries should be given priority and properly regulated by legislation and placed under the appropriate department (ministry) and for universities to offer social work programmes.

Abstract: French

En Afrique francophone et au Cameroun, les approches pédagogiques occidentales (françaises) ont façonné l'éducation et la formation en travail social. Ce chapitre avait pour objectif d'examiner l'éducation et la formation en travail social en Afrique francophone, en mettant l'accent sur le cas spécifique du Cameroun. La collecte de données a été réalisée à travers une revue de la littérature et des échanges personnels avec un responsable principal du travail social et un représentant du Ministère de l'Enseignement Supérieur et de la Recherche Scientifique. Les résultats mettent en évidence que l'éducation en travail social a été confrontée à des périodes instables marquées par la fermeture et la réouverture des institutions de formation. Les orientations et les pratiques françaises demeurent présentes dans le programme actuel du travail social. En comparaison avec les normes mondiales de l'éducation en travail social, le cursus souffre de certaines lacunes dans des domaines essentiels, ce qui peut entraîner des déficiences dans certaines compétences en travail social chez les diplômés. Parmi les obstacles de l'éducation en travail social au Cameroun, on peut citer l'absence d'un organisme d'accréditation et d'un cadre législatif, semblables à ceux existant dans la plupart des pays francophones. Pour promouvoir une éducation en travail social ancrée dans la culture africaine plutôt que dans la culture française, Il est recommandé que l'éducation en travail social au Cameroun et dans les autres pays francophones soit priorisée et réglementée de manière appropriée par la législation, et placée sous l'égide du département (ministère) approprié et que les universités mettent en place des programmes de travail social.

Introduction

There is a dearth of literature on social work education and training in Francophone Africa and Cameroon in particular. Cameroon has a population of over 26 million inhabitants and is located within the central African sub-region. The country has an unusual colonial history, having been colonised by three colonial powers (Germany, France, and Britain), and it is unique with two international languages, French and English, as official languages (Dike et al., 2010; Ngoh, 2019). Despite having been colonised by three colonial powers, social work education in Cameroon like other Francophone African countries was significantly influenced by French ideologies and practices. In these countries, individuals who wished to be trained as social workers in the 1960s and 1970s had little option but to go abroad, mostly to France for training. They were thus trained using curricula that had France orientations without any African values.

The goal of social work as a profession is to enhance human wellbeing and help meet basic and complex needs of all people, particularly the vulnerable and those in poverty, to improve their quality of life (Bang and Balgah, 2022). To effectively achieve this goal, social workers need certain knowledge and competencies, which can be gained only through education and training. According to Moulabuksh and Zarar (2021), social work professional knowledge can be categorised into five knowledge forms that include theoretical, empirical, procedural, practice wisdom, and personal knowledge. These can be placed broadly in three areas of knowledge of social work education and include theories/models, methods of intervention, and processes that are involved in interventions. The International Federation of Social Work [IFSW] (2020) adopted the Global Standards for Social Work Education and Training with the aim of ensuring global consistency and adherence to the values and policies of the profession, amongst others. Accordingly, it is expected that all social work programmes core curricula should be organised into social work in context and social work in practice, which are interdependent and dynamic (IFSW, 2020). The social work context, such as the case of Cameroon, is about understanding critical socio-structural inadequacies, traditions, beliefs, social welfare policies, sustainable peace, and justice, among others. The Global Standards also specify that social work programmes must prepare students for social work in practice and practice education (placement) to acquire certain knowledge and competencies. Similarly, research and scholarly activity as well as the people (educators, students, and service users) are also described as areas of focus for social work education and training.

It is the responsibility of the social work training institutions to bestow this knowledge and competencies on their students to be effective social work practitioners. The quality of social workers reflects the eminence of education and training received, and it is expected that social work curriculum development experts should take into consideration these key generic knowledge areas and competencies. There are also expectations that African social work curriculum should be indigenised and/or Africanised. The Association of South African Social Work Education Institutions [ASASWEI] (2016, p. 2) refers to indigenisation as 'making something more native and the transformation of ideas, education, and training to suit local cultures and reformulating in indigenous terms, so that it takes on an indigenous 'look and feel'. Africanisation is 'understood to be equivalent to indigenisation, but specifically within an African context' while decolonialisation in simple term is 'a process of undoing the negative effects of colonialism' (ASASWEI, 2016, pp. 23) with the desire to reclaim one's heritage or culture. Social work education and training should be structured to deal with specific conditions and cultures of the local people. Africanising the social work education and training will produce social workers who are not alienated from their communities and are sensitive to the challenges facing Africans and Africa.

This chapter therefore attempts to examine social work education and training in Francophone Africa with Cameroon as a case study. As a result, of the paucity of literature on this topic, we had personal communications with one graduate of the current social work training institution in Cameroon and the other from the Ministry of Higher Education and Scientific Research, and we gave them, anonymously, pseudonyms of Mbe and Amougu, respectively. The next section gives an overview of education and training in Francophone Africa, followed by the evolution of social work education in Cameroon. To appraise the current social work education in Cameroon, we examine social work curriculum at the National School of Administration and Magistracy (École Nationale d' Administration et Magistracie [ENAM]), which is the only school offering social work education and training in Cameroon for top civil servants (social workers). Finally, the conclusion and recommendations are presented.

Social Work Education in Francophone Africa

Social work education in Francophone Africa began in the 1960s with the help of France. Francophone Africa refers to countries belonging to a population using French as its first or sometimes second official language (International Federation of Social Workers [IFSW], 2020). Out of the 25 African countries that are members of the International Federation of Social Workers, 13 are from Francophone Africa. These include Cameroon, Niger, Mali, Democratic Republic of Congo, Morocco, Senegal, Sudan, Togo, Guinea, Benin, Burundi, Djibouti, and Congo, with a total population of 300 million inhabitants (Asamoah and Umoren, 2016; IFSW, 2020).

Although the Cairo School of Social Work in Egypt was the first school of social work in Africa, established in 1937 (Healy, 1999; Lekane and Asuelime, 2017), the profession did not take root until the 1960s. The first social work training was in 1961 when the government of Burkina Faso opened a training programme for 'social helpers' as an annex to the National School of Public Health. The training was later expanded to different levels of social work training in 1973. In 2005, the Burkina Faso National Institute of Social Work Training (INFTS) (Institute National de Formation en Travail Sociale) was established and modelled on French knowledge and pedagogy (IFSW, 2020; Canavera et al., 2018). This was followed by the establishment of similar professional schools across Francophone countries. Some of these schools took the character of pre-service and in-service social work training. Presently, most of the social work programmes are offered at the diploma and certificate levels with a few offering a four-year Bachelor of Social Work, two-year masters, and three-year doctorate degrees (Lyons, 1999; IFSW, 2020).

Given the variety of terminologies that describe the fields of action and the scarcity of literature, tracing the history of social work education in Francophone Africa is not an easy task. Some of these terminologies include *Protection Sociale, Service Sociale, and Action Sociale* (respectively, Social Protection, Social Service and Social Action). Schools of social work also have different appellations and include names such as Institut D'enseignment Social, Institut de Formation Social, École de Service Social, École des Aides Sociales and Centre d'Enseignment Paramedical (Healy, 1999, 2001). The French government used the social work training centres established on French models instead of universities to create top civil servants (social workers). This was to perpetuate French (Western) orientation of social work education and training and maintain their presence in Francophone Africa (Lyons, 1999; Asamoah and Umoren, 2016; Umoren, 2016). These training centres operated as professional schools, many of which are still functioning in most of these countries and follow the system of professional schools in France. After graduation, graduates of these schools are automatically absorbed into the public service as civil servants (*fonctionnaires*) with many benefits such as better salaries, retirement benefits, and children's allowances. While those from universities except in Cameroon are employed in the public service but as contract workers (*contractuelles*) with limited benefits (Mbe, 2023).

The French social welfare programmes, which emphasised medico-social programmes, were introduced in Francophone African training centres during the colonial era. These programmes were inherently curative and community development oriented. The focus of a curative approach is to ameliorate the effects of social problems on an individual, community, or group basis rather than tackling the root causes and empowering those affected. These colonial orientations of social work education and practice are still prevalent in Francophone countries, and Cameroon is a case in point. This also portrays the low recognition of social work as a profession in these countries compared to some African English-speaking countries. In the later, social work is legally recognised and valued as other professions, and it is properly regulated by established accreditation bodies and professional associations (Spitzer, 2019).

The history of social work in any African country will be incomplete without acknowledging the critical role played by mutual aid societies and the extended African family. These mutual aid societies were in existence in Africa before the coming of the colonial powers, including France, the coloniser of French-speaking African countries. Without any form of social work education and training, they assisted family members affected by death, sickness, disability, old age, or unemployment, among others. Some of the mutual aid societies were family or kin-based, cultural and/or religious-based (such as rotating credit societies [stokvel] (Giacomucci, 2021). The African extended family operated as a social welfare system, which addresses the social welfare needs of a sizeable number of their members who lack social protection during hardships, such as sickness, bereavement, and destitution (Nhapi and Dhemba, 2020). Those without financial means supported other extended family members with moral support, especially during times of bereavement where their physical presence was appreciated (World Bank, 2019). These values still dominate life in Francophone Africa and the rest of the African continent alongside formal social work practice.

In Francophone African countries, the activities of mutual aid societies, missionaries from Europe (France) and other parts of the world, and the colonisation of the continent contributed to the emergence and development of social work education and training as well as formal social work practice (Tusasiirwe, 2022). The missionaries preceded the colonisers and their primary role was focused on addressing the religious and spiritual needs of Africans (Mudzanire, 2022). This is because they saw Africans as primitive and backward and as worshippers of idols rather than the Supreme God. In addition to these religious and spiritual needs, the missionaries established vocational training schools and engaged in almsgiving and community work. In providing social services, these missionaries functioned as informal social workers (Lyons, 1999; Mudzanire, 2022). This informality arose because they did not receive any formal social work education and training. Without the necessary social work knowledge and competencies, and coupled with their Western ideologies and education, these missionaries offered social services without considering the sociocultural realities of the Africans. As a result, this conflicted with some social-cultural values such as hospitality, chastity before marriage, and respect for the elderly, which guide the behaviour of every member of African households. Today, there are criticisms of the dominance of Western hegemonic educational theories and models within African social work curricula and practice. This is because the training does not prepare social workers to adequately address the unique problems of the populace. Hence, the call for the decolonialisation of social work curricula and the introduction of indigenisation and Africanisation (African theories and models based on their culture or heritage) (Nhapi and Dhemba, 2020; Tusasiirwe, 2022).

However, despite the increase in social work education in Francophone Africa, the vital components of instruction remain largely conservative and underdeveloped with many of the educators trained in France (Canavera et al., 2018). They have therefore shaped their curricula based on French models with little regard for the sociocultural and spiritual realities of their fellow citizens. Mupedziswa (2020) maintains that although these Francophone African countries have schools that are affiliated with the International Association of Schools of Social Work, the approach of social work education and practice that was introduced by France, and which remains in force in many of the countries, is largely focused on a curative or remedial approach. It is mainly reactive and deals with the symptoms and not the real causes of problems. These countries' curriculum developers have not heeded the call for decolonialisation of social work education and training in Africa and are unable to reclaim their heritage or culture from the dominance of French culture. They have failed to embrace social development as a theory that was developed in a unique form in South Africa and serves as a foundation of the welfare approach meant to address large-scale poverty and promote critical and radical social work as well as a strengths perspective as the critical edge through which developmental social work operates (ASASWEI, 2016; Tusasiirwe, 2022). Social work education and training in these countries continues to be on a neo-colonial path. The remedial approach adopted by many of the training institutions is based on the principles underlying remedial services and does not serve the needs of the majority of the countries' inhabitants. The approach ignores concerns of a more developmental nature, such as unemployment, homelessness, illiteracy, and disease, while concentrating on individual pathologies (Umoren, 2016).

Evolution of Social Work Education and Training in Cameroon

Cameroon social workers were initially trained in France where they obtained their bachelor's degrees in social work (*Travail Social*). In the early years (around the 1970s and 1980s), scholarships were awarded to study social work in France (Tanga, 2004; World Bank, 2017). On return to Cameroon, they were integrated into the public service and were called inspectors of social affairs (*Inspecteurs des Affaires Sociales*). Those from English-speaking Cameroon enjoyed the same privilege, but their social work qualifications had to be evaluated at the Ministry of Higher Education and Scientific Research, Department of Equivalent Services, a process that takes years, which leads to frustration (Tanga, 1994; World Bank, 2019). Those with masters and doctorate degrees in social work from abroad (France and other countries) were employed and integrated and called senior inspectors of social affairs (*inspecteurs principal des affaires sociales*).

Social work education and training in Cameroon have gone through rough stages of closures and reopening. The first professional school of social work was opened in Yaoundé in the 1970s called École Nationale des Assistants des Affaires Sociales (ENAAS, its French acronym) and the English equivalent called the National School for Social Welfare Workers (IFSW, 2020). Rather than being affiliated to a university, the school, as other professional schools in Cameroon, was placed under the control of a government ministry. In the 1970s, the training of social workers was under the Ministry of Social Affairs, and later the Ministry of Social and Women's Affairs from the 1990s to date. This is contrary to other countries where the training of social workers is incorporated in their national Departments of Education and Training (Tanga, 2004). According to Mbe (2023), the training of social workers followed the French system of competitive entrance examinations into different levels of the profession. The first level was called Category C for social assistants, *Assistants Sociales*, and to be admitted, candidates needed at least a pass in the General Certificate of Education at the Ordinary Level, *Breveté*. The second, Category B1, *Assistants Principal des Affaires Sociales* – Senior Assistant Social Workers, where candidates must possess at least a pass in one subject at the General Certificate of Education Advanced Level, the French equivalent of *Probatoire*. The last level was for candidates with a pass in at least two subjects at the General Certificate of Education Advanced Level, the French equivalent of *Baccalaureate*.

Entrance examinations into all professional schools in Cameroon including social work are organised by the Ministry of Public Service and Administrative Reform. The training of social workers for each of the levels was two years (Amougu, 2023). The governments of other Francophone countries such as Chad, Central African Republic, Benin, Gabon, and Niger, were sending students to be trained at the École Nationale des Assistants des Affaires Sociales (ENAAS) in Yaoundé. The governments of these countries sent their students to train in ENAAS because that was the only social work training institute in the region (Amougu, 2023). After training, the social workers are posted to different divisions and subdivisions of the different provinces (now called regions) throughout the country to service vulnerable populations. While the Ministry of Public Service and Administrative Reform was responsible for recruitment of candidates through competitive entrance examinations, the Ministry of Social and Women's Affairs took responsibility for posting and allocation of social work responsibilities and supervision (Mbe, 2023). The advantages of professional schools are that students receive monthly stipends and are guaranteed employment after successful completion of the programme.

The adoption of the structural adjustment programme of the Bretton Woods institutions (World Bank and the International Monetary Fund) by Cameroon, led to the closure of the social work training school (ENAAS) in the early 1990s as the country embarked on retrenchment of workers, including social workers. Consequently, Cameroon, with a population of about 26 million people, had a total of only 1,308 social workers as of 2019 (Waha, 2021). In Cameroon, the opening of professional schools, just as those in social work, depends on the Head of State through a presidential decree(s). Between 1992 and 2004, the Ministry of Public Service and Administrative Reform, on the instructions of the Head of State, undertook a two-year training of inspectors of social work (social workers with lower qualifications and other civil servants) at the National School of Administration and Magistracy (École Nationale d'Administration et Magistracie – ENAM).This training is for senior social workers to assume leadership positions within the Ministry of Social and Women's Affairs (Republic of Cameroon, 2022). The training of social workers at ENAM again resumed after a presidential decree from 1996. Instead of allowing universities to offer social work programmes, this higher institution (ENAM) is charged with the training of top civil servants (social workers) . In 2006, a presidential decree created the National Institute of Social Work (Institut National du Travail Social (INTS), another professional school that is yet to go operational.

There are seven state universities in Cameroon and three new ones established by presidential decree in 2021. However, none of these state universities, including a plethora of new private universities established by Christian missions and individuals as well as groups, offer social work education programmes. This reflects the perception of social work education and training in government circles in the country (Amougu, 2023). There are probably two reasons why no single university in the country is offering education and training for social workers. First, the government's lack of political will to regulate social work as a profession and, second, the system of professional schools adopted and fashioned on French models and approaches (Mbe, 2023). If universities were to train social workers, graduates will not be integrated into the public service because of the country's system of professional schools, such as ENAM. This has stifled the establishment of many programmes at universities because of the fear that their graduates might not find jobs in the public service.

Social Work Curriculum at the National School of Administration and Magistracy (ENAM)

Social work education and training curriculum was initially designed by inspectors of social work, who were trained in France assisted by the Swiss and French experts who also supported with teaching in the early years (World Bank, 2017; Mbe, 2023). ENAM is the only school to date that trains top civil servants such as administrators, taxation and customs inspectors, and social work inspectors. ENAM is not affiliated with any university; rather, it is a stand-alone professional school. The training of social work inspectors at ENAM (Cycle A or Category A) takes two years and embodies theoretical training and fieldwork block placement for six months (three months per year). To be admitted into the Inspector of Social Work Division of ENAM only civil servants who are social workers (social workers – Category B1 with five years working experience, and senior social workers, Category B2 with three years of experience) are considered. Also, it is open to other civil servants from other ministries who have obtained authorisation from the Ministry of Public Service and Administrative Reform. Recruitment is through written and oral examinations (Amougu, 2023). After successful completion, the graduates are awarded with a Diploma (Certificat de Scolarité). The curriculum for social work education and training is determined by the Ministry of Social and Women's Affairs (Amougu, 2023). There is no accreditation body to ensure that social work has acceptable levels of performance, integrity, and quality that entitles it to the confidence of the educational community and the public it serves. However, the social work curriculum shows social work in context and social work in practice, as required by the IFSW (2020). Table 16.1 shows the social work curriculum at ENAM.

Table 16.1 Social Work Curriculum at National School of Administration and Magistracy (École Nationale d'Administration et Magistracie – ENAM)

No.	Subject	No.	Subject
1.	Counselling	13.	Sociology
2.	Social case work	14.	Psychology
3.	Social group work	15.	Social science research methods
4.	Community organisation	16.	Statistics
5.	Social [work] administration	17.	Economic development
6.	Programmes and project management	18.	Women and development
7.	Delinquency and criminality	19.	Civil law
8.	Childcare / welfare	20.	Penal code
9.	Probation	21.	Administrative writing
10.	Elderly	22.	Computer studies
11.	Mental disability	23.	French
12.	Rehabilitation of the disabled	24	Field work placement

Source: Mbe, 2023 – ENAM transcript (many courses translated from French)

Table 16.1 shows the different courses that are taught at ENAM for the two-year period of inspectors of the social work programme. According to Mbe (2023), the social work curriculum at ENAM bears little change from what was designed and taught at ENAAS, Yaoundé. The curriculum is dominated by Western theories and philosophies. Emphasis is laid on curative and residual social work practice and social work administration (Mbe, 2023). Some of the courses do not show specific issues that are covered but are broadly coined as disciplines (sociology, psychology, civil law, statistics, etc.). The question one might ask is: what about sociology, psychology, and statistics? The curriculum reflects a resemblance of the transplanted French programmes that were designed to solve the problems of highly industrialised urban problems with little regards to African and Cameroonian realities (UNICEF, 2021). One of the authors of this chapter went through social work training in the late 1980s, at the now defunct ENASS (closed in the early 1990s) and bears testimony to the fact that the curriculum offered at ENAM according to Table 16.1 is not much different from that which was taught in the 1980s. The content of the courses as revealed by Mbe (2023) has not changed much.

Cameroon is a bilingual country with two official languages (two distinct cultures) and a dominant population of Christians and Muslims with more than 250 lingos (Ngoh, 2019). This diverse nature of the country is not reflected in the curriculum, although it might be argued that this might be embedded in one of the courses. However, the finding of Mbe (2023) reveals the contrary, which speaks to the type of training and curriculum that continued to be modelled along French cultural practices and values while ignoring Cameroon's socioeconomic, spiritual, and cultural realities. Compared to other social work curricula across the globe and compared to the Global Standards for Social Work, one can argue from reading the titles of the courses that there is little or nothing regarding comparative welfare policies either in the North or in the South. Similarly, it is doubtful whether the curriculum covers national, regional, and international instruments pertaining to social issues. Also absent in the curriculum is social work theory, which is a core component of social work education. These have been confirmed by Mbe (2023), who recently graduated from ENAM. Across the world, titles of social work courses should immediately tell anyone the possible topics that are taught in each course rather than disciplinary names, some of which are displayed in the ENAM curriculum. The title of one of the courses is Rehabilitation of the Disabled. The word 'Disabled' gives a bad connotation to people with disability. Another course, Mental Disability, which is a type of disability, could fall under the Rehabilitation of the Disabled (more appropriately the Rehabilitation of People with Disability). Mbe (2023) also maintains that the library is void of current social work textbooks, with only a few obsolete ones. In addition, there is no digital library and no available databases where students and staff can access modern and current social work textbooks and journals. Mbe further revealed that many depend on Google for reading materials from the West, except for Cameroon law (civil and penal) and language courses. Consequently, the teaching materials and methods do not encourage creativity and innovation. According to Spitzer (2019), imported social work education materials are inappropriate and, in most cases, irrelevant in the African context.

Mwansa (2010) corroborates and states that schools of social work in Africa (like ENAM) continue to rely on knowledge from outside Africa. Hence, the dynamic nature of social work is ignored in these training programmes. Understandably, the bulk of the staff members are non-social workers with no social work qualifications, and fieldwork supervisors are not trained to undertake field work supervision, which is the backbone of social work education and training (Tanga, 2013; Mbe, 2023). The curriculum, as it is, has serious implications for practice and service delivery by graduates of this institution.

Although social science research method is taught at ENAM, lecturers scarcely publish papers in journals nor do they attend conferences to keep abreast of the latest developments in social work, such as the current calls for decolonialisation of social work education and practice and the adoption of African approaches. There is no motivation or sponsorship for publication and conference attendance. The importance of research cannot be overemphasised as it is used to inform practice decision-making and articulate how practice experience informs research and evaluation decisions. Mwansa (2010) aptly maintains that research is paramount if responses that are locally relevant and appropriate to problems such as poverty, unemployment, and conflict. This also poses problems for social work graduates when it comes to evidenced-based practice. With such a curriculum, graduates might find themselves deficient in some social work competencies, such as professional identity, social policy issues, assessment, and evaluation of social work interventions.

Social work education and training in Cameroon have been beneficial to many who have been employed at the United Nations agencies and other international non-governmental organisations because of their bilingual training (English and French) compared to others from countries with similar populations. Cameroon has also attracted other foreign nationals to be trained at ENAM with financial and diplomatic gains for the country, such as its transformation into a regional giant.

Conclusion

Social work education and training in Francophone Africa and Cameroon has had its own share of colonial dominance, especially in curriculum design and implementation. Social work education and training in Cameroon has been 'on and off' trajectory. ENAM, which is a professional school with different training divisions for top civil servants, is the only school that offers social work training for a duration of two years. Unfortunately, the curriculum is still dominated by French (Western) theories and models as if they are universal and transcend all cultures while ignoring the sociocultural realities of Cameroonians. This could lead to graduates not being proficient in some vital social work competences as stipulated by the Global Standards for Social Work Education and Training. Although the current social work curriculum at ENAM has some deficiencies, some graduates have benefitted from the training through international employment opportunities. The absence of legislative regulation of social work as a profession has compounded the education and training of social workers as well as social work practice in Cameroon. Even though social work education and training is currently offered only at ENAM, the absence of basic social work training for lower qualifications, as in the case of universities, is worrisome.

Recommendations

1. The basic education and training of social workers at the lower echelon in Francophone countries, in general, and in Cameroon, in particular, should be resumed with a new curriculum that reflects the aspirations of the citizens and their sociocultural diversity, practices, and values. A transformation from French-centric to Afro-centric curriculum and indigenisation of some relevant Western knowledge and values should be encouraged.
2. Relevant departments or ministries in Cameroon and other Francophone countries should draft legislation that will regulate social work training and practice.
3. All the state and private universities within this region and in Cameroon should be encouraged to establish social work programmes, which should be under the tutelage of the relevant department or ministry with an accreditation authority to oversee their functioning.

Further Reading

Canavera, M., Akesson, B., Landis, D., Armstrong, M. and Meyer, E. (2020) 'Mapping social work education in the West Africa region: Movements toward indigenisation in 12 countries' training programmes', *International Journal of Social Welfare*, 29(2), 83–95. DOI: 10.1111/ijsw.12372.

Ibrahima, A. B. and Mattaini, M. A. (2019) 'Social work in Africa: Decolonizing methodologies and approaches', *International Social Work*, 62(2), 799–813. DOI: 10.1177/0020872817742702.

References

Amougu, A. B. (2023) 'Personal communication', February 20, 2023.

Asamoah, Y. W. and Umoren, N. (2016) 'Social work development in Africa: Encouraging best practice', *International Journal of Scientific and Engineering Research*, 7(1), 191–203.

Association of South African Social Work Educators [ASASWEI] (2016) *Decolonising of Social Work Education in South Africa: A Report Emerging from a Series of Workshops Held in September 2021*. Pretoria: ASASWEI.

Bang, H. N. and Balgah, R. (2022) 'The ramification of Cameroon's Anglophone crisis: Conceptual analysis of a looming complex disaster emergency', *Journal of International Humanitarian Action*, 7(6), 2–25.

Canavera, M., Akesson, B. and Landis, D. (2018) 'Social service workforce training in the West and Central Africa Region'. Available from www.file:///C:/Users/gekobi/Downloads/UNICEF-WCARO-Social-Work-Mapping-FINAL-17-August-2014.pdf. Date Accessed: 02 August 2022.

Dike, M., Rebecca, D. N., Mark, M. and DeLancey, W. (2010) *Historical Dictionary of the Republic of Cameroon*. MD: The Scarecrow Press, Inc.

Giacomucci, S. (2021) *Social Work, Sociometry, and Psychodrama: Experiential Approaches for Group Therapists, Community Leaders, and Social Workers Phoenix*. Springer.

Healy, M. L. (1999) 'International social work curriculum in historical perspective', in Ramanathan, C. S. and Link, R. J. (eds.) *All Our Future: Principles and Resources for Social Work Practice in a Global Era*. Boston, MA: Brooks/Cole, 14–29.

Healy, M. L. (2001) *International Social Work: Professional Action in an Interdependent World*. New York: Oxford University Press.

International Federation of Social Workers [IFSW] (2020) 'Definition of social work', *Journal of Scientific and Engineering Research*, 7(1), 191–203.

Lekane, G. M. and Asuelime, L. E. (2017) 'One country, three colonial legacies: The politics of colonialism, capitalism and development in the pre-and post-colonial Cameroon', *African Journal of Contemporary History*, 42(1), 134–153.

Lyons, K. (1999) *International Social Work: Themes and Perspectives*. Burlington: V.T. Ashgate Publishing.

Mbe, J. M. (2023) 'Personal communication', January 25, 2023.

Mudzanire, S. (2022) 'A missiological investigation into the role of the Church of Christ's medical missions as transformational development in Mashoko, Zimbabwe'. Available from file:///C:/Users/Downloads/mudzanire_missiological_2022.pdf. Date Accessed: 29 May 2023.

Mupedziswa, R. (2020) 'Building a successful career in social work: Issues, prospects, and challenges', *African Journal of Social Work*, 10(2), 1–8.

Moulabuksh, M. and Zarar, R. (2021) 'Professional social work practice international and Pakistan perspective', *Pak, Journal of International, Affairs*, 4(4), 434–447.

Mwansa, L. J. (2010) 'Challenges facing social work education in Africa', *International Social Work*, 53(1), 129–136. DOI: 10.1177/0020872809348959.

Ngoh, J. V. (2019) 'Cameroon 1884–Present (2018): The history of a people'. Available from https://www.tandfonline.com/doi/abs/10.1080/17532523.2022.2047284?journalCode=rahr20. Date Accessed: 09 September 2022.

Nhapi, T. G. and Dhemba, J. (2020) 'Embedding the developmental approach in social work education and practice to overcome poverty: The case of Southern Africa', *Greenwich Social Work Review*, 1(1), 11–20.

Republic of Cameroon (2022) 'decree no. 2022/003 of 5 january 2022 to set up universities'. Available from https://www.prc.cm/en/news/the-acts/decrees/5620-decree-no-2022-003-of-5-january-2022-to-set-up-universities. Date Accessed: 10 October. 2022.

Spitzer, H. (2019) 'Social work in East Africa: A mzungu perspective', *International Social Work*, 62(2), 567–580.

Tanga, P. T. (1994) 'Appraisal of community development activities in Momo division of the republic of Cameroon'. B. Sc. [social work and community development] Dissertation. University of Nigeria, Nsukka, Nigeria (unpublished).

Tanga, P. T. (2004) 'Social welfare policy towards female-headed households in Cameroon' PhD'. Thesis. University of KwaZulu-Natal, Durban, South Africa (unpublished).

Tanga, P. T. (2013) 'The challenges of social work practice training in Lesotho', *Social Work Education: International Journal*, 32(2), 157–178.

Tusasiirwe, S. (2022) 'Is it indigenisation or decolonisation of social work in Africa? A focus on Uganda', *African Journal of Social Work*, 12(1), 1–11.

United Nations Children Fund [UNICEF] (2021) *The State of the World's Children*. New York: UNICEF.

University of Social Responsibility Network (2022) 'Education and action for a sustainable future'. Available from https://usrsummit2022.org/. Date Accessed: 10 June 2022.

Waha, E. (2021) 'Social workers, trainings and employers in humanitarian crisis'. Available from https://www.facebook.com/541845809323789/posts/1804158449759179/?_rdc=1&_rdr. Date accessed: March 23, 2022, Facebook.

World Bank (2017) 'Country partnership framework for the Republic of Cameroon for the period FY17-FY21'. Available from http://documents.worldbank.org/curat ed/en/480711490925662402/pdf/CPF-CM-Boad/. Date Accessed: 13 June 2022.

World Bank (2019) 'Social safety nets: Lessons from rich and poor countries'. Available from http://newsletters.worldbank.org/newsletters/listarticle. Date Accessed: 05 September 2022.

Yiman, A. (1990) *Social Development in Africa 1950–1985*. Aldershot: Avebury.

17
A CASE STUDY OF THE EMERGING SOCIAL WORK SECTOR IN GUINEA, WEST AFRICA

Marissa Kaloga and Abdoul Karim Camara

Abstract: English

A coastal country in West Africa, Guinea is home to 13 million people and ranks 175 out of 189 countries on the United Nation's Human Development Index. While the majority of West African nations have a recognised social work sector, Guinea has only a small number of trained social workers. In response to the Ebola epidemic, there is increased governmental interest in developing a sector of university-educated social workers to address the complex social issues the country faces. Using data gathered through a Fulbright research grant, the authors of this case study communicate the most recent developments in professionalising social work in Guinea, and they consider them through a framework of transmission, indigenisation, and authentisation. This includes the redevelopment of a tertiary level social work training programme, a new national policy to employ social workers in the public service, and the expansion of professional social work organisations to support the creation of a professional social work sector.

Introduction

Social work as a sector emerged across the African continent in the 1960s as more and more nations asserted independence from colonisation (Chitereka, 2009). In a 1974 report on social work education in Africa (Association for Social Work Education (ASWEA), 1974), seven countries in West Africa had already established social work degree programmes. This has increased in recent decades, with 14 of the 15 ECOWAS (Economic Community of West African States) countries hosting social work education programmes, and Nigeria alone hosting 15 social work training schools and institutes (Canavera et al., 2014). A UNICEF (United Nations Children's Fund) funded report in 2014 (Canavera et al.) highlighted significant developments in the social work sector across West and Central Africa and provided extensive analysis of the educational programmes supporting the development of professional social work. Guinea is absent from this report; its only social work degree programme having closed that same year. This reflects the reality that while almost all countries in West Africa have a social work education programme and sector, as of 2022 Guinea does not. Multiple actors in Guinea continue to push for a functional social work sector, and the authors have endeavoured to provide an accurate depiction of these efforts in this case study.

The current gaps in Guinean social work provide an opportunity to reflect on the ways in which globalised social work theories and norms, dominated by Western approaches, interact and impact domestic social work sectors in the Global South. Previous research into the indigenisation of social work in West Africa has examined how countries, including Ghana, Nigeria, and Burkina Faso, have engaged with social work (Kreitzer, 2012; Ugiagbe, 2015; Canavera and Akesson, 2018). This research, alongside a broader base of literature from Global South scholars, provides a strong evidence base that Western-generated or internationalised social work theories and practice frameworks may be insufficient to address the needs of contexts like West Africa (Gray and Hetherington, 2013; Yunong Xiong, 2008; Ng and Sim, 2006). However, as of writing, there is no available literature that explores the Guinean social work context, which is unique within the region. This research contributes to addressing this gap in the literature, with the hope that additional scholarly work will continue to expand the knowledge base in this area.

This paper uses a qualitative case study methodology and a framework for analysis that draws upon Walton and El Nasr's (1988) ideas on indigenisation and authentisation to explore the multiple areas required for professionalisation, developing concurrently in Guinea. We ask the following research questions: What is the current state of the social work profession in Guinea? How can the sector best develop to address the unique needs of the Guinean population?

Social Work, Colonisation, and Globalisation in Guinea

The development of social work in Guinea cannot be explored in the current context without first recognising the historical impact of colonisation in Africa, as well as the ways in which African nations have asserted their independence. France has had a presence in the region they named Guinea since the 1600s, but it began aggressive colonisation during the 'scramble for Africa' in the 1800s (Ginio and Sessions, 2016). The colonisation of Guinea did not happen peacefully, with significant resistance to imperialism by a large African army led by Samory Touré, who fought the French for 20 years until his capture in 1898 (d'Andurain, 2021). The current territorial border is a European creation, and it does not follow traditional ethnic or geographic boundaries of the people indigenous to this region; the most prominent ethnicities are Malinké, Foula, and Sousou, the historical lands of which extend across Guinean national boundaries (Goerg, 2011).

French colonisation was characterised by rhetoric that expressed a desire to 'civilise' Africans by making them more European, and the reality of that effort involved violence and exploitation enacted upon people living in the Guinean territory (Ginio and Sessions, 2016). Social, health, and education services were largely administered by French Catholic missionaries in this Muslim country (Foster, 2015) and contributed to the dismantling of traditional kinship-based helping systems and indigenous social development approaches (Ibrahima and Mattani, 2019; Burke and Ngonyani, 2004). In this manner, the traditional governance and social structures that existed prior to imperial expansion were systematically replaced with Western models throughout the colonisation period.

Following World War II, African independence leaders put pressure on France to end colonisation, which culminated in a referendum in 1958 where French colonies claimed their sovereignty (Ginio and Sessions, 2016). Guinea, led by future President Sekou Touré – Grandson of Samory Touré – took a strong stance to distance itself from France, choosing complete independence rather than maintaining ties. France retaliated quickly, extracting all French professionals and civil servants as well as any mobile equipment (Brittanica, 2022). Because colonization had previously dismantled indigenous social and governance structures, this was devastating to the newly independent Guinea.

The historical legacy of colonization continues to impact Guinea today, and is further exacerbated by the effects of globalization, which can be understood across both economic and cultural spheres (Ife, 2013). Economically, Guinea is an export led economy, continuing the economic patterns established during colonization whereby foreign countries import raw materials from Guinea. Recent economic growth has come largely through the expansion of extractive bauxite mining operations (Africa Development Bank (AfDB), 2021). Cultural globalisation, also referred to as McDonalization (Ife, 2013), affects the country through the import of foreign commercial goods, clothing styles, beauty standards, music, and cultural norms. Globalisation has also brought positive developments, in particular Internet connectivity, which has enabled communication and access to international resources and information.

As with other issues of globalisation, the globalisation of professional social work must be viewed through a critical lens, in particular given its history in Guinea. If the social work profession as understood globally lies on a foundation of Western modernist traditions, it is culturally bound and not without bias. In this environment it is crucial not to accept 'the Americanisation of social science over locally relevant ideas (Rankopo and Osei-Hwedie, 2011, p. 144) in the context of Guinean social work education.

Transmission, Indigenisation, or Authentisation?

The social work profession in Guinea is thus tied up between the roots in colonisation in the 20th century and the relationship with globalisation in the 21st century. However, both the past and the present demonstrate that Guineans stalwartly value their independence and continue to harbour a diversity of resilient and dynamic traditional values and cultural practices. The uneasy balance between traditional social development and externally driven social welfare models is explored in social work indigenisation literature. Sewpaul (2006) acknowledges the impacts of globalisation on the local level and gives credence to the complexly intertwined histories of the European and African continents. Ibrahim and Mattani (2019) also acknowledge that globalisation has profoundly altered the socioeconomic and political contexts within which African nations operate, making a return to fully traditional structures impossible. Gray and Allegriti (2002) describe this as a 'post-colonial global society' (p. 11).

There is no removing or dismissing past damage done by colonisation and the current mixed bag of globalisation. However, in the current era the metaphorical distance between local and global continues to be erased. In this context, a purely local solution is insufficient as it does not give heed to the international influences on local issues. Thus, there is a continued need to engage with existing social work paradigms, but to do so in a way that respects and represents Guinean values, norms, and culture. Walton and El Nasr (1988), in their article on indigenisation of social work in Egypt, provide three possibilities for engagement with the global profession of social work: transmission, indigenisation, and authentisation. They describe transmission as an imitation of the dominant models of social work originating from Western anglophone countries. Indigenisation of social work, a concept first used at the 1972 International Congress of Schools of Social Work, involves adapting externally developed theories and practices to local contexts. Third, authentisation involves the creation of fully domestically created social work theories and practices derived from knowledge generated in local contexts. These approaches to social work development are particularly salient in a West African context, where countries have followed diverse paths in their development of a social work sector (Canavera et al., 2020).

The idea of indigenisation can be understood from multiple perspectives. Some have conceptualized indigenisation as a post-modern construct (Gray and Allegriti, 2002), created in response to the effects of globalisation; that indigenisation exists as a response to colonisation. Other authors of indigenisation research write that this approach strikes an effective balance between articulating and embodying traditional practices while simultaneously challenging the dominant social work discourses (Ibrahim and Mattaini, 2019). The authors hold that both perspectives have merits and can be useful in the analysis of Guinea's current social work sector. We conceptualise this as a continuum, shown in Figure 17.1, from fully externally generated social work theories and practices to fully domestically generated social work theories and practices, placing transmission, indigenisation, and authentisation across this spectrum. The case study elaborated below will present a multi-faceted narrative of the development of social work in Guinea and subsequently apply this framework to provide insight into opportunities for further development of this sector.

Methods

The growth of a formal social work sector is a complex endeavour, and includes development in policy, education, research, and practice. And, while there is some literature on the development of social work in sub-Saharan Africa, the West African region remains 'vastly under-represented in scholarship and policy' (Canavera et al., 2020, p. 83). Of the existing literature, much of it focuses on Ghana (Canavera and Akesson, 2018), an Anglophone country with little ethnic, cultural, or religious similarity to Guinea. Francophone West Africa is markedly absent from global discussions of social work practice and education, with a correlating 'large chasm in the literature' (ibid., p. 469) in social work.

Guinean social work is not included in academic literature, thus the research presented here is exploratory in nature. To support authentisation in social work research, Gray and Allegritti (2002) propose writing and teaching from indigenous case studies. Following this directive, the authors chose a qualitative case study design using a single instrumental, exploratory methodology, as described by Stake (2005); the authors engage with a context with limited academic coverage, leading to the choice of a constructivist approach that 'allows for a holistic understanding of a phenomenon within real-life contexts from the perspective of those involved' (Boblin, 2013, p. 1268). Our approach resonated with Stake's constructivist assumptions, shown in Table 17.1 adapted from Boblin et al. (2013).

The data for this paper were collected by the authors between 2018 and 2022, as part of the first author's Fulbright Grant and the second author's Master's thesis from the Catholic University

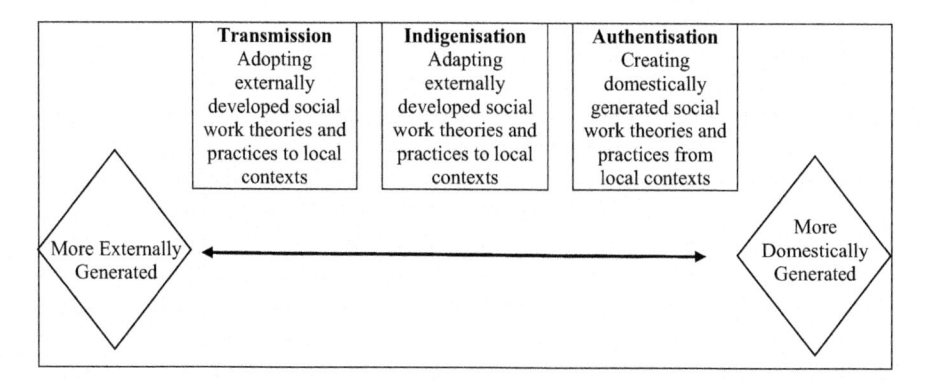

Figure 17.1 Transmission, indigenisation, and authentisation Continuum, adapted from Walton and El Nasr, 1988

Table 17.1 Constructivist Case Study, Adapted from Boblin et al. (2013)

Philosophical Assumptions	Constructivist Assumptions	As Applied to this Case
Ontology	Reality is subjective, a phenomenon is understood holistically.	The professionalisation of Guinean social work is understood holistically across multiple areas.
Epistemology	Researcher has prolonged engagement with the context, decreasing the distance between researcher and researched.	The second author is a Guinean social worker currently working in practice, and the first author has long-standing familial relationships in Guinea.
Axiology	Values and context are accepted as part of the analysis	The social work profession globally finds areas of overlap based on shared values. As such, values are an integral aspect of indigenisation of social work in Guinea.
Methodology	Inductive stance, using a naturalistic paradigm	The authors collected data in situ, and they had access to hardcopy documents unavailable online, as well as oral histories not included in written texts.

Table 17.2 Qualitative Data Sources

Data	Qualitative Data Types	Data Sources, Examples Provided
Primary	Participant Observation	First Author: 2018–19; Second Author: 2018–22
	Ethnographic Field Notes	First Author: 2018–19
	Informational Interviews	First Author: 2018–19; Second Author: 2018–22
	Email, Phone, and Text Exchanges	2018–22
Secondary	Newsletters, Newspaper Articles, Websites, Reports	ANAS-Guinée, Guinee Matin, Guinee Actuelle, Facebook Groups, University websites, AGTS,
	Programme Documents	CENAFOD, UNICEF, Jean Paul II Centre Nationale
	Policy Documents	de Formation Sociale Appliquee – Curriculum A/2006 no 1241/MET-FP/CAB;

of West Africa. The authors worked collaboratively to gather evidence from diverse primary and secondary qualitative data sources in both English and French, as detailed in Table 17.2.

Through an iterative qualitative analysis process, information from secondary textual and primary oral sources were woven together over three years to build a holistic understanding of the past and current development of social work education. Textual sources of information used include online news articles, newsletters, policy documents, non-governmental organisations (NGO) reports, programme documents, and relevant websites. These documents, while useful, provide an incomplete picture of social work's trajectory in Guinea. To weave these textual sources together, we used several methods. First, both authors were participant observers, working in the social work sector in Guinea during the time this data were collected. Second, a purposive sampling approach to identify n = 17 key informants involved in the social work sector. These key informants were interviewed in their professional capacity, and provided first-hand accounts of events to ensure accuracy and fill gaps in textual data. Interviews were not audio recorded; the first author recorded detailed field notes to document relevant information. While we were building this case study, we continued to communicate with these key informants to verify information. Through this process, we established a narrative of the past and current development of social work education in Guinea, triangulating the information gleaned from textual sources with data from the key informant interviews.

Through this process, the authors built a comprehensive narrative of the development of social work in Guinea. The emerging account was multi-faceted and expanded to include intersecting areas of social work sector that emerged as critical in the development of social work education in Guinea, namely Policy, Research, and Practice associations. To explore potential avenues for further development of the sector, the authors then applied the indigenisation continuum informed by Walton and Abu Nasr's (1988) paper. The analysis offered an opportunity to gather and present disparate pieces of information in an accessible and coherent format, as there is little written material available, in particular, online. The subsequent results detail the developments within the social work sector in Guinea across the areas of Policy, Education, Research, and Practice associations.

There is currently no formal ethics review process in Guinea that oversees social work research. To ensure ethical oversight, the researchers maintained open communication with Université General Lasana Conté a Sonfonia's Laboratoire d'Analyse Socio-Anthropologique de Guinée (LASAG) and Catholic University of West Africa, where the second author was supervised for their Master's Degree in Project Management and Development. No personal information was collected or retained as part of the dataset for this case study.

Results

Policy

The social work sector was officially established by the Guinean government in 2006 through a collaboration between the Ministry of Social Affairs, the Promotion of Women and Children (MASCFE), and the Ministry of National Education and Scientific Research (MENRS), with financial and technical support from UNICEF and the African Centre of Training for Development (CENAFOD). The policy document, A/2006 no 1241/MET-FP/CAB supported the creation of an 'Assistance Sociale' programme at L'École Nationale de la Santé de Kindia (ENSK), The National School of Health in Kindia. This policy is critical in establishing what the social work role is, in particular, in environments where development and aid workers associated with NGOs and international agencies are prevalent and provide similar services (Canavera et al., 2020). The enactment of this policy led directly to the development of the first social work education programme in Guinea.

Education

While there has been some mention of a social work training programme in the 1990s (CENAFOD, 2008) the first comprehensive university level social work degree programme began at École Nationale de la Santé de Kindia, National Health University of Kindia (ENSK) located approximately 130km outside the capital city of Conakry. The mandate for a social work programme was established in the 2006 policy that recognized the social work profession, and the development of the training and curriculum was supported in the following year by the Italian Guineo Fund for the Reconversion of Debt (FOGUIReD) in collaboration with the MASCFE and CENAFOD. Originally, this partnership envisaged the social work programme housed in the Jean Paul II Hospital's National Center for Applied Social Training, known locally as Jean Paul II, or JP2. However, the FOGUIReD programme was slated for completion in 2008, and as JP2 was not yet ready to host students the decision was made to locate the programme in Kindia (Dente, 2013, p. 16). In their report on the first year of activities, CENAFOD noted that they sought to do a literature review but were not able to find a document or report on social work training in Guinea (2008). Thus, the creators of the first social work programme engaged with both national and international experts to develop a degree. The social work programme at ENSK operated from 2007 to 2014, granting social work diplomas to a total of 83 students in five cohorts. While graduates from this programme reported that there was initial enthusiasm about the social work degree, it slowly lost students to a nursing programme operating on the same campus. This was attributed to the lack of a social work sector; graduates of the programme could not find jobs in the field because there was no awareness or recognition of the profession and they believed they had a better chance at finding a job with a different degree.

There are several social service related training programmes currently in operation, including the Social and Family Economics programme at University of Labé, the Education Science degree with a specialisation in social work from the Institut Supérieur des Sciences de l'Éducation, and Psychology specialisations at Universities in Kankan and Sonfonia. However, since 2014, Guinea has not had a tertiary social work programme. This same year, Guinea also saw the outbreak of the Ebola virus. Many of the social workers trained at ENSK mobilised to provide social support in infected areas, for example with the reintegration of recovered family members who were facing stigmatisation. The mobilisation of social workers in the Ebola epidemic created a broader recognition of the profession, and an awareness in government ministries of the critical role of social support in epidemic situations (Desclaux and Toure, 2018).

International organisations in Guinea during the Ebola epidemic noted the lack of social workers in Guinea. A UNICEF report included Guinea's lack of a social work sector, with no social workers employed by the government (Brooks, 2016). During their involvement in Guinea, UNICEF wrote that they:

> adopted a 'build back better approach' by rebuilding, or building, the social worker workforce. As part of the Child Protection response, the Governments were supported to increase the number of social workers with an additional 120 in Guinea. The mid-level follow-up support system was strengthened with experienced officers at the county/district/prefecture level, supported further by NGOs. *Training new social workers was on an emergency basis and limited to a few days,* but the intensity of their experience in the Ebola response provided them with an experience that, with the right support, will contribute to them becoming solid practitioners (p. 35, emphasis added).

Given the critical needs for social support during the Ebola epidemic, the condensed approach of the UNICEF social work training is understandable. However, with no national social work programme operating in the country since 2014, the only option for education comes in the form of short-term trainings funded and often delivered by international organisations. For example, in 2020 UNICEF Guinea supported the training of 40 social workers in the area of child protection (Diallo, 2020). While these workshops serve a valuable purpose for continuing education of practicing social workers, they do not provide the necessary education needed to establish a Guinean social work sector. Provision of short-term trainings delivered by international NGOs in the absence of a comprehensive national social work training programme risks continuing to transmit Western-based approaches with no formalised mechanism for Guinean-led opposition or innovation. Other examination of West African social work education sectors mirrors this finding, with Canavera et al. writing:

Currently, outside training programmes provided by NGOs and international organizations are issue-based and fail to cover basic social work principles. Abbreviated training of this nature results in a piecemeal approach to education, precluding holistic understanding of key issues and solutions (2020, p. 90).

The social work training centre at JP2 is progressing towards offering a degree granting programme. During 2018–2019, leadership explored potential collaborations with universities to provide general undergraduate curriculum requirements and be the official degree granting institution. However, these efforts did not culminate in an accord.

The approved three-year social work curriculum was provided in hard copy to the authors (MASPFE and MENRS, n.d.), and it includes a detailed explanation of the purpose and objectives of the programme. To support this curriculum, included as Appendix A, the first author provided a series of trainings in 2019 to an interdisciplinary group of scholars and practitioners chosen as potential social work lecturers in the developing programme. These efforts to reestablish a tertiary social work programme continue, but they face multiple barriers. As noted in Canavera et al. (2020), a major issue with much of African social work education is the lack of nationally relevant study materials. Thus, while the topics of study in the curriculum were chosen with deliberate care, there are currently no Guinean social work texts available. JP2 is an ideal institutional host for the social work field placements required in the training programme because of its diverse placement opportunities, including a hospital and cancer clinic, emergency services, a migrant recovery centre, a fistula recovery ward, geriatric support services, and an extensive pre-school programme. However, the lack of existing social workers suggests that field supervision activities will need further development to be an effective praxis for students. These and other operational issues impede the launch of tertiary social work education in Guinea.

Professional Associations

With tertiary education in social work education currently unavailable, Guinean social workers in practice are supporting the development of the sector in their country by organising into professional associations. These professional associations provide important links to professional development education for existing social workers. The first professional social work organisations, NAJASOGUI (New Guinean Association of Young Social Workers) and AASOGUI (Association of Guinean Social Workers), were created in 2007 by the initial cohorts of social work students in the ENKS programme, but the organisations did not have external support and ceased in 2008. Currently there are two recognised social work professional organizations operating, Association National des Assistants Sociaux-Guinée (ANAS-Guinée, National Association of Guinea Social Workers) and Association Guinéene des Travailleurs Sociaux (AGTS, Guinean Association of Social Workers). The development of these two parallel groups provides an illustration of the tension between domestic and international influences in the Guinean social work sector.

AGTS (2017) was officially founded in 2016, and it became a part of the International Federation of Social Work (IFSW) in 2017. This organisation has engagement externally with IFSW member countries and attended the 2019 IFSW African regional conference as a representative of Guinea. This highlights their engagement with international social work bodies. The statutes and code of ethics of AGTS do not demonstrate specific contextualisation to the Guinean context, and they are reflective of globalised social work values. The choice to pursue organization through alignment with the IFSW ethical principles, as shown in Table 17.3, connects AGTS with external social work networks.

Table 17.3 Alignment between AGTS and IFSW ethical principles

AGTS* Code of Ethics: Principles (2017)	IFSW* Global Social Work Statement of Ethical Principles (2018)
• Respect for the dignity and inherent worth of all people	1. Recognition of the inherent dignity of humanity
• Pursuit of social justice	3. Promoting Social Justice
• Service to humanity	(no corollary identified)
• Integrity in the exercise of the profession	9. Professional Integrity
• Confidentiality in the exercise of the profession	8.2 Social workers must recognise that the use of digital technology and social media may pose threats to the practice of many ethical standards including but not limited to privacy and **confidentiality**…
• Competence in the exercise of the profession	9.2 Social workers must hold the required qualifications and develop and maintain the required skills and **competencies** to do their job

* AGTS: Association Guinéene des Travailleurs Sociaux (AGTS, Guinean Association of Social Workers), IFSW: International Federation of Social Work

This is contrasted with ANAS-Guinée (2022), which was formalized in 2019 and is led by Guinean trained social workers currently practicing in the country. This organisation has been active on the ground in multiple domains, and it communicates regularly to its members via a Facebook page[1], as well as via newsletters that provide updates and information to practicing social workers in Guinea. ANAS-Guinée has been highly visible in the public arena in promotion of the social work sector (Bah, 2019), performing a grassroots advocacy role as a professional organisation sitting outside of government institutions. For example, in 2019 the Guinean government took an important step in creating general recognition of the social work profession by introducing 120 social work positions in the public service, thus potentially creating demand for a social work degree programme. However, ANAS-Guinée wrote in an open letter to the prime minister that trained social workers were not occupying the majority of these positions (Guinée Matin, 2019). This is important, in particular due to the role that the ENSK-trained social workers had in providing critical psycho-social support in Ebola-affected areas during the 2014 epidemic (Madou, 2019).

The parallel development of these two organisations provides an illustrative example of the different paths that social work sector development can take, and the ways that the globalised social work profession interacts with locally generated initiatives. AGTS as an organisation has aligned with an international body (IFSW), which has provided them with opportunities to access knowledge and connections outside of the country. However, the organisation has not developed strong links with the social work sector initiatives in Guinea. Conversely, ANAS-Guinée is a domestically generated organisation created specifically for the needs of Guinean social workers. The organisation has strong ties to the small population of professional social workers, and it has been effective at domestic advocacy. However, the organisation is not accessible outside of Guinea and, as such, does not have links to the same external opportunities as AGTS. The authors reflected on this situation, and they posit the question: what is the role of international bodies like IFSW in supporting indigenous social work associations like ANAS-Guinée, which may not be as clearly aligned with global social work norms but that are responding to local contexts?

Research

Social work specific research is not available in Guinea, which is unsurprising due to the current absence of degree granting programmes in this subject. The public university system includes Université General Lansana Conté – Sonfonia, which houses the central sociology, anthropology, geography, law, business, and related departments. Université Gamal Abdel Nasser is the public university that houses health sciences programmes. Faculty in these universities collaborate regionally and internationally to produce published research. Regional universities with social science programmes and some research active faculty include Université Julius Nyeréré of Kankan, Université de Labé, and Université de Kindia. In addition to public universities, there is a sector of private universities that offer diverse programmes of study at varying levels, some of which generate social science–related research. Of note is Université Kofi Annan, Guinea's oldest private university that has a strong reputation within the country. Research institutes outside of health are rare, with the notable exception of CIRD, Centre Internationale de Recherche et Documentation (CIRD, 2015) established in 2015. A timeline of events discussed in this section is provided in Table 17.4.

While externally published articles and reports are limited, it is important to note that there is a significant amount of research already completed as a part of requirements for university research degree programmes. However, this work is often retained by the university in the form of hardcopy theses in library repositories. In the case of Guinea's main social science university, UGLC Sonfonia, these documents are not catalogued or digitised, making the majority of Guinean generated social science knowledge largely inaccessible to practicing social workers. Research theses dating from the 2000s back to the 1950s are currently retained, and they could provide an extraordinary resource for Guinean social workers looking for relevant research materials to inform local social work practice.

Discussion

The results section addresses the first research question by providing a holistic examination of the current state of the social work profession in Guinea and highlights the interconnectedness of education, policy, research, and professional associations in both the creation and the development of the social work sector. The second research question asks how this sector can best develop to address the unique needs of the Guinean population. The continuum in Figure 17.2 is a useful lens through which to consider the future development of Guinea's social work sector. Rather than consider the sector as a whole, the four arenas of policy, education, research, and practice can be seen at different points on this continuum. While there will be aspects of each transmission, indigenisation, and authentisation, in all of these areas, our discussion focuses on the most likely path forward for Guinean social work. While authentisation of social work is rhetorically the ideal approach to generating a Guinean-specific model of social work *ceteris paribus*, Guinea will likely not have the economic, political, or human capital to take this approach across all areas of professionalisation.

Transmission of Policy

The two policies explored in this article, the recognition of the social work profession and the establishment of public service social work roles, can be understood as a transmission of Western social work norms. The governmental structure in Guinea draws from the French model, and the inclusion of a cadre of publicly funded social workers likewise reflects the French orientation to social work development. In the current context, it is unlikely that these governmental structures

Table 17.4 Social Work Sector Timeline in Guinea

Event	Date	Involvement
1st cohort begins social work programme at ENSK	2004	ENSK
Creation of the social assistance sector through decree A/2006 n°1241/MET-FP/CAB of March 22, 2006 creating the social work sector and the ENSK educational programme in Kindia	2006	UNICEF, African Training Center for Development (CENAFOD)
1st cohort completes social work programme at ENSK	2007	ENSK
Creation of the first NGO of social workers (ANASOGUI)	2007	1st student cohort
Creation of the second NGO of social workers (AASOGUI)	2008	2nd student cohort
Validation of the guide and training programme for social workers	2009	CENAFOD
5th and last cohort completes social work programme at ENSK	2014	ENSK
Trained social workers respond to communities during the Ebola epidemic	2014-2016	
Guinean Association of Social Workers (AGTS) joins IFSW	2017	AGTS, IFSW
'Train the trainers' sessions for social work programme at JP2's National Center for Applied Social Training	2019	Ministry of Social Action, JP2
Merger of ENSK social work associations into ANAS-Guinée	2019	Graduated social workers
Guinea government establishes social work roles in the public service	2019	Ministry of Social Action
Trained social workers protest lack of employment in public services roles	2019	ANAS-Guinée
Social workers respond to communities during the COVID-19 epidemic	2020	
Guinean government in contact with social workers regarding public service roles	2022	
JP2 continues to pursue a social work programme		
ANAS-Guinée provides grassroots support to professional social workers		

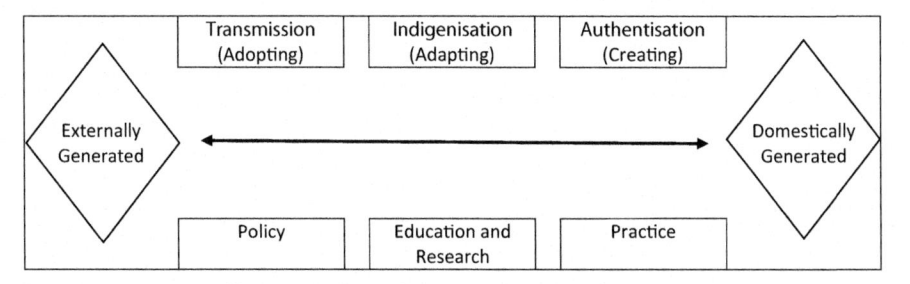

Figure 17.2 Transmission, indigenisation, and authentisation of social work in Guinea

and approaches to policy will change to reflect a traditional Guinean approach to governance, meaning that the bureaucratic structure of the social work policy realm will continue to reflect an overall transmission approach in the future, even if the content of the policy is more reflective of Guinean contexts.

Indigenisation of Education and Research

The domestically created social work educational sector has shown that an indigenisation approach is preferred, adapting social work theories and methods created elsewhere to the Guinean context. The original ENSK degree programme in Kindia reflects this, as the curriculum was developed by both national and international experts keen to incorporate externally generated social work ideas into uniquely Guinean models of practice. The JP2 social work programme uses a similar approach, blending coursework using international social work approaches with an understanding that Western models may not be appropriate in a Guinean context. One objective in the approved curriculum is to:

> Develop specific theoretical and practical training in social service, capitalizing on and promoting the traditions and cultures of both Guinea and the sub-region, within the framework of social policies and poverty reduction strategies (p 11).

The strong influence of international organisations and interests in Guinea leads the authors to believe that social work education cannot be entirely domestically derived. The larger international systems, theories, and influences of globalisation that impact Guinea are necessary to understand in order to effectively practice in a local context, even if a social worker chooses to use Guinean-specific practice-models.

As the JP2 social work programme continues to develop, leadership can benefit from West African regional expertise to guide their efforts at indigenisation of curriculum, rather than relying on European or American approaches. Possible partners from Francophone nations include Burkina Faso's Institut National de Formation en Travail Social *(*INFTS*)*, Côte d'Ivoire's Institut National de la Formation Sociale (INFS), and Senegal's École Nationale des Travailleurs Sociaux Spécialisés (ENTSS).

Research

There is no existing body of Guinean social work research and a limited number of West African resources (Canavera et al., 2020), creating a large gap in knowledge on the ways that this region's educational institutions have effectively contextualised social work theory and practice. However, Guinean universities do have repositories of domestic research that have not been widely disseminated. This large body of interdisciplinary Guinean social science knowledge, while not social work specific, is a valuable and locally created resource to inform the developing sector. Future Guinean social work research would do well to build from these foundations, rather than relying wholly on externally generated sources, whether Western or African. A well-resourced digitisation project that results in a catalogued inventory of Guinean materials could vastly improve the ability of social work researchers to translate existing studies into contextualised, evidence-informed practice frameworks.

It is also important to underscore that globally recognised higher education systems existed in West Africa prior to European contact, most notably Sankoré University in Timbuktu, Mali (Shuriye and Ibrahim, 2013).

Authentisation of Practice

The ENSK-educated social work practitioners have already taken steps to create a Guinean specific model of social work practice, most notably through ANAS-Guinée's advocacy and organisational actions. These grassroots efforts reflect an observed tendency towards authentisation in practice, looking inward rather than outwards for models to create positive change. After careful review of the data gathered for this case study, the authors posit that authentisation of social work in Guinea will likely be led by practitioners in the field. Engaging with a diversity of ethnicities, communities, languages, and kinship structures, practitioners will need to innovate rather than rely on existing globalised models in order to find effective methods to promote wellbeing according to Guinean values. It will be important for supportive institutions, such as JP2, UNICEF, IFSW, CENAFOD, MASPFE, and MENRS, to demonstrate their support of this important contribution to Guinean social work knowledge. Collaboration to disseminate theories, frameworks, case studies, and stories of impact will support the development of a social work sector that privileges Guinean-led progress.

Conclusion

The development of the social work sector in Guinea has lagged behind other West African nations. However, this offers an opportunity for Guineans to reflect on what social work should be in their country, learning from the journeys of other Global South countries' social work sector development. The past era of colonisation and the current era of globalisation are tied to social work's historical connection to Guinea, and these relationships are important to acknowledge. Social work administered by missionaries during colonisation has been damaging to people in Guinea, and globalised social work norms may not always be advantageous to the unique social environments across the country. Given this background, the current state of social work in Guinea continues to be in flux. Government and International NGO partners have collaborated in the past to launch a social work programme, but it was not sustainable. Now, the students of that programme are strong advocates for the social work sector, engaging with government ministries to relaunch a degree programme at Jean Paul II National Centre for Applied Social Training in Conakry. Strong supporters, including the Ministry of Social Action and Promotion of Women and Children and UNICEF, have identified social work as an important factor in Guinea's efforts to promote wellbeing and reduce poverty and will continue to support sector development.

The future of Guinea's social work sector is uncertain; however, the interplay between indigenous and external theories and practices will continue. It is important for Guinean social work practitioners and future instructors to reflect deeply on the kind of sector they want to create; Will it be a replica of globalised social work models, reflecting a Western-oriented base? Will it be a purely indigenous model of social work practice, drawing from the strong social base of the multiple cultures coexisting in the country? Or will it be a balance of locally generated knowledge, informed but not dominated by a diversity of international influences reflecting the globalised world? The decision likely lies in the hands of practitioners, who embody the values and theories of social work in their daily practice with the Guinean people.

Notes

1. The Facebook site is free or reduced to access via common internet providers in Guinea. As such, it is a very popular and accessible platform for information dissemination across the literate population.

Recommendations

1. Social work education needs to be engaged alongside the development of the sector to support career pathways for graduates. Professional associations, social welfare policy, and institutional partnerships are all needed to support positive educational outcomes for social work.
2. International aid organisations have an interest in promoting social work training. However, the provision of short-term training in emergency situations is insufficient to address complex social issues. These organisations should focus efforts on supporting locally led, sustainable, comprehensive social work education that builds national capacity that can respond when emergencies arise.
3. While this chapter advocates for practice models and educational materials that draw from local contexts and knowledge, the implications of globalisation and prior colonisation on the lives of individuals and families must also be addressed. As such, the development of social work education in Guinea should ensure both micro and macro issues are addressed, balancing the local with the global.

Further Reading

Canavera, M., Akesson, B., Landis, D., Armstrong, M., and Meyer, E. (2020). Mapping social work education in the West Africa region: Movements toward indigenization in 12 countries' training programs. *International Journal of Social Welfare*, 29(1), 83–95.

Tusasiirwe, S. (2023). ***Decolonising and Reimagining Social Work in Africa: Alternative Epistemologies and Practice Models***. Taylor & Francis.

Acknowledgements

The Authors Would Like to Acknowledge the Support of the Staff of Jean Paul II Hospital's National Centre for Applied Social Training and Anas-Guinée for Their Support of This Research.
Funding Declarations.
The Field Work for This Case Study Was Funded by a 2018/2019 Fulbright US Scholar Programme Grant 8033-GV, Social Work Specialization.

References

African Development Bank Group (2021). ***African Economic Outlook 2021 – From Debt Resolution to Growth: The Road Ahead for Africa***. African Development Bank. https://www.afdb.org/en/documents/african-economic-outlook-2021

AGTS (2017). ***Association Guineen des Travailleurs Socials***. International Federation of Social Work. https://www.ifsw.org/member-organisation/guinea/.

ANAS-Guinée (2022). Association National des Assistants Sociale – Guinee. https://www.facebook.com/anasguinee/.

Association for Social Work Education in Africa (ASWEA) (1974). *Curricula of Schools of Social Work and Community Development Training Centres in Africa* (No. Document 7). ASWEA. http://www.historicalpapers.wits.ac.za/?inventory_enhanced/U/Collections&c=124935/R/AG3303-2-3.

Bah, H. (2019). Humanitaire : Les rôles d'assistant social débattus en conférence de presse. *Guinea, 360*. https://guinee360.com/07/08/2019/humanitaire-les-roles-dassistant-social-debattus-en-conference-de-presse/.

Boblin, S. L., Ireland, S., Kirkpatrick, H., andRobertson, K. (2013). Using Stake's qualitative case study approach to explore implementation of evidence-based practice. *Qualitative Health Research, 23*(9), 1267–1275.

Brittanica (2022). Sekou Toure, President of Guinea. https://www.britannica.com/biography/Sekou-Toure.

Brooks, A. (2016). *Care and Protection of Children in the West African Ebola Virus Disease Epidemic: Lessons Learned for Future Public Health Emergencies*. UNICEF. https://resourcecentre.savethechildren.net/pdf/final-ebola-lessons-learned-dec-2016.pdf/.

Burke, J., and Ngonyani, B. (2004). A social work vision for Tanzania. *International Social Work, 47*(1), 39–52.

Canavera, M., andAkesson, B. (2018). Supervision during social work education and training in Francophone West Africa: Conceptual frameworks and empirical evidence from Burkina Faso and Côte d'Ivoire. *European Journal of Social Work, 21*(3), 467–482.

Canavera, M., Akesson, B., and Landis, D. (2014). *Social Service Workforce Training in the West and Central African Region*, Final Report. UNICEF, CPC Learning Network. http://www.cpcnetwork.org/wp-content/uploads/2014/10/UNICEF-WCARO-Social-Work-Mapping-FINAL-27-November-2014.pdf

Canavera, M., Akesson, B., Landis, D., Armstrong, M., and Meyer, E. (2020). Mapping social work education in the West Africa region: Movements toward indigenisation in 12 countries' training programmes. *International Journal of Social Welfare, 29*(1), 83–95.

Centre africain de Formation pour le Developpement (2008). Projet d'appui a la promotion et au renforcement de l'assistance sociale en Guinee. https://cnoas.org/wp-content/uploads/2020/02/out-13-1.pdf.

Chitereka, C. (2009). Social work in a developing continent: The case of Africa. *Advances in Social Work, 10*(2), 144–156.

Dente, F. (2013). *Nuove dimensioni del servizio sociale*. Maggioli editore.

Desclaux, A., and Touré, A. (2018). *Quelle 'préparation' aux dimensions sociales des épidémies en Afrique ? Une expérience de formation à Conakry*. Medecine et sante tropicales, John Libbey Eurotext. ff10.1684/mst.2018.0749ff. ffhalshs-02099204f.

Diallo, A. S. (2020). *L'UNICEF appuie le Ministère de l'action Sociale pour la formation de 40 travailleurs sociaux*. UNICEF Guinee. https://www.unicef.org/guinea/recits/lunicef-appuie-le-minist%C3%A8re-de-laction-sociale-pour-la-formation-de-40-travailleurs-sociaux.

Foster, E. A. (2015). 'Theologies of colonization': The catholic church and the future of the French empire in the 1950s. *The Journal of Modern History, 87*(2), 281–315.

Ginio, R., and Sessions, J. (2016). *French Colonial Rule*. Oxford Bibliographies. https://www.oxfordbibliographies.com/view/document/obo-9780199846733/obo-9780199846733-0029.xml.

Goerg, O. (2011). Couper la Guinée en quatre ou comment la colonisation a imaginé l'Afrique. *Vingtième Siècle. Revue d'Histoire, 111*(3), 73–88. https://doi.org/10.3917/vin.111.0073.

Gray, M., and Allegritti, I. (2002). Cross-cultural practice and the indigenisation of African social work. *Social Work-Stellenbosch, 38*(4), 324–336.

Gray, M., and Hetherington, T. (2013). Indigenisation, indigenous social work and decolonization: Mapping the theoretical terrain. *Decolonizing Social Work*, 25–43.

Guinee Matin (2019). *Lettre ouverte au PM: Les assistants sociaux tirent à boulets rouges sur le ministère de l'action Sociale*. Guinee Matin. https://guineematin.com/2019/07/18/lettre-ouverte-au-pm-les-assistants-sociaux-tirent-a-boulets-rouges-sur-le-ministere-de-laction-sociale/.

Ibrahima, A. B., and Mattaini, M. A. (2019). Social work in Africa: Decolonizing methodologies and approaches. *International Social Work, 62*(2), 799–813.

Ife, J. (2013). *Community Development in an Uncertain World*. Cambridge University Press.

Kreitzer, L. (2012). *Social Work in Africa: Exploring Culturally Relevant Education and Practice in Ghana*. University of Calgary Press.

Madou, M. M. (2019). *Conakry: Des assistants sociaux exigent leur intégration à la function publique*. Guinee actuelle. http://guineeactuelle.com/conakry-des-assistants-sociaux-exigent-leur-integration-a-la-fonction-publique.

Ministere des Actions Sociales De la Promotion Feminine et de L'Enfance (MASPFE) & Ministere de l'Education National et de la Recherche Scientifique (MENRS) (n.d.). Programmeme de formation en assistance sociale.

Ng, G. T., and Sim, T. (2006). Globalization, indigenisation, and authentisation in social work. *Asia Pacific Journal of Social Work and Development*, *16*(1), 1–5.

Rankopo, M. J., and Osei-Hwedie, K. (2011). Globalization and culturally relevant social work: African perspectives on indigenisation. *International Social Work*, *54*(1), 137–147.

Sewpaul, V. (2006). The global-local dialectic: Challenges for African scholarship and social work in a post-colonial world. *British Journal of Social Work*, *36*(3), 356–380. https://doi.org/10.1093/bjsw/bcl007.

Shuriye, A. O., and Ibrahim, D. S. (2013). Timbuktu civilization and its significance in Islamic history. *Mediterranean Journal of Social Sciences*, *4*(11), 696. https://www.richtmann.org/journal/index.php/mjss/article/view/1359.

Stake, R. E. (2005). Qualitative case studies. In N. K. Denzin and Y. S. Lincoln (Eds.), *The Sage Handbook of Qualitative Research* (3rd ed., pp. 443–466). Sage.

Ugiagbe, E. O. (2015). Social work is context-bound: The need for indigenisation of social work practice in Nigeria. *International Social Work*, *58*(6), 790–801.

Walton, R. G., and Abo El Nasr, M. M. (1988). Indigenisation and authentisation in terms of social work in Egypt. *International Social Work*, *31*(2), 135–144.

Yunong, H., and Xiong, Z. (2008). A reflection on the indigenisation discourse in social work. *International Social Work*, *51*(5), 611–622.

Appendix A

	Subjects	Year	Points
I	*Supporting Subjects*		*340*
1	French	1	72
2	English	1	108
3	Computer Science	1	108
4	Environment	1	52
II	*Foundational Subjects*		*1152*
A	Sociology		234
a	General Sociology	1	50
b	Urban and Rural Sociology	2	92
c	Sociology of Deviance and Cultural Anthropology	3	92
B	Psychology		234
a	General Psychology	1	50
b	Developmental Psychology	2	92
c	Social Psychology and Pathology	3	92
C	Research Methodology		108
a	Methodology	2	108
D	Health Sciences		118
a	Hygiene	1	36
b	Social Medicine	1	36
c	Occupational Medicine	2	46
E	Law		234
a	General Law	1	50
b	Criminal Law	1	30
c	Administrative Law	2	50
d	Social Law	2	50
e	Legislation	3	24
f	Conventions/Treaties	3	30
F	Social Policy		104
a	Guinea's Social Policy	2	34
b	Comparative Policy	2	34
c	Social Service Organizations	3	36
G	Economics		120
a	Social Solidarity Economy	2	15
b	Economic andSocial Geography	2	15
c	Administrative andFinancial Management	2	60
d	Health Economics	3	30
III	*Social Service Subjects*		*396*
1	Principles and foundations	1	108
2	Methods and techniques in social work 1	2	108
3	Methods and techniques in social work 2	3	108
4	Child Welfare	3	72
IV	*Internships*		*920*
1	Discovery Internship	1	214
2	Professionalization Internship	2	252
3	Integration Internship	3	454

Appendix A: Approved Social Work Curriculum, Jean Paul II National Center for Applied Social Training

18
CULTURE AND ETHNICITY IN MEDICAL SOCIAL WORK

Lessons for Future Directions for Social Work Curriculum Transformation in Kenya

Wilkins Ndege Muhingi, Ajwang' Warria, and Edwine Jeremiah Otieno

Abstract: English

Medical social work acknowledges the basis for psychosocial challenges, ill health, and cultural elements as influencing practices related to wellbeing. Attention to the cultural context of wellbeing is crucial in ensuring the provision of culture-sensitive and transformative client-friendly intervention. This chapter aims to contribute to the social work curriculum in Kenya, shedding light on important but often understated roles of ethnicity and culture in psychosocial interventions as well as training of medical social workers. This chapter explores the issues of culture and ethnicity in medical social work practice and training. Many individuals in Kenya value their families' cultural-emotional strength and social support; they source home/ herbal remedies and consult traditional healers, often impacted by low resource levels. Furthermore, the focus on advanced health planning may not always be culturally relevant as there is a huge focus on being present-oriented, with taboos related to discussions around ill health, death, and disability. The training for medical social workers in Kenya needs to strengthen the aspect of cultural and ethnic diversity issues, and there is a need for culturally sensitive training.

Abstract: Luhya

Igasi yo bukonyi mulihonyi imanyilitsa manyangano ngi tsinganagani nende kusanga, kudaka vulamu nende vindu vilombaga mwima gulondekana nende limenya lilahi. Kuvika tsinganagani ku havundu hi miima mulimenya lilahi kunyariza kuleta kwi tsinganagani ku mwima nende ligirung'anyi lilahi ku vakonywaa. Muliango yigu gwenyanga kumenda ku libanga lyo vusominyi vya vi ingasi ya vakonyi mukivara cha Kenya. Muliango yigu gumeedanga kwanguhiza kugerihitsa kurondekana nende vurahi vutavoleka vyu mwima nende tsihili zianga vandu mu vukonyi vurondekananga nende tsinganagani nende kusanga. Muliango yigu gukaviritsanga vindu vilondekana nende miima nende tsihiri mu ligiza lya vandu vakonya kuhonya. Vandu vingi mukivara cha Kenya valola vulahi nende zinguru tsi miima jireta ku migizi jyavo nende kukonyana vene. Vandu vataveye nende miandu vatumikiranga tsinyasi zi kimwamu kandi vanyola vukonyi vya vashi vimisara nende vasalisi. Kumeda ku yaga, kuhennzelitsa nende kubanga kunyola vuhonyi kunyara

DOI: 10.4324/9781003314349-21

kuvura kurondekana nende miima. Ni kigira vayazirira vuhonyi vywayitsi kandi gunyara kuvaa mujiru kumoroma ku vulware, likutsa nende vulema. Kwigiza vakonyi vukuhonya mukivara cha Kenya kwenyeka kudinyiritsi ling'ana lyi miima nende tsihiri tsingano tsinyingi nende mang'ana gajyo, kurwayago, kuganaganange kwigitsa kurondanga miima gya vandu.

Abstract: Kiswahili

Kazi ya kijamii ya matibabu inatambua chanzo cha changamoto za saikolojia ya jamii, magonjwa pamoja na vipengele vya kiutamaduni vinavyohusiana na ukuaji bora wa binadamu. Ni muhimu kuzingatia utamaduni wa jamii husika ikiwa unalenga kufanikisha utoaji wa huduma yenye kudhamini maslahi ya jamii. Sura hii inalenga kuchangia katika kufanikisha mtaala wa huduma ya jamii nchini Kenya. Inaangazia umuhimu wa kikabila na kiutamaduni ambao hupuuzwa katika kukabiliana na changamoto za saikolojia ya jamii pamoja utoaji wa mafunzo kwa wahudumu wa afya kwa jamii. Sura hii inatalii masuala ya kiutamaduni na kikabila katika kutoa mafunzo na huduma ya afya kwa jamii. Watu wengi nchini Kenya wanadhamini sana uwezo wa hisia za kitamaduni zinazotokana na familia zao pamoja na uungwaji mkono wa jamii; wao hutafuta kinga ya mitishamba na ushauri wa waganga ambao huwa ghali mno kwao kiwango cha kukosa uwezo wa kugharamia. Hata hivyo, matibabu ya kisasa huenda yasiwe muhimu kwao kwa kuzingatia mtazamo wa jamii; watu wengi wanaenda na majira ya kisasa japo kuna itikadi nyingi zinazohusiana na masuala ya magonjwa, vifo na ulemavu. Utoaji wa mafunzo kwa wahudumu wa afya ya jamii nchini Kenya unafaa kutilia mkazo suala la mwingliano wa kiutamaduni na kikabila kwani ni muhimu katika kutoa mafunzo yanayotilia maanani utamaduni wa watu.

Introduction

Culture encompasses 'all aspects of the way of life associated with a group of people' (Healey et al., 2019 p. 40). Literature once reflected a misunderstanding to exclusively denote practice with or give precedence to ethnicity or race, despite the fact that the National Association of Social Work (NASW), the largest international professional organisation for social work, has a standing definition that defines culture as inclusive of all groups beyond ethnicity or race (Melendres, 2022 citing Fellin, 2000; Johnson & Munch, 2009; Reisch, 2008; Yan Wong, 2005). Cultural humility is a related term that means a social worker getting a chance to step away from the notion of being experts to being lifelong learners when it comes to enhancing their self-awareness.

Ethnicity is increasingly being recognised as a component of social work, as seen by its rising inclusion in the field's educational system (Urh, 2011). The term 'ethnicity' is relative and has no univocal definition. Ethnicity is a special form of social categorisation (Gabbert, 2006 citing Barth, 1969). Frederic Barth's classic definition provides a first clue:

> A categorical ascription is an ethnic ascription when it classifies a person in terms of his basic, most general identity, presumptively determined by his origin and background.
> *(Barth, 1969, p.13)*

Gehlert and Browne (2012) explain that medical social work owes its origins to changes in 'demographics population during the 19th and early 20th centuries, attitudes about how the sick should be treated, including where treatment should occur; and attitudes toward the role of social and psychological factors in health' (p. 5). For this reason, Ida Cannon invented medical social work after extensive research at Massachusetts General Hospital (MGH) and the Simmons School of

Social Work (Muhingi and Machani, 2022). During earlier times, medical social workers were involved in:

> (1) the securing of information to enable an adequate understanding of the general health problem of the patient; (2) interpretation of the patient's health problem to himself, his family, and community welfare agencies; and (3) the mobilizing of measures for the relief of the patient and his associates. (Gehlert Browne, 2012, p. 11)

Over the years, the field has grown, and the diversity in the field is both exciting and challenging (Egede, 2006). For instance, a diversity of roles has emerged for social workers (Umoren, 2016). The areas that draw practices and opportunities from inter- and transdisciplinary collaborations are unprecedented in the profession (Eklund, 2008). Social workers and other professionals are on the cutting edge of new health-relevant programmes and practices, with social workers frequently in top leadership roles in these efforts, and this is the case in Kenya at the moment. For example, medical social workers are involved in providing genetic counseling and mental health treatment, coordinating hospice and palliative care, working with communities to develop better access to cancer care and clinical trials, advocating for and writing improved health-relevant policies, developing health programmes and practices, and conducting research that provides an evidence base for effective practice in social work and other professions (Gehlert and Browne, 2012; Egede, 2006; Malinga and Mupedziswa, 2009).

Modern social work that applies social work theories, methods, and strategies to the medical industry is known as medical social work. Frequently complex and requiring numerous sorts of support at once, the needs of the sick are rarely simple. A medical social worker may be helpful in circumstances of decisional conflict, such as when two or more clinically appropriate options have advantages and hazards that patients value differently or shared decision-making (Peterson, 2012). According to Browne (2019, citing Dhooper, 1994), medical social work, also known as health social work, has a dual focus on improving social structures, known as choices, that have benefits and harms that patients value differentially.

Many countries have passed laws and rules to support the development of medical social work practice. By assisting patients in getting access to healthcare, social workers in Kenya, for instance, contribute to the implementation of the health laws and the Children Act of 2022. Medical social workers take part in social-economic assessments, home visits and follow-ups, reintegrating abandoned patients into the wards, NHIF sensitisations, support groups, and caregivers forum, sensitising on gender-based violence cases stigma and discrimination, developing a case management plan for all vulnerable patients and documenting appropriate social/intervention provided, placing abandoned children in the wards, and placing patients in homes (Public Service Commission, 2020). Evidence-based practice, which is lacking in this social task, is necessary.

Medical social workers should apply evidence-based practice, which is integral to the rising importance of social work in health. They work with patients from different cultural backgrounds. Kenyan medical social workers are sometimes forced to employ heuristics where formal knowledge is not applicable and where patient health matters are embedded in cultural beliefs of patients, who hold different beliefs and customs. Hence, understanding culture is very important in solving their problems (Chelogoi et al., 2020). The higher socioeconomic classes have better access to healthcare than the lower socioeconomic classes. It is the role of the medical social worker to address health inequalities. As the profession is focused on improving people's wellbeing through practice that targets interrelationships among systems and people, medical social workers, through social and economic assessment, can improve the health of the patients (Althumali, 2021).

Medical social work combines evidence to practice and concerted and strategic efforts of academic, social work, professional social work organisations as well as health social work research to promote healthcare. Despite the huge benefits of medical social work in healthcare settings in the country, there is still a gap in the literature, and few studies have been done to promote medical social work. The growth of the perspective of the social determinants of health has fostered a crucial place for medical social work. As a profession, medical social workers have long understood the importance of multiple life dimensions and experiences as they affect human wellbeing across the life cycle and have built their practice on such a perspective. As other health professions catch up in this area, medical social work's contributions can be very influential in helping to prevent the reinvention of the wheel in both healthcare and disease prevention.

Historical Development of a Focus on Culturally Competent Practice

A focus on culturally competent practice initially arose as a result of recommendations made by the counseling and psychology professions. There was a worry that professionals were not getting the training they needed to work effectively with a clientele that was becoming more diverse. As a result, a request for standards was made, with the result being a definition of what makes a counselor with cultural competence in terms of their beliefs and attitudes, knowledge, and abilities (Sue et al., 1992). The beliefs/attitudes dimension included sensitivity in being willing to refer a client to practitioners of the same race and culture as the client, self-awareness of one's cultural roots, biases one might hold about those who are culturally different, comfort with the client's cultural differences, and comfort with one's own cultural roots.

Understanding the influence of sociocultural dynamics on the treatment of minorities required knowledge of a particular cultural group's values, beliefs, and norms as well as awareness of potential obstacles preventing a minority person from accessing mental health services. The capacity to send and receive a wide range of verbal and nonverbal communications as well as use of cultural syntonic methods were among the skills that were developed. Ten years later, these guidelines became culturally sensitive counseling traits that emphasised the attitudes, information, and abilities necessary to cultivate one's own self-awareness, client understanding, and ability to deliver effective interventions (Sue et al., 1992). Following the development of that model, specific steps a practitioner would need to follow to develop cultural competency were articulated (Arredondo et al., 1996).

In essence, social work has borrowed from developments within counseling and psychology in order to define the components of a culturally competent approach. Lum (1999) may have made the most significant contributions to the social work field's creation of the cultural competence construct. His description of cultural competency as the capacity to comprehend the culture and cultural practices within the framework of a client's sociocultural milieu is consistent with the social work generalist and ecological perspectives. Lum (1999) has developed a framework to more fully specify how a social worker could go towards the development of cultural competency. His framework includes four tools, which he describes as follows:

1. Development of personal and professional awareness of ethnic persons and events that have been a part of the upbringing and education of the worker.
2. Acquisition of knowledge related to culturally diverse practice.
3. Development of skills to work with multicultural clients.
4. Ongoing discovery of new facts about multicultural clients through inductive learning.

Further development, for example, in studies show that there is still little structured orientation to a new culture, and social workers feel judged and experience significant cultural differences. They propose improving the process of transition in their practice to include having a systemic approach to learning about the bicultural environment, provision of mandatory bicultural work induction, and providing cultural supervision once in practice (Staniforth Connor, 2023).

Understanding Concepts of Ethnicity and Culture

The term 'ethnicity' is relative and has no univocal definition. It can be defined ethnicity 'as a group of people with a common cultural or national tradition' (The Oxford English Dictionary, n.d, p. 1194). In health, 'ethnicity' is capricious and polemically used in studies on health disparities. Schlesinger and Devore (1995) have defined minimum standards for maintaining, collecting, and presenting data on race and ethnicity. This includes ethnic categories, 'focus on community or tribe; racial categories: this entails skin colour. The concept of ethnicity is an attempt to differentiate racial groups further; however, like race, it carries its own historical, political, and social baggage. The current definition of ethnicity is arbitrary and ill-defined' (Hamer et al., 2020). For example, in Kenya, there are different ethnic groups. Kenya has more than 40 ethnic groups. The groups are differentiated by the language they speak and their geographical location.

The concept of culture as distinct from ethnicity has been proposed as a better explanation for differences in health behaviour and outcomes. The definition and conceptualisation of culture vary across disciplines (Egede, 2006; Chelogoi et al., 2020). The United States Department of Health and Human Services Office of Minority Health (2001) defines culture as language, thoughts, communications, acts, customs, beliefs, values, and institutions of racial, ethnic, religious, and social groups that result from integrated patterns of human behaviour. According to King, Bokore, and Dudziak (2017), culture in the context of health behaviour is defined as unique shared values, beliefs, and practices that are directly associated with a behaviour or indirectly associated with a behaviour or influence acceptance and adoption of the health education message. Although culture is a valid explanatory variable for racial and ethnic differences in health outcomes, researchers must recognise that knowing someone's ethnic identity or national origin does not reliably predict beliefs and attitudes. Rather, it is more important to specify the cultural traits being tested and include appropriate measures that capture such cultural traits (King et al., 2017).

Culture, rather than ethnicity, is proposed as a better explanation for health behaviour differences. Culture is defined as shared patterns of behaviour and beliefs within racial, ethnic, and social groups (Spitzer, 2019). Culture influences health education messages and behaviours, and it is transmitted across generations (King et al., 2017). However, researchers should not assume beliefs and attitudes based on ethnic identity or origin but should measure specific cultural traits (King et al., 2017). Definitions and conceptualisations of culture vary across disciplines (Egede, 2006; Chelogoi et al., 2020).

Ethnicity, Culture, and Medical Social Work Training

The social work education process is characterised by a multicultural perspective (Mungai et al., 2014). It forces people to become more conscious of their own viewpoints and to accept the legitimacy of other cultural viewpoints. Even though social work is concerned with racial injustice, the multicultural approach utilised in social work teaching does not necessarily address this issue. After the civil rights movement, a multicultural approach emerged that addresses the marginalisation of non-dominant communities (Schoorman Bogotch, 2010). Its key areas of interest include equitable pedagogy, bias reduction, and content integration. Accordingly, the multicultural approach has a lot to offer social work education, but Schoorman and Bogotch (2010) argue that it may overemphasise group differences rather than the underlying factors that give rise to them. The pursuit of social justice can become difficult as a result. Social workers are in a good position to create and put into practice destigmatising initiatives due to their understanding of communities and enduring social concerns. Social workers can encourage other interested parties to employ powerful tactics to combat stigma for example those associated with mental illness at the macro, mezzo, and micro levels (Kiwanuka, 2012).

Social work training in Kenya corresponds with Dominelli's (2009) three generic roles: maintenance, emancipator, and therapeutic. To aid in social workers' understanding of the social environment, they cover five major courses, including human behavior, social welfare policy, research, practice methods, and field practicum (Onyiko et al., 2017). Social workers advocate for patients' rights, advise on legal procedures, and address stigma. Therapeutic interventions include counseling for mental health and disabilities.

Thabede (2008) notes that the cultural aspect of social work, particularly in medical social work, has been overlooked. Social work training should be tailored to align with the cultural philosophies of the people it serves. Kenyan societies have their own guiding philosophies that influence how they perceive health and respond to health issues. Incorporating cultural elements, such as religion, into medical social work training is crucial to promoting cultural competency among medical social workers. Althumali (2021) points out that tensions can arise when patients or their families impose their religious and social values on staff during treatment. A social worker's understanding and appreciation of their patient's culture can significantly affect their response to treatment. Therefore, it is important to recognise and integrate cultural values into social work practices and education.

According to Gehlert and Browne (2012), social workers in any geographical area are likely to encounter some patients who consider religion important, attend worship services weekly, and pray daily. Culturally competent medical social work practice requires that social workers be prepared to understand and take account of these realities. In Kenya, this aspect has been taken into consideration but in a biased way. Social work training is imbued with the religious beliefs of the training institutions, for instance, Christian-sponsored institutions tend to train their student in Christian philosophy. It has jeopardised cultural competence during general social work and also medical social work practice as medical social workers may advise patients against traditional beliefs. Traditional beliefs have spiritual and psychological values that promote the social and mental health of the patient.

Despite modern medicine, patients often still rely on traditional practices for health purposes, including traditional medicine and spiritual leaders. This is particularly true among certain communities in Kenya, such as the Luo, who believe in illnesses that cannot be treated by modern medicine, including *Sihoho* and *Kwer*. Similarly, the Luhya community believes that a child's name can lead to illness if not endorsed by spirits, while the Kamba community believes in illnesses caused by witchcraft, or *Kamote*. For medical social workers, understanding these traditional health beliefs is crucial to addressing health's social and cultural aspects. Incorporating traditional health belief knowledge into the medical social work curriculum can help social workers be more culturally relevant when dealing with patients. Doing so empowers medical social workers to address patients' cultural and spiritual values and preferences, which can affect their response to treatment.

Another important aspect of culture is the organisation of ethnicity. The social and political are still based on African philosophy. Oduor (2014) explains the African philosophical concepts of Ubuntu, African Socialism, and African communitarianism. Should inform social work curriculum. For instance, the African Ubuntu recognised that a person becomes human within the larger context of society. In Kenya, medical social workers are consulted to waive the medical fee for patients who cannot pay. While traditional resource mobilisation is embedded in Ubuntu, the ability to provide moral and financial support is usually ignored. These traditional African perceptions of life can be formalised into theories. Already they inform people's behaviour. In addition, they have led to the development and the emergence of Pan-Africanism, consciencism, negritude, socialism, African humanism, and scientific socialism (Ikechukwu, 2016), although we do not wish to discuss these philosophical concepts as they are beyond the scope of the chapter. Adoption of the concepts aids in developing relevant cultural curricula and deviating from professional imperialism.

Kenya has recently witnessed rapid development in the healthcare field based on the Western medical model. When it comes to the diagnosis and management of chronic diseases, the Western medical model has a fairly reductionist perspective on health. Choosing an appropriate medicine or surgical intervention to remove the problematic body part or organ is frequently necessary when dealing with the proper management of the illness for which the patient exhibits a symptom. However, Howland (2020) observes that cultural healing remains significant due to skepticism of biomedicine among the people. The scholar explains that herbal medicine and traditional healers remain integral to the health system. The choice of treatment or healthcare is believed to be informed by patients' beliefs and values. Besides, Western medicine is a system in which doctors and other healthcare professionals see patients and treat their symptoms through prescription medications, surgical operations, various forms of therapy, and radiation (Althumali, 2021). The Western model of healthcare incorporates multidisciplinary teams. Disciplines such as medicine, social work, nursing, and other allied health professionals comprise interprofessional teams in the Kenyan healthcare sector. Chelogoi et al., 2020; Ross, 2008 detail the history and origins of the Western model of social work practice in the United Kingdom from a philanthropic activity to an organised profession.

Medical social workers play a significant role in ensuring successful healthcare services (Egede, 2006). To ensure the efficiency and effectiveness of the healthcare sector, cooperation between medical staff and social workers is essential given the current environment in which standard practices can conflict with established social and behavioural norms (National Association of Social Workers, 2011; Ross, 2008). Medical social workers can bridge the gap between patients' social, cultural, and economic needs and medical treatment while providing regular support in managing life events (Malinga & Mupedziswa, 2009; Krüger and Lewis, 2011). There is a clear connection between the medical social workers' willingness to adapt to limitations imposed by cultural norms and positive caregiver-patient results. Medical social workers routinely provide patients with support in managing life events (Zelnick et al., 2018; Gehlert and Browne, 2012; Chelogoi et al., 2020).

Medical Social Workers Practice

Malinga and Mupedziswa (2009) state that within hospitals, culturally competent practice presupposes an understanding of the sociocultural meanings attached to illness and disability and the people likely to be consulted concerning providing healthcare and restoring wellbeing. Many Kenyan ethnic groups are known to consult with traditional healers in preference to or in conjunction with Western, allopathic healthcare professionals. Studies on indigenous health and medicine among Kenyan ethnic communities across all religions allude that the plurality of reasons surrounding decision-making is complex (Spitzer, 2019; Ross, 2008; Onyiko et al., 2017), but it is clear that many people often use indigenous healing; improvements in the regulation of both formulas and practice would assist people to access more effectively. In addition, the spiritual and the religious nature has socialised and maintained the common cognitive inertia that illness is attributed to 'disorders to spiritual factors, punishment and superstitious beliefs' (Howland, 2020 p 199). Therefore, the patients perceive that only through tradition can they be cured.

According to Ross (2008), treating illnesses associated with spirits, bad omens, or being bewitched involves using natural substances, prayer and rituals, and procedures designed to restore equilibrium. In his analysis, the scholar observes that the community embraces medical pluralism. They would sometimes combine both biomedicine and traditional medicine. It suggests collaboration between formal and traditional healthcare practitioners and why people consulted with traditional healers. It is believed that medical social workers are positioned to address the issue and avoid conflict between the patient and the doctor. For this reason, medical social work professionals are essential in facilitating healthcare services and promoting the wellbeing of marginalised patients. Medical social work practice in any healthcare setting requires knowledge of culture, ethnicity and behaviour; social, economic, and cultural institutions; and the interaction of all these factors. Social work practice occurs in various contexts, but essentially it happens in both primary and secondary settings (Egede, 2006).

According to Muhingi and Machani (2022), medical social work has widened its scope. The field entails oncological social work, palliative care, psychiatric social work, geriatric social work, and comprehensive care centres/social work with people living with HIV/AIDS. In addition, Malinga and Mupedziswa (2009) explain that the hospital setting is secondary, essentially because the core business in such settings is the treatment of patients suffering from various ailments by medical personnel. Further, the scholars allude that in both primary healthcare settings and secondary healthcare settings, medical social work professionals often encounter enormous challenges, and these tend to be acute in developing countries, in particular, due to resource constraints and lack of culturally competent skills (Malinga & Mupedziswa, 2009).

Nkomo (2017) concurs that sociocultural beliefs influence health choices, a notion anchored on the health belief model. These beliefs may influence the need to use various healthcare providers. By understanding patients' belief systems, medical social workers can effectively meet the needs of hospital patients. A study by Zelnick et al. (2018) showed that patients' sociocultural beliefs in a healthcare setting influence adherence to drugs and treatment of TB. Further analysis showed that African traditional and cultural beliefs were reported to be affordable and enable people to connect with their ancestral spirits. Close relatives and traditional healers played an important role during illness and recovery. The scholar recommended that medical social workers always engage with patients and other multidisciplinary team members for a holistic patient care approach. Medical social workers should communicate to understand their patients holistically.

Muhingi and Machani (2022) note that the emergence and continued growth of the sub-field of medical social work implied that treatment is both physiological and holistic. Kodom (2022) points out that medical social workers practice at the micro, meso, and macro levels and have been involved in policy decisions and social aspects of health related to the pandemic. The scholar notes that medical social workers are trained in; crisis management, advanced care planning, case management, problem-solving, and policy development relevant to addressing the COVID-19 pandemic. Medical social workers were involved in hospitals, mental health facilities, nursing homes, and clinics during the pandemic. The combination of skills from social and medical perspectives gives medical social workers professional efficacy in handling social problems associated with individual health (Egede, 2006; Chelogoi et al., 2020; Howland, 2020). However, in Kenya medical social work is mainly practiced in healthcare settings, and its scope and relevance are rarely understood and appreciated (Muhingi and Machani, 2022). Medical social work has been detrimental in addressing psychosocial treatment and has been at the forefront in providing health justice and empowering and promoting patients' wellbeing at hospitals. Medical social workers act as gatekeepers and resource persons. They assess and provide referrals to patients when they need them. For example, connecting HIV patients to the psychosocial organisation and dealing with gender-based violence issues (Zelnick et al., 2018; Umoren, 2016; Althumali, 2021).

Culturally Sensitive Medical Social Work Practice

There are many layers of culture present in the helping process, and social workers act within a particular cultural framework. Most social workers in Western contexts are assimilated into a professional social work culture that values people, respects their ability or potential to make their own decisions and judgements, acts autonomously, etc., starting with their social work education and being shaped by the practice context. Such independent thought and behavior is viewed within this value framework as admirable, worthy of pursuit, a goal of the helping process, and a gauge of client success. Therefore, even within social work cultures, there are circumstances in which group or family interests, when taken into consideration, generate a supportive environment for individual decisions, which must be considered rather than individual interests.

When we think of culture, the interactions between the worker and the client or community are crucial. In addition to our professional culture and the beliefs we have chosen, there is also our culture and the culture of the organisations or environments in which we work or operate. There is what is frequently referred to as academic culture in universities. If you operate from a strengths viewpoint, you might find that the medical culture is very different from your professional culture if you were a social worker working in a hospital context (Gray Allegritti, 2003). Sometimes it is much easier to describe someone else's culture than to describe one's own.

Ethnic-Sensitive Social Work Practice

According to Spitzer (2019), for models to be ethnically sensitive, he suggests that, for the most part, these models emphasise differences in cultural norms. Of course, the multifaceted approach to ethnic-sensitive practice is needed, and professional imperialism is discarded. The people's culture and beliefs must also inform the philosophical foundation. An earlier use of the term was introduced by McMahon and Allen-Meares (1992). To answer the question 'is social work racist?' these authors reviewed segments of the social work literature and concluded that 'ethnic-sensitive practice ultimately focuses on change in the social worker, not the client nor the client's external conditions'. Thus, by itself, without regard for the client's social and economic contexts, ethnic-sensitive practice reinforces the racist conditions that oppress clients. It is a distortion of the approach introduced initially by the present authors and subsequently reiterated (Gehlert and Browne, 2012). Emphasis on simultaneous attention to psychological and systems change strategies was and remained an integral focus of the approach.

Cross-Cultural Social Work Practice

The social work literature includes views on cross-cultural practice from modernist, postmodern, psychoanalytic, intersubjectivist, and sociopolitical perspectives. Dean (2001) offers an informative review of these viewpoints. The modernist perspective, which is still held in high regard in the clinical community, has its origins in static conceptions of ethnicity and culture that are based on ethnological and anthropological studies, wherein people belonging to one culture are assumed to have certain key characteristics in common. According to this viewpoint, doctors may create a schema that enabled them to communicate 'more professionally' with group members.

The postmodern perspective emphasises the constantly shifting and developing nature of cultural identities, which calls for social workers to be 'informed not-knowers' (Laird, 1998, p. 30), conscious of their cultural baggage, and capable of separating themselves as much as possible from their own cultural biases in order to avoid impeding their efforts to get to know one another. A psychological approach to cross-cultural therapy treatment is taken by the psychoanalytic intersubjectivist position, which emphasises the clinician's self-knowledge (Foster, 2001). An 'inevitable' component of the therapeutic exchange is the blend of information and emotions that social workers bring to their work with clients on conscious and unconscious levels (Gerhardt et al., 2001). Together with the client's thoughts and feelings, this creates a multi-leveled field of interaction where the client and social worker collaborate to create meaning. Deep unconscious feelings are triggered by race, culture, and ethnicity, and these feelings 'become matters for projection by both patient and therapist, usually in the form of transference and countertransference' (Comas-Diaz Jacobsen, 2001, p. 625).

Conclusion

Social work has borrowed from developments within counseling and psychology in order to define the components of a culturally competent approach. According to Lum (1999), cultural competency is the capacity to comprehend the culture and cultural practices within the framework of a client's sociocultural milieu and is consistent with the social work generalist and ecological perspectives. Culturally competent practice presupposes an understanding of the sociocultural meanings attached to illness and disability and the people likely to be consulted concerning providing healthcare and restoring wellbeing. Many Kenyan ethnic groups are known to consult with traditional healers in preference to or in conjunction with Western, allopathic healthcare professionals. Studies on indigenous health and medicine among Kenyan ethnic communities across all religions allude that the plurality of reasons surrounding decision-making is complex, but it is clear that many people often use indigenous healing; improvements in the regulation of both formulas and practice would assist people to access more effectively.

Medical social work training may benefit from increasing or incorporating cultural competence and ethnicity knowledge to effectively equip trainees who may later become culturally sensitive professionals. A medical social worker may be helpful in circumstances of decisional conflict where two or more clinically appropriate options have advantages and hazards that patients value differently or when collaborative decision-making is used (Peterson, 2012).

Recommendations

1. The curriculum should also prepare medical social work students on culture and ethnicity. It is recommended that professionally trained medical social workers who have practice experience be engaged in developing and implementing the culture and ethnic-sensitive curriculum. This will enable sharing of their experiences to benefit the learners.
2. Kenya's social work curriculum developed and implemented by training institutions should prioritise cultural and ethnic diversity issues to equip medical social workers to work with diverse populations. This can be achieved by integrating cultural competency training and

education in traditional healing practices. Trainers, practitioners, and learners must acknowledge the impact of cultural elements on clients and provide culturally sensitive care, value traditional healing practices, and educate themselves about clients' cultural backgrounds.
3. A modernist vision of skill identification and development serves as the foundation for a cultural-competence approach to diversity education. Although it makes the erroneous assumption that cultural competency can be reduced to a set of discrete skills that can be acquired and mastered through linear instruction, we recommend that our Kenya medical social work curriculum is designed to identify and outline skills that will produce culturally competent medical social workers.

Further Reading

Weaver, Hilary N., 2000. Culture and professional education. *Journal of Social Work Education*, 36(3), pp. 415–428. DOI: 10.1080/10437797.2000.10779019.

References

Althumali, N., 2021. *Culture and Medical Social Work Practice in Saudi Arabia*. Nottingham Trent University.

Barnhart, S., Benner, K., Latimer, A. and Pope, N., 2023. Considerations in preparing social work students to thrive in health care settings. *Journal of Teaching in Social Work*, 43(1), pp. 116–133.

Carol, S., 2012. *From Jerusalem to the Lion of Judah and Beyond: Israel's Foreign Policy in East Africa and Beyond*. iUniverse.

Chelogoi, D.N., Jonyo, F.O. and Amadi, H., 2020. The influence of socio-cultural factors in access to healthcare in Kenya: A case of Nairobi County, Kenya. *Journal of Social and Political Sciences*, 3(3), pp. 328–347.

Comas-Díaz, L. and Jacobsen, F.M., 2001. Ethnocultural allodynia. *The Journal of Psychotherapy Practice and Research*, 10(4), p. 246.

Egede, L.E., 2006. Race, ethnicity, culture, and disparities in health care. *Journal of General Internal Medicine*, 21(6), pp. 667–669.

Eklund, H., 2008. *Ubuntu: An Analysis of the Political Rhetoric of a Traditional Concept in Contemporary South Africa*. School of Culture and Media.

Gehlert, S. and Browne, T. eds., 2011. *Handbook of Health Social Work*. John Wiley & Sons.

Hamer, K., McFarland, S., Czarnecka, B., Golińska, A., Cadena, L.M., Łużniak-Piecha, M. and Jułkowski, T., 2020. What is an 'ethnic group' in ordinary people's eyes? Different ways of understanding it among American, British, Mexican, and Polish respondents. *Cross-Cultural Research*, 54(1), pp. 28–72.

Howland, O., 2020. Fakes and chemicals: Indigenous medicine in contemporary Kenya and implications for health equity. *International Journal for Equity in Health*, 19(1), pp. 1–12.

Ikechukwu, O.B., 2009. African theories of development and the reality of underdevelopment. *International Journal of Development and Economic Sustainability*, 4(4), pp. 12–19.

King, R.U., Bokore, N. and Dudziak, S., 2017. The significance of Indigenous knowledge in social work responses to collective recovery: A Rwandan case study. *Journal of Indigenous Social Development*, 6(1), pp. 37–63.

Kodom, R.B., 2022. The role of social work in the healthcare settings during the COVID-19 pandemic in Africa. *International Social Work*, pp. 1–6.

Krüger, C. and Lewis, C., 2011. Patient and social work factors related to successful placement of long-term psychiatric in-patients from a specialist psychiatric hospital in South Africa. *African Journal of Psychiatry*, 14(2), pp. 120–130.

Malinga, T. and Mupedziswa, R., 2009. Hospital Social work practice in Botswana: Yesterday, today and tomorrow. *Journal of Social Development in Africa*, 24(1). DOI: 10.4314/jsda.v24i1.54266.

Muhingi, W.N. and Machani, S.O., 2022. Medical social work in Kenya: Scope, relevance, and utility. *The International Journal of Social and Development Concerns*, pp. 17–31.

Mungai, N.W., Wairire, G.G. and Rush, E., 2014. The challenges of maintaining social work ethics in Kenya. *Ethics and Social Welfare*, 8(2), pp. 170–186.

Nkomo, T.S., 2017. The influence of socio-cultural beliefs in Chris Hani Baragwanath academic hospital (Chbah): A social work perspective. *Open Journal of Social Sciences*, 5(8), pp. 46–59.

Oduor, R.M., 2014. A critical review of Leonhard Praeg's A report on Ubuntu. *Thought and Practice*, 6(2), pp. 75–90.

Onyiko, K., Nzau, J. M. and Ngendo, A., 2017. The relevance of social work education for social development in Kenya. *Research on Humanities and Social Sciences*, 7(10), pp. 86–96.

Peterson, K.J., 2012. Shared decision making in health care settings: A role for social work. *Social Work in Health Care*, 51(10), pp. 894–908.

Public Service Commission, 2020. *Revised Scheme of Service for Medical Social Workers*. Public Service Commission.

Ross, E., 2007. Traditional healing in South Africa: Ethical implications for social work. *Social Work in Health Care*, 46(2), pp. 15–33.

Schlesinger, E.G. and Devore, W., 1995. Ethnic sensitive social work practice: The state of the art. *The Journal of Sociology and Social Welfare*, 22(1), p. 29.

Spitzer, H., 2019. Social work in East Africa: A mzungu perspective. *International Social Work*, 62(2), pp. 567–580.

Thabede, D., 2008. The African worldview as the basis of practice in the helping professions. *Social Work/Maatskaplike Werk*, 44(3), pp. 233–245.

Umoren, N., 2016. Social work development in Africa: Encouraging best practice. *International Journal of Scientific and Engineering Research*, 7(1), pp. 191–203.

United States. Office of Minority Health, 2001. *National Standards for Culturally and Linguistically Appropriate Services in Health Care*. US Department of Health and Human Services, Office of Minority Health.

Zelnick, J.R., Seepamore, B., Daftary, A., Amico, K.R., Bhengu, X., Friedland, G., Padayatchi, N., Naidoo, K. and O'Donnell, M.R., 2018. Training social workers to enhance patient-centered care for drug-resistant TB-HIV in South Africa. *Public Health Action*, 8(1), pp. 25–27.

PART 3

Embedding Field Practicum into Social Work Education

19
SOCIAL WORK FIELD PRACTICUM
Experiences, Challenges, and Perspectives from Malawi

Agnes Gogo Wizi-Kambala

Abstract: English

Social work field practicum is the very heart of social work training. It is the vehicle through which students practice the skills, knowledge, and values taught in class. International global standards for social work education require students to undergo rigorous training in the field in order to learn the fundamental dimensions of professional social work with individuals, families, groups, and communities. This chapter examines the context of social work field practicum in Malawi, where social work is a relatively young profession. The chapter notes that despite being in its developing stages, social work field practicum is making strides in Malawi. Students have the opportunity to practice in different settings under the guidance of their university and agency supervisors. However, as the chapter notes, a myriad of challenges face the social work field practicum. They include limited orientation, inadequate time for practicum, lack of resources, poor student assessment, and non-recognition of social work as a profession. The chapter suggests that for the future success of social work education in Malawi, significant interventions that involve both universities and agencies need to be put in place to improve the field practice situation and to thoroughly prepare students for professional practice.

Abstract: Chichewa

Kwa omwe akuchita maphunziro a zakasamalidwe ka anthu, kuyesera ntchitoyi ndi gawo limodzi lofunika kwambiri mkatikati mwa maphunziro awo. Ophunzira akapita kukayesera ntchitoyi m'maboma ndi m'mizinda, amakhala ndi mpata ogwiritsa ntchito maluso osiyanasiyana omwe iwowa amaphunzira mkalasi. Motsatira ndondomeko yomwe idakhazikitsidwa ndi bungwe loyang'anira anthu ogwira ntchito za kasamalidwe ka anthu pa dziko lonse la pansi, aliyense amene akupanga maphunziro a za kasamalidwe ka anthu akuyenera kukhala ndi nthawi yokwanira yoyesera ntchito yi, ndi cholinga choti aphunzire zinthu zina zofunikira kwambiri pantchitoyi. Cholinga cha kafukufuku uno ndikuyang'ana mozama momwe ndondomeko yotumiza ophunzira a za kasamalidwe ka anthu kukayesera zomwe akuphunzira nkalasi ikuyendera mdziko la Malawi. Kafukufukuyu wapeza umboni wokwanira kuti ngakhale maphunziro a zakasamalidwe ka anthu sadakhazizike kwenikweni mdziko la Malawi, ntchito yophunzitsa ophunzira kagwiridwe koyenerera ka ntchito yao mu njira yoyesera ikuyenda bwino. Mwa zina, ophunzirawa amapatsidwa mwayi ogwira ntchito mmalo osiyanasiyana pansi pa upangiri wa aphunzitsi awo aku sukulu za ukachenjede, komanso akuluakulu ena omwe amayang'anira mmalo ogwira ntchito amenewa. Ngakhale izi zili chonchi, kafukufuku uno wapeza umboni wokwanira kuti ndondomekoyi ili ndi mavuto ambiri ndipo ena mwa iwo ndi awa: kuchepa kwa nthawi yowakonzekeretsa ophunzira pa zoyenera kukachita akapita m'maboma ndi m'mizinda, kuchepa kwa nthawi yomwe ophunzirawa amakhala akugwira ntchito yoyesera ntchito yawoyi, kusowa kwa zipangizo zogwirira ntchito, komanso kuti ntchito ya zakasamalidwe ka anthu siiyamikiridwa kwenikweni m'dzikoli. Ngati ntchito yophunzitsa ophunzira a zakasamalidwe ka anthu ingapite patsogolo mdziko la Malawi, zitengera sukulu za ukachenjede komanso ma bungwe kuikapo mtima kuti ophunzira amene amapita kukayesa maphunziro awo mma bungwe wo aphunzitsidwe mokwanira.

Introduction

In the social work profession, field practicum (also known as practice education, field instruction, field education, field practice, and field placement) is regarded as the very centre or the signature pedagogy of professional social work education (Wayne et al., 2010; Earls Larrison and Korr, 2013; Boitel and Fromm, 2014). To this, Bogo (2015) concurs that 'the ability of social work education to graduate ethical, competent, innovative and effective social workers is highly dependent on the quality of the field experience' (p. 317). Tanga (2013) defines field practicum as a component of social work training where students are placed in agencies or organisations to undertake real social work practice, handling cases at micro, mezzo and macro levels with the guidance and supervision of trained fieldworkers, who ideally are social workers. Global standards for social work education and training jointly set by the International Association of Schools of Social Work (IASSW) and the International Federation of Social Workers (IFSW) emphasise that field practicum should be well integrated into the curriculum in preparing students with the knowledge, values, and skills needed for ethical, competent, and effective practice (Ioakimidis and Sookraj, 2021).

Various social work scholars and practitioners from across the globe (Walker et al., 2008; Dhemba, 2012; Eltaiba and Ndoye, 2018) have acknowledged the practical usefulness of field practicum on the future functioning and competencies of social work graduates. Field practicum offers a crucial space where students obtain the opportunity to integrate and contextualise things learnt in class (Flanagan and Wilson, 2018) and test their learning in real-life situations (Walker et al., 2008) while fostering their reflective skills (Eltaiba and Ndoye, 2018). By working with various service user groups in different contexts, students are also able to actively and carefully consider and reconsider their beliefs and practices. All these reasons justify the emphasis on field practicum in the training of social workers. This chapter examines the context of social work field practicum in Malawi. Specifically, the chapter explores the actual approaches to field practicum among selected universities in Malawi. In discussing the nature of field practicum, the chapter also focuses on the challenges experienced in field practicum. In the final stage, the chapter suggests solutions to the challenges encountered in field practice in Malawi, highlighting that the experiences would be similar to other African settings.

The Sociopolitical Context of Social Work in Malawi

Malawi is a relatively small, developing country located in southern Africa with an estimated population of 19.8 million people (National Statistical Office, 2020a). Malawi's population is predominantly rural, with over 84% of the population living in rural areas who rely on subsistence agriculture for their livelihood (National Statistical Office, 2020b). The socioeconomic situation of Malawi has left a majority of people living in poverty where inequality and social injustice are common. This has further been complicated by the burden of disease, such as HIV/AIDS, as well as climate change. The latter has worsened the occurrence of natural hazards, such as floods, droughts, and strong winds, which have all contributed to the increase in the frequency of disasters in Malawi (Mwalwimba, 2020). Further, Malawi has often witnessed social conflicts between indigenous and immigrant groups (National Statistical Office, 2021). Such challenges, among others, call for the need for well-trained social work practitioners who can practically and professionally assist individuals, families, groups, and communities to navigate life. Social workers in Malawi, as in other developing countries, offer services that will respond to needs related to widespread poverty, marginalisation, and social exclusion (Gray et al., 2017). Social workers work alongside those involved in agricultural, water, sanitation, and infrastructural development programmes in an effort to encourage improvements in people's wellbeing (Gray et al., 2018).

The Historical Context of Social Work Field Practicum in Malawi

Like in most African countries, social work in Malawi predates colonial times. In those times, social welfare was mainly organised through informal systems of family and community institutions (Kakowa, 2016; Imaan et al., 2021). Later, during the British colonial administration of Malawi (1891–1964), missionaries drove social work activities by offering social welfare services such as education and health (Sindima, 1992; Imaan et al., 2021). After independence in 1964, the government of Malawi took over the provision of social welfare services, and the social welfare system was institutionalised, thereby requiring effort of social workers as the lead professionals in the provision of social welfare services (Kakowa, 2016; Imaan et al., 2021). This development necessitated the establishment of Magomero College under the then Ministry of Local Government, which in 1978 introduced a certificate programme in social welfare that produces social welfare assistants (SWAs) to meet the rising demands for social welfare services in the communities (Kakowa, 2016).

In 2006, the Catholic University of Malawi was established and became the first tertiary institution in Malawi to offer a degree in social work. Following this, several other universities introduced degree programmes in social work. As of March 2023, four universities are accredited by the Malawi National Council for Higher Education (NCHE) to offer four-year degree programmes in social work (National Council for Higher Education, 2022). These universities (three private and one public) are: Catholic University of Malawi, Daughters of Mary Immaculate-St John the Baptist University, and Millennium University (all of which are private universities) as well as University of Malawi (a public university). They all operate within policy frameworks that govern higher education in Malawi generally, as there is none specifically on social work education. This has seen different social work curricula across the four universities as there is a lack of minimum standards for the education and training of social workers in Malawi. This also applies to the way that the field practicum is approached.

In line with global standards for social work education and training (Ioakimidis and Sookraj, 2021), the four universities offering degree programmes in social work send students on field practicum. Common agencies for field practicum in Malawi include social welfare agencies, hospitals, corrective institutions, childcare institutions, and community-based organisations. They can either be governmental or non-governmental agencies, where students get the opportunity to exercise both direct and indirect practice. In direct practice, social work students focus on person-to-person contact with individuals, families, small and larger groups, and communities (Rooney et al., 2017; Okoye and Ebimgbo, 2022). On the other hand, in indirect practice, students are involved in performing services on behalf of other people in contexts such as administering, designing, and evaluating programmes, developing procedures to improve the delivery of services, and performing management duties (Okoye and Ebimgbo, 2022).

Block field placements are the most common approach to field placement in Malawi. In the block field placement, students undergo their classroom exercises for some time to acquire the necessary social work skills and competences; they are then placed in social service agencies with an approved learning plan for a length of time, which can be a whole academic semester or during long vacations (Dhemba, 2012; Okoye and Ebimgbo, 2022). Depending on logistics as devised by the universities, block field placements in Malawi are either dedicated to a whole academic semester or during long holidays (about six to eight weeks). This is unlike other universities in the world, such as American universities, which prescribe the number of hours a student should spend on field practicum (CSWE, 2022). However, the practicum pattern followed by each of the four universities in Malawi is unique to that particular university, differing from others in terms of duration, supervision, and assessment. The sections below focus on practicum patterns at two major schools of social work that dedicate at least an academic semester to field practicum, namely, the University of Malawi and the Catholic University of Malawi.

Field Practicum at the University of Malawi

The social work programme at the University of Malawi was introduced in the Department of Sociology in 2012. Since the inception of the programme, social work students at the university have been undergoing field practicum, which is organized at three levels: at the end of first year, students go on a two-week observational placement at an agency of their choice. This observational placement is meant to introduce the students to social work practice and also prepare them for second-year modules such as Introduction to Social Work Practice, and Assessment, Planning and Intervention that focus on professional social work practice (Department of Sociology, University of Malawi, 2012).

The second level of field placement comes in the first semester of the third year, when students undergo a 16-week (or one semester) placement. The practicum coordinator at the university is responsible for liaising with the students in finding practicum placements at an organisation in a district of their choice, depending on the objectives of the department (Department of Sociology, University of Malawi, 2018). For this practicum, students usually go to mental health hospitals, community-based childcare centres, reformatory centres, and district social welfare offices. This placement is meant to enable students to put social work theory, skills, values, and ethics learnt in the two years of study into real-life situations through hands-on experiences on various aspects of social work (Department of Sociology, University of Malawi, 2012). Students therefore assist individuals, groups, families, and communities to overcome various social problems they may be going through.

The last placement, which also lasts for 16 weeks, comes in the final year after the completion of all course work. While students are free to go to the same district and work with the same agency they worked with in the previous practicum, most students prefer to gain experience in a different setting, hence, doing this practicum in a different agency and district. On top of indicating their preferred district, students are expected to submit a proposal with a detailed justification of their learning needs and the context in which they would like to work (for example, within child protection, elderly care, or community development), including their expected contributions to the agency (Department of Sociology, University of Malawi, 2018). Students are therefore matched with an agency which meets their learning needs.

During the two 16-week practicums, an agency is expected to assign a supervisor to the students. The responsibility of the supervisor is to take the student through the day-to-day learning processes. Following a given assessment tool, the supervisor makes direct observations of the student's work with service users and, in the process, assesses their performance. The assessment mainly focuses on the students' demonstration of social work knowledge and skills and their ability to apply theory into practice as well as other competences, such as student's commitment to work, including their creative and innovative contributions to the agency (Department of Sociology, University of Malawi, 2018).

Apart from the agency supervision and assessment, the department also conducts its own assessment of students on practicum. Social work lecturers visit the students on practicum twice during their 16-week stay at the agency. The visits are (normally) scheduled mid-way through the placement and a week before the end of practicum. Students are assessed on their ability to independently handle cases, observance of social work ethics, and competence in handling dilemmas in practice. This assessment is done through one-on-one interviews with a university supervisor as well as through a review of various documentation, such as case records, daily journal entries, and reports. In addition, students are assessed through written critical reflections of different aspects of their practice. Among other things, students reflect on areas of strengths, weaknesses, supervision, as well as ethical dilemmas encountered in practice. For the second practicum, in addition to the general supervision, students are assessed through a written report on the outcomes of what they proposed prior to allocation for placement (Department of Sociology, University of Malawi, 2018).

Practicum at the Catholic University of Malawi

The Catholic University of Malawi opened in 2006. The Social Work programme was among its pioneer programmes. Students in the programme follow the block pattern of field practicum, undertaking it in the second semester of their final year for 12 weeks (Department of Social Work, Catholic University of Malawi, 2016a). This allows students to complete all theoretical courses before they go on practicum.

Similar to the University of Malawi, the Catholic University of Malawi allows students to choose a district of preference, and thereafter the head of the social work department who is also the practicum coordinator identifies suitable agencies. Students go on practicum at primary healthcare centres, district councils through district social welfare offices, early childhood development centres, courts, and mental health hospitals as well as various faith-based and non-governmental organisations that offer social welfare services to children, youth, the elderly, persons with disabilities, and people with HIV/AIDS. Students on practicum are under the watch of a practice supervisor, who is a member of the agency responsible for guiding them and monitoring their progress. The students play a number of roles, including, but not limited to, brokering, educating, mediating, case management, and being probation officers (Department of Social Work, Catholic University of Malawi, 2016b).

Students' progress and performance in the field are jointly evaluated by the practice supervisors and university supervisors. Practice supervisors are provided with assessment tools, which they use to assess a student's ability to reconcile theory with practice, their commitment to work, as well as their ability to communicate in an organisational setup. For university assessment, lecturers from the social work department at the Catholic University of Malawi visit the students twice during practicum. These visits are normally scheduled at six weeks (mid-Point) and at 11 or 12 weeks (end point). During the mid-point visit, through one-on-one interviews, students are assessed on

Table 19.1 Patterns of Field Practicum in Malawi

University	Yr 1	Yr 2	Yr 3	Yr 4
University of Malawi	2 Weeks (Observation)	/	16 weeks	16 weeks
Catholic University of Malawi	/		/	12 Weeks

their abilities to apply evidence-based social work interventions, in particular, their ability to individually handle cases, their skills in integrating specific social work theories in practice, and their competence in report writing within the organisational context and beyond (Department of Social Work, Catholic University of Malawi, 2016b).

The students are also expected to submit one report of a case they individually handled. In the case report, they are expected to demonstrate their application of the process, ethics, and theories and methods which they learnt in class. Lastly, as is the case with their counterparts at the University of Malawi, the students are expected to write a reflective report on their learning at the agency. Students reflect upon various roles they played at the agency, personal factors that prompted their learning, and relationship with service users as well as the challenges they faced (including ethical dilemmas) and the procedures as well as decisions made towards resolving them. In this report, students also evaluate the performance of the agency, focusing on its strengths and weaknesses in aiding the students' learning (Department of Social Work, Catholic University of Malawi, 2016b).

Best Practices during Field Practicum: Student Support in Field Placement

Supporting and enhancing student experience is critical to students' success in higher education (Bartram, 2009). Global standards for social work education and training recognise student support as among the most important responsibilities of universities during field practicum (Ioakimidis and Sookraj, 2021). Both the University of Malawi and the Catholic University of Malawi offer support to students before the commencement of, and during, practicum placements.

Securing Placements

Prior to practicum, securing places for field practicum is one of the key areas where students need support (Muchinako and Muridzo, 2015). This is particularly a challenge in countries where social work is relatively young and still developing, like Malawi. The number of agencies does not usually correspond with the number of students who need to be accommodated for field practicum. However, at both the University of Malawi and the Catholic University of Malawi, students are supported with finding places for practicum. In particular, students are given the opportunity to choose a district where they would like to do their practicum (Department of Sociology, University of Malawi, 2018; Department of Social Work, Catholic University of Malawi, 2016b). Students choose a district depending on a number of factors, including availability of accommodation closer to the agency and easy transportation from their place of lodging to the agency, which they have to personally cater for as both universities do not cover students' personal expenses during field practicum. Students' choice of a practicum district is also influenced by the availability of social work/welfare agencies that students admire, and sometimes the desire for a lifetime experience in a district where they have never lived. It is upon choosing the district when the universities, through their practicum coordinators, allocate students to particular agencies in the student's district of choice (Department of Sociology, University of Malawi, 2018; Department of Social Work, Catholic University of Malawi, 2016b). This practice is very helpful as students do not have to labour in finding places for practicum all by themselves.

Pre-Departure Orientations

Prior to leaving the university for practicum, social work students need to undergo an orientation exercise to discuss a number of issues pertaining to the practicum covering the code, norms, and expectations of this teaching/learning opportunity, including details regarding documentation of field practicum, types of records, and their submission (Bragg et al., 2020). Both the University of Malawi and the Catholic University of Malawi offer pre-departure orientation seminars to support students prior to practicum commencement. These seminars are regarded as a key aspect for ensuring that students are able to successfully undertake placement. At both institutions, day long seminars are conducted by departmental members at which students are instructed on what to expect during the practicum. They are also appraised of the university's expectations from the practicum. Students are given an orientation on preparing learning objectives, entering a new community, filing daily reports, writing case studies and reflective reports, and general conduct during practicum (Department of Sociology, University of Malawi, 2018; Department of Social Work, Catholic University of Malawi, 2016b).

Challenges of Social Work Field Practicum in Malawi

As social work is an emerging profession in Malawi, field practicum faces a number of challenges. The sections below explain these challenges.

Limited Field Practicum Curriculum

A clearly defined curriculum is associated with learning and teaching being manageable and focused (Dhemba, 2012). While the University of Malawi has a dedicated course focusing on practice in second year, the Catholic University of Malawi relies on pre-departure orientation seminars to prepare students for the practicum. Despite being important (Bragg et al., 2020), the preparation seminars are held in one day at both universities, meaning that students are required to absorb a lot of information in a single day. Although students are given fieldwork manuals, they often find it hard to understand some important sections, especially on the assessment process, as the manuals are not comprehensive enough. This calls for extensive pre-departure seminars where the manuals can be explained in detail. The universities should also consider reviewing the manuals so that they provide valuable and well-detailed reference material on practicum expectations, standards, procedures, and assessment standards/criteria (Ioakimidis and Sookraj, 2021).

Inadequate Time Allocated to Practicum

The IFSW and IASSW recommend that social work practicum be sufficient in duration and complexity of tasks and learning opportunities to ensure that students are prepared for professional practice (Ioakimidis and Sookraj, 2021). The two universities have different time allocations to their block placements. While students from the University of Malawi go on a two-week practicum observation at the end of their first year, followed by two block (16 weeks) placements in years three and four, students from the Catholic University of Malawi go on practicum only in year four, after doing all the course work. An obvious advantage of at least two block placements is that students obtain varied experiences, which prepares them to function in a wider range of social work settings when they qualify; a single placement, on the other hand, limits the student particularly in developing countries where resources are scarce and deprivation is widespread (Dhemba, 2012). In addition, the timing of the practicum at other institutions such as the Catholic University of Malawi at the end of the four years means there is no time for the students to learn and develop their skills from previous field practicum. The students do not get back on campus to share experiences with their peers.

Limited Assessment from University and Agency Supervisors

In social work field education, student assessment is a critical component as it encourages the development of reflective and critical learning (Crisp and Lister, 2002; Tapp et al., 2012). Global standards for social work education and training require universities to ensure that there are clear and transparent policies, procedures, and guidelines for supervising, monitoring, and evaluating student progress and performance in the field (Ioakimidis and Sookraj, 2021). In Malawi, university supervisors (who in this case are social work lecturers) visit students twice for assessment in the course of their 12 or 16 weeks of block field placement. However, these visits are not enough to give a true reflection of students' performance during practicum. Agency (or practice) supervisors come in handy as they spend more time with the students at the agency. Both universities discussed in this chapter value the feedback that they get from supervisors at the different agencies. Despite the IASSW and IFSW requiring that agency supervisors should be qualified and experienced social workers (Ioakimidis and Sookraj, 2021), most supervisors in the agencies do not have any social work qualifications although they perform the roles of a social worker. In other places, unqualified agency supervisors have been associated with making assumptions on student performance without really checking if the students are ensuring proper service delivery (CSWE, 2015).

To overcome the problems of limited supervision, the IASSW and IFSW encourage the provision of orientation and ongoing support, including training and education of practice supervisors (Ioakimidis and Sookraj, 2021). In the same vein, the University of Malawi has initiated a training programme for practice educators to support, supervise, and assess their social work students during field practicum (Walker et al., 2008). Since 2016, when the first training for practice educators was conducted, at least 80 supervisors from different agencies across the country have been trained. However, the number of practice educators is very small compared to the number of students who go out on practicum as the same practice educators, on top of their daily duties, are expected to supervise students from other universities who are placed in their agencies.

Lack of Recognition of Social Work as a Profession

Social work in Malawi is barely recognised as a profession as there is no legal mandate to recognise and protect the profession (Joseph, 2020). Government registration and regulation are two key processes for raising social workers' professional standing, ensuring effective interventions, and protecting clients from harmful practice (DeAngelis and Monahan, 2012). The lack of a legal framework in Malawi has seen most of the tasks that should have been implemented by social workers being executed by non-social workers, who sometimes use the *social worker* title (as is the case with the agency supervisors). This is also evidenced in practicum, as students who are studying other programmes compete with social work students for placement and interventions.

Efforts to regulate the social work profession in Malawi began in 2015 when the Association of Social Workers in Malawi (ASWiM) was established to promote, protect, coordinate, and advance the social work profession. Amongst its core activities, ASWiM has been working alongside the government, civil society organisations, and academia towards the establishment of the Council of Social Workers, a legally mandated body that, once instituted, will exercise general supervision and control over training and practice of social work in Malawi (Joseph, 2020). The bill towards the establishment of this council was submitted to the Office of the President and Cabinet in 2020, but it has yet to be discussed in parliament. In the absence of such a law, the impacts on practicum for social work students will continue to be felt. In neighbouring countries like Zambia and Zimbabwe where the regulatory framework has been passed, minimum standards for social work training and education have been adopted as well as controlling and regulating of social workers through annual registration and licensing (Bohwasi and Chidyausiku, 2021; IFSW, 2022).

Limited Resources

Resources such as office space to accommodate incoming clients, stationery for filing cases and reports, as well as transport to visit clients are crucial in social work field practicum. The IFSW and IASSW recommend schools of social work ensure that adequate and appropriate resources are made available to students (Ioakimidis and Sookraj, 2021). These are for the purpose of meeting the needs of the practice component of social work programmes. Social work field placements in Malawi are often marred by a lack of necessary basic resources, which, when available, enhance students' experiences. The influx of students doing non-social work degrees in predominantly social work settings for practicum, for example, has left most of the host organisations with limited office space and resources to cater to both full-time workers and the students on practicum. Due to the limited social work settings available in Malawi, most organisations usually welcome more students than they can provide space and resources for. This affects students' operations, as they sometimes fail to do home visits because of lack of transport or they have to help clients in the presence of other (social) workers due to limited office space. Students are thus made to breach the very principles of social work, such as privacy and confidentiality (ASWiM, 2019), that they are meant to uphold.

Conclusion

Social work in Malawi is still under development. The first degree programme for social work was introduced in Malawi only in 2006. In this context, the nature of field practicum is such that it also reflects the challenges that the profession faces. This chapter has discussed the status of social work field practicum in Malawi by specifically focusing on the University of Malawi and the Catholic University of Malawi, both of which have four-year social work programmes. It has been noted that while these universities operate different patterns for fieldwork, the grounding of the practicum is similar. This is particularly applicable for student support as they depart for and navigate through practicum. However, as the chapter has highlighted, there are challenges faced in field practicum that affect students' learning. Such challenges include limited orientation, inadequate time for practicum, lack of resources, poor student assessment, and non-recognition of social work as a profession. To improve students' experience in field practicum and for the future success of social work education in Malawi, this chapter recommends that significant interventions need to be put in place by universities and agencies to improve the field practice situation and, hence, by so doing thoroughly prepare students for professional practice.

Recommendations

1. Increasing engagement and partnership among universities, agencies, and students so that all three are aware of their responsibilities during practicum, including scaling up training for practice educators to ensure that students obtain the necessary and relevant supervision during field placement.
2. Coming up with innovative means of doing field practicum that do not require students to be in an office or to use expensive resources.
3. Introducing in the curriculum a taught course on field practicum for students to give them a good grounding before undertaking their first practicum experience. In addition, field practicum manuals need to be updated and in greater detail.

Further Reading

Dhemba, J. (2012). Fieldwork in social work education and training: Issues and challenges in the case of Eastern and Southern Africa. *Social Work and Society*, 10(1), 1–16.

Okoye, U.O. & Ebimgbo, S.O. (2022). Contextualising social work fieldwork practicum: Innovations, challenges, and perspectives from Nigeria. In R. Baikady et al. (eds) *The Routledge Handbook of Social Work Field Education in the Global South*. London: Routledge, 329–342.

References

ASWiM (2019). *Code of Ethics for Social Workers in Malawi. Association of Social Workers in Malawi-ASWiM*. https://www.ifsw.org/wp-content/uploads/2018/01/ASWIM-Code-of-Ethics-2019-1.pdf.

Bartram, B. (2009). Student support in higher education: Understandings, implications and challenges. *Higher Education Quarterly*, 63(3), 308–314.

Bogo, M. (2015). Field education for clinical social work practice: Best practices and contemporary challenges. *Clinical Social Work Journal*, 43(3), 317–324.

Bohwasi, P.M. & Chidyausiku, W. (2021). The Zimbabwean model of social work regulation: Process and lessons for other countries. *African Journal of Social Work*, 11(5), 322–333.

Boitel, C.R. & Fromm, L.R. (2014). Defining signature pedagogy in social work education: Learning theory and the learning contract. *Journal of Social Work Education*, 50(4), 608–622.

Bragg, J.E. *et al.* (2020). Preparing students for field education using innovative field labs and social simulation. *Field Educator*, 10(2), 101–121.

Crisp, B.R. & Lister, P.G. (2002). Assessment methods in social work education: A review of the literature. *Social Work Education*, 21(2), 259–269.

CSWE (2015). *2015 Educational Policy and Accreditation Standards, Council for Social Work Education*. https://www.cswe.org/accreditation/standards/2015-epas/.

CSWE (2022). *2022 Educational Policy and Accreditation Standards, Council for Social Work Education*. https://www.cswe.org/accreditation/.

DeAngelis, D. & Monahan, M.J. (2012). Professional credentials and professional regulations. *The Profession of Social Work: Guided by History, Led by Evidence*, 91–104.

Department of Social Work, Catholic University of Malawi (2016a). *Undergraduate Curriculum for the Award of Bachelor of Social Science (Social Work)*. Chiradzulu, Malawi: CUNIMA Press.

Department of Social Work, Catholic University of Malawi (2016b). *Fieldwork Manual*. Chiradzulu, Malawi: CUNIMA Press.

Department of Sociology, University of Malawi (2012). *Bachelor of Social Science in Social Work Programme Document*. Zomba, Malawi: University Printing Press.

Department of Sociology, University of Malawi (2018). *Social Work Field Practicum Manual*. Zomba, Malawi: University Printing Press.

Dhemba, J. (2012). Fieldwork in social work education and training: Issues and challenges in the case of Eastern and Southern Africa. *Social Work and Society*, 10(1), 1–16.

Earls Larrison, T. & Korr, W.S. (2013). Does social work have a signature pedagogy? *Journal of Social Work Education*, 49(2), 194–206.

Eltaiba, N. & Ndoye, A. (2018). The effectiveness of field education in social work education: A student perspective. *Advances in Social Work and Welfare Education*, 20(1), 170–184.
Flanagan, N. & Wilson, E. (2018). What makes a good placement? Findings of a social work student-to-student research study. *Social Work Education*, 37(5), 565–580.
Gray, M. *et al.* (2017). The role of social work field education programmes in the transmission of developmental social work knowledge in Southern and East Africa. *Social Work Education*, 36(6), 623–635.
Gray, M. *et al.* (2018). The expansion of developmental social work in Southern and East Africa: Opportunities and challenges for social work field programmes. *International Social Work*, 61(6), 974–987.
IFSW (2022). *The Social Workers' Association of Zambia Act, Passed, International Federation of Social Workers*. https://www.ifsw.org/the-social-workers-association-of-zambia-act-passed/.
Imaan, L.M. *et al.* (2021). Evolution of social welfare and social work in Malawi. *Social Welfare and Social Work in Southern Africa*, 99–119.
Ioakimidis, V. & Sookraj, D. (2021). Global standards for social work education and training. *International Social Work*, 64(2), 161–174.
Joseph, S. (2020). Professionalisation of social work in Malawi. *The Nation*. https://mwnation.com/professionalisation-of-social-work-in-malawi/.
Kakowa, F. (2016). Nurturing professional social work in Malawi. *African Journal of Social Work*, 6(2), 1–6.
Muchinako, G.A. & Muridzo, N.G. (2015). Challenges faced by University of Zimbabwe social work students on fieldwork attachment. *Journal of Sociology*, 3(7), 1–12.
Mwalwimba, I. (2020). Assessing vulnerability trends and magnitudes in light of human responses to floods in Karonga District, Malawi. *International Journal of Science and Research (IJSR)*, 9(4), 938–945.
National Council for Higher Education (2022). *Annual Report of the Council for Higher Education in Malawi*. Lilongwe, Malawi: NCHE.
National Statistical Office (2020a). *2018 Malawi Population and Housing Census: Population Projection 2018–2050 Report*. Lilongwe, Malawi: NSO. https://mppn.org/malawi-multidimensional-poverty-index-report/.
National Statistical Office (2020b). *The Fifth Integrated Household Survey (IHS5) 2019–2020*. Lilongwe, Malawi: NSO. http://www.nsomalawi.mw/index.php?option=com_content&view=article&id=230&Itemid=111.
National Statistical Office (2021). *Malawi Multidimensional Poverty Index Report | MPPN*. Lilongwe, Malawi: NSO. https://mppn.org/malawi-multidimensional-poverty-index-report/.
Okoye, U.O. & Ebimgbo, S.O. (2022). Contextualising social work fieldwork practicum: Innovations, challenges, and perspectives from Nigeria. In R. Baikady et al. (eds) *The Routledge Handbook of Social Work Field Education in the Global South*. London: Routledge, 329–342.
Rooney, G.D. *et al.* (2017). *Direct Social Work Practice: Theory and Skills*. London: Cengage Learning.
Sindima, H. (1992). *The Legacy of Scottish Missionaries in Malawi*. New York: Edwin Mellen.
Tanga, P.T. (2013). The challenges of social work field training in Lesotho. *Social Work Education*, 32(2), 157–178.
Tapp, K., Macke, C. & McLendon, T. (2012). *Assessing Student Performance in Field Education: The Field Educator, Field Educator*. https://fieldeducator.simmons.edu/article/assessing-student-performance-in-field-education/.
Walker, J., Crawford, K. & Parker, J. (2008). *Practice Education in Social Work: A Handbook for Practice Teachers, Assessors and Educators*. Exeter: Learning Matters.
Wayne, J., Bogo, M. & Raskin, M. (2010). Field education as the signature pedagogy of social work education. *Journal of Social Work Education*, 46(3), 327–339.

20
DEARTH OF STANDARD SOCIAL WORK AGENCIES FOR FIELD PRACTICUM

Barrier to Social Work Pedagogy in Nigeria

*Chinyere Onalu, Chinwe Nnama-Okechukwu,
Patricia Agbawodikeizu, and Ngozi Chukwu*

Abstract: English

The prerequisite for a standard social work practice agency for students' field practicum in the Nigerian social work pedagogy is that it should be staffed by trained social workers who will adequately play the role of field supervisors to guide students on field practicum. However, it appears that this critical aspect of social work pedagogy is being harmed by lack of standard social work practice agencies and skilled agency supervisors. Information for this chapter was obtained largely through key informant interviews with four social work educators and focus group discussions with 20 undergraduate social work students. Participants' lived experiences revealed current realities and challenges with fieldwork placement within the Nigerian social work educational system. A revelatory theme that emerged from the study, however, suggests innovative strategies for a sustainable social work education in Nigeria. We recommend provision of Nigerian-based fieldwork instructional guides and periodic retraining of social work educators.

Abstract: Igbo

Ihe dị mkpa maka ezi ụlọ ọrụ na-ahụ maka ọzụzụ nnwale ụmụ akwụkwọ amụmamụ mwulite obodo na nkụzi na ọmụmụ amụmamụ mwulite obodo na Naijiria bụ na ọ ga-abụ nke nwere ndị a zụrụ nke ọma n'amụmamụ mwulite obodo, bụ ndị ga-arụ ọrụ ndị nlekọta iji duzie ụmụ akwụkwọ na-agabiga ọzụzụ nnwale. Ka ọ sila dị, ọ dị ka ihe mmekpa ahụ mpaghara a dị mkpa na nkụzi na ọmụmụ amụmamụ mwulite obodo bụ ụkọ ezi ụlọ ọrụ na-ahụ maka ọrụ amụmamụ mwulite obodo na ndị nlekọta ma ihe ekwe na-akụ. Ozi e jiri hazie isi nke a sitekariri n'ajụjụ ọnụ a gbara ndị e sitere n'aka ha nweta ọkpụrụkpụ ozi bụ ndị nkụzi amụmamụ mwulite obodo mmadụ anọ na otu mkparịta ụka ajụjụ ọnụ ụmụ akwụkwọ nọ n'amụmamụ mwulite obodo mmadụ iri abụọ. Ihe ndị so n'ọrụ nchọcha a gabigara n'onwe ha mere ka a hụta ọnọdụ na ihe ịma aka n'ihu dịịrị iziga ọzụzụ nnwale n'usoro agụmakwụkwọ amụmamụ mwulite obodo na Naijiria ugbu a. Ka o sila dị, nchọpụta nchọcha a mere ka a hụta usoro ọhụrụ ndị ga-eme ka nkụzi na ọmụmụ amụmamụ mwulite obodo guzosie ike na Naijiria. Anyị na-atụnye aro ka e nwee akwụkwọ nduzi maka ime ọzụzụ nnwale nke gbadoro ụkwụ na Naijiria na ọzụzụ ndị nkụzi amụmamụ mwulite obodo kwa mgbe kwa mgbe.

Introduction

Field practicum is arguably the most essential aspect of social work pedagogy. Globally, social work education is based on a unified curriculum that includes both theory and practical/fieldwork components (International Associations of Schools of Social Work [IASSW] and International Federation of Social Workers [IFSW], 2004). It includes a theoretical component taught in the classroom as well as field-based education to integrate academic and practical experience. Students can participate in field practicum to gain experience, learn new skills, and participate in the delivery and development of social work services (Mohimuddin, 2019). It allows students to align their theoretical knowledge and learning with the needs of clients. It also allows students to respond appropriately to clients' needs and to be well grounded in general (social work) practice, with knowledge, understanding, and skills in a variety of settings (Dhemba, 2012).

According to the literature, fieldwork has always been an essential component of social work education (Tippa and Mane, 2018a). Tippa and Mane go on to argue that preparing students to become professional social workers requires not only academic fitness, but also evidence-based knowledge, field-tested skills, and a wealth of hands-on experience. Thus, Dhemba (2012) summarises that providing sound theory in a classroom setting is just as important as fieldwork experiences. However, applying the theoretical content covered in the classroom to real-life situations has been observed to be fraught with difficulties, such as divergent knowledge of fieldwork and its types, scarcity of standard agencies, shortage of competent social workers, and supervision by unskilled agency supervisors, amongst others. This section examines existing theoretical and empirical discourses on fieldwork and its challenges.

Fieldwork as a Concept

Fieldwork, according to Dhemba (2012), is the precursor to social work education and an experiential form of learning and practice. Tippa and Mane (2018a) support this viewpoint by describing the historical antecedent of social work education as apprenticeship by the Charity Organisation Society of America, and arguing that social work education emerged from practical field training. Fieldwork, according to Ajibo et al. (2017), is an opportunity for students to align theoretical knowledge and learning with the needs of society, and it allows students to take responsibility for addressing people's problems. It is an experiential form of teaching and learning that takes place in a variety of settings and provides an opportunity to understand a people's needs against the backdrop of prevailing cultural traditions and values. According to social work scholars, field practicum is the pedagogy of social work education that allows students to sharpen and develop their skills for competent practice outside of the classroom (Levy et al., 2022; Omorogiuwa, 2016).

Types of Fieldwork

Fieldwork is classified based on its form and duration structures. According to Dhemba (2012), most social work training institutions use one of four types of fieldwork: block, concurrent, combined concurrent and block, and in-service placements. Block and concurrent fieldwork are the most common types of field placement used in many social work institutions in Nigeria (Okoye and Ebimgbo, 2022). Regardless of the type of fieldwork available in social work institutions, the IASSW and IFSW global standards state that 'Field education should be sufficient in duration and complexity of tasks and learning opportunities to ensure that students are prepared for practice' (Sewpaul and Jones, 2004, p. 496).

Block Fieldwork

A block fieldwork placement is a continuous full-time commitment of a social work student after the completion of coursework at a fieldwork agency for a period ranging from at least one month to one year, depending on the institution (Dhemba, 2012). This model offers students the opportunity to take the knowledge and skills learnt in the classroom and apply them to real-world hands-on learning in the internship (Okoye and Ebimgbo, 2022). Its advantages include:

1. A fully immersive learning experience with excellent client continuity and exposure to learning opportunities.
2. There is no interruption to the field experience due to coursework, missed experiences, or other classroom responsibilities (Wilson, 1981). As a result, learning is faster and intense (Henton, 1995; Wilson, 1981).

Its major disadvantages include fewer opportunities for integrating classroom learning and practice and less time to develop client relationships (Henton, 1995).

Concurrent Fieldwork

Concurrent fieldwork requires students to devote full time to both classroom learning and practical components. It enables students to be placed with various organisations that address various societal issues. Students visit their placement agencies twice or three times per week, spending at least eight hours per visit (Mohinuddin, 2020). In Nigeria, students visit their agencies two to three days per week (Okoye and Ebimgbo, 2022). Concurrent fieldwork has the following benefits:

1. It allows for the immediate application of classroom theory to practice (Tippa and Mane, 2018b).
2. It is an effective method for integrating theory and practice because the student can immediately apply classroom learning in a practice setting and, in turn, bring field learning into the classroom (Wilson, 1981).

Concurrent placements have several disadvantages, including fewer placement sites available to students, particularly in rural areas, and fewer agencies available in urban areas (Hamilton and Else, 1983), denying students the opportunity to practice and learn in rural areas where social work services are most needed (Desai, 2019). It is less adaptable, particularly for part-time students. Furthermore, it is associated with general as well as context-specific structural challenges that affect fieldwork students, social work educators, and fieldwork supervisors (Desai, 2019); for example, requiring students to report their fieldwork experiences to their training institution and the agency supervisor (Tippa and Mane, 2018b). Despite the disadvantages associated with concurrent fieldwork placement as observed in other contexts, this form of fieldwork placement in Nigerian higher institutions allows a varied proportion of time to be devoted to both classroom and field learning activities (Okoye and Ebimgbo, 2022). This allows students to retain knowledge from both learning experiences and improves their practice skills. Furthermore, concurrent placement allows students to share ideas about their pending cases with their peers while also receiving directions or instructions from the supervisors (Okoye and Ebimgbo, 2022).

Challenges of Fieldwork

Fieldwork practice, in whatever form it takes, has been observed to face a number of challenges. According to studies, there are fewer resources available to guide fieldwork education when compared to academic learning (Hesham, 2016; Okoye and Ebimgbo, 2022; Tippa and Mane, 2018b). According to these scholars, there is a lack of written text on field instruction by Nigerian social work institutions to guide social work educators, students, and field supervisors, which limits their understanding of fieldwork from a setting specific practice standpoint. Furthermore, in low- and middle income countries (as in Egypt), most schools of social work appoint new graduate students or new employed members with little or no fieldwork training, skill, or competence to take on fieldwork education or practice supervision (Hesham, 2016). These have implications for the quality of fieldwork training provided to students by their placement agencies. Students in Nigeria are assigned to various agencies for their field practicum. However, the majority of these training agencies are staffed by non-social workers who lack social work training and have academic backgrounds in sociology, psychology, counselling, and law but who serve as field supervisors to the students in training (Onalu and Okoye, 2022). Okoye (2014) also notes that there are few social work agencies where students can do fieldwork. Because the few available agencies are not staffed by trained social workers, agency supervisors lack the expertise to adequately guide students and may engage in unethical practices. As of 2011, an estimated 12,000 social workers worked in government agencies in Nigeria (Canavera et al., 2014); social work services provided in these agencies are solely staffed by the government, and social workers cannot practice independently (Okoye and Ebimgbo, 2022). These have a negative impact on the nature of the practical training that students receive.

Dearth of Standard Fieldwork Agencies in Nigeria

The dearth of a standard in fieldwork agencies within the Nigerian social work educational system has not been a common narrative in most studies in social work education in Nigeria. Discourses frequently centre on the dominance of Western pedagogy, indigenous knowledge, curriculum updates, indigenisation debate, and the future of social work education (Agbawodikeizu, et al. 2022; Nnama-Okechukwu et al., 2022; Onalu and Ingram, 2022). However, very few studies have examined this deficiency (Okoye and Ebimgbo, 2022). The challenges posed by a lack of standard social work fieldwork are examined through the lived experiences of undergraduate students and social work educators in this chapter.

The University of Nigeria, Nsukka [UNN] Experience

We asked a small group of social work students and educators from the University of Nigeria, Nsukka to provide an overview of the lack of standard agencies for fieldwork practicum, how it affects social work pedagogy in Nigeria, and how to overcome the challenges. We used focus group discussions with the social work students and key informant interviews with the educators. The questions were designed to be both reflective and forward thinking. We purposefully selected third and final year students for the focus group discussion based on their participation in fieldwork practicum for the previous three to four years as well as four educators with first-hand knowledge of the effects of field practicum agencies on social work pedagogy. We used semi-structured interviews to elicit information from the participants. Based on their responses, we identified four thematic areas:

- Perspectives of fieldwork.
- Challenges students face during field practicum.
- Effects of a dearth of standard fieldwork agencies and supervisors.
- Suggestions to overcome challenges students encounter during fieldwork practicum.

Perspectives of Fieldwork

Knowledge of Fieldwork

The participants demonstrated excellent subject knowledge, given their levels of social work education and years of experience as social work educators. They believed that fieldwork practicum provided an opportunity to investigate the validity of theory taught in the classroom. One of the participants stated:

> Fieldwork simply means putting into practice all the theoretical knowledge being taught in class by our lecturers. The theoretical which includes the social work values, ethics, practice standards, knowledge base, ethical principles, and skills are put in practice with the assistance of a professional in the field. (final year student, female)

Another participant corroborated these assertions:

> Fieldwork is just a formal arrangement that gives social work students the opportunity to put to practice everything they have been taught in class by their instructors. It is an essential fragment of social work practice that places students in social work agencies where they encounter and treat real life cases in the course of their study and the experience they gathered during this period will help them to handle cases when they graduate. (social work educator, male)

According to the participants, fieldwork allows social work students to meet with clients and address the nature, causes, and solutions to real-life problems using knowledge, skills, techniques, ethics, and values learned in the classroom. The concurrent, block, and in-service methods of fieldwork practicum were mentioned by the participants. Currently, at the University of Nigeria, the concurrent fieldwork model was chosen because it allows students to practice what they learned in class while it is still fresh. In concurrent practicum, students are placed in different agencies or organisations and their time is divided between classroom learning and fieldwork experiences. Students are expected to be in the agency for two days per week and to take classes three days. Concurrent field placement allows students to share ideas about upcoming cases with peers while also receiving instructions from supervisors.

A participant defined block fieldwork as 'the type in which the students finish up the theoretical aspect of their study completely before going to agencies to practice the knowledge and skills they have accumulated over time'. Here, a period of time is given for the student to engage in fieldwork just like industrial training; students spend a period ranging from at least one month to six months in the agency depending on the institution. In-service training according to one of them, 'is a situation where social workers undergo training and practice while they work. It gives the social workers the opportunity to learn more and that can be achieved with the aid of professionals at the field'.

Challenges Social Work Students Face during Fieldwork Practicum

Dearth of Standard Agencies

The participants were of the view that there are limited standard social work agencies in Nsukka. They stated that 'aside two or three social work agencies which is being manned by non-professionals, majority of the social work students are being posted to the university hostels, market places, and even mechanic village'. Another participant said:

> It is obvious that almost if not all the agencies we are posted to are not social work oriented. Even when they are, their work cultures are always in conflict with social work principles and there tends to be disconnect in opinions shared by student social workers and the agencies. (final year student, male)

The agency's purpose and work culture may not align with social work principles, ethics, and values, making it difficult to avoid becoming involved in unethical practices as a result of poor field exposure.

Lack of Trained Social Workers as Agency Supervisors

Many agencies, according to the participants, lack trained social workers as supervisors, making appropriate field guidance and integration of theoretical and practical knowledge impossible. According to them, this is a major stumbling block in the chariot of the social work profession in Nigeria. They complained that their field experiences did not correspond to what they learned in lectures. According to participants, this has made practicum difficult for students because those who should be supervising their practicum know nothing about social work practice methods; they cannot give what they do not have. For example, when students are assigned to schools, most principals and teachers want to turn social work students into classroom teachers, which falls outside the scope of practicum because school social workers are not classroom teachers. Conflicts frequently arise as a result of this, and students are frequently demoralised. As narrated by a final year female participant: 'I was once posted to a primary school and the moment I told the teachers that I am not meant to teach, I became a 'lazy social worker' who just comes to look at pupils and go'. Even when there are no conflicts, students have no one to supervise their intervention with their clients because their supervisors are not trained social workers. According to a participant:

> Lack of professionals as supervisors in the agencies makes it impossible for us to practice effectively in the field, due to the fact that we cannot take difficult cases to them because they are not professionals and may not be able to handle the cases. (third year student, male)

The importance of supervision in social work education has been emphasized (Miller et al., 2017). Non-trained social work agency supervisors undermine this critical aspect of social work pedagogy by rendering supervision ineffective for students in training.

Problem of Fieldwork Report Writing

We wanted to know if fieldwork report writing, which is a crucial aspect of social work field practicum, is difficult for student social workers. Some participants mentioned that two factors should be considered when writing a fieldwork report. The first is that students sometimes have nothing to write because they have done nothing in the field, and, second, some students struggle to reconcile their fieldwork with appropriate theories required to present a comprehensive report. In essence, report writing is always intimidating to students, especially those who have not learned the fundamental principles of report writing. According to one of them:

> At times it is really challenging to write report due to the fact we start some cases that we are not able to handle because we don't know the theories or skills to apply in solving the problem. For instance; in Nsukka Social Welfare, social workers are not allowed to handle any case there, the cases are being handled by the welfare officer who is not even a trained social worker. (final year student, female)

Students at UNN who work with any type of clientele system must write detailed fieldwork reports about their experiences using the log book. This, along with the attendance list, is used by the agency supervisor to evaluate the students' performance in their respective agencies, and it is then submitted to the students' class instructors on a weekly basis for assessment and corrections. This comprehensive field report is used for each academic session's final evaluation of the student. The Department of Social Work has a field practicum report template. The template must include the following sections: visit purpose, observation, content, impression, workers' role, and next plan of action.

Effects of Dearth of Standard Fieldwork Agencies and Supervisors

Incompetent Social Workers

All participants agreed that the absence of standard social work agencies and the use of non-professionals as agency supervisors can result in the production of social workers with limited experience and knowledge. It has had a negative impact on how social workers handle cases even after they graduate. According to a male educator: 'It breeds incompetence. When students have no practical experience, and lack supervision, they cannot boast of being competent social workers in future'.

Non-Professional Social Work Supervisors in Fieldwork Agencies

Non-professionals serving as agency supervisors and non-social work agency staff, according to participants, have an impact on the role students play in their fieldwork agencies. These agency supervisors make things difficult for students. This is due to lack of understanding of social workers' roles and expectations in the field, the guidelines and ethical standards of social work. One of the final year students summarised the students' perspectives as follows:

> Most often, the roles they assign to us are not meant for social workers, and when we refuse to play these roles, trying to enlighten them that that is not what we are meant to do, they will see it that we are not doing anything, and during evaluation, they will evaluate us poorly. (third year student, female)

Having non-professionals as agency supervisors most often reduces the efficiency of social work students in those agencies as well as creates conflict during field practice. For example, social work students posted to medical centres are sent to meet patients' relatives only for hospital bills. They believe that it is the reason the students were sent to their clinics. In some instances, those posted to motherless babies' homes were made to mop dirty floors, feed babies, and wash diapers according to educators. Because these agency supervisors are not trained social workers, they frequently entice or persuade students to violate their ethical standards, such as taking over teaching duties from teachers at various schools (agency). They sometimes force student social workers to compromise their values by contributing money to interventions.

Suggestions to Overcome Challenges Students Encounter during Fieldwork Practicum

Participants in the study proposed incorporating report writing into social work curriculum, reorienting agency supervisors, and hiring more trained social workers in the fieldwork agencies. Unlike in many high-income countries, professional social workers are rarely hired in Nigeria because social work services in Nigeria are solely provided by the government. This means that the government is Nigeria's sole employer of social workers. Regarding report writing, one of the participants stated:

> It is of paramount importance that report writing should be added into social work curriculum in order to have a peculiar standard of report writing, and as well inculcate in students the knowledge of proper writing report. (final year student, female)

The participants urged that field training be included as part of an industrial training experience for a set period of time. They stated that various training institutions should provide adequate assistance to students in order to bridge the gap between theory and real-life practice. They recommended that students visit agencies located outside of their study institutions, particularly during the holidays, to ensure that they are properly handling real-life cases. Students' classroom instructors at the University of Nigeria, Nsukka, for example, used to be with them by 7:00 a.m. every Tuesday and Thursday to ensure that they all got to their various agencies on time. Although school supervisors visit these agencies twice per academic session, participants suggested that they visit them as frequently as possible. These frequent visits will allow students and agency supervisors to receive guidance and assess their performance while pursuing the placement's objectives. To avoid making things difficult for social work students, some participants suggested that agency supervisors receive periodic orientation/training on social work roles. Similarly, social work educators should hold regular seminars and conferences to educate agency supervisors on social work principles and their responsibilities as supervisors.

Field Practicum and Social Work Education

Social work field practicum is an integral facet of social work education in Nigeria because of the connectivity it provides between the theoretical classroom learning and practical settings in different social agencies. Given the structures of social work fieldwork practicum found in African studies (Shokane et al., 2016), this chapter revealed a good understanding of these structures: block, in-service, concurrent fieldwork, and a combination of the two. Whether it is block, in-service, or concurrent fieldwork, fieldwork practicum provides an opportunity to investigate the validity of theory taught in the classroom. It also exposes social work students to experiences that expand their knowledge and expertise in social work education and practice. According to research on social work education in Africa, field work practicum provides an opportunity for social work students to align theoretical knowledge and learning with societal needs (Okoye and Ebimgbo, 2022). Such convergence serves as a foundation for a strong professional structure in the practice and education of social work in Africa.

Fieldwork placement in social agencies exposes social work students to real-life situations, is the foundation for understanding human behaviour in the social environment in preparation for professional practice at the micro, macro, or messo levels. Knowledge of concurrent field work practice in Nigeria was evident in students' narratives, given their two days weekly visits to various social agencies both within and outside the university community and three days weekly classroom lectures. This means that their time is split between classroom learning and practical field experience in order to promote competence and professional development.

The chapter also looked into the difficulties of field practicum. Worryingly, field work agencies lacked field work practicum standards. Non-social workers staff these few agencies, and supervisors are frequently not professional social workers (Okoye, 2014). While social work students are occasionally placed in agencies with qualified social work supervisors, the vast majority are not. However, few studies have looked into this deficiency (Okoye and Ebimgbo, 2022). With few available social work agencies and the need for professional practice skills development, students are frequently left with the option of placement in only a few available social agencies that are often referred to as 'not standard'. In this context, social agencies are said to be 'not standard' if they are not focused on social work. Placement in social agencies such as hotels, markets, and automobile workshops where agency supervisors are not professional social workers raises some concerns about social worker training for professional practice. An automobile workshop provides students with the opportunity to understand conflict management, networking skills, and other life skills. While placement of social work students in social agencies in Nigeria provides an opportunity for students to model professional practice by practicing skills with clients, it is critical to address challenges associated with their scarcity for social work practice in Nigeria.

Assigning students to agencies that are not social work–oriented or where work cultures are in conflict with social work principles and ethics leads students to lose the opportunity to apply classroom theories first-hand. Students are undoubtedly given the opportunity to model methods of dealing with clients in practical situations under supervision by social work–oriented organisations. This scenario supports and promotes the apprenticeship model, which is the foundation of fieldwork education and allows students to learn by doing. This is still a significant challenge for fieldwork education in Nigeria (Okoye and Ebimgbo, 2022). Due to the lack of suitable agencies, the scope of fieldwork education is limited, resulting in the use of what is available even when it is challenging. As a result, social work students may graduate without having had any contact with real social agencies during their four years of professional training in the university.

Future Trends for Sustainable Fieldwork Practice

Dearth of Standard Social Work Agencies for Field Practicum

As it raises the question of their suitability, this is a discourse that should constantly occupy major discourses of social work educators in Nigeria. Social work educators in Nigeria are encouraged to conduct evidence-based research in order to find novel ways to provide students with enriched learning and practical experiences for a more sustainable future (Levy et al., 2022). Part of the engagement entails stimulating thought, advocacy, and action on the implementation of the legislation and regulation as enshrined in the Nigerian Council of Social Work (Establishment) Act, 2022. This was accented by the Federal Government of Nigeria (FGN) on 6 December 2022 (FGN, 2022) to guide the social work profession in Nigeria. The future of social work education in Nigeria must be sustainable in order to provide students, practitioners, and social work educators with the motivation to promote a sustainable future in viable communities by leaving no one behind (Nnama-Okechukwu et al., 2022).

Report Writing

Field education may present some challenges to both students and supervisors, but it is an excellent opportunity for a learner to apply classroom knowledge to the practice of social work through effective report writing. Report writing presents unique challenges for social work students. As part of the learning experience, challenges encountered in the field must be communicated to the classroom supervisor via report writing. Report writing includes reports on the process of the field event, case assessment, application of theory to real-life situations, and how social work students engaged in the problem-solving process. Report writing was found to be difficult for social work students, who indicated: 'students sometimes have nothing to write because they have done nothing in the field'.

Access to academic materials from evidence-based studies that chart the path of social work in various areas of social work practice can assist social work students in understanding how to apply theory in real-life situations (Chukwu et al., 2022; Onalu et al., 2020). However, how many students have access to these scholarly materials in order to improve their report writing and social work practice within their agency? Report writing is essential for student social workers because it provides evidence that can be used to make practice decisions using scientific methods designed in an ethical manner. With Onalu and Okoye (2021), Onalu and Ingram (2022), and Nnama-Okechukwu and Maclaughin (2022) calling for a curriculum update in social work education, it is pertinent that report writing be added to the social work curriculum in order to have a uniform standard as well as instill in students the knowledge of effective report writing through reading academic materials. Formal reports are essential for documenting students' case studies in their various agencies, and it can serve as a communication tool for both agency and classroom supervisors for monitoring and evaluation.

Conclusion

This chapter reveals the scarcity of standard social work agencies in Nigeria for field practicum. While it identified a number of challenges, it is critical to chart a new course of action to promote national standards in fieldwork practicum in social work education. One example is the requirement for field training to be completed as part of an industrial training experience for specified periods of time, particularly during vacations. This has been reported in order to promote real-life case studies in appropriate social agencies (Onalu and Okoye, 2021; Nnama-Okechukwu and McLaughlin, 2022). There is a need to rethink fieldwork placement in social work education in Nigeria in order to aid the development of more innovative strategies, such as assigning social work students to communities and agencies in their locality during vacations. Such participation could help students connect with the reality of human behaviour in the social environment.

Recommendations

1. Organising regular trainings for fieldwork agency supervisors and agency staff on the roles that social work students are expected to play at the agencies, ethics to guide practice, and field practicum skills. Periodic retraining can be held remotely by videoconferencing. Academics

train students through regular fieldwork presentation seminars in the classroom, in which students present challenges and issues in their agencies and get appropriate feedback.
2. Field training as part of an industrial training experience for specified periods of time, particularly during vacations.
3. Provision of fieldwork instructional guides and texts written by social work educators for Nigerians.

Further Reading

Ajibo, H., Mbah, F. and Anazonwu, N. (2017). Field work practice in social work. In U. Okoye, N. Chukwu and P. Agwu (eds.). *Social Work in Nigeria: Book of Readings*. 104–113. Nsukka: University of Nigeria Press.

Okoye, U.O. and Ebimgbo, S.O. (2022). Contextualizing social work field practicum: Innovative challenges and perspective in Nigeria. In *Routledge Handbook of Social Work Education in the Global South*. https://www.taylorfrancis.com/chapters/edit/10.4324/9781003270119-28/contextualising-social-work-fieldwork-practicum-uzoma-okoye-samuel-ebimgbo.

References

Agbawodikeizu, P., Levy, S., Ekoh, P., Chukwu, N. and Okoye, U.O. (2022). Religion and spirituality as a core module in social work education in Nigeria: Perspectives of social work educators. *Journal of Religion and Spirituality in Social Work: Social Thought*, 41(4), 333–350. https://www.tandfonline.com/doi/full/10.1080/15426432.2022.2089316.

Ajibo, H., Mbah, F. and Anazonwu, N. (2017). Field work practice in social work. In U. Okoye, N. Chukwu and P. Agwu (eds.). *Social Work in Nigeria: Book of Readings*. 104–113. Nsukka, Nigeria: University of Nigeria Press.

Canavera, M., Akesson, B. and Landis, D. (2014). Social service workforce training in the West and Central Africa Region, final report. https://www.researchgate.net/publication/266392250_Social_Service_Workforce_Training_in_the_West_and_Central_Africa_Region.

Chukwu, N.E., Agwu, P.C., Ajibo, H.T. and Aronu, N. (2022). Challenges faced by informal caregivers of patients in a Nigerian hospital and implications for social work. *Journal of Social Work*, 22(5), 1189–1206. https://journals.sagepub.com/doi/pdf/10.1177/14680173221077371.

Desai, K.T. (2019). Concurrent fieldwork training and supervision in social work: Challenges and solutions in the context of Barak Valley, Assam. In R. Nair, S. Juvva and V.V. Nadkarni (eds.). *Field Instruction in Social Work Education: The Indian Experience*. 1–26. London: Routledge India. https://doi.org/10.4324/9780367810320.

Dhemba, J. (2012). Fieldwork in social work education and training: Issues and challenges in the case of eastern and southern Africa. *Social Work and Society*, 10(1), 1–16.

Federal Republic of Nigeria (2022). *Nigerian Council for Social Work (Establishment) Act, 2022*. Lagos: FGN.

Hamilton, N. and Else, J. (1983). *Designing Field Education: Philosophy, Structure, and Process*. Springfield, IL: Thomas Press.

Henton, D. (1995). Block and concurrent field: Contrasting models for social work field education. Paper presented at a summer seminar, Case Western Reserve University, Cleveland, OH.

Hesham, S.A. (2016). Issues and challenges of social work practicum at developing countries in comparable with developed countries. *Egyptian Journal of Social Work*, 2(1). https://ejsw.journals.ekb.eg/article_8760_941a1176bed65c115d23878340b48e05.pdf.

IASSW and IFSW (2004). *Global Standards for the Education and Training of the Social Work Profession*. Bern: Switzerland: Sage.

Levy, S., Okoye, U.O. and Ingram, R. (2022). Making the 'local' visible in social work education: Insights from Nigeria and Scotland on (Re) balancing and Contextualising Indigenous and international knowledge. *British Journal of Social Work*, 1–19.

Miller, J., Deck, S., Conley, C. and Bode, M. (2017). Field practicum supervision perspectives about social work licensing: An exploratory study. *Field Education*, 7(1), 1–18.

Mohinuddin, M.D. (2020). Types of field practicum in social work. https://www.sweducare bda.com/2020/01/types-of-field-practicum-in-social-work.html.

Nnama-Okechukwu, C., McLaughlin, H. et al. (2022). Indigenous knowledge and social work education in Nigeria: Challenges and need for sustainable development. *International Social Work*. https://doi.org/10.1177/00208728221098511.

Nnama-Okechukwu, C.U. and McLaughlin, H. (2022). Indigenous knowledge and social work education in Nigeria: Made in Nigeria or made in the west?. *Social Work Education: International Journal*. https://doi.org/10.1080/02615479.2022.2038557.

Omorogiuwa, T.B.E. (2016). Field education an integral component of social work education: Student perception of the learning process. *Benue State University Journal of Education*, 16(1), 221–228.

Okoye, U.O. (2014). Indigenizing social work education for better social services provisioning in Nigeria. In G.E.D. Omuta (ed.). *Perspective on Social Services in Nigeria*. 883–895. Ibadan: HEBN Publishers Plc.

Okoye, U.O. and Ebimgbo, S.O. (2022). Contextualizing social work field practicum: Innovative challenges and perspective in Nigeria. In R. Baikady, S.S.M. Varoshini and M. Rezaul Islam (eds.). *Routledge Handbook of Social Work Education in the Global South*. https://www.taylorfrancis.com/chapters/edit/10.4324/9781003270119-28/contextualising-social-work-fieldwork-practicum-uzoma-okoye-samuel-ebimgbo.

Onalu, C.E., Chukwu, N.E. and Okoye, U.O. (2020). COVID-19 response and social work education in Nigeria: Matters arising. *Social Work Education*, 39(8), 1037–1047. https://doi.org/10.1080/02615479.2020.1825663.

Onalu, C. and Ingram, R. (2022). The contribution of Western pedagogy and knowledge in the development of social work education in Nigeria: A coin of two sides. *Social Work Education*. https://doi.org/10.1080/02615479.2022.2052039.

Onalu, C. and Okoye, U. (2022). Social Justice in Nigeria: It is time to update social work curriculum and make social justice part of the course title. Available at: https://socialwork.ubc.ca/news/social-justice-in-nigeria.

Onalu, C.E. and Okoye, U.O. (2022). Teaching and practicing social work in Nigeria: Challenges and prospects. *Journal of Social Work in Developing Societies*, 4(1), 68–83.

Sewpaul, V. and Jones, D. (2004). Global standards for social work education and training. *Social Work Education*, 23(5), 493–513. https://doi.org/10.1080/0261547042000252244.

Shokane, A.L., Neumutandani, V. and Budeli, N.J. (2016). Challenges faced by fourth year social work students during field practice at a rural-based university. *AFFRIKA: Journal of Politics, Economics and Society*, 66, 133–162.

Tippa, N.G. and Mane, S. (2018a). Problems and prospects of field work training in social work education: A review. *Innovare Journal of Social Sciences*, 6(1), 1–4. https://core.ac.uk/download/pdf/234676025.pdf.

Tippa, N.G. and Mane, S. (2018b). The role of fieldwork training in social work education: A review. *Review of Research*, 7(10), 1–4.

University of Nigeria Nsukka Academic Planning Unit (2020). *Population of Students in the Department of Social Work*. Nsukka, Nigeria: UNN Academic Planning Unit.

Wilson, S.J. (1981). *Field Instructors: Techniques for Supervisors*. New York: Free Press.

21
SITUATIONAL ANALYSIS OF SOCIAL WORK FIELD PRACTICE IN TANZANIA MAINLAND

Meinrad Haule Lembuka

Abstract: English

The aim of the chapter was to conduct a situational analysis on social work field practice in Tanzania mainland through the social work schools Tanzania Association of Social Workers and Association of Schools of Social Work. The findings revealed that the Department of Social Welfare provides technical support to social work education as a government organ, all social work training's curricula have accommodated field instruction courses and field practice, there is a shortage of qualified social work instructors, and all social work trainings conduct field work practice. However, the challenge remains with the social work field placement agencies as most of the intended field agency supervisors are non-social workers and others are under-qualified compared to the students. The shortage of social workers necessitates that non-social workers supervise social work students. Moreover, in field work students are placed in lower and routine tasks rather than management and macro practice. It is recommended that there should be staff capacity-building, an effective connection made between the social work training institutions and field practice agencies, and establishment of a social work education council.

Abstract: Muhtasari

Lengo kuu la chapisho hili ni kufanya uchambuzi wa kina juu ya utekelezwaji wa elimu ya vitendo wakati wa mafunzo ya ustawi wa jamii (amara jamii) nchini Tanzania kwa kuangalia vyuo husika, chama cha wataalam wa ustawi wa jamii (TASWO) na chama cha vyuo vinavyotoa elimu ya ustawi wa jamii (ASSWOT).

Tafiti mbalimbali zimeonyesha kuwa Idara Kuu ya Ustawi wa jamii (DSW) ambayo ni Idara kuu ya Selikari ndio msimamizi wa mkuu wa uratibu wa huduma na elimu ya ustawi wa jamii nchini Tanzania kwa mujibu wa sheria na miongozo mbalimbali, hivyo basi Idara ya Ustawi wa jamii imekuwa ikitoa miongozo na ushauri wa kitaalam kuhakikisha kuwa mitaala yote ya elimu ya ustawi wa jamii imejumuisha elimu kwa vitendo. Japokuwa vyuo vyote vinavyotoa elimu ya usatwi wa jamii vinazingatia elimu kwa vitendo lakin kwa upande mwingine utekelezaji wa elimu kwa vitendo umekuwa ukikabialiana na changamoto mbalimbali ikiwemo upungufu wa walimu walionasifa stahiki na wakati mwingine wasimamizi wa wanafunzi wa vitendo katika taasisi husika hawajosomea mambo ya ustawi wa jamii. Pia, wakati mwingine taasisi huwapangia wanafunzi wa elimu ya vitendo majukumu ya madogo au ya kiutendaji zaidi ambayo hayahusiani na huduma za ustawi wa jamii.

Chapisho hili limetoa mapendekezo ya kujengea uwezo waalimu wa ustawi wa jamii na wasimamizi wa wanafunzi wa vitendo, pia kuongezwa mahusuiano ya karibu kati ya vyuo vya ustawi wa jamii na taasisi zinazopokea wanafunzi wa vitendo. Mwisho TASWO kwa kushirikiana na Idara kuu ya Ustawi wa jamii kufanikisha upatikanaji wa sheria na baraza la kusimamia elimu na huduma za ustawi jamii nchini Tanzania.

Introduction

The chapter presents a situational analysis of social work field practice concerning the Tanzania mainland. Tanzania is a union of two countries known as Tanganyika and Zanzibar Island that took place on 26 April 1964 (United Republic of Tanzania, 2012). Like the rest of Africa, social work education in Africa has a colonial heritage having been imported from the Western world, especially Europe, in the last century (Mwansa, 2011; Mupedziswa, 2001). Just like other African countries, social work education in Tanzania mainland is a colonial product and the process of indigenisation is still gaining momentum in dealing with African problems. Field education is considered the signature pedagogy in social work. 'Signature pedagogy represents the central form of instruction and learning in which a profession socialises its students to perform the role of practitioner' (CSWE, 2008, p.4).

The transformation history of social work education and fieldwork practice in Tanzania mainland began in the early 2010s when the country experienced a mushrooming of social work schools. Then in 2010 the Tanzania Association of Social Workers (TASWO) and other key stakeholders envisioned having a special committee to standardise social work programmes and fieldwork practice in Tanzania through the Tanzania Emerging Schools of Social Work Programme (TESWEP) under the first chairman, Daud Chanila. TESWEP was later transformed into the Association of Schools of Social Work in Tanzania (ASSWOT). Overtime, TASWO and ASSWOT jointly have been working with national and international social work key stakeholders to standardise social work education through developing and reviewing social work curricula and creating a fieldwork practice manual since 2015 (TASWO, 2015).

Social work field practice, which is also known as field instruction, field placement, field education, practicum, or internship, is therefore an integral component of social work education (Dhemba, 2012). Social work education comprises classroom-based learning, which is twinned with social work field practice as a mandatory learning process for competence-based practice. For producing competent social workers to deal with complex and multiple social problems, a social work student must undergo social work field practice to link classroom theories and knowledge with actual real-life situations, which concurrently shape the professional identity of the student social worker. Social work is a competence-based profession, like medical doctors, mechanical engineers, and pilots, that demands competence-based training (ASSWOT, 2018).

Overview of Social Work Field Education in Africa

The first social work school to be established in Africa was the South African Jan Hofmeyer College in 1924, followed by the Egyptian Higher Institute for Social Work in Cairo established in 1946 and, in Ghana, the School of Social Welfare Accra had its humble beginnings around 1946. According to Midgley (1981), social work education institutions have continued to increase in Africa with an increase of social work workforce due to multiple social problems caused by globalisation and its impacts. The various social work education and training institutions in Africa have offered a diversity of programmes and certainly not all of them have offered high-quality qualifications in social work training. Spitzer and Twikirize (2014) note that some institutions could not be regarded as professional schools of social work because of the nature of their offerings and the lack of core competence of social work. while other institutions are mostly dominated by other disciplines, such as community development, social administration, and public administration, with no core courses in social work and, above all, no fieldwork practice for social work students (Mupedziswa, 2001). Thus, in Africa discrepancies are evident in terms of training standards of different institutions. There are also variations in the extent to which these different institutions conform to international standards, guidelines, and expectations (Mupedziswa, 2001; Spitzer, 2019).

Various scholars at different times have identified similar challenges associated with choice of placements in social work education and training institutions in Africa:

- Shortage of suitable staff in agencies (i.e. to supervise students).
- Competition for a limited number of places for fieldwork.
- Limited opportunities to explore suitability of agencies which take students.
- Lack of suitable accommodation for students and supervisors.
- Lack of financial resources, which limits the placement choices (Mupedziswa, 2001; Aamoah, 1994; ASWEA, 1982).

The above challenges have been confirmed by researchers who conducted a study of 25 social work institutions in southern and eastern Africa (Hochfeld et al. 2009). While these challenges might be experienced in both urban and rural areas, they are prevalent and acute mostly in rural rather than urban areas. The study of Hochfeld (2009) confirms the existence of similar challenges for social work field practice in southern and eastern Africa, as presented in the following summary.

- The problem of a shortage of suitable staff to supervise students in agencies, for example, is mostly a rural phenomenon. In many African countries, the vast majority of trained personnel prefer to work in urban areas, partly because of the 'urban biased' nature of the education system they went through, but also because most employment opportunities are concentrated in urban areas and so is the infrastructure.
- Lack of proper accommodation for students and supervisors may be both an urban and a rural problem, but it is more acute in the rural situations. Generally, students going on urban placements can easily arrange to stay with relatives and/or friends, but such an arrangement is for obvious reasons possible only on very rare occasions in rural settings.
- A concern about competition for a limited number of social work fieldwork agencies while the demand for placement is too high especially in an urban compared to a rural area. This is because fieldwork in many African countries is concentrated in urban areas. As education and training institutions in Africa have grown and expanded, it has become more and more difficult to find placements for students.
- The limited budgets for fieldwork training have also made it virtually impossible to send students to places that are too far away and scattered all over the countryside. Safari (1986) echoes this concern and explains that it is the prohibitive costs involved that make it difficult for institutions in Africa to consider rural placements.

- Njau (1986) also expresses reservations about using rural placements, especially due to the distances involved. She notes that the distance between some rural agencies and the social work training institutions (which are mainly urban-based) makes it difficult for trainers to identify suitable rural fieldwork agencies and fieldwork supervisors, and they therefore prefer to place students in nearby agencies where communication and effective supervision can be carried out. Yet as the number of social work education institutions increases, there will be a need to focus on rural placements as urban placements cannot absorb everyone.

Background to Social Work Field Practice in Tanzania Mainland

Social work field practice in Tanzania mainland commenced in 1973 when the first social work training school was established under Parliament Act No. 26 of 1973, known as the National Social Welfare Training Institution, which was later renamed the Institute of Social Work (ISW) under Parliament Act No 2002 (ISW, 2020). Despite being the single social work training institution in the country, ISW remarkably and unquestionably embraced the social work field practice through its accredited social work curricular and institutional field practice manual that provided social work students with opportunities to integrate classroom knowledge and theories with practice (Department of Social Work [DSW], 2013). For more than 30 years (1973–2005), the country retained a single social work training school with its traditional fieldwork practice that influenced social work training, but in the 2010s other social work training schools emerged all over the country. The mushrooming of social work training came to the attention of the Department of Social Welfare under the Ministry of Health and Tanzania Association of Social Workers (TASWO), which in 2011 established a special committee to coordinate and standardise social work education as well as social work field practice (Ngondi, 2013).

Until 2010 there was no specific organisation to standardise social work training and fieldwork practice apart from the Department of Social Welfare's section on social welfare training, which supervised and monitored mainly governmental social work training institutions, namely, the Institute of Social Work and Kisangara Social Welfare Institute. The revival of the Tanzania Association of Social Workers (TASWO) in 2010 influenced the formulating of a special committee to coordinate, standardise, and promote social work education in Tanzania through the Tanzania Emerging School of Social Work Programme (TESWEP, 2013). TESWEP was later changed to an association and was registered on 26 September 2015 as the Association of Schools of Social Work in Tanzania (ASSWOT). ASSWOT has continued the work done by TESWEP, i.e., standardisation of social work curricula and field work practice aimed at producing quality professional social workers in Tanzania who will deliver quality social welfare services not only to support the socioeconomic and political welfare of society, but also to ensure a harmonious environment for development. To date, both TASWO and ASSWOT emphasise that assessment (formative and summative) is a core feature of social work field education for competent social work students regarding indigenisation and cultural values in the Tanzania context (Shigongo et al., 2015).

To date, ASSWOT has initiated a number of social work education stakeholders' consultative meetings that have included key stakeholders such as schools of social work, social work clients, employers, relevant accreditation bodies, and professional bodies in Tanzania for the improvement of social work field practice. These key stakeholders were considered key for both the indigenisation process of social work field practice and for standardisation (ASSWOT, 2015). Furthermore, both TASWO and ASSWOT have succeeded in advocating for standardised social curricula and integration of field work practice requirements to the two major national accreditation bodies, namely, the National Accreditation Council for Technical Education (NACTE) and the Tanzania Commission of University (TCU) regarding indigenisation of social work education in the country.

In the Tanzanian context, social work field education is practiced through concurrent fieldwork and block fieldwork. During block fieldwork, students learn full time in the field under an experienced and qualified social worker. On the other hand, under concurrent placements, a student's time is divided between classroom learning and fieldwork experiences. Essentially, students are expected to be present in the agency for two or three days per week and to take classes for two or three days. However, ASSWOT recommends students at NTA level 4, 5, and 6 (certificate and diploma) undertake block fieldwork training for the duration of 60 days as mandatory. Hence, the rationale for developing a manual to guide block fieldwork practice (ASSWOT, 2017).

Therefore, this chapter presents a critical analysis of current social work field-work practice in Tanzania mainland in ten social work schools, TASWO and ASSWOT. Social work education is practical-based, and, thus, field placement is a core component that meets a global standard and that makes room for contextualisation with the local environment and local cultural values.

Methodology

According to Boyd et al. (2015), decomposition is a general approach to solving a problem by breaking it up into smaller ones and solving each of the smaller ones separately, either in parallel or in sequence. The breakdown of complex concepts into their simpler concepts means that its logical structure is displayed. Therefore, the chapter uses a documentary review method and desk research method to make intended analysis of social work field education and practice in the Tanzanian mainland context. A systematic procedure was used for reviewing or evaluating documents, both printed and electronic (computer-based and Internet-transmitted) material. Like other analytical methods in qualitative research, document analysis requires that data be examined and interpreted in order to elicit meaning, gain understanding, and develop empirical knowledge (Corbin and Strauss, 2008). Table 21.1 shows several social work training institutions available in Tanzania.

Table 21.1 represents ten social work training institutions in Tanzania whose reports were used to enrich the development of this chapter and it was observed that there were varieties of

Table 21.1 Sample of Social Work Training Institutions in Tanzania

	Cert. Social Work	Diploma Social Work	BA Social Work	Postgrad. Diploma Social Work	MSc Social Work	PhD Social Work
Institute of Social Work						
Open University of Tanzania						
University of Dar es Salaam						
Mbalizi Institute of Health Sciences						
Kaliua Institute of Community Development						
Hubert Kairuki Memorial University						
Kigoma Training College						
Mwenge Catholic University						
Kampala International University of Tanzania						
Sengerema Health Institute						

Source: ASSWOT, 2021

social work programmes offered by each institution from certificate to doctor of philosophy. It was observed that only one institution offers the doctor of philosophy in social work, which is the Open University of Social Work, two institutions offer a masters of social work, two institutions offer a postgraduate diploma in social work, five institutions offer bachelor degrees in social work, nine institutions offer a diploma in social work, and another nine institutions offer certificates in social work.

Key Actors of Social Work Practice in Tanzania Mainland

Since the introduction of social work education in the early 1970s, fieldwork practice has been a collaborative relationship among the training institutions, the community of social work agencies, social work professionals, and students. The main actors in fieldwork include departments of social work, fieldwork coordinators, fieldwork consultants, social service agencies, agency supervisors, and social work students. The roles of each actor need to be properly understood from the onset in order to facilitate a meaningful organisation and an effective experience of fieldwork (ASSWOT, 2017).

Department of Social Welfare (DSW) under the Ministry of Health

The Department of Social Welfare is a government organ responsible for supervision and coordination of social welfare services in the country and is fully committed to provide technical support to social work education and practice. The Department of Social Welfare strives to ensure the quality of social welfare service provision in the country by providing relevant support to TASWO and ASSWOT in developing a standardised social work fieldwork manual for non-degree, undergraduate, and postgraduate social work programmes in the country (Mabeyo, 2014). For a competent social welfare workforce and quality social welfare provision, the Department of Social Welfare in collaboration with other stakeholders is committed to seeingthat social work field practice remains a fundamental aspect of social work education that provides students with the opportunity to apply the theoretical foundations of the profession to the practice arena (ASSWOT, 2017).

Association of Schools of Social Work in Tanzania (ASSWOT)

ASSWOT is a registered association with registration number SA19637 under the Societies Act (CAP. 337 R.E. 2002); which came into existence after a proliferation of schools offering social work education, including field work practice. It started as Tanzania Emerging Social Work Education Programme (TESWEP) under the umbrella of TASWO which brought together twelve schools offering (and intending to offer) social work education in Tanzania. At the moment, the association is made up of more than twelve schools offering social work education at different levels of study (ASSWOT, 2018).

Tanzania Association of Social Workers (TASWO)

TASWO advocates for quality social work training through implementing social work field practice in all social work training institutions. It facilitates curricular development or review with an emphasise on the importance of fieldwork for all training, including certificate, diploma, bachelor's degree, and postgraduate studies (Zena, 2014). The main goal of social work field practice among all social work training institutions and field placement agencies in the country is on generic skill development through contact with the client system, linking classroom theories and knowledge with actual practice and development of values and attitudes consistent with the profession of social work as well as personal development (Csiernik et al, 2004).

Department (Unit) of Social Work

Each social work training institution has an independent department of social work that has overall responsibility to ensure that the fieldwork is conducted in a manner that is both professional and practical. The department should, among other roles, ensure that students are placed in appropriate fieldwork settings or agencies, specify areas of social work interventions that students must be exposed to and actively involved in during placement, help students develop a learning contract that outlines students' learning goals, and provide supervisors and agencies with guidelines to help them supervise students (Buhori, 2015). According to the Ministry of Health Community Development Gender, Elderly and Children (MoHCDGEC), the Department of Social Work is responsible for ensuring that technical support is made available to students and agency supervisors in working together and where resources allow. Meetings with agency supervisors will be arranged from time to time to ensure that agencies understand and appreciate their roles and that they give their best to the students (MoHCDGEC, 2017).

Social Work Fieldwork Coordinator

Each social work school appoints one social work field coordinator who handles the administrative and logistic issues for the fieldwork placements and attends to issues that require clarification and guidance. For complicated cases, the Head of Department will be consulted for guidance and support. Agency supervisors and students can contact the fieldwork coordinator whenever the need arises. The coordinator is charged with responsibility of planning and managing all issues related to field practice education within the department. They handle questions, concerns, and problems of the students, agency supervisors, and academic supervisors (Buhori, 2015; MoHCDGEC, 2017). The coordinator is also responsible for providing guidelines for supervisory content. They are also responsible for maintaining an up-to-date database of agencies where placements can be secured and, where possible, to negotiate contracts with such agencies for long-term partnerships with the department in the pursuit of field practice education (Buhori, 2015).

Fieldwork consultant (Academic Supervisor)

Each student is assigned a consultant or academic supervisor from the department. It is recommended that students meet or contact their supervisors prior to the commencement of fieldwork and keep in constant touch with them throughout the duration of the placement. The consultant will arrange one face-to-face supervision visit at the site/agency where the student is placed. Supervision is not a policing/surprise visit but a prearranged meeting for purposes of supervision. The consultant checks on the progress of the student as well as providing the agency supervisor with guidelines where necessary to help them supervise the students. The consultant from the department advises the agency supervisor and together they evaluate the student's work. The academic supervisor is responsible for submitting the final assessment results to the Head of Department for onward consideration by the department (Buhori, 2015; MoHCDGEC, 2017).

Social Welfare Service Agency

The social welfare service agency or social work settings are pre-identified agencies or organisations that qualify for social work student field practice with a qualified social work or social welfare workforce to supervise. These agencies are responsible for giving students appropriate educational, administrative, and supportive environments throughout their fieldwork. They provide each student with a letter of introduction stating that she or he is placed at the agency for fieldwork for a specified period, and they sign the field practice agreement form (Buhori, 2015). They also ensure provision of adequate space, support, and other resources needed by the students. Notwithstanding the practical realities within some agencies, an agency should be able to provide appropriate physical arrangements for students, such as office and desk space, use of telephones, interviewing rooms, and recording facilities where these are needed. Also, they assign a supervisor for each student doing fieldwork in that particular organisation and ensure that the supervisor is available for the duration of each student's placement. It is advisable that the agency supervisor possesses the technical ability and personal qualities necessary for successful student supervision (MoHCDGEC, 2017).

Agency Supervisor

The agency supervisor should be a member of the staff of the organisation where the student is doing his/her fieldwork. He/she is responsible for the overall day-to-day supervision and guidance of the student. In some organisations there are specific staff designated to manage students on field practice while in others supervision is an additional role handled alongside the member of staff's core businesses. Agencies and students need to appreciate this fact and therefore make use of the time the agency supervisor dedicates to supervision wisely. The specific roles of the agency supervisor include identifying appropriate opportunities within the agency where a student can be engaged to secure exposure to as wide a range of activities as possible. This should be done within the framework of the agency's normal work schedules and activities (MoHCDGEC, 2017).

Social Work Students

Students play a vital role in ensuring that the fieldwork exercise is successful and thus they become vital stakeholders by ensuring their active participation right from the beginning in securing placements that are appropriate for social work education. Students should follow the guidelines and procedures provided in the manual in selecting the agencies and after securing the placement, the student has the responsibility to report to the respective training institution fieldwork coordinator about the placement as well as submit a copy of the acceptance letter duly signed by the responsible person in the agency. Lastly, a social work student is responsible for reporting to the agency/organisation of placement and for making sure that the field placement is fully completed according to the social work objectives (MoHCDGEC, 2017).

Challenges Facing Social Work Field Practice in Tanzania Mainland

The ASSWOT Report (2017) shows that social work placement students are generally assigned with routine tasks that are more clinical or involved in direct social work, rather than exposure to preventive tasks. Lack of enough social work experts in the field work agencies influence the generalisation of tasks given to social work field placement students from certificate to postgraduate students. Also, these routine tasks are micro social work practice, and, as a result, the social work schools and fieldwork agencies unknowingly are continuing to produce generalist social workers (Buhori, 2015). For instance, most were assigned routine tasks of micro level, including client assessment, case management, customer care and inquiry, and psychosocial intervention, providing referral and linkage to clients and arranging and attending official meetings. For those working in a medical setting, it was observed that social work fieldwork students are given a task to explain problems to clients and client systems in non-medical, and participating in rounds with other medical team in the hospital wards (Spitzer and Twikirize, 2014).

The analysis shows that despite several shortfalls in social work field practice in Tanzania mainland there is a common standard of practice that is acceptable across the social work training institutions. The social work field practice experience is structured as a continuum of learning and provides students with an opportunity to gain experience in a social work setting, receive regular professional supervision, and engage in a dynamic process towards the development of being a professional generalist practitioner (ASSWOT, 2015). The relevance of the students' learning goals to the setting, the quality of field instruction, the connection of theory to case material, the students' input regarding practicum sites, and the preparation of and support to field instructors were all found to be predictors of student satisfaction while in practicum (Spitzer, 2019).

During ASSWOT needs assessment with key stakeholders in 2015, it was reported that employers and policymakers pointed out a lack of competence in handling different cases during practice. However, this was reported to be limited to some institutions. Furthermore, policymakers reported that in some colleges, students are poorly trained, which was evident through their poor performance during the fieldwork placement at the social work agencies. If the curricula are not uniform or social work academic staff across social work institutions are not competent, it should be expected that differences in skills among social work students (ASSWOT, 2017) will be apparent.

The duration of social work field placements vary according to the level of study, but it was observed that weaknesses exist in some institutions in implementing curricular especially for one-year social work training where some training institutions minimise the duration of field placement. An inadequate number of teaching staff and a too short duration of the course to cover both theory and field work practice were reported to affect certificate and diploma-level social work training competence (ASSWOT, 2017). The duration of time for placement of each student at the fieldwork agency is determined on the basis of the level of study; for example, for the master's degree in social work (MSW), students are required to spend in the field a minimum of 90 days for MSW students in the foundation year or PGDSW (i.e., students pursuing MSW without social work background). For MSW students in the advanced year (i.e., students pursuing MSW with social work background), the minimum number of days is 60 (ASSWOT, 2017).

Professionals reported that there is an inadequate number of qualified teachers in some social work training institutions who can stress the importance of social work practice as well as provide professional supervision (TESWEP, 2012). Despite an increased number of social work training schools, there are inadequate human resources in terms of qualified social work academicians who are trained to teach social work professionally in the country (MoHCDGEC, 2017). The above observations suggest a few issues; first, there might be inconsistency in implementation and supervision of social work field practice across institutions. Second, it highlights the incompetence of teachers and the weaknesses of teaching and field work practice across institutions that could affect the social work field practice.

Annual reports from ASSWOT (2017) have shown that faculty members reported that there is a shortage of special teaching and learning facilities for students with special needs in both classrooms and at fieldwork placement agencies. Despite having a national policy and legislation on disability that emphasises the user-friendly environment for people with disabilities in public services, some social work training institutions and fieldwork agencies fail to accommodate the special needs of fieldwork students. The reported missing facilities include flip braille books, hearing supporting devices, special sign language devices and software (ASSWOT, 2017). The lack of enough facilities to accommodate people with disabilities in social work field practice affects the learning objectives for some students with special needs in the country.

After many years of social work field practice, only in 2017 was the fieldwork practicum manual for certificate and diploma-level education in social work prepared by the Ministry of Health, Community Development, Gender Elderly and Children, with expertise provided by ASSWOT and other stakeholders. The field-work manual aims to harmonise field-work practice across the nation among social work fieldwork actors at different agencies. The ministry has the role and responsibility of assessing and improving the quality of curricula for social welfare programmes as well as of supervising standards regarding education and training in the social welfare profession. It is envisioned that the manual will serve as a useful resource to facilitate greater understanding of fieldwork practicum among the various parties involved, namely, the student, the fieldwork supervisor, field consultants, the agency, and the social work training institutions (MoHCDGEC, 2019). The field practice manual has been adopted by training institutions, and social work field practice has noticeably improved.

The Hubert Kairuki Memorial University (2020) reported on concerns about the competence of social work fieldwork students observed by social work key stakeholders in noting that students lack some social work competences during fieldwork practice. Calls were made to place more emphasis on training in ethics, leadership, management, customer care, report writing skills, advocacy, and crisis interventions which were perceived to be central to social workers. They mentioned competencies are the key issues that are supposed to be addressed in the social work classroom and during fieldwork practice (HKMU, 2020). This implies that such important components of competencies are missing in some institutions.

Conclusion

The lack of a social work education council in Tanzania mainland to regulate social work education has lessened the quality of social work training and fieldwork practice in the country, which could enforce indigenisation and uniform standards of social work education and fieldwork practice. Experiences in other African countries have shown that where a social work education council has been established, no social work education standard is compromised.

Recommendations

1. The need for more indigenisation of social work curricular and fieldwork practice manuals that reflect African context and involvement of all local stakeholders during curricular development or review.
2. There is an urgent need for mapping of social field practice agencies that have quality social work practice and qualified social work competence to supervise social work field practice students. Social work training institutions and respective social work field agencies need to engage in a memorandum of understanding or contract covering such fieldwork practice to increase the commitment of both sides.
3. Social work curricular and fieldwork practice should also prepare students in macro-level practice with regard to the current global shift in practice from remedial welfare policies to an emphasis on preventive and developmental policies and practices. It is recommended that developing or reviewing social work curricula in Africa should include developmental social work.

Further Reading

Zena, M. (2014). *Professional Social Work in East Africa; Development of Social Work Education and Practice in Tanzania*. Kampala: Fountain Publishers.

References

Asamoah, Y. (1994). *'Challenges to social work around the World: Africa'. Centre for International Social Work: Inaugural Conference*. Storrs: University of Connecticut, 6.

Association of Schools of Social Work (2015). *Field Work Manual; Master Level*. Dar es salaam (Unpublished).

Association of Schools of Social Work (2017). *Annual Report*. Dar es salaam (Unpublished).

Association of Schools of Social Work (2018). *Situational Analysis Report*. Dar es salaam (Unpublished).

Association of Schools of Social Work in Tanzania- [ASSWOT] (2017). *Annual Report*. Dar es salaam (Unpublished).

Association of Schools of Social Work in Tanzania [ASSWOT] (2018). *Situational Analysis Report*. Dar es salaam (Unpublished).

Association of Social Work Education in Africa (ASWEA) (1982). *Survey of Curricula of Social Development Training Institutions in Africa*. Addis Ababa, Ethiopia: ASWEA.

Boyd, S., Xiao, L., Mutapcic, A. and Mattingley, J. (2015). *Decomposition Methods, Notes for EE364B*. Stanford, CA: Stanford University Press, 1–36.

Buhori, J. A. (2015). *The Post Graduate Fieldwork Manual and Guideline*. The Open University of Tanzania (Unpublished).

Corbin, J. and Strauss, A. (2008). *Basics of Qualitative Research: Techniques to Developing Grounded Theory* (3rd ed.). Los Angeles, CA: Sage.

Council on Social Work Education (2008). *Educational Policy and Accreditation Standards*. http://www.cswe.org/.

Csiernik, R. and Karley, M.L. (2004). The experience of social work practicum: Activities in the field. *Currents: New Scholarship in the Human Services*, 3, 1–24.

Department of Social Welfare (2013). Annual Progressive Report Presentation on National Stakeholders Meeting, Morogoro (Unpublished).

Dhemba, J. (2012). Fieldwork in social work education and training: Issues and challenges in the case of eastern and Southern Africa. *Social Work and Society International Online Journal*, 10(1), 1–16.

Hall, N. (1990). Social work training in Africa: A fieldwork manual. *Harare: Journal of Social Development in Africa*, 6(1), 33–45.

Hochfeld, T.; Mupedziswa, R.; Chitereka, C. and Selipsky, L. (2009). *Developmental Social Work Education in Southern and East Africa*. Johannesburg, South Africa: Centre for Social Development in Africa, University of Johannesburg.

Hubert Kairuki Memorial University (2020). *Needs Assessment Report for Establishment of Master of Social Work Program-Dar es Salaam* (Unpublished).

Institute of Social Work (2014). *Master of Social Work Fieldwork Manual*. Dar es salaam: Kijitonyama Institute of Social Work (Unpublished).

Mabeyo, Z. (2014). *Professional Social Work in East Africa; Development of Social Work Education and Practice in Tanzania*. Kampala: Fountain Publisher.

Midgley, J. (1981). *Professional Imperialism: Social Work in the Third World*. London: Heinemann.

MoHCDGEC (2017). *Situation Analysis Report for Standardization of NTA Level 4, 5 And 6 of Social Work Curricula*. Dar es salaam: URT.

MoHCDGEC (2019). *Standardised Social Work Curricular for NTA Level 4, 5 and 6*. Dar es salaam: URT.

Mupedziswa, R. (1992). Africa at the crossroads: Major challenges for social work education and practice towards the year 2000. *Journal of Social Development in Africa*, 7(2), 19–38.

Mupedziswa, R. (2001). The quest for relevance towards a conceptual model of development social work education and training in Africa. *International Social Work*, 44(3), 285–300.

Mwansa, L.K. (2011). Social work education in Africa: Whence and whither? *Social Work Education*, 30(1), 4–16.

Njau, W.P. (1986). Social development training with special reference to rural fieldwork. In J. Hampson and B. Willmore (eds), *Social Development and Rural Fieldwork*. Harare: School of Social Work, 13–20.

Safari, J. (1986). The role of fieldwork in the training of social workers. In J. Hampson and B. Willmore (eds), *Social Development and Rural Fieldwork*. Harare: School of Social Work, 27–33.

Spitzer, H. (2019). Social work in East Africa: A mzungu perspective. *International Social Work*, 62(2), 567–580.

Spitzer, H. and Twikirize, J.M. (2014). PROSOWO: A project to professionalize social work in East Africa. In H. Spitzer, J.M. Twikirize and G.G. Wairire (eds), *Professional Social Work in East Africa: Towards Social Development, Poverty Reduction and Gender Equality*. Kampala, Uganda: Fountain, 1–11.

Tanzania Association of Social Workers [TASWO] (2015). *Annual General Report*. Dar es salaam (Unpublished).

Tanzania Emerging School of Social Work Programme [TESWEP] (2012). *General Meeting; Annul Report*. Dar es salaam (Unpublished).

Tanzania Emerging School of Social Work Programme [TESWEP] (2013). *TESWEP General Meeting; Annul Report*. Dar es salaam (Unpublished).

Tanzania Emerging School of Social Work Programme [TESWEP] (2014). *TESWEP Annul Report*. Dar es salaam (Unpublished).

United Republic of Tanzania (2012). *Assessment of Social Welfare Workforce Report*. Dar es salaam (Unpublished).

Zena, M. (2014). *Professional Social Work in East Africa; Development of Social Work Education and Practice in Tanzania*. Kampala: Fountain Publisher.

22
THE IMPORTANCE AND CHALLENGES OF SOCIAL WORK FIELD EDUCATION
The University of Benin Experience

Tracy B.E. Omorogiuwa

Abstract: English

The place of social work in enhancing societal welfare cannot be separated from field education, which is a vital part of social work training. Field practicum offers students with information and opportunities to tackle and resolve issues in practice. Given that it is an essential element in the social work curriculum, field education is crucial in students' learning competence. This chapter aims to explore the structure of the social work field experience and the need to seriously look into the practice methods in order to promote the worth of field experience. This chapter discusses that social work field education is fraught with limitations arising from insufficient field agencies to the engagement of students in activities not related to their field experience. The chapter therefore concludes that core stakeholders/departmental administrators should liaise with other social service organisations to create a platform for training and retraining of key staff to ensure effective practical experiences for students. The chapter thus highlights the crucial implications for departmental administrators to improve the quality of field practice training.

Introduction

This chapter seeks to explore the place and importance of field practicum in the context of Nigerian social work education. The contribution that field work has in providing a practical experience for students to apply their knowledge and sharpen their skills is discussed and the need for trained and effective supervisors to ensure the quality of these opportunities is recommended.

Location of the University of Benin

University of Benin is a public research university located in Benin City, Edo State, southern Nigeria. The University of Benin has dedicated instructors draw from a strong contemporary curriculum and their own practical experience. The Department of Social Work at the University of Benin, Nigeria, is committed to social work education that prepares graduates who can promote social justice in different sociocultural contexts. We are leaders in social work education, committed to social justice, human rights, and equity. We work with groups who have been marginalised and produce research that has real impact on the community. Our teaching team, drawn from a range of professional and research backgrounds, works with our students to help them reach their full potential and equip them to enter a range of professional roles focused on children, adults, families, and communities.

Field Education, an Integral Component of Social Work

This section focuses on field education as a learning process that contributes to acquiring effective social work education. Quality social work education develops the learning process of field education. As part of the requirement for acquiring the professional degree in social work, field education, which is an integral component of social work education, helps to complement theories, principles, and skills learned in the classrooms (Omorogiuwa, 2021). Thus, it gives students the opportunity to experience solving issues in the field and giving them a clue to the practice situation. Research indicates that field education is an essential element of social work education, as the training in social work of a professional requires a combined curriculum of theory and field experience (Bogo, 2005 2015). Field practicum, as Gitterman (1989, p. 78) explains, 'transforms knowledge and understanding into practice, principles, and behaviors'. Field education as a vital tool of social work is central to the education of social work students' and not an extra-curricular activity (Fortune et al. 2001). Field placement represents a milestone of accomplishment and an opportunity for learning and growing professionally while making a difference in the lives of others.

According to Aristotle, 'for all things we have to learn before we can do them, we learn by doing them' (as quoted in Birkenmaier Berg-Weger, 2007, p. 11). Research indicates that 'field practice, is also conterminously referred to as field practicum, field instruction, field placement, field education, or simply fieldwork in social work literature, forms an important part of social work education and training' (Amadasun, 2021, p. 2). To Bogo (2015), field education is the aspect of social work education, which involves the actual utilisation of knowledge and abilities acquired during classroom learning to the practice setting where students are taught to reflect on practical issues by social workers. Whilst Savaya et al. (2003) point out that field practicum is centered on the value of development. Therefore, students are expected to improve and develop both in theory and in field experiences. Field practicum is extremely important for upcoming social workers because it allows them to work in a professional setting to establish and demonstrate social work skills, implement theories and practices learned in and out of the classroom, and build a sense of dedication to the profession and ethical standards. Working with social welfare agencies, non-profit organisations, government entities, or any other institutions that assist people, groups, or communities in improving their social functioning or coping with challenges is another significant component of field practicum for students (Garthwait, 2021).

It is a time for students to apply the knowledge, values, and skills gained in the classroom as a means towards integration, internalisation, and mastery (Damskey, 2011). Field education that links competences learning in practice classes and applied in the field provides additional training for students on placement and supervisions in development of learning objectives that reflect the social work practice. In social work education, field education is crucial to the acquisition of practice skills knowledge and it is important to the completion of social work degree, irrespective of the progress in classroom courses (Reisch and Jaman-Rohde, 2000; Hick and Swain, 2007). Research establishes that field education enables students to test and integrate learning in the classroom and practice settings, assess the effectiveness of interventions, strive for competence, contend with injustices, and acquireprofessional practice.

The social work education at the University of Benin utilises an extensive number of service agencies in Benin City, Edo State, as well as nationally. The development of a suitable practicum placement is a collaborative effort between the university, student, and agency to maximise the student's learning potential. Placements are sought in agencies that offer a varied practice experience in terms of kinds of interventions and types of systems that the student works with (e.g., individuals, groups, families, community involvement, and organisational change), exposure to interprofessional teamwork, non-traditional approaches to practice, and innovative settings for social workers. The practicum at the University of Benin is not just another work experience, but it is also an educational learning experience. Thus, the field practicum training provided to students equips them with the skills they need to achieve their academic objectives and beyond. It gives students the chance to put theory into practice, to build real employability abilities, and to establish significant relationships in the field.

It is pertinent for students to have the opportunity to practice what they learn under a supervised setting while carrying out statutory social work tasks involving legal interventions, providing services to users' groups, in a way that takes account of values and diversities. Field education creates opportunities of ensuring that the social work practitioners of the future are equipped to practice autonomously and responsibly and show effective respond to the complex and changing needs of clients. As an integral part of social work education and practice, field education makes connection between students' world of knowledge and practice a reality (Nobel, 2001). Most especially, field experiences refine social work education and practice realities. New patterns of social work education and practices are shaped through field education. The field is a mechanism for the transfer of knowledge between the school environment and the practice environment; the knowledge acquired from the field serves as feedback by promoting learning and advancement in curriculum development (Larger and Robbins, 2004). In field education students make transition from the abstract to the real through experimental learning. That is, the field is a process of transforming practical experiences into knowledge skills and senses (Miller et al. 2005). The field creates an opportunity for student to demonstrate theories learned and develop skills – to test their capacities to be a proficient professional in practice situations.

Raskin (1994) affirms that an important priority in field education is learning activities, which helps students connect ideas with practice situations. Learning activities are crucial to students' performance outcome in the field. Active participation of students in learning activities in field placements gives students the opportunity to put into practice skills and acquired knowledge; this, in turn, gives them satisfaction, the zeal to provide assistance and to assume role-taking. Students' effective learning in social work education is enhanced when students have a focus to link their practice with realities. An effective learning in the field should include different learning activities and that the learning from the instructors in the field helps students to link theory with practice as concepts and issues are better explained in real-life situations and are connected (Fortune et al. 2001).

The students who are exposed to learning in the field develop more zeal in task accomplishment and feel themselves more fulfilled than those who are not (Omorogiuwa, 2021). As students are being prepared for later practice, they are expected to acquire vital knowledge through field education; of importance in social work education is the issue of what students do while on field placement. Students are sent for field education for their practice experience. With routine supervision by professionally trained social workers; the students who are sent out on placements are expected to be equipped with the essential knowledge and skills needed for practice situations.

Research on field education constitutes an integral component of social work education, conducted in Benin City, and it establishes that the field creates an opportunity for students to demonstrate theories learned and develop skills and test their capacities to be proficient professionals in practice situations (Omorogiuwa, 2016). This implies that leaning activities during practicum affect students' perception of field education. Similarly, Raskin (1994) notes that an important priority in field education is the learning activities that helps students connect ideas with practice situations as learning activities are crucial to students' performance outcome in the field. This is because when students are being prepared for later practice, they are expected to acquire vital knowledge through field education. Of importance in social work education is the issue of what students do while on field placement. Hence, the field is a process of transforming field experiences into knowledge skills and senses as it allows students to make the transition from abstract to real through experimental learning. The students come to appreciate certain learning activities with field learning than others. Learning from instructors was, however, related to high positive perception as opposed to other learning activities. To Fortune et al. (2001), learning 'from the field instructors in the field helps students to link theory with practice as concepts and issues are better explained and connected; giving room for feedback. Amadasun (2021) indicates that there are four groups engaged in the social work field education, which are the students, agency-based field instructor/supervisor, the university field liaison/supervisor, and the field education coordinator. Garthwait (2021) affirms the need for these parties, recapping that the acknowledgement of and devotion to their tasks are basic to the achievement of the aim of field education.

Types of Field Practicum at the University of Benin

There exist various types of field experience. The traditional method, which is still employed, involves students' placement in organisations/agencies in communities (Savaya et al. 2003; Amadasun, 2021). However, Liu (2013) affirms that the most regular categories of field education involve block placement, where it is mandatory for students to complete entire coursework before proceeding with field placement of four to five days weekly in agencies. The rotational type of practicum enables students to move through two alternations or occasionally three before the end of a placement. Birkenmaier et al. (2012) assert that the rotational type of field practicum, which is a substitute for the traditional type, has often been adopted in past years. Further, they establish that the rotational method helps to expand the variety of training students obtain, given the rotation of placement in different units of an agency or at various agencies.

Moreover, the community-centre type of practicum has been embraced by a number of social work institutions, as it requires students' engagement within the communities to recognise issues as well as the need to advance micro-, mezzo-, and macro-intervention strategies (Omorogiuwa, 2016). Research asserts that the community-centre model has developed in collaboration with communities and organisations/agencies, which centres on developmental values and supporting the community, while simultaneously aiding as a base for students' practice-oriented training (Du Plessis, 2011). Social work field practice helps learners develop their interpersonal relationships and understand their clients in relevant aspects. This level of understanding includes and is not limited to understanding their behavior and developing skills to deal with diversity at a personal level. Field practice equips learners with character development skills and develops their character and ability to deal with problems on a personal level. Learners' professional competencies to deal with challenges and the development of a community at a micro level are also developed during their time in the field (Rollins, 2020).

The primary focus of community social workers is to provide services and to acquire a better understanding of how to handle people in the community, especially during crises such as pandemics or in the case of bandit attacks or political instability. The learners become equipped to develop their attitudes and behaviors to maintain the integrity and serve the community without bias. This enables them to overcome their prejudices and tendentious points of view, building their responsibility to defend the oppressed without looking into their beliefs (Amadasun, 2021). The theoretical practices learned about integrity and services are incorporated into internships and practicum.

Field education also enables trainees to understand the requirements of a community and its development. It leads to a knowledge of the challenges affecting society and equips learners with skills and techniques that can be used to deal with social problems at all levels. Learning the strategies that can be used to ensure management of shared resources and educating society on the harmonious utilisation of the resources shared in the community is obtained through field education. Most social workers consider problem-solving and service the core of social work, which mainly involves helping a large population by solving a single root problem.

According to Garthwait (2021), field practicum equips learners with the core values of service to society, competencies, integrity, social justice, dignity and value, and the usefulness of others in balancing nature and the interrelationship of people and nature. The learners are equipped with strategies of retrospectively identifying the cause of a given problem and learning how to solve that given problem. The competencies of the learners to identify a shared concern in a marketplace are evaluated, and their ability to develop strategies to solve the problem using either a single strategy or combined strategies.

Harris and Boys (2021) point out that social work education demands a social work curriculum that ensures that students will be equipped with the knowledge to be able to fight for and advance human rights. Many techniques are made more efficient when paired with knowledge of the judicial system and processes, as human rights cannot be fully fulfilled unless they are safeguarded by law. Because advocacy is an integral part of social work practice, social work education gives students a firm fundamental grasp of the legislative branch. Field practicum exposes learners to organisations and structures of the social agency to solve problems in society, equipping them with knowledge of the power possessed by such organisations in promoting human rights as well as social, environmental, and economic rights (Department of Social Work, 2021). An internship in such organisations allows the learner to understand how the theoretical legal procedures are carried out in such organisations. During such training, the location, structures, and correct protocols to solve a given problem are also obtained. The exposure enables students to familiarise themselves with the dynamics of society and the trends in changes in society; hence, broadening the learners' knowledge of human rights and ability to solve human rights violations (Amadasun, 2021).

Issues and Challenges in Social Work Field Education

Amadasun (2021) asserts that few professions devote adequate time and vigor to field practice compared to social work. Although some studies on social work field practicum provide far-reaching evidence of supervision (Reichelt and Skjerve, 2000), students' assessment and review of their engagements during placement, and practice methods utilised by field instructors, research on social Work field practice experience in Nigeria is limited (Omorogiuwa, 2016). This situation requires attention, since field practice is the mark of instruction and stands at the core of social work training (Homonoff, 2008; Wayne et al., 2010; Larrison and Korr, 2013; Omorogiuwa, 2016). To Bogo (2015, p. 317), 'the ability of social work education to graduate ethical, competent, innovative, effective clinical social workers is highly dependent on the quality of the field experience.' Given that institutions of higher education need a way to determine whether field practicum experience meets estalblished standards as well as knowledge of the issues confronting students' during placement (Omorogiuwa, 2016; Amadasun, 2021), students assessment during field experience in social work programmes offers a thoughtful lens in which the value of practice can be determined and plans are made for future practice and achieving competencies. Thus, this section explores the issues and challenges of field placement in Nigeria through the lens of social work students.

Examination of social work field education through the experience of social work students needs to earnestly look into the practice methods in order to improve the quality of the field experience. Sometimes, social work field education is fraught with irregularities ranging from insufficient field agencies to engagement of students in activities not related to their field experience (Omorogiuwa, 2021). Concerns about inadequate human service agencies are disturbing. This is not only because of the shortage of social service organisations per se, but also because of the artificial blockade of such agencies that require advance payments as a precondition to offer training to students. Such exploitative behavior is capable of rendering the field practicum training component of social work disempowering and disillusioning to many students who are desirous of learning.

The inadequate human service agencies in Benin City, Nigeria, and their exploitative behavior are novel, but hardly surprising. This position is highlighted in light of widespread poverty and poor remuneration, which, taken together, culminates in official corruption (United Nations Development Programme [UNDP], as cited in Amadasun, 2021). This tendency to shift the burden onto other groups (in this case, social work students) is a pervasive phenomenon in Nigerian society. The involvement of social work students in irrelevant assignments, such as running errands, housekeeping, and cleaning, constitutes a cause for serious concern. This is so because if students are to meet the standards of their counterparts in other parts of the world, they should be fully grounded in knowledge of pertinent job specifications in terms of responding to the needs of our clients; system. Clients' system as used here includes individuals, families, groups, organisations, and communities.

Inadequate Human Service Agencies

Human services are an integrative set of welfare programmes ranging from counseling and healthcare to shelter and food and are delivered by non-profit organisations and the government to contribute to the wellbeing of societies by offering a wide range of support and assistance to families and individuals (Omorogiuwa, 2021). Human service agencies refer to the institutions offering the humanitarian service mentioned; healthcare, food, counseling, shelter, and other services (Hasenfeld, 2010). Humanitarian services is a field that focuses on improving service delivery mechanisms by focusing on the effectiveness of direct services and accessibility, transparency, and collaboration among individuals and organisations involved in service delivery. Humanitarian service systems are at the heart of almost every employee in human services. These service professionals operate in a range of settings, including care facilities and halfway homes; rehabilitative mental impairment; community-based mental health centers; child, family, and youth assistance organisations; alcoholism; family violence; drug abuse; and aging initiatives (Omorogiuwa, 2021). The categories of persons served and the job titles and responsibilities vary widely based on the workplace.

Nigeria's social services are offered by government agencies as stipulated under the statutory laws of the federal state of Nigeria. They are mandated as part of efforts to improve social welfare.

Other non-governmental organisations (NGOs) in Nigeria are involved in improving social welfare. These agencies include the NOK social intervention center, the Rotary Club, Lion's Club, and the Young Women's Christian Association (YWCA). In addition, the Jaycees provide humanitarian services to the poor and to underprivileged, homeless children, seniors, and physically and mentally impaired people, in offering services and programmes that reduce delinquency, illiteracy, poverty, and unemployment. With the high population of Nigeria, these agencies may be overwhelmed in offering these humanitarian services. Several agencies provide services to the underprivileged in the community, and trainee budgets are rarely considered (Fortune et al., 2001).

Inadequate human service agencies refer to insufficient agencies to cover social welfare needs in a given community or region. Social welfare programmes are often underdeveloped, underfunded, and underutilised in Nigeria. The resources available are severely inadequate compared to the number of people who seek assistance. Unlike wealthy countries, Nigeria lacks welfare benefits, which are a critical component of contemporary institutions. Child abandonment, criminality, kidnapping, cultism, drug trafficking, divorce, HIV/AIDS, and the difficulty of single parenting are serious societal concerns requiring prompt action (Ahmed et al., 2017). The inadequate social service agencies and the logistics involved in training lead to several organisations considering offering field education.

Engaging Students in Non-academic Activities during Field Practicum

Non-academic work refers to activities' students do outside of class to improve their abilities, such as internships, volunteer work, and extracurricular activities. Under social work field education programme, students can work in different settings, such as community development, hospice, psychiatric, etc. There are several steps/ways to involve students in field practicum based on the students learning agreement and level of skills required; however, these have to be disseminated so that a social worker's core values and principles are imparted to the learners. Thus, ensuring that students learning agreement, code of conduct during field placement, mission and vision of the service while in the field is not compromised or violated (Amadasun, 2019; Omorogiuwa, 2021).

The various stakeholders in fieldwork are thus required to be committed to offering field training to the learners without interfering with the organisation's routine activities and to giving the learners as much exposure as needed. The supervisor should gauge the student's ability to evaluate the confidentiality of a given study set and knowledge regarding the community structure (Choi et al., 2021). The legal requirements and rights regarding a problem at hand and the ability of learners to engage in problem-solving without jeopardising the client, organisation, or learner are indicators of a successful field practicum. The techniques involved in field practicum are observational, where the learners observe how the social workers acquire hands-on experience in the field. This helps them understand the social work structure and build their essential skills and knowledge of the traits of an undertaking by observation. Observational learning can be incorporated with hands-on real-life exposure so as to build confidence and critical thinking skills (Dennison et al., 2007). The ability of learners to relate to different organisations' dynamic structures and frameworks is a comparative method of offering field practicum. It may involve the learners taking part in several interrelated organisations and solving similar problems (Amadasun, 2019).

Students may be involved in a human rights organisation to defend the affected people in a dispute and offer services to the less privileged in the community. Several governmental and non-governmental organisations may not be ready to take on the learners in field practicum based on the sensitivity and the scope of the activities involved in the field; this has been seen in cases of humanitarian services (Dennison et al., 2007). Students benefit from social work field education in various ways, including obtaining pride in achieving more complex tasks; acquiring knowledge of specialties among participants; securing better treatment, greater responsibility, and respect from supervisors; and achieving improved general comprehension and skill advancement. The quantity of time students spend in homogeneously grouped settings and an excessive workload, and the perceived social/emotional stresses that may be taken, are some of the disadvantages (Tebb et al., 1996).

Conclusion

This chapter testifies to the important place of fieldwork in contributing to the training of social work students as extremely vital to effective social work practice. This chapter explores the structure of the social work field experience and the need to earnestly look into the practice methods in order to promote the worth of field experience. There exist insufficient field agencies and lessened engagement of students in activities not related to social work field experience. It also exposes the need for integrative seminars to enable students to receive feedback about their experiences at fieldwork placement. The chapter therefore concludes that core stakeholders/departmental administrators should liaise with other social service organisations to create a platform for training and retraining key staff to ensure effective practical experiences for students.

Implications for Schools of Social Work Administrators

Based on the analysis in this chapter, implications are made to schools of social work administrators and field education coordinators in Nigeria to anticipate the occurrence of such encounters among students during their field practicum.

1) As core stakeholders in the preparation of the next generation of social workers, departmental administrators could create an avenue to liaise with other social service organisations that are desirous of imparting genuine knowledge to students. Fortunately, virtually all states in Nigeria have an abundance of statutory and voluntary organisations that are more than willing to thoroughly share their experience with students (Amadasun, 2021). These organisations range from being faith-based to social development–oriented and are open to partnership with departments of social work in the country.

2) Social work administrators/field education coordinators in conjunction with social service administrators or instructors could work together to create a platform for training and retraining key staff so that the issue of engaging students in frivolous tasks (which are not helpful to their professional development) is drastically reduced. As administrators and educators, we are answerable for ensuring that students become fully proficient following their graduation. One way in which such synergy may be concretised is through pre- and post-placement integrative seminars (Omorogiuwa, 2011). By facilitating seminars involving key faculty members and agency staffs, the issue of discontent by social work students with their field practice experience may be adequately addressed.

Recommendations

1. The improvement on practicum model that match developmental social work.
2. The prospect of co-supervision in field practicum
3. Possibility of initiatives to strengthen students' relationship with agency supervisors.

Further Reading

Garthwait, C. I. (2021). *Social Work Practicum: Preparation for Practice* (8th ed). NJ: Pearson Education Inc.

References

Ahmed, H. G. et al. (2017). 'Social welfare scheme; A neglected component of public health care services in Nigeria', *MOJ Public Health*, 5(3), 101–104.

Amadasun, S. (2019). 'Mainstreaming a developmental approach to social work education and practice in Africa? Perspectives of Nigerian BSW students', *Social Work and Education*, 6(2), 196–207.

Amadasun, S. (2021). 'Is the signature pedagogy still worthwhile? An empirical study of field practice experience among social work students in Nigeria', *Social Work Education*, 40(2), 229–243.

Birkenmaier, J. and Berg-Weger, M. (2007). *The Practicum Companion for Social Work: Integrating Class and Field Work*. New York: Allyn and Bacon.

Birkenmaier, J. et al. (2012). 'Knowledge outcomes within rotational models of social work field education', *Journal of Gerontological Social Work*, 55(4), 321–336.

Bogo, M. (2005). 'Field instruction in social work: A review of the research literature', *The Clinical Supervisor*, 24(1–2), 163–193.

Bogo, M. (2015). 'Field education for clinical social work practice: Best practices and contemporary challenges', *Clinical Social Work Journal*, 43(1), 317–324.

Choi, M. J. et al. (2021). 'Predictors of job satisfaction among New MSWs: The role of organizational factors', *Journal of Social Service Research*, 47(4), 458–472.

Damskey, M. (2011). *Social Work Field Placement*. Arizona: Northern Arizona University.

Dennison, S. T. et al. (2007). 'Students' perceptions of social work: Implications for strengthening the image of social work among college students', *Social Work*, 52(4), 350–360.

Department of Social Work (2021). *Social Work Field Education Manual: A Guide for Field Experience*. Benin City: Department of Social Work, University of Benin.

Du Plessis, C. (2011). 'Fourth-year Social Work Students' Experiences Relating to Their Social Work Practical Training at a Service-Learning Center of an Open and Distance Learning University'[Unpublished Master's thesis]. University of South Africa. http://hdl.handle.net/10500/4799.

Fortune, A. E. et al. (2001). 'Student learning processes in field education: Relationship of learning activities to quality of field instruction, satisfaction, and performance among MSW students', *Journal of Social Work Education*, 37(1), 111–124.

Garthwait, C. I. (2021). *Social Work Practicum: Preparation for Practice* (8th ed). NJ: Pearson Education Inc.

Gitterman, A. L. (1989). 'Field instruction in social work education: Issues, tasks and skills', *Clinical Supervisor*, 7(1), 77–91.

Harris, E. M. and Boys, S. K. (2021). 'Legal education for human rights work: Social work practicum students in forensic placements', *Journal of Human Rights and Social Work*, 6(1), 41–48.

Hasenfeld, Y. (2010). 'The attributes of human service organizations', *Human Services as Complex Organizations*, 2, 9–32.

Hicks, H. and Swan, P. (2007). 'Direct, facilitate enable the juxtaposition of the duty of care and the duty of disclosure in social work field education', *Social Work Education*, 26(1), 69–85.

Homonoff, E. (2008). 'The heart of social work: Best practitioners rise to challenges in field instruction', *The Clinical Supervisor*, 27(2), 135–169.

Larger, P. and Robbins, V. (2004). 'Guest Editorial: Field education: Exploring the future, expanding the vision', *Journal of Social Work Education*, 40(1), 3–11.

Larrison, T. and Korr, W. (2013). 'Does social work have signature pedagogy?', *Journal of Social Work Education*, 49(2), 194–206.

Liu, M. et al. (2013). 'Challenges in social work field education in China: Lessons from the western experience', *Social Work Education*, 32(2), 179–196.

Miller, J. et al. (2005). 'Field education Students and field instructors' perception of the learning process', *Journal of Social Work Education*, 19(1), 2–16.

Nobel, C. (2001). 'Researching field practice in social work education: Integration of theory and practice through the use of narratives', *Journal of Social Work*, 1(3), 347–360.

Omorogiuwa, T. B. E. (2011). 'The place of integrative seminar in social work education: The University of Benin experience', ***Knowledge Review: A Multidisciplinary Journal***, 23(4), 29–34.

Omorogiuwa, T. B. E. (2016). 'Field education an integral component of social work education: Students' perception of the learning process', ***Benue State University Journal of Education***, 16(1), 221–228.

Omorogiuwa, T. B. E. (2021). 'Overview, principles and objectives of field education'. In ***Social Work Field Education Manual: A Guide for Field Experience***. Benin City: Department of Social Work, University of Benin, 4–24.

Raskin, M. S. (1994). 'The Delphi study in field instruction revisited: Expert consensus on issues and research priorities', ***Journal of Social Work Education***, 30(1), 75–89.

Reichelt, S. and Skjerve, J. (2000). 'Supervision of inexperienced therapists: A qualitative analysis', ***The Clinical Supervisor***, 19(2), 25–43.

Reisch, M. and Jarman-Rohde, L. (2000). 'The future of social work in the United States: Implications for field education', ***Journal of Social Work Education***, 36(2), 201–214.

Rollins, W. (2020). 'Social worker–client relationships: Social worker perspectives', ***Australian Social Work***, 73(4), 395–407.

Savaya, R. et al. (2003). 'Congruence of classroom and field instruction in social work: An empirical study', ***Social Work Education***, 22(3), 297–308.

Tebb, S. et al. (1996). 'A renaissance of group supervision in practicum', ***The Clinical Supervisor***, 14(2), 39–51.

Wayne, J., Raskin, M. and Bogo, M. (2010). 'Field education as the signature pedagogy of social work education', ***Journal of Social Work Education***, 46(3), 327–339.

23
FIELD PRACTICUM IN SOCIAL WORK EDUCATION
The Ethiopian Experience

Demelash Kassaye

Abstract: English

The profound importance of field practicum in social work education is to help students learn in a professional setting, demonstrate skill, and integrate the theories and practices learned in and out of the classrooms. Fieldwork practicum is, therefore, a hallmark of social work to advance the values and practices of social work education. The primary objective of this chapter is to present the views of students, agency liaisons, and instructors' on field practice in Ethiopia. The study selected informants purposively based on their knowledge and affiliation with the field practicum. The findings show that students learn social work in culturally sensitive settings, working with diverse and at-risk populations. It further shows that it introduces and teaches them about indigenous knowledge and the value of helping people in real-life situations. However, the learning process is affected by a lack of commitment from the instructors' side, weak supervision of the agency liaisons, and students' hesitancy. The lack of mutual understanding of shared values between actors in field practicum has been identified as the source of challenges and suggests developing a new curriculum across Ethiopia.

Abstract: Amharic

በሶሻል ዎርክ ትምህርት የመስክ ልምምድ ዋናው አላማ ተማሪዎች በክፍል ውስጥ የተማሩአቸውን የንድፈ ሀሳብ እውቀቶች በእውኑ አለም ምን አንደሚመስሉ ለማየት የሚረዳቸውን መልካም አጋጣሚ መፍጠር ሲሆን ለሶሻል ዎርክ ትምህርት መሰረትም ነው። ስለዚህ የመስክ ልምምድ የሶሻል ዎርክ እሴቶችንና ተግባራትን የበለጠ ለማጎልበት የሚረዳ የሙያው ወሳኝ ክፍል ነው ተብሎ ይወሰዳል። የዚህ ምዕራፍ ዋናው ዓላማ የሶሻል ዎርክ ተማሪዎችን፣ ከተቋማት የሚመደቡ ቱተሮችንና የሶሻል ዎርክ ትምህርት ቤት መምህራንን እይታ ከመስክ ትምህርት አንጻር ማየት ነው። ጥናቱም ከመስክ ልምምድ ትምህርት ጋር ቅርበትና እውቀት ያላቸውን መረጃ ሰጭዎች ለይቶ መርጧል። የጥናቱ ግኝትም ተማሪዎች በብዙ ባህልና ልማዶች ውስጥ እንዴት መስራትና ለአደጋ ተጋላጭ የሆኑ የተለያዩ ሰዎችን መርዳት እንደሚቻል ለመረዳት አስችሎአቸዋል፤ ከዚህ በተጨማሪ በእውነታው አለም ውስጥ ያለውን ተጨባጭ ሁኔታ ከግምት ውስጥ አስገብቶ ርዳታ የሚፈልጉ ሰዎችን እንዴት መርዳት እንደሚችሉም አስተምሮአቸዋል። የሀገር በቀል እውቀቶችን ፋይዳም እንዲረዱ ረድቶአቸዋል። ነገር ግን የመስክ ትምህርት ሂደቱ ተግዳሮቶች ያጋጠሙት ሲሆን መነሻቸውም

276 DOI: 10.4324/9781003314349-27

የመምህራን ትኩረት ማነስ፣ ከተቋማት የሚመደቡ ረዳቶች ክትትል የሏና ተማሪዎች ለሙስክ ልምምዱ የሚሰጡት ትኩረት አነስተኛ መሆን ናቸው። ጥናቱ በመስክ ልምምድ ላይ የሚሳተፉ ወሳኝ ሰዎች የሶሻል ዎርክ እሴቶችን በእኩል ደረጃ ያላመረዳት ለተግዳሮቶቹ መነሻ መሆናቸውንም ለይቶአል። በመጨረሻም የሶሻል ዎርክ መምህራንን፣ የስርዐተ ትምህርት ቀራጮችንና ተቋማትን አንድ ላይ በማገናኘት በስራ ላይ ያለውን ካሪኩለም በመከለስ አዉዱን የዋጀ ካሪኩለም ቢዘጋጅ የሚል ምክረ ሀሳብ ሰጥቶአል።

Introduction

The primary objective of this chapter is to examine and reflect on social work field practicum in Ethiopia's social work education. Hamilton and Else (1983), define fieldwork in social work as a consciously planned set of experiences occurring in a practice setting designed to move students from their initial level of understanding, skills, and attitudes to levels associated with autonomous social work practice. The definition indicates that knowledge complemented by practice will last with the professionals. The chapter describing the learning outcomes of field practice in social work education confirms that it is decisive to meet the demand of producing professionals skillful in managing social problems at macro and micro levels. As is defined in various field practicum guidebooks (Field Practicum Manual, 2015), the main aim of assigning students to fields where human service is provided emphasises the necessity of integrating theoretical lessons obtained from classrooms with field practicum. To this end, the School of Social Work at Addis Ababa University developed a curriculum meeting the standards of global social work field practice (Field Practicum Manual, 2015). This chapter aims not to provide an exhaustive array of theories or issues to cover every unique practicum situation; rather, it provides insights into understanding the views and the critical reflections of actors engaged in the realisation of the curriculum. As noted by Nadesan (2020) and Bell and Anscombe (2013), field placement is a platform designed such that students will be engaged in testing the theories learned in classrooms with practices in their academic endeavors and gather additional knowledge, skills, and values to enhance their professional competencies in social work. Considering this, Shardow and Doel (1996, p. 6) observe that the two contexts for learning about cooperative practice, class, and fieldwork must be integrated, comprehensive, and mutually consistent. They further claim in substantiating the components that, besides creating the opportunity for students to explore reality, gives ample room to extract the needs of society. The curriculum designed for the undergraduate programmes of social work gives ample space for students to experience the realities that exist in real-life situations. Students learn to value that knowledge is complemented and refined by practice. In addition, the chapter provides data on the views and perspectives of actors in field practice and suggests a viable way forward for social work education in Ethiopia. It further deals with the founding elements of social work and its profound importance to connect learners with experiences. Likewise, studies examining the challenges of implementing field practicums in the school system are rare and scant. This chapter is, thus, projected to fill that gap and share with Africans and others the experiences gained from field practicum from an Ethiopian's point of view.

An Overview on Education in Ethiopia

Ethiopia is a country located in the Horn of Africa and one of the oldest countries in the world. It is a landlocked sovereign state bordered by Eritrea to the north, Sudan to the west, South Sudan to the southwest, Kenya to the south, Somalia to the east, and Djibouti to the northeast. It is the second most populous country in Africa. It became prominent in modern world affairs first in 1896, when it defeated colonial Italy in the Battle of Adwa, and again in 1935–1936, when it was invaded and occupied by fascist Italy. Ethiopia was among the first independent nations to give moral and material support to the decolonisation of Africa and the growth of Pan-African cooperation. Ethiopians are ethnically diverse, with the most significant differences based on linguistic categorisation. It has had its own alphabet and calendar since ancient times. Before Ethiopians were introduced to modern education, there were religious schools where children learned to write and read Ethiopian phonics and letters. Until the early 1900s, formal education was introduced under a system of religious instruction organised and presented under the aegis of the Ethiopian Orthodox Church. Church schools prepared students for ordained ministry as well as other religious duties and positions. In the process, these schools also provided religious education to the children of the nobility and the sons of a limited number of tenant farmers and servants associated with elite families. The main aim of the schools was to produce children to serve the Ethiopian churches, which required people who could write and read Ethiopian letters. Teachers in the schools were well known for their long years of experience in instructing children and serving the Ethiopian Orthodox Church.

Ethiopia was ruled by kings until the Socialist Military Government (Derg) came to power ousting the emperor and his subordinates in 1974, and it remained in power until 1991. Derg was socialist and promised to better serve the interests of the masses and alter the constitution with the aim of establishing a socialist society (Zewdie, 2000). Marxist-Leninist philosophy was the central theme that guided the country's political, economic, and social life. During the Derg government, this was the only time in Ethiopian history that education was conceptualised as an essential means to secure political power. As a result, the curriculum during this period was highly politicised and students were obliged to take courses in political education (Tekeste, 1990). Under the new rulership, it was difficult to transition from traditional models of education to modern and secular forms, as there were significant obstacles (Birhanu and Demeke, 1995). Some argue that the problems arose from the conservative attitude of church leaders and nobility. However, Ethiopia became a federalist state in 1991 when the Ethiopian People's Revolutionary Democratic Front (EPRDF) came to power and introduced the idea of 'self-determination for the nationalities', up to and including secession, devolving political, administrative, and economic power to ethnically defined regional states. Following the establishment of the new government in 1991, the constitution of the Federal Democratic Republic of Ethiopia recognised 10 regional states and two city administrations.

Social Work Education in Ethiopia

The first schools of Social Work in Africa opened in countries such as South Africa, Egypt, and Algeria between the years 1924 and 1942 (Mwansa, 2011). The historical development of social work in Africa has been significantly impacted by the international emergence and the long-lasting implications of contact with the West. As noted by Helmut (2014), colonialism and its concomitant mechanisms of modernisation in the post-colonial period have had a considerable impact on the way social work is conceptualised in Africa today. Social work in Africa has unique characteristics and specific forms of handling problems that are entirely different from experiences in the industrialised world. Moreover, colonialism fostered a deeply rooted belief that Western ideas and concepts were superior and irrevocable (Midgely, 2010). The significant problem encountered from Western dominance is that the unique characteristics of social work in Western communities are largely inappropriate in the African context.

The history of social work in Ethiopia is related to the opening of higher educational institutions. To mention a few, the first higher education institution in Ethiopia was Abadina Police

College, the then Ethiopian Police College, which opened to train police officers in 1946. Later, the first University College of Addis Ababa, then the Emperor Haile Sellasie I University was opened in 1951. The School of Social Work in Ethiopia was opened in 1959, eight years after the opening of the university. It was undertaken under a joint effort between the Ministry of Public Health and the United Nations Technical Assistance Board. The aim was to address the demand for trained personnel in medical social work to facilitate social services in medical facilities. The school started with a nine-month programme, which was later developed into a two-year diploma programme. In 1961, it was transferred to the Faculty of Arts at Haile Selassie I University and developed the four-year programme to offer a bachelor's degree in social work. However, the School was banned by the Socialist Military Government (Derg), when it came to power in 1974 (Robel, Demelash, and Tanja, 2021). The ban followed the decision of other Marxist-Leninist–oriented governments in post-colonial Africa (Noyoo and Tanja, 2019), which preferred handing over the responsibility of social service delivery to their respective mass-based organisations, such as socialist women's and youth groups. Consequently, the Derg regime rationalised its action of banning it by pointing out that it is a profession devastating the morale and participation of the productive youth, hence endangering the country's sovereignty and independence (Robel et al., 2021). The socialist government argued this was the only response to address human needs, including social welfare services (Stout, 2009). However, the new government that came into power after the ousting of the Derg government in 1991 launched a new era for social work in Ethiopia. The rebirth of social work at Addis Ababa University in 2004 led to the rapid expansion of social work across the country. Addis Ababa University, as the pioneer in promoting the profession opened various programmes, including a Masters in Social Work programme (MSW) in 2004, a doctoral degree in social work in 2006, and a Bachelor in Social Work programme (BSW) in 2008. Currently, three public universities – Jima University, Gondar University, and Bahr Dar University – and two private universities – Saint Marry University and Unity University –offer BSW and MSW programmes.

The mission of social work, as described by the National Association of Social Workers (NASW) 'is to enhance human well-being and help meet the basic human needs of all people with particular attention to the needs and empowerment of people who are vulnerable, oppressed, and living in poverty' (NASW, 1999, p. 1). The International Federation of Social Workers defines the purpose of social work as including the promotion of social change and the empowerment and liberation of people to enhance wellbeing (IFSW 2000, p. 1). Reviews of the definition further note that the mission of social work is to maintain a focus on marginalised peoples and their empowerment but add an emphasis on global and cultural sensitivity (Bidgood, 2003). The rebirth of social work education in Ethiopia came about after a series of meetings held between Ethiopian and American professors. The professors from abroad played a significant role in the reopening of the programme with MSW in developing the curriculum and teaching the first and second batches of students. The school began with graduate students and later developed to include doctoral students. Currently, the school offers both graduate and undergraduate programmes.

Moreover, the curriculum of BSW and MSW requires students to complete field practicum as a course prerequisite. Students are deployed for field practice in an organisation where social and human services are delivered. They work at all levels of society – from individuals and families to small groups and associations, communities, and organisations and at both governmental and non-governmental organizations. Moreover, the placement procedure considers the areas where people are at risk – those in conflict with the law, welfare organisations, civic society, clinics and hospitals, family courts, differently abled populations, and rural and urban sections of society. The field education in graduate and undergraduate programmes helps prepare generalist practitioners with three-unit modules for every year of the study level. The cumulative effects of learning social work in class and interpreting the values in field practice are worth noting in introducing the profession as a helping one. The international standard for practice set by IASSW and IFSW for social work practicum for undergraduate programmes is at least 400 hours to 1,000 hours of practice that can equip students with the social work skills, knowledge, values, and attitudes to help vulnerable social groups and the promotion of social justice. Students pursuing their BSW degree are required to spend at least 45 days and 360 hours each year in the field in addition to completing subjects in class, according to the curriculum. The field practicum allows the students to plan and implement various programmes. Fieldwork in social work is primarily a learning process and effective only if it facilitates learners to apply their knowledge to the situation.

Conceptual Framework, Teaching Paradigms, and Practical Implications

This chapter argues that field practicum is a comprehensive approach and the backbone of social work. Social work values, theories, and practices offer the opportunity to meaningfully provide professional services for marginalised/vulnerable groups. Professionalising services reduces the clumsiness and challenges of people making ethically informed decisions about how to act in each case. Students' enrolment in field practicum means learning skills, rendering services, and participating in the provision and development of social work services. The benefits they score from field practicum will enable them to understand the profession's purposes, values, and ethics. By doing field practicum, students acquire insights into various aspects of human life and confront a range of problems people experience in Ethiopia in their daily lives, which is unique to the social work profession. Social work is, thus, the field that has a practical element integrated into it, and the profession helps students test their theoretical knowledge learned in class and learn more about the field. Moreover, it fosters integration of empirical and practice-based knowledge and promotes professional competence development in enabling the people in need of help to become self-sufficient. On the one hand, it prepares students with the skills and knowledge to become professional social workers and exercise the responsibility of addressing people's problems. Thus, fieldwork is an essential instrument for developing the roles and responsibilities of diverse groups in the community to achieve social development. On the other hand, field practicum is a dynamic course that challenges students to apply social work knowledge, skills, and values within an organisational context. Meanwhile, studies conducted on social work field practicum in Ethiopia are inadequate, and carrying out extensive research is relevant to identify the challenges and the extent to which students are assisted to examine the reality in the real-life situation in Ethiopia and Africa in general.

The field practice curricula, as stated by Hutchings (1990), impart the capacity to perform, to put what one knows into practice (p. 1). However, Kramer (1998) emphasises that to help students to become capable and competent practitioners requires that they have training in self-awareness, knowledge acquisition, and skill building. Shebib (2003) further notes that practitioners need to have skills in four areas: relationship building, exploring or probing, empowering, and challenging. An essential additional skill is the ability to gain and utilise knowledge from practice (Dorfman, 1996). The curriculum of field practice asserts that students taking the course will be skilful in assessing the needs of client systems, especially the vulnerable populations from open community, neighbourhood formal or informal groups, and those in conflict with the law, welfare organizations, civic society, clinics and hospitals, family courts, networks of positive people, differently abled populations as well as rural-urban sections of society. The overarching objective of intervention will be to work towards improving the quality of life and promoting participatory development and social justice. In the process, they will learn how to apply the knowledge, skills, and professional value base taught in the classroom into their supervised field practice. Faculty as well as the fieldwork placement agencies jointly provide supportive supervisory inputs to train students and incrementally build their professional identity from the first to the third year. On the other hand, in an inductive mode, learning from field practicum will also be utilised in teaching relevant theory in courses. It is organised based on the knowledge requirements of real-world settings with an intensive time of practice.

Paradigm of Constructivism in Social Work Field Education

In the teaching and learning process, some favour the constructivists' paradigm, while others stress positivist thinking to help their students learn. Constructivism is based on the idea that people are active in constructing their own knowledge and determine reality using their own experiences. Constructivism is crucial in the course to understand the facets as an educator because it influences the way all the students learn. The paradigm is, therefore, concerned in defining the way knowledge is produced. As Windschitl (1999) notes, constructivism is based on the belief that learners work to create, interpret, and recognise knowledge in individual ways: 'these fluid intellectual transformations occur when students reconcile formal instructional experiences with their existing knowledge, with the cultural and social contexts in which ideas occur, with a host of other influences that mediate understanding' (Windschitl, 1999, p. 752). Gordon (2009) suggests that teachers promote experiences that require students to become active learners in the learning process. Freire (1970) notes that learning requires the active participation of students, and that knowledge arises out of a shared process of inquiry, interpretation, and creation. More specifically, Gorden cites Dewey (1988) in pointing out that genuine knowledge derives not in the abstract, but rather by integrating thinking and doing, by getting the mind to reflect on the act. Another element in pragmatic constructivism is attributed to Freire (1970), namely, a notion that complements the importance of problem-solving education, where the teacher is no longer the one who only teaches, but one who also learns through dialogue with the students. Likewise, students in this prospect are not only learners, but also take over the responsibility of being a co-teacher in the learning process. In Ethiopia, the approach taken in social work education is to let the students interpret the theoretical lessons learned in class based on the reality of worldviews. Freire's model reflected in this review advocates social work field education in co-teaching in Ethiopian field education. By doing this, students are engaged in actualising the pedagogical approach, Freire has stressed the profound importance of students' active participation during field practice.

Integrating Theory and Practice in Social Work

Different reviews made to show the relationship between theory and practice strongly confirm the profoundness of creating the platform to attest the compatibility of social work in the real world. Its importance is indisputable in the real world in viewing the theories covered in classroom as being representative of the real world. A review of the literature on the integration of theory and practice within the social work discipline uncovers several studies that found that graduates of social work degree programmes felt that their classwork had not adequately prepared them for real-world practice (Clapton and Cree, 2004). Thompson (2000) strongly suggests that 'there is an unacceptable gap between theory and practice, a disjuncture between what is taught or learned and what is practiced.... Theory has come to be seen as the preserve of the academic and practice as the domain of the practitioner' (p. 84). Remarks of Clapton and Cree (2004) place emphasis on the subject and conclude that there is a need for learning models that integrate theory and practice in ways that bring the field into the classroom as well as take the classroom into the field. They further note that the goal expected to appear at the end should be pursued throughout the student's educational experience.

Method of the Study

The qualitative research method was employed to understand the case in depth. It is the strategy selected to allow people to reflect their views in multiple ways. Creswell (2009) states that, in the constructivist paradigm, meanings are subjective, and individuals give the definition based on their experience. According to Creswell (2013), in social constructivism the meanings developed from the subjective understanding of the participants are multiple and differ from each other. To extract the challenges and views of students, liaisons and instructors who support field practice, its process, and implementation, the study considered the constructivist worldview as a guide to explore the participants' views. To this end, informants were selected using purposive sampling, and nine students, five liaisons working in clinical and community services, and six faculty supervisors were identified. To meet the benefits Mack et al. (2005), describes in probing the subjective understanding, perspective, and opinions of the participants on how they define the situation, in-depth interviews were employed. It was initially produced in Amharic and translated into English. Items in an in-depth interview were crafted to gather views and perceptions of the interviewees on field practice in general. Furthermore, the author interviewed all of them, with each interview lasting around 1.5 hours. Data collected from the interview were subject to thematic analysis. Coding, categorising, giving meaning, and identifying themes were applied in the data analysis process at the end. As mentioned in the previous sections, the prime objective of this chapter is to fill in the gaps that are untapped and contribute to the existing body of knowledge on field practicum.

Findings

The findings of the study include the views of students, challenges in the learning process, culture sensitive and indigenous knowledge, views of liaisons and supervisors, and the commitment and determination of faculties.

Views of Students on Field Practicum

Field practicum is one of the required criteria and covering the hours of the total credit to graduate is mandatory. Moreover, it exposes students to knowledge, skills, and values of work in respecting the working procedures, ethical standards, and operational frameworks of different organisations. Students gain credit in the field practicum in testing their competence in the practical world. Bearing this in mind, the following evidence is summed up:

> Third-year students are placed in human and social service organizations three times each year. From the field practicum, they learn more about social work in real-life situations. However, they critique the theories discussed in class are not matching with the realities on the ground. It is because the social work curriculums are copied from developed nations. It means not customized as per the socio-cultural realities of the country, as reflected by the students.

Besides the drawbacks mentioned above students added:

> Field practicum is worth noting in social work education. The curriculum clearly states that the objective is to get students to learn social work in practice. By taking the course, they learn various skills, such as skills of communication and solving community problems.

Students are placed in organisations where human and community services are delivered. They reflected that field education helped them to obtain knowledge from real-life situations. Nevertheless, indigenising the curricula derived from developed nations with home-grown knowledge is crucial to make the learning process more productive.

Challenges in the Learning Process of Field Practicum

Challenges in field practicum are reported to be of several types. They arise from the staff and agency liaisons where students are assigned. Students discussed the challenges in mentioning the commitments to strict supervision and mentoring.

> The school of social work at Addis Ababa University (AAU) signed the Memorandum of Understanding (MoU) with welfare organizations, civic society, clinics and hospitals, and family courts to deploy students for field practice. They were assigned in the hospital where patients are receiving clinical treatments. The liaison assigned to facilitate in the hospital introduced them with the ethical principles and working procedures that they must comply. However, the liaison was not mentoring us daily, and thus unable to get further consultation on matters aligned with social work in clinics. We are unlucky not to have learned more about clinical social work from her experience as the agency liaison.

Overall, students were not happy with the mentorship from the liaisons being too loose. They said that they are not even fair in evaluating students' performance and give exceedingly high grades whether they are present or absent. The main problem, as reflected by the students, refers to the fact that they see mentoring students as their second job.

Culture-sensitive Field Practice and Indigenous Knowledge

Students placed in governmental and non-governmental agencies take various courses, such as community development, clinical social work, and social work methods and practice, before deployment. The course aims at endowing students with the required knowledge and skills to manage a diversity of cultures, social norms, and religious domains. In this regard, the following prospect is made:

> Social work comprises courses addressing concepts dealing with culture, environment, and social norms. Knowledge of diverse nature of culture, religion, and social norms is said to deliver professionally sound services. Because social work is a culturally sensitive profession, requesting everyone to at least know about the area to provide professionally renowned services. The agencies where they are located accommodate people with diverse interests arising from their cultural and religious backgrounds. The knowledge emanating from these is undoubtedly valuable to often make indigenous knowledge part of the curricula.

Additional points were made in supporting the abovementioned ideas:

> The field practicum is a course designed to relate students to reality on the ground. It is an eye-opening experience to meet people for the first time as a student. The benefit of field practice relates to learning how to foster relations with people having diverse interests, cultural backgrounds, and norms. In addition, it equips them with skills of problem-solving and communication. The students have praised the benefits they were able to secure in relation to knowing the value of culture to help clients accordingly.

The curriculum in field education is developed based on the courses covered in classrooms. The courses share values stated in human interaction, culture, environment, and social norms. The aim is indeed to prepare graduates to be informed about real contexts that exist in the social system in delivering professionally heightened services.

Views of Liaisons and Supervisors of Field Practicum

Liaisons in the field practicum are those members of the organisations to which students are assigned. An agreement entered with agencies forces all to act accordingly. The signatories are responsible for advising students in the apprenticeship. The following are some of the interviewees' reflections on the role supervisors and agency liaisons play in field practice.

> We as liaisons and supervisors are assigned to closely observe students' performance in field practice. From experience, we were able to lean that it is decisive to students' knowledge and skill in solving problems. It is undeniable fact that there are drawbacks from the liaisons side in strictly following and reporting the students' performance to the instructor from the school.

The agency liaisons are lenient in following students' performance in field practicum. It has been one of the causes contributing a lot to achieving less. They have commented on the importance of intensive mentorship to shape students and teaching in the life course of field education.

Developing Independent learning

Independent learning is a learning process students do on their own rather than relying solely on the materials teachers hand them. Students in field practicum take ownership of their educational path by setting their own goals and objectives to meet the end. To put it simply, it is when students set goals and monitor and evaluate the impact of field practicum to manage their motivation towards learning.

> Students develop independent learning because it engages them through their presence at field placements to provide services to needy. Those who are there are true with diverse interests requiring the critical looking of students into that. Letting them think independently about solutions and evaluating the outcome in alleviating the problem helps them later too. Instructors favouring interactive learning are suitable to the field practice with the belief to enhance students' independent learning.

The benefits students cultivate from the learning process in field practicum bring a relative advantage to undoubtedly develop self-reliance in learning. As pointed out above, they commented on the importance that the instructors with the teaching methods of interactive learning in their teaching paradigm helped students develop the modality of independent learning.

Faculty Commitment to Field Practicum

Field practicum will be successful only if the faculties are committed and give high priority to learning from practice. The role of faculties in field practice is irrevocable in the teaching and learning process. To this end, they are expected to regularly check students' presence in the agencies through attendance and other mechanisms. Reluctance of faculty to do this and less attention paid yields less success.

> Staff in the school of social work are with above fourteen years of teaching experiences. They believe that field practice helps students learn how to solve problems in a diverse society. The manual of the field practice stated the jobs and responsibilities of agency liaisons and field supervisors in clear terms. Both follow similar manuals validated in 2004. However, students condemn the staff for their improper treatment and guidance. It is, of course, impossible to create a problem-free zone, but it is possible to minimize the magnitude of the problem.

In support of the lack of commitment observed from the faculties:

> The unique demand to make the field practicum productive in bringing attitudinal change among students is the faculty's commitment to supervising the students' performance in the clinics, hospitals, courts, and community service organizations. It may be a hasty generalization to say that most faculties are careless and barren of changing the attitudes of students in social work through field practice. However, they are reckless to mentor the same as in class.

From the above comments, one can learn that instructors who have teaching experience over fourteen years. They teach in the school with the belief that field practice is a backbone to enhance the professional competence of social work in helping people with multiple interests. But their commitment to strictly mentor students is yet under question.

Conclusion

The primary objective of this chapter was to critically examine the perspective of actors enrolling in the field practicum of social work education at the School of Social Work, Addis Ababa University. Social work education was started during the regime of the emperor and closed for a while by the Socialist Government of Derg, which seized power in 1974. Derg was socialist-oriented to better serve the interests of the masses and alter the constitution towards establishment of a socialist society (Zewdie, 2000). Marxist-Leninist philosophy was the leading philosophical thought in advancing the socioeconomic and political development of the country. The curriculums during this period were highly dominated by the philosophical ideology of promoting the concept of proletariat and socialism. Social work in Africa is dominated by western perspectives, practices, and philosophy of education. Moreover, colonialism fostered a deeply rooted belief that western ideas and concepts were superior and irrevocable of emulation (Midgley, 2010). The international standard of practice set by IASSW and IFSW for social work practicum for undergraduate programmes is expected to cover 400 hours to 1,000 hours with the aim of endowing students with the social work skills, knowledge, values, and attitudes to help vulnerable social groups and the promotion of social justice. Students pursuing their BSW degree are required to spend at least 45 days and 360 hours each year in the field in addition to completing subjects in class, according to the curriculum.

Field practicum is vital in social work education to meet students with the reality on the ground. It also helps them test their competence to determine social work as a lifelong career. As explained by Friedlander (1963), fieldwork aims to integrate the academic knowledge, practical understanding, and personal skills of the students through personal contact and give guidance to clients. His opinion is in conjunction with the perspectives of agency liaisons and instructors assigned to field practice. Students expressed their views by pointing out that they are not getting proper support and mentorship from the liaisons and the instructors. The report summarised the perspectives of students, liaisons, and instructors' points of view and agreed upon the pitfalls that caused the field practicum to lag a bit in achieving the expected outcomes. Students perceive the result of field practicum differs from their expectations because of various facts encountered at the time of application. They take it for granted that they can have fun and relax. It is a course where they can score high grades and make up for their deficit in terms of marks for graduation. Agency liaisons are not seeing the field practicum as their regular job and consider it a burden for nothing. Instructors have failed to strictly follow students under their supervision to achieve duties and responsibilities. On the other hand, students agreed on the relevance of field practicum in pointing out that it is so helpful to enhance the skill of identifying and solving community problems in a diverse group. They further noted that they cultivate indigenous knowledge and learn the potential advantage one can secure pursuant to the cultural values and social norms functioning in the community. The chapter called the attention of educators and social work professors to spend some time developing empirically designed programmes that can produce professionals well equipped with the social work values and theories enriched through field practicum. The field practicum is said to be the backbone of social work in giving students the qualifications they need to run the professional service at micro, meso, and macro levels.

Recommendations

1. The Ethiopian schools of social work should conduct an extended form of review to identify the gaps and fill them in to increase the capacity of field education in producing students physically and psychologically ready to challenge problems in the real world.
2. It is recommended that African social work give major emphasis to field practicum to produce students equipped with the necessary knowledge and practical skills to solve social problems.
3. Association of Schools of Social Work in Ethiopia and Africa should unite to develop an Ethiopian and African curriculum promoting indigenous knowledge to bring radical change on the educational system in the era of the post-colonial period.

Further Reading

Donald, C., Barbara, T. and Richard, M. (1992). *The Social Work Practicum: A Student Guide*. Peacock Publishers.

Freire, P. (1970). *Pedagogy of the Oppressed* (Original work published 1970). Translated by Myra Bergman Ramos. New York, NY: Continuum.

References

Bell, K. and Anscombe, A. (2013). International field experience in social work: Outcomes of a short-term study abroad Programmeme to India. *Social Work Education*, 32(8), 1032–1047.

Bidgood, B., Holosko, M. and Taylor, L. (2003). A new working definition of social work practice: A turtle's view. *Research on Social Work Practice*, 13(3), 400–408.
Birhanu, D. and Demeke, M. (1995). Education for production in Ethiopia. In W. Hoppers, D. Clapton, and V. Cree (eds.) *Integration of Learning for Practice: Literature Review. Learning for Effective and Ethical Practice*. Edinburgh: Scottish Institute for Excellence in Social Work Education. http://www.iriss.org.uk/files/LEEP11 litRev.pdf.
Creswell, J. (2009). *Research Design: Qualitative, Quantitative, and Mixed Methods Approach* (3rd ed.). London: SAGE Publications.
Creswell, J. (2013). *Qualitative Inquiry and Research Design: Choosing among Five Approaches* (3rd ed.). London: SAGE Publications.
Dewey, J. (1988). The quest for certainty. In J. A. Boydston (ed.) *The Latter Works, Vol. 4: 1929* (p. 30). Carbondale, IL: Southern Illinois University Press.
Dorfman, R. A. (1996). *Clinical Social Worker: Definition, Practice, and Vision*. New York, NY: Brunner/Mazel.
Field Practicum Manual (2015). *Bachelor of Social Work (BSW) Field Practice Manual*. School of Social Work, Addis Ababa University. Unpublished.
Freire, P. (1970). *Pedagogy of the Oppressed* (Original work published 1970) Translated by Myra Bergman Ramos. New York, NY: Continuum.
Friedlander, W. (1963). *Introduction to Social Welfare*. India: Prentice Hall of India (Private) Limited.
Gordon, M. (2009). Toward a pragmatic course discourse of constructivism: Reflections on lessons from practice. *Educational Studies*, 45(1), 39–57.
Hamilton, N. and Else, J. (1983). *Designing Field Education: Philosophy, Structure, and Process*. Springfield, IL: Charles C. Thomas.
Helmut, S. (2014). *Social Work in African Contexts: A Cross-Cultural Reflection on Theory and Practice*. Kampala, Uganda: Fountain Publisher.
Hutchings, P. (1990). *Assessment and the Way It Works: Closing Plenary Address, Association of Higher Education Conference on Assessment*. Washington, DC.
International Federation of Social Workers (IFSW) (2000). *New Definition of Social Work*. Berne: International Federation of Social Workers.
Kramer, B. (1998). Preparing social workers for the inevitable: A preliminary investigation of a course on death, grief, and loss. *Journal of Social Work Education*, 34(2), 211–227.
Mack, N., Woodsong, C., MacQueen, K., Guest, G. and Namey, E. (2005). *Qualitative Research Methods: A Data Collector's Field Guide*. Family Health International (FHI).
Midgley, J. (2010). The theory and practice of development social work. In J. Midgley and A. Conley (eds.) *Social Work and Social Development. Theories and Skills for Development Social Work* (pp. 3–28). Oxford: Oxford University Press.
Mwansa, L. (2011). Social work education in Africa: Whence and whither? Social work education. *The International Journal*, 30(1), 4–16.
Nadesan, V. (2020). Social work supervision in a developing country: Experiences of students. *Indian Journal of Social Work*, 81(3), 263–282.
National Association of Social Workers (NASW) (1999). *Code of Ethics*. Washington, DC: NASW Press. http://www.naswc.org/publs/code/.asp.
Noyo, N. and Tanja, K. (2019). *Decolonizing Social Work Practice and Social Work Education in Postcolonial Africa*. London: Routledge.
Robel, A., Demelash, K. and Tanja, K. (2021). *Overcoming the Socioeconomic Impacts of the Coronavirus Pandemic: Social Work Practice and Postcolonial Reflections from Ethiopia*. London: Springer.
Shardlow, S. and Doel, M. (1996). *Practice Learning and Teaching*. Basingstoke: Macmillan.
Shebib, B. (2003). *Choices: Counseling Skills for Social Workers and Other Professionals*. Boston, MA: Allyn and Bacon.
Stout, C. E. (2009). *The New Humanitarians: Inspiration, Innovations, and Blueprints for Visionaries*, Vol. 2. Westport: Praeger.
Tekeste, N. (1990). *The Crisis of Ethiopia Education: Some Implications for Nation Building*. Uppsala, Sweden: Uppsalo University.
Thompson, N. (2000). *Theory and Practice in Human Services*. Buckingham: Open University.
Windschitl, M. (1999). The challenges of sustaining a constructivist classroom culture. *Phi Delta Kappon*, 80, 751–757.
Zewdie, M. (2000). *A Study Guide for Curriculum Implementation and Evaluation*. Addis Ababa University. Unpublished Teaching Materials for the Course Educ.676.

24
FAMILY GENOGRAM AS AN EXPERIENTIAL METHOD TO ENHANCE TRAINING IN SOCIAL WORK PRACTICE IN BOTSWANA

Tumani Malinga

Abstract: English

Social work education and training furnishes students with knowledge, skills, and requisite tools for practice. However, studies in Africa have indicated that there are gaps in social work curricula due to over-reliance on didactic teaching methods. Studies have argued the need to have practice courses that can equip students with knowledge and skills for competent and elective practice. This chapter promotes the use of a family genogram as an experiential teaching tool in social work practice courses in Botswana to impart knowledge, skills, and techniques in working with families. The experiential method is proposed as a 'bridge between knowing what and applying how, connecting the doing with theoretical knowledge'. The benefits are that it helps students to understand and conceptualise concepts, enhances communication between lecturer and student; and promotes student self-understanding and self-introspection. Due to its benefits, it is recommended that social work educators in Africa adopt experiential teaching methods for practice courses to allow for self-understanding, introspection, and reflection. Also, educators should adopt student-centred and participatory learning to allow for collaboration instead of students being passive learners.

Introduction

Social work is a practice-based profession and an academic discipline that promotes social change and development, social cohesion, and the empowerment and liberation of people (International Federation of Social Workers (IFSW), 2014). As a practiced-based profession social work requires a combination of both theoretical and practical learning. These two components carried out within the university classroom and outside through field placement in social work–based agencies are critical for preparing students to become professional social workers (Papouli, 2014). Social work education should have a curriculum that provides a field education component since academic courses alone are not enough to prepare social work professionals (IFSW, 2020). Social work students are expected to engage in field practice during their training as a way of exposing them to reality and giving them an opportunity to practice what they have learnt in the classroom. Field practice is rich in that it provides students with the 'opportunity to deepen their knowledge about the social work profession through active participation in it' (Papouli, 2014 5).

However, new social work graduates in the United Kingdom (UK) have reported a hard clash with reality, labelled as a 'Baptism of Fire' when they first joined the workforce (Bates et al., 2010, p. 152), or 'a reality shock' (Jack and Donnellan, 2010, p. 309), despite having engaged in field practice. On one hand, it has been reported that there is a lack of statutory placement and exposure to legal interventions in the UK (Bates et al., 2010). On the other hand, issues of accountability as a qualified professional, as opposed to being a student, were raised as concerns (Jack and Donnellan, 2010). Similar sentiments were raised by Kang'ethe (2014) who reported that social workers in Botswana and South Africa are not adequately trained to handle contemporary development challenges. Jongman and Tshupeng (2020) also argue that some social workers in Botswana are not competent to handle casework.

To ensure that social work professionals effectively fulfil their mandate, to enhance human wellbeing and functioning, with particular attention to the needs and empowerment of people who are vulnerable, oppressed, and living in poverty, there should be context-based and alignment between social work practice and the needs of the local people as well as relevance through using appropriate strategies and methodologies in teaching (Mupedziswa and Sinkamba, 2014). A good fit of the social work professional should be emphasised in the education and training of social workers. This is so because social work education and training furnishes students with knowledge, skills, and an appreciation of local philosophy and requisite tools of the trade for contextualised practice (Mupedziswa and Sinkamba, 2014). They further argue that relevance should start with education to better inform practice in any given context.

It is critical therefore, for social work students to have a realistic understanding of what they are taught in the classroom by linking it with real-world experiences. This can be done through introducing experiential learning methods in the classroom, such as constructing and analysing family genograms. As argued by IFSW (2020), such methods can expose students to, and equip them with, knowledge and values for ethical, competent, and elective practice. Students need this initial preparation since, during field practice, they work with real clients, in real settings, and need to ensure they are able to support clients and work from an anti-oppressive perspective that is culturally relevant.

Tham and Lynch (2014) report that students wished for practice courses that prepare for, and expose them to, practical skills. In such courses, they can learn how family and childhood experiences have an impact on individuals' attitudes, beliefs, values, personalities and behaviours (Cournoyer, 2016) and how it can influence practice. Cournoyer (2016, p 36) further states that 'unless you are keenly aware of the influence of your family experiences, you may inadvertently or unconsciously play out a family role or pattern in your work with clients and colleagues'. It is on this premise that this chapter adopts, describes, and promotes the use of family genogram as a teaching tool in social work practice courses to impart knowledge, skills, and techniques in working with families.

This chapter proposes the use of family genograms as an experiential method to support effective teaching and learning in practice courses, a way to make certain that students are equipped with the necessary skills even before they embark on field practice. Including family genograms in practice courses exposes students to the reality that social work practice is not only focused on the individual, but also has a collective orientation in assessing and addressing family dynamics, relationships, and challenges. Intergenerational family genograms is a method 'to become aware of how our families influence us' (Cournoyer, 2016, p. 36). Even though this is deemed a Western model, Mupedziswa and Sinkamba (2014, p.145) argue that it can be helpful as some of these Western models and approaches have been 'tested, and tried with universal appeal and application'.

Social Work Education

Social work education prepares students to be competent and ethical professional social workers. One of the objectives of the Global Standards for Social Work Education and Training is to 'ensure that the next generation of social workers have access to excellent quality learning, opportunities that also incorporate social work knowledge deriving from research, experience, policy and practice' (IFSW, 2014). Social work curriculum 'should prepare students to understand the interconnectedness of practice at all levels – individual, family, group, organization, community, etc. (i.e., micro, mezzo, macro) (IFSW, 2014). This broader understanding will help students to become critical, ethical and competent practitioners'.

In Africa, social work education and practice can be traced back to the colonialisation era. As a result, social work education and practice were inherited from Western ex-colonial power (Veta and McLaughlin, 2022). Despite this inheritance setting the foundation of the social work profession in the African continent, limitations have been observed. One limitation is that the theories and methods used are foreign to the African context and its people (Twikirize and Spitzer, 2019). Based on this premise, Veta and McLaughlin (2022) propose that African social work education and practice should adopt the 'person and environment' framework as it addresses problems from the root cause. This framework adopts the intrapersonal and social interactions, among other factors, to improve clients and their environment (Monkman, 1991). This chapter therefore proposes the use of the 'person and environment' framework where social work educators in Africa are encouraged to adopt the use of experiential learning methods, such as the family genogram, as opposed to relying only on the didactic teaching method.

A didactic teaching method is where the student is a passive learner and the educator controls the content (Friedman, 2008). A didactic teaching method limits trainees in developing the cultural awareness and sensitivity that is crucial for practice (Warkentin, 2017). As knowledge, attitudes, and skills are imparted to students during their training, adopting experiential methods ensures knowledge and skill development (Warkentin, 2017).

The need to ensure that social work in context and in practice components are considered simultaneously in training to ensure that graduates have relevant exposure is also emphasised (IFSW, 2020). In addition to these components, attention should also be paid to the methods of instruction to ensure fully rounded social work graduates. One way of achieving this, as this chapter argues, is the use of the family genogram as an experiential method in teaching. The importance of ensuring that students are knowledgeable and appreciative of their own family of origin relationships through drawing their own family genograms is emphasised as a way of instilling skills and techniques as well as ensuring that students are better prepared mentally for practice (Cournoyer, 2016).

Botswana Context

Botswana is a landlocked country in sub-Saharan Africa with a population of about 2.3 million (Statistics Botswana, 2021). The population is concentrated in the southeastern and eastern regions of the country (Statistics Botswana, 2021). There are many ethnic groups, and, amongst them, there are eight principal groups: Bangwato, Bakwena, Bangwaketse, Bakgatla, Barolong, Batlokwa, Balete, and Batawana, and smaller groups are incorporated amongst the principal groups. Botswana is a culturally homogenous country as all the groups have similar basic beliefs and customs (Dryden-Peterson and Mulimbi, 2017).

Botswana secured its independence from Britain on 30 September 1966. At independence, Botswana was one of the poorest countries in Africa, with a GDP per capita of about US$70. Pre-colonial times Botswana had strong traditional social structures consisting of the extended family and communal support guided by the spirit of Ubuntu. The family structure in Botswana has experienced some changes due to social changes that have prevailed since independence. The extended family, which provided closely knit communities for social support, is slowly being replaced by nuclear and single-parent families. As a result, Botswana has encountered challenges, such as economic disparities, poverty, and crime, among others (Murray and Parsons, 2016). The family system has also been adversely affected as shown by family conflicts, divorce, and other dynamics that have hampered the standard of living and wellbeing of families (Mupedziswa et al., 2021). The government, however, has continued its efforts to intensify and improve the standard of living through comprehensive social protection and welfare programmes (BIDPA and World Bank, 2013), which are at the core of the work of social work professionals, who engage in assessments and development of interventions to address family and community challenges.

Social Work Training in Botswana

Social work training in Botswana was introduced in 1985 at the University of Botswana (UB), where it equips students with emerging knowledge, technology, skills, and techniques to develop their confidence and potential through a variety of innovative and time-tested pedagogical activities. The Social Work Department offers a two-year diploma, four years bachelor, full-time and part-time masters, and doctorate in social work degrees. Undergraduate training is generalist and specialisation is for graduate programmes (Department of Social Work, 2009). In training students, the Social Work Department at UB adheres to international professional standards, and it includes two primary components: theory and fieldwork practice. The theory component is offered in class-based activities while fieldwork practice is where students are placed for block placements across the country in social work–based agencies. The fieldwork component provides practical experience to strengthen the links among knowledge, skills, and practice (Department of Social Work, 2021). Since social work is an applied discipline, it is imperative that students integrate classroom learning with fieldwork (Kealey, 2010).

Over the years, social work has had to deal with complex social problems in the country, as the country experienced the breakdown of the traditional welfare practices that have always cushioned the majority of those faced with challenges. On that note, there has been a need for professional social workers with competencies to deal with these modern-day challenges. The Department of Social Work at the University of Botswana has as its mandate training competent social workers who can engage in direct practice, group work, community service organisation/development, social action, social work research, and social administration. Since social work training was introduced, the Department of Social Work has continued to improve the curriculum to ensure that it not only relies on the didactic teaching method, but also adopts the 'intentional learning' that encourages active and blended learning (University of Botswana, 2008).

Family Genogram

The concept of genogram was first introduced by Bowen in his family systems model in the 1970s (Stagoll and Lang, 1980). In the 1980s, McGoldrick and Gerson promoted the use of genograms in clinical settings in their publication *Genograms: Assessment and Intervention* in 1985. Family genograms provides a graphic representation of parties involved and a chronology of critical events and themes, and it illustrates that individual problems are linked to how family systems interact (Huss and Kapulnik, 2021). It also provides a visual of hereditary patterns and psychological factors that punctuate relationships (McGoldrick, 2016; McGoldrick et al., 2020). In addition, it represents relationship patterns within a family (McGoldrick et al., 2020). Through a family genogram, a hypothesis about an individual's psychosocial characteristics and family patterns can be developed (McGoldrick et al., 2020). They show graphic records of families' membership and interpersonal relationships, map family systems, and provide understanding of recurring patterns within the family structure, themes, and events, and they illustrate the history of traumas, deaths, and transitions over generations using universal symbols (Huss and Kapulnik, 2021; McGoldrick, 2016). They also reveal intergenerational transmission of family patterns (McGoldrick et al., 2020), family history, as well as promoting cultural knowledge (McGoldrick et al., 2011). It has to be noted that even though the original concept of family genogram was concentrated on the emotional characteristics of relationships in the family, broadly, genograms can be used for contextual factors and how they influence family functioning (Puhlman et al., 2023).

Case Study 1 is used to illustrate how the basic genogram symbols are used to depict a family's demographic information, Figure 24.1 and Figure 24.2 show how the family members relate to each other.

Case Study 1

Lesogo, a 15 year old, was referred to the Letsema JSS social worker after he was caught smoking marijuana in the school toilets by a teacher on duty. Lesego is the first born of three children. Lesego admitted that he started smoking marijuana when he was 13 years old and that his parents recently found out about his smoking habit. His relationship with his mother Nora (43 years) has

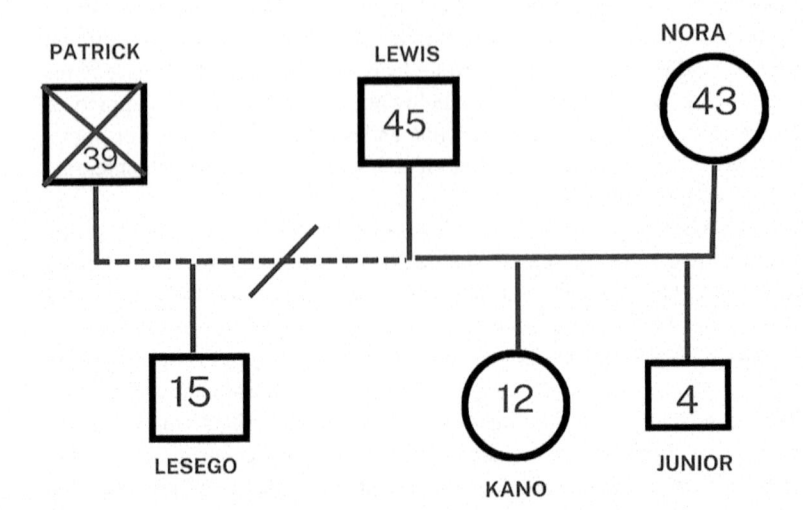

Figure 24.1 Lesego family genogram with demographic data

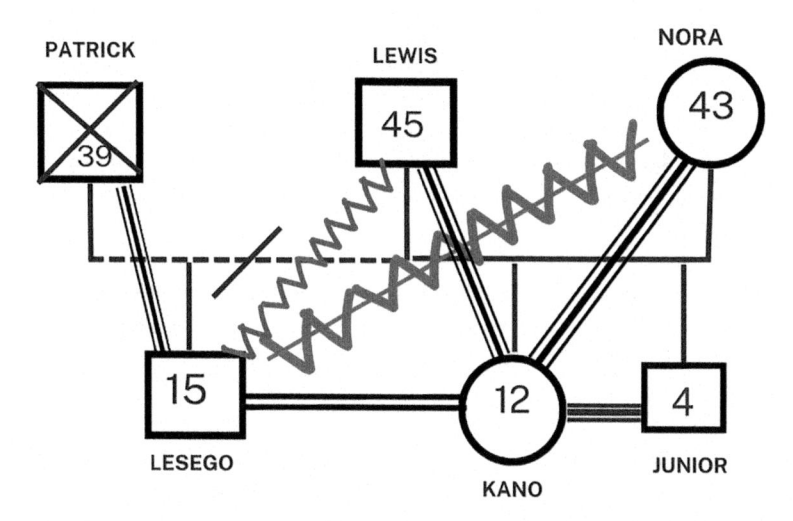

Figure 24.2 Lesego family genogram showing demographic information and relationships

become sour. He does not have a good relationship with his stepfather Lewis (45 years). He said that he feels excluded from the family because he is so uncomfortable around them. He would rather be alone in his room or in the neighbourhood with his friends. He said that he does not talk a lot to his mother anymore because she lets relatives know about his smoking habit and his poor performance at school. He reported that he has one 12-year-old sister, Kano, and a four-year-old half-brother, Junior. He said that Kano is doing well at school and she is the family's favourite. He reports that he resents his sister as she is the family's favourite. He said that sometimes he misses his 'real' father, Patrick, who died after a short illness when he was seven years old. He said that his father would be 46 now if he were alive. His father and mother stayed together but were not married. His mother married Lewis when Lesego was 10 years old. Lesego reports that he is not close to his stepfather as he is always reprimanding him.

Family genogram benefits have been well documented. A family genogram is a diagram illustrating emotional processes in the family (McGoldrick et al., 2020: Puhlman et al., 2023), which explore the history of intergenerational family relationships and dynamics, and it can serve as an assessment and intervention tool (DeMaria, 2013; McGoldrick, 2016; McGoldrick et al., 2016). They record family history over a period of three or more generations and gather information about the family (McGoldrick et al., 2020). They can provide an understanding of family relationships as well as the biopsychosocial environment within the family (Majhi et al., 2018). Constructing family genograms with clients provides an opportunity to engage with and enrich the therapeutic alliance and develop rapport with clients as well as allowing the client to explore their own family background, social interactions, and relationships (Mackay, 2015). In sum, a family genogram is an assessment tool that provides a comprehensive structure of one's family background, patterns, relationships, and interactions. Even though the use of a family genogram in practice is not common in Botswana, it is beginning to gain traction as practice courses in the University of Botswana are emphasising its use.

Use of Family Genogram in Teaching and Learning

Adopting experiential class exercises is encouraged as they assist students to understand concepts, and they also serve as a basis for reflection and learning (Foster et al., 2021). The characteristics include experiences, reflections, and a learner-centred focus. As proposed by experiential learning theory (ELT) whose underpinnings are on experience to guide educational innovation (Kolb and Kolb, 2017), experiential learning is an educational tool that uses different styles of acquiring knowledge and skills applications. It incorporates knowledge acquisition and application; or what Askeland (2003) refers to as a 'bridge between knowing what and applying how – connecting the doing with theoretical knowledge'. Slavich and Zimbardo (2012, p.594) describe the importance of experience in learning as:

> Experiential lessons provide students with an opportunity to experience concepts first-hand and, as such, give students a richer, more meaningful understanding of course concepts and of how they operate in the real world…They enhance the affective quality of the course content.

ELT is an experience-based learning process, which is centred on the learning cycle and which has four main learning phases, namely, Concrete Experience, Reflective Observation, Abstract Conceptualisation, and Active Experimentation (Kolb, 2014). These phases give the students an opportunity to be exposed to concrete activities and to reflect on their experiences during learning (Kolb and Kolb, 2014). Foster et al. (2021) further illustrate that it helps build new knowledge through the interaction of student's prior knowledge and experiences. This model emphasis is on reflection based on experience. In the social work profession, reflection is critical as it offers an opportunity for one to review one's own experience to make positive changes and improve practice.

An Experiential Class Exercise: Constructing a Family Genogram

As outlined in the experiential learning phase, to gain applied knowledge, students have to engage in constructing a family genogram. Such an exercise can allow students an opportunity to be actively engaged in their learning. As indicated in the experiential learning theory, this phase one includes using the concrete experience that the student would have acquired during lectures and assigned readings (Kolb, 2014). Preparing a family genogram requires one to collect the necessary information from family members. It might require one to interview several family members to ensure that they get the correct information concerning dates of events and activities that have occurred over the years. McGoldrick et al. (2020) formulated a comprehensive standardisation for constructing and interpreting genograms. Below are the steps for constructing a family genogram:

1. Collect three generations family information: dates of birth, deaths, marriage, divorce, etc. This involves tracing the family of origin on both the maternal and paternal sides back to grandparents.
2. Constructing at least a three-generation family genogram. There are universal symbols that are used in constructing family genograms (McGoldrick et al., 2020). There are symbols that represent the sex and lines to show family relationships.
   - Males are drawn on the left side whereas females are on the right side.
   - A spouse is drawn close to his/her current partner.
   - Older child is always from the left to the right side following the horizontal line.
3. The diagram visually displays generational relationships, history, and records demographic data and main events and transitions that the family has experienced. Within the symbols,

dates of birth and death are captured or the current age. The symbol can also capture genetic diseases, still births, and other information that can be deemed necessary to provide clarity to the family story (McGoldrick and Gerson 1985).

Upon completion of their family genograms, students can be asked to reflect on the diagram to make sense of it (Kolb, 2014). As per the ELT phase two – reflective observation – they process the engagement of collecting and constructing their family genogram. This is an opportunity for self-introspection and self-understanding on the part of the student. Phase three of ELT involves abstract conceptualisation. This is where there is a lecture on concepts, analysing and understanding family processes. Based on the reflective observation of the diagram, students have to engage in identifying concepts and apply them to their family situation. On phase four, active experimentation, they use information from lectures, and class readings linking it with what is going on in their families to see if it is or not applicable in their family settings (Kolb, 2014). As explained by the ELT, there is no end to this process, but it facilitates students appreciating the link with information from lecturers and readings (Kolb, 2014).

Adopting family genograms as an experiential class exercise in training social work students helps them appreciate it as a helpful tool in exploring the cultural context in the society through their own families as well as understanding family functioning and family processes (Puhlman et al., 2023). This is so as the family exists within the broader society that subscribes to certain cultural patterns. McGoldrick et al. (2020) illustrate that using family genograms allows for assessing the informal family networks and how they have influenced family functioning. Individuals are also asked to identify themselves ethnically so that they can recognise the continuities and discontinuities in their history and to identify the themes of cultural identity in their families (McGoldrick et al., 2020). Family genograms as an experiential training tool provide an opportunity for students to examine and appreciate their own cultural identities to promote cultural awareness and sensitivity (Hardy and Laszloffy, 1995).

Engaging students as collaborators in the learning process through constructing and analysing their own family genograms allows them to draw from their own experiences, which improves learning. When students engage in drawing their family genogram and analysing them, they develop self-understanding, which is critical in practice as it avoids an individual acting out unresolved personal issues with clients (Cournoyer, 2016). This exercise allows students to be sensitive to clients' experiences in practice (Cournoyer, 2016). As family genograms track family history from a systematic perspective, it can allow for students' personal growth as they prepare for practice (McGoldrick et al., 2020).

Benefits of Family Genogram as a Teaching Tool

Constructing family genograms as a teaching tool in social work practice courses has benefits. It allows for lecturer awareness of student characteristics and enhanced communication between lecturer and student as well as and student self-understanding and self-introspection. These are discussed below.

Awareness of Student Personal Characteristics and Enhanced Communication between Lecturer and Student

Constructing and analysing family genograms provide an opportunity for the lecturer to get to know the students' personal characteristics. As a result, it facilitates and improves communication between lecturer and students. In discussing the genogram with the students, the lecturer can better understand the challenges and problems that students are faced with in their families that need to be attended to. Also, knowing student personal characteristics can help the lecturer to vary learning approaches that can be accommodative to diverse students. This therefore can facilitate learning as the lecturer gets to know the student's background and how their past and family experiences can influence learning (Cournoyer, 2016).

In such cases, students can be encouraged to seek counselling to process and address their problems. Cournoyer (2016) argues that the instructor should be actively engaged in creating a conducive learning environment that encourages students to explore their experiences and beliefs. As the lecturer engages with the student discussing their family genogram, it facilitates awareness of familial patterns as its focus is on family patterns and relationships, which then can serve as an intervention tool for students (Warkentin, 2017). As the family history is virtually displayed and is discussed between the student and the lecturer, dysfunctional family patterns can be identified, and such insights might promote healing and growth and facilitate learning (Warkentin, 2017).

Furthermore, as illustrated by Dykes and Green (2015), participatory learning methods, where there are exercises allowing students to reflect, are favoured by students. Such exercises are commended in social work education as they encourage learning and critical thinking skills (Hussain et al., 2011). Dykes and Green (2015) further illustrate that real-world issues (as illustrated by students drawing their family genograms and analysing them) is a better way to train social work students for practice. Active learning through experiences and reflection is found to be more beneficial as students are able to construct new knowledge and skills (Foster et al., 2021).

Self-Understanding and Self-Introspection

Allowing students to draw their own family genogram can afford them an opportunity to engage in self-introspection and enhance self-understanding, which is critical in the social work profession (Cournoyer, 2016). At the most, social work students have to be aware that their own ideologies, based on their family background, can interfere with professional practice. This awareness can help them to exercise self-control in certain professional encounters. As indicated in the National Association of Social Workers (NASW), Standard 2, social workers recognise and appreciate the importance of being aware of one's own cultural identity and experiences in cross-cultural practice. Through self-introspection and understanding, they can identify their own characteristics that they might need to work on as they train to work with diverse families. This activity can be a way to help students envision and understand their family system, events, relationships, transitions, and family history and how these have influenced them and how it can influence them in practice. They also obtain an opportunity to map out problems at the individual level (Guerin et al., 1996), which can later be applicable when working with families. As illustrated by Cournoyer (2016), once clinicians are trained and allowed to explore facets of themselves, they realise their own assumptions, biases, limitations, and strengths and are better prepared to be competent in their practice as they can address any identified limitations and biases through this exercise and work on resolving any issues in their life to avoid countertransference later on with clients. This self-awareness and the opportunity to work on the negative traits can help reduce harm to clients later on when they are service providers.

Conclusion

This chapter explored the use of the family genogram as a teaching tool in a social work practice course. The discussion illustrated that utilising a family genogram as an example of experiential learning has benefits for students. The exercise facilitates self-understanding as students explored themselves through examining their family history, experiences, and relationships. Moreover, course content was enhanced as the students were able to link the concepts learnt in the classroom with real-world experiences. As students engaged in self-disclosure through sharing their family genogram, lecturers are able to better understand students and vary their teaching approaches to cater to their diverse learning needs. There was also enhanced communication between lecturers and students. This practical exercise gave students a cohesive image and practical example of what is involved in using family genograms when working with families.

Recommendations

1. Social work educators in Botswana, and Africa, should use active teaching and learning methods, such as family genograms, to enhance learning outcomes as they prepare social workers for practice.
2. Curriculum for social work education in Africa should consider adopting and contextualising Western models and techniques for effective teaching and learning.
3. As the family genogram adopts the systematic perspective, African social work educators should emphasise this during training to allow students to appreciate the importance of all systems in influencing individual and family functioning.

Further Reading

Kolb, A. Y. and Kolb, D. A. (2017). Experiential learning theory as a guide for experiential educators in higher education. *Experiential Learning and Teaching in Higher Education*, *1*(1), 7–44.

McGoldrick, M.; Gerson, R. and Petry, S. S. (2020). *Genograms: Assessment and Intervention* (4th ed.). New York: WW Norton and Company.

Power, T. A. (1989). *Family Matters: A Layperson's Guide to Family Functioning*. Meredith: N.H. Hathaway Press.

References

Askeland, G. A. (2003). Reality-play--Experiential learning in social work training. *Social Work Education*, *22*(4), 351–362.

Bates, N.; Immins, T.; Parker, J.; Keen, S.; Rutter, L.; Brown, K. and Zsigo, S. (2010). 'Baptism of fire': The first year in the life of a newly qualified social worker. *Social Work Education*, *29*(2), 152–170.

BIDPA and World Bank (2013) *Botswana Social Protection Assessment Report*. Gaborone: Ministry of Finance and Development Planning.

Cournoyer, B. R. (2016). *The Social Work Skills Workbook*. Belmon, CA: Cengage Learning.

DeMaria, R.; Weeks, G. R. and Hof, L. (2013). *Focused Genograms: Intergenerational Assessment of Individuals, Couples, and Families*. London: Routledge.

Department of Social Work (2009a). *Graduate Handbook*. Gaborone: University of Botswana.

Department of Social Work (2009b). *Undergraduate Handbook*. Gaborone: University of Botswana.

Department of Social Work (2021). *Fieldwork Manual*. Gaborone: University of Botswana.

Dryden-Peterson, S. and Mulimbi, B. (2017). Pathways toward peace: Negotiating national unity and ethnic diversity through education in Botswana. *Comparative Education Review*, *61*(1), 58–82.

Dykes, G. and Green, S. (2015). Learning profiles of social work students: Who are you and how should this influence my teaching? *Social Work/Maatskaplike Werk*, *51*(4), 577–598.

Foster, M. K.; Taylor, V. F. and Walker, J. L. (2021). *Experiential Exercises in the Classroom*. Northampton, MA: Edward Elgar Publishing.

Friedman, B. D. (2008). *How to Teach Effectively – A Brief Guide*. Chicago, IL: Lyceum.

Guerin, P. J.; Fogarty, T. F.; Fay, L. F. and Kautto, J. G. (1996). *Working with Relationship Triangles: The One-Two-Three of Psychotherapy*. New York: Guilford Press.

Hardy, K. V. and Laszloffy, T. A. (1995). The cultural genogram: Key to training culturally competent family therapists. *Journal of Marital and Family Therapy*, *21*(3), 227–237.

Huss, E. and Kapulnik, E. (2021). Using creative genograms in family social work to integrate subjective and objective knowledge about the family: A participatory study. *Research on Social Work Practice*, *31*(4), 390–399.

Hussain, M. A.; Mehmood, A. and Sultana, M. (2011). An inquiry into benefits of reflective practice in open and distance learning. *Turkish Online Journal of Distance Education*, *12*(2), 51–59.

International Federation of Social Workers [IFSW] (2014). Global definition of social work. https://www.ifsw.org/what-is-social-work/global-definition-of-social-work/.

International Federation of Social Workers [IFSW] (2020). Global standards for social work education and training. https://www.ifsw.org/global-standards-for-social-work-education-and-training/#practiceeducation.

Jack, G. and Donnellan, H. (2010). Recognising the person within the developing professional: Tracking the early careers of newly qualified child care social workers in three local authorities in England. *Social Work Education*, *29*(3), 305–318.

Jongman, K. and Tshupeng, M. (2020). Unregulated social work practice in Botswana: A risk to professional integrity and clients' welfare. *Journal of Education, Society and Behavioural Science*, *33*(4), 1–10.

Kang'ethe, S. M. (2014). Exploring social work gaps in Africa with examples from South Africa and Botswana. *Journal of Social Sciences*, *41*(3), 423–431.

Kealey, E. (2010). Assessment and evaluation in social work education: Formative and summative approaches. *Journal of Teaching in Social Work*, *30*(1), 64–74.

Kolb, A. Y. and Kolb, D. A. (2017). Experiential learning theory as a guide for experiential educators in higher education. *Experiential Learning and Teaching in Higher Education*, *1*(1), 7–44.

Kolb, D. A. (2014). *Experiential Learning: Experience as the Source of Learning and Development*. Place of Publication: FT Press.

Mackay, B. (2015). Genograms or housework. *New Zealand Journal of Counselling*, *35*(2), 41–45.

Majhi, G.; Reddy, S. and Muralidhar, D. (2018). The use of family genogram in psychiatric social work practice. *Open Journal of Psychiatry and Allied Sciences*, *9*(2), 98–102.

Mascolo, M. F. (2009). Beyond student-centered and teacher-centered pedagogy: Teaching and learning as guided participation. *Pedagogy and the Human Sciences*, *1*(1), 3–27.

McGoldrick, M. (2016). *The Genogram Casebook: A Clinical Companion to Genograms: Assessment and Intervention*. New York: WW Norton and Company.

McGoldrick, M.; Carter, E. A. and Garcia-Preto, N. (2011). *The Expanded Family Life Cycle: Individual, Family, and Social Perspectives* (4th ed.). Boston, MA: Pearson Allyn and Bacon.

McGoldrick, M. and Gerson, R. (1985). *Genograms in Family Assessment*. New York: Norton.

McGoldrick, M.; Gerson, R. and Petry, S. S. (2020). *Genograms: Assessment and Intervention* (4th ed.). New York: WW Norton and Company.

Monkman, M. M. (1991). Outcome objectives in social work practice: Person and environment. *Social Work*, *36*(3), 253–258.

Mupedziswa, R. and Sinkamba, R. P. (2014). Social work education and training in Southern and East Africa: Yesterday, today and tomorrow. *Global Social Work*, 141–153.

Mupedziswa, R. *et al.* (2021). Standard of living, well-being and community development: The case of Botswana. In Ryan Merlin Yonk (ed.) *Improving Quality of Life: Exploring Standard of Living, Wellbeing, and Community Development*. https://www.intechopen.com/online-first/standard-of-living-well-being-and-community-development-the-case-of-botswana.

Murray, A. and Parsons, N. (2016). The modern economic history of Botswana. In Z. Konczacki, J. Parpart and T. M. Shaw (eds.) *Studies in the Economic History of Southern Africa: Volume 1: The Front Line States* (pp. 159–199). London: Routledge.

National Association of Social workers (n.d.). Standards and Indicators for cultural competency in social work practice. https://www.socialworkers.org/LinkClick.aspx?fileticket=PonPTDEBrn4%3D.

Papouli, E. (2014). Field learning in social work education: Implications for educators and Instructors. *Field Educator*, *4*(2), 1–16.

Power, T. A. (1992). *Family Matters: A Layperson's Guide to Family Functioning*. New Hampshire: Hathaway Press.

Puhlman, D.; Shigeto, A.; Murillo-Borjas, G. A.; Maurya, R. K. and Vincenti, V. B. (2023). Qualitative genogram analysis: A methodology for theorizing family dynamics. *Journal of Family Theory and Review*, 1–16.

Slavich, G. M. and Zimbardo, P. G. (2012). Transformational teaching: Theoretical underpinnings, basic principles, and core methods. *Educational Psychology Review*, *24*(4), 569–608.

Stagoll, B. and Lang, M. (1980). Climbing the family tree: Working with genograms'. *Australian Journal of Family Therapy*, *1*(4), 161–170.

Statistics Botswana (2021). *Botswana Population and Housing Census: Populations of Towns, Villages, and Associated Localities*. Gaborone, Botswana: Government Printer.

Tham, P. and Lynch, D. (2014). Prepared for practice? Graduating social work students': Reflections on their education, competence and skills. *Social Work Education*, *33*(6), 704–717.

Twikirize, M. J. and Spitzer, H. (2019). *Preface. Social Work Practice in Africa: Indigenous and Innovative Approaches* (pp. xiii–xiv). Kampala: Fountain Publishers.

University of Botswana (2008). *University of Botswana Learning and Teaching Policy*. Gaborone: University of Botswana.

Veta, O. D. and McLaughlin, H. (2022). 'Social work education and practice in Africa: The problems and prospects. *Social Work Education*, 1–12.

Warkentin, B. (2017). Teaching social work with groups: Integrating didactic, experiential and reflective learning. *Social Work with Groups*, *40*(3), 233–243.

25
RETHINKING SOCIAL WORK EDUCATION IN SOUTH AFRICA AMIDST THE COVID-19 PANDEMIC

Suggestions for Innovative Fieldwork Practice

Thabisa Matsea

Abstract: English

The COVID-19 pandemic has brought about unprecedented challenges for social work education in South African institutions of higher learning. Fieldwork practice, also known as practicum, is a critical component of social work education that affords students an opportunity to integrate theory with practice by applying all methods of intervention using the values, complex practices, and skills of the social work profession. It not only exposes students to various social environments, but also prepares them for the reality in which they will practice. Many universities have adopted, since the outbreak of the COVID-19 pandemic, hybrid forms of teaching, but fieldwork practice is difficult to implement in hybrid form. Thus, fieldwork practice is experiencing multi-layered challenges that are hindering the life-changing experiences for students. Whilst COVID-19 imposes challenges on social work education, it also creates opportunities to review the curriculum and create innovative ways of delivering fieldwork practice. The chapter examines the need for a shift in the delivery of fieldwork practice to accommodate current and future changes that affect the traditional delivery. It acknowledges the importance of adopting a pedagogy that embraces technology while suggesting consideration of other ways of delivery where the use of technology is not possible.

Abstract: IsiXhosa

Ubhubhane iCovid-19 uze nemingeni engumnqa kwimfundo yezentlalontle kumaziko anemfundo enomsila kwilizwe loMzantsi Afrika. Umsebenzi ogxile kuqhelaniso, nowaziwa ngokuba licandelo lokuziqhelisa kwizifundo, lelona candelo lingundoqo kwizifundo zobuntlalontle, nelinika abafundi ithuba lokudibanisa ingcingane (ithiyori) nemeko yokuziqhelanisa ngokomsebenzi, ngokubandakanya zonke iindlela zongenelelo kusetyenziswa iinqobo zemilinganiselo, iimeko zokuziqhelanisa ezixananazileyo, kuquka nezakhono zomsebenzi wobuntlalontle. Oku akubakrobisi nje kuphela abafundi kwimimandla eyahlukileyo yentlalo, koko kubalungiselela nenkqu yemeko abaza kusebenza kuyo. Ukusukela mhla kwagqabhuka ubhubhane weCovid-19, uninzi lweeyunivesithi zamkela iindlela ezintlandlu-mbini zokufundisa, kodwa kwaphawuleka ukuba olu hlobo lwemfundo entlandlu-mbini lunzima xa kufikelela ekufundisweni kwemisebenzi yokuziqhelanisa. Ngenxa yoku ke, umsebenzi wokuziqhelanisa uye ujongane nemingeni eyahlukeneyo, mingeni leyo ikhangeleka isisithintelo ekubeni abafundi bazuze amava anokuza notshintsho kubomi babo. Nangona iCovid-19 isiza nemingeni kwimfundo yezentlalontle, ikwadala namathuba okuhlaziywa kwekharityhulam kwanokuyilwa kweendlela eziphuhlileyo zokunikezelwa kwemfundo yokuziqhelanisa. Esi sahluko sihlola sikwacubungula isidingo sotshintsho kwindlela ekunikezelwa okanye ekufundiswa ngayo imfundo yokuziqhelanisa, oku kusenziwa ngeenjongo zokulungiselela utshintsho olugqubayo nolwexesha elizayo oluchaphazela iindlela zantlandlolo zokufundisa. Olu phando luyakwamkela ukubaluleka kokusetyenziswa kwendlela yokufundisa engabuchasiyo ubuchwepheshe bale mihla, kodwa ikwanika neengcebiso malunga nokwamkelwa nokusetyenziswa kwezinye iindlela zokufundisa eziveza kunzima okanye kungelula ncam ukusetyenziswa kobuchwepheshe okanye iteknoloji.

Introduction

Globally, the impact of the COVID-19 pandemic on many aspects of life, including education, has been widely documented. The outbreak of the COVID-19 pandemic forced governments to put in place measures to flatten the curve of the virus. However, precautionary and preventive measures adopted to mitigate the spread of the virus and reduce its impact halted many activities, resulting in significant disruptions that exacerbated existing inequalities (Walter and Shenaar-Golan, 2022) while posing new challenges to the scientific community (Sonuga-Barke, 2021). This resulted in considerable collateral damage that posed new challenges to social work education and practice as their activities involve direct communication and physical contact with other people (Kurzman and Maiden, 2014; Phelan, 2015).

Social workers interact with individuals, groups, and communities at the micro, mezzo, and macro levels with the aim of bringing social change and improving their wellbeing. The understanding of the person-in-environment approach assists social workers to come up with an intervention strategy that can bring change in people and society as well as promote self-reliance (Dhemba, 2012). The ability of social workers to perform their professional duties is firmly rooted in social work education as it prepares and empowers them with the necessary skills. Social work education equips students with knowledge, values, and skills to intervene at the points where people interact with their environments in order to promote and improve social wellbeing (Rambaree, 2020; South African Qualification Authority [SAQA], 2012). It also enables them to work with diverse groups of people using anti-oppressive and non-discriminatory approaches to empower communities to challenge structural sources of poverty and inequality (SAQA, 2012; Nunev, 2019; Pack and Brown, 2017).

Following the suspension of educational activities, working and studying conditions changed as many universities and other educational institutions resorted to online teaching and learning to save the academic year. Mirick and Davis (2021) assert that social work programmes were caught off-guard as many did not have contingency plans in place. These changes presented challenges as there was no body of literature to consult about the delivery of social work education, transition to online instruction or remote service delivery, and navigation of placement disruptions. The social work curriculum contains fieldwork, which is a compulsory practical component aimed at assisting social work students to acquire skills and competencies crucial for professional practice. The practical nature of fieldwork makes it difficult to offer online (Azman et al., 2020). Fieldwork has been described as the signature pedagogy of the social work profession that can be mastered through the integration of theory to practice (Council of Social Work Education, 2008; Dhemba, 2012).

There have been reported challenges in fieldwork education in South Africa. These include the limited number of available agencies for student placements, shortage of social work supervisors, limited office space, and the unwillingness of the available supervisors to supervise or mentor social work students (De Bie et al., 2020; Nadesan, 2020a; Shokane et al., 2016). COVID-19 exacerbated the situation, resulting in a crisis state as placing students became risky and impossible in some instances. The COVID-19 pandemic not only exacerbated challenges associated with fieldwork, but also amplified the limits of online teaching and learning in social work education. However, social work educators are left with no choice but to radically change by adopting new approaches for teaching.

This chapter aims to examine the impact of the COVID-19 pandemic on social work fieldwork practice. It explores how students should be prepared for practice in such situations. It aims to find out how the implementation of fieldwork practice capacitates students to participate in real-world situations. The chapter argues that there is a need for a shift in the delivery of social work education, hence the need to create innovative ways of delivering fieldwork practice in future pandemics. Drawing from the lessons learned since the outbreak of the COVID-19 pandemic, it acknowledges the importance of adopting a pedagogy that embraces technology while suggesting consideration of other ways of delivery where the use of technology is not possible.

Social Work Education in South Africa

Social work education in South Africa is offered at universities as a generalist degree to prepare students to work with clients in various settings upon completion. Except for one university that offers social work as a part-time study, South African universities offering a Bachelor of Social Work (BSW) degree offer a four-year full-time qualification. The offering of the BSW complies with the National Qualification Framework (NQF), which is a framework within which the South African Qualifications system recognises and organises qualifications across a range of professions with a set of guidelines according to which student achievements are registered (Spolander et al., 2011). Additionally, the BSW programme must meet 16 core social work knowledge areas as set out in the higher education framework (Council on Higher Education [CHE], 2015 South African Qualifications Authority [SAQA], 2015). Thus, social work students are required to complete both theory and practical modules to be awarded the BSW qualification. The purpose of the qualification is to ensure that students acquire knowledge, skills, and values resulting in well-rounded graduates who contribute meaningfully to enhance the quality of life for all, especially vulnerable populations.

The South African Council for Social Services Professions (SACSSP) is a regulatory body that determines, guides, and exercises authority regarding matters affecting social service education and training. Social work students are required to register with the council in their second year of study to allow them to interact and intervene in cases involving clients in various communities (SACSSP, 2012a). It is from this level that social work students are exposed to real-life social issues through fieldwork in which they are expected to integrate theory and practice.

Although basic elements of fieldwork are anticipated to be similar in all South African institutions of higher learning, how it is implemented differs from one institution to the other. At the institutional level, students do fieldwork from first up to fourth-year levels. During the first year of study, students visit various organisations in which social workers render services. This helps them to understand the roles and functions of social workers in these organisations. In the second-year level, students get an opportunity to interact with clients for the first time and provide intervention in various cases if they are registered with SACSSP. The second-year level is crucial in determining the students' ability to apply social work values, principles, and skills. The students' interaction with clients continues until the fourth-year level, which is the final year of study. Fourth-year fieldwork is, however, different from that of other levels because students are placed in various social services agencies for four months, after which they are expected to produce a portfolio of evidence that contains various reports and related aspects indicating what the student has done to address the core standards of the BSW and achieve the learning outcomes.

The Significance of Fieldwork Practice

Work-integrated learning (WIL) is fast gaining popularity as a way of equipping graduates with the necessary skills for the workplace. Billet (2009) defines WIL as learning that is aimed at developing students' capacities by providing them with opportunities to participate in real-world situations. Fieldwork is a discipline-specific term for WIL in social work. Unlike other disciplines, social work has exposed students to real-life situations with the aim of integrating theory with practice since its inception (Wrenn and Wrenn, 2009). In other words, students get to apply to the field what they have learned in class. Fieldwork practice is mandatory to achieve all the graduate attributes in South Africa (CHE, 2015). Universities offering social work learning have a responsibility to place students in organisations that are viewed as appropriate agencies for social work practice. In most instances, students would identify a preferred place of attachment that is closer to their homes, or which would expose them to more learning experiences.

Research shows that fieldwork is beneficial to both the student and the placement agency. Some of these benefits include exposure to different social environments (Mishra, 2014), firsthand experience with various social ills, and understanding the connection between people and their environment, (Johnson et al., 2012). Exposure to the work environment helps students to develop professionalism as well as work ethics (Panda and Nayak, 2012; Johnson et al., 2012) and the ability to work collaboratively with other professionals (Pare and Maistre, 2006). Fieldwork also exposes students to the organisational culture and how qualified social workers conduct themselves in addressing various aspects of practice. Most importantly, they acquire an opportunity to use various methods of intervention under the supervision of a qualified social worker.

Fieldwork practice provides students with an opportunity to actively participate in professional activities and allows them to internalise professional values, beliefs, and perspectives (Dhemba, 2012; Panda and Nayak, 2012). In addition, it enables students to interact and collaborate with other professionals whose activities overlap with their profession (Garraway and Morkel, 2014). Fieldwork exposes students to a range of authentic experiences such as different social environments that provide them with the opportunity to have firsthand experience of various social problems and understand the connection between people and their environment (Billet, 2009; Johnson et al., 2012; Mishra, 2014). It also allows students to make mistakes and learn from them (Garraway and Morkel, 2014). The presence of students in the agency benefits the agency by having extra hands. Given that students are exposed to new literature with evidence-based practices, they often come up with new ideas. This helps the agency to reflect on current practices and improve service delivery (Pare and Maistre, 2006).

Despite these positive aspects, fieldwork can pose challenges that hinder the integration of theory into practice in South Africa. These challenges can be attributable to students or supervisors' incapacity, the environment in which students are placed, and the incapacity of agency supervisors or their willingness to supervise (Pare and Maistre, 2006; Garraway and Morkel, 2014). In South Africa, supervision plays a crucial role in facilitating the learning process during fieldwork. For instance, good supervision during fieldwork not only focuses on theory and practice, but also facilitates opportunities for the development of students and the professional self (Dykes and Green, 2015). This means that supervisors should be knowledgeable about the environment and resultant situations in which students are placed (Budeli, 2018). Findings of a study that highlighted the supervision experiences of students and their interactions with field placement supervisors from three field instruction programmes in South Africa showed mostly negative recollections of supervision experiences as some students were left unsupervised (Nadesan, 2020b).

The fact that students bring with them new ideas from the most recent literature poses a challenge for people who have long been in the field. Thus, some people who are comfortable with routine work may not be open to new ideas, making it difficult for students to introduce any changes (Pare and Maistre, 2006). Garraway and Morkel (2014) talk of unfair power relations that may disincentivise learning as supervisors may use their authority to intimidate students and prevent them from introducing new ideas. Common to most agencies is the unavailability of supervisors due to other work commitments or unwillingness to provide support and guidance to students (Billet, 2009) or lack of supervisory skills (Dhemba, 2012). As a result, students fail to integrate theory into practice because they have difficulty understanding theory (Carelse and Dykes, 2013).

The Impact of the COVID-19 Pandemic on Social Work Education

South Africa was not spared from the disruptions of the COVID-19 pandemic, which forced many countries into a state of emergency, hence adopting precautionary measures to flatten the curve. The country recorded the first case of COVID-19 in March 2020 after which the president declared a national state of disaster as provided for in the Disaster Management Act 57 of 2002. Thus, a 21-day national lockdown, which restricted the movement of people, was implemented. This implies that people were forced to adapt to a new normal as social distancing measures and restrictions on gatherings for any purpose were put in place to slow the spread of the virus. These changes challenged all forms of traditional face-to-face education, including social work as adherence to regulations resulted in school closures (Safodien, 2021). As the virus spread, the national lockdown was extended, resulting in uncertainties and extensions of academic sessions. Thus, to save the academic year, while also ensuring the safety of all those involved (Hodges et al., 2020), many institutions were compelled to shift their usual operations and introduce new ways of engaging students by adopting virtual and hybrid learning initiatives (Tanga et al., 2020).

There has been a growing use of technology in practice (Dombo et al., 2014), with many universities adopting blended learning. The COVID-19-enforced shift to full use of online platforms was not without challenges as many instructors and students lacked the competencies required for online learning (Mirick and Davis, 2021). Zimba et al. (2020) acknowledge the benefits of blended learning in fostering student engagement and providing social work students with many options to support their learning preferences but are concerned about the inequalities that impact successful outcomes among South African students. Thus, over-dependency on technological devices, unreliable Internet service, insufficient space and privacy at home, non-availability of a suitable place of work, insufficient equipment, and lack of proper technical support (Lischer et al., 2021; Rapanta et al., 2020) are among challenges faced by South African students from disadvantaged backgrounds. Additionally, these challenges were exacerbated by poor connectivity and exorbitant prices of data (Dube, 2020; Aruleba and Njere, 2022).

While the shift to online platforms somehow yielded some positive outcomes with regards to teaching and learning there were significant disruptions in social work fieldwork. Since social work is a practice-based discipline, the BSW programme requires students to complete a certain number of hours to obtain enough credits to acquire a degree (Mirick and Davis, 2021). The strategies adopted to prevent the spread of the COVID-19 pandemic prevented students from obtaining the prescribed hours due to the unavailability of placement organisations. Although many organisations that provide essential services remained open during lockdowns, they were forced to make the difficult choice of either including students as part of the essential workforce to meet clients' needs or protecting them. Thus, many organisations opted to protect their permanent workforce and clients by not admitting any students or terminating those who were already placed (Council on Social Work Education, 2020a). The universities were in a difficult position as they were confronted with the dilemma of either cancelling fieldwork practice, postponing it indefinitely, or continuing, with the risks to the health of students, supervisors, and clients. Given the concerns about social work programmes that do not foster the necessary skills and knowledge required for practice (Morley and Stenhouse, 2021; Alpaslan, 2019), cancellation of fieldwork would lead to disruptions in the number of hours required for the BSW, resulting in the production of ill-prepared graduates.

SACSSP held and facilitated meetings with universities and other stakeholders to guide social work programmes in making decisions to save the academic year while prioritising the safety of students, educators, social workers, and clients. Many universities made modifications to academic courses and fieldwork. For instance, in levels such as the first year, which does not require intensive fieldwork practice, online presentations were provided on specific topics. For other levels, the required number of field hours and contact with groups were reduced while allowing remote-based field activities to count as in-person contacts. Due to the uniqueness of circumstances among rural, semi-rural, and urban-based universities, each university was granted an opportunity to use its discretion in terms of conducting fieldwork practice.

Although all South African universities faced challenges, it is important to note that the experiences were different depending on location. For the historically disadvantaged institutions (HDIs), which are institutions that are mostly rural-based and poorly resourced as they were deprived of funding during the apartheid era (Atkinson, 2014), placing students during the COVID-19 pandemic was extremely challenging. Rural-based universities are disadvantaged because practice placements are limited and offer a narrower range of learning opportunities for social work students. Although placements in semi-rural and rural areas are unique in terms of observing protocols of entry and embracing indigenous healing practices, lack of available and accessible placement settings results in students sharing placements or traveling long distances to their placements (Nadesan, 2019).

Due to the limited number of non-governmental organisations in rural areas, universities place many students in the Department of Social Development (DSD) and few in Correctional Services (DSC). DSD has focused its attention most recently on statutory services such as foster care, thus providing limited opportunities for professional training (Nadesan, 2020a). Placement of students in these governmental organisations was difficult during the COVID-19 pandemic as compliance with regulations and social distancing forced them to allow a certain number of people indoors. Given the shortage of office space, many organisations opted for rotation of staff. Thus, accommodating students was not a priority and in cases where students were placed, supervision was a challenge as supervisors would barely be available, leaving social work students without any learning experiences. In organisations where there were limited social work supervisors, many students would not receive supervision as required. As discussed in the following section, this necessitates the determination of how best the use of new forms of teaching and learning can be supported without compromising the values of social work.

Innovative Ways to Conduct Fieldwork

The pandemic transformed social work education and practice, thereby necessitating the adaptation of older practices while creating new instructional tools to meet the needs of students and all those involved (Lischer et al., 2021). It introduced a 'chicken and egg' situation as the effects it has directly or indirectly affect social work education and practice. The COVID-19 pandemic marked therefore a turning point in social work education that needed to be embraced and adopted without compromising the guiding principles and values of the social work profession. It is a recognition of the need to change the way things are done without ignoring ethical practices that, if not taken into consideration, would compromise the fieldwork practice, resulting in ill-equipped social work graduates.

Given the concern about the unemployability of social work graduates due to the inability to integrate theory with practice, among other challenges (Alpaslan, 2019), the COVID-19 pandemic has created an opportunity for a review of social work curricula to ensure that students are equipped with the required knowledge, understanding, and skills needed in the profession of social work (Laidlaw et al., 2020). Smith and Rasool (2020) assert that student social workers are trained to be change agents that support wellbeing by addressing the needs of individuals, families, groups, and communities through interventions that support social justice and social cohesion. This requires institutions offering social work education to come up with innovative ways of conducting practicum that will enable students to develop competencies to advocate against social injustices aimed at social transformation (Moore et al., 2018) and restoring the value of human rights that have been exploited (Laidlaw et al., 2020).

With COVID-19 pandemic regulations not allowing in-person interactions, adopting virtual approaches seemed the best option to ensure that students gain practical learning experiences. However, there have been concerns about the effectiveness of online teaching versus traditional teaching for fieldwork practice as in-person learning is a preferred method when preparing students for practice (Levin et al., 2018). Shirodker (2022) suggests conducting online workshops to empower students with knowledge of certain social problems after which tasks with related themes should be assigned to students. Kourgiantakis and Lee (2020) concur that the use of virtual platforms for practice-based learning in the form of voluntary simulation-based learning activities provides students with opportunities to develop social work practice competencies.

While the use of video and other virtual platforms is beneficial, these may not be practical in some contexts. In the South African context, Turton and Schmid (2020) note that many university students are from disadvantaged backgrounds and lack the financial and technological resources to engage meaningfully in the virtual learning process. The concerns highlighted above remain hindrances to meaningful participation in virtual fieldwork learning, thereby affecting the students' ability to meet the degree requirements. Transitioning to virtual platforms affects not only students on practicum, but also the clients with whom they interact. For instance, interaction with virtual platforms requires a level of literacy and accessibility to gadgets (Mehta and Briskman, 2022), but due to illiteracy and inequalities among South Africans, many clients may not be able to use gadgets relevant for video calling nor have access to such gadgets (David et al., 2018). This is despite the increase in use and ownership of mobile phones in South Africa (Miyajima 2020) whereby many rural households and low-income earners have access to a mobile phone. It was also found that those who do not own mobile phones have access since they share with someone else. This presents an opportunity to use mobile phones to improve access to social service delivery.

Since many organisations have no prior experience in virtual or telephone social service provision, this requires students and their supervisors to be creative and inventive. It also requires a level of tactfulness as dealing with new clients in a virtual platform could be difficult compared to those who are familiar with the student or social worker since there is an existing trust (Mehta and Briskman, 2022). Students, fieldwork coordinators, and supervisors can develop remote learning plans, especially for remote and rural communities, with schedules for various activities that are aimed at providing support and educating clients. Given students' familiarity with and use of technology, they can use text messages or social media platforms, such as WhatsApp, Facebook, and Twitter, for group work with young people. In addition, students can set up speed dial for their older clients. Many mobile phones have speakers that can be activated when interacting with more than one person. This means that students can also use mobile phones for family sessions or a meeting with a group of stakeholders. This shifts the paradigm by allowing students to plan and execute their plans. Students acquire skills they would not have been exposed to in traditional fieldwork and, most importantly, contribute to knowledge creation while also taking charge of their learning.

Conclusion

This chapter discussed the innovative ways to deliver social work field practicum during health pandemics and related crisis situations. The sudden transition to online learning because of the COVID-19 pandemic affected social work education, including students and educators on various levels. The pandemic has served as an eye-opener that created a new normal for the universities, resulting in adoption of technology for social work education. It has demonstrated that digital literacy is a necessity for both educators and students. However, it is also important to acknowledge that the total transition from in-person or blended learning to online platforms cannot be achieved overnight and may not even be possible, especially for unequal societies such as South Africa. While there is a high possibility of returning to traditional teaching and learning, this does not mean that the experiences gained cannot be incorporated into teaching and learning. The rapid advances in technology that led to the adoption of virtual approaches or blended teaching and learning created opportunities for use in various fields of study and social work as a people-centred profession is not immune to these changes. However, the use of technology and its effectiveness in fieldwork require further research. Given the exposure that both educators and students gained, a blended approach should be adopted for delivering theoretical and practical components of social work education, provided this is done in an ethical, practical, and responsible manner. This includes acknowledging that many students from disadvantaged backgrounds may not be able to afford the required gadgets for online teaching and learning.

Recommendations

1. Universities should review the curriculum and structure it in such a way that future social workers are proactive rather reactive to address multi-dimensional challenges that remain an issue in Africa.
2. Considering opportunities created by COVID-19, infusing technologies in social work curricula to enable social work profession engagement with the current technologies is crucial.
3. Practicing social workers should receive further skills training to enable them to provide effective supervision to technologically advanced students during fieldwork practice and increase accessibility for their clients in remote areas of many African countries.

Further Reading

Gad, S. (2022). E-learning and social work education during COVID-19. *Public Organization Review*, 23(1), 343–364. https://doi.org/10.1007/s11115-022-00613-0.

References

Alpaslan, N. (2019). Promoting social work graduates' employment through the social work curriculum: Employers' perspectives on the employability of UniSA's newly qualified social workers. *Social Work*, 55(3), 341–358.

Aruleba, K. and Jere, N. (2022). Exploring digital transforming challenges in rural areas of South Africa through a systematic review of empirical studies. *Scientific African*, e01190.

Atkinson, D. (2014). *Rural-urban linkages: South Africa Case Study*. Working Paper Series N° 125. Working Group: Development with Territorial Cohesion. Territorial Cohesion for Development Program. Santiago, Chile: Rimisp.

Azman, A.; Singh, P. S. J.; Parker, J. and Ashencaen Crabtree, S. (2020). Addressing competency requirements of social work students during the COVID-19 pandemic in Malaysia. *Social Work Education*, 39(8), 1058–1065. doi.org/10.1080/02615479.2020.1815692.

Billett, S. (2009). Realizing the educational worth of integrating work experiences in higher education. *Studies in Higher Education*, 34(7), 827–843.

Budeli, J. (2018). Supervision during social work fieldwork practice: A case of the University of Venda. In: Shokane, A. L.; Makhubele, J. C. and Blitz, L. V. (eds) *Issues Around Aligning Theory, Research and Practice in Social Work Education* (pp. 237–260). Cape Town: AOSIS (Pty) Ltd.

Carelse, S. and Dykes, G. (2013). Integration of theory and practice in social work: Challenges and triumphs. *Social Work/Maatskaplike Werk*, 49(2), 164–181.

Council for Higher Education (2015). *Higher Education Qualifications Sub-framework: Qualification Standard for Bachelor of Social Work*. Pretoria: Council for Higher Education.

Council for Social Work Education (2008). Educational policy and accreditation standards. http://www.cswe.org/File.aspx?id=41861.

Council on Social Work Education (2020a). CSWE and commission on accreditation statement. https://www.cswe.org/CSWE/media/AccredidationPDFs/COA-Field-ReductionUpdate-05-09-2020.pdf [31.

David, A.; Guilbert, N.; Hino, H.; Leibbrandt, M.; Potgieter, E. and Shifa, M. (2018). *Social Cohesion and Inequality in South Africa*. Cape Town: SALDRU. UCT.

De Bie, A.; Chaplin, J.; Vengris, J.; Dagnachew, E. and Jackson, R. (2020). Not 'everything's a learning experience': Racialized, indigenous, LGBTQ, and disabled students in social work field placements. *Social Work Education*, 40(6), 756–772. DOI.org/10.1080/02615479.2020.1843614.

Dhemba, J. (2012). Fieldwork in social work education and training: Issues and challenges in the case of Eastern and Southern Africa. *Social Work and Society*, 10(1), 1–16.

Dombo, E. A.; Kays, L. and Weller, K. (2014). Clinical social work practice and technology: Personal, practical, regulatory, and ethical considerations for the twenty-first century. *Social Work in Health Care*, 53(9), 900–919. DOI.org/10.1080/00981389.2014.948585.

Dube, B. (2020). Rural online learning in the context of COVID-19 in South Africa: Evoking an inclusive education approach. *Multidisciplinary Journal of Educational Research*, 10(2), 1–24. DOI.org/10.4471/remie.2020.5607.

Dykes, G. and Green, S. (2015). Learning profiles of social work students: Who are you and how should this influence my teaching?. *Social Work*, 51(4), 577–598.

Garraway, J. and Morkel, J. (2014). Learning in practice through a CHAT lens. In: Bozalek, V.; Ng'ambi, D.; Wood, D.; Herrington, J. and Hardman, J. (eds) *Aand Amory, A. Activity Theory, Authentic Learning and Emerging Technologies: Towards a Transformative Higher Education Pedagogy* (pp. 22–31). London: Routledge.

Hodges, C.; Moore, S.; Lockee, B.; Trust, T. and Bond, A. (2020). The difference between emergency remote teaching and online learning. *Educause Review*, 27, 1–12.

Johnson, E. J.; Bailey, K. and Padmore, J. (2012). Issues and challenges of social work practicum in Trinidad and Tobago and India. *Caribbean Teaching Scholar*, 2(1), 19–29.

Kourgiantakis, T. and Lee, E. (2020). Social work practice education and training during the pandemic: Disruptions and discoveries. *International Social Work*, 63(6), 761–765. https://uk.sagepub.com/en-gb/journals-permissions.

Kurzman, P. A. and Maiden, R. P. (2014). *Distance Learning and Online Education in Social Work*. London: Routledge.

Laidlaw, K.; Cabiati, E.; Henriksen, O. and Shore, C. (2020). Preparing students for social work practice in contemporary societies: Insights from a transnational research network. *European Journal of Social Work*, 23(6), 1–12. DOI.org/10.1080/13691457.2020.1793108.

Levin, S.; Fulginiti, A. and Moore, B. (2018). The perceived effectiveness of online social work education: Insights from a national survey of social work educators. *Social Work Education*, 37(6), 775–789.

Lischer, S.; Schmitz, S. C.; Krüger, P.; Safi, N. and Dickson, C. (2021). Distance education in social work during the COVID-19 pandemic: Changes and challenges. *Frontiers in Education*, 6, 1–12. DOI.org/10.3389/feduc.2021.720565.

Mehta, R. and Briskman, L. (2022). COVID and social work voices from India and Australia: Strategic and meaningful solidarities for global justice. In: dos Santos Gonçalves, M.; Kleibl, T.; Noyoo, N.; Gutwald, R.; Lutz, R. and Twikirize, J. (eds.) *The Coronavirus Crisis and Challenges to Social Development: Global Perspectives* (pp. 3–15). Switzerland: Springer Nature.

Mirick, R. G. and Davis, A. (2021). Supporting social work students during the COVID-19 pandemic. *Journal of Teaching in Social Work*, 41(5), 484–504. doi.org/10.1080/08841233.2021.1978612.

Mishra, P. J. (2014). Social work field practicum: Opportunities with challenges. *International Journal of Multidisciplinary Approach and Studies*, 1(5), 288–295.

Miyajima, K. (2020). Mobile phone ownership and welfare: Evidence from South Africa's household survey. SSRN, 3758055.

Moore, M.; Ballesteros, J. and Hansen, C. J. (2018). The role of social work values in promoting the functioning and well-being of athletes. *Journal of Social Work Values and Ethics*, 15(2), 48–61. https://jswve.org/download/15-2/articles15-2/48-Well-being-of-athletes-JSWVE-15-2-2018-Fall.pdf.

Morley, C. and Stenhouse, K. (2021). Educating for critical social work practice in mental health. *Social Work Education*, 40(1), 80–94. DOI.org/10.1080/02615479.2020.1774535.

Nadesan, V. S. (2019). *A Systems Analysis of Field Instruction in Social Work Education*. PhD thesis. University of Johannesburg.

Nadesan, V. S. (2020a). Challenges of social work students from historically disadvantaged universities during placements in semi-rural areas in South Africa. *Southern African Journal of Social Work and Social Development*, 32(3), 1–17. DOI.org/10.25159/2415-5829/6509.

Nadesan, V. S. (2020b). Social work supervision in a developing country: Experiences of students. *The Indian Journal of Social Work*, 81(3), 263–282. DOI.ORG/10.32444/IJSW.2020.81.3.263-282.

Nunev, S. T. (2019). Club forms of activities and creation of educational environment promoting the development of social work students. *Social Work Education*, 39(3), 1–16. DOI.org/10.1080/02615479.2019.1627309.

Pack, M. and Brown, P. (2017). Educating on anti-oppressive practice with gender and sexual minority elders: Nursing and social work perspectives. *Aotearoa New Zeal and Social Work*, 29(2), 108–118. https://anzswjournal.nz/anzsw/article/view/279.

Panda, B. and Nayak, L. M. (2012). Strengthening field work practicum in social work education. *Social Work Chronicle*, 1(2), 14–30.

Pare, A. and Maistre, C. L. (2006). Active learning in the workplace: Transforming individuals and institutions. *Journal of Education and Work*, 19(4), 363–381.

Phelan, J. E. (2015). The use of e-learning in social work education. *Social Work*, 60(3), 257–264. DOI.org/10.1093/sw/swv010.

Rambaree, K. (2020). Environmental social work: Implications for accelerating the implementation of sustainable development in social work curricula. *International Journal of Sustainability in Higher Education*, 21(3), 557–574. DOI.org/10.1108/IJSHE-09-2019-0270.

Rapanta, C.; Botturi, L.; Goodyear, P.; Guàrdia, L. and Koole, M. (2020). Online university teaching during and after the Covid-19 crisis: Refocusing teacher presence and learning activity. *Postdigital Science and Education*, 2(3), 923–945. DOI.org/10.1007/S42438-020-00155-Y.

Safodien, M. (2021). Social work 4.0? the fourth Industrial Revolution and social work education: A South African perspective. *Social Work*, 57(3), 257–271.

Shirodker, M. V. (2022). Community-based fieldwork during Covid 19 pandemic. *Revista Review Index Journal of Multidisciplinary*, 2(1), 36–40.

Shokane, A. L.; Nemutandani, V. and Budeli, N. J. (2016). Challenges faced by fourth year social work students during fieldwork practice at a rural-based university. *AFFRIKA Journal of Politics, Economics and Society*, 6(1), 133–163.

Smith, L. and Rasool, S. (2020). Deep transformation toward decoloniality in social work: Themes for change in a social work higher education program. *Journal of Progressive Human Services*, 31(2), 144–164. DOI.org/10.1080/10428232.2020.1762295.

Sonuga-Barke, E. J. (2021). 'School of hard knocks'–what can mental health researchers learn from the COVID-19 crisis? *The Journal of Child Psychology and Psychiatry, and Allied Disciplines*, 62(1), 1–4. https://doi.org/10. 1111/jcpp.13364.

South African Council for Social Service Professions (2012a). Policy guidelines for course of conduct, code of ethics and the rules for social workers. http://www.sacssp.co.za/website/wp-content/uploads/2012/06/Code-of-Ethics.pdf.

South African Qualifications Authority [SAQA] (2012). Registered qualification: Bachelor of social work. http://regqs.saqa.org.za/view Qualification.php?id=23994.

South African Qualifications Authority [SAQA] (2015). *Qualification Standard for Bachelor of Social Work, Council of Higher Education*. Pretoria: SAQA.

Spolander, G.; Pullen-Sansfacon, A.; Brown, M. and Engelbrecht, L. (2011) Social work education in Canada, England and South Africa: A critical comparison of undergraduate programmes. *International Social Work*, 54(6), 816–831.

Tanga, P.; Ndhlovu, G. N. and Tanga, M. (2020). Emergency remote teaching and learning during COVID-19: A recipe for disaster for social work education in the Eastern Cape of South Africa? *African Journal of Social Work*, 10(3), 17–24.

Turton, Y. and Schmid, J. (2020). Transforming social work: Contextualised social work education in South Africa. *Social Work/Maatskaplike Werk*, 56(4), 367–382.

Walter, O. and Shenaar-Golan, V. (2022). Modified focusing as a contemplative pedagogy in an MSW research course. *Social Work Education*, 41(4), 472–484.

Wrenn, J. and Wrenn, B. (2009). Enhancing learning by integrating theory and practice. *International Journal of Teaching and Learning in Higher Education*, 21(2), 258–265.

Zimba, Z. F.; Khosa, P. and Pillay, R. (2021). Using blended learning in South African social work education to facilitate student engagement. *Social Work Education*, 40(2), 263–278.

26
BEING A STUDENT SOCIAL WORKER DURING ACADEMIC DISRUPTIONS IN SOUTH AFRICA

What Do We Need to Prepare for Practice?

Marichen van der Westhuizen, Ronel Davids, and Violet Adonis

Abstract: English

Prior to the COVID-19 pandemic, a need for supported education practices in social work education and training in South Africa was highlighted. Previous studies reported on students' educational and psychosocial challenges, including demands of the social work profession experienced during fieldwork placements. This chapter reports on a qualitative study that explored how the pandemic further contributed to these educational and psychosocial challenges for final year student social workers. The findings reported on identified students' educational needs in becoming competent and confident social worker graduates and the psychological support needed to address mental health issues impacting their readiness for practice that became apparent during the pandemic. Academic resources and key role-players required to support them to prepare for practice were identified as technological resources and contact and access to lecturers and social work supervisors. The critical reflections on learning and teaching during the COVID-19 pandemic by participating students supported the recommendations made in this chapter regarding adaptations needed in fieldwork modules to ensure preparedness for practice when academic life is disrupted.

Abstract: IsiXhosa

Ngaphambi kobhubhani we-COVID-19, imfuno yemfundo exhaswayo kwimfundo yentlalontle kunye noqeqesho eMzantsi Afrika yaphawulwa. Izifundo zangaphambili zinike ingxelo malunga nemingeni yezemfundo kunye neengqondo zabafundi bezentlalontle, ezibandakanya iimfuno zomsebenzi wentlalontle ofunyenwe ngexesha lokufakwa komsebenzi. Esi sahluko sinikela ingxelo ngophononongo lomgangatho oluphonononge ukuba lo bhubhani ube negalelo njani na ngakumbi kule mingeni yezemfundo neyengqondo yabafundi boonontlalontle abakunyaka wokugqibela. Iziphumo ezichazwe kwiimfuno zemfundo zabafundi ezichongiweyo ukuze babe ngababphumeleleyo kunye nokuzithemba koonontlalontle, kunye nenkxaso yengqondo efunekayo ukujongana nemiba yempilo yengqondo echaphazela ukulungela kwabo ukuziqhelanisa nokuye kwabonakala ngexesha lobhubhani. Iingcinga ezibalulekileyo zokufunda nokufundisa ngexesha lobhubhani we-COVID-19 ngabafundi abathatha inxaxheba zixhase izindululo ezenziwe kwesi sahluko malunga nohlengahlengiso olufunekayo kwiimodyuli zomsebenzi wangaphandle ukuqinisekisa ukulungela ukuziqhelanisa xa ubomi bokufunda buphazamisekile.

Introduction

An alarming student dropout rate at South African higher education institutions (HEIs) has been reported (Moodley and Singh, 2015) due to, among others, institutional barriers as well as personal and social challenges (Van Breda, 2017). Previous studies among student social workers that identified educational and psychosocial challenges affecting studies (Van Breda, 2017; Dykes and Green, 2015) do not, however, indicate how the identification of needs has guided the development of discipline-specific holistic-supported education practices in South Africa. Furthermore, additional challenges experienced during the COVID-19 pandemic must be considered and included when holistic-supported education practices are being developed.

This chapter is based on the findings of a study that explored final year student social workers' experiences during the pandemic and their perspectives regarding what is needed to be prepared for practice when their academic lives are disrupted. The aim was to identify key aspects, resources, and role-players to be included in a holistic-supported education framework for social work fieldwork modules at a South African university.

Background

In a post-colonial and post-apartheid South Africa, the lingering influences of the past injustices in academia cannot be ignored (Prinsloo, 2016). In the context of Higher Education (HE), the so-called Africanising of our approach to curricula and student support becomes essential to contribute to the development of a just society (Tamburro, 2013; Republic of South Africa, 2013). Sadly, Van Breda (2017) and Prinsloo (2016) assert that recent events at universities do not only show students' dissatisfaction with ongoing colonial practices and student fees, but also portray their dissatisfaction with society. Van Breda (2017) argues that academic practices must acknowledge that students not only face educational challenges, but also experience significant adversity in their families and communities that may contribute to mental health problems (Maluleke, 2018; Bantjes et al., 2017). These adversities include poverty, exposure to crime, violence and substance abuse, inequality, financial burdens, a lack of access to technology expected by universities, gender discrimination, social exclusion, and unhealthy lifestyles (Van Breda 2017; Aldiabat et al., 2014). The need to provide holistic support to address educational, psychological, physical, intellectual, spiritual, and emotional needs to mitigate the impact of socioeconomic challenges on students, especially for students who are less likely to receive the support they need, is illuminated (Tamburro, 2013).

In terms of educational challenges, a high number of students who enter South African universities do not have the required study skills and strategies to succeed in HE (Council of Higher Education [CHE], 2013). In addition, Siyengo (2015) found that first-generation students experience added stressors that include academic language, the requirements of the academic curricula, as well as co-curriculum activities. It must be considered that the majority of South African students are first-generation students, described as 'underprepared, coming from impoverished backgrounds in terms of economic strength, poor schooling and socio-cultural resources, and using English as an additional language' (Dykes and Green, 2015, p. 577). This points to the influence of a person's environment on learning to be addressed through context-relevant supported education practices.

Considering the legacy of the apartheid era, Sommer and Dumont (2011) concur that students who attend the so-called historically disadvantaged institutions in South Africa experience further challenges to be acknowledged and included in educational support practices. These authors argue that while equity in access to HE has been attained, equity in graduate output has not been attained when the disparities in dropout and graduation rates of students from historically disadvantaged and advantaged groups are compared (South Africa, 2019). Maringe and Osman (2016) go further to argue that students from disadvantaged communities mostly attend historically disadvantaged institutions, and they find it harder to access employment opportunities because of the perceptions of inferior learning and teaching practices at such universities. Likewise, as HEIs focus on maintaining and pursuing global trends in performance and competition for rankings and throughput rates (Mayet, 2016), so does the need for supported education and social support increase. As such, HE was identified as a sector requiring reform in the National Development Plan 2030 (National Planning Commission, 2011). The focus has largely been on curriculum transformation and inclusivity and not on the identification of supported education needs to support student retention and throughput that include preparation for practice. Furthermore, when we speak about a decolonial practice, we need to consider the complexities of students' holistic needs and their lived experiences.

Apart from socioeconomic and educational challenges, mental health challenges among South African university students are common and may result in suicide, the second-leading cause of death among university students (Jung, 2021; World Health Organisation, [WHO], 2019; September, 2018). Jung (2021) and Khaldoun et al. (2014) identified reasons behind mental health issues among students as a result of social change in a post-school environment, stressful academic conditions, financial burden, a lack of access to technology expected by universities, gender discrimination, social exclusion, and unhealthy lifestyles, among others. These authors identify depression, anxiety, and stress as the most prevalent mental health disorders among South African university students, particularly among female students (Johnson et al. 2019).

On the one hand, Khaldoun et al. (2014) conclude that South African universities should develop tools that support students to address those stressors that put academic and personal development at risk. On the other hand, Siyengo (2015) notes that HEIs should empower students by linking them with professional and personal resources to develop coping strategies so that they can successfully complete their studies. These two viewpoints are linked by Sommer (2013), who reports on the psychosocial factors that need to be acknowledged when providing student support in terms of help-seeking behaviour, academic motivation, self-esteem, perceived stress and academic overload, test anxiety, and self-efficacy.

The Strategic Policy Framework on Disability for the Post-School Education and Training System proposes that HEIs consider 'physical, mental, intellectual, developmental or sensory impairments' to be accommodated through learning and teaching practices and contexts that support the full development of human potential (South Africa, 2018,: p. 28). Fleming et al. (2018), however, assert that students' disclosure, especially with regard to mental health challenges, is needed to ensure reasonable accommodation within an academic setting. While institutional structures such as student support centres provide different forms of support, it remains unclear how programmes can include supported education practices to enhance students' holistic wellbeing and development and preparation for practice.

Challenges for Student Social Workers Experienced in Fieldwork Modules

Social work, as a helping profession, has to do with direct services to those in need to nurture holistic growth towards the development of potential (Graf et al., 2014). Dârjan and Thomita (2014) assert that direct service requires academic knowledge and skills and personal attributes such as compassion and objectivity, which can affect professionals in positive and negative ways. As such, the standards for a bachelor of social work degree in South Africa include Self vis-à-vis professional practice as a core knowledge requirement, focusing on the development and consolidation of a professional identity to understand the Self as an important intervention instrument (CHE, 2015). Therefore, education and training need to include an awareness of students' psychosocial profile to provide them with effective support to prepare for their careers.

Prior to the pandemic, Dykes and Green (2015) highlighted a need among student social workers to participate actively in learning activities, to relate academic work with real-life social experiences, for lecturers to respond to their emotional reactions, to create debriefing opportunities, and to be empowered to effectively engage with self-assessments. HEIs, in line with the regulations to control the spread of the coronavirus, had to adhere to the protocols relevant to the different lockdown levels (Ramaphosa, 2020). This included a move to emergency online learning and teaching practices. Due to the various waves of infections, no timeframes could be determined to plan for a return to campus. An understanding of how the pandemic further affected experiences of learning and teaching in fieldwork modules is required to identify what is needed to prepare student social workers for practice during emergency online learning and teaching, and also in a post-pandemic context.

COVID-19 Pandemic as an Academic Disruption

Traditional residential social work education and training primarily use face-to-face practices while including some technology-based learning and teaching activities (Bosch et al., 2020; Ubah et al., 2019). During the pandemic, these practices had to move rapidly to an online platform. Chetty and Pather (2015) highlighted prior to the pandemic that the inequalities in primary and secondary education systems resulted in students from disadvantaged South African communities being underprepared for online learning and teaching in tertiary settings due to, among others, a lack of exposure to technology in school settings. As such, the previous divide between historically advantaged and disadvantaged institutions became more visible during the pandemic (Dwolatzky and Harris, 2020).

Viewed as the heart of social work education and training, fieldwork modules require direct activities where students are able to integrate what they have learned into practice. Within fieldwork modules, supervision sessions create space for students to reflect on how the social issues they encounter in practice impact them, on the one hand, and how their own real-life experiences influence their responses, on the other hand (Schmidt and Rautenbach, 2016). Dhemba (2012) and Shokane et al. (2016) argue that these modules are, however, underemphasised, and that there is a need to explore how fieldwork modules can be developed to ensure high-quality preparation practice. Van der Westhuizen et al. (2021) and Kourgiantakis and Lee (2020) argue that while blended-learning in fieldwork modules has been described as effective, more research is needed to understand how students' learning needs can be accommodated on online platforms. Online learning and teaching in fieldwork modules during the pandemic can guide a discovery of what can be used post the pandemic (Kourgiantakis and Lee, 2020) to prepare for future academic disruptions (Amadasun, 2020).

Supported Education as a Framework for Holistic Development

Supported education interventions were developed by researchers in Germany and the Netherlands, and Bantjes et al. (2017) argue for exploring how both face-to-face and online interventions could be tested in and adapted to the South African context.

Korevaar and Hofstra (2018) describe typical academic barriers to be addressed through holistic and context-related support in terms of cognitive and illness-related barriers, social and emotional challenges, and environmental influences. The concern regarding disparities between historically advantaged and disadvantaged communities and institutions (South Africa, 2019) is acknowledged by supported education, as it aspires to ensure social justice. Hofstra and Korevaar's (2016) framework for supported education caters for diverse needs to provide all students with an opportunity to reach their potential. The philosophy of supported education in HE includes that choice is fundamental and that students take control of their vulnerability, their environment, and their future. Students explore and identify their learning needs and, in return, are assisted to acquire skills and resources to achieve their academic goals. The unique needs of students are catered for by means of individualised support by a variety of role-players within the HEI and the community. In this way, supported education aligns well with Africanised developments in HEIs, as it includes the principles of fairness, equality, worthiness, and rights and responsibilities applicable to all as well as the acknowledgement of different needs and capabilities (Meckled-Garcia, 2011).

The need for context-relevant research to identify key aspects, resources, and role-players to include in a discipline-specific supported education framework (Bantjes et al., 2017) is based on the viewpoint that the psychosocial wellbeing of student social workers will impact their ability to provide quality care to members of the South African society (Dârjan and Thomita, 2014). Within this understanding, vulnerable students should be provided with structures and support systems to empower them to excel academically with the aim to prepare them for practice.

Theoretical Framework

This chapter is underpinned by the developmental approach to education and training, where students' life experiences are acknowledged. Van Breda (2017) explains that while challenges such as academic stress, diversity, and poverty are visible, HEIs should also become aware of non-visible challenges that have an impact on student success. The holistic nature of a developmental approach to education and training could include any positive or traumatic event that influences the student financially, emotionally, spiritually, intellectually, and/or socially. When this is acknowledged, it becomes possible to provide students with a context-relevant learning and teaching framework where they can develop on all levels needed for career preparation as a form of life preparation (Johnson et al., 2019; Henrico, 2015).

By addressing holistic needs of students, HEIs show a genuine interest in student development and success. The long-term aim is to develop an intrinsic motivation and desire for life-long learning (Hofstra and Korevaar, 2016) by not approaching students as victims lacking the ability to change and to take responsibility for themselves and others. Instead, it looks at students exposed to educational and psychosocial challenges as survivors; providing them with opportunities, knowledge, and skills to grow in all areas of their lives and enhancing their full potential (Barkley and Major, 2020).

It is imperative to include students' voices when holistic supported education practices are being designed and implemented (Prinsloo 2016). This standpoint guided the formulation of the research questions: What are the educational and psychosocial needs of fourth-year student social workers that emerged during the COVID-19 pandemic? What resources and role-players need to be included in a supported education framework to address their needs to respond to academic disruptions while preparing them for practice?

Research Methodology

A qualitative approach was followed and supported by contextual and explorative research designs. Purposive non-probability sampling was used to select the participants in this study. Inclusion criteria were fourth-year student social workers at a university in the Western Cape of South Africa who could report on their experiences during the pandemic that affected them in terms of preparation for practice. All fourth-year student social workers at the university were informed about the nature of this study and requested to participate. Twenty students gave informed consent for voluntary participation. Journaling was used as the method to access qualitative data through a reflection on experiences, thoughts, and understanding of the research topic (Hayman et al., 2012). Semi-structured open-ended questions were provided to the participants to guide their reflections. The journals were used to conduct a thematic analysis, using Tesch's (in Creswell, 2014) step-by-step framework.

Ethics included voluntary participation and informed consent. Although participation in this study was voluntary, the sensitive nature of exploring psychosocial needs was acknowledged. Therefore, debriefing opportunities were arranged to be accessible. Anonymity, privacy, and confidentiality were ensured through the use of pseudonyms, the storage of data on a password-protected computer, and a collective presentation of data (Halej, 2017).

The primary limitation of this study was that it included only one university, representing a historically disadvantaged context. While the findings could be generalised to other HEIs, findings could be different when the same methodology is employed at previously advantaged universities.

Key Themes

Educational and psychosocial challenges, resources, and role-players represent the main themes of the findings.

Educational Challenges

The participants felt underprepared regarding competencies to engage with service users, impacting their readiness to enter practice. 'Feeling unprepared is a major challenge for me'. 'It (online learning and teaching) impacted on our readiness to go into the field as there are still several areas which could be improved on'. They mentioned a concern regarding the application of knowledge and skills due to a lack of face-to-face engagements: 'The pandemic has robbed us of our practical experience which was going to be beneficial for acquiring skills and experience that we were going to apply in practice.' 'I am not adequately prepared for the field due to little practical experience'. This left them anxious: 'There is an increased sense of fear and anxiety'. A student expressed a feeling of being less confident and disadvantaged: 'I am feeling less confident because the social work profession is based on working with clientele therefore it is important to build confidence from practical experience. However, with the lack of that I am left feeling disadvantaged'.

A full online learning experience created a sense of loss regarding opportunities to build confidence and skills to prepare students for practice (Sarbu and Unwin, 2021; Phelan, 2015). Truell and Crompton (2020) confirm that not being able to access fieldwork settings led to a lack of confidence and field readiness. As such, online learning seems not to translate well for students in developing confidence and professional competencies (Apgar and Cadmus, 2022). In this regard, Van der Westhuizen et al. (2021) propose consideration of a blended-learning approach.

Psychosocial Challenges

Landa et al. (2021) explain emotional challenges during the pandemic as heightened anxiety and depression due to the pandemic itself, academic stresses, and reduced access to psychosocial support. Participants reported: 'There were many emotional challenges that we faced, and therefore not able to focus on work; creating mental health issues, such as anxiety and depression'. They referred to the fear of infection that impacted their ability to engage with studies and mental health: 'Panic and anxiety are created as people are anxious to be infected with the Covid-19 virus'. 'I began experiencing panic attacks due to the overwhelming situation I am faced with'. 'Mentally I am not prepared to be out in the field because of the fear of getting the virus'. A participant explained the link between psychological and educational challenges as follows: 'My self-efficacy, my motivation and procrastination, my stress, and my anxiety all affected my psychological state'.

Working online and restrictions in movement were highlighted as aspects impacting on emotional wellbeing: 'Sitting in front of a laptop all day in one space is draining and demotivating. Pairing that along with restrictions is a recipe for disaster as students had no alternative way of releasing stress'. Heightened anxiety levels (Apgar and Cadmus, 2022) and the negative effect of the pandemic on the mental health of South African university students due to isolation and disconnectedness from peers (Visser and Law-Van Wyk, 2021) have been reported. This was confirmed by the participants: 'Being separated from classmates for a while, I realised that the relationship is no longer as connected as it used to be'. They expressed how this affected their academic experiences: I feel disconnected and find it challenging to work'. 'Feeling disconnected from the learning experience'. These descriptions highlight that the restrictions on physical contact challenged students both emotionally and academically (Fegert et al., 2020; Apgar and Cadmus, 2022).

Furthermore, home circumstances challenged students during the pandemic: 'People drink and party all the time. It is very distracting, you can hardly focus on anything'. 'Many had to endure staying in homes which were overcrowded or busy throughout the day which made focusing on academics merely impossible'. 'Those students with difficult family circumstances or relationships found it increasingly hard to work from home and adequately prepare for the field'. These descriptions point to students being challenged to find a balance between home and academic lives, impacting on their development and preparation for practice (Landa et al., 2021).

Resources Needed

A substantive shift of resources is required to ensure that students are supported to successfully engage with online learning and teaching (Perumal et al., 2021; Landa et al., 2021). The participants raised concerns about a lack of access to resources that impacted their learning: 'Not having the resources e.g. laptop, electricity'. 'Not having stable WIFI connection'. 'I needed a laptop to access classes and do assignments… I was not able to afford data'.

Interestingly, only one student referred to mental support resources needed: 'The resources that students needed were mental support'.

The Role-players

Lecturers and supervisors were identified as vital role-players in preparing students for practice: 'The supervisor and lecturers are the main role-players from whom we need support in preparing for practice'. Supervisors are employed by the university to provide on-campus, in this case online, supervision in fieldwork modules.

Modelling was identified as a key role of the lecturer: 'Lecturers help students in modelling how their profession works, to help students understand and improve academically'. The participants highlighted that lecturers should be aware of students' contextual realities: 'Lecturers need to understand the circumstances of students during COVID-19'. 'Lecturers should ask students how they are coping'. 'They should understand our challenges'.

The students referred to the supervisors as both a role-player and a resource to support them emotionally: 'The supervisor plays an important role in providing support to students when academics are overwhelming'. 'Supervisors also provide guidance to help students overcome the challenges that they are faced with'. 'Not only do they help in the process of providing educational support, but they also offer emotional support and advice'.

While emotional support was needed prior to the pandemic (Dykes and Green, 2015), this became more accentuated during the pandemic (Mirick and Davis, 2021), further accentuating the need to include contextual realities in learning and teaching practices. During a pandemic, it was evident that students would be challenged, but it is also important to be aware of individual times of crisis (Berger and Calderon, 2014). A student asked that both physical and emotional/mental challenges should be taken into consideration: 'Not just physical challenges where a medical certificate is required'. Another participating student referred to a need to be referred to resources when needed: 'A personal therapist … as this will ensure that one's well-being stays adhered to'.

The findings were used to reflect on what this means in terms of holistic and supported education to enhance the preparation of students for practice.

Conclusion

This discussion explored students' experiences during the pandemic to make recommendations for social work education and training during academic disruptions. The findings point to an overlap between educational and psychosocial challenges experienced by students. The lack of exposure to fieldwork settings left students feeling disadvantaged and underprepared. This resulted in fear and anxiety to enter practice. The lack of access to devices and socioeconomic and home circumstances led to further anxiety and becoming demotivated. The need for support to access resources was described in terms of a lack of devices, electricity, and data, and a need to have access to emotional support. The latter was related to the role of lecturers and supervisors. The participants accentuated the importance of awareness and consideration of their contextual realities and to be referred to relevant support systems to address these challenges.

The findings relate to Rybska and Blaszak's (2020) reference to three pillars of holistic education to be considered during academic disruptions. First, the *internal world* has to be included in terms of ensuring inclusiveness and participation to support internalised engagement with what students learn, and how they apply this in practice. Second, the *external world* is considered when learning and teaching activities are enhanced through social interactions that support exchanges of ideas and shared problem-solving. Third, *internal values* need to be explored and related to professional principles and values and an understanding of the Self as an intervention tool (cf. CHE, 2015). During times of crises, such as pandemics, these pillars could be supported by technology.

For example, using breakout rooms on the online platform, reflections and individual sessions, albeit online, with lecturers and supervisors, and online simulation activities.

Recommendations

It is recommended that a supported education framework includes:

1. Lecturers and supervisors collaborate to assess academic and psychosocial needs within the supervision component of the fieldwork modules. The outcomes of the assessments are accommodated through reflective practices where students identify how their own vulnerabilities and realities affect preparedness for practice, and included in individual development plans (Hofstra and Korevaar, 2016).
2. The development of a resource list within the HEI (internal) and the community (external) is essential for student referrals to access academic and psychosocial support.
3. Technology through blended-learning can ensure (1) preparedness for emergency online learning and teaching, and (2) skills to use technology in practice.

The recommendations are aimed to support the development of a holistic supportive learning and teaching environment and content towards personal and professional development to prepare students for practice.

Further Reading

Ajibo, H., Mbah, F. and Anazonwu, N. (2017). 'Field work practice in social work', in U. Okoye, N. Chukwu, and P. Agwu (eds.) *Social Work in Nigeria: Book of Readings* (pp. 104–113). Nsukka: University of Nigeria Press Ltd.

Czerniewicz, L., Agherdien, N., Badenhorst, J., Belluigi, D., Chambers. T., Chili, M., de Villiers, M., Felix, A., Gachago, D., Gokhale, C., Ivala, E., Kramm, N., Madiba, M., Mistri, G., Mgqwashu, E., Pallitt, N., Prinsloo, P., Solomon, K., Strydom, S. et al. (2020). 'A wake-up call: Equity, inequality and Covid-19 emergency remote teaching and learning', *Post-Digital Science and Education*, 2(3), 946–967.

References

Apgar, D. and Cadmus, T. (2022). 'Using mixed methods to assess the coping and self-regulation skills of undergraduate social work students impacted by COVID-19', *Clinical Social Work Journal*, 50(1), 55–66.

Aldiabat, K. M. *et al.* (2014). 'Depression among university students in South Africa', *Universal Journal of Public Health*, 2(8), 209–214.

Amadasun, S. (2020). 'Social work and the Covid 19 pandemic: An action call', *International Social Work*, 63(6), 753–775.

Bantjes, J. *et al.* (2017). 'Global study aims to unpack mental health issues facing university students', *University of Cape Town News*. https://www.news.uct.ac.za.

Barkley, E. and Major, C. H. (2020). *Student Engagement Techniques: A Handbook for College Faculty* (2nd ed.). Hoboken, NF: Jossey Bass.

Berger, R. and Calderon, O. (2014). 'Helping those who learn to help: Addressing stress during a community disaster', *Reflections: Narratives of Professional Helping*, 20(2), 17–25.

Bosch, C. *et al.* (2020). 'Cooperative learning as a blended learning strategy: A conceptual overview', in IGI Global (ed.) *Emerging Techniques and Applications for Blended Learning in K-20 Classrooms* (pp. 65–87). IGI Global.

Chetty, R. and Pather, S. (2015). 'Challenges in higher education in South Africa', in J. Condy (ed.) *Telling Stories Differently. Engaging 21st Century Students Through Digital Storytelling* (pp. 1–7). Stellenbosch: SUN Media.

Council on Higher Education (CHE) (2013). *Report of the Task Team on Undergraduate Curriculum Reform in South Africa. Discussion Document*. Pretoria: South African Council for Higher Education.
Council for Higher Education (CHE) (2015). *Qualification Standard for Bachelor of Social Work*. Pretoria: South African Council for Higher Education.
Creswell, J. W. (2014). *Research Design: Qualitative, Quantitative and Mixed Methods Approaches* (4th ed.). Thousand Oaks, CA: Sage.
Dârjan, I. and Thomita, M. (2014). 'Helping professionals: The bless and the burden of helping', Paper presented at The Second World Congress on Resilience: From Person to Society. West University of Timisoara, Romania, May 2014.
Dhemba, J. (2012). 'Fieldwork in social work education and training: Issues and challenges in the case of Eastern and Southern Africa', *Social Work and Society*, 10(1), 1–16.
Dwolatzky, B. and Harris, M. (2020). 'SA Education: A national reset is needed and mass internet access is the only way forward', *The Daily Maverick*. https://www.dailymaverick.co.za/article/2020-07-02-sa-education-a-national-reset-is-needed-and-mass-internet-access-is-the-only-way-forward/.
Dykes, G. and Green, S. (2015). 'Learning profiles of student social workers: Who are you and how should this influence my teaching?', *Social Work/Maatskaplike Werk*, 51(1), 577–598.
Fegert, J. *et al.* (2020). 'Challenges and burden of the coronavirus 2019 (COVID-19) pandemic for child and adolescent mental health: A narrative review to highlight clinical and research needs in the acute phase and the long return to normality', *Child and Adolescent Psychiatry and Mental Health*, 14(1), 1–11.
Fleming, A. *et al.* (2018). 'Treatment-seeking college students with disabilities: Presenting concerns, protective factors, and academic distress', *Rehabilitation Psychology*, 63(1), 55–67.
Graf, E. *et al.* (eds) (2014). *Discourses of Helping Professions*. Amsterdam: Benjamins.
Halej, J. (2017). *Ethics in Primary Research (Focus Groups, Interviews and Surveys). United Kingdom and Scotland: Equality in Higher Education*. Equality Challenge Unit (ECU).
Hayman, B. *et al.* (2012). 'Journaling: Identification of challenges and reflection on strategies', *Nurse Researcher*, 19(3), 27–31.
Henrico, K. (2015). *An Appreciative Self-Management Coaching Programme to Facilitate the Wellness of Somatology Therapists*. Bloemfontein: University of Free State.
Hofstra, J. and Korevaar, L. (eds.) (2016). *Supported Education Toolkit*. Groningen: Research and Innovation Centre for Rehabilitation.
Johnson, J. *et al.* (2019). 'Teaching the whole student: Integrating wellness education into the academic classroom', *Student Success*, 10(3), 92–103.
Jung, C. (2021). *Why Does It Take A Pandemic to See the Real Pandemic – Mental Health?* Pretoria: Arbinger Institute.
Khaldoun, M. A. *et al.* (2014). 'Depression among university students in South Africa', *Universal Journal of Public Health*, 2(8), 209–214.
Korevaar, L. and Hofstra, J. (2018). *Supported Education Training Manual*. Groningen: Research and Innovation Centre for Rehabilitation.
Kourgiantakis, T. and Lee, E. (2020). 'Social work practice education and training during the pandemic. Disruptions and discoveries', *International Social Work*, 63(6), 761–765.
Landa, N. *et al.* (2021). 'Education in emergencies: Lessons from COVID-19 in South Africa', *International Review of Education*, 67(1–2), 167–183.
Maluleke, R. (2018). 'StatsSA quarterly Labour force survey: Q2:2018. Statistics South Africa'. http://www.statssa.gov.za/publications/P0211/Presentation_QLFS_Q2_2018.pdf.
Maringe, F. and Osman, R. (2016). 'Transforming the post-school sector in South Africa: Limits of a skills-driven agenda', *South African Journal of Higher Education*, 30(5), 120, 140.
Mayet, R. (2016). 'Supporting at-risk learners at a comprehensive university in South Africa', *Journal of Student Affairs in Africa*, 4(2), 1–12.
Meckled-Garcia, S. (2011). *Human Rights or Social Justice? Rescuing Human Rights from the Outcomes View: Working Paper 30*. London, UK: London University College: School of Public Policy.
Mirick, R. G. and Davis, A. (2021). 'Supporting social work students during the COVID-19 pandemic', *Journal of Teaching in Social Work*, 41(5), 484–504.
Moodley, P. and Singh, R. J. (2015). 'Addressing student dropout rates at South African Universities', *Alternation Special Edition*, 17, 91–115.

National Planning Commission (NPC) (2011). *National Development Plan: Vision for 2030*. Pretoria: Office of the Presidency.

Perumal, N. *et al.* (2021). 'Autoethnographic view of South African social work educators during the COVID-19 pandemic: Highlighting social (in)justice', *Social Work/Maatskaplike Werk*, 57(4), 393–406.

Phelan, J. E. (2015). 'The use of e-learning in social work education', *Social Work*, 60(3), 257–264.

Prinsloo, E. H. (2016). 'The role of the humanities in decolonising the academy', *Arts and Humanities in Higher Education*, 15(1), 164–168.

Ramaphosa, C. (2020). 'Coronavirus: President Ramaphosa announces a 21-day lockdown', *INSESSION: Official Newspaper of the Parliament of the Republic of South Africa*, 1(9), 1–16.

Republic of South Africa (2013). *White Paper for Post-school Education and Training: Building A Expanded, Effective and Integrated Post-school System*. Pretoria: Government Printers.

Rybska, E. and Blaszak, M. (2020). 'Holistic education – A model based on three pillars from cognitive science. An example from science education', *Issues in Early Education*, 2(49), 1–16.

Sarbu, R. and Unwin, P. (2021). 'Complexities in student placements under COVID-19: Moral and practical considerations', *Frontiers in Education*, 6(654843), 1–8.

Schmidt, K. and Rautenbach, J. V. (2016). 'Field instruction: Is the heart of social work education still beating in the Eastern Cape?', *Social Work/Maatskaplike Werk*, 52(4), 589–610.

September, J. (2018). 'Campus suicide'. https://www.wits.ac.za/news/latest-news/in-their-own-words/2018/2018-10/campus-suicide.html.

Shokane, A. L. *et al.* (2016). 'Challenges faced by fourth year social work students during fieldwork practice at a rural-based university', *AFFRIKA Journal of Politics, Economics and Society*, 6(1 and 2), 33–163.

Siyengo, N. (2015). *The Educational and Psychosocial Experiences of First-Generation Students in Higher Education*. Master of Education Dissertation in Educational Support. Stellenbosch University, Stellenbosh.

Sommer, M. M. (2013). *Psychosocial Factors Predicting the Adjustment and Academic Performance of University Students*. Doctor of Philosophy In Psychology Thesis. University of South Africa, Pretoria.

Sommer, M. M. and Dumont, K. (2011). 'Psychosocial factors predicting academic performance of students at a historically disadvantaged university', *South African Journal of Psychology*, 41(3), 386–395.

South Africa (2018). *Strategic Policy Framework on Disability for the Post-school Education and Training System*. Pretoria: Department of Higher Education and Training.

South Africa (2019). *Towards a 25-Year Review of Democracy: 1994–2019*. Pretoria: Government of South Africa. Department of Planning, Monitoring and Evaluation.

Tamburro, A. (2013). 'Including decolonization in social work education and practice', *Journal of Indigenous Social Development*, 2(1), 1–16.

Truell, R. and Crompton, S. (2020). 'To the top of the cliff: How social work changed with COVID-19', http://www.ifsw.org/to-the-top-of-the-cliff-how-socialwork-changed-with-covid-19.

Ubah, I. J. A. *et al.* (2019). 'Blended learning approaches at higher education institutions to prepare mathematics pre-service teachers for practice: A review of literature', Paper presented at The International Conference on Education: Rethinking Teaching and Learning in the 21st Century: African Academic Research Forum. Pretoria, 16–18 September 2019.

Van Breda, A. D. (2017). 'Students are humans too: Psychosocial vulnerability of first-year students at the University of Johannesburg', *South African Journal of Higher Education*, 31(5), 246–262.

Van der Westhuizen, M. A. *et al.* (2021). 'A reflection on the use of technologies in social work practical modules within the South African context', *Journal of Education for Sustainable Development*, 16(1), 54–73.

Visser, M. and Law-van Wyk, E. (2021). 'University students' mental health and emotional wellbeing during the COVID-19 pandemic and ensuing lockdown', *South African Journal of Psychology*, 51(2), 229–243.

World Health Organization (WHO) (2019). 'Mental health'. https://www.who.int/health-topics/mental-health#tab=tab2.

PART 4

Knowledge Exchange between the Global South and the Global North

27
PRIORITISING INDIGENOUS KNOWLEDGE IN SOCIAL WORK EDUCATION THROUGH EXPERIENTIAL LEARNING

Narratives from Social Workers

Rita Adoma Parry, Elizabeth Onyedikachi George, and Catherine Suubi Kayonga

Abstract: English

Social work education in Africa has been criticised as being Eurocentric, with little done to centre the socio-cultural context and peculiarity of Africa. The ontology, epistemology, theories and practice models of social work in many African institutions appear to be deeply rooted in Eurocentric hegemony and individualism considered superior to African communalism and being. This has resulted in the relatively notable absence of indigenous knowledge in African social work scholarship and students going into professional practice with knowledge far removed from the everyday realities of the African people. This chapter aims to identify opportunities for effective social work education in Africa that highlights indigenous knowledge and draws on narratives from social workers from Ghana, Nigeria, Uganda, Ethiopia and Zambia, with fieldwork experiences in both Africa and Europe. Findings show the importance of and opportunities in experiential learning, through field practicum, exchange programmes, and balancing a heavily theorised western education model with everyday African experiences that are capable of dealing with the unique challenges Africans face. To encourage indigenisation of social work practice in Africa, we recommend that researchers and practitioners collaborate in developing a modern framework based on home-grown philosophies across the African continent that can promote efficient service provision.

Abstract: Luganda

Eby'enjigiriza by'embeera z'abantu mu Africa binenyezebwa nti byekubiira nnyo ku ludda lwe'kizungu; kitono nnyo ekikoleddwa okwesigamya enjigirirza yaabyo ku buwangwa n'enjawulo eriwo wakati wa bazungu n'abaddugavu. Ebyenkula, entegeera, era n'ebyokwefumitiriza mu byembeera z'abantu mu matendekero mangi mu Africa kirabika gasimba nnyo essira ku busukulumu era n'obwansiwa mukange ebirowoozebwa nti birina enkizo ku nkola y'abaddugavu eyanakalyaako ani. Kino kiretedde amagezi g'abaddugavu okuba nga gakozesebwa kitono mu misomo gy'embeera z'abantu era nga abayizi baagyo bakola emirimu gyaabwe nga bakozesa amagezi agatakwatagana na mbeera z'abaddugavu. Musuula eno ekigengedererwa kwekuzuula ebisoboka okukolebwa okulaba nga bakola ku mbeera za bantu mu baddugavu basosowoza amagezi g'obuwangwa agabaddugavu nga enkola mu Ghana, Uganda, Ethiopia ne Zambia yekenenyezebwa era ngenkola mu Africa ne Europe nayo etaganjulwa. Ebyokunonyereza biraga omugaso oguli mu kugenda mu nsiike, okuwanyisiganyanga ebinonyerezebwaako nga kigendererwa okukendeeza ku kwefumitiriza okwesigamye ku bazungu era nokulaba nti embeera ezabulijjo ez'abaddugavu zisibwaako essira era ng'okunonyereza okukolebwa kiriganyura abaddugavu mu kusoomozebwa kwonna kwebasannga. Okunyikiza amagezi ganansangwa agabaddugavu mukola ku bantu mu Africa twagala abanonyereza era n'abo abakola ku mbeera z'abantu bakolaganire wamu mukukiriza entendeka ey'omulembe nga yesigama ku birowoozo bya bantu ba Africa weefa yenkana ng'ekigendererwa kwekutumbula n'okukulakulanya embeera za bantu.

Introduction

Social work education in Africa is committed to training practitioners who will be able to intervene in the life situations of Africans, especially those who are in vulnerable and marginalised situations. Africa remains one of the most vulnerable continents in the world with social, economic, and environmental challenges. The continent has suffered years of colonisation, wars and instability, poverty, hunger, etc. The plethora of Africa's problems makes the social work profession particularly crucial due to its commitment to promoting social change and development, social cohesion, and the empowerment and liberation of (African) people (International Federation of Social Workers (IFSW), 2014). However, social work education and practice in Africa are faced with several challenges that make the profession unable to deliver on its core mandate.

Social work has its roots in Western colonialism and capitalism which centre more on individualism and modernism that are distinct from African realities of collectivism and shared destiny. The Western philosophical background continues to dominate the ontology, epistemology and methodology of social work education and practice in Africa. Meanwhile, western concepts have not helped the social work profession to solve the social ills of Africa because they fail to account for the local and cultural realities of Africans. Consequently, many social workers after their training become unrecognised in their countries, unemployed, or migrate to other Western countries where their acquired education will be relevant, and they can get better careers (Veta and McLaughlin, 2022).

Social work education in Africa has therefore been challenged to shift from its Western-centred theorisation and orientation to embrace locally and culturally relevant indigenous approaches that are meaningful to the needs of the people it seeks to help. Following the criticisms and recommendations, African scholars have continuously explored the best possible ways to improve social work education and practice. Mwansa (2010) particularly notes that there should be a synthesis of the already existing Western theories and African cultural values that are appropriate to Africans.

One less emphasised aspect of social work education when it comes to indigenisation is field practicum. This is where budding social work students are exposed to the real-world situations through practice placements to work with various social work service user groups, organisations, and communities. The findings from our study support the argument that the field practicum area of social work education holds much promise for indigenising social work education in Africa. Reflecting on our backgrounds as social workers who have received social work education in both Africa and Europe, we believe that there is much to learn from both worldviews to this effect.

Therefore, this chapter draws on findings from a virtual qualitative study (semi-structured interviews) we conducted via Zoom on the experiences of 12 social workers from Ghana, Nigeria, Ethiopia, Zambia, and Uganda, who have received social work education in both Africa and Europe. Thus, they understand how indigenous knowledge applies in both contexts, especially in social work education and field practicum, a criterion that was important for the analysis of collected data and our reflection on reciprocal learning.

We discuss the evolution of social work practice and education in the South, experiences of field practicum with regards to indigenisation and the criticisms/challenges associated with achieving practising indigenous social work in the continent of Africa. Emphasising the importance of reciprocal learning between the North and the South in our study, we discuss some best practices in both contexts worthy of emulation to promote global social work practice. Lastly, we make some recommendations for the development of an up-to-date indigenous framework by us and for us to promote contextual social work practice in Africa.

Evolution of Social Work Education in Africa

Social work practice has seen tremendous evolution in Africa since its inception. It is tenable to argue that the practice of social work existed in Africa even before colonialism. That is, Africans were already catering for each other's welfare through the family clan system and community. Initially, colonialism provided the sociopolitical environment in which the social work profession was formed in Africa (Mwansa, 2011). The profession was modeled after the welfare system of the colonial countries like Britain and France that were more industrialised (Shawky, 1972). Also, the evolution of social work in Africa prominently featured missionaries whose arrival in Africa even preceded the colonialists (Umoren, 2016). The missionaries significantly shaped the ethical and moral foundation of African social work through their teaching of mostly Christian virtues like respect, charity, caregiving, and non-violence, among others. Moreover, their commitment to social-infrastructural development like building schools has contributed to education in Africa.

In Zambia, social work sprang up as a result of industrialisation and urbanisation, where social welfare services were introduced to safeguard the wellbeing of employees, while in Ghana social services began in 1939 as a result of an earthquake and in 1946 as part of efforts to care for the needs of veterans of the Second World War (Association of Social Work Education in Africa [ASWEA], 1974; Mwansa, 2011). In Togo and Sierra Leone, social welfare ministries were introduced in 1974, and similar departments were established in countries like Nigeria, Tanzania, Senegal, Ethiopia, Kenya, Ivory Coast, Madagascar, and Cameroon (Mwansa, 2011, cited in ASWEA Documents, 1973 and 1974). While in South Africa, social work was introduced to offer services to the white population (Association of Social Work Education in Africa [ASWEA], 1974; Mwansa, 2011).

Higher education social work institutions started in South Africa between 1931 and 1934 in Stellenbosch, Cape Town, and Pretoria (Gray et al., 2014). The initiation of schools of social work then followed in other African countries like Egypt in 1936, Algeria in 1942, Ghana in 1945, Zambia in 1950, Uganda in 1954, Tanzania in 1958, Ethiopia in 1959, Burkina Faso in 1960, and Tunisia and Zimbabwe in 1964 (Gray et al., 2014). The established social work schools emphasised colonial models in the education of higher learning and only provided basic skills or technical training instead of a full-fledged social work profession at the time (Gray et al., 2014).

Field Practice in Social Work Education

Social work as a professional discipline is anchored in a unified curriculum consisting of both theory and fieldwork components. Tracing the history of social work education (as recorded in Europe and North America), it is evident that fieldwork has almost always been integral to social work education and training. Social work education started in Europe and North America in the last quarter of the 19th century with its history dating back to the era of the Charity Organisation Societies when students learned social work by apprenticeship (Dhemba, 2012). As apprentices, students learnt by doing, obtaining firsthand knowledge of what it meant to work with people in poverty and other adverse conditions, through applied philanthropy (Dhemba, 2012). By the end of the 19th century, social work gradually evolved from the apprenticeship method with the launching of the first social work training in 1898 (Dhemba, 2012). This was a summer school established at the New York City Charity Organisation Society (Durst, 2010). Six years later, in 1904, the society established the New York School of Philanthropy, which offered eight months' training in social work (Durst, 2010). Further to these developments, George (1982) asserted that Mary Richmond, an early social work practitioner, teacher, and theoretician, advocated for complementing field learning with academic education. He also observed that early in social work education, students spent about half of their academic time in field settings.

The fieldwork component of social work education, which the CSWE considers the 'signature pedagogy' of social work, focuses on connecting 'the theoretical and conceptual contribution of the classroom with the practical world of the practice setting' (Council on Social Work Education (CSWE), 2008, p. 8). It stands as an integral part of the training process for social workers as it allows students to put into practice concepts and theories they have been taught in the classroom (Dhemba, 2012; Moorhouse, 2013). However, it is not a reality that fieldwork is prioritised or devoid of challenges in social work training institutions in Africa. For example, due to the lack of importance given to fieldwork (Kaseke, 1990; Mupedziswa, 1997), students are sometimes not given adequate time in the field to complete cases or even engage fully with service users; as can be confirmed by Iwuagwu's (2014) study carried out among undergraduate social work students in a Nigerian university, and Dhemba's (2012) study among students and agency supervisors in institutes of social work in Tanzania, Lesotho, and Zimbabwe . Of the challenges facing fieldwork education in Africa, the fit of the theoretical focus and practice guidelines to the field practice is of particular significance to this chapter. Since students are expected to put into practice what has been taught in the classroom and are usually assessed by their utilisation of standard social work theories, models, and frameworks in their practice and subsequent report writing, the field practice is limited to the scope of what is taught in the classroom.

Literature shows that social work education in Africa relies heavily on Western models, theories, guidelines, and standards, although there has been an effort on the continent recently to indigenise and Africanise social work education and practice (Turton and Schmid, 2020; Twikirize and Spitzer, 2019). However, social work education in Africa is still dominated by Western values and knowledge, which also influences how students learn and what knowledge and theories are being put to practice.

Indigenising Social Work Education in Africa

Understanding the concept of indigenisation is vital as we investigate its existence in African social work practice. Some scholars associate the idea of indigenisation with Africanisation and anti-colonisation (Gray et al., 2014). Gray (2005232) describes indigenisation as a facet that involvee articulating local cultures and demarcating how they differ from Western traditions and cultures (Gray, 2005). Therefore, the decolonisation of social work education in Africa through indigenisation is envisaged to improve the impact of the social work profession in Africa since the Western models have not been considered effective in Africa (Gray et al., 2014).

Despite the influences of workshops and conferences, social work education and the profession have not been free of colonial influence (Mabvurira et al., 2018). To deliver practical, sustainable, and socially accepted services that benefit the African contextual problems, African educators and scholars have pointed out the need to intently draw on the broad wealth of indigenous knowledge (Twikirize and Spitzer, 2019). Social values represented in the form of language, rituals, music, art, dance, cultural spaces, riddles, idioms, folklore, oral traditions, and taboos (Mawere, 2015) are the aspects that can be fused into social work education to uphold the value systems of the communities (Twikirize and Spitzer, 2019).

In 1972, the Association for Social work Education in Africa launched projects to indigenise teaching materials, for example, the use of group work case studies in lectures, community development, and role-plays that were adopted from practical cases in countries like Uganda, Zambia, Mauritius, Sierra Leone, Ethiopia, Togo, Tanzania, Ghana, Malawi, Mauritius, Kenya, and Madagascar (Gray et al., 2014). In South Africa, since the Western models of social work practice and education were also deemed unfit and inappropriate, South African educators and practitioners have come forward to emphasise community-based approaches to tackle problems such as injustice and poverty since this accords well with the holistic African values of family, community, and nature (Turton and Schmid, 2020). Furthermore, the need for more research within Africa stands as a prerequisite to creating indigenous knowledge to be applied to the school curriculum and community since tAfrican knowledge and values currently remain undocumented (Mwansa, 2011). Besides, a continental forum remains a fundamental arena that can be used to engage social work professionals in Africa to define, discuss, and shape the future of the profession, including the standard operating practices of social workers within the continent (Mwansa, 2011).

Balance between Indigenisation and Globalisation

The introduction of social work in Africa is criticised for its inappropriateness in meeting the needs of the African community because its inception was based on Western values and knowledge incompatible with the problems of the most deserving people in Africa (Mwansa, 2011). Thus, to achieve optimum impact, social work practitioners in Africa anticipated embracing those values and norms compatible with the people's way of life.

Despite the momentum gained by the concept of indigenisation among social work scholars and students in Africa, criticisms of indigenisation practices have also been made and acknowledgement of the need to deeply sieve the practices (Twikirize and Spitzer, 2019) that can be included in indigenisation due to the presence of some brutal practices like female genital mutilation and patriarchy that are deeply embedded in people's ways of living. Blindly adhering to only Western values or indigenous knowledge without an assessment of their relevance may stagnate the impact of social practice. Thus, pioneers of indigenisation of social work in Africa need to scrutinise both the Global North and the Global South value systems to devise harmonised, developmental knowledge that will enhancethe profession's impact on the community.

Challenges to Achieving Indigenisation

Social work practice and education have often been criticised for a lack of local and authentic approaches and appropriateness to the African continent (Turton and Schmid, 2020). As scholars strive to make relevant the practices of the social work profession within the African context, some hindering factors have also been deliberated, including challenges in the acquisition of funds to execute association activities and the lack of laws, continental bodies, and structures for uniform governance of the profession within the African continent (Shawky, 1972; Mwansa, 2011). Entry into the profession by practitioners without any social work skills and yet practise as if they were trained social workers pose a threat to the profession's progress (Hochfeld et al., 2009; Mwansa, 2011).

Also, it is quite interesting that the Ubuntu philosophy is known by several different names in Africa such as *Ubudehe* in Rwanda, *obuntu-bulamu* in Uganda, *Nn)boa* in Ghana, *Iddir* and *Eko* in Ethiopia, among others, which are all associated with principles such as reciprocity and fair sharing of resources that are synonymous with the social work principle of promotion of social justice (Twikirize and Spitzer, 2019). However, one may question why African societies are fighting issues of poverty, social injustices, drug addictions, security, and healthcare despite our inherent practices of looking out for each other. In this regard, Twikirize and Spitzer (2019) argue that indigenous practices have placed much emphasis on community-based practices, which represent the meso-level practice of social work; neglecting micro- and macro-level approaches to service provision. Conversely, we agree with the assertion that globalisation is impacting communities and, as a result, indigenous practices have proved to be inadequate to deal with the multiplicity of social problems and to improve the standard of living for our local communities. Thus, indigenisation seems to be achieving little success, making it hard to replicate in other societies or even in the North.

Further still, challenging Western methodologies, pedagogical strategies, and knowledge may not be welcomed by the Western world since the indigenisation of social work in Africa is mainly attributed to shunning Western practices in favour of adopting culturally relevant practices and methodologies (Manomano et al., 2020).

Reciprocal Learning between the Global North and the Global South

After discussing the importance of indigenisation and the challenges that come with the process of achieving it in Africa, we discuss the importance of reciprocal learning between the Global North and the Global South. Lutz et al. (2021) assert that it is imperative that practitioners in the Global North and Global South embrace the contradictions and contextuality that characterises social work practice rather than their dependence on the universal or contextual tenets of the profession. Based on our experiences of social work in the North and South, we argue that knowledge about social work practice in both contexts is different, yet globally available, and can be adapted to apply to practice or education locally. Thus, through our reflections we have come to the realisation that knowledge of these two perspectives is relevant for global exchanges in a process that Lutz et al. (2021, p.18) define as 'interwoven social work'. In practical terms, this is an opportunity to incorporate local and global social work practices/standards that ensure that professionals are connected globally, yet act or think locally in applying indigenous knowledge in our local contexts (Gray et al., 2008; Nuttman-Shwartz and Ranz, 2014). Consequently, there may be less chances of reproducing colonial social work processes while embracing ongoing emancipation in both contexts; something that is achievable when the South learns from the experiences of the North and vice versa. We discuss some of these best practices below.

South Learning from the North

As Africans championing the indigenisation of social work practice in our local communities, it is important to acknowledge that the problems that social work seeks to tackle in the West are similar to those in developing countries, except that social work in the North is structured in terms of formal structuring of organisations that enhance their problem-solving processes (Rankopo and

Osei-Hwedie, 2010) and the varying degree of the problems. They further posit that the impact of globalisation has caused many people in developing countries, including in Africa, to wish to live up to the trends like those in the developed North. Thus, it is necessary for social workers to acknowledge the fact that as much as African social work should be one where the people involve themselves and identify with local values, we can adopt the structuring of our organisations to meet the rapidly changing environment with the aim of improving the standards of living of our service-users (Rankopo and Osei-Hwedie, 2010).

Results from our study revealed that the ability to adapt the organisational structures of African social work goes beyond the ability of social workers and constitutes a challenge based on the lack of professionalisation of the practice in our countries. This means that African countries must continually advocate for macro-level policies that will establish social work as a recognised profession with its body of regulations, organisational structure, adequate funding, and leadership positions that will ensure the practice will thrive in meeting global standards (Baffoe and Dako-Gyeke, 2013; Rankopo and Osei-Hwedie, 2010). Only after we have achieved this will social work practice feature robust problem-solving institutions, methods, and programmes necessary to meet the diverse social problems in Africa.

Also, in agreement with the assertion of Lutz et al. (2021) that social work practice in the South focuses on human development where people are the agents of development, another best practice worth learning from the North is for social work practice in Africa to focus on problem prevention. Inferring from our study results, we suggest that once again as a macro-level need, policymakers develop the essential policies and conditions that aim mostly at prevention and only secondarily at intervention. This can be achieved when we empower the service users in relationships and communities to promote the scope of individual capabilities and opportunities at the meso and micro levels in the face of an availability of development-related strategies and infrastructure.

North Learning from the South

First, as a characteristic of Southern social work, the North can learn from the principle of heterogeneity that underpins advocacy for a practice that aims at promoting integration, adaptation, localisation, and authenticity as well as being culturally appropriate and relevant (Gray et al., 2008). Social work in the North, as described by Röh (2020), regards itself as being universal and context independent, which may not be entirely true as they have their own challenges of developing culturally relevant interventions for indigenous, minority, immigrant, and refugee communities (Rankopo and Osei-Hwedie, 2010). For example, the Aboriginals in Australia, the Maori in New Zealand, the Roma people in Europe, and the First Nations people in Canada as well as refugees and minority groups have been at the negative receiving end of having mainstream societies impose their values and systems on them without a recognition of differences in culture (Gray et al., 2008; Twikirize and Spitzer, 2019).

Rather than holding on to universal principles of doing social work without giving attention to the variations among service--users, learning from the social work of the South can be effective for practice in the North. This will be relevant in giving attention to 'the taken for granted' assumptions on the deep meanings different groups attach to commonalities in their culture; consequently, it will help in devising culturally relevant solutions for diverse populations as well as finding a balance between local and global standards (Gray et al., 2008; Rankopo and Osei-Hwedie, 2010; Lutz et al., 2021).

Second, social work in the North could improve its degree of involvement with service-users and community organising strategies to find solutions for problems. We refer to findings from our study as being consistent with criticism of the methods used in handling casework and community development. Social work practice in the North is seen as one that lacks empathy and responsiveness towards local conditions and the living conditions of 'extended families' or emphasises the importance of 'communities' (Mupedziswa, 1993, p.159). African social work practice recognises the importance of community, including village, neighbourhood, and extended families, rather than stressing the individualism that characterises the North. To encourage the North to consider this perspective, Osei-Hwedie (1996) notes the benefits of social work focused on the community as an approach by which an individual can find character and expressions of the self within the group.

While one may argue that the North recognises the importance of human relations in the community through the use of theories such as systems/ecological theories, the extent to which this is used in problem-solving and prevention of individual problems such as mental health challenges arising from individualism is debatable. It is no wonder that the IFSW has adopted the Ubuntu principle as its guide in service delivery for the next decade to prove how an African 'homegrown' philosophy synonymously stands for humanity, neighbourly love, and community spirit (Lutz et al., 2021).

Accordingly, like the Ubuntu principle, community experiences and consciousness are believed to play a role in the social, political, and religious-spiritual facets of society, which highlights an obligation towards, and the assimilation of, people in the community based on shared respect, acknowledgement of, and respect for human dignity as stipulated in the global standards for social work practice (Lutz et al., 2017). For individualistic communities in the North, building this sense of belonging and responsibility may be necessary to increase the level of empathy with which practitioners work (Lutz et al., 2021), especially in efforts to avoid ethical dilemmas arising from emotional involvement with service-users. On the other hand, when people look out for each other, it may improve their psycho-social wellbeing and be used as alternatives to problem-solving, which may often seem very trivial but are very important in social work practice.

Conclusion

To conclude, notwithstanding the assertion that progressive indigenous practices in Africa are signs of a healthy and connected society because of their roles in community organising and recognition for families, clans, communism, and volunteerism (Flick et al. 2002). Concepts such as Ubuntu and other related concepts in the South have also been criticised for been preoccupied with community mobilisation, with a disregard for other aspects of social work, such as individual casework, social policy, and the development of national welfare states (Mupedziswa et al., 2019). Thus, they have proved to be entirely incapable of solving modern social problems, inability to matching globalisation trends, and incurring gaps in their problem-solving approaches (Mupedziswa et al., 2019). It is in this vein that emphasis must be placed on the need for reciprocal learning between the North and the South in the quest to develop creative thinking to modify existing philosophies and advance appropriate theories and practice frameworks that can efficiently solve modern and diverse social problems on the micro, meso, and macro levels of social work practice.

Recommendations

Recognising the pros and cons of applying indigenous practices to social work in the South, we recommend the following:

1. First, we corroborate Mupedziswa et al. (2019) the call for African social work academics, researchers, and practitioners to collaborate in developing a modern framework for home-

grown philosophies like Ubuntu and its related concepts in different languages across the African continent and their contribution to efficient service provision.

2. Second, we recommend the mainstreaming of indigenous practices into national social protection schemes. Transforming indigenous best practices such as the *Ubudehe* and *Akabondo* (cluster model) from Rwanda and Uganda, with a cultural emphasis on mutual support between people, into social protection schemes. Because these practices serve as the foundation for their survival, there will be joint ownership, which will make the schemes sustainable and effective in tackling their socioeconomic problems (Twikirize and Spitzer, 2019).

3. Last, we recommend that African social workers continue to advocate for the professional recognition of social work practice in the South. Attaining a professional status would facilitate our ability to learn from the developed organisational structures in the North. It will also boost the confidence of practitioners in negotiating terms of engagement with international organisations/actors operating in Africa with regards to prioritising working with local staff over foreign staff on projects to assist communities in Africa.

Further Reading

Ayim, M., Abdullah, A., Bentum, H., Amponsah, E. B., Cudjoe, E., and Manful, E. (2023) 'Contributing to indigenous social work practice in Africa: A look at the cultural conceptualisations of social problems in Ghana'. *African Journal of Social Work and Social Development*, 30(1), pp. 1–18.

Mogorosi, L. D. (2018) 'Social work and indigenisation: A South African perspective'. *Southern African Journal of Social Work and Social Development*, 30(1), p. 1. https://doi.org/10.25159/2415-5829/2393.

Shokane, A. L., and Masoga, M. A. (2018) 'African indigenous knowledge and social work practice: Towards an afro-sensed perspective'. *Southern African Journal of Social Work and Social Development*, 30(1). https://doi.org/10.25159/2415-5829/2320.

References

Association of Social Work Education in Africa (ASWEA) (1974) *Case Studies of Social Development in Africa*. Addis-Ababa, Ethiopia: ASWEA Information Centre.

Baffoe, M., and Dako-Gyeke, M. (2013) 'Social problems and social work in Ghana: implications for sustainable development'. *International Journal of Development and Sustainability*, 2(1), pp. 347–363.

Council on Social Work Education (2008) 'Educational policy and accreditation standards'. https://www.cswe.org/accreditation/standards/2022-epas/ [Accessed on 28 November 2022].

Dhemba, J. (2012) 'Fieldwork in social work education and training: Issues and challenges in the case of Eastern and Southern Africa'. *Social Work and Society International Online Journal Social Work & Society*, 10(1), pp. 1–16.

Durst, D. (2010) 'A comparative analysis of social work in Vietnam and Canada: Rebirth and renewal'. *Journal of Comparative Social Work*, 2(2), pp. 2–12.

Flick, M., Bittman, M., and Doyle, J. (2002) *The Community's Most Valuable [Hidden] Asset – Volunteering in Australia Sydney.* New South Wealses: University of New South Wales (Social Policy Research Centre).

George, A. (1982) 'A history of social field instruction: Apprenticeship to instruction'. In B. W. Sheafor and L. E. Jenkins (eds.) *Quality Field Instruction in Social Work: Programme Development and Maintenance*. New York, NY: Longman, pp. 37–59.

Gray, M. J. (2005) 'Dilemmas of international social work: Paradoxical processes in indigenisation, universalism and imperialism'. *International Journal of Social Welfare*, 14(3), pp. 231–238. https://doi.org/10.1111/j.1468-2397.2005.00363. x.

Gray, M. J., Coates, J., and Yellow Bird, M. (2008) 'Introduction'. In M. Gray, J. Coates, and M. Yellow Bird (eds.) *Indigenous Social Work Around the World: Towards Culturally Relevant Education and Practice*. Aldershot: Ashgate, pp. 1–12.

Gray, M. J., Kreitzer, L., and Mupedziswa, R. (2014) 'The enduring relevance of indigenisation in African social work: A critical reflection on ASWEA's Legacy'. *Ethics and Social Welfare*, 8(2), pp. 101–116. https://doi.org/10.1080/17496535.2014.895397.

Hochfeld, T., Selipsky, L., Mupedziswa, R., and Chitereka, C. (2009) 'Developmental social work education in Southern and East Africa'. *Bunting Road Campus Auckland Park, Johannesburg: Research Village, House*, 9.

IFSW (2014) *Global Definition of Social Work*. International Federation of Social Workers (ifsw.org).

Iwuagwu, A. O. (2014) *Perception of Field Work Practicum among Undergraduate Social Work Students: A Study of Social Work Department*. Nsukka: University of Nigeria.

Kaseke, E. (1990) 'A response to social problems in developing countries in Hall, N. Social work training in Africa: A fieldwork manual'. *International Journal of Policy and Research*, 21(1), pp. 13–20.

Kreitzer, L. (2012) *Social Work in Africa: Exploring Culturally Relevant Education and Practice in Ghana*. Calgary, Canada: University of Calgary Press.

Lutz, R., Inkje, S., Stauss, K., and Alexander, A. (2017) 'Border thinking in social work: The role of indigenous knowledge in the development of relations between the Global North and the Global South'. *Transnational Social Review*, 7(2), pp. 188–205.

Lutz, R., Kleibl, T., and Neureither, F. (2021) 'Social work of the South: Political, anti-colonial, environmental'. *Socialnet International*, 9 June 2021. https://www.socialnet.de/international/papers/social-work-of-the-south-political-anti-colonial-environmental.html [Accessed on 4 July 2022].

Mabvurira, V., Jabulani, C., Makhubele, F., and Matlakala, K. (2018) 'Exploring language as an impediment to or a resource for the indigenisation of social work education'. *The Social Work Practitioner-Researcher*, 30(1), pp. 1–20. https://doi.org/10.25159/2415-5829/2973.

Manomano, T., Nyanhoto, R., and Gutura, P. (2020) 'Prospects for and factors that militate against decolonising education in social work in South Africa'. *Critical and Radical Social Work*, 8(3), pp. 357–370. https://doi.org/10.1332/204986020X16019188814624.

Mawere, M. (2015) 'Indigenous knowledge and public education in sub-Saharan Africa'. *Africa Spectrum*, 50(2), pp. 57–71. https://doi.org/10.1177/000203971505000203.

Moorhouse, L. M. (2013) 'How social work students perceive their field work supervision'. An Unpublished Thesis. Massey University, Manawatu, New Zealand.

Mupedziswa, R. (1993) *Social Work in Africa: Critical Essays on the Struggle for Relevance. Draft Manuscript*. Harare, Zimbabwe: School of Social Work.

Mupedziswa, R. (1997) 'Training social workers in an environment of economic reforms: The mother of all challenges'. *Social Work/Maatskaplke Werk*, 33(3), pp. 233–243.

Mupedziswa, R., Rankopo, M., and Mwansa, L. (2019) 'Ubuntu as a Pan-African philosophical framework for social work in Africa'. In J. M. Twikinze and H. Spitzer (eds.) *Social Work Practice in Africa Indigenous and Innovative Approaches*. Fountain Publishers, Vol. 1, pp. 21–38.

Mwansa, L. J. (2010) 'Challenges facing social work education in Africa'. *International Social Work*, 53(1), pp. 129–136.

Mwansa, L. J. (2011) 'Social work education in Africa: Whence and whither?' *Social Work Education*, 30(1), pp. 4–16. https://doi.org/10.1080/02615471003753148.

Nuttman-Shwartz, O., and Ranz, R. (2014) 'A reciprocal working model for fieldwork with international social work students'. *The British Journal of Social Work*, 44(8), pp. 2411–2425. http://www.jstor.org/stable/43688069.

Osei-Hwedie, K. (1996) 'The indigenisation of social work practice and education in Africa: The dilemma of theory and method'. *Social Work/Maatskaplike Werk*, 32(3), pp. 215–225.

Osei-Hwedie, K., and Boateng, D. (2018) 'Do not worry your head: The impossibility of indigenising social work education and practice in Africa'. *Southern African Journal of Social Work and Social Development*, 30(3). https://doi.org/10.25159/2415-5829/3978.

Rankopo, M. J., and Osei-Hwedie, K. (2011) 'Globalisation and culturally relevant social work: African perspectives on indigenization'. *International Social Work*, 54(1), pp. 137–147. https://doi.org/10.1177/0020872810372367.

Shawky, A. (1972) 'Social work education in Africa'. *International Social Work*, 15(3), pp. 3–16. https://doi.org/10.1177/002087287201500302.

Turton, Y., and Schmid, J. (2020) 'Transforming social work: Contextualised social work education in South Africa'. *Social Work*, 56(4), pp. 367–382. https://doi.org/10.15270/56-4-880.

Twikirize, M. J., and Spitzer, H. (eds.) (2019) *Social Work Practice in Africa: Indigenous and Innovative Approaches*. Kampala, Uganda: Fountain publishers, pp. 1–257.

Veta, O. D., and McLaughlin, H. (2022) 'Social work education and practice in Africa: The problems and prospects'. *Social Work Education*. https://doi.org/10.1080/02615479.2022.2029393.

28
AN INTERNATIONAL UNIVERSITY PARTNERSHIP TO SUPPORT THE SOCIAL SERVICE WORKFORCE AND STRENGTHEN THE CHILD PROTECTION SYSTEM IN GHANA

Bree Akesson and Magnus Mfoafo-M'Carthy

Abstract: English

Common perceptions of children in Africa tend to focus on poverty, famine, and war. There has been less attention given to the successes of African countries that have aimed to improve the lives of children. One such success is Ghana, which is a regional and continental leader in child protection issues and continues to nurture a robust social service workforce. Yet, there exists some detachment in the implementation of child welfare laws and practice. To address this gap, there has been a recent global movement to address child protection issues by strengthening child protection systems and specifically social work education. This chapter uses a process evaluation to examine an international university partnership between a Global North Canadian university and a Global South Ghanaian university to integrate child protection knowledge into the university curriculum and to produce the next generation of social service workers. This chapter chronicles the development and structure of the partnership, discusses the opportunities and challenges faced, and suggests a future agenda to support the endogenous strengths inherent within Ghanaian universities to work towards improving the status of children and families and to serve as a model for other African contexts.

Introduction

Within Africa, and specifically West and Central Africa, Ghana is a leader in addressing issues related to children. For example, in 1989, the Ghana National Commission on Children was established to promote the general welfare and development of children and to coordinate all essential services for children in the country. As the first country in sub-Saharan Africa to endorse the

Convention on the Rights of the Child (United Nations, 1989) in 1990, Ghana has spearheaded other major international regulations on child protection, for instance, the African Charter on the Rights and Welfare of the Child, which was signed in 1997 and ratified in 2005. In 1998, Ghana passed the Children's Act and has been at the forefront of instituting legislation against harmful traditional practices, such as child marriage and female genital mutilation.

Despite this strong legislative history aimed at protecting children, there is still a gap between policy and practice, and a lack of understanding of community approaches to deal with children and family welfare issues in Ghana. Children are still subjected to varying forms of violations, including sexual abuse, exploitation, family violence, child marriage, child labour, and institutionalisation (Global Affairs Canada and UNICEF, 2015). As such, there is a need to bridge this gap between policy and practice by strengthening the child protection system. Since social service workers, including social workers, are at the forefront of child protection, strengthening the social service workforce is a promising approach that can positively impact the child welfare system.

This chapter details a project aimed at strenthening the social service system and its related workforce in Ghana. According to the Global Social Service Workforce Alliance (Global Social Service Workforce Alliance, 2015), the social service system consists of 'interventions, programmes and benefits that are provided by governmental, civil society and community actors to ensure the welfare and protection of socially or economically disadvantaged individuals and families' (p. 5). While acknowledging that there are a wide range of workers engaged in work within the social service system, this chapter refers to 'social service workers' to generally include a variety of workers – paid and unpaid, governmental and non-governmental –including social workers, social service workers, social work administrators, social assistants, child protection professionals, child protection workers, front-line workers, paraprofessional social service workers, and other types of workers who staff the social service system in Ghana. (For details on the range of social service workers in Ghana, please see Canavera et al., 2014)

This chapter will describe a partnership between a Global North Canadian university and a Global South Ghanaian university to integrate child protection knowledge into the university curriculum and to produce the next generation of social service workers. The following pages chronicle the development and structure of the partnership, discuss the challenges and opportunities faced, and suggest a future agenda to support the endogenous strengths inherent within Ghanaian universities to work towards improving the status of children and families within the country.

Growing Movement towards Strengthening Child Protection in Ghana

A 2011 study led by Child Frontiers to assess Ghana's child protection system concluded that the implementation of child-targeted programmes in Ghana had previously yielded marginal results for children largely due to the lack of a national policy framework for the delivery of comprehensive child and family welfare services. Subsequent studies commissioned by UNICEF (2012) and the Government of Ghana (2014) found that Ghana lacked a national policy framework for the delivery of comprehensive services for children and families. Ideas and practices supporting children's wellbeing were not consistent from the child, family, community, and traditional levels through to the governmental and supra-governmental levels. These studies found that Ghanaian communities have clear and strong ideas of what is necessary for child wellbeing and what is required on a community and family level. However, they also found that there were difficulties in coordinating among the different levels of the child protection system and that the levels often struggled to understand and trust one another. The studies noted that while Ghana was far ahead of its West African neighbours in this regard, there were often insufficient funds allocated to support the workforce and its services in difficult times, such as those of economic transition. This practice of under-resourcing made such tasks as community and family support, regulation of child labour, as well as protection from sexual abuse and other adversities spotty in some places (Canavera et al., 2020). The recommendations called for the development of a child and family welfare policy to provide a comprehensive framework and an enabling environment to strengthen the country's child welfare system.

The Child Frontiers (2011) study also noted that the lack of detailed guidelines, policies, and procedures were major factors restricting child welfare professionals, such as social workers and social service workers, from carrying out their mandates in line with the 1998 Children's Act. They identified that protocols currently in place lacked culturally appropriate or sensitive approaches and failed to consider traditional practices by families and community leaders. The gaps in scope and content of these protocols provided opportunities for the development of curriculum and training programmes to enhance service delivery by practitioners and in support of the child and family welfare policy.

This chapter will elaborate on one approach to support the child protection system through Ghana's higher education system, with a specific focus on a project that aims to educate future social service workers at the University of Development Studies (UDS) in northern Ghana. Before describing the project, we will first describe the history and challenges of North-South cooperation in Ghana's higher education system.

Higher Education in Ghana and North-South Cooperation

University Collaboration in Ghana

Academic and research collaborations among institutions of higher learning are becoming the global norm. This trend is due to the North-South cooperation where educational institutions in the Global North or Global South are realising the importance of collaborating with other institutions (Gyamera, 2016; Kok et al., 2017). International collaborations result in numerous benefits not just for faculty members and students, but also for universities and the countries involved. Participants benefit from access to communication channels with a variety of experts. The collaborative opportunity provides students and faculty with the capacity to study and work at the international level. In addition, participants have the opportunity to learn from other knowledge centres and cultures.

In the 1980s, many universities from the Global North started establishing partnerships with universities in Ghana. At this time, Ghana had only three public universities: University of Ghana, University of Cape Coast, and the Kwame Nkrumah University of Science and Technology. Most of these collaborations were driven by the goals of further developing Ghanaian universities and improving their quality of education. Over the years, these agreements and partnerships have expanded to include almost every field of study at nearly all tertiary institutions in Ghana, including 15 public, 10 technical, and almost 50 private universities. Most Ghanaian universities now have special offices solely responsible for international partnerships.

Child Protection in Ghanaian Higher Education

Not an esoteric philosophical construct, child protection relates to virtually every aspect of Ghanaian society. It is therefore perplexing that it is not a central facet of society and part of everyday discourse. Child protection reduces risks to children's wellbeing, makes children's rights to protection a reality, and restores hope and dignity in the lives of children and families. Children are also foundational to families, which are the building blocks for a healthy society.

Higher education is a natural entry point for promoting child protection knowledge. This ensures that students who will become social service workers upon graduation are taught the solid foundations of child protection through rigorous course content. Through the process of curricula integration, child protection is no longer viewed as a specialised field, but rather falls under the purview of a wide range of disciplines that engage in social service work. Infusing child protection concepts into university curricula in Ghana has the potential to improve the delivery of child protection services in every sector of society. Graduates of these institutions have the opportunity to apply their acquired skills in their homes, places of employment, communities, and society.

Indigenisation and Knowledge Development in Ghana

Scholars have argued for the adoption of indigenous ways of knowing, which tend to focus more on the traditional African culture rather than on the Western norm (Forkuor et al., 2019; Ibrahima and Mattaini, 2019; Naami and Mfoafo-M'Carthy, 2023). But despite this emphasis, it is not always the reality. For example, in Ghana, a country with a colonial past, much of the academic discourse tends to originate in the Global North (Forkour et al., 2019; Naami and Mfoafo-M'Carthy, 2023). This is due, in part, to the fact that the majority of the advanced degrees of Ghanaian faculty are from the Global North.

There has been a failure to sustain the indigenisation of training and practice of academics in the Global South, particularly Africa. African academics have been highly influenced by Global North exposures, strategies, and training, and therefore they tend to prioritise this kind of knowledge. It is therefore necessary to challenge intellectuals in the Global South to embrace indigenous ways of knowing. That is, there must be mechanisms to ensure that African content is a main component of knowledge production.

One way to ensure that both indigenous knowledge and Ghanaian ways of conceptualizing child protection are honored is to create a partnership – not just in name, but in practice – between entities with the shared goal of strengthening the social service workforce and child protection systems in Ghana. Driven by Ghanaian ways of knowing, the partnership blended African and Global North approaches and models to ensure that the outcomes were reflective of the Ghanaian context while ensuring that the outcomes were relevant to national child protection efforts.

Project Overview

The goal of this chapter is to provide an overview of a two-year university collaboration between a Global North Canadian university (Wilfrid Laurier University) and a Global South Ghanaian university (University of Development Studies) to improve the child protection system in Ghana using higher education as a means to access the social service workforce, specifically those who engage in child protection issues.

This chapter uses process evaluation as a method by which to better understand the implementation of this project. Focusing on a programme's operations, implementation, and service delivery, a process evaluation is used to consistently assess how a programme is being implemented (Saunders et al., 2005). As the name indicates, this method is *process*-focused as opposed to *outcome*-focused, which is relevant to the university partnership that is the focus of this chapter. As we will describe in the following pages, the partnership underscores the importance of emphasising concepts of Ghanaian-specific child protection within the existing culturally relevant curriculum (rather than exporting models from the Global North) to promote a cadre of social service workers skilled in engaging in relevant and effective child protection practice in Ghana.

Goals of the Project

UNICEF Ghana established and supported a partnership between the Faculty of Integrated Development Studies (FIDS) at the University of Development Studies (UDS) and Wilfrid Laurier University's (WLU) Faculty of Social Work (FSW) with the aim of integrating child protection knowledge into the faculty and developing a stand-alone certificate course in child protection. Faculty members from UDS and WLU were the main collaborators of the project. All faculty members from UDS were Ghanaian, while the two faculty members from WLU were American-Canadian (Akesson) and Ghanaian-Canadian (Mfoafo-M'Carthy). This chapter is written from the perspective of the two WLU faculty members. According to the partnership agreement facilitated by UNICEF, WLU was tasked with delivering technical input and peer support, while UDS faculty members provided input into the goals of the project, participated in all project activities, and served as important arbiters of conveying knowledge about child protection to the target audiences.

In addition to supporting the professional development of faculty members, this project had multiple target audiences: students who intended to graduate into careers in the social service workforce (for the curriculum mainstreaming) and current practising social service workers who were focusing on child protection issues (for the certificate course). The intention was that if these two groups directly benefitted from the project, then the indirect impact would be more far-reaching to children, families, communities, and Ghanaian society.

Description of Project Activities

Initial Field Visit

In the first year of the project, we engaged in an initial in-person partnership meeting at the UDS campus to become oriented with the project. A major goal was to meet with stakeholders and solicit their input regarding the project and any potential challenges that might arise. We also took the opportunity to answer any questions about the scope and objectives of the project to determine how we could best support FIDS/UDS. Finally, we worked closely with FIDS/UDS to develop an action plan to keep us on track to complete the project within two years.

Baseline Survey

One of the first partnership activities was to develop a baseline survey to better understand the level of knowledge, attitudes, and behavior on child protection of the faculty members and students of FIDS/UDS. The focus of the baseline survey was to establish a level of understanding of child protection issues to measure future improvements in child protection knowledge for faculty members and students. The survey also served as a tool by which to identify gaps in child protection issues, which would point to areas of focus. The survey sampled 63 faculty members and 270 students across all four-year cohorts. The baseline survey was critical for informing the project's first faculty development workshop held at the end of the first year of the project in Damongo, Ghana.

The Damongo Workshop

Child Protection Foundations Using a Workshop

Participants included all faculty members from FIDS/UDS. Driven by the interests and recommendations of the participants, the week-long Damongo Workshop dedicated the first two days to learning about basic child protection knowledge. Because these child protection concepts tended to be born from a Global North perspective, the content was considered and grappled with the Ghanaian context. In other words, debate and disagreement weres encouraged when discussing topics such as how to define childhood, the role of the family, child development approaches and theories, early childhood development, and child rights. Ghanaian-specific understandings of child protection among the faculty participants were highly valued within the process. All activities sought to elicit faculty participants' own professional and personal experiences, in order to ensure that the content was relevant to the context, but also resonated with the faculty participants on a personal level. We entered the process with an understanding that the project would be successful only if the faculty participants saw their own experiences reflected in the content and had a sense of ownership over the material. Such a commitment to Ghanaian-specific child protection issues among faculty members would inevitably positively impact the students who would eventually enter into the social service workforce upon graduation.

Also at the request of the faculty participants and to further enhance faculty development, child protection topics were taught using a range of active learning strategies that we modeled for the faculty participants to engage them as learners but also to show how they might use these techniques in their own classrooms. Active learning strategies reflected Ghanaian practices of collectivity, interconnectedness, and reciprocity (Naami and Mfoafo-M'Carthy, 2023). For example, 'buzz groups' are a cooperative learning technique that uses small discussion groups to work on a specific task about a specific topic. And 'gallery walks' used small and group discussion techniques to actively engage participants as they walk together through a space to share ideas, respond to questions, or devise problem-solving ideas. According to the faculty participants, these active teaching and learning approaches were a welcome contrast to the 'sage on the stage' technique where a professor lectures in front of the classroom, transmitting knowledge down to students who passively absorb the material.

The child protection skills taught in the first two days of the Damongo Workshop were basic. Many faculty participants noted that this was the first time they had heard about or discussed these issues. Yet, child protection cannot be taught in two days. We found a potential challenge moving forward regarding how to increase the level of knowledge of faculty participants so that they would be able to go more in-depth into the important child protection issues, especially as related to the Ghanaian context. We wanted to avoid a superficial or oversimplified understanding of child protection, which will not be effective or sustainable for a system-strengthening approach. Therefore, we provided faculty participants with a range of child protection resources that they could access at their own pace and apply in their future teaching.

Course Redesign and Integration of Child Protection Content

The third and fourth days of the Damango Workshop focused on the course redesign process to integrate the newfound child protection knowledge into the FIDS/UDS curriculum. The faculty participants engaged in multiple exercises aimed at evaluating existing courses and determining how child protection issues could be effectively and meaningfully integrated into these courses. The main activity during this part of the workshop was the development of an individual course concept map. We facilitated a process of peer review – from both within each department and then from the faculty as a whole – to ensure that there was no over-duplication of concepts within departments. For example, we wanted to avoid a student learning the same concept in the first through fourth years, yet not broadening their understanding of the concept and its application during that time. These two days emphasised the importance of ensuring alignment among intended learning outcomes, active teaching and learning methods that reflected a Ghanaian approach, and formative/summative assessments.

Through a process of modelling, faculty were taught: elements of a course outline; Bloom's taxonomy of learning (1956); mapping course concepts; identifying where child protection issues can be integrated into the curriculum; developing and reviewing course learning objectives; different assessment and teaching methods; alignment among learning objectives, assessments, and teaching and learning methods; and teaching/learning/assessment techniques. This part of the workshop culminated in a micro-teaching exercise, where each department was invited to present a brief lesson to their peers, resulting in imaginative and creative approaches that reflected the teachers' differing styles and cultures. The observing faculty participants were encouraged to provide constructive feedback to their presenting peers.

Curriculum Mapping and Review

The final two days of the Damongo Workshop were dedicated to assessing how child protection knowledge could be integrated into the entire FIDS/UDS curriculum in a meaningful way. Faculty participants reviewed how their individual courses fit into the larger FIDS/UDS vision for teaching and learning. Each department also developed a future curriculum assessment plan to ensure that the process developed at this workshop was carried forward as a consistent mechanism within their individual departments and within the whole FIDS/UDS system. Faculty participants were asked to identify any existing resources and gaps for future curriculum development and child protection mainstreaming activities. The workshop ended with faculty participants revisiting the learning objectives that they had developed on the first day. Using stickers to vote, faculty participants indicated whether these objectives had been met during the course of the workshop.

In the course of the curriculum mapping process, we emphasised how the process was designed to ensure that child protection concepts are not merely repeated in the same way as a student progresses through a programme. Rather, it was important that the faculty participants communicated how certain child protection concepts would be taught and expanded upon from first-year through fourth-year courses.

The Wa Workshop
Module Design for Standalone Certificate Programme

At the end of the second year of the project, we participated in a third and final field visit to Wa, in the Upper West Region of northern Ghana to conduct another faculty development workshop with the same faculty participants from the Damongo Workshop but focusing on the following two tasks: (i) to design modules for a Ghanaian-specific standalone certificate programme for social service practitioners, and (ii) to develop monitoring and evaluation mechanisms for the mainstreamed courses and the standalone certificate programme.

The first part of the Wa Workshop focused on developing new modules for the standalone certificate programme. As a first step, faculty participants participated in a learner analysis to better understand the types of students who would enrol in a standalone certificate programme. Activities challenged faculty participants to consider how the diversity of these learners might influence how the modules would be designed. The categories that the faculty participants focused on included general aptitude or ability to succeed in the course; reading, writing, and basic computer skills; percentage of students entering the course with prerequisite knowledge; motivation to learn in the course; attitudes towards subject matter; potential anxiety level in the course; comfort level with different teaching and learning activities; and cultural diversity.

The faculty participants then conducted a context analysis, a method used to better understand the multiple contextual factors that might affect how the modules were delivered and how the individual modules (and the certificate programme more broadly) were situated within the programme, faculty, institution, and the learning environment in general. In this case, the context analysis considered both the FIDS/UDS environment as well as the larger socio-cultural-political context of Ghana. Some of the advantages of conducting a context analysis in the course design process included: (i) analysing the context would help define the course content; (ii) designing a course in an appropriate context would greatly enhance teaching and learning; and (ii) doing the analysis had the potential to pinpoint factors that participants were unsure of or needed to find out more. It also uncovered challenges participants would have to deal with in their course design.

On the second day of the workshop, faculty participants focused on designing their certificate course modules. Faculty participants engaged in the activities learned from the Damongo Workshop, specifically the concept map. This not only reinforced learning from the Damongo Workshop but also assisted faculty participants in thinking through what content they would focus on for the modules. After working in groups to develop a concept map, faculty participants reviewed the concept maps and content for each module and provided peer feedback. Faculty members were then asked to work in their groups to develop module learning outcomes that would feed into the module assessment plan. The faculty members developed a draft module design plan and presented their modules to the whole group to elicit both oral and written feedback on how to revise and move forward with the module design.

What emerged was a uniquely Ghanaian perspective on child protection. Faculty participants were able to develop a curriculum that centred on child welfare in the Ghanaian context. They were able to inculcate traditional and indigenous views of child protection in their teaching. For instance, on the topic of child abuse, they identified, addressed, and integrated nuances from a Ghanaian viewpoint. Based on the evaluation of the project, the faculty participants acknowledged that even just knowledge of the topic reduced risks to children's wellbeing, making children's right to protection a reality.

Monitoring and Evaluation Mechanisms

The final day of the Wa Workshop was devoted to developing monitoring and evaluation methodologies for both the mainstreamed courses and the standalone certificate modules. Faculty-participants discussed different ways of evaluating the mainstreamed courses and the certificate modules. They were encouraged to evaluate the course by assessing the workload, content, and diversity of teaching and learning activities. They also discussed how courses could be evaluated through formative evaluations using culturally relevant approaches, such as small group discussions, rather than more traditional methods, such as surveys or tests. Ultimately, faculty-participants were encouraged to envision Ghanaian-specific approaches that determine if students are learning what they should be learning.

To ensure that each syllabus is an effective part of the broader department and faculty, faculty-participants discussed how they would engage in a programme review and enhancement process. Faculty-participants reviewed the department-level curriculum map that they used in the previous Damongo Workshop. They revisited the concept of a curriculum map, defining it as a process wherein the curriculum is examined for its alignment against the department or faculty goals or outcomes. The principle behind the process is that each required course or component within the programme should make a defined contribution towards the overall curriculum. This is especially relevant with many courses, including new child protection material. The faculty members discussed how curriculum mapping could also be used to evaluate how child protection topics have been effectively integrated across the curriculum.

Faculty participants also learned direct and indirect methods of assessing if one's department or programme is successful. They explored how to use a variety of qualitative and quantitative assessment methods to ensure that programme learning outcomes have been achieved. Finally, they learned how to identify, prioritise, and implement actions to enhance the curriculum and improve student learning.

Reflection and Conclusion

There have been many project successes. For example, at the conclusion of the project and in the subsequent years, FIDS/UDS faculty members felt that child protection concepts had been meaningfully integrated into the FIDS/UDS curriculum, which was one of the main goals of the project. This, in turn, means that students were exposed to these concepts and therefore are more likely to turn that knowledge into action to positively address child protection issues as social service workers. We hoped that the child protection concepts would grow with the students. Students should be exposed to concepts of child protection in their first year at the university so that their knowledge of child protection will expand each year of their studies. However, robust monitoring and evaluation mechanisms are needed in order to ascertain the true impact.

Nevertheless, short-term project funding makes it difficult to sustain programmes. Despite efforts to design projects to ensure sustainability, when funding runs out projects may stall and fall short of their goals. This project took place over the course of two years, which all involved parties agreed was too short to fully achieve meaningful project impact. The often glacial pace of academia, especially the longer-term processes of developing curricula, makes meeting goals and achieving impact within two years difficult. For example, the project funding ended before the standalone certificate programme could be fully implemented. Quite simply, more resources were needed to ensure its success. FIDS/UDS is currently seeking additional funding to make this aspect of the project a reality.

There also continues to be a dearth of Ghanaian- or African- specific resources related to child protection. A lack of child protection materials is compounded by overworked faculty and under-resourced teaching and research needs. Hence, there is an overreliance on child protection materials from the Global North. The lack of Ghanaian- or African-specific content makes it difficult for Ghanaian faculty members to make meaningful connections between child protection issues and their own scholarly and teaching interests. Therefore, another positive outcome of the project was the collation of an edited collection of work around child protection in Ghana, led by professors from FIDS/UDS. The book, *Social Change and Child Protection in Ghana: Concepts, Theories and Empirical Discourses* (Gasu et al., 2023), adds an important voice to the Ghanaian- and African-specific academic literature.

Ultimately, this project encouraged productive discourse on child protection for faculty members so that they could efficiently learn the concepts and see how the concepts applied to their teaching, research, and everyday lives. Therefore, faculty members were encouraged and supported to engage in child protection–related research and academic activities that were aligned with their own knowledge base and competencies, while also making attempts to expand their understanding of new and unexplored topics related to child protection. Rather than simply teaching for the sake of teaching, faculty members ensured their syllabi reflected their own

Ghanaian-specific knowledge and experience in order for them to have ownership of the material. If the syllabi were meaningful for the faculty members, then the syllabi content would become meaningful for the students and the students' future practice as social service workers. For example, after completing the child protection foundations sessions during the Damongo Workshop, one faculty member noted how child protection concepts could be applied to his research focus area in a way that he had never thought of before. The learning and integration of new child protection concepts can invigorate faculty members' research agendas. The positive reverberations of a social service workforce strengthening project has the potential to make a huge impact. One enthusiastic professor can impart their passion for a child protection issue to a classroom of students each of whom will one day become critical members of the social service workforce.

Recommendations

1. To support child protection efforts, child protection elements should be integrated into academic curricula across Africa. This initiative should be spearheaded by local African scholars who are well versed in child protection issues at the local and global level and coordinated with government-supported initiatives. Methods of engagement may include university partnerships (Global South-Global North, in addition to Global North-Global South), national and regional conferences, academic journal and book projects, and knowledge and resource hubs.
2. African scholars in all disciplines related to the social service workforce should be encouraged to collaborate to ensure knowledge production regarding child protection is African-centred and culturally relevant. This will be successful only if local knowledge is unearthed, unpacked, and understood. This could be accomplished using the same methods listed in the previous point with a focus on indigenous ways of conceptualising child protection issues in Ghana.
3. Faculty members should be supported and provided with adequate resources (e.g., written materials, appropriate remuneration, access to technology) so they can capably teach and promote child protection elements within existing curricula. If funding for these resources is time-limited, then sustainability plans should be developed and implemented.

Further Reading

Ayim, M., Abdullah, A., Bentum, H., Amponsah, E., Cudjoe, E., and Manful, E. (2021) 'Contributing to indigenous social work practice in Africa: A look at the cultural conceptualizations of social problems in Ghana'. *Qualitative Social Work*, 22(1), 1–17. https://doi.org/10.1177/14733250211055487.

Frimpong-Manso, K., and Mawudoku, A. (2017) 'Social work practice in child and family welfare'. In M. Gray (Ed.), *The Handbook of Social Work Social Development in Africa*. Routledge International Handbooks.

Twikirize, J., and Spitzer, H. (2019) *Social Work Practice in Africa: Indigenous and Innovative Approaches*. Fountain Publishers.

References

Bloom, B.S. (1956) *Taxonomy of Educational Objectives: The Classification of Educational Goals*. New York, NY: David McKay Company, Inc.

Canavera, M., Akesson, B., and Landis, D. (2014, August) *Social Service Workforce Training in the West and Central Africa Region*. New York, NY: CPC Learning Network and UNICEF.

Canavera, M., Akesson, B., Landis, D., Armstrong, M., and Meyer, E. (2020) 'Mapping social work education in the West Africa region: Movements toward indigenisation in 12 countries' training programmes'. *International Journal of Social Welfare*, 29(1), 83–95. https://doi.org/10.1111/ijsw.12372.

Child Frontiers. (2011) *Report of the Mapping and Analysis of Ghana's Child Protection System*. Kowloon, Hong Kong: Child Frontiers.

Forkuor, J.B., Ofori-Dua, K., Forkuor, D., and Obeng, B. (2019) 'Culturally sensitive social work practice: Lessons from social work practitioners and educators in Ghana'. *Qualitative Social Work*, 18(5), 852–867. https://doi.org/10.1177/1473325018766712.

Gasu, J., Nkegbe, P.K., and Galaa, S.Z. (Eds.). (2023) *Social Change and Child Protection in Ghana: Concepts, Theories and Empirical Discourses*. Accra, Ghana: Woeli Publishing Services.

Global Affairs Canada and UNICEF. (2015). 'Building a national child protection system in ghana: from evidence to policy and practice'. https://www.socialserviceworkforce.org/system/files/resource/files/Ghana_CP_system_case_study.pdf.

Global Social Service Workforce Alliance (GSSWA). (2015) *The State of the Social Service Workforce 2015 Report: A Multi-country Review*. Washington, DC: GSSWA.

Government of Ghana (GoG). (2014) *Child Protection Baseline Research Report*. Ghana: GoG Ministry of Gender, Children and Child Protection (supported by UNICEF).

Gyamera, G.O. (2016) *Internationalisation in Ghana's Higher Educational Institutions*. The Association of Commonwealth Universities. https://www.acu.ac.uk/membership/membercommunities/internationalisation/articles/internationalisation-ghana/.

Ibrahima, A.B., and Mattaini, M.A. (2019) 'Social work in Africa: Decolonizing methodologies and approaches'. *International Social Work*, 62(2), 799–813. https://doi.org/10.1177/0020872817742702.

Kok, M.O., Gyapong, J.O., Wolffers, I., Ofori-Adjei, D., and Ruitenberg, E.J. (2017) 'Towards fair and effective North-South collaboration: Realising a programme for demand-driven and locally led research'. *Health Research Policy and Systems*, 15(1), 96. https://doi.org/10.1186/s12961-017-0251-3.

Naami, A., and Mfoafo-M'Carthy, M. (2023) 'Exploring African-centered social work education: The Ghanaian experience'. *Social Work Education*. https//doi.org/10.1080/02615479.2023.2174507.

Saunders, R.P., Evans, M.H., and Joshi, P. (2005) 'Developing a process-evaluation plan for assessing health promotion program implementation: A how-to guide'. *Health Promotion Practice*, 6(2), 134–147. https://doi.org/10.1177/1524839904273387.

UNICEF. (2012) *Mapping and Analysis of Ghana's Child Protection System*. Accra, Ghana: UNICEF Ghana.

United Nations. (1989) *Convention on the Rights of the Child*. New York, NY: Author.

29
SOURCES OF KNOWLEDGE TRANSFER BETWEEN THE GLOBAL SOUTH AND THE GLOBAL NORTH IN SOCIAL WORK EDUCATION

Peninah Kansiime, Sharlotte Tusasiirwe, and Diana Nabbumba

Abstract: English

This chapter draws on the authors' collective experiences of social work education and knowledge mobility as social work students, researchers, and educators in three countries in the Global North. It discusses knowledge transfer through four channels: social work education, research, academic publication, and digital information-sharing platforms. It promotes co-constructed knowledge sharing to facilitate decolonisation and recommends a review of social work curricula globally to ensure they examine the origins of knowledge taught in light of the international definition's thrust towards local and cultural relevance and the Global Agenda's embrace of *Ubuntu* in its first theme to strengthen social solidarity and global connectedness. In so doing, it recommends the inclusion of indigenous teaching methods, knowledge, and research frameworks to foster social work's engagement with Indigenous Peoples' issues, noting a premier role for the profession's international education body in leading the decolonising thrust in social work education.

Abstract: Swahili

Waandishi wameandaa sura hii kutokana na uzoefu wao wa pamoja wa elimu ya ustawi wa jamii na uhamishaji wa maarifa kama wanafunzi, watafiti, na watoaji elimu ya ustawi wa jamii katika nchi tatu zilizopo Kaskazini mwa dunia. Inajadili uhamishaji wa maarifa kupitia njia nne: elimu ya ustawi wa jamii, utafiti, machapisho ya kitaaluma, na majukwaa ya kidijitali ya kupeana habari. Inakuza kushirikishana kwa maarifa yaliyojengwa kwa pamoja ili kuwezesha kuondoa ukoloni inapendekeza uchunguzi wa mitaala ya ustawi wa jamii duniani kuhakikisha inachunguza asili ya maarifa yanayofundishwa kwa kuzingatia ufafanuzi wa kimataifa kuelekea umuhimu wa kitamaduni na Agenda ya Kimataifa kukumbatia Ubuntu katika mada yake ya kwanza kuimarisha mshikamano wa kijamii na muunganisho wa kimataifa. Kwa kufanya hivyo, inapendekeza kujumuishwa kwa njia za asili za kufundisha, maarifa, na mifumo ya utafiti ili kukuza ushirikiano wa ustawi wa jamii na masuala ya watu wa asili, kwa kubainisha jukumu kuu la shirika la elimu ya kimataifa la taaluma hiyo katika kuongoza msukumo wa kuondoa ukoloni katika elimu ya ustawi wa jamii.

Introduction

For over a century, social work's Eurocentric roots have influenced education, research, and practice, prompting cries of professional imperialism and calls for cultural relevance, indigenisation, and, more recently in response to processes of globalisation and internationalisation, decolonisation (Gray, 2005; Gray et al., 2013a, 2013b; Tusasiirwe, 2019). In recognition of this, an addendum to the international definition of social work suggests the 'definition may be amplified at national and/or regional levels' (International Association of Schools of Social Work (IASSW) and International Federation of Social Workers (IFSW), 2014). We interpret this as recognition of cultural diversity and other ways of knowing and doing than Western ways. However, dominant theories and models from the Global North continue to overshadow indigenous knowledge from the Global South (Dumbrill and Green, 2008). Midgley (2008) believed that his work on *professional imperialism in the third world* had prompted efforts to promote reciprocity in social work education through academic exchange programmes between northern and southern schools. As social workers from the Global South, who have benefitted from academic exchanges in Sweden, England, and Australia, we concur with Midgley's (2008) claims about unidirectional knowledge flows southwards. In this chapter, we draw on our personal autobiographies (Coffey, 1999) and life histories (Plummer, 1983) to reflect on our experiences of knowledge mobility through an analysis of four avenues of knowledge transfer and their challenges: social work education, research, academic publication, and digital information-sharing platforms.

We concur that knowledge travels with the movement of 'people, practices, institutions, ideas, [and] technologies' (Jöns et al., 2017, p. 1), moving 'between different contexts and positions, within and between societies' (Andersson and Fejes, 2010, p. 203). With increased worldwide migration and digital connectivity, one might expect a rapid transfer of knowledge across contexts, but our collective experience as Black social work students and educators has shown that this is often not the case, with the biggest barrier to knowledge mobility encountered in social work education due, inter alia, to the continued dominance of Whiteness and Eurocentric knowledge, values, and ideals in social work (BlackDeer and Ocampo, 2022). The growing number of international students and opportunities for academic exchanges and sabbaticals has led, over the years, to increased understanding of cultural diversity and the cross-fertilisation of ideas. One wonders then why there is continued dominance of knowledge from the Global North, despite cross-disciplinary studies of knowledge transfer.

The global migration of about 281 million people by mid-2020 (United Nations Department of Economic and Social Affairs, Population Division, 2020) highlighted the need for social work education to embrace knowledge from other contexts, given the movement of people is a crucial conduit for knowledge acquisition and transfer that is beneficial to home and host countries. McAuliffe (2021) observes that the only way to redress Western scientific colonialism in Australia was to listen to, and learn from, indigenous groups. Gray (2016) refers to the need for social workers to think globally and locally, and act globally and locally, indicating the need for cognisance of the origins and adaptability of knowledge. Understanding the problems and needs of people in an increasingly globalised and diverse world means social workers everywhere need to learn about other contexts and cultures and understand the struggles of relevance encountered in southern contexts. In the discussion that follows, we consider four channels of knowledge transfer: social work education, research, academic publishing, and digital information-sharing platforms, in light of our experience in Uganda, England, Sweden, and Australia, first as students, then as educators.

Channels of Knowledge Mobility

Human mobility is a phenomenon that spans centuries and, according to some authors, is a vehicle of knowledge transfer (Andersson and Fejes 2010; Jöns et al., 2017). According to Williams and Graham (2014), migrants comprise diverse groups of people, including 'international students, highly skilled workers, economic migrants, retirees, refugees, nomads, those within global care chains and those whose unauthorised status leave[s] them vulnerable to all sorts of human rights violations, including slavery' (p. i1). Australia is a popular destination for skilled professionals and international students from the Global South, with social work listed among the 44 priority occupations on the country's skilled occupation list (Department of Home Affairs, 2022). Thus, social work is a migration route to Australia for people from diverse countries and, as such, constitutes a channel for the transfer of knowledge from various contexts. Coming from Uganda, we are beneficiaries of this migration pathway, having become social work educators on completion of our PhDs at different Australian universities. Like many other African skilled migrants, we moved to Australia to pursue an education, find jobs, and improve opportunities for ourselves and our families (Mwanri et al., 2021). We came to learn and to share our indigenous Ugandan knowledge in Australia. Our Ugandan, Swedish, and English social work education hinged on Eurocentric frameworks that, in the main, were dissonant from what we encountered in social work practice in Uganda (Tusasiirwe et al., 2022). This, however, gave us an opportunity to analyse and advocate the need for the decolonisation of the profession through recognition and use of indigenous knowledge.

Decolonisation theory sees indigenous knowledge as an important tool of resistance and a valuable resource for a reimagined culturally appropriate, courageous, and respectful decolonised social work (BlackDeer and Ocampo, 2022). It advocates a reclamation of untapped ancestral knowledge developed from centuries of observation, experience, familiarity with, and understanding of the ecosystems that have survived the onslaught of European colonisation and imperialism. Like Australian indigenous knowledge, ours is also wisdom and knowledge passed on through, inter alia, proverbs, wise sayings, tongue twisters, stories and storytelling, songs, poetry, rituals, and traditional environmental knowledge (Chilisa, 2012; Wa Thiong'o, 1986). Indigenous knowledge and education is not a thing of the past; it constitutes African people's lived experience in the present, where ancestors have an important influence (Abur and Mugumbate, 2022). Tascón and Ife (2020) have been scathing of social work's 'whiteness' and devaluation of indigenous knowledge, which they labelled 'epistemicide' (p. 2). Decolonisation theorists, like ourselves, see our role as disrupters of 'epistemicide' by incorporating non-Eurocentric worldviews and knowledge systems in social work education, practice, and research. Decolonisation seeks to reimagine alternatives to Eurocentric knowledge by bringing indigenous social work knowledge to the fore. In the next section, we discuss the transfer of knowledge through education, which Goode et al. (2021) describes as the best launching pad to revamp the profession and deconstruct oppressive structures.

Decolonising the Social Work Curriculum and Teaching Approach

Sharlotte (Author 2) designed an introductory social work course for domestic and international students at Western Sydney University, where she brings the value of learning from diverse knowledge systems to inform Australian social work (Lerner, 2021). As indicated in the course outline, she uses a decolonised approach, encouraging students to share their knowledge and experience to enrich understanding on how diverse cultures and contexts can inform social work, including professional ethics and practice models (BlackDeer and Ocampo, 2022). Within her caring pedagogical model, Sharlotte sees education as a mutual learning process, where students and educators exchange knowledge to deepen understanding. She values reflective learning and encourages students to share their cultural knowledge and perspectives and, in so doing, explain their relevance to local contexts in Australia and elsewhere. The International Federation of Social Workers (IFSW) (2022) notes that the need to share knowledge is in line with the United Nations (2015) Sustainable Development Goals; it falls under the domain of partnership, a key tenet in social work. According to the IFSW (2022), 'to partner means sharing knowledge and insights and collaboratively and coherently creating and establishing solutions' (n.p.) to contemporary social problems. This could not happen if the knowledge and views of people from the Global South were minimised and dismissed.

From our lived experiences as social work students and educators in Uganda, Sweden, England, and Australia, we found little appreciation of the need for epistemological diversity in conceptualising and teaching 'what social work is'. In multicultural contexts like Australia, social work remains stubbornly white (Tascón and Ife, 2020). A social work curriculum and practice dominated by Whiteness hampers knowledge mobility and the reimagining of social work: 'By applying only white social work knowledge, [people are] forced to assimilate into the white world and alternative knowledge systems that may be more significant for the lived experience of the people with whom they work are [denied]' (Tascón and Ife, 2020, p. 2). This was not only unjust but also was at loggerheads with the profession's social justice claims (BlackDeer and Ocampo, 2022). Hence, decolonising the curriculum through knowledge sharing and mobility in Australia, as elsewhere, was a social justice pursuit.

A decolonised curriculum has been well received by the students from our institutions, whom we have challenged to explore their cultural identity and to reimagine social work as befitted their cultural context. The aim of the decolonised approach is not to impose one worldview or to 'whiten' or 'blacken' the curriculum; it is about supporting students, who are becoming social workers, to always think of what is culturally appropriate for the people with whom they will be working. With the magnitude of the crises being faced around the world, there is no one-size-fits-all social work applicable to every country or community. What is needed are social workers able to reimagine ideas to address crises and prevent further crises, by applying culturally appropriate responses. To enable reimagining, some students have confronted the thinking that Western social work was the norm, noting ethnic ways of doing social work. We have conducted these conversations in culturally safe spaces borrowing from Aboriginal practices of deep listening and yarning (Bessarab and Ng'andu, 2010).

In a decolonising approach, the classroom is a platform for exchanging knowledge that students find enriching. As one student from the 2021 class noted, 'the exchange of cultural information helped me to gain insight of different countries and traditions followed and how they can work towards the issues'. The students experienced a decolonising approach as enabling genuine and deep reflection about self and connection to culture, particularly for domestic students with an Anglo background in Australia. At the start of the unit, domestic students tended to claim that they did not have a culture but encouragement from the educators helped them start their journey of self-exploration. A decolonising pedagogical approach prioritises the care, encouragement, reciprocity, and nurturing of students (Gatwiri, 2018). These values are embodied in our African philosophies, like Ubuntu, transmitted to us through our socialisation (Tusasiirwe et al., 2021). They are consistent with a decolonising educational approach that encourages knowledge sharing and transmission. Since social work's international definition's thrust is towards local and cultural relevance and the Global Agenda of Social Work and Social Development's (IASSW, IFSW, and International Council on Social Welfare (ICSW) (2020) first theme is *Ubuntu: Strengthening Social Solidarity and Global Connectedness*, it is incumbent on schools of social work across the world to examine the origins of Ubuntu. This will, of necessity, lead to an awareness of its source in African indigenous knowledge, philosophy, and values (Abur and Mugumbate, 2022; Mupedziswa et al., 2019). Failure to do this would amount to the hijacking of a pivotal African indigenous concept in a disrespectful way, without understanding its true import and meaning. It would also signal a tokenistic approach to cultural diversity and desire to maintain the status quo of Whiteness in the social work curriculum (Gatwiri, 2018; Lerner, 2021).

Students come to social work wanting to make a difference in people's lives (Goode et al., 2021), and, therefore, social work educators need to challenge them to think of culturally appropriate ways to do this without undermining their motivation. Thus, we encouraged the introduction of indigenous cultural knowledge in the classroom, as well as reflexivity on the forces shaping this knowledge. Students learnt how context shaped knowledge and that Western models, methods, ethics, and values were not universal (Gray, 2005). This allowed for the emergence of culturally relevant and contextually informed approaches to social work practice. So culturally diverse were our social work classrooms that students shared and learnt about culturally appropriate social work in many areas of practice. In one example, they emphasised the relevance of traditional healers in the Global South, where they were authoritative figures in clients' lives. Students believed it would be best for social workers to engage with, and not work against, traditional healers, if they were to yield good mental health outcomes for their clients. In Tascón and Ife's (2020) terms, decentring 'whiteness' in the classroom in this way provided an excellent opportunity for the cross-fertilisation of knowledge. Students learnt that all knowledge had value, and none was superior or inferior to another.

There were some challenges, however, in using this approach, especially for social work educators from the Global South entering the Global North as skilled migrants. Like most migrants of colour, they encountered resistance, racism, discrimination, and isolation during resettlement that could affect their employment prospects in Australia, for example (Mwanri et al., 2021). One of the authors of this paper observed the reluctance by the Department of Social Work at the university where she completed her PhD to employ PhD students from the Global South as sessional educators, even when they had academic and practice experience in social work. Interestingly, schools of social work at some other universities were keen to employ them as adjunct lecturers. This problem of limited opportunities was not unique to Australia, with Fulton et al. (2016) writing that it occurred in countries like Canada, the United Kingdom, and the United States. Schools of social work should accept that social workers from overseas have a wealth of knowledge and experience to contribute (Abdelkerim and Grace, 2012).

Decolonising Social Work Research

Social work research was another channel of knowledge transfer we used, and that we continue to use. Some international students come to Australia having secured PhD scholarships to conduct supervised research projects, often on social problems in their home countries. We received various scholarships to pursue graduate studies in social work at the Masters level in Sweden and England and PhD level in Australia. Our PhD research projects focused on Uganda. Peninah's (Author 1) thesis involved a study on male survivors of conflict-related sexual violence (Kansiime, 2020). Diana examined ecological social care responsibility in rural Uganda (Nabbumba, 2022), while Sharlotte explored decolonising social work practice based on older women's experiences (Tusasiirwe, 2019). One of Peninah's supervisors was very knowledgeable about the African context having been born and worked there, whereas the supervisors of the other two authors all came from a Western context, which, at times, caused challenges, for example, in choosing contextually relevant theories and research methodologies.

Nevertheless, our supervisors provided intellectual guidance and support throughout the research process through regular supervisory meetings that promoted knowledge building and transfer. Research has indicated that many students have limited agency in choosing the topics for their projects (Tran and Vu, 2018). This was not our experience. In fact, Diana's (Author 3) supervisors encouraged her to draw on her lived experience in Uganda and explain how different the social care context was from Australia's and how the policies were relatively new compared to Australia with its vast policies and formalised, well-structured aged-care system. They encouraged her to provide detailed accounts for non-African and international readers to gain a better understanding of social care in rural Uganda. They positioned her as more knowledgeable of the Ugandan context than they were and enhanced her agency, providing a platform for knowledge sharing, shaping, and reconstruction to create an original contribution to international knowledge. In this way, Diana showed her supervisors why certain theoretical and analytical frameworks did not fit the Ugandan context. For example, Diana attempted various policy analysis methods like discourse analysis, critical policy analysis (CPA), and the policy triangle framework (Bacchi, 2009; Fairclough, 1992; Walt and Gilson, 1994) before convincing her supervisors that trace analysis (Sevenhuijsen, 2004) was the most viable approach to the first stage of her multi-stage PhD thesis. Such caring and respectful supervisory experiences shaped agency and knowledge sharing from South to North and fostered a multidirectional flow of knowledge between academics in the Global North and PhD students from the Global South. It also facilitated indigenous people's engagement with social work, as well as respectful research on indigenous people's issues (Bessarab and Ng'andu, 2010; Chilisa, 2012; Gray et al., 2010).

Some authors highlighted that Western social work research models threatened to undermine indigenous research methods (BlackDeer and Ocampo, 2022; Lerner, 2021). Bessarab and Ng'andu (2010), for example, claimed that indigenous methodologies had been criticised for not being bona fide research methodologies, when they explored the concept of yarning as a research tool among two indigenous communities, one in Botswana and the other in Western Australia. The fact that yarning, for example, facilitated in-depth discussions and dissipated the power gap between researchers and participants made everyone involved a giver and receiver of knowledge (Bessarab and Ng'andu, 2010). Thus, researchers should leverage its importance, especially when researching non-Western communities but, as Chilisa (2012) highlights, many social work courses on research methods and methodologies draw mainly on non-African texts in teaching Western approaches as 'the legitimate' way of doing research.

Additionally, academics in Western universities, who did not include literature from authors in the Global South on their reading lists, were effectively spurning this knowledge, putting it out of the reach of students in these institutions of higher learning. Thus, with these challenges, disrupting *epistemicide* in research required students from the Global South to be courageous and to assert their indigenous knowledge, drawing on their creativity and remembering to design PhD research projects that drew on the cultural perspectives of the local people they were researching (Tusasiirwe, 2019).

From Sharlotte's experience, indigenous African languages were very important to help researchers adapt research methods embedded in African worldviews and ways of knowing, for example. Such methods included one-on-one or group conversations following African oral storytelling traditions, where local people shared stories with the intention of imparting life's lessons. Such conversations were non-hierarchical, allowing for the co-production of knowledge (Tusasiirwe, 2019). Drawing from indigenous African worldviews and ways of knowing also informed ways of doing ethical research that valued long-term relationships, hospitality, mutual caring, and concern about the welfare of those being researched, among others (Abur and Mugumbate, 2022). These indigenous perspectives on ethics went beyond the Western ways of conceptualising ethics and sometimes contradicted the seemingly top-down ways of demonstrating ethics epitomised in Western-oriented ethical review boards (Mugumbate and Mtetwa, 2019). Overall, students from the Global South doing research must assert that what they know is critical, understandable, and respectful of the people being researched and their perspectives, instead of copying and pasting Western methodologies that might not be suitable to the context.

Also, knowledge from the Global South, including research findings, could be disseminated through participation in school workshops, conferences, networking activities, seminars, and webinars organised by professional associations that increased the scope of knowledge mobility. Research indicated that these engagements were essential in personal development, especially in cultivating communication skills, independence, and confidence and developing long-term professional networks (Nguyen and Robertson, 2020). During their candidature, the authors were required to present at various graduate research forums, which provided a platform to showcase their research and share knowledge of sociocultural phenomena that differed from the Australian context with which most audiences were familiar.

We were accorded opportunities to serve as sessional academics at various institutions during our PhD candidature. Such opportunities were the norm and have been documented elsewhere (Nguyen and Robertson, 2020), even though two of the authors' host social work departments were not keen to provide this platform. During their engagement with students, the authors provided African examples and asked students to share cases from their cultural contexts, thereby using classroom spaces as platforms for knowledge sharing. The authors also included literature on indigenous knowledge on the reading lists, with the hope that this would, in turn, influence book and journal editors and publishers, and librarians and other academic stakeholders, to engage in the decolonising process through the promotion of indigenous knowledge – through, inter alia, academic publishing and library purchasing (Chilisa, 2012; Gatwiri, 2018). University social clubs and community volunteering projects also presented opportunities to share social work knowledge from educators' home countries.

Like other international students, social work students from the Global South experienced other common challenges that could hinder them from sharing knowledge. These included discrimination, racism, and marginalisation (Dovchin, 2020), social isolation, new cultures, idiomatic language, and new learning methods (Harrison and Ip, 2013). Peninah and Sharlotte recalled moments in class, while pursuing graduate social work study in Sweden, that depicted some of these hindrances to knowledge mobility. These moments involved heated debates on critical issues in social work marked by different cultural perceptions. They recall a class facilitated by a visiting lecturer from the Global South that was brought to a halt, due to a heated debate on differing cultural and religious perceptions on gender and sexuality. Students from both sides (Global North and Global South) seemed unwilling to accept each other's point of view and the result was the loss of an opportunity to foster critical thinking and decolonise knowledge on those issues (Gray, 2005). Such scenarios represented a minimisation and rejection of other ways of knowing (Lerner, 2021). Scenarios of this nature might scare students from the Global South from critically assessing and opposing myths held by the Global North about them, or even challenging beliefs that they might further disadvantage social work clients in the Global South. In such cases, students effectively failed to prioritise the advancement of knowledge, instead opting to preserve their personal identity and resilience. For social work to benefit from knowledge mobility, therefore, classrooms should be safe environments for 'transformative education', where everyone could scrutinise their 'ideological beliefs, biases and prejudices, and our own conformity to the status quo' (Gatwiri, 2018, p. 184).

Academic Publications

Knowledge mobility from the Global South to the Global North was not only limited to human, academic, student, or skilled workforce migration. Technologies also fostered knowledge mobility through publication and Internet-based platforms. The *African Journal of Social Work*, *South African Journal of Social Work and Social Development*, and *Social Work/Maatskaplike Werk*, as well as the Africa Social Work Network (ASWNet) are all essential platforms fostering knowledge mobility from the Global South to the Global North, as their primary focus is the dissemination of knowledge on social work practice, research, and education in the African region. These journals are easily accessible via Google Scholar and the African Journal Online database. Social workers across the world, especially in the Global North, should embrace, and make use of, these journals to learn and understand different African indigenous social work ideologies and how they have been used to overcome social problems and advance social and economic sustainability among African populations.

Digital Information-Sharing Platforms

While acknowledging the 'brain drain' from the Global South, due to human mobility, with Peninah's help, Sharlotte established the Ekyooto platform to facilitate the sharing and exchange of social work knowledge, lived experiences, and decolonising stories of social work, as well as stories of decolonising self and other lived experiences (Ekyooto, 2022). According to the website, 'Ekyooto is a Runyankole/Luganda word for a fireplace which, in African oral storytelling, is a place/space where stories are told, knowledge and wisdom shared, thus shaping individuals and communities' (Ekyooto, 2022). The platform aims to mobilise people from all over the world through Zoom, Facebook, and WhatsApp to initiate discussions on contemporary social issues and come up with indigenous strategies on how to address them.

There are other such platforms, including the one provided by the ASWNet, which, according to its website, 'creates, aggregates and disseminates information and resources to facilitate Social Work and Development on the African continent' (ASWNet, 2021). In 2022, the platform hosted two post-colonial researchers, educators, and advocates of indigenous methodologies: Professor Bagele Chilisa from Botswana and Professor Johnnie Wycliffe Frank Muwanga-Zake, during the Ubuntu Annual Lecture. In her address, Professor Chilisa spoke about many of the issues on knowledge mobility this chapter addresses, including the need to 'promote documentation, uptake and testing of innovative techniques from the Global South, and build new theories, frameworks and approached based on the global South experiences' (Chilisa, 2022).

Conclusion

This chapter has shown that the decolonisation of social work education, research, and practice is a work in progress across the globe. It highlighted three African social worker educators' (teaching in the Global North) continual struggle to bring indigenous approaches to the fore in a context dominated by Whiteness and Western social work knowledge. To address the unbalanced mobility of social work knowledge, it suggested channels to facilitate the flow of knowledge from the Global South to the Global North through the social work curriculum, arguing that learning across these two worlds would bridge gaps in mutual learning and knowledge exchange. It provided examples of knowledge mobility drawing on the authors' direct experiences as social workers from the Global South studying, researching, and teaching in the Global North. It presented social work education as an important channel for the decolonisation of social work knowledge and highlighted several platforms to support knowledge transfer.

Recommendations

Considering our collective experience recounted herein, we would like to end with some recommendations on decolonising social work education in light of the Global Agenda's thrust towards strengthening social solidarity and global connectedness in the name of Ubuntu.

1. First, we recommend an examination of social work curricula globally to ensure that social work educators and students embrace and learn from and about diverse cultural perspectives. Examining the origins of the knowledge taught is a good place to start in introducing students to social work.
2. Second, we recommend that a commitment to decolonising social work education requires the inclusion of indigenous teaching methods and field placements, along with indigenous knowledge and research frameworks pertinent to particular contexts.
3. Lastly, social work's premier international education organisation, the IASSW, should be at the forefront of this decolonising thrust to incorporate indigenous knowledge and research frameworks into social work education. A cultural shift of this nature would influence academics to prescribe Indigenous literature for their courses.

Acknowledgments

We are very grateful to Emeritus Professor Mel Gray from the University of Newcastle, Australia, for her useful input in the development of this manuscript. We are also grateful for the academic scholarships from the various academic institutions that we have been privileged to attend.

Further Reading

Gatwiri, K. (2018) 'Leaning into the discomfort and embracing the disruption: A Freirean approach to (de)colonised social work teaching in Australia', *Whiteness and Education*, 3(2), 182–197, viewed on 27 November 2022, DOI: 10.1080/23793406.2019.1573644.

References

Abdelkerim, A. A., and Grace, M. (2012) 'Challenges to employment in newly emerging African communities in Australia: A review of the literature', *Australian Social Work*, 65(1), 104–119, DOI: 10.1080/0312407X.2011.616958.

Abur, W., and Mugumbate, J. R. (2022) 'Experiences of Ubuntu and implications of African philosophy for social work in Australia', *Advances in Social Work and Welfare Education*, 23(2), 21–37, https://search.informit.org/doi/10.3316/informit.571057635557631.

Andersson, P., and Fejes, A. (2010) 'Mobility of knowledge as a recognition challenge: Experiences from Sweden', *International Journal of Lifelong Education*, 29(2), 201–218, DOI: 10.1080/02601371003616624.

Africa Social Network (2021) 'Home', viewed on 27 November 2022, https://africasocialwork.net/.

Bacchi, C. (2009) *Analysing Policy*. Wales, North South: Pearson Higher Education AU.

Bessarab, D., and Ng'andu, B. (2010) 'Yarning about yarning as a legitimate method in indigenous research', *International Journal of Critical Indigenous Studies*, 3(1), 37–50, DOI: 10.5204/ijcis.v3i1.57.

BlackDeer, A. A., and Ocampo, M. G. (2022) '#SocialWorkSoWhite: A critical perspective on settler colonialism white supremacy, and social justice in social work', *Advances in Social Work*, 22(2), 720–740, https://doi.org/10.18060/24986.

Chilisa, B. (2012) *Indigenous Research Methodologies*. London: Sage.

Chilisa, B. (2022) *Decolonising Research and Evaluation Methodologies: Challenges and Opportunities*. Power Point Slides, Ubuntu Annual Lecture, Africa Social Network.

Coffey, A. (1999) *The Ethnographic Self: Fieldwork and the Representation of Identity*. London: SAGE Publications, Limited.

Department of Home Affairs (2022) 'Priority migration skilled occupation list', viewed on 17 May 2022, https://immi.homeaffairs.gov.au/visas/employing-and-sponsoring-someone/sponsoring-workers/pmsol.

Dovchin, S. (2020) 'The psychological damages of linguistic racism and international students in Australia'. *International Journal of Bilingual Education and Bilingualism*, 23(7), 804–818, DOI: 10.1080/13670050.2020.1759504.

Dumbrill, G., and Green, J. (2008) 'Indigenous knowledge in the social work academy', *Social Work Education*, 27(5), 489–503, https://doi.org/10.1080/02615470701379891.

Ekyooto (2022) 'Ekyooto: Decolonising social work-Uganda', viewed on 10 July 2022, https://www.ekyooto.obuntu-ledcommunityinitiative.org/.

Fairclough, N. (1992) 'Discourse and text: Linguistic and intertextual analysis within discourse analysis', *Discourse and Society*, 3(2), 193–217. https://doi.org/10.1177/0957926592003002004.

Fulton, A., Pullen-Sansfaçon, A., Brown, M., Éthier, S., and Graham, J. (2016) 'Migrant social workers, foreign credential recognition and securing employment in Canada: A qualitative analysis of pre-employment experiences', *Canadian Social Work Review/Revue Canadienne de Service Social*, 33(1), 65–86, https://doi.org/10.7202/1037090ar.

Gatwiri, K. (2018) 'Leaning into the discomfort and embracing the disruption: A Freirean approach to (de)colonised social work teaching in Australia', *Whiteness and Education*, 3(2), 182–197, DOI: 10.1080/23793406.2019.1573644.

Goode, R. W., Cowell, M., McMillan, D., Deinse, T. V., and Cooper-Lewter, C. (2021) 'Preparing social workers to confront social injustice and oppression: Evaluating the role of social work education', *Social Work*, 66(1), 39–48, viewed 23 October 2022, https://doi.org/10.1093/sw/swaa018.

Gray, M. (2005) 'Dilemmas of international social work: Paradoxical processes in indigenisation, universalism and imperialism', *International Journal of Social Welfare*, 14(3), 231–238, https://doi.org/10.1111/j.1468-2397.2005.00363.x.

Gray, M. (2016) 'Think globally and locally, act globally and locally': A new agenda for international social work education', in Taylor, I., Bogo, M., Lefevre, M. and Teater, B. (eds.) *The Routledge International Handbook of Social Work Education*, pp. 3–13. London: Routledge.

Gray, M., Coates, J., and Yellow Bird, M. (eds.) (2010) *Indigenous Social Work around the World: Towards Culturally Relevant Education and Practice*. Aldershot, Hants: Ashgate.

Gray, M., Coates, J., Yellow Bird, M., and Hetherington, T. (2013a) 'Introduction: Scoping the terrain of decolonization', in Gray, M., Coates, J., Yellow Bird, M. and Hetherington, T. (eds.) *Decolonizing Social Work*, pp. 1–26. Aldershot, Hants: Ashgate.

Gray, M., Coates, J., Yellow Bird, M., and Hetherington, T. (eds.) (2013b) *Decolonizing Social Work*. Farnham, Surrey: Ashgate.

Harrison, G., and Ip, R. (2013) 'Extending the terrain of inclusive education in the classroom to the field: International students on placement', *Social Work Education*, 32(2), 230–243, https://doi.org/10.1080/02615479.2012.734804.

International Association of Schools of Social Work (IASSW) and International Federation of Social Workers (IFSW) (2014) 'Global definition of social work', viewed on 01 March 2022, https://www.iassw-aiets.org/global-definition-of-social-work-review-of-the-global-definition/.

International Association of Schools of Social Work (IASSW), International Federation of Social Workers (IFSW), and International Council on Social Welfare (ICSW) (2020) '2020 to 2030 global agenda for social work and social development framework: Co-building inclusive social transformation', https://www.iassw-aiets.org/global-agenda/.

International Federation of Social Workers (IFSW) (2022) 'Social work and the United Nations sustainable development goals (SDGS)', viewed on 25 November 2022, https://www.ifsw.org/social-work-and-the-united-nations-sustainable-development-goals-sdgs/.

Jöns, H., Meusburger, P., and Heffernan, M. (eds.) (2017) *Mobilities of Knowledge*. Springer International Publishing AG.

Kansiime, P. (2020) *Social Work with Male Survivors of Conflict-Related Sexual Violence in Uganda: The Experiences of Practitioners and Their Intervention Methods* (Doctoral dissertation. University of Newcastle, Australia).

Lerner, J. E. (2021) 'Social work the "white way": Helping white students self-reflect on a culture of whiteness in the classroom and beyond', *Social Work Education*, 41(4), 605–624, https://doi.org/10.1080/02615479.2020.1868422.

McAuliffe, D. (2021) 'Claiming and expanding social work knowledge in the international space', *Australian Social Work*, 74(4), 391–393, DOI: 10.1080/0312407X.2021.1945731.

Midgley, J. (2008) 'Promoting reciprocal international social work exchanges: Professional imperialism revisited', in Gray, M., Coates, J. and Yellow Bird, M. (eds.) *Indigenous Social Work Around the World: Towards Culturally Relevant Education and Practice*, pp. 31–45. Burlington, VT: Ashgate Publishing.

Mugumbate, J., and Mtetwa, E. (2019) 'Reframing social work research for Africa's consumers of research products: A guiding tool', *African Journal of Social Work*, 9(2), 52–58, https://www.ajol.info/index.php/ajsw/article/view/192200/181314.

Mupedziswa, R., Rankopo, M., and Mwansa, L. (2019) 'Ubuntu as a Pan-African philosophical framework for social work in Africa', in Twikirize J. M. and Spitzer, H. (eds.) *Social Work Practice in Africa Indigenous and Innovative Approaches*, pp. 180–200. Kampala, Uganda: Fountain Publishers.

Mwanri, L., Anderson, L., and Gatwiri, K. (2021) 'Telling our stories: Resilience during resettlement for African skilled migrants in Australia', *International Journal of Environmental Research and Public Health*, 18(8), 3954, DOI: 10.3390/ijerph18083954.

Nabbumba, D. (2022) *Examining Responsibility Allocation within the Social Care System for Older People in Rural Uganda: An Ecological Systems Approach* (Doctoral dissertation, La Trobe), https://doi.org/10.26181/19532632.v1.

Nguyen, M. N., and Robertson, M. J. (2020) 'International students enacting agency in their PhD journey', *Teaching in Higher Education*, 27(6), 814–830, DOI: 10.1080/13562517.2020.1747423.

Plummer, K. (1983) *Documents of Life. An Introduction to the Problems and Literature of a Humanistic Method*. London: Allen and Unwin.

Sevenhuijsen, S. (2004) 'Trace: A method for normative policy analysis from the ethic of care', in Sevenhuijsen, S. and Svab, A. (eds.) *The Heart of the Matter. The Contribution of the Ethic of Care to Social Policy in Some New EU Member States*, pp. 13–46. Ljubljana: Peace Institute.

Tascón, S. and Ife, J. (2020) *Disrupting Whiteness in Social Work*. New York: Routledge.

Thiong Wa'o N (1986) *Decolonising the Mind : The Politics of Language in African Literature*. London, England: James Currey.

Tran, L. T. and Vu, T. T. P. (2018) 'Agency in mobility: Towards a conceptualisation of international student agency in transnational mobility', *Educational Review*, 70(2), 167–187, https://doi.org/10.1080/00131911.2017.1293615.

Tusasiirwe, S. (2019) *Stories from the Margins to the Centre : Decolonising Social Work Based on Experiences of Older Women and Social Workers in Uganda*. Penrith, NSW: Western Sydney University.

Tusasiirwe, S., Kansiime, P., Eyaa, S., Namisango, F., and Bulamu, N. (2021) 'Living and revitalizing Ubuntu: Challenges of passing on Ubuntu values to the younger generation and attempted strategies to overcome them', in Mukuni, J. and Tlou, J. (eds.) *Understanding Ubuntu for Enhancing Intercultural Communications*, pp. 85–101. IGI Global, DOI: 10.4018/978-1-7998-7947-3.ch008.

Tusasiirwe, S., Nabbumba, D., and Kansiime, P. (2022) 'Religion and spirituality in social work in Uganda: Lessons for social work education', *Social Work Education*, 1–18, DOI: 10.1080/02615479.2022.210424.

United Nations Department of Economic and Social Affairs, Population Division (2020) International Migration 2020 Highlights (ST/ESA/SER.A/452).

Walt, G., and Gilson, L. (1994) 'Reforming the health sector in developing countries: The central role of policy analysis', **Health Policy and Planning**, 9(4), 353–370, viewed 21 March 2022, http://www.jstor.org/stable/45089160.

Williams, C., and Graham, M. (2014) 'A world on the move: Migration, mobilities and social work', **British Journal of Social Work**, 44(1), i1–i17, https://doi.org/10.1093/bjsw/bcu058.

30
SOCIAL WORK EDUCATION AND BLACK AFRICAN DIASPORA
Explorations in the Republic of Ireland

Washington Marovatsanga and Paul Michael Garrett

Abstract: English

Somewhat different in focus to other chapters in the book, here we primarily dwell on the Black African diaspora in the Republic of Ireland. In this context, the chapter draws attention to the views of social work educators and our main interest is their perceptions in relation to four thematic concerns: social work education and theoretical perspectives; praxis; organisational structures within the capitalist racial state; neoliberalism. These interviews cannot, of course, be regarded as 'representative' of the 'field' of social work education in Ireland. Nonetheless, what the remarks of the respondents illustrate are certain interesting tendencies that signal causes for concern, and they also hint at directions for possible future studies. We reflect on such issues and also highlight other recent developments, including the 2021 launch of the Irish Association of Social Workers (IASW) 'Anti-Racism Strategy'.

Abstract: Muhtasari

Tofauti kidogo na sura nyingine kwenye kitabu hiki, hapa tunaangalia kwa undani waafrika walioopo ughaibuni hapa Ayalendi. Kufuatilia hawa sura hii inatilia mkazo maoni ya wakufunzi wa elimu ya ustawi wa jamii na tunafuatilia mitazamo yao katika maeneo manne muhimu: elimu ya ustawi wa jamii: mtaala wake, na jinsi mipangilio na taratibu zilivyo ndani ya dola ya kibepari na ubaguzi wa rangi; na mfumo wa uhuria. Mahojiano tuliyofanya hayawezi kuchukuliwa kama uwalishi wa sekta nzima ya ustawi wa jamii Ayalendi.Pamoja na hivyo majibu ya waliojibu maswali yanaonyesha mwenendo fulani unaoashiria mambo muhimu yakuzingatiwa, na pia yanatoa mwelekeo kwa tafiti nyingine za baadaye. Tunatafakari juu ya haya mambo na pia kuangalia maendeleo mengine ya karibuni, pamoja na kuanzishwa kwa mkakati wa kupingga ubaguzi wa rangi wa Umoja wa Wafanyakazi wa Ustawi wa Jamii wa Ayalendi.[1]

Introduction

This book is clearly focused on African social work education. However, in this chapter we suggest that it is also vital that we are attentive to the Black African diaspora and its engagement with questioning circulating around how the profession structures its approach to the curriculum and wider issues pivoting on pedagogy. Matters pertaining to curriculum development – and, indeed, failures to evolve teaching programmes – are tremendously important for the Black African diaspora. Education is immensely significant because it serves to transmit (or challenge) 'received ideas' within particular fields (Rojek et al., 1988). That is to say, what is taught is not merely of significance within the walls of the university; rather, how the curriculum is constructed directly impacts on practice and on the experience of racialised minorities, such as Black Africans. Problems are already apparent in this regard. If, for example, we note research findings relating to social work with children and families in Ireland it becomes apparent that Black African families are 'about seven times more likely to face child protection proceedings than are indigenous Irish people, and this figure is likely to be greater if the "mixed" category includes one African parent, as we have observed it often does. Eastern Europeans are about 1.5 times as likely as Irish people to face the child care courts' (Child Care Law Reporting Project, 2015, p. 14). Such findings, in the area of child protection, reflect the fact that Black African service users, in Europe, are disproportionately represented in 'social problem' categories and this has generated disquiet and controversy.

In some quarters, not unreasonably these developments have prompted a questioning of social work's ethical commitment to repudiate 'discrimination' and 'oppression' and to uphold the 'dignity' and 'worth' of every person (see, for example, Onyejelem, 2017). Such concerns echo, in complex ways, those of US scholars and commentators who point to the fact that African American children and their families are disproportionately targeted by child protection services (Roberts, 2014). Discussing a not dissimilar situation in the United Kingdom, relating to the experience of Nigerian parents, Okpokiri (2021) refers to the fears of such parents being caught 'parenting-while-Black'. Literature from Canada similarly reveals that Black parents feel that their parenting practices are unfairly targeted by child welfare agencies and this contributes to the overrepresentation of Black children in the care system (Adjei and Minka, 2018).

Nevertheless, there are also emerging signs of a greater interest in social work's positioning and the appropriateness (or otherwise) of its intervention strategies when working with those who are not only visibly different, but who also may have culturally distinct worldviews and belief systems. The launch of the Irish Association of Social Workers (IASW) 'Anti-Racism Strategy', in February 2021, may herald a progressive departure (IASW, 2021). Indeed, the motif 'Black lives matter' must become a more focal and defining feature of social work in the future (Michael and Joseph, 2021).

The chapter will begin with brief reference to the interviews that are at the core of our contribution. We will then move on to refer to the four chief themes that our respondents discussed. We will then conclude with a short discussion on some of the key messages conveyed in this research endeavour.

Listening to Social Work Educators

In what follows, we draw attention to the views of four social work educators (Table 30.1). These respondents are central to the empirical work that we will discuss in the chapter.

All our respondents self-describe as 'White Irish'. At the time the interviews were conducted – by the first author – there was no Black African social work educators employed on full-time contracts in the Irish university sector. The individual, one-to-one interviews took place prior to the onset of the COVID-19 pandemic and its related physical distancing measures. Occurring between May 2017 and March 2018, they were conducted in-person and 'face to face'. The chapter is derived from a much larger research project encompassing the views and opinions of front-line social workers. Issues pertaining to methodology are also featured in the main publication derived from this research endeavour (Marovatsanga and Garrett, 2022).

Table 30.1 The Four Social Work Educators

Pseudonym	Race/Ethnicity	Approximate Age
Kim (F)	White Irish	Early 40s
Michael (M)	White Irish	Late 40s
Thomas (M)	White Irish	60s
Tina (F)	White Irish	50s

The focus is on the respondents' perceptions in relation to four main themes: social work education and theoretical perspectives; praxis; organisational structures within the capitalist racial state; neoliberalism.

Social Work Education and Theoretical Perspectives

All of these educator respondents agreed that their cultural and racial background – and, perhaps what Bourdieu (2003 [1977]) would term their 'habitus' – was a significant factor in determining their orientation to social work education and the theoretical approaches that they taught. The focal response was captured by Michael:

> It is impossible to escape one's own cultural background and socialisation. It is an inevitable factor. Indeed, much of the conventional underlying social theory is rooted within a Western cultural perspective.

Three of the four educators interviewed felt that, in recent years, social work education had not adequately changed in order to respond to issues of 'race' and ethnicity. The fourth one, Kim, argued there was very little the educators could do beyond instructing their students to treat people equally and in a humane manner based on the available teaching resources. She continued:

> It could, however, mean what we are teaching is not solid enough to unsettle or make our students 'unlearn' prior negative conceptions of equality of 'races'/cultures they bring to college with them from their homes and communities.

Equality studies tended to be taught from a perspective that did not critique or radically question the dominance of Eurocentric epistemologies and practice methods. Some even dismissed the teaching of 'anti-oppressive practice' as not going far enough to interrogate the history and origins of the oppression in that it tended to ignore the structural and racialised oppression embedded in social institutions. Michael maintained that it was crucial to recognise that 'diversity' does not merely signal a willingness to enroll culturally diverse students:

> That is the easy bit! The real challenge is to make the course itself culturally diverse. The challenge there is that you must relativise the dominant hegemony and admit into equal or at least respectful consideration diverse discourses and practices. That is very problematic for academics trained within the hegemonic discourse and is very unsettling to Western assumptions of superiority...These assumptions of dominance and superiority are very much grounded in claims to be 'scientific'.... Other discourses, especially those from 'less advanced' cultural groups, can be categorised as instances of 'culture' and 'diversity', but not as equally valid claims on 'truth' itself.

Some respondents suggested there was universal gender oppression/inequality dynamic at play and it was far more challenging to be a woman *and* to be Black within the field of social work. Some also pointed to how a more individualistic, career-orientated 'lean-in' feminism may have helped some White women attain a measure of 'equality' (see also the compelling critique of this strand of feminism in Fraser, 2013). They also viewed most Black African societies and cultures as continuing to be more patriarchal than Western ones. For example, Michael commented:

> Many African cultures appear more 'patriarchal' than Western 'liberal' ones. This can raise questions for Black African female students when addressing issues …. In my experience, so far, most if not all of the Black African female students are critical of patriarchy. However, western individualism is not an obvious 'good' thing either.

Tina maintained:

> Yes, you can think of all the oppressions that are gender based – it's worse when you add the colour Black. From what my female Black students say, even with racism and Afrophobia, women are disproportionately targeted in terms of physical violence and verbal abuse as the Black men are considered naturally violent in the minds of most White Irish people and are therefore perceived as likely to retaliate in kind if attacked.

The educators main responses to the notion of 'cultural competence' identified with Strier's (2004) definition and they all acknowledged the nature of the 'competences' required for intercultural communication: attention to prosody (different accents), proxemics, (distance from a person when speaking), gestures, and facial expressions (eye contact as well as cognitive competences). They did not, however, believe such models alone would make practitioners respond better to 'cultural others'. Thomas argued:

> 'Cultural competence' and 'intercultural competence' I think primarily suggest a capacity to recognise and then respond to cultural difference. This is wrapped up, for me, in the concept of attempting to understand each person in terms not only of their individuality, but also of their gender, ethnicity, culture and so on. It is difficult to fully evaluate how successful I and my colleagues have been in creating a 'culturally open learning environment' at this college. I suspect we cannot ultimately escape our underlying assumptions.

All the respondents reported that it 'made sense' to teach different worldviews emanating from the Global North *and Global* South as this would be entirely in keeping with democratic tenets and notions of inclusivity. Doing so would also be consistent with the social justice imperatives and would be aligned with efforts to 'decolonise' social work education (Gray et al., 2013; Kleibl et al., 2019). Tina commented:

> The only recommendation I can make is to teach both Black African and European perspectives in the classroom. This should be easily done. Teaching only one worldview from one 'race' in my view amounts to some form of racism…perhaps even 'epistemic racism' or 'cultural oppression'.

Indeed, this remark resonates from Fricker's perception that a person or group might find their 'intellectual courage' inhibited or eroded because of being routinely treated as a subject or subjects lacking in knowledge and the capacity to know (Fricker, 2007, p. 49).

All four respondents agreed that these 'differences' were largely underpinned by notions of the liberal Enlightenment and logical positivism as manifested through the philosophy of 'individualism' (see also Garrett, 2024). This, the social work educators suggested, often clashed with Black African philosophies which are often rooted in a more 'collectivist' and 'communal' approach to life. For example, the Black African philosophy of Ubuntu is rooted in the understanding that a person is entirely constituted as a 'self' through their relationship with others. One of the respondents described Ubuntu philosophy, as defined by Swanson (2007), as suggesting that personal 'strength' comes from community support with a sense of dignity and identity achieved through mutualism, empathy, generosity, and community commitment. The often-cited African adage 'it takes a village to raise a child' is aligned with the 'spirit' and intent of Ubuntu and a humble 'togetherness' is perceived as a source of 'solidarity in crisis times (Swanson, 2007). Old age is frequently viewed as degeneration in Western culture. In contrast, within most Black African cultures, the elderly are often valued for their life-long experientially acquired wisdom.

Praxis

The educator respondents were unanimous that the presence of Black African and other minority ethnic students 'enriched' class discussions, and, in the process, some of them confided that they themselves had also learned 'something new' or had their earlier misconceptions 'clarified'. For example, Kim maintained:

> Yes, we have Black African students in each of our programme stages/years. I think this has been quite positive for everyone. I'm not aware of any difficulties that have arisen. I think it has enriched our programme and made us all more alert to cultural difference and assumptions.

In contrast, and reflecting some of the emerging research and conversations occurring amongst Black African students, Tina confided:

> While we do our best to paint a picture that in academia that we are more enlightened and hence more tolerant, sometimes there have been difficulties in hearing what Black African students are saying due to their heavy accents, particularly those from West Africa. Equally, sometimes you get a sense they are not challenging what is said in class, no matter how offensive...maybe this is related to cultural taboos about challenging authority or just out of fear that the White lecturer/White students will be offended. Perhaps there is concern too about how their response may be used against them. I just don't know. This may not, though, apply to all Black social work students.

Thomas added:

> The Black students I have taught are very cautious how they get involved in discussions. They try to be as polite as possible and usually use their own experiences/ stories and what they have heard, but they wait for White students to speak first, like they're 'testing the waters'. Most of the mature ones have poor computer literacy/typing skills and are often slow in completing assignments. Their excuse has often been they had no access to home computers in their countries of origin. Moreover, some work to send money to family members back home despite being on a 'full-time' course.

Organisational Structures within the Capitalist Racial State

The organisational structures housing social work are, of course, immensely significant in terms of how they shape the provision of services. Our engagement with this theme was also influenced by the 'racial state' conceptualisation used by Lentin (2007). She maintains that the contemporary state promotes 'racial categorisation and identification' and that it shapes 'national identities' by 'legislating on immigration controls and citizenship rights' (Lentin, 2007, p. 614). Such practices can be associated with what is often termed 'institutional racism' and the embedding of patterns of discrimination within all the distinctive 'fields' of the racial state (see also Policante and Garrett, 2022). Hence, spheres such as welfare, education, the law and policing, arts and culture, housing and, of course, social work are shaped accordingly (Garrett, 2015). Our main refinement of the racial state conceptualisation is to seek to ground it in the symbolic and material fabric of *capitalism*. Hence, our preference for *capitalist* racial state aims to highlight how states' imperatives are also capitalist imperatives that are triggered and sustained in order to increase the surplus value derived from – and stolen from – the working class. Whatever the colour of our skin, most of us are exploited by capital, even though the rate of exploitation may differ on account of our skin colour (and gender) and our roles and functions within a capitalist world system and the complex social orders that it gives rise to and maintains.

Most of the academic respondents admitted they found it 'uncomfortable' talking about or teaching racism within their organisational setting and that is was more convenient and easier to discuss the need to 'treat all people equally and fairly' in the context of teaching 'human rights', 'equality studies', and generic 'anti-oppressive' and 'anti-discriminatory' theory. When asked about specific teaching on racism and anti-racism, Tina stated:

> This depends on how comfortable the individual lecturer is talking about issues of 'race'/ racism. Some of us are obviously embarrassed and prefer to give the impression that, as Irish people, we can never be seen in the same light as perhaps the English or other Europeans with a colonial and racist history. The fact that we teach social work values professing humanitarian ethos of equality and repudiate any form of oppression means we are duty bound to expose structural issues such as 'institutional racism' and neoliberal racism manifested in punitive social policy such as Direct Provision (DP) [hotel-style accommodation holding, and regulating the lives of, asylum seekers awaiting judgement on their status] and the Habitual Residence Condition (HRC) [which ensures that housing and welfare services can only be provided if an applicant is able to show that they meet stipulated residence conditions] (se also Dalikeni, 2021; Harmon and Garrett, 2015). In other words, it's 'politically correct' for social work lecturers to be heard condemning any form of injustice as that accords with their mandate. The question perhaps is beyond what we teach [and should focus on] how many of us, as lecturers, have joined the street protests to, for example, press for the end or DP or to end the deportation of children, previously taken into 'care', when they turn eighteen?

All of the respondents felt that that the often relentlessly 'negative' past and present images of Black Africa and its inhabitants influenced how Black African social work service users are perceived today (Fanon, 1989 [1959]). They largely attributed this to biased teaching of the history of early European colonialism and, not infrequently, the appropriation of the Bible and scripture to suggest that it was appropriate to maintain a hierarchy of 'races' (Tsri, 2016). The White 'race' is at the apex with a 'primitive' Blackness, variously evoked as 'child-like' and 'dependent' and/or and 'evil' at the bottom (McClintock, 1995). Respondents also believed that the current global media focus on poverty as exclusive to Black Africa (as represented in international aid advertisements) implies that 'poverty has one colour' and that 'colour is Black'. In a politically convenient way, and entirely in tune with the neoliberal project, this presentation also erases the plight of the millions of impoverished White people residing is the so-called developed Western world and in ostensibly 'rich countries' such as the United States (see also Garrett, 2002).

All the social work educators cited possible cultural misunderstandings, poverty, and shortcomings due to policies (failing to reflect the presence of other cultures) as the chief reasons for the disproportionate number of Black African children in 'care' mentioned at the outset of our chapter. Kim said:

> Four factors I think contribute to the high number of Black African children being taken into care namely: (1) cultural misunderstandings (2) poverty and socioeconomic disadvantage and (3) 'institutional racism' and, I think, (4) the ethnocentric design of child welfare systems impacts negatively on the equitable assessment of Black African families. I would like to also add that Black African children are at risk of becoming overrepresented in the child protection system in Ireland when ethnocentric, rather than culturally appropriate assessment criteria, are used to judge whether 'maltreatment' has occurred. 'Culture' is more at risk of taking the blame for overrepresentation in the child protection system than 'institutional racism' where organisational practices and policies, such as the Children First national guidelines (Department of Children and Youth Affairs, 2017), preserve only the dominant culture. It is important that 'culture' is not mistaken for 'maltreatment' and that 'maltreatment' is not mistaken for 'culture'.

Three of the respondents believed that increased racism targeting Black Africans was attributable to being 'more visibly different' than, say, Eastern European migrant workers. One respondent maintained:

> Most people are unaware that majority of older Irish people could have been irreparably indoctrinated by the 'pennies for Black babies' collections [in church parishes and schools in the 1960s and 1970s], yet this possibly fostered an enduring mind-set about Black Africans' 'dependency'. Ireland was also part of the White world despite itself being colonised. [As a consequence, it was] also subjected to prevailing socialisations of White supremacy prevalent in the western hemisphere for centuries. [All of this was] further reinforced by missionaries who sent back home stories of 'Black savages' who needed to be 'saved from themselves'. Do not forget that in the Bible and scripture 'Black' is also often equated with death, decay, sin and so on. [Such deep-rooted ideas have not been adequately] contested in our inherited constructions.

Thomas remarked:

> Afrophobia is not just an Irish problem...it is on the rise in most Western countries disguised as the 'ultra-nationalism' of right-wing parties. It's similar, in some ways, to new forms of cultural racism like 'Islamophobia' and both are often expressed through policies that seek to retreat from multiculturalism. The pretext is that multiculturalism as an ideal is impractical given the huge cultural differences. What is not highlighted, though, is that such sentiments and movements mostly thrive in situations of declining economic conditions with visibly different often getting the blame.

All agreed that these organisations such as CORU – the Irish social work regulatory body – and the Irish Association of Social Workers (IASW) played a key role in setting 'basic standards' and fulfilling a 'watchdog' role in maintaining some semblance of uniformity in education and practice. The respondents were critical of these bodies for not 'taking the lead' in energetically pressing for more diversity in the social work curricula, student recruitment, and relevant training to ensure students (that is to say, future practitioners) get exposure to working in *all* our communities. Some even saw CORU as seeking to shape and control the intellectual and political allegiances of practitioners (Garrett, 2021).

Neoliberalism

All of the social work educator respondents suggested that Black African service users were more 'at risk' of having their lives undermined by the impact of the neoliberal regime of capital accumulation and the pernicious social order that it generates (Brockmann and Garrett, 2022). This included their lacking 'proper' information, not understanding the welfare system and the impact of 'institutional racism': this third element included exclusion from the labour market through discrimination or being more 'at risk' of being the first to be 'let go' following neoliberal moves to 'slim down' workforces (Garrett, 2019).

These educators also maintained that the 'negative' media presentation of Black Africans could be perceived as having deleterious consequences in term of the wider public debates on immigration, asylum seekers, and refugees. Thomas, for example, argued:

> I'm not sure I'm influenced by this. However, there is no doubt that the current focus on migration and the political responses are a very important backdrop to our life at present. This clearly is an issue we must pay attention to and firmly address using the core humanist values of social work as a frame of reference.

Michael differed slightly:

> While it's true that some media has influenced the public perception of Blacks and asylum seekers negatively, it is also true that not all media have done that. Some sections of the media have run some 'positive stories' highlighting how asylum seekers have defied the difficult situations and worked hard to be successful citizens. It could be just that the 'negative stories' have been highlighted by those with an agenda against immigrants.

In keeping with the idea that large-scale immigration is a recent experience in Ireland and the country may still have a lot to learn from other jurisdictions with longer histories of immigration, Kim argued that there is a:

> need for an integration policy encompassing policies on education, health, social welfare, housing, public and civic participation and so on. The current understanding of integration policy is often confused with immigration policy that seeks to control who has access to enter, and live in, Ireland. There should be a clearly defined policy with programmes that link in with all other services and perhaps a new social work role of resettlement social worker, specialising in supporting new arrivals beyond refugees and asylum seekers might be considered.

The other policy reform, suggested by Tina, was to commence a thorough and ongoing 'decolonisation' of much of what is taught within the Irish educational system:

Policy reform interventions should also take cognisance of and address emerging research evidence suggesting there is value in other cultural ways and methods. However ... there is need to go beyond changing what we teach and unlearning old ways of thinking and teaching new perspectives. A policy framework that targets changing the entrenched 'habitus' of practitioners and institutions through 'conscientisation' is more sustainable and effective long-term solution. More importantly, the contradictions of neoliberal hegemony need to be exposed.

Conclusion

Attentive to the comments of our respondents, we need to recall that Ireland is situated within a western European sociocultural context still saturated in historical and contemporary notions of Western racial and cultural superiority. When applied to social work, such a neo-colonial ideological orientation is entirely at odds with the profession's rhetorical egalitarian claims (Garrett, 2024). More conceptually, this may reveal a good deal about what Bourdieu (2003 [1977]) might term embedded 'doxic' knowledge that is difficult to question.

In this context, de Sousa Santos (2014) suggests that the sociology of 'emergences' can potentially help us to see that the prevailing oppressive social order is not 'natural' – or, indeed, imbued with 'permanence' – and can be changed through human agency that seeks to counter silencing and exploitation with activism. The conceptualisations of this Portuguese intellectual remind us, therefore, that which currently exists canonically is not the only way of understanding the social world. Alternative and more socially and economically progressive forms of knowledge, formerly subjected to historical enforced absences, can always begin to emerge. In this sense, social work teaching might begin to try to furnish examples of knowledge systems whose absence has been historically enforced. Certainly there are hints that social work students in Ireland are beginning to think in politically insightful ways about how other intersecting concerns can be harnessed to a struggle against racism. This was reflected in the summer of 2021 with the emergence of the #Fees Must Fall campaign. Influenced by a similarly titled campaign in South Africa, the core demand of the Irish students was for a reduction of fees on social work courses with a circulated motion stating:

Whilst recognising that there is great variability in fees throughout the state, we call on directors of social work programmes and associated staff to advocate that universities in Ireland reduce fees. This is important because such a move would:

a. be a very practical measure rooted in a commitment to developing anti-racist practices and it is congruent with social work values associated with social inclusivity and combatting social exclusion.
b. potentially open up access to such programmes for members of Black and ethnic minority communities, such as Irish Travellers, who are frequently unable to afford the cost of current fees on account of structural racism and discrimination that undermines their, and the families, ability to afford to embark on social work studies.
c. potentially help to transform the composition of the social work workforce by introducing more students, and subsequently practitioners, who are not white and middle class.
d. aid the efforts of working-class class students who are also presently largely excluded from applying to social work programmes because of expensive fees and the additional costs associated with fieldwork placements.

In contrast to the progressive and combative politics reflected in this motion, our respondents expressed concern that the way that social work is taught lays insufficient emphasis on the political nature of the profession. This was blamed for 'turning out' graduates who had little, if any, interest in critical politics and this rendered them largely neoliberal compliant and averse to dissent (Fenton, 2018). Underpinning this chapter, therefore, is something of a 'call' for social work to view critical praxis as a way of disrupting the current orthodoxies (Garrett, 2021). This might be done, by, for example, beginning to politically exploit the tensions inherent within the rhetoric of 'fundamental rights', 'human rights', and so on. In this context, it is noteworthy that 'human rights' have been cynically and crassly expunged from Irish social work's ethical code (CORU, 2019).

Social work practice and education in Ireland and elsewhere needs to be comprised of a workforce that is racially and culturally diverse. Whilst essential, this does not necessarily mean that social work – as institution, field, and discipline – will become more benign and beneficially responsive to the needs of the Black African diaspora. The situation is much more complex and it is sociologically and politically naïve to conclude that recruitment of more Black African educators and practitioners is a magic bullet 'solution'. Based in Scotland, Bowes and Dar (2000) suggest that White social workers lack knowledge of minority ethnic communities or have difficulties working with them. These practitioners also view such work as risky given they may unintentionally offend service users and this might prompt accusations of their being labelled 'racist' (Bowes and Dar, 2000). This is confirmed by Burman *et al.* (2004), who reveal that White social workers intervening with South Asian families in child protection cases express similar anxieties and tend to withdraw from this work and unduly rely on their Black colleagues. Given these findings, it is not unlikely that newly trained and recruited Black social work practitioners might find themselves exclusively working with more 'difficult cases' within Black and minority ethnic ghettoised enclaves.

If we are to prompt fundamental changes within the field of social work, these will not be triggered simply by recruiting more Black African social workers and educators. Rather, there needs to be a more encompassing strategy that reorientates the field to truly address the needs of the Black African people and others who are (dis)similarly exploited and rendered voiceless. This would entail substantial economic transformations, the dispossession of the super-rich and – at present a pressing requirement in Ireland – a major public housing programme. That is to say, major changes relating to the teaching of 'race' and racism within social work education need to occur as part of a more encompassing transformative programme strategy intent on remaking the state and its economic and social imperatives (Garrett, 2021).

Even within the narrow field of social work, it is important to recognise the constraints hampering new ways of working. As our respondents make apparent, certain reductive and stereotypical perceptions of Black Africans continue to haunt the social work imaginary. This factor aside, we can also observe that a more in-depth engagement with Black African families, by both White and Black African practitioners, demands that social workers undertaking the job day-in and day-out produce more immersive and time-consuming assessments. This involves reactivating something of a traditional social work emphasis on heightened attentiveness, intensive listening, clear communication, and relationship building.

Recommendations

1. We need a form of social work that is grounded in a willingness to question, and oftentimes dissent from, established paradigms and canonic streams of thought within the profession (Garrett, 2021). In an Irish context, 'Afro-Hibernian lifeworlds' are pluralistic and com-

plex and social work services must begin to engage with those inhabiting and creating such worlds in a much more nuanced and informed way.
2. When working with Black Africans, White social work educators often have no knowledge or lack familiarity with relevant ethnic cultures. Ironically, this may be connected to the gradual, but uncritical, adoption of arid 'cultural competence' models derived from, for example, the United States. There is, of course, nothing wrong in critically adopting foreign models, but these must deepen and expand our thinking, not stupefy us.
3. To promote a form of social work more attuned to the definition of the profession provided by the International Federation of Social Workers (2014), neoliberal imperatives and ways of perceiving the world need to be questioned and confronted. Racism and epistemological shortcomings (within and beyond social work education) can be understood only if they are related to material and economic concerns.

Further Reading

Marovatsanga, W. and Garrett, P. M. (2022) *Social Work and the Black African Diaspora*, Bristol: Policy Press.
Michael, L. (2016) 'Afrophobia, ENAR Ireland'. https://static.rasset.ie/documents/news/afrophobia-in-ireland.pdf.

Notes

We are grateful to Dr. David Nyaluke (University College Dublin) for his kind assistance with the translation.

References

Adjei, P. B. and Minka, E. (2018) 'Black parents ask for a second look: Parenting under 'white' child protection rules in Canada', *Children and Youth Services Review*, 94, 511–524.
Bourdieu, P. (2003 [1977]) *Outline of a theory of Practice*, Cambridge: Cambridge University.
Bowes, A. and Dar, N. (2000) 'Researching social care for minority ethnic older people: Implications of some Scottish research', *British Journal of Social Work*, 30(3), 305–321.
Brockmann, O. and Garrett, P. M. (2022) 'People are responsible for their own individual actions': Dominant ideologies within the neoliberal Institutionalised social work order', *European Journal of Social Work*, 25(5), 880–893.
Burman, E., Smailes, S. L. and Chantler, K. (2004) '"Culture" as a barrier to service provision and delivery: Domestic violence services for minoritised Women', *Critical Social Policy*, 24(3), 332–357.
Child Care Law Reporting Project (2015) 'Final report'. https://www.childlawproject.ie/wp-content/uploads/2015/11/CCLRP-Full-final-report_FINAL2.pdf.
CORU (2019) 'Social workers registration board code of professional ethics'. https://www.coru.ie/files-codes-of-conduct/swrb-code-of-professional-conduct-and-ethics-for-social-workers.pdf.
Dalikeni, C. (2021) 'Child-rearing practices: Cross cultural perspectives of African asylum-seeking families and child protection social workers in Ireland', *European Journal of Social Work*, 24(1), 8–20.
de Sousa Santos, B. (2014) *Epistemologies of the South*, London: Routledge.
Department of Children and Youth Affairs (2017) 'Children first guidance'. https://www.tusla.ie/uploads/content/Children_First_National_Guidance_2017.pdf.
Fanon, F. (1989 [1959]) *Studies in a Dying Colonialism* (Trans. H. Chevalier), London: Earthscape.
Fenton, J. (2018) 'Putting old heads on young shoulders', *Social Work Education*, 37(8), 941–954.
Fraser, N. (2013) *Fortunes of Feminism*, London: Verso.
Fricker, M. (2007) *Epistemic injustice*, New York: Oxford University Press.
Garrett, P. M. (2002) 'No Irish need apply: Social work in Britain and the history and politics of exclusionary paradigms and practices', *The British Journal of Social Work*, 32(4), 477–494.

Garrett, P. M. (2015) 'Words matter: Deconstructing "welfare dependency" in the UK', *Critical and Radical Social Work*, 3(3), 389–406.

Garrett, P. M. (2019) 'Revisiting "The Birth of Biopolitics": Foucault's account of neoliberalism and the remaking of social policy', *Journal of Social Policy*, 48(3), 469–487.

Garrett, P. M. (2021) *Dissenting Social Work: Critical Theory, Resistance and Pandemic*, London: Routledge.

Gray, M., Coates, J., Yellow Bird, M. and Hetherington, T. (eds.) (2013) *Decolonizing Social Work*, Farnham: Ashgate.

Garrett, P. M. (2024) 'What are we talking about when we are talking about "decolonizing" social work?', *British Journal of Social Work*, 27 February. https://doi.org/10.1093/bjsw/bcae018.

Harmon, A. and Garrett, P. M. (2015) 'It's like Weber's "iron cage": Irish social workers' experience of the habitual residence condition (HRC)', *Critical and Radical Social Work*, 3(1), 35–52.

International Federation of Social Workers (2014) 'Global definition of social work'. http://ifsw.org/get-involved/globaldefinition-of-social-work/.

Irish Association of Social Workers (IASW) (2021) 'A new way forward: Dismantling racism in 21st-century Irish social work – ISAW anti-racism strategic plan 2021–2023'. file:///C:/Users/0103674s/Downloads/IASW%20Anti%20Racist%20Strategy%202021-2023.pdf.

Kleibl, T., Lutz, R., Noyoo, N., Bunk, B., Dittmann, A. and Seepamore, B. (eds.) (2019) *The Routledge Handbook of Postcolonial Social Work*, London and New York: Routledge.

Lentin, R. (2007) 'Ireland: Racial state and crisis racism', *Ethnic and Racial Studies*, 30(4), 610–627.

Marovatsanga, W. and Garrett, P. M. (2022) *Social Work with the Black African Diaspora*, Bristol: Policy Press.

Michael, L. and Joseph, E. (eds.) (2021) *The Sociological Observer: Black Lives Matter*, Maynooth, Ireland: Sociological Association of Ireland. https://www.sociology.ie/uploads/4/2/5/2/42525367/sociological_observer_2.pdf.

McClintock, A. (1995) *Imperial Leather: Race, Gender and Sexuality in the Colonial Conquest*, London: Routledge.

Okpokiri, C. (2021) 'Nigerian parents have fears of "parenting-while-Black" in Britain', *The Conversation*, 6 January. https://theconversation.com/nigerian-parents-have-fears-of-parenting-while-black-in-britain-152197.

Onyejelem, C. (2017) 'Tusla "biased against" ethnic families', *Metro Éireann*, 1 March. http://www.metroeireann.com/news/810/tusla-biased-against-ethnic-families-social-workers-claim-care-rates-for-african-children-disproportionately-high.html.

Policante, E. and Garrett, P. M. (2022) 'The "medieval castle approach": Social work and the Irish and Swiss asylum-seeking processes', *Critical and Radical Social Work*, 26 July. doi.org/10.1332/204986022X16546739159218.

Roberts, D. E. (2014) 'Child protection as surveillance of African American families', *Journal of Social Welfare and Family Law*, 36(4), 426–437.

Rojek, C., Peacock, G. and Collins, S. (1988) *Social Work and Received Ideas*, London: Routledge.

Strier, J. (2004) 'Intercultural competencies as a means to manage intercultural interactions in social work', *Journal of Intercultural Communication*, 7(1), https://www.immi.se/intercultural/nr7/stier.htm.

Swanson, D. M. (2007) '*Ubuntu*: An African contribution to (re)search for/with a 'humble togetherness', *Journal of Contemporary Issues in Education*, 2(2), 53–67.

Tsri, K. (2016) 'Africans are not black: Why the use of the term "black" for Africans should be abandoned', *African Identities*, 14(2), 147–160.

31
SOCIAL WORK AND PRACTICE EDUCATION, DECOLONISATION AND UBUNTU

Making Connections in Malawi

Janet Walker, Simon Cauvain, Felix Kakowa, and Anstance Fometu

Abstract: English

As a relatively new profession in Malawi, the challenges for establishing social work as a profession are being driven by the social work community. Outlining the political, economic, and social issues impacting the development of professional social work, this chapter will outline the strengths, weaknesses, opportunities, and challenges impacting on current and future developments for social work practice and education. The chapter examines the impact of colonisation and a concern for decolonisation, as indigenous worldviews, epistemologies, knowledge, and dialogues evident in teaching and learning, as indicated through education rooted in the principles and practice of Ubuntu. Drawing on the authors' experiences of training qualified social workers as practice educators in Malawi, this chapter examines 'practice education' through a colonisation-decolonisation lens of knowledge and practice and the emerging issues for decolonised and developmental social work for student learning in practice. It examines how decolonisation and Ubuntu can bring an alternative critical angle to teaching and learning for social work educators and for practice educators and their role with student social workers. It highlights the implications for knowledge exchange, as a multidirectional process; as critical for consideration of global challenges, and their impact on local practice; and as a critical, reflective process.

Abstract: Chichewa

Monga ntchito yatsopano ku Malawi, zovuta zokhazikitsa ntchito za chisamaliro cha anthu zikuyendetsedwa ndi gulu la anthu ogwira ntchitozi. Pofotokoza za ndale, zachuma ndi chikhalidwe cha anthu zomwe zimakhudza chitukuko cha ntchito za chisamaliro ch anthu, mutuwu udzalongosola mphamvu, zofooka, mwayi ndi zovuta zomwe zimakhudza zomwe zikuchitika panopa komanso zamtsogolo za ntchito yachisamaliro cha anthu ndi maphunziro ake. Izi zikuwonetsa kufunikira kozindikira kugwirizana kwa banja, dera ndi chilengedwe monga magwero a chidziwitso komanso kuchotsa utsamunda, monga malingaliro adziko, mamvekedwe, chidziwitso, ndi zokambirana zowonekera pophunzitsa ndi kuphunzira, mwachitsanzo monga momwe zimasonyezedwera kupyolera mu maphunziro ozikidwa pa mfundo ndi machitidwe a Ubuntu. Pogwiritsa ntchito zomwe alembi adakumana nazo pophunzitsa anthu ogwira ntchito zochisamaliro cha anthu kuti akhale othandizira kuphunzitsa ntchitoyi mmadera ku Malawi, mutu uno ukuwunika 'maphunziro a ntchito za chisamaliro cha anthu m'madera kudzera mu chidziwitso ndi machitidwe a chitsamunda - ufulu ndi zomwe zikutulukapo za kuchotsa utsamunda komanso ntchito ya chisamaliro cha anthu yotukula miyoyo kwa ophunzira ntchitoyi m'madera. Mutuwu ukuyang'ana momwe kuchotsa maganizidwe autsamunda ndi ubuntu zingabweretse njira ina yofunikira pakuphunzitsidwe ka kwa aphunzitsi a, ogwira ntchito zachitsamaliro cha anthu, komanso kwa ophunzitsa m'madera pamene agmira ntchito yawo. Mutuwu ukuwunikira zotsatira za kupitiriza kwa maphunziro a aphunzitsi a ntchito zachisamaliro cha anthu m'madera a m'Malawi, komanso zomwe zingakhudze maiko ena.

Introduction

Malawi is a landlocked, developing country in southern Africa with a population of 19,130,000, which is expected to double by 2038 (World Bank, 2022). With a gross domestic product per capita of $407, Malawi is one of the poorest countries in the world, with the economy heavily dependent on agriculture and vulnerable to climatic shocks, for example, flooding. The majority of the population are based in rural areas. About 50% of the population are below the age of 18 years of age, meaning that the country has few income earners and, hence, a high dependency ratio (Destatis, 2021). This fact, coupled with a poor performing agricultural sector as the main source of national revenue, results in 62% of the population experiencing multidimensional poverty (National Statistical Office (NSO) et al., 2021) and many related social problems, for example, food insecurity, gender inequality, and a need for social protection for many groups of people. With the majority of the population living in poverty and unprecedented rapid urbanisation experienced by the country since attaining independence in 1964, developmental social work and social work in general was perceived as important in alleviating social problems and empowering the poor to promote their wellbeing (Imaan et al., 2021).

Social work education in Malawi dates back to 1964 when Magomero College, a training institution under the then Ministry of Local Government, introduced a certificate programme in community development mainly targeting Malawi Young Pioneers. The Young Pioneers were an elite wing of the League of Malawi Youth, a nationalist movement of the then ruling Malawi Congress Party (MCP) (Phiri, 2000). In 1966, the Malawian government established the Ministry of Community and Social Development that inherited Magomero College and the certificate course. The growing need for social welfare services within the communities led to the incorporation of more social work modules into the curriculum and, in 1978, the College introduced a full-fledged certificate programme in social welfare, which produced Social Welfare Assistants (SWAs).

In 2006, the Catholic University of Malawi introduced a four-year bachelor's degree programme in social work, followed in 2010 by DMI-Saint-John of God the Baptist University's opening of a School of Social Work with three bachelors' degree programmes, namely, Community Development, Human Resource Management, and Social Work. However, the Ministry of Gender, Children, Disability and Social Welfare (MoGCDSW) had little say on the curriculum, these being private universities. The ministry collaborated with the University of Malawi, the public university, United Nations Children's Fund (UNICEF) and United States Agency for International Development (USAID) to introduce a social work degree programme at Chancellor College, with the first cohort enrolled in 2013. Some private universities have also introduced four-year bachelor's degree programmes in rural and community development.

Malawi's National Social Welfare Policy (Government of Malawi, 2015) states that social welfare in Malawi has a philanthropic background that precedes the colonialisation of 1891. This was mostly through traditional structures, which, like in most African societies, used kinship, extended family structures, and traditional leadership to support the vulnerable members of their communities (Avendal, 2011). Later, missionaries arrived in the country and established churches, which, apart from the religious teachings, offered education, health, alms, and counselling services to the communities. In a way, they functioned as informal social workers (Darkwa, 1999).

There has always been a working relationship between the government through the Social Welfare Department and Civil Society Organisations (CSOs) comprising community-based organisations (CBOs), local and international non-governmental organisations (NGOs), and religious organisations. The main providers of social welfare support have been the MoGCDSW; Ministry of Health, Ministry of Economic Planning and Development, Ministry of Labour; and Ministry of Youth and Sports. Social workers in Malawi are the lead professionals in the provision of social welfare services. They generally fall under MoGCDSW. The Department of Social Welfare in the ministry has a policy mandate of coordinating all social welfare activities. This, of course, does not mean that all components of social welfare fall within it.

Other key players include the other directorates of the ministry such as the Community Development, Child Affairs, Gender Affairs, Disability and the Elderly departments (Kakowa, 2016). At the implementation level, the key players are Social Welfare Officers (SWOs), Social Welfare Assistants (SWAs), Community Development Officers (CDOs), Community Development Assistants (CDAs), and, of late, the Community Child Protection Workers (CCPWs) (Government of Malawi, 2015). Most of these positions are held by para-social workers, trained up to certificate level while top positions are mostly held by non-social work professionals due to an inadequate supply of professional social workers. However, just as in NGOs, the situation is improving, with more professional social workers taking up top positions. Social workers in Malawi work within the confines of specific policy and legislation contained in various Acts of Parliament, Policy Guidelines, and Plans of Action that have been developed for different categories of the population.

Whilst the number of social workers in Malawi with relevant degrees is limited, estimated to be about 700 social workers employed in relevant posts, the impetus for professionalisation and development is seen as critical for social work by social workers. The efforts to professionalise social work in Malawi began in 2018 with a working group consisting of MoGCDSW, in collaboration with social workers and the university academics and relevant partners (for example, United Nations Children's Fund (UNICEF) Malawi, and Supporting Social Work in Malawi (SSWIM). Following stakeholder conferences held in 2018 and 2019, the Association of Social Workers in Malawi (ASWM) – Bungwe La Ogwira Ntchito Zachisamaliro cha Anthu m'Malawi – was established, with the aim of professionalising and regulating the social work profession in Malawi. Drafting a government bill that would lead to the establishment of the Council for Social Work in Malawi, which would regulate social work education and practice, was central to this effort.

A key part of the momentum to professionalise social work is to develop and strengthen social work education, based on a continuing need to develop and synthesise the requirements of the social work programme curricula and content in Malawi. The social work curricula in Malawi have not been harmonised and are not coordinated, apart from the normal accreditation process conducted by the National Council for Higher Education (NCHE). Universities such as the Catholic University of Malawi, University of Malawi, DMI St. John of God University, Lilongwe University, and Millennium University offer four-year degree programmes. In some cases, there are variations in modes of offering the programmes. For example, the Catholic University and

DMI St. John of God University also have weekend classes, while the University of Malawi has a block-release programme in addition to the regular generic programme. Under the block release programme students attend face-to-face classes for three weeks in a semester after which they learn through online platforms for the remainder of the semester. Magomero College has a curriculum that is two-staged. Completion of the first year only accounts for a certificate in social work while completion of the two years of the programme results in a diploma award.

The Regional Psychosocial Support Initiative (REPSSI) in collaboration with the University of KwaZulu Natal (UKZN), South Africa, introduced a certificate programme, Community Based Work with Children and Youth (CBWCY), which targeted volunteers and front-line staff in social welfare agencies, working with children and youth (REPSSI, 2011). The programme extended social work training to cadres that were not normally enrolled in universities because students did not require a secondary school leaving certificate. Whilst the programmes on offer demonstrate an eclectic approach to supporting social welfare training, and to developing qualified social workers and workers to work in communities, it remains fragmented and, therefore, there are inconsistencies in approaches.

In an effort to strengthen social work practice education in Malawi, the University of Malawi introduced a Practice Educator (PE) training in collaboration with Supporting Social Work in Malawi (SSWiM) and Association of Social Workers in Malawi (ASWiM). Practice educators are social work practitioners that supervise, teach, and assess social work students on practice learning placements (also referred to differently in other countries, for example, field practicums), as extended opportunities to gain firsthand experience of social work practice and make a recommendation to the awarding institution whether a student is 'fit to practise at the point of qualification'. The initiative strengthens students' ability to learn from practicum by providing these well-trained Practice Educators to mentor the students in practice. A strong practice learning environment is vital to the training of effective social workers because they graduate from the training institutions not only with theoretical knowledge but also with relevant practice skills and knowledge (Stone, 2016; Veta and McLaughlin, 2022). Owing to the infancy of the profession in Malawi, students are able to be located in agencies that emphasise community and indigenous approaches and still be able to apply contemporary social work practices through the support of the Practice Educators. Whilst on placements, students were therefore able to assimilate academic models and theories with practice approaches and support greater collaboration between the university and social work practice.

A particular aspect of the programme has been to work alongside participants to construct the discourses and narratives around practice contexts in Malawi and exploring the roles and responsibilities of the PE's. This ensures that the PE programme acknowledges the African and, more specifically, Malawian, context through principles of adult learning. Thus, a particular feature of the PE training in Malawi has been an exploration of the work of Freire (2000). Freire's political, intellectual, and pedagogical project aims at promoting a more just and humane world through praxis that seeks to counter dominant ideologies in practice and theory (Bolin, 2019). The facilitators understand that the content of the programme has to be decolonised to be in tandem with Malawian practice contexts, allowing for the identification of critical social work activities and associated learning and development opportunities for social work students to support positive action for change and development. The training targets practising social workers and is designed in such a way that the participants are considered to possess knowledge of the practice settings and relevant indigenous, as well as theoretical, knowledge of interventions. Concepts are therefore introduced, and knowledge and approaches are negotiated through group work activities that amalgamate lived experiences and internationally recommended procedures and processes.

The Legacy of Colonisation, Decoloniality, and Ubuntu

Brutal incursions and slave trading in East Africa under Omani rule, followed by Yao settlers selling captives to the Portuguese, devastated Malawian societies during the 19th century. Lake Malawi provided a trade route, previously used for gold and ivory, to Kilwa and ultimately slave markets in Zanzibar. David Livingstone, the missionary born in Blantyre, Scotland, arrived in Malawi in 1859. Bearing direct witness to the devastation of slavery, he believed, with the support of the British government, that civilisation (colonisation), commerce, and Christianity would provide the solution. Livingstone is credited with contributing to the eventual abolition of East African slavery through published descriptions of the atrocities following his return to Britain in 1864. Missionaries returned in 1875 aiming to educate, support peace, and end slavery. Whilst it is argued that eventual success in achieving these aims was established, subjugation and brute force were instrumental facilitators. Migrant labour, in response to colonial taxation, led to a fragmentation of traditional Malawian family structures with many Malawians leaving to work in the squalid conditions of mineral mines in South Africa (McCracken, 2012).

The European colonial legacy in Malawi, named Nyasaland between 1907 and 1964, is deep-rooted. English is the widely spoken official language of Malawi with indigenous languages belonging to the Bantu group, Chitumbuka spoken in the north, and Chichewa, 'Malawi's mother tongue' (Tembo and Oltedal, 2015), in the central and southern regions. The Christian-led endeavours of colonising missionaries were arguably functioning as social workers (Darkwa, 1999).

Western colonial expansion created a world system with unequal power relations and assumed principles of knowledge and understanding of how the world is and should be. This system dictated the organising of economy and political authority. Global inequalities have been produced by racial, class, gender, sexual, religious, pedagogical, linguistic, aesthetic, ecological, and epistemological power hierarchies that operate in complex and entangled ways on a worldwide scale. Colonialism reinforces social order through the dominance of class, race, and heterosexual and gendered power structures, and it is recognised as having Western-centric, Christian-centric, capitalist, and patriarchal characteristics that deny the epistemic diversity of the world (Grosfoguel, 2011).

Decoloniality is contested, complex, and highly political, and the associated structural challenges across many levels of society mean it will take years of action to make lasting change. It involves confronting historical realities of colonial violence, dehumanisation, and the historical context of 500 years of history (Bhambra et al., 2018). Social work is arguably a colonial profession built upon Western principles, values, and psychological and sociological knowledge. This uncomfortable 'truth' requires an individual and collective ability to reflect on and question the core of what social workers personally and professionally value. This can be an unsettling, confusing, and disturbing experience. Decolonisation begins with 'the self' (Bell et al., 2019), with intellectual curiosity, and with tolerance and critical reflection on world paradigms, personal prejudices, the colonial legacy, concepts of white privilege, power, oppression, racism, dehumanisation, and struggle for social justice and equity.

Malawian and UK social workers share more than a global definition of social work. They work within challenging and rewarding environments to protect those most vulnerable and in need of protection and support. There are, however, many practical differences. Malawian policy is identified as adopting a fragmented and uncoordinated approach and delegates responsibility to families themselves (Tembo and Oltedal, 2015). In this familiarised approach within a patriarchal society, social workers rely on the male (husband/father) as the head of the family to consent to interventions, including the removal of a child for protection. State provision, for example, orphanages are described as 'deplorable' and not in the best interests of children' (Tembo and Oltedal, 2015,: p. 15). Poverty and lack of state resources limit options beyond the extended family for child protection.

The Ubuntu Philosophy

Ubuntu is an ancient African philosophy that means 'being self through others' and is interpreted to mean 'I am because of who we all are' (Mugumbate and Nyanguru, 2013). It represents a humanistic existential philosophy rooted in concepts of community and kindness where land, body, mind, and spirit are interconnected. The concept reminds social workers to recognise and critically engage with universal social work knowledge and systems, for example, human rights, social justice, and specific social work knowledge and skills, for example, local knowledge and practices (Twikirize and Spitzer, 2019). This should ultimately lead to culturally responsive social work practice, and, when combined with the decolonisation movement, it provides a critically informed approach to teaching practice education in Malawi.

Practice Educator Programme: Voices of Malawian Social Workers

Malawi presents some stark challenges when it comes to social work concerns, as one of the world's least developed countries. As in other sub-Saharan African countries, social work in Malawi is relatively young, with a shortage of frontline qualified social workers, particularly at the district level (Tempo and Oltedal, 2015). Education for social work is one of the key priorities for Malawi in efforts to increase the number of professionally qualified social workers and to support and improve the services available to vulnerable people and their families (Global Social Services Workforce Alliance, 2016). Education for social work has been heavily focused on theoretical learning in the universities, largely based on Western models (Kakowa, 2016). However, there has been increasing recognition that opportunities to prioritise placements for students in social work practice, known variously as fieldwork, practicums, internships, and attachments, for example. Supporting the development and application of theories, skills, and values in and for practice and social work responses should be a key component of the curriculum (Kakowa, 2016).

Fieldwork placements are described as a signature pedagogy for social work education (Cornell-Swanson, 2012), and they highlight the importance of relevant fieldwork placements to the development of culturally appropriate knowledge for practice (Osei-Hwedie, 1993). This is seen as being a critical component to consolidate and further student learning in education for undertaking social work in Malawi. The identification of a practice educator, variously identified as a field educator (Australian Association of Social Workers, 2008), field instructor (Council on Social Work Education, 2008), field supervisor, and a supervisor, practice educator (The College of Social Work, 2012a), is viewed as fundamental. A practice educator is a social worker who mentors, supports, and supervises the students learning in practice in helping students to use and acquire professional knowledge, intervene skilfully, and apply skills to demonstrate professional values as well as to ensure that the student is supported in learning and reflecting on their practice. In effect, they could be said to be making a significant contribution to the stewardship of the profession. The authors of this chapter have worked together to deliver a five-day Practice Educator Programme to social workers in Malawi to support this ambition.

Positioning the Voices of Social Workers as Practice Educators

The challenges for social workers are complex and require critical knowledge, skills, and values to guide and sustain practice with individuals, families, and, especially, communities. Social workers have developed and maintained respectful professional relationships in working with others, for example, in addressing issues of power and empowerment. Practice needs to draw on the distinct knowledge, practices, and ways of living and doing within specific communities (Gray, 2017;

Van Breda and Sekudu, 2019; Twikirize and Spitzer, 2019). This acknowledges that 'as human beings we are all embedded in societies and dependent on their socio-political, economic and cultural structures and conventions' (IASSW/IFSW, 2018:1). The voices below, used with their permission, and using their real first names, are those of Malawian social workers undertaking the Practice Educators Programme, recorded as an opportunity to highlight their experiences and practice. Matthew expresses the difficulties and sensitivity required in entering into the lives of others.

> It's kind of a challenge to be honest because trying to be involved in the life of someone else as a 'stranger' is difficult – but it poses a positive challenge. (Matthew)

As Moses highlights for those engaged in social work practice, motivation is high, with a critical focus on strengths-based practice with communities.

> Social work in Malawi is a most rewarding job because each and every day as a social worker I am helping the vulnerable population ... being in the system to make an impact to people who are vulnerable is really the most generous thing I can ever do as a person ... [we] try to empower the community so they can sustainably empower themselves as well. (Moses)

Social workers recognise their growing importance as a professional group in contributing to supporting, alleviating, and advocating for vulnerable people and communities. The environment in which social work is practiced is complex, featuring a range of challenges and undertaken with limited resources. However, ethical practice with a focus on empowering others and rights-based practice is seen as critical. Social workers are seen as ideally situated in working with other professionals to resolve social concerns. This requires social workers to have a strong sense of what social work can provide and the ability to communicate that vision in the work that they do.

> What we are saying social work is not just a chaotic process or haphazard happening, it is a profession. Because I am a social worker I can plan and bring the best to client ... the future looks bright. When we started social work in Malawi there were a few schools and a few social workers. [Now we are] building our capacity ... with service users ultimately to benefit to get the profession the attention it deserves, and we represent our people and communities better. (Robert)
>
> I work in a district office. At the moment I am working with victims of disaster, distributing resources ... raising awareness with the community as having access to food as a right ... they do not need to pay for this, nor be abused, or give sexual favours for the food – not be harmed in anyway. They should be able to have their rights upheld. [I am] working with others [e.g., police] to advocate for the people. It's exciting to work with people; they are open to this and open to working with us. (Isaac)

The positive contribution and possibilities for social work in Malawi are evident. Founded on indigenous and innovative models of practice, this acknowledges the importance of working at both a micro and macro level to make a difference in the lives of people and in the communities in which they serve.

> Social work is having a greater impact in Malawi ... It is now that people are realising the importance of social work in Malawi because when they see us working hand-in-hand [with

vulnerable people] trying to alleviate poverty, in the community they see we are making a difference. (Elisabeth)

Positioning Social Workers as Practice Educators

The priority, for social work education in Malawi has been to identify and develop social work practitioners as practice educators, as critical to supporting, supervising, and assessing social work students in local practice settings (UNICEF/Global Social Services Workforce Alliance, 2019). This gives, for example, the opportunities to apply local examples, materials, and sources to teach social work students to support an appreciation of the fact that local models, approaches, and practices are relevant and essential for decolonial social work.

The interface between the university, practice, and the practice educator as a collaborative effort was seen as critical to support the development and success of placements and, ultimately the development and strengthening of social work across Malawi.

> I'll put things in perspective. Where I work [with street children, I am an] advocator, an activist, an educator, a researcher … a counsellor. But beyond that as social worker I have to work with the community... and also, at a higher-level influence policy change … and as an activist. (Robert)

Cultural competence, understanding cultural and traditional ways of addressing welfare (Kreitzer, 2012), and cultural humility, namely, to learn about and acknowledge knowledge limitations (Harindranathan et al, 2021; Veta and McLaughlin, 2021) are highly relevant for social work practice. Contextual, localised approaches to helping, once accepted and practiced locally, are essential for professional social work helping.

> [The future of Malawian social work is] very bright if we learn how to 'hold hands' – to speak in one language [to achieve] better chances for all our people, for our communities, working in all areas and represent and empower people and communities so that we can make people know what can be achieved by all of us by working together. *(Hannah)*

Supporting social work students in understanding the implications of a post-colonial lens for their social work practice in placements needs to develop through putting students in a variety of placements, with opportunities for community-level action, such as supporting self-help projects and community-level developments. Placements in practice need to focus on 'community' as sources of strength and knowledge (Mupedziswa, 2001), understanding that services reside not only in formal structures such as government, non-governmental organisations (NGOs), and International NGOs, but also in family, traditional structures, and community, including self-help efforts. This is situated in the understanding that community elders, older people, and community members are strong and credible sources of knowledge, support, and services for social work practice

Practice educators have a vital role to play in supporting students to highlight and question learning and knowledge, and finding their place in the community, identifying gaps as they practice and filling in those gaps with local contextual and experiential knowledge.

> Structured, supportive and regular supervision is crucial … We need to develop a practice curriculum that supports preparation before they come; during the placement; and what needs to be taken into the future. Issues of supportive reflection is vital. (Chisangalalo)

This can mean being pragmatic and identifying practices that work for the local people, using the local norms, values, and resources and support systems, although they may be different from government-identified services. Students need to demonstrate a willingness and ability to work with local, non-formal actors, such as elders and opinion leaders. Students need to demonstrate sensitivity to local helping systems and recognise that these are relevant and accessible in the local context, although they may appear different from the structured education they have received. Students need to identify and structure issues and problems in the local context and draw up a plan of action, not only focusing on the broader government policies and processes, but also reflecting local options and solutions accessible to rural communities and citizens.

Assessing students' reflection on local approaches, identifying areas of improvement and or conflict with formal processes, and questioning the basis of that conflict in the context of cultural, professional, and Ubuntu ethics can point the way to oversome contested ideological spaces.

Knowledge Exchange and the Decolonial Context of Teaching and Learning in Practice Education

Knowledge sharing and exchange provide invaluable opportunities to share and learn from each other. Concepts of indigenisation, as the inclusion of traditional, indigenous, local, pluriversal, and communal knowledge (Yellow Bird, 2006); localisation, as the adaptation of social work to make it relevant to the social realities of a local context (Healy and Link, 2011); and pluriversification, as the belief that people of different beliefs, backgrounds, and lifestyles can coexist in the same society and participate equally, underpin our reflections and actions on processes that modify imported ideas and practices in order to bring them into harmony with the local cultural context and specific colonial experiences.

We have been able to explore the global impact of social work and the influence of shifting political ideology on individuals, communities, and citizens. This includes the current sociopolitical ideology of 'progressive neoliberalism', particularly in the Global North, as the 'undeserving' narrative focussing on the individual and their apparent failing (Brown, 2021; Fenton, 2021; Carey, 2022). The ability to look beyond individual ontology as a moral stance in which deficits and weaknesses are portrayed in the individual and which focuses on the historical, political, structural, and systemic inequality and injustice of poverty are critical. This requires reframing poverty as a violation of human rights with social work practice as playing a crucial role in advancing social justice (Krumer-Nevo, 2020). The chronic and systematic impact of poverty and ultra-poverty on people and communities in Malawi is evident. Social work practice in Malawi has a greater focus on practice that identifies and works with the strengths of communities, with a concern for social protection and social development. This acknowledges the importance of drawing on theory and practice that reflect the history, context, culture, and identity of Africa, in general, and Malawi, in particular. This reflects the philosophy of Ubuntu with its values of interconnectedness, inclusion, and interrelationships informing and shaping the direction of interventions (Wright and Jayawickrama,2020).

The challenge for facilitators to train Malawian social workers using decolonialised content was significant and important. As argued, Malawian social work began through colonial endeavours, and Malawian social work courses are influenced by, and have been developed from, Western knowledge dominated by white European and American scholars. This mix of influences, entwined with unconscious bias, implied a requirement for self-reflection, a checking of motivation, and an understanding of trainee learning needs before designing a supporting programme of learning.

Adopting reflexive, critical, and intellectually curious approaches (Freire, 2000) essentially underpinned a collaborative approach toward a co-produced practice education course. Acknowledging complicity with coloniality and the legacy of social injustice (Bell et al., 2019) was, and remains, a humbling and uncomfortable experience that exposes ignorance and need to become alive to power, privilege, and the potential to oppress. Freire provided a philosophical framework within which the course, and the presence of the facilitators, were communicated. The following quotation was shared and explored in the opening presentation of the Practice Educator Training Programme.to ensure all present were clear on the intent for a shared teaching and learning experience, 'Whoever teaches learns in the act of teaching, and whoever learns teaches in the act of learning' (Freire, 2000:31). This opened a dialogue that explained that the facilitators were developing an understanding of coloniality, in social work and Malawian contexts, and letting that understanding inform actions within an iterative human relational teaching and learning process.

Conclusion

The challenges for citizens and communities, especially the impact of multidimensional poverty and, consequently, for social work practice in Malawi, are considerable (World Bank, 2022). Social workers view themselves as critically placed to respond to social needs and are dedicated and enthusiastic about their work and its possibilities. They are held in high esteem by the people and communities they serve. The 'grass roots' of social work are situated in direct practice with the citizens and the communities they serve, with clear evidence of the strength of the social work profession and the dedication of its practitioners to community work, community action, and social development with citizens. Critically, social work in Malawi has increasingly been seen as supporting diverse and culturally relevant experiences in local cultural contexts, as being active and intentional, and as engaging with increasing awareness and empathic understanding of the complex ways individuals interact within systems and institutions in the Malawian context.

Recommendations

1. Recognising the historical impact, and continuing impact, of post-colonial engagement requires critical consideration and reflection on knowledge and relationships and on the endurance and efficacy of power relationships (Sewpaul, 2006). Social workers as practice educators have highlighted the critical role they have in incorporating indigenous perspectives and practices into the social work curriculum, including knowledge, skills, and values.
2. As a response to decolonial social work and as a demonstration and application of Ubuntu, a number of attributes need to be developed in the student as essential qualities, skills, and traits we would expect to be demonstrated by a social work student in a practice placement. Local and indigenous ways of life should largely inform and shape their practice, and knowledge of these provides an opportunity to support individuals and communities in realising their potential.
3. Attention should be given to the possibilities of harmful solutions embedded in local cultures and contexts, but this danger must be understood and analysed using local understanding rather than through a comparison with Western-oriented social work. Such disputed approaches should be renegotiated with local communities and elders, and a non-harmful intervention co-designed with local individuals and social workers working together.

Further Reading

Kakowa, F. (2016) 'Nurturing Professional Social Work in Malawi'. *African Journal of Social Work*, 6(2). Available from: https://www.ajol.info/index.php/ajsw/article/view/150260.

Kleibl, T., Lutz, R., Noyoo, N., Bunk, B., Dittmann, A. and Seepamore, B. (2019) *The Routledge Handbook of Postcolonial Social Work*. London: Routledge.

Spitzer, H., Twikirize, J. M. and Wairire, G. G. (eds) (2014) *Professional Social Work in East Africa. Towards Social Development, Poverty Reduction and Gender Equality*. Uganda: Fountain Publishers.

References

Avendal, C. (2011) 'Social Work in Ghana: Engaging Traditional Actors in Professional Practices'. *Journal of Comparative Social Work*, 6(2), 106–124.

Banks, S. (2020) *Ethics and Values in Social Work* (5th ed). London: Macmillan. Red Globe Press.

Bell, D., Canham, H. and Fernéndez, J. S. (2019) 'Retrospective Autoethnographies: A Call for Decolonial Imaging for the New University'. *Qualitative Inquiry*, 26(7), 1–11.

Bhambra, G., Gebrial, D. and Nisancioglu, K. (eds) (2018) *Decolonising the University*. London: Pluto Press.

Bolin, T. (2019) 'Paulo Freire: The Global Legacy'. *Educational Philosophy and Theory*, 51(5), 537–539.

Brown, C. (2021) 'Critical Clinical Social Work and the Neoliberal Constraints on Social Justice Mental Health'. *Research on Social Work Practice*, 31(6), 644–652.

Carey, M. (2022) 'The Neoliberal University, Social Work and Personalised Care for Older People'. *Ageing and Society*, 42(8), 1964–1978.

Chigangaidze, R. K. (2021) 'Defending the African Philosophy of Ubuntu and Its Place in Clinical Social Work Practice in Mental Health: The Biopsychosocial and Ecological Systems Perspectives'. *Social Work in Mental Health*, 19(4), 276–288.

Cornell-Swanson, L.-V. J. (2012) 'Towards a Comprehensive Signature Pedagogy in Social Work Education'. In Nancy L. Chick, Aeron Haynie and Regan A. R. Gurung (eds.) *Exploring More Signature Pedagogies*. Sterling, VA: Stylus Publications, 203–216.

Darkwa, O. (1999) 'Continuing Social Work Education in an Electronic Age: The Opportunities and Challenges Facing Social Work Education in Ghana'. *Professional Development: The International Journal of Continuing Social Work Education*, 2(1), 38–43.

Destatis (2021) *Malawi Statistical Country Profile*. Berlin: Federal Statistical Office of Germany.

Fenton, J. (2021) 'The "Undeserving" Narrative in Child and Family Social Work and How It Is Perpetuated by "Progressive Neoliberalism": Ideas for Social Work Education'. *Societies*, 11(4), 123.

Freire, P. (2000) *Pedagogy of the Oppressed*. New York, NY: Continuum Books. (Originally published 1970).

Global Social Services Workforce Alliance (2016) *The State of the Social Services Workforce 2017 Report: A Review of Five Years of Workforce Strengthening*. Global Social Services Workforce Alliance: Available from: https://www.socialserviceworkforce.org/resources

Government of Malawi (2015) *National Social Welfare Policy: Promoting Social Inclusion and Human Dignity*. Lilongwe: MOGCDSW.

Gray, M. (ed) (2017) *The Handbook of Social Work and Social Development in Africa*. London: Routledge.

Grosfoguel, R. (2011) 'Decolonizing Post-colonial Studies and Paradigms of Political Economy: Transmodernity, Decolonial Thinking and Global Coloniality'. *Transmodernity*, 1(1) Available from: https://escholarship.org/uc/item/21k6t3fq.

Hantrais, L. (2004) *Family Policy Matters: Responding to Family Change in Europe*. Bristol: Policy Press.

Harindranathan, P., Addo, R., Koers, G. and Para-Perez, L. G. (2021) 'Developing Cultural Humility in an International Social Work Classroom'. *Social Work Education*, 41(5), 787–800.

Harms-Smith, L. and Rasool, S. (2020) 'Deep Transformation towards Decoloniality in Social Work: Themes for Change in a Social Work Higher Education Programme'. *Journal of Progressive Human Services*, 31(2), 144–164.

Healy, L. M. and Link, R. J. (eds) *Handbook of International Social Work: Human*.

Imaan Mwayi, K., Wizi, A., Nkhata Kabunduli, D. and Sr Tambulasi, V. (2021) 'Evolution of Social Welfare and Social Work in Malawi'., In Ngangwa Noyoo (ed.) *Social Welfare and Social Work in Southern Africa*. South Africa: African Sun Media, 99–121.

International Association of Schools of Social Work(IASSW)/International Federation of Social Workers (IFSW) (2018) 'Global Social Work Statement of Ethical Principles'. Available from: https://www.iassw-aiets.org/archive/ethics-in-social-work-statement-of-principles/.

Kakowa, F. (2016) 'Nurturing Professional Social Work in Malawi'. *African Journal of Social Work*, 6(2). Available from: https://www.ajol.info/index.php/ajsw/article/view/150260.

Kreitzer, L. (2012) *Social Work in Africa: Exploring Culturally Relevant Education and Practice in Ghana*. Calgary, Alberta: University of Calgary Press.

Krumer-Nevo, M. (2020) *Radical Hope: Poverty Aware Practice for Social Work*. Bristol: Policy Press.

McCracken, J. (2012) *A History of Malawi 1859–1966*. New York, NY: Boydell and Brewer, Inc.

Mugumbate, J. and Nyanguru, A. (2013) 'Exploring African Philosophy: The Value of Ubuntu in Social Work'. *African Journal of Social Work*, 3(1), 82–100.

Mupedziswa, R. (2001) 'The Quest for Relevance: Towards a Conceptual Model of Developmental Social Work Education and Training in Africa'. *International Social Work*, 44(3), 285–300.

National Statistical Office (NSO) (Malawi). In: collaboration with the Ministry of Economic Planning and Development and Public Sector Reforms, with support from United Nations Development Programme and Oxford Poverty and Human Development Initiative (OPHI) (2021) *Malawi Multidimensional Poverty Index*. Zomba, Malawi: NSO.

Osei-Hwedie, K. (1993) 'The Challenge of Social Work in Africa: Starting the Indigenisation Process'. *Journal of Social Development in Africa*, 8(1), 19–30.

Phiri, K. M. (2000) 'A Case of Revolutionary Change in Contemporary Malawi: The Malawi Army and the Disarming of the Malawi Young Pioneers'. *Journal of Peace, Conflict and Military Studies*, 1(1), 1–15.

Regional Psychosocial Support Initiative (REPSSI) (2011) *REPSSI Strategy: 2011–2015*. Randburg, ZA: REPSSI.

Sewpaul, V. (2006) 'The Global-Local Dialectic: Challenges for African Scholarship and Social Work in a Post-colonial World'. *British Journal of Social Work*, 36(3), 419–434.

Stone, C. (2016) 'The Role of Practice Educators in Initial and Post Qualifying Social Worker Education'. *Social Work Education*, 35(6), 706–718.

Tembo, M. J. and Oltedal, S. (2015) 'Social Work and Families in Child Welfare in Malawi: Social Workers Considering When Placing a Child outside the Home'. *Journal of Comparative Social Work*, 10(1), 50–72.

Twikirize, J. M. and Spitzer, H. (eds) (2019) *Social Work Practice in Africa. Indigenous and Innovative Approaches*. Oxford: Fountain Publishing.

United Nations Children's Fund (UNICEF)/Global Social Services Workforce Alliance (2019) *Guidelines to Strengthen the Social Services Workforce for Child Protection*. New York, NY: UNICEF.

Veta, O. D. and McLaughlin, H. (2022) 'Social Work Education and Practice in Africa: The Problems and Prospects'. *Social Work Education*. DOI: 10.1080/02615479.2022.2029393.

World, Bank (2022) *The World Bank in Malawi*. Washington, DC: World Bank.

Wright, J. and Jayawickrama, J. (2020) 'We Need Other Human Beings in Order to be Human': Examining the Indigenous Philosophy of Umunthu and Strengthening Mental Health Interventions'. *Culture, Medicine and Psychiatry*, 45(4), 613–628.

Yellow Bird, M. (2006) 'Terms of Endearment: A Brief Dictionary for Decolonizing Social Work with Indigenous Peoples'. In Mel Gray and John Coates (eds.) *Indigenous Social Work around the World. Towards Culturally Relevant Education and Practice*. London and New York, NY: Routledge, 275–292.

32
CHALLENGES AND PROSPECTS FOR INTEGRATING INTERPROFESSIONAL EDUCATION AND COLLABORATIVE PRACTICE (IPECP) INTO SOCIAL WORK EDUCATION ACROSS CULTURES

*Abigail Adubea Mills, Doris A. Boateng,
Sevaughn Banks, and Felicia Tuggle*

Abstract: English

The social work profession has always emphasised the need to collaborate with other professionals to achieve holistic outcomes for clients. However, in many social work programmes, this emphasis has not been commensurate with curriculum structure to prepare students for interprofessional practice. In Africa, social work students and their professional allies are rarely put together for interprofessional education (IPE) purposes, and, in other parts of the world, few social work institutions offer IPE opportunities for their students. The World Health Organisation (WHO) is promoting IPE as critical pedagogy for future health workers; thus, students from healthcare disciplines and healthcare professionals tend to be more involved in IPE programmes than are social workers. As part of efforts to promote interprofessional education and collaborative practice (IPECP) among social workers, faculty from three universities in Ghana and the United States of America collaborated to develop an IPECP curriculum. Centred around the Ubuntu philosophy, the curriculum was designed to provide cross-cultural interprofessional learning opportunities for social work and allied health students. This chapter provides an overview of IPE in Africa and the United States. It offers insights into the curriculum design process, and makes some recommendations from lessons learned.

Introduction

Social workers are by nature collaborators, team builders, and community builders. The profession has, since its inception, emphasised the need for collaboration with other professionals to achieve holistic outcomes for clients (Kobayashi and Fitzgerald, 2017; Rubin et al., 2018). As a result, social work education is increasingly embracing interprofessional education (IPE) and collaborative practice (CP) as pedagogical and practice strategies for addressing interrelated social issues across systems (Adamson et al., 2020; Ashcroft et al., 2018). The International Association of Schools of Social Work (IASSW) Standards for Global Social Work Education and Training stipulate that education programmes curricula must include sufficient knowledge of related occupations and professions to facilitate interprofessional collaboration and teamwork (IASSW, 2020). Despite the curricula stipulation and emerging practice, effective interprofessional collaboration can be difficult to realise in practice as it has not been met with commensurate curriculum structure to prepare students for interprofessional practice (Deichen Hansen et al., 2020; Rubin et al., 2018). Interprofessional education and collaborative practice (IPECP) have, however gained significant attention in the health sector, with the World Health Organisation (WHO) promoting it as critical pedagogy for preparing future health workers (WHO, 2010).

Anecdotally, although, interprofessional collaboration occurs in all social work practice settings (for example, schools, healthcare, criminal justice, child and family welfare, among others), interprofessional education in social work curricula around the world leans heavily in the field of healthcare. This may be because the most accepted definition of IPE adapted from the Interprofessional Education Collaborative and the World Health Organisation states: 'interprofessional education occurs when two or more professions learn with, about, and from each other to enable effective collaboration and improve health outcomes' (WHO, 2010).

The greatest representation of professionals involved in interprofessional education (IPE) are from nursing/midwifery, the allied health professions, doctors, and social workers (Rodger and Hoffman, 2010). However, whereas the social work profession has traditionally supported, and continues to support, interdisciplinary practice to optimise outcomes for clients, only a few social work training institutions afford students the opportunity to experience IPE curriculum involving other health professionals (Kobayashi and Fitzgerald, 2017; Rubin et al., 2018). Kobayashi and Fitzgerald (2017, p. 738) rightly assert:

Creating and offering IP opportunities for social work students will serve as important steps toward gaining support for the inclusion of social workers as essential participants in IP healthcare teams. By becoming partners in IP education, social work educators may also begin to address the challenge of building a bridge from IP social work education to IP social work practice.

In this chapter, the challenges and prospects for integrating IPECP into the curricula of three university units of social work in Ghana and the United States of America are explored. The authors further share their experience in collaborating to co-develop a course titled, Interprofessional and Collaborative Applied Global Health Practice (IPCAGHP) situated in the three universities with which the authors of this chapter are affiliated, one in Ghana and two in the United States. The course was developed with a focus on cross-cultural educational experience for social work students as well as students from nursing, pharmacy, and occupational therapy to have IPECP experiences. Due to rigid administrative mechanisms (on the part of the Ghanaian institution) and the outbreak of the COVID-19 pandemic, the course could not be implemented at all three universities.

However, the course development process turned out to be a learning curve for all the authors as they worked together across cultures and university systems. The authors catalysed Ubuntu, a dominant African philosophy (Africa Social Work Network, 2020) while working together. According to Mugumbate and Chereni (2020), Ubuntu social work includes reciprocity and sharing, respect and empowerment, equitable distribution of resources, promotion of social justice, and economic progress (p. viii). Educators and practitioners can recognise their interconnectedness and operationalise Ubuntu values, such as teamwork and collaboration, solidarity, and mutual respect (Mayaka and Truell, 2021), through alignment with the Global Agenda for Social Work and Social Development 2020–2030. In the spirit of Ubuntu, the authors collaborated with each other for an entire academic year.

Collaboration consisted of reviewing and discussing IPECP initiatives at their respective universities, professional and national support of IPECP in Ghana and the United States, assessment of student learning outcomes, and consideration for each other's work schedules and different time zones. Authors structured task meetings via Zoom, shared responsibilities for co-designing the curriculum, stored and shared files via a web-based shared folder, discussed sociocultural and systems-based realities that needed to be considered, and established outcome measures and accountability to keep the course development on track. Guided by Ubuntu values, the IPCAGHP course aspires to develop and enhance social work students' confidence and competencies to collaborate effectively in interprofessional teams. Social work was the anchor of the course, while simultaneously focusing on health and wellbeing.

Interprofessional Education and Collaborative Practice in Social Work Education in Africa

As a continent with varying economies, a huge disease burden, and the lowest density of healthcare professionals, Africa is well situated to benefit from interprofessional education and collaborative practice, with social workers in the healthcare delivery system (Aluttis, 2014; Crisp and Chen, 2014). Undeniably, social workers play various roles within the healthcare system in Africa, though their contributions are often not recognised by 'traditional' healthcare personnel. In Ghana, for example, major public hospitals have designated 'social welfare offices' staffed by professional social workers who provide various services to patients, such as discharge planning, conducting social inquiries about patients (where required), and assisting victims of domestic violence cases who report at the hospitals. However, social workers are notably not considered as part of the healthcare delivery team (Dako-Gyeke , 2018; Kodom, 2022). This is possibly due to the fact that, although social work has articulated a longstanding vision that supports IPE, social work students and their professional allies are rarely included in IPE learning opportunities. Greater collaboration between social work and healthcare professionals is necessary to prepare professionals in these fields to meet the current complex demands of healthcare and patient care needs in Africa.

Global scans of IPE implementation reveal it is utilised to varying degrees across various income-economies (Rodger and Hoffman, 2010; Sunguya et al., 2014). Although literature regarding IPECP in Africa is scant, some countries, such as Ghana, Egypt, South Africa, Ethiopia, Algeria, Uganda, and Namibia, are highlighted as having some form(s) of IPECP occurring within their healthcare systems (Rodger and Hoffman, 2010; Sunguya et al., 2014). Furthermore, some studies conducted on the African continent support the fact that most healthcare students and professionals have positive attitudes towards IPECP and collaborative practice (Dassah et al., 2022; Kithuci et al., 2022; Hlongwa and Rispel, 2021; Quartey et al., 2020; Keith, 2014).

What is clearly missing though is the lack, or minimal involvement, of social work students and professionals in these IPECP programmes. While a few studies in Ghana highlight examples of IPECP opportunities and perceptions about IPE, most of these studies focus on students from various 'traditional' healthcare disciplines (Dassah et al., 2022; Keith, 2014; Quartey et al., 2020). For example, in the Ghana Cross-Cultural Healthcare Immersion (GCCHI) described by Keith (2014), the international students who participate in the programme come from various disciplines, including social work, physician assistants, occupational therapy, dental hygiene, pharmacy, and physical therapy. However, the Ghanaian participants are primarily from 'traditional' health disciplines in Ghana. This is one example of the social work profession not given due recognition within IPECP programmes. This could partly be because social workers have not succeeded in asserting their professional status within healthcare systems in Africa, or, conversely, healthcare systems do not respect or recognise social workers as professional collaborators. Embracing IPECP in social work curriculum and practice would ensure that social work students have sufficient knowledge of interprofessional collaboration as mandated in the International Association of Schools of Social Work Global Standards for Social Work Education and Training (IASSW, 2020).

Another challenge is that most healthcare professionals do not possess sufficient knowledge about the role of social workers in the management of health outcomes for patients and how they can collaborate effectively. These challenges could be attributed to little to no IPE opportunities during the educational training of social workers and healthcare professionals in Africa. Lack of knowledge about the competencies of other professionals within the healthcare system creates a lacuna that could impact the receptiveness of IPECP in Africa. Closely related to the constraints in the implementation of IPECP in Africa highlighted above is the rigid nature of the existing curricula in most higher education institutions in Africa, which often makes it almost impossible to modify to allow students from across various disciplines to participate in IPE. Even where IPE may occur, if it is not made mandatory for the students under consideration, only a few of them may experience it, leaving out an entire cadre of professionals being trained. In most instances, curricula are designed such that students do not have the flexibility to take courses across disciplines. Although social work students may get placed in healthcare settings for their fieldwork, their experiences are often limited to what the facility considers to be within the remit of social work practice, and often they are not considered part of the patient's team of health professionals. Despite these challenges, there are numerous opportunities that can be harnessed within the African continent to make IPECP an enduring reality.

The establishment of the Africa Interprofessional Education Network (AfrIPEN, see www.afripen.org) in 2015 offers hope in instituting Interprofessional Education and Collaborative Practice (IPECP) as an integral part of training the health workforce and to function effectively within health systems on the African continent (Botma and Snyman, 2019; Nyoni , 2020). There will be learning across disciplines, as social work students and professionals learn and incorporate relevant values of other health professions into their profession and vice versa. Furthermore, the Africa Interprofessional Education Network (AfrIPEN) has broadened its networking base by opening membership to individuals from diverse backgrounds, including service user organisations and advocacy groups; student organisations; institutions involved in health and/or social care service provision; professional boards/regulators for health and social service provision; ministries of health, social services, and higher education. This broad network of people provides an avenue for IPECP to be better understood, appreciated, and implemented in Africa. The fact that some African countries, like Ghana, already recognise the importance of social workers in the delivery of healthcare provides a good leveraging point for social work training institutions to assert the importance of social work students in IPECP programmes.

Furthermore, the co-development of the Interprofessional and Collaborative Applied Global Health Practice course by the authors demonstrates the cross-cultural opportunities that exist for promoting IPECP in social work education in Africa and around the world. As the leading social work training institution in Ghana, there is an opportunity for the University of Ghana to consider implementing this course as an interdisciplinary programme for social work and health sciences students. Finally, while there are periodic training programmes organised for social work field placement supervisors, there must be deliberate efforts to train field supervisors in interprofessional collaboration so it is not only known and appreciated in theory, but also dynamically integrated into social work curricula in Africa.

Interprofessional Education and Collaborative Practice in Social Work Education in the United States of America

The Council on Social Work Education (CSWE) incorporated interprofessional practice into its curricular guidelines in 2012 through its Educational Policy and Accreditation Standards (EPAS) and became an institutional member of the Interprofessional Educational Collaborative (IPEC) in 2016. The EPAS standards mandate interprofessional training be incorporated into each social work programme's explicit curriculum. The CSWE 2022 EPAS standards stipulate social work students should understand the value of evidence derived from interprofessional approaches and sources and apply this knowledge in culturally responsive assessments, interventions, and evaluation with clients and constituencies, including individuals, families, groups, organisations, and communities. Students are also expected to recognise beneficial outcomes that may require interprofessional and inter-organizational collaboration. The advantages of IPE centre around students gaining better understandings of their own disciplines and roles as well as appreciating the roles and functions of other disciplines, valuing interprofessional learning, and working more effectively within teams to perceive multidisciplinary teamwork as positive for themselves and patient/ client outcomes.

In the United States, interprofessional collaboration occurs in almost all social work practice settings, but it occurs heavily in the field of healthcare. As has been indicated earlier in this chapter, this is possibly a reflection of the WHO's dominant interest in the field, which includes their definition of healthcare. Around the same time the World Health Organisation outlined the definition for IPE and published its Framework for Action on Interprofessional Education and Collaborative Practice (WHO, 2010), a major health reform policy was signed into legislation in the United States. The Protection and Affordable Care Act (ACA) included funds for innovative programmes that supported and integrated healthcare approaches to improve access to services and simultaneously address physical and mental healthcare needs (Kuramoto, 2014). This led to an integration of traditional medical care with social services addressing behavioural and social determinants of health as social workers were called upon to apply their values, principles, and skills to respond holistically to the multiplicity of the client needs (Gehlert, 2011; Stanhope et al., 2015). The new workforce and educational funding opportunities that came with ACA resulted in interprofessional education in social work curricula leaning heavily towards healthcare and social workers in the United States having a major presence in the healthcare field as members of interprofessional teams.

Social workers fulfil multiple roles and functions on interprofessional teams, so it is important that social work students be exposed to an interprofessional environment and understand the importance of interdisciplinary collaboration before they commence professional practice. Social work education is central to preparing future practitioners for interprofessional care and collaborative practice. For social work students, early introduction of IPE during a generalist curriculum can shape attitudes and values of these emerging professionals and instil a collaborative attitude. Introducing IPE early in the social work curriculum and providing low-risk opportunities for students to be supported in their development of interprofessional skills, values, and ethics; roles and responsibilities; communication'; and teamwork is an important aspect of preparing social work students for practice in diverse and interdisciplinary practice settings like healthcare. The communication, teamwork and collaboration, and conflict resolution skills social workers need to be excellent members of interprofessional teams are the same skills they need to be excellent social workers.

Despite the multiple benefits of including social work in IPE, there are a few barriers that need to be overcome to optimise social work's engagement in IPE. While barriers such as scheduling, differing accreditation standards, and faculty capacity exist within and across institutions, virtual experiences may provide comparable benefits to in-person experiences (Watts et al., 2022). Educational technologies such as online learning, distance technologies, networking innovations, and simulation approaches are overcoming traditional barriers to interprofessional learning related to time and space. There has also been substantial international commitment to lead curriculum and pedagogical changes to better respond to the need for transformative collaborative models of care (Rubin et al., 2018).

As USA-based social work programmes endeavour to cultivate cultural awareness and global consciousness through internationalisation and decolonisation of social work curriculum, and African social workers continue to advocate for indigenisation of social work education and practice, opportunities to integrate interprofessional education and collaborative practice in social work curriculum across cultures through Global North and Global South partnerships are rife. Working together, social work educators in the Global North and the Global South can facilitate cross-border educational discussion about how the values and competencies of the social work profession meet the changing needs of healthcare service delivery and explore the benefits and challenges of different healthcare models and the impact different models play in addressing social determinants of health. Social work's person-in-environment paradigm aligns with the IPECP model and, thus, social work educators should place a high priority on IPE, given the important role social workers play within the health and social service systems and a rapidly globalising society.

Cross-Cultural Knowledge Exchange in Social Work Education

Drawing from the Ubuntu theme of the Global Agenda for Social Work and Social Development (2020–2030), the opportunities to consciously integrate IPECP in social work education in Africa are vast. As explained by Mayaka and Truell (2021), Ubuntu is a philosophy that unearths the 'values of justice, responsibility, equality, collectiveness, relatedness, reciprocity, love, respect, helpfulness, community, caring, dependability, sharing, trust, integrity, unselfishness and social change' (p. 651). Although the philosophy of Ubuntu is reflected in several words from different African cultural groups, Ubuntu is globally the most popular term (Mayaka and Truell, 2021). Ubuntu emphasizes 'people's identities are continuously developing in the context of their reciprocal relationships with others, and thereby, through supporting and nurturing others, one's own identity and life quality are enhanced' (Mayaka and Truell, 2021, p. 651). The dominance of the Ubuntu worldview in global social work presents an opportunity for IPECP to be embraced among professionals and students across various disciplines, as IPECP encapsulates several values embedded in Ubuntu, such as collectiveness, community, and social change.

This section details the guiding philosophy and processes the authors went through in developing the Interprofessional and Collaborative Applied Global Health Practice (IPCAGHP) course that was to be implemented in Ghana and the United States. Social work was the anchor, while simultaneously focusing on health and wellbeing. The course was guided by three core goals. Goal one was to facilitate social work students' awareness of their roles and team members' expertise to address outcomes for clients within global human service systems. This is to encourage students to maintain a climate of shared values, ethical conduct, and mutual respect among team members and clients. Goal two was to incorporate opportunities for social work students to communicate with diverse client systems in addressing common biopsychosocial conditions in a responsive, responsible, respectful, and compassionate manner with team members. Goal three was to prepare social work and students in allied professions to apply the values and principles of team science in prevention, assessment, diagnosis, intervention, and treatment of clients. In so doing, social work students would demonstrate cultural humility, appreciate different perspectives, and deconstruct social, political, and economic systems and institutions that maintain and perpetuate oppression and marginalisation of vulnerable people.

The IPCAGHP course includes seven knowledge competencies, four skill competencies, and three value competencies. In Table 32.1 the traditional standards for social work education and training, Ubuntu philosophy, and 2023 proposed IPECP core competencies have been aligned to the IPCAGHP course. At the end of the course, students, through classroom integration combined with practicum, will be able to demonstrate these competencies.

Lessons Learned

The collaborative process, guided by the philosophy and practice of Ubuntu, proved to be insightful. What posed the major challenge was the global shutdown related to the COVID-19 pandemic. This meant that the social work faculty were unable to implement the IPCAGHP course as planned at the time. However, several lessons learned illuminated the importance and need for continued and expanded interprofessional social work partnership, strategic alignment between social work education and healthcare, and clear delineation of roles between social work and healthcare students. Fundamental to the social work profession is the conceptualisation and practice of praxis where social work students dialogue with each other, demonstrate their learning through implementation and experience in the classroom or field, and then reflect upon their strengths and challenges (Morgaine and Capous-Desyllas, 2020; Miley, 2017; Freire, 2000). Social work students tend to appreciate interprofessional collaboration with allied professionals (Banks et al., 2019 2020; Tuggle et al., 2022). The students' experiences are consistent with the authors' own experiences in developing the course and gave impetus to design the IPCAGHP course to facilitate social work students' awareness of global human service systems; incorporate opportunities for social work students to work with clients and constituents; and prepare social work and healthcare students to practice collaborative prevention, assessment, diagnosis, intervention, and treatment of patients/clients, using advocacy and social change skills.

The whole experience of collaborating to develop the IPCAGHP course helped to advance the authors' knowledge and understanding of social work education in Africa and the United States. Although the authors did not get the opportunity to fully implement the course, there was an enriching learning experience wherein the principles of reciprocity, mutual respect, communitarianism, intercultural awareness, collaborative decision-making, integrity and competence, and the use of technology were demonstrated. When the authors conceived the idea to develop

Table 32.1 Competencies for the Interprofessional and Collaborative Applied Global Health Practice (IPCAGHP) Course

Knowledge Competencies

IPCAGHP Course Competencies	Ubuntu Philosophy	IPE Competencies
Define the four competencies of interprofessional collaborative practice (i.e., roles and responsibilities, values, and ethics, interprofessional communication, teams, and teamwork)	*Sharing and cooperation*: Students define how they will cooperate in their collaborative efforts to communicate effectively in teams to resolve common social work problems.	Use the knowledge of one's own role and team members' expertise to address health outcomes.
Articulate medical conditions in special populations	*Unity of humanity*: Students learn about medical conditions though acknowledging, 'I feel for you, your problems are my problems' (Brock-Utne, 2016).	
Memorise components of three theoretical approaches and/or practice frameworks	*Theory application*: Students research Ubuntu, the overarching theory that describes African social work (Mugumbate and Chereni, 2020) and articulates its components.	
Name at least three local or governmental policies that address the health of people afflicted with medical conditions in Ghana	*Humanitarianism*: Students respect a diversity of perspectives in what it means to be human in the law and verbally conveys these definitions.	
Engage in discussion about client intersectionality and the nexus of power, privilege, and oppression	*Social justice and fairness*: Students contend that any course of social action and intervention should treat individuals equally.	
Compare their knowledge of health service agencies operations in Ghana and the United States	*Human dignity*: Students compare benevolence systems and concepts of equal treatment, human rights, and tolerance towards insiders and outsiders (Murenje, 2020).	
Use reflection and self-regulation to manage personal values and maintain professionalism in practice situations	*Morality*: Students demonstrate morality (Brock-Utne, 2016) and ethics (Mabvurira, 2020) in social work practice.	

Skill Competencies

IPCAGHP Course Competencies	Ubuntu Philosophy	
		Communicate in a responsive, responsible, respectful, and compassionate manner with team members.
		Apply values and principles of team science to adapt one's own role in a variety of team settings.

(*Continued*)

Table 32.1 (Continued)

Knowledge Competencies

IPCAGHP Course Competencies	Ubuntu Philosophy	IPE Competencies
Apply theoretical knowledge acquired in the classroom and transfer theoretical knowledge into practice skills while working with patients in healthcare settings	*Ubuntu*: Students transfer their knowledge of Ubuntu theory (an authentic individual human being is part of a larger and more significant relational, communal, societal, environmental, and spiritual world) from the class to practicum.	Work with team members to maintain a climate of shared values, ethical conduct, and mutual respect.
Apply practice knowledge acquired in the classroom and transfer practice knowledge while working with patients in healthcare settings	*Integrity and competence*: A good social worker should possess the qualities of *munhu/umuntu* which is the person with acceptable behaviour (Mabvurira, 2020). Students work within their social work scope of practice in the classroom and in practicum.	
Synthesise interprofessional competencies while networking with service agencies to implement a community health fair	*Divinity and do no harm*: Students evaluate and embody the term 'divine', directing their social work practice away from harm towards good, including the earth and environment (Chigangaidze et al., 2022; van Breda, 2019).	
Express how agencies' goals and outcomes converge and/or diverge knowledge and practice skills.	*Collaborative decision-making*: Students de-centre the individual as the prime unit of analysis, and centre relationships between people to meet goals and objectives.	
Values Competencies		
IPCAGHP Course Competencies	**Ubuntu Philosophy**	
Appreciate healthcare services systems that are like and different from those in their home country	*Communitarianism*: Students value their interconnectedness with clients and individuals who are a part of a family, families that are a part of a community, and communities that are part of the environment, which is part of a larger spiritual community (Mugumbate and Chereni, 2020; van Breda, 2019). This cycle is important and should be respected in the decision-making and delivery of health care services to global patients.	
Appreciate exchange of ideas and philosophies with global practitioners	*Reciprocity*: Students value the phrase, 'umuntu ngumuntu ngabantu', a person is a person through other people (van Breda, 2019); the worldview of seeing oneself through others (Chigangaidze, 2022) through global dialogue and collaboration.	
Articulate the importance of data-informed agencies and communities in decreasing and resolving preventable negative health outcomes through evidence-based practice and policy	*Technology*: The application of Ubuntu is now worldwide with Ubuntu software developed in the United States of America and is based on the sharing tenet of Ubuntu (Mumgumbate and Nyanguru, 2013). The open-source desktop operating system powers millions of PCs and laptops around the world (Ubuntu.com). Students and professionals can conscientiously purchase and use the software to solve social work's most pressing challenges.	

the course, there was great interest in learning if, and how, IPE was integrated into social work education across cultures. The authors were eager to learn about what happens in each other's contexts and to make the course as culturally relevant as possible. Using technology, the authors created a shared folder on OneDrive where collaborative documents were placed for team contributions to be accessible in real time. The authors also used Zoom to hold live monthly meetings to discuss course content and implementation strategies. There was active participation of all authors' voices, mutual respect, dependability, and collaboration, notwithstanding the challenges in implementing the course. All these experiences fostered and deepened understanding and appreciation of the Ubuntu principles that would be transferred to students as they take the course.

Overall, this experience enhanced the authors' global connectedness and commitment to working together to co-design and co-build social work curriculum. The IPCAGHP course promotes a global interprofessional community of professionals across cultures and advances Ubuntu philosophy and principles.

Suggested Course Activities

1. Discuss, in small groups, some of the social work practice settings where IPECP would be required/useful.
2. List three other professionals with whom social workers can collaborate for IPE, both in title and in function.
3. Identify two interprofessional organisations that promote IPE within social work and discuss its alignment with their mission.
4. Draft a policy brief to advance IPECP in social work education.
5. Suggest ways of broadening IPECP to incorporate more allied professions in schools, healthcare, criminal justice, child and family welfare, and others
6. Identify three ways the Ubuntu competencies (Table 32.1) can manifest in social work education and IPECP.

Recommendations

The action-oriented recommendations presented in this section are guided by lessons learned during the design and partial implementation of the course and the World Health Organisation's Framework for Action on Interprofessional Education and Collaborative Practice (2010). The recommendations are consistent with the International Association of Schools of Social Work (IASSW) Global Standards for Social Work Education and Training (2020), which mandates social work education programmes to ensure students have sufficient knowledge of related occupations and professions to facilitate interprofessional collaboration and teamwork (p. 11). To inscribe IPEC into social work curricula, the authors recommend:

1. National and international social work organisations provide funding, training, and marketing to assist programmes to build the infrastructure required to institutionalise interprofessional education experiences in social work curricula.
2. Social work deans, directors, and department heads mitigate barriers to interprofessional education courses and experiences caused by scheduling, curriculum rigidity, and meeting space.

3. Social work faculty engage with faculty from other disciplines on campus and in the global community to identify opportunities for students to participate in in-person or virtual interprofessional education and collaborative practice experiences that strengthen interprofessional competency in the domains of teams and teamwork, roles and responsibilities, ethics, and values, and communication.

Further Reading

Kobayashi, R., and Fitzgerald, C. (2017) 'Teaching note – Asserting social worker's role in developing an interprofessional education project'. *Journal of Social Work Education*, 53(4), 737–743. https://doi.org/10.1080/10437797.2017.1284627.

Mayaka, B., and Truell, R. (2021) 'Ubuntu and its potential impact on the international social work profession'. *International Social Work*, 64(5), 649–662. https://doiorg.spot.lib.auburn.edu/10.1177/00208728211022787.

References

Adamson, K., Ashcroft, R., Langlois, S., and Lising, D. (2020) 'Integrating social work into interprofessional education: A review of one university's curriculum to prepare students for collaborative practice in healthcare'. *Advances in Social Work*, 20(2), 454–472.

Africa Social Work Network (ASWNet) (2020) 'The Ubuntu philosophy'. Available at https://africasocialwork.net/ubuntu-social-work/ (Accessed: 22 June, 2022).

Aluttis, C., Bishaw, T., and Frank, M. W. (2014) 'The workforce for health in a globalized context–global shortages and international migration'. *Global Health Action*, 7(1), 23611.

Ashcroft, R., McMillan, C., Ambrose-Miller, W., McKee, R., and Brown, J. B. (2018) 'The emerging role of social work in primary health care: A survey of social workers in Ontario family health teams'. *Health and Social Work*, 43(2), 109–117.

Banks, S., Stanley, M., Matthew, W., and Brown, S. (2019) 'Simulation based interprofessional education: A nursing and social work collaboration'. *Journal of Nursing Education*, 58(2), 110–113.

Banks, S., Tuggle, F., and Coleman, D. (2020) 'Standardization of human rights–based workforce induction curriculum for social work field supervisors'. *Journal of Human Rights and Social Work*. https://doi.org/10.1007/s41134-020-00152-y.

Botma, Y., and Snyman, S. (2019) 'Africa interprofessional education network (AfrIPEN)'. *Journal of Interprofessional Care*, 33(3), 274–276. https://doi.org/10.1080/13561820.2019.1605236.

Brock-Utne, B. (2016) 'The Ubuntu paradigm in curriculum work, language of instruction and assessment'. *International Review of Education*, 62(1), 29–44. https://doi.org/10.1007/s11159-016-9540-2.

Chigangaidze, R. K., Mafa, I., Simango, T. G., and Mudehwe, E. (2022) 'Establishing the relevance of the Ubuntu philosophy in social work practice: Inspired by the Ubuntu world social workday, 2021 celebrations and the IFSW and IASSW's (2014) global definition of social work'. *International Social Work*, 66(1), 6–20. https://doi.org/10.1177/00208728221078374.

Council on Social Work Education (CSWE) (2012) 'Social work and integrated behavioral healthcare project'. Available at https://www.cswe.org/Centers-Initiatives/Initiatives/Social-Work-and-Integrated-Behavioral-Healthcare-P.

Crisp, N., and Chen, L. (2014) 'Global supply of health professionals'. *New England Journal of Medicine*, 370(10), 950–957.

Dako-Gyeke, M., Boateng, D. A. and Mills, A. A. (2018) 'The Role of social work in the provision of healthcare in Africa'. In N. Nortjé, J. De Jongh and W. A. Hoffman (Eds.), *African Perspectives on Ethics for Healthcare Professionals, Advancing Global Bioethics 13* (pp. 107–118). Springer. ISBN 978-3-319-93230-9.

Dassah, E. T., Norman, B. R., Dzomeku, V. M., Opare-Addo, M. N., Asare, O., Buabeng, K. O., and Adu-Sarkodie, Y. (2022) 'Implementation and outcomes of interprofessional education programme among health care students and practitioners in Ghana'. *Preprints*. https://doi.org/10.21203/rs.3.rs-1617788/v1.

Deichen Hansen, M., Holland, M. M., and Munn, J. (2020) 'Teaching note—A call for social work education modification: Moving toward a model of interprofessional education'. *Journal of Social Work Education*, *56*(3), 595–601.

Freire, P. (2000) *Pedagogy of the Oppressed*. Bloomsbury.

Gehlert, S. (2011) 'Conceptual underpinnings of social work in health care'. In S. Gehlert and T. Browne (Eds.), *Handbook of Health Social Work* (2nd ed., pp. 1–22). Hoboken, NJ: Wiley.

Hlongwa, P., and Rispel, L. C. (2021) 'Interprofessional collaboration among health professionals in cleft lip and palate treatment and care in the public health sector of South Africa'. *Human Resources for Health*, *19*(1), 1–9.

International Association for Schools of Social Work (IASSW) (2020) 'Global standards for social work education and training'. Available at https ://https://www.iassw-aiets.org/wp-content/uploads/2020/11/IASSW-Global_Standards_Final.pdf.

Keith, J. (2014) *The Role of an International Cross Cultural Interprofessional Healthcare Immersion Programme in Doctor of Physical Therapy Education: An Educational Case Report*. University of New England Case Report Papers. Available at http://dune.une.edu/pt_studcrpaper/16.

Kithuci, R. K., Makworo, D., Mutisya, A., Simba, J., and Mburugu, P. (2022) 'Attitudes towards interprofessional education and associated factors among faculty at the college of health sciences in a public university in Kenya: A cross-sectional study'. *The Pan African Medical Journal*, *42*(4). https://doi.org/10.11604/pamj.2022.42.4.32732.

Kobayashi, R., and Fitzgerald, C. (2017) 'Teaching note – Asserting social worker's role in developing an interprofessional education project'. *Journal of Social Work Education*, *53*(4), 737–743. https://doi.org/10.1080/10437797.2017.1284627.

Kodom, R. B. (2022) 'The role of social work in the healthcare settings during the Covid-19 pandemic in Africa'. *International Social Work*. https://doi.org/10.1080/208728211070525.

Kuramoto, F. (2014) 'The Affordable Care Act and integrated care'. *Journal of Social Work in Disability and Rehabilitation*, *13*(1–2), 44–86. https://doi.org/10.1080/1536710X.2013.870515.

Mabvurira, V. (2020) 'Hunhu/Ubuntu philosophy as a guide for ethical decision making in social work'. *African Journal on Social Work*, *10*(1), 73–77.

Mayaka, B., and Truell, R. (2021) 'Ubuntu and its potential impact on the international social work profession'. *International Social Work*, *64*(5), 649–662. https://doiorg.spot.lib.auburn.edu/10.1177/00208728211022787.

Miley, K. K., O'Melia, M. W., and DuBois, B. L. (2017) *Generalist Social Work: An Empowering Approach* (8th ed.). Pearson.

Morgaine, K., and Capous-Desyllas, M. (2020) *Anti-oppressive Social Work Practice* (2nd ed.). San Diego, CA: Cognella.

Mugumbate, J. R., and Chereni, A. (2020) 'Now, the theory of Ubuntu has its space in social work'. *African Journal of Social Work*, *10*(1), v–xvii.

Murenje, M. (2020) 'Ubuntu and xenophobia in South Africa's international migration'. *African Journal on Social Work*, *10*(1), 95–98.

Nyoni, C. N., Pietersen, E., and Reitsma, G. (2020) 'Interprofessional education and collaborative practice. Report on the activities of AFriPEN'. Available at Interprofessional-education-and-collaborative-practice.pdf (researchgate.net) (Downloaded: 17 January, 2023).

Parmer, A. (2014) 'Methods of social work and its role in understanding the team climate and team effectiveness for organizational development'. *Journal of Sociology and Social Work*, *2*(1), 303–318.

Quartey, J., Dankwah, J., Kwakye, S., and Acheampong, K. (2020) 'Readiness of allied health students towards interprofessional education at a university in Ghana'. *African Journal of Health Professions Education*, *12*(2), 86–89.

Rodger, S., Hoffman, J., and S. (2010) 'Where in the world is interprofessional education? A global environmental scan'. *Journal of Interprofessional Care*, *24*(5), 479–491.

Rubin, M., Konrad, S., Nimmagadda, J., Scheyett, A., and Dunn, K. (2018) 'Social work and interprofessional education: Integration, intersectionality, and institutional leadership'. *Social Work Education*, *37*(1), 17–33. https://doi.org/10.1080/02615479.2017.1363174.

Stanhope, V., Videka, L., Thorning, H., and McKay, M. (2015) 'Moving toward integrated health: An opportunity for social work'. *Social Work in Health Care*, *54*(5), 383–407. https://doi.org/10.1080/00981389.2015.1025122.

Sunguya, B. F., Hinthong, W., Jimba, M., and Yasuoka, J. (2014) 'Interprofessional education for whom? —Challenges and lessons learned from its implementation in developed countries and their application to developing countries: A systematic review'. *PLoS One*, 9(5), e96724.

Tuggle, F. J., Watts, S., Sewell, J., and Slay, J. (2022) 'Learning together to work together: Introducing interprofessional education in the generalist curriculum.' *Journal of Health Science and Education*, 6(4). https://doi.org/10.0000/JHSE.1000228.

Watts, S. O., Tuggle, F. J., Sewell, J., Slay, J. L., Ellison, K. J., and Frugé, A. D. (2022) 'Achievement of interprofessional competencies in live and virtual community clinics: A comparative study'. *Nurse Education Today*, 119. https://doi.org/10.1016/j.nedt.2022.105578.

World Health Organization (WHO) (2010) 'Framework for action on interprofessional education and collaborative practice'. Available at http:// www.who.int/hrh/resources/framework_action/en/.

INDEX

Note: Page numbers in *italics* and **bold** refer to figures and tables, respectively.

Abo El Nasr, M. M. 201, 202, *203*, 205
ACA *see* Affordable Care Act
actors, informal social work 31–32
Addis Ababa University 77
Affordable Care Act (ACA) 386
Africa: disaster risk management policy 159; social workers/social work profession 157; *see also specific country*
Africa Interprofessional Education Network (AfrIPEN) 385
African Child Policy Forum 126
African family theory 57
African Independent Churches (AIC) 97
African Indigenous Knowledge Systems (AIK) 49–55; integration in social work curriculum 52–55, **53–54**; Western knowledge and 51–52
Africanisation 191
African Journal of Social Work 353
African Network on Prevention and Protection against Child Abuse and Neglect (ANPPCAN) 108
African Social Work Network (ASWNet) 57
African strength theory 56–57
African Traditional Religion (ATR) 87, 91
African Union (AU) 159; Agenda 2063 157, 159, 162, 184, 185; ARSDRR 159
Africa Regional Strategy for Disaster Risk Reduction (ARSDRR) 159
Afrikaans 66
Afrocentricity 55–56
Agenda 2063 (African Union) 157, 159, 162, 184, 185
agents, informal social work 31–32
AIK *see* African Indigenous Knowledge Systems
Allegritti, I. 202, 203

America Counsellors' Association 166
Anti-Racism Strategy 358, 359
antiretroviral therapy (ART) 76
apartheid 63
Asamoah, M. K. 101, 102
ASASWEI *see* Association of South African Social Work Education Institutions
Association for Social Work Education in Africa 329
Association of Schools of Social Work in Africa (ASSWA) 99
Association of Schools of Social Work in Tanzania (ASSWOT) 120–121, 123, 125–127, 255, 257–259, 261–263
Association of Social Workers in Malawi (ASWiM) 373
Association of South African Higher Education Institutions (ASASWEI) 99
Association of South African Social Work Education Institutions (ASASWEI) 191
associations, informal social work 31–32
ASSWA *see* Association of Schools of Social Work in Africa
ASSWOT *see* Association of Schools of Social Work in Tanzania
ASWNet *see* African Social Work Network
Australia 348

Bantu Education Act 1952 63
biopsychosocial-spiritual assessment 76
Black African Diaspora in Ireland 358–367; neoliberalism and 365–366; overview 358–359; racism against 363–365; social work education 360–362
Boblin, S. L. 203, **204**

INDEX

Bohwasi, P. 182–183
Botswana 288; family genograms *see* family genograms; social work training 291
Bourdieu, P. 360, 366
brain drain 353
Browne, T. 218–219, 222

Cairo School of Social Work in Egypt 191
Cameroon: colonial history 190; ENAM curriculum **195**, 195–197; evolution of social work education and training 193–195; population 190; structural adjustment programme 194
Canadian Counselling and Psychotherapy Association (CCPA) 167; ethical code standards 167–169
Cannon, I. 218–219
Carelse, S. 98, 100
Catholic University of Malawi 233, 234, 235–238, 371, 372–373; *see also* field practicum in Malawi
CBWCY *see* Community Based Work with Children and Youth
Chancellor College of Malawi 371
channels, knowledge mobility/transfer 348
child abuse and neglect 108–109
Child Frontiers 336–337
child protection: concept 108; factors affecting 111–112; traditional African society 109–110
child protection in Ghana 335–344; Damongo Workshop 339–341; indigenous knowledge and 338; movement towards 336–337; Wa Workshop 341–343
child protection in Nigeria 111–115; challenges 114–115; family-based care 113; institutional care 113–114; legislation 112
Child Protection Sub-Sector (CPSS) 111
children: abuse *see* child abuse and neglect; vulnerable 107
Child's Rights Act (CRA) 112
Christians/Christianity in South Africa 96–98
Coetzee-de Vos, G. 66
collaborative practice (CP) 383
colonialism 3, 63, 64, 65, 68, 191; early European 363; money economy in Zimbabwe 182; reinforcing social order 374; social work profession 327; Western ideas and concepts 278, 285, 326, 347
communal mobilisation, informal social work and 30
communicable disease outbreaks in South Africa 152–162; competencies and value standards for **161**, 162
Community Based Work with Children and Youth (CBWCY) 373
community determination 88
community development officers 126
competencies for cyber counselling 167, 170–176

computer applications for cyber counselling 167–168
constructivism 281
context-relevant research 315
Convention on the Rights of the Child 336
Council of Social Workers Zimbabwe (CSWZ) 185
Council on Social Work Education (CSWE) 386
COVID-19 pandemic 3, 300–307; as an academic disruption 314–315; adapting to challenges by 134–135; disaster management responses to 160, 162; higher education institutions and 130; impact on social work education 304–306; innovative fieldwork practice 306–307; IPCAGHP and 383; online learning and *see* online learning in South Africa; post-traumatic stress among nurses 158–159, **159**, *159*; protective behavioural protocols 166; social justice 133–134; social services to vulnerable populations 157–159, *158*
cross-cultural social work practice 225–226
cultural adaptation 15
cultural competence 361, 377
cultural humility 218, 377, 388
cultural identities 226
culturally competent practice 220–221
culturally relevant curriculum for Nigeria 13–22; ethics and 19–20; ethnicity and 20–21; indigenising 15–16; literature review and findings 16–21
culturally sensitive medical social work practice 225
cultural others 361
culture: concept 218, 221; medical social work training and 221–223
curriculum development 122–123
cyber counselling 165–176; competencies 167, 170–176; computer applications 167–168; defined 167; ethical code standards 167–169

Damongo Workshop 339–341
Dean, R. G. 225–226
decoloniality 374
decolonisation 8–9, 64–66, 278, 329; AIK and 55; concept 63, 191; curriculum 99, 387; ecosocial approach 44; indigenous knowledge and 348; knowledge mobility and 348
Department of Social Welfare 259
Department of Social Work, University of Benin, Benin City 89
Desmond, C. 110–111
development, concept of 180
developmental social work in Zimbabwe 180–182
didactic teaching method 290
digital divide 146–148
digital information-sharing platforms 353
disaster management responses to COVID-19 pandemic 160, 162

396

INDEX

disaster risk management: Africa's policy framework for 159; South Africa's policy framework for 159–160
DMI-Saint-John of God the Baptist University of Malawi 371, 373
Dykes, G. 98, 100

Ebonyi State University, Abakaliki 89
École Nationale d'Administration et Magistracie (ENAM) 194–196
École Nationale des Assistants des Affaires Sociales (ENAAS) 193, 194, 196
ecosocial approach 37–46; curriculum with ecosocial content 41–43; decolonising and indigenising 43–44; environmental sustainability 44–45; overview 38–40; Ubuntu philosophy and 41
ecosocial worldview 40–41
education: access to 143; delivery of 143; supported 315; UNESCO on 142; *see also* social work education
employment opportunities 123–124
ENAAS *see* École Nationale des Assistants des Affaires Sociales
ENAM *see* École Nationale d'Administration et Magistracie
epistemicide 348, 351–352
ethical code standards for cyber counselling 167–169
ethics: culturally relevant curriculum 19–20
Ethiopia: education in 277–278; faith and spirituality in 77–84; field practicum 280–285; Socialist Military Government 278; social work education 77–84, 278–280
Ethiopian Experience 276
Ethiopian People's Revolutionary Democracy Front (EPRDF) 77
ethnicity: concept 218, 221; culturally relevant curriculum 20–21; medical social work training and 221–223
ethnic-sensitive social work practice 225
extended family 19, 27, 58, 332, 372, 374; African family theory 57; Botswana 291; care/caregiving by 113; kinship 31; as long-established institution 110; social welfare projects 110, 157, 192; Western civilisations 110

Faculty of Integrated Development Studies (FIDS) 339
faith and spirituality 74–84; biopsychosocial-spiritual assessment 76; defined 75–76, 87–88; in Ethiopia 77–84; identity formation 77; meaning of 87–88; in Nigeria 86–93
family: extended *see* extended family; informal social work and 30–31; recognising and prioritising 110–111

family genograms 289–290, 292–296; awareness of personal characteristics 295–296; case study 292–293; concept of 292; constructing 294–295; self-introspection 296; self-understanding 296; as teaching tool 295
#FeesMustFall student protests 64, 99
field practicum 255–257, 328; block 244; challenges 245; concept 243; concurrent 244–245; as an integral component of social work education 267–269; as a learning process 267; significance of 303–304; types 243–245; at the University of Benin 269–273
field practicum in Ethiopia 280–285; challenges 283; faculty commitment to 285; independent learning 284–285; indigenous knowledge 283–284; liaisons and supervisors 284; views of students on 282–283
field practicum in Malawi 231–239; agencies for 233; block field placements 234; Catholic University of Malawi 235–236; challenges 237–239; duration 237–238; historical context 233–235; limited assessment 238; limited curriculum 237; student support 236–237
field practicum in Nigeria: agency supervisors 247; challenges 247–249; dearth of standard agencies 247; incompetent social workers 248; non-professional social work supervisors 248–249; overcoming challenges 249; perspectives 246; report writing 247–248, 251; social work education 249–250; sustainable, future trends 250–251
field practicum in Tanzania Mainland 255, 257–263; academic supervisor 260; agency supervisor 261; background 257–258; challenges 261–263; coordinator 260; department 260; social welfare service agency 261; students 261
fieldwork 244–245
fieldwork placements 375
Francophone Africa 190; medico-social programmes 192; missionaries 192–193; social welfare programmes 192; social work education in 191–193; social work training centres 192; *see also* Cameroon

Gehlert, S. 218–219, 222
gender-based violence (GBV) 132, 133
genograms *see* family genograms
Ghana: child protection in 335–344; collaborations among universities 337; indigenisation and knowledge development 338; IPCAGHP course 386; social welfare offices 384; university collaboration 337
Ghana Cross-Cultural Healthcare Immersion (GCCHI) 385
Global North 330–332; *see also* reciprocal learning
Global Social Service Workforce Alliance 336

Global South 330–332; *see also* reciprocal learning
Global Standards for Social Work Education and Training (IASSW) 383, 385
Gray, M. 14, 15, 18, 131, 179, 202, 203, 328–329, 347–348
Guinea, social work in 200–213; academic literature 203; authentisation 203, *203*, 212; education 205–207; French colonization 201–202; gaps in 201; globalisation and 202–203; indigenisation 202–203, *203*, 211–212; overview 200–201; policy 205; professional associations 207–208, **208**; research 209; transmission 202, 203, *203*, 209, 211, *211*

health care in Kenya 223
higher education: COVID-19 pandemic and 130–131
higher education in Ghana: child protection *see* child protection in Ghana; collaborations among universities 337
historically Black universities (HBU) 132
historically White universities (HWU) 132
HIV/AIDs 76
Hochfeld, T. 182, 256
Hubert Kairuki Memorial University 263
Hubert Kairuku Memorial University (HKMU) 121

IASSW *see* International Associations of Schools of Social Work
Ife, J. 348, 350
indigenisation 15–16, 328–330; ASASWEI on 191; challenges 329–330; globalisation and 329
indigenous knowledge 121–122
indigenous knowledge systems (IKS) 180; language and 66
informal social work 26–35; actors, associations, and agents 31–32; associated structures and 31; communal mobilisation and 30; conceptualisation 27; critique 32–33; families and 30–31; features characterizing 28; formal intervention 34; grassroot mechanisms and 29–30; kinship and 31; knowledge production on 33; learning included in education curriculum 33–34; mutuality and reciprocity 30; overview 26–27; pervasive continuity 28–29; recommendations 33; religion and 31; social relations and 31; spirituality and 31
Information Communication Technologies (ICT) 143
Institute of Social Work 120
institutional racism 363
International Associations of Schools of Social Work (IASSW) 14, 156, 165–166, 182, 232, 237–239, 244, 280, 285, 354; Francophone African schools and 193; Global Standards for Social Work Education and Training 383, 385

International Federation of Social Work (IFSW) 134, 165–166, 190; ethical statement of principles 180–181
Interprofessional and Collaborative Applied Global Health Practice (IPCAGHP) 386, 388–391; competencies for **389–390**; COVID-19 pandemic and 383; cross-cultural educational experience 383; Ubuntu values and 384
interprofessional education (IPE) 383
interprofessional education and collaborative practice (IPECP) 382–391; in Africa 384–386; overview 382–384; in United States 386–387
IPCAGHP *see* Interprofessional and Collaborative Applied Global Health Practice
IPECP *see* interprofessional education and collaborative practice
Ireland *see* Black African Diaspora in Ireland
Irish Association of Social Workers (IASW) 359, 365; Anti-Racism Strategy 358, 359
isiZulu 5, 67

Jan Hofmeyr College 65
journaling 316

Kampala International University (KIU) 121
Kaseke, E. 182, 183
Kenya 217; Children Act of 2022 219; cross-cultural social work practice 225–226; culturally sensitive medical social work practice 225; ethnic-sensitive social work practice 225; guiding philosophies 222; health care in 223; medical social workers practice 223–225; modern medicine 222; religious beliefs 222; social work training 222–223
kinship 31; *see also* informal social work
knowledge mobility/transfer 346–353; academic publications 353; channels 348; curriculum and teaching approach 349–350; decolonisation and 348; digital information-sharing platforms 353; research 350–353

Lachman, P. 108–109
Lake Malawi 374
Lange, L. 68–69
League of Malawi Youth 371
Lombard, A. 41, 124, 125, 179, 184

Machani, S.O. 224–225
Magomero College, Malawi 233, 371, 373
Malawi 231; burden of disease 233; economy 371; field practicum in 231–239; gross domestic product per capita 371; as a landlocked developing country 371; population 233, 371; practice education and educators in 373, 375–379; social welfare 372; sociopolitical context 232–233; University of Malawi 233–238, 371

INDEX

Malawi Congress Party (MCP) 371
Malawi Young Pioneers 371
Malinga, T. 223–224
Mandela, Winnie Madikizela 65
Mangaung Metropolitan Municipality, Free State, South Africa 157–159
Manyama, W. 119, 121, 123, 124, 126
Massachusetts General Hospital (MGH) 218
Masters in Social Work (MSW) 77–80, 83, **121**, 262, 279
Mauda, L. T. 96–98, 101
Mbe, J. M. 191, 194, 196
McLaughlin, H. 181, 290
medical social work 218–219; cross-cultural practice 225–226; culturally sensitive practice 224–225; ethnicity, culture and training of 221–223; ethnic-sensitive practice 225; evidence-based practice 219–220
Midgley, J. 14, 256, 347
Ministry of Gender, Children, Disability and Social Welfare (MoGCDSW) 371, 372
Mugumbate, J. R. 182–183, 384
Muhingi, W.N. 224–225
Mupedziswa, R. 122–123, 124, 193, 223–224, 332–333
Muslims 75
mutuality, informal social work 30
Mwansa, L. J. 196–197

National Accreditation Council for Technical Education (NACTE) 258
National Association of Social Work (NASW) 218
National Human Rights Commission of Nigeria 112
National Qualification Framework (NQF) 302
National Social Protection Policy Framework for Zimbabwe (NSPPF) 183
National Social Welfare Policy of Malawi 372
National Student Financial Aid Scheme (NSFAS) 145
neoliberalism 365–366; progressive 378
New Partnership for Africa's Development (NEPAD) 109
Ngwu, C. N. 18–19
Nigeria 242; child protection in 111–115; cultural diversity 87; cultural heritage 87; culturally relevant curriculum for 13–22; curriculum contents 89; ethnic groups 87; faith and spirituality in 86–93; fieldwork in *see* field practicum in Nigeria; population 87; religion(s) in 87, 89, 90; religious beliefs 87; social work education and practice 89–93; *see also* University of Benin, Benin City, Nigeria
Nkala, N.Z. 133–134
nuclear family 110

Oduor, R.M. 222–223
Ojo, E. 66, 68
online learning in South Africa 130; assessment opportunities 136–137; challenges 149; digital divide 146–148; financial implications 144–145; lessons learnt 138; plagiarism 148; student support 137–138; theory classes 135–136
Open University of Tanzania 120
Orthodox Christians 75
outcome-focused method 338

pastors in social work counselling 100–102
Patel, L. 14, 57, 132, 181, 182
pervasive continuity 28–29
post-traumatic stress among nurses 158–159, **159**, *159*
practice education in Malawi: course 379; decolonialised content 378; knowledge sharing and exchange 378; teaching and learning in 378–379
Practice Educator Programme in Malawi 375
practice educators in Malawi 373, 375–379; social work practitioners as 377–378; voices of social workers as 375–377
Probation and School Attendance Compliance Officer programme 183
process-focused method 338
progressive neoliberalism 378
proselytising 88
Psychotherapy and Counselling Federation of Australia (PACFA) 166–167

racial segregation system 63
racial state: capitalist 363–365; conceptualisation 363; *see also* racism
racism 363–365
Rawls, J. 133, 134
reciprocal learning 330–332; North learning from South 331–332; South learning from North 330–331
reciprocity, informal social work 30
Regional Psychosocial Support Initiative (REPSSI) 373
religion 75–76
REPSSI *see* Regional Psychosocial Support Initiative
research 209; knowledge mobility/transfer 350–353

Save the Children 112
School of Social Work at Addis Ababa University 75, 77, 78
School of Social Work in Johannesburg 65
secularism 76
Sendai Framework for Disaster Risk Reduction 2015–2030 (SFDRR) 157; Programme of Action (POA) for 159

INDEX

Sewpaul, V. 124, 125
Simmons School of Social Work 218–219
Sinkamba, R. P. 124, 290
Smith, L. 64, 306
Sobantu, M. 133–134
Social Work Code of Ethics 88
social work education 1–4; colonialisation and 290; constructivism 281; curriculum 288–289, 290; evolution of 327; field practice *see* field practicum; indigenisation *see* indigenisation; integrating theory and practice 281–282; *see also specific African country*
Social Workers Act of Zimbabwe 185
social workers/social work profession 2–3, 153–154; in Africa 157; in South Africa 157–162
Social Work/Maatskaplike Werk 353
South Africa: Christians/Christianity in 96–98; colonialism 63, 65; communicable disease disasters *see* communicable disease outbreaks in South Africa; COVID-19 *see* COVID-19 pandemic; decolonisation 65, 68–69; epistemic injustice 68, 69; epistemological access 68–69; experiential knowledge 69; #FeesMustFall student protests 64, 99; higher education in 63; online learning in *see* online learning in South Africa; racial segregation and discrimination 63; social work assessment 98–99; social work education in 64–69, 99–102, 131–133; student social workers *see* student social workers; translanguaging 65–68; Western knowledge 68; White Paper on Social Welfare 68; White population 63
South African Council for Social Services Professions (SACSSP) 132, 133, 148, 152, 160, 302, 303, 305
South African Council of Social Service Profession 65
South African Journal of Social Work and Social Development 353
Spitzer, H. 123–124, 125, 127, 180, 181, 196, 225, 256, 330
Stellenbosch University 65
student social workers: challenges for 314; educational challenges 316–317; psychosocial challenges 317; resources needed 317; role-players 318
supported education 315–316
Supporting Social Work in Malawi (SSWiM) 373
Sustainable Development Goals (SDGs) 108

Tanzania 118–127; challenges 124; Child Law of 2009 126; colonial government 119; community development officers 126; conflicts of interest 126; curriculum development 122–123; employment opportunities 123–124; field practicum 125–126; historical perspective 119–121; indigenous knowledge 121–122; opportunities 121–124; poor working environment 126; post-independence period 1961–2020 119–121; regulatory organ 124; scheme of service and workers' development 125; social workers 124–126; social work organisations in 127; transferring welfare services from one ministry to another 126–127; universities 121
Tanzania Association of Social Workers (TASWO) 123, 127, 255, 257, 258, 259–260
Tanzania Commission of University (TCU) 258
Tanzania Emerging Schools of Social Work Programme (TESWEP) 127, 255, 257, 259
Tanzania Mainland 254
Tascón, S. 348, 350
TESWEP *see* Tanzania Emerging Schools of Social Work Programme
translanguaging 65–68; as a pedagogy 66–67
Twikirize, J. 33, 41, 123–124, 127, 181, 256, 330

Ubuntu 56, 375, 383–384; ecosocial approach and 41; IPCAGHP and 384; IPECP and 387
Ubuntu: Strengthening Social Solidarity and Global Connectedness 350
UKZN *see* University of KwaZulu Natal
United Nations Children's Fund (UNICEF) 371
United Nations Convention on the Rights of the Child (UNCRC) 108
United Nations/International Organizations (UN/IO) 78
United Nations Sustainable Development Goals (UNSDG) 1, 2, 178
United States: Affordable Care Act (ACA) 386; IPECP in 386–387; social work programmes 387
United States Agency for International Development (USAID) 371
University Language Board (ULB) 67
University of Benin, Benin City, Nigeria 89, 266–273; engaging students in non-academic activities 272–273; human service agencies 271–272; issues and challenges 270–271; location 266–267; types of field practicum 269–270
University of Benin Experience 266
University of Calabar, Calabar 89
University of Dar es Salaam 120–123
University of Development Studies (UDS) 339
University of Fort Hare (UFH) 144
University of Ilorin, Nigeria 89
University of KwaZulu Natal (UKZN) 67, 373; Language Policy 67; ULB 67
University of Limpopo (UL) 144
University of Malawi 233–238, 371

INDEX

University of Nigeria, Nsukka 89, 245–246

Veta, O. D. 181, 290
vulnerable children 107
vulnerable populations, social services during COVID-19 to 157–159, *158*

Walton, R. G. 201, 202, *203*, 205
Wa Workshop 341–343
Western colonial expansion 374

White Paper on Social Welfare (1997), South Africa 68
Wilfrid Laurier University (WLU) 339
World Health Organisation (WHO) 383

Zimbabwe 178–185; colonialism and 182; developmental social work 180–182; overview 179–180; socioeconomic trajectory and 182–185
Zvomuya, W. 133, 135, 138

Taylor & Francis Group
an informa business

Taylor & Francis eBooks

www.taylorfrancis.com

A single destination for eBooks from Taylor & Francis with increased functionality and an improved user experience to meet the needs of our customers.

90,000+ eBooks of award-winning academic content in Humanities, Social Science, Science, Technology, Engineering, and Medical written by a global network of editors and authors.

TAYLOR & FRANCIS EBOOKS OFFERS:

A streamlined experience for our library customers

A single point of discovery for all of our eBook content

Improved search and discovery of content at both book and chapter level

REQUEST A FREE TRIAL

support@taylorfrancis.com

Routledge
Taylor & Francis Group

CRC Press
Taylor & Francis Group